Dvornik, Francis, 1893-
Photian and Byzantine ecclesiastical studies / Francis Dvornik. -- London : Variorum Reprints, 1974
[472] p. : 1 ill., port. ; 23 cm. (Collected studies series ; 32)
Facsimile reprint of 22 articles originally published between 1930 and 1973.
English and French.
Includes bibliographical references and index.
1. Photius I, Saint. Patriarch of Constantinople, ca. 820-ca. 891. Add., ess., lects. 2. O.E. Church. Add., ess., lects. I. Title.

Amongst other Variorum Reprints:

JU. KULAKOVSKIJ
Istorija Vizantii I, II & III
Kiev 1913, 1912 & 1915 editions

N.L. TUNICKIJ
Monumenta ad SS Cyrilli et Methodii successorum vitas resque gestas pertinentia – Sergiev Posad 1918 edition

E. KALUŽNIACKI
Werke des Patriarchen von Bulgarien Euthymius (1375-1393)
Aus der panegyrischen Litteratur der Südslaven (One set)
Vienna 1901 editions

I.E. TROITSKIJ
Arsenij i Arsenity
Serialized articles – St Petersburg 1867-72

O. HALECKI
Un empereur de Byzance à Rome
Warsaw 1930 edition

In the Collected Studies Series:

FRANÇOIS HALKIN
Martyrs Grecs. IIe-VIIIe s.

MARIUS CANARD
L'expansion arabo-islamique et ses répercussions

DONALD M. NICOL
Byzantium: its ecclesiastical history and relations with the western world

JOHN MEYENDORFF
Byzantine Hesychasm: historical, theological and social problems

AUGUST HEISENBERG
Quellen und Studien zur spätbyzantinischen Geschichte

JEAN DARROUZÈS
Littérature et histoire des textes byzantins

KENNETH M. SETTON
Europe and the Levant in the Middle Ages and the Renaissance

Photian and Byzantine Ecclesiastical Studies

The Rt. Reverend Monsignor Francis Dvornik

Francis Dvornik

Photian and Byzantine Ecclesiastical Studies

VARIORUM REPRINTS
London 1974

ISBN 0 902089 68 4

Published in Great Britain by
VARIORUM REPRINTS
21a Pembridge Mews London W11 3EQ

Printed in Switzerland by
REDA SA
1225 Chêne-Bourg Geneva

VARIORUM REPRINT CS32

CONTENTS

This volume contains a total of 472 pages

PREFACE

I welcomed the kind invitation from Mrs Eileen Turner to choose a number of studies from my bibliography that she wished to reprint in the *Variorum Reprints* Series of Collected Studies, which has already rendered valuable service to Byzantine scholarship. I chose twenty-two studies which in many ways complete my major works on the Photian Schism and on the history of the Eastern Churches, but excluded those dealing with these problems because they are to be found in more complete form in my major works. I have not found it necessary to make any changes in my findings in this selection. Some of the papers not only correct but allay the apprehensions of several of my critics. The study on "National Churches and the Church Universal" (1944) reflects the debates I held with both Anglican and Catholic clergy in London during the war and in the post-war period. A few of the ideas we discussed in an oecumenical spirit were echoed favorably in some of the sessions of the Second Vatican Council. Although all the hopes expressed in this short essay have not been fulfilled, I have left it unchanged as homage to the clergy of the Church of England who shared them with me. I have limited my choice to studies which are not easily accessible to scholars, and have omitted others including the study on "Constantinople and Rome", which was published in *The Cambridge Medieval History* (1966), and which are readily available. I hope that the reprinting of these works will be of service to students of Eastern Church History.

FRANCIS DVORNIK

Dumbarton Oaks, May 1974

PHOTIACA

I

LETTRE A M. HENRI GRÉGOIRE

A PROPOS DE

MICHEL III ET DES MOSAIQUES DE SAINTE-SOPHIE

Mon cher Ami,

Permettez-moi d'attirer votre attention sur deux homélies du patriarche Photius, qui, me semble-t-il, apportent une éclatante confirmation à vos surprenantes découvertes sur le règne et la personne de l'empereur Michel III. La première a été prononcée en présence de l'empereur Michel III et de Basile, le 29 mars 867, à l'occasion de l'inauguration de l'image de la sainte Vierge placée devant l'iconostase de Sainte-Sophie (Aristarches, *Φωτίου λόγοι καὶ ὁμιλίαι*, Constantinople, 1900, II, *ὁμ. ογ'*, p. 294 : *ὁμιλία λεχθεῖσα ἐν τῷ ἄμβωνι τῆς μεγάλης ἐκκλησίας τῷ μεγάλῳ σαββάτῳ, ἐπὶ παρουσίᾳ τῶν φιλοχρίστων βασιλέων, ὅτε ἡ τῆς θεοτόκου ἐξεικονίσθη καὶ ἀπεκαλύφθη μορφή*). On y trouve un passage qui, me semble-t-il, est important pour l'histoire de la décoration intérieure de Sainte-Sophie. Voici ce que Photius y dit (*l. c.*, p. 300 sq. : *Ταύτην τὴν ἡμέραν εἴ τις ὀρθοδοξίας ἀρχὴν καὶ ἡμέραν, ἵνα μηδὲν ὑπέρογκον εἴπω, καλέσειεν, οὐκ ἂν ἁμάρτοι τοῦ δέοντος. Καὶ γάρ, εἰ καὶ βραχὺς ὁ χρόνος, ἐξ οὗ τῆς εἰκονομαχικῆς αἱρέσεως ἀπηθαλώθη τὸ φρόνημα, καὶ τὰ τῶν ὀρθῶν δογμάτων εἰς πάντα τῆς οἰκουμένης περιηυγάσθη τὰ πέρατα, βασιλικῷ καὶ θείῳ προστάγματι φρυκτωρούμενα, ἐμὸν καὶ τοῦτο καλλώπισμα· τῆς γὰρ αὐτῆς θεοφιλοῦς βασιλείας ἀγώνισμα.*

Ἀλλ' οὖν, ἐπείπερ ὁ τῆς οἰκουμένης ὀφθαλμός, ὁ περιώνυμος οὗτος καὶ θεῖος ναός, οἱονεὶ τὰ τῆς ὁράσεως ἐκκεκολαμμένος μυστήρια ἐσκυθρώπαζε, τῆς γὰρ εἰκονουργικῆς ἀναστηλώσεως οὔπω ἀπειλήφει τὸ δικαίωμα, ἀμυδρὰς τοῖς προσιοῦσι τὰς ἀκτῖνας ἠφίει τῆς ὄψεως, καὶ στυγνὸν ἐπὶ τούτοις τὸ τῆς ὀρθοδοξίας ἐδείκνυτο πρόσωπον.

Ces paroles ne semblent-elles pas indiquer que Sainte-Sophie, même après le rétablissement de l'orthodoxie, était restée pendant très longtemps privée des saintes images que les empereurs iconoclastes avaient fait détruire, que la réinstallation des icones dans la principale église avait demandé un certain temps et que Photius et Michel III y étaient pour quelque chose? Le fait serait assez inattendu pour bien des gens et projetterait une lumière nouvelle sur l'histoire de la liquidation de l'iconoclasme ainsi que sur la figure de Michel III, « l'empereur impie ». Qu'on se rappelle d'ailleurs les hésitations de Théodora avant le rétablissement de l'orthodoxie et la politique de réconciliation pratiquée par le gouvernement de Théodora et de Théoctiste, que je me suis efforcé de mettre en lumière dans mon dernier ouvrage sur les *Légendes de Constantin et de Méthode.* Il semble, en tout cas, qu'en 867, les icones n'étaient pas encore très nombreuses à Sainte-Sophie, car, à la fin de son homélie, le patriarche a formulé, sous la forme d'une prière, le vœu que les empereurs persévèrent dans cette pieuse entreprise (*l.c.*, p. 307) : *Δίδου δὲ καὶ τοὺς διὰ σοῦ λαχόντας τῶν ἐπὶ γῆς βασιλεύειν καὶ τὰ ὑπόλοιπα τοῦ νεὼ τοῖς ἱεροῖς μορφώμασι καθιερῶσαι.*

La seconde homélie me semble encore plus importante pour la confirmation de votre thèse. Elle a également été prononcée à Sainte-Sophie en présence de Michel et de Basile dans une circonstance très solennelle, c'est-à-dire à l'occasion de l'inauguration d'un monument en l'honneur des empereurs, vainqueurs de toutes les hérésies (*l. c.*, II, *ὁμ. οδʹ*, p. 314-326 : ... *ὁμιλία λεχθεῖσα ἐν τῷ ἄμβωνι τῆς ἁγίας Σοφίας, ἡνίκα τοῖς ὀρθοδόξοις καὶ μεγάλοις ἡμῶν βασιλεῦσι, Μιχαὴλ καὶ Βασιλείῳ, ὁ κατὰ πάσης αἱρέσεως ἐστηλογραφήθη θρίαμβος*).

Cette homélie semble refléter la grande joie et l'orgueil des Byzantins de 867, qui voyaient leur Empire à l'apogée de sa puissance, après les victoires sur les Pauliciens, sur les Arabes, sur les Bulgares, et après les succès que l'orthodoxie avait remportés, à l'intérieur, sur les derniers restes des hérésies — surtout sur l'iconoclasme, définitivement mort et enterré — et, au dehors, chez les Arméniens, chez les Bulgares, les Moraves et les Russes. Voici comment Photius y apostrophe Michel III (*l. c.*, p. 314-317) : *Ἦν ἄρα ἐκ πολλοῦ γεγηρακὼς ὁ χρόνος, καὶ νέαν οὐκ ἔχων ὠδῖνα, καθ' ἣν ἀκμάζων ἐθάρρει σεμνύνεσθαι, μόναις δὲ ταῖς παλαιαῖς ἐγκεκυφὼς ἐκείναις, καὶ λαμπρὸν οὐδὲν οὐδὲ γενναῖον εἰς τόκον ἔχων νεανιεύσασθαι, τὰ αὐτὰ φέρων κύκλῳ περιήει στρεφόμενος, ἐκείνων μόνῃ τῇ φορᾷ φιλοτιμούμενος, ὃν ὁ φθάσας ἐμέτρει τὴν γένεσιν, καὶ ἃ τὴν χάριν ἀνθεῖν οὐκ ἐδίδω νεάζουσαν. Νῦν δὲ δι' ἑνὸς ἀνδρὸς εὐσεβοῦς καὶ καινῶν καὶ γενναίων ἔργων ἀθλητοῦ καὶ νεαζούσαις ὠδῖσιν ἐγκαλλωπίζεται, καὶ τὸ γῆρας αὐτοῖς ὀνείδεσιν ἀποδύεται, οἵά περ τόκον εὐγενῆ τε καὶ κράτιστον καὶ τῶν ἄλλων καλῶν ἀνθοῦντα τὰς χάριτας, ὑπὸ φωτὶ τῆς ἀληθείας πᾶσιν εὐτυχήσας, ἐπιδείξασθαι · εἰ δὲ καὶ ῥητόρων ἤνεγκε φοράν, μετρεῖν εἰδότων τοῖς λόγοις τὰ πράγματα, καὶ τῷ μεγέθει τῶν ἔργων συμπαρατείνειν τῆς γλώσσης τὴν δύναμιν, εἰς ὁλόκληρον ἂν αὐτῷ τὰ τῆς ἀκμῆς καὶ τὰ τῆς ἀνανεώσεως ἐκρατύνετο. Νῦν δὲ οὐ βραχυτάτῳ μέρει ζημιούμενος τοῖς μὲν παροῦσι καὶ θεαταῖς, κἂν μηδεὶς ἐφέστηκε τοῖς δρωμένοις ῥήτωρ, οὐδὲν ἧττον γεγονὼς ἐνακμάζων δεικνύει τὸ τέλειον· ὅσοι δὲ τοῦ βίου γενεαῖς ὑστέραις προκύψουσι, τούτοις δ' ἄρα τὴν ἐν τοῖς λόγοις μνήμην οὐκ ἔχων δωρήσασθαι, εἰς γῆρας, οἶμαι, πάλιν, ἢ νόσον, ἢ τὰ τοιαῦτα διαβληθήσεται · πράξεων μὲν γὰρ μετριάζουσαν σεμνότητα λόγοι φιλοῦσι παρρησιάζεσθαι, δειλίᾳ δὲ καὶ συστολῇ καταδύονται, ὄγκον αὐτοῖς πραγμάτων ὁρῶντες ἐπιφερόμενον, καὶ κατορθωμάτων μεγέθη προκείμενα. Ἐντεῦθεν κἀγὼ σιγᾶν ἐβουλόμην, καὶ τῶν ὑπὲρ λόγον ἔργων τὸ μέγεθος τῇ ἀτονίᾳ μὴ καθυβρίσαι τοῦ λέγοντος, τὸν τοῦ ἡττηθῆναι φόβον πρὸ τοῦ παθεῖν τὴν ἧτταν αὐτῷ προβαλλόμενος εἰς ἀσφάλειαν. Ἀλλ' ἐπειδήπερ αὐταὶ παρεστήκασιν αἱ πράξεις, καὶ τὸ λαμπρὸν τῶν ἔργων κατ' ὀφθαλμοὺς ἕστηκεν ἁπάντων, οὐκ ἐν μεγάλῳ τὰ τῆς ζημίας οἶμαι πεπεῖσθαι, τὸ ἔλαττον ἀποφερομένης τῆς διηγήσεως · τὰ γὰρ δρώμενα τὸ λεῖπον ἀναπληρώσει, καὶ τὸ ἐνδέον τοῦ λόγου ἡ ὑπεροχὴ σαλπίσει τῆς πράξεως.*

Ἀλλὰ γὰρ λαμπροὺς μέν ἐστιν ἰδεῖν αὐτοῦ τοὺς ἐν πολέμοις ἄθλους καὶ τὰς νίκας καὶ τὰ τρόπαια, ὧν χρόνος οὐδείς, ἐξ οὗ τῆς βασιλείας οὗτος διέκυψεν, ἄγονος ἔμεινεν. Ἐμοὶ δὲ τούτων καταλέγειν οὐδὲν εἰς σπουδὴν ἥκει · καὶ γὰρ οὐδὲ γνώμης μᾶλλον ἢ ῥώμης ταῦτα, καὶ τούτων οὐδετέρας μᾶλλον, ἢ τῆς εἰς ἄδηλον ἀναφερομένης αἰτίας ἐπὶ πολλῶν πολλάκις ἐλέγχθη δεικνύμενα. Οὐ μὴν οὐδὲ πόλεων τῶν μὲν πολεμίων ἀνδραποδισμοὺς καὶ μεταναστάσεις, οἰκοδομὰς δὲ καὶ ἀνοικισμοὺς τῶν φίλων · οὐδ' ὅτι φαιδρῷ καὶ μειδιῶντι προσώπῳ τοῖς ἐντυγχάνουσιν ὁμιλῶν, καὶ τὸν τύραννον φόβον εἰς πόθον ἑκούσιον ἁρμοζόμενος κατήφειαν πᾶσαν ἀπὸ παντὸς προσώπου ἀφείλετο, πατὴρ μᾶλλον πατρίδος ἢ δεσπότης καλεῖσθαι φιλοτιμούμενος, οὐ κατὰ τοὺς παλαιοὺς ἐκείνους, Κῦρον καὶ Αὔγουστον, ὧν ὁ μὲν Περσῶν ὁ δὲ Ῥωμαίων ἄρξας ἐπὶ πρᾳότητι καὶ φιλανθρωπίᾳ δόξαν ἔλιπον τῷ πλήθει, πρὸ τῶν ἔργων τὰς κλήσεις ἀρυσάμενοι, ἀλλ' ὡς ἂν ὁ πρέπων ἐπιστατεῖ λογισμός, πρὸ τῶν ὀνομάτων ταῖς πράξεσι σεμνυνόμενος· ἀλλ' οὐδ' ὅτι χρυσοῦ ῥέουσαν τὴν χεῖρα τῇ πολιτείᾳ προέτεινεν, ὡς οὐδεὶς ἄλλος πενίαν ἐξ οἰκίας οὕτως αὐτὸς ἐλάσας ταύτην τοῦ πολιτεύματος· καὶ πόλις ἡ βασιλίς, καὶ τῷ πλούτῳ βασιλεύουσα διὰ μιᾶς βασιλικῆς δεξιᾶς εἰς πάντας τοὺς ὑπηκόους τὰ τῆς εὐδαιμονίας ἐξήπλωσεν· οὐδὲν οὖν τούτων ἀριθμεῖν ἐμὴ μελέτη καὶ σπούδασμα, κἂν καὶ αὐτὴν ἔχωσιν ἐφεστῶσαν αὐτοῖς καὶ μάρτυρα τὴν ἀλήθειαν· οὐδὲ γὰρ οὐδὲ πομπικός τις ἐγώ, καὶ τέρψεις ἐκ λόγων τοῖς ἀκροαταῖς τεχνάζων χαρίζεσθαι, ὥσπερ ὕλην μᾶλλον, ἃ παρέρχομαι· οὐ μὴν οὐδὲ πρὸς ἐπαίνους ἄγων τὴν γλῶσσαν γυμνάζεσθαι, καὶ τοῦ θεάτρου κρότους ἐκτρίβειν τοῖς ῥήμασιν· ὅ τε γὰρ τοῦ βίου τρόπος καὶ τὸ τῆς ἱερωσύνης δικαίωμα οὐκ οἶδε τούτοις ἐναποδύεσθαι, οὐδ' ὅτε νεὼς αὐτῷ καὶ οἰκοδομημάτων ἱερῶν ἱεραὶ φροντίδες εἰς ἀνέλπιστον προελθεῖν πρᾶξιν καὶ κάλλος ἀνίκητον ἐξενίκησαν...

Nous trouvons ici tous les éléments dont l'imagination populaire a besoin pour créer des *τραγούδια* et des chants épiques : un grand empereur, victorieux, courageux, bon administrateur, populaire, sachant parler au peuple et faire un généreux emploi de ses richesses, pieux, plein de sollicitude pour les églises — un vrai « père de la patrie ». Voilà le témoignage d'un contemporain, et ce témoignage ne saurait être rejeté... Photius appelle Michel III, dans un autre passage (*l. c.*, p. 320), *ὁ πιστὸς ἡμῶν καὶ μέγας βασιλεύς* ; il semble savoir que la vie privée de Michel ne fut pas toujours, dans sa jeunesse, à l'abri de tout reproche, et qu'au début de son règne, il se laissait volontiers remplacer dans la gestion des affaires publiques par un autre — Bardas, sans doute. C'est pour cela que ce texte m'a paru intéressant pour vous et que je me suis permis de vous le signaler. Ces homélies ont été découvertes et traduites en russe par P. Uspenskij, en 1864 déjà. Le commentaire d'Uspenskij est parfois trop touffu ; il faut se méfier de certaines exagérations auxquelles l'entraîne son ardeur orthodoxe ; mais, au fond, il a vu juste.

et il est surprenant que, malgré ce qu'il en a dit, ces deux homélies n'aient pas obtenu l'attention qu'elles méritent, à mon avis. C'est à vous, mon cher Ami, de les examiner et de dégager ce qu'elles apportent de nouveau et d'intéressant.

Prague.

II

ÉTUDES SUR PHOTIOS

I

Photios, Marin et Formose.

Dans notre étude sur le « deuxième schisme » de Photios (1), nous nous sommes efforcé de mettre en lumière les relations entre le patriarche Photios et les successeurs de Jean VIII. Nous avons conclu que tous les papes postérieurs à Jean VIII se sont conformés à la ligne de sa politique orientale et que personne parmi eux n'est revenu sur la reconnaissance de Photios comme patriarche de Constantinople. Tous ces papes regardaient aussi les ordinations de Photios comme valides. Nous nous sommes limité à faire valoir seulement les arguments qui nous ont paru les plus décisifs, en remettant, comme nous l'avons répété à plusieurs reprises dans notre étude, une discussion approfondie de ces problèmes à plus tard, car nous préparons un travail d'ensemble sur le schisme de Photios.

Pourtant, l'étude du Père V. Grumel, *La liquidation de la querelle photienne* (2), dans laquelle le savant Assomptioniste veut compléter et corriger certaines de nos déductions, nous force à anticiper une fois de plus sur la publication de notre livre et à exposer aux spécialistes les raisons pour lesquelles nous nous croyons autorisé à maintenir notre point de vue. Nous ne voulons revenir ici que sur les faits essentiels où les idées du savant critique s'éloignent le plus des nôtres, nous réservant de traiter quelques détails de moindre importance en une autre occasion.

(1) *Byzantion*, t. VIII, 1933, pp. 425-474.
(2) *Echos d'Orient*, t. 37, 1934, pp. 257 et suiv.

Photios et Marin.

Reprenons d'abord les relations entre Photios et le premier successeur de Jean VIII, Marin. Tout en étant d'accord avec nous sur le point essentiel, M. Grumel veut pourtant prouver que si Marin n'avait pas rompu avec Photios, reconnu par Jean VIII, c'était bien à contre-cœur. Il regrettait au fond cette reconnaissance de la part de son prédécesseur et il s'abstenait délibérément d'entrer en contact avec le patriarche qu'il continuait à détester, et cela malgré la lettre que Photios lui avait adressée après le concile de 879-880 et dans laquelle il lui avait offert son pardon et son amitié. Les différends qui ont existé entre Marin et Photios durant le premier patriarcat de ce dernier sont invoqués comme une preuve certaine que telle aurait été aussi l'attitude de Marin durant le second patriarcat de son adversaire.

Nous pensons pourtant qu'il ne faut pas exagérer l'importance de ces différends. Il est vrai que Marin a joué, lors du concile de 869-870, un rôle de premier plan. Si tous les détails sur sa conduite à l'égard du patriarche condamné, qu'Anastase, le traducteur des Actes, nous rapporte, sont vrais, Marin prenait son rôle à Constantinople très au sérieux. N'oublions pourtant pas que même le futur pape Jean VIII, alors archidiacre d'Adrien II, avait signé les Actes du synode de Rome qui précédait le concile de Constantinople et qui devait justement donner à Marin et à ses collègues, chargés de représenter le Saint-Siège au concile, les instructions que Marin s'appliqua à observer à la lettre avec tant de conviction. Jean approuvait certainement alors aussi les décisions de ce concile et pourtant il oublia plus tard qu'il avait, lui aussi, joué un rôle important dans la condamnation de Photios et il se réconcilia avec lui. Pourquoi Marin, devenu pape, devait-il garder son animosité contre Photios ?

Il est vrai que la signature de Marin manque dans les Actes du synode de Rome de 879 qui avait précédé le concile photien et dans lequel on s'était prononcé pour la réhabilitation de Photios. Mais est-il vraiment permis de tirer de cette absence des conclusions aussi graves ? Marin était-il alors à Rome ? Il semble possible, en effet, qu'il remplissait alors encore les fonctions d'évêque de Cère, car il n'apparaît dans les fonctions d'archidiacre à Rome qu'en 880, comme nous allons le voir tout à l'heure.

Les conclusions de M. Grumel seraient recevables si on pouvait démontrer que Marin désapprouvait tout à fait la politique de son prédécesseur. Le changement d'attitude à l'égard de Formose, condamné par Jean VIII, prête à croire, au premier abord, que Marin voulait rompre définitivement et sur toute la ligne, avec la politique de son prédécesseur. Tant qu'on croyait à une excommunication de Photios par Marin, on disait même que l'ordination de Marin comme évêque de Cère de la part de Jean VIII avait pour but d'éloigner pour toujours Marin de Rome et de lui couper la route vers la dignité suprême. Marin aurait dû se résoudre à ce triste sort tant que vivait Jean VIII. Mais, celui-ci mort, il aurait donné immédiatement sa démission de son siège, en prétendant qu'il avait été forcé d'accepter la dignité épiscopale, pour pouvoir aspirer à la papauté (1). Devenu pape, Marin se serait alors vengé de Jean VIII en détruisant les effets de sa politique orientale surtout.

Pourtant, cette interprétation des faits n'est pas conforme à la réalité. Jean VIII avait, en effet, ordonné Marin évêque de Cère. Mais, rien ne prouve que c'était parce qu'il sentait en lui un adversaire et qu'il voulait l'empêcher de devenir pape et de détruire son œuvre politique. Au contraire, tout semble indiquer que Jean VIII, de sa propre initiative ou sur la demande de Marin, avait relevé ce dernier de ses fonctions en réclamant ses services à Rome. C'est peut-être encore la même année qu'a eu lieu à Rome le synode précédant le concile de 879-880.

En effet, Jean VIII a confié deux importantes missions à un évêque Marin qu'il appelle « arcarius sedis nostrae ». La première était auprès de Charles III en mars 880 (2) et l'autre en 882 auprès de l'évêque de Naples, Athanase (3). Il est à remarquer que, à la première occasion, le pape ne men-

(1) C'est aussi l'opinion de J. Duhr, *Le pape Marin* Ier dans *Recherches de sciences religieuses*, t. 24, 1934, pp. 200-206.

(2) *M.G.H.*, Ep. VI, p. 200.

(3) *M.G.H.*, Ep. VI, p. 265.

tionne pas le siège de cet évêque Marin. Ce fait est d'autant plus significatif que le pape nomme bien le siège du compagnon de Marin — *episcopus Senogaliensis*. Dans l'autre occasion, le siège de Marin n'est pas non plus mentionné. Cette omission n'est pourtant pas aussi significative qu'on l'a dit à l'occasion de la première, car le compagnon de Marin pendant cette ambassade n'était qu'un laïque — *Sico, egregius vir*.

On connaît à cette époque encore un autre évêque Marin, celui de Città di Castello, qui a signé les Actes du synode de Ravenne en 877 (¹). Ce n'est certainement pas à lui que le pape aura confié ces deux missions, car ce personnage nous est inconnu par ailleurs. C'est sans doute au futur pape Marin, alors évêque de Cère, qui avait déjà rempli à plusieurs reprises les fonctions d'ambassadeur sous Nicolas Ier et Adrien II. Pour profiter de ses services, Jean VIII lui avait fait abandonner son siège et lui avait confié à Rome l'office d'archidiacre.

Il est inadmissible qu'un homme qui jouait un rôle aussi important sous Jean VIII ait pu être hostile à sa politique. Jean VIII n'aurait jamais donné sa confiance à quelqu'un qui aurait été hostile surtout à sa conception de la politique orientale, conception à laquelle il tenait tant.

Remarquons d'ailleurs que si Jean VIII avait ordonné Marin évêque de Cère pour lui couper la route vers une dignité plus haute, il aurait agi directement contre ses propres institutions. Dans un synode romain qui a eu lieu entre 871-878, donc à l'époque où il aurait ordonné Marin, Jean VIII rappelait aux évêques la défense d'employer de pareils procédés à l'égard de leurs diacres ou archidiacres (²).

Ce fut justement cette confiance de Jean VIII qui désigna Marin comme candidat à la papauté en décembre 882. Parce qu'il remplissait auprès de Jean l'office si important d'archidiacre et parce qu'il n'exerçait plus les fonctions d'évêque, Marin fut élu pape.

C'est ainsi qu'on peut expliquer les deux versions diffé-

(1) Mansi, XVII, 342.

(2) F. Maassen, *Eine römische Synode*, Wien, 1878, chap. xvii, p. 20.

rentes de la cinquième partie des Annales de Fulda. En effet, l'un de ces continuateurs est scandalisé de voir Marin, évêque de Cère, changer de siège, en dépit des prescriptions canoniques alors en vigueur; l'autre pourtant attribue à Marin, lors de son élection, simplement le caractère d'archidiacre (1).

Citons encore un dernier fait qui nous semble particulièrement probant pour notre thèse. Marin, devenu pape, avait gardé comme bibliothécaire Zacharie d'Anagni (2), le même qui remplissait ces fonctions sous Jean VIII. Or, c'était justement Zacharie qui était à la Curie romaine le plus solide soutien de la politique grécophile, car il était un fidèle ami de Photios.

Il est inconcevable que Marin aurait conservé Zacharie comme bibliothécaire, s'il avait gardé sa vieille hostilité contre Photios et s'il n'avait pas approuvé la politique grécophile de son prédécesseur.

C'est d'ailleurs le même Zacharie qui semble avoir exercé une certaine influence à la cour pontificale même sous le pape Étienne V, qu'il avait élevé, jusqu'à sa mort en 891. Si cette supposition de Lapôtre (3) est vraie, on comprendrait mieux pourquoi la politique pontificale à l'égard de l'Orient était restée si favorable sous les trois successeurs de Jean VIII.

Les choses étant ainsi, nous ne pouvons plus invoquer le

(1) *M.G.H.*, SS., I, pp. 397, 398. — J. Duhr, *l.c.*, pp. 205, prétend que Marin s'était démis, et qu'il ne reprit ses fonctions d'archidiacre à la curie qu'après la mort de Jean. Pourtant, plus haut, p. 202, il reconnaît que déjà le pape Jean VIII, en le chargeant d'une mission à Vergola, l'avait appelé évêque et arcarius, fonction qui a été, ordinairement remplie, à la curie romaine, par l'archidiacre. M. Duhr ne s'était pas aperçu de cette contradiction, qui surprend un peu dans un article de quelques pages, et qui illustre bien l'embarras dans lequel se trouvaient les historiens qui s'occupaient de l'affaire de Marin.

(2) C'est Zacharie qui écrivit la lettre de Marin « pro monasterio Saviniensi ». *P.L.*, vol. 126, col. 970.

(3) *Le souper de Jean le Diacre*, dans *Mélanges d'archéologie et d'histoire*, t. XXI, 1901, pp. 333 et suiv. D. Amelli a publié dans le *Spicilegium Casinense*, I, 381, une lettre attribuée à Étienne V et qui insinue que Zacharie prenait une part active à la vie de l'Église même sous le pontificat d'Étienne V.

fait que Marin n'avait pas envoyé une lettre synodique au patriarche de Constantinople comme preuve que Marin désapprouvait la politique de Jean VIII à l'égard de Photios qu'il continuait à détester. En effet, cette omission peut être expliquée par des raisons plus naturelles. La réhabilitation de Formose, dans les premiers mois du pontificat de Marin, a certainement suscité une certaine agitation à Rome, car Formose n'avait pas seulement des amis à la Curie, mais aussi des ennemis. Ces troubles obligeaient le nouveau pape à donner toute son attention aux affaires romaines. La mort de Marin a été probablement précédée par une maladie qui a empêché l'exécution de plus d'un projet du pape. C'est pour cela que son successeur Adrien III se hâta d'expédier sa lettre synodique à Constantinople dans les premiers jours de son pontificat pour que ce long délai ne fît pas à Constantinople une fâcheuse impression. Nous ne savons pas ce que cette lettre contenait. Le nom de Marin semble y avoir été mentionné, car la réponse de l'empereur Basile y fait allusion. La lettre d'Adrien donnait donc peut-être même la raison pour laquelle Marin n'avait pu envoyer sa lettre synodique.

Nous nous sommes vu obligé de dire ceci pour la défense de la mémoire de ce pape. En effet, rien ne nous autorise à prétendre que le pape romain était moins généreux et moins noble que le patriarche de Constantinople et qu'il n'avait pas assez de force morale pour sacrifier ses sentiments personnels aux besoins de l'Église qu'il gouvernait. Plus nous étudions l'histoire de cette période, plus nous sommes convaincu que les papes, de Jean VIII jusqu'à Jean IX, ne changèrent pas leur ligne politique à l'égard de l'Orient d'après leurs sentiments personnels. La politique pontificale suivait toujours une ligne droite, inaugurée par le grand Jean VIII et inspirée par l'idée de réparer les fautes reconnues et de conserver l'unité de toute l'Église.

Photios et Formose.

Nous croyons avoir suffisamment mis en lumière, dans notre dernière étude sur le deuxième schisme de Photios, les relations entre ce dernier et le pape Formose. Après avoir examiné les principales sources qui nous en parlent, nous avons conclu que le pape Formose n'avait pas rompu avec l'Église de Constantinople à cause de ses idées sur les ordinations photianistes. Formose a fait, il est vrai, une démarche à Constantinople pour liquider le schisme « ignatien », mais son initiative n'ayant pas abouti, il en resta là sans aller plus loin.

Nous regrettons aujourd'hui d'avoir réservé alors à plus tard la discussion des quelques écrits latins du xe siècle concernant la reconnaissance des ordinations formosiennes et où on trouve — nous le savions déjà à l'époque où nous écrivions notre étude — quelques mentions vagues sur les relations entre Formose et Photios.

Il s'agit des écrits des deux ecclésiastiques napolitains Eugenius Vulgarius et Auxilius. Eugenius avait publié vers 907 une défense de Formose sous le titre *De causa Formosiana libellus*, et un autre écrit en forme de dialogue (1). Auxilius, originaire probablement de l'empire franc, mais vivant à Naples, publia vers 908 deux écrits qui avaient le même but : *In defensionem sacrae ordinationis papae Formosi*, et *Libellus in defensionem Stephani episcopi* (2). Deux autres traités suivirent vers 911 (*De ordinationibus a Formoso papa factis*, et *Infensor et defensor*) (3). Cette série d'écrits formosiens est close par un traité anonyme, *Invectiva in Romam pro Formoso papa*, (4) publié probablement en 914.

Or, on trouve dans le premier traité d'Auxilius un passage qui se rapporte à la reconnaissance de Formose par l'Église de Constantinople et qui a été récemment invoqué comme preuve pour la thèse que le pape Formose, tout en désirant ramener la paix à l'intérieur de l'Église de Constantinople, bouleversée par le schisme « ignatien », a abouti, à la fin, à une nouvelle rupture entre Rome et Byzance, rupture sur laquelle on ne seraitrevenu qu'après le concile de Ravenne (898), convoqué par le pape Jean IX pour reconnaître les ordinations

(1) E. Dümmler, *Auxilius und Vulgarius*, Leipzig, 1866, pp. 117-139. Mabillon, *Vetera analecta*, 1723, pp. 28-31.
(2) Dümmler, *ibid.*, pp. 58 et suiv.
(3) *P.L.*, vol. 129, 1061-1102.
(4) E. Dümmler, *Gesta Berengarii*, Halle, 1871.

de Formose (1). Voici le passage en question : « Nos autem eandem ordinationem idcirco ratam et legitimam esse non ambigimus, quia, ut supra ostensum est, sanctorum patrum scriptis et exemplis instituta dinoscitur. Insuper et auctoritate venerandae synodi concorditer roborata monstratur : cui synodo non solum sanctae Romanae ecclesiae praesules, verum etiam Francorum archiepiscopi, episcopi, presbiteri, diaconi apud Ravennatem urbem interfuisse noscuntur. Nihilominus autem et Constantinopolitana ecclesia hanc ordinationem complexa dominicae pacis concordiam regulariter fovet ».

En ce qui concerne l'interprétation de ce passage, il nous semble tout au moins exagéré d'y voir, la preuve catégorique que la reconnaissance de Formose par Constantinople ait eu lieu après le concile de Ravenne. La structure de la phrase n'autorise nullement, à notre avis, une pareille conclusion. Justement, le terme *nihilominus*, sur lequel veut se baser cette interprétation erronée, n'indique aucunement, à notre avis, une suite temporelle. L'auteur ne veut que citer, à la fin de son argumentation, encore un cas qui est capable de confirmer sa thèse : « Pareillement, l'Église de Constantinople elle-même, ayant embrassé — complexa — cette ordination, favorise régulièrement la concorde de la paix du Seigneur ».

Pour trouver la valeur exacte de ce passage, il ne suffit pas de l'étudier isolément, mais on doit respecter aussi le contexte et l'esprit dans lequel cet ouvrage a été composé. On doit également fouiller les autres écrits formosiens pour voir si on ne pourra y trouver des passages analogues qui autoriseraient une pareille interprétation, car tous ces traités proviennent du même milieu. C'est ce que notre savant contradicteur a, malheureusement, omis de faire.

En ce qui concerne le passage en question, la mention de l'Église de Constantinople, à cet endroit, ne doit pas nous surprendre. N'oublions pas que l'auteur provenait de l'Italie du Sud, probablement de Naples, où on s'intéressait aux affaires grecques et où l'opinion de l'Église de Constantinople comptait pour quelque chose.

(1) V. Grumel, *l. c.*, p. 285, 286.

Or, on trouve dans les traités d'Auxilius encore quelques autres allusions aux choses grecques, allusions qui illustrent bien cette mentalité des gens de Naples du xe siècle. En un autre endroit du même traité, Auxilius cite une chronique grecque (1), et plus loin (2), il fait allusion à ses connaissances de la langue grecque. En parlant de son protégé, l'évêque Étienne (3), il souligne que celui-ci parlait et écrivait couramment non seulement le latin, mais aussi le grec. Enfin, dans le traité sur les ordinations du pape Formose (4), Auxilius mentionne la persécution des Juifs inaugurée par l'empereur Basile Ier, mention qui complète les renseignements que nous tirons des sources byzantines.

On trouve de pareilles allusions à l'Église grecque, même dans l'ouvrage de Vulgarius. En voici une particulièrement curieuse (5) : « Ponamus igitur duos Nicolaum et Formosum et, ut fertur, unus probus, alter reprobus, unus pius, alter impius, quis eos sacravit, quis ad astra provexit, nisi Roma? Etenim Grecia nesciebat Formosum, Francia Nicolaum. Pietatis autem instinctu uterque Romam venit, vota reddidit, papam uti deum requisivit... Ordinatus fuit Nicolaus sanctus et iustus, quid pertinet ad Grecos? Unde laudandi ex hoc? Positus Formosus : quid peccavit Thracia? Vestra est quippe causa : vos vestrum ponitis, aut bonus, aut malus sit, per vos fit... ». Si on employait une pareille méthode, on pourrait presque citer ce passage aussi comme preuve que les Grecs n'ont pas reconnu Formose comme pape. Si on prend pourtant ce passage dans son ensemble, on voit bien que ce n'est pas cela que l'auteur veut dire.

Cette allusion à Byzance dans l'affaire de Formose devient pourtant encore plus curieuse, si on parcourt le texte qui précède immédiatement notre passage. L'auteur dit : « Patet enim ratio quia, dum omnis mundus in suo stet statu omnisque ecclesia sub Christi militet optentu, sola ecclesia Romana peragit, unde post omnium ecclesiarum ordinatio tabescit ».

(1) *L. c.*, p. 67 (chap. 7).
(2) *L. c.*, p. 92 (chap. 11).
(3) *L. c.*, p. 99 (chap. 3).
(4) *L. c.*, p. 109 (chap. 39).
(5) *L. c.*, p. 119 (chap. 1).

Cette idée de Vulgarius est reprise par l'auteur anonyme de l'*Invectiva in Romanam ecclesiam*, qui dit (1) : « Mirum tamen et valde mirandum est, cum omnes ecclesie tam cismarine quam transmarine in proprio statu permaneant, sola Romana ecclesia procellosis a fluctibus navitas suos mortis proximos redundat ». On voit bien que les deux auteurs pensent ici même à l'Église de Constantinople. On comprendrait mal cette allusion si Byzance avait refusé de reconnaître l'ordination de Formose et s'il avait fallu un acte spécial pour l'amener à cette reconnaissance.

Un autre passage du même écrit de l'anonyme semble vouloir exclure une pareille hypothèse d'une façon plus catégorique encore (2) : « Totus ergo mundus et omnes eius christiane fidei habitatores contra te clament (O Roma) : quia omnes decepisti et ipsa decepta es. Constantinopolis namque, Sicilia, tota Italia, Gallia, Germania, in quarum spaciis metropolitani, qui subfraganeos episcopales cetus sue consecrationi vindicant, degere videntur, adversus te causantur et querelantur, quia nullus metropolitanus consecracionem facere potest, nisi a sede apostolica pallium sumat. A quo ergo Bisancium, quae Constantinopolis vocatur (!?), Ravenna, Forum Iulii, Mediolanum, Hebrudunum, Arelatum, Lugdunum, civitas Remorum, Colonia, Magontia cetereque urbes metropolitane nisi ab apostolica potestate pallium sumant? *Si ita est, ut prodis, totus poene mundus per annos XXX in ruina positus est*, non solum ad dampnationem corporum, verum eciam, quod deterius est, ad detrimentum animarum. »

Comment l'auteur aurait-il pu opposer Constantinople à Rome, dans une apostrophe aussi passionnée, si cette Église avait émis sur l'ordination de Formose les mêmes doutes que Rome? N'oublions pas qu'il s'agit d'écrits polémiques auxquels les adversaires pouvaient répondre par leurs propres arguments. Les défenseurs de Formose et de ses ordinations ne pouvaient donc pas employer des arguments aussi fragiles.

Comme l'auteur compte les trente ans que dura ce triste

(1) E. Dümmler, *Acta Berengarii*, *l. c.*, pp. 137-138.
(2) *L. c.*, p. 148-149.

état de choses depuis Marin Ier (1), qui avait réhabilité Formose, on doit bien supposer, d'après le contexte, que les Églises énumérées dans ce passage reconnaissaient toutes — contrairement à celle de Rome — pendant toute cette période, Formose et ses ordinations. L'auteur peut bien citer les grandes métropoles de l'Occident, car le cas de Formose paraît avoir touché presque exclusivement Rome et le patrimoine de S. Pierre où vivaient presque tous ceux qui avaient été ordonnés par Formose.

Ces fréquentes allusions à Constantinople dans les écrits des défenseurs de Formose, semblent indiquer qu'ils connaissaient bien les relations de celui-ci avec l'Église de Constantinople qui l'avait reconnu comme pape et qui n'était plus revenue depuis sur cette reconnaissance (2).

D'ailleurs nous disposons, encore d'un document de la même époque qui montre d'une façon claire et précise que Formose n'avait pas provoqué, par son attitude dans la liquidation du schisme ignatien, une nouvelle rupture entre Byzance et Rome. C'est le rapport de Flodoard sur l'échange de correspondance entre Formose et Folco, archevêque

(1) Cf. ce que dit Dümmler, *l. c.*, p. 67, sur ce calcul et sur l'époque de la composition de l'ouvrage.

(2) On ne trouve dans ces écrits qu'une allusion directe à l'affaire de Photios et d'Ignace. L'auteur anonyme, en énumérant les cas de réhabilitation d'évêques condamnés pour certaines raisons, nomme aussi l'affaire de Zacharie (*l.c.*, p.151 : Nicolaus papa Zachariam episcopum pro eo, quod Constantinopolim directus Phocium invasorem subito e laico clericum factum et per ecclesiasticos ordines improvise ad patriarchatum Constantinopoleos provectum approbavit, et Ignatium patriarcham, virum sanctum et iustum reprobavit, in sua sinodo merito dampnavit, sed Adrianus papa eum in pristinum ecclesie sue statum revocavit. » L'auteur ne mentionne ici Photios qu'en passant. Le fait qu'il ne cite pas, parmi ces exemples, la réhabilitation de Photios par Jean VIII s'explique si on lit tout le passage. L'auteur cite les cas universellement connus de l'histoire ancienne de l'Église, mais quand il arrive aux temps modernes il se limite à énumérer uniquement les exemples récents dans l'Église occidentale. N'oublions d'ailleurs pas que le nom de Jean VIII rappelait aux formosiens la première condamnation de leur héros. Auxilius (*l. c.*, p. 66, chap. 6) énumère à peu près les mêmes cas sans citer l'exemple de Zacharie. Également dans « Infensor et def. », Mabillon, *l. c.*, chap. 21, p. 47.

de Reims. Comme ce passage est très important pour notre investigation, il faut le donner ici en entier (1) :

« Cui rescribens idem papa Formosus monet, eum compati debere Romanae ecclesiae atque imminenti eius subvenire ruinae nec ei suam praesentiam denegare ; adiungens, hereses undique ac scismata pullulare, nec qui ad resistendum occurreret esse. Dicitque, longo retroacto tempore perniciosas hereses Orientem confundere, et Constantinopolitanam ecclesiam nociva scismata perturbare ; simul etiam regionis Affricanae legatos insistere, responsa petentes pro dudum exorto inter episcopos ipsarum provinciarum scismate. Diversarum quoque partium legationes diversa responsa petentes instare. Cuius rei gratia generalem sinodum die Kalendarum Martiarum indictionis undecimae se inchoare disposuisse, ad quam eundem remota omni dilatione admonet festinare, ut colloquendo largius de his valeant pertractare et affluentibus ad consulta singula respondere... Miserat etiam alias pro hac eadem sinodo celebranda pridem huic quoque presuli nostro litteras, quam decrevisse se asserit incipere mediante Maio mense indictionis decimae. In quibus litteris fatetur, Italiam tunc semel et secundo horrida bella perpessam et pene consumptam, Orientalium vero partium se deflere vesanam heresim in Christum Jesum blasphemiam conicientem... »

Ce témoignage nous paraît confirmer d'une façon quasi absolue la thèse exposée dans notre dernière étude, c'est-à-dire que sous Formose la paix entre les deux Églises continua à exister et que l'infructueuse tentative de Formose pour liquider le schisme « ignatien », à l'intérieur de l'Église byzantine, n'avait nullement fait empirer les relations entre Rome et Byzance. En effet, Formose ne parle ici que d'un schisme à l'intérieur de l'Église byzantine. Nous ne comprenons pas comment on peut contester le poids d'un tel témoignage. Si M. Grumel (2) a raison de dire qu' « on comprendra bien mieux les plaintes du pontife, si la discorde intérieure de l'Église byzantine dont le Saint-Siège, au fond, ne souffre aucun dommage, se complique d'une rupture, beaucoup plus

(1) *Flodoardi Historia Remensis ecclesiae*, lib. IV, *M.G.H.*, SS., XIII, p. 559.

(2) *L. c.*, p. 269.

grave, de cette Église et de son chef avec l'Église romaine », pourquoi donc le pape n'est-il pas plus explicite? Pourquoi ne souligne-t-il pas davantage l'importance de la chose? Si le pape tenait tant à avoir les représentants de l'Église franque à ce concile — et on voit bien qu'il y tenait, car, n'ayant pas reçu de réponse à sa première invitation, il avait remis d'un an la convocation du concile — pourquoi ne leur aurait-il pas expliqué la gravité de la situation de l'Église entière pour les décider à effectuer le long voyage de Rome? Et si M. Grumel trouve étrange « qu'un concile d'Occident soit invité à délibérer sur un schisme purement intérieur de l'Église byzantine », il oublie que ce schisme ne devait pas constituer le seul objet des délibérations du concile projeté. Le pape énumère toute une série de questions qui touchaient les affaires occidentales avant tout. Le schisme byzantin n'y apparaît donc pas au premier plan. D'ailleurs, Formose n'était pas le premier qui aurait voulu avoir l'épiscopat franc à Rome pour délibérer avec lui non seulement sur les affaires occidentales, mais aussi sur les affaires orientales. Nicolas avait essayé à deux reprises de convoquer un pareil concile à Rome, mais son projet n'avait jamais pu être réalisé (1).

Le savant Assomptioniste émet, au même endroit, quelques doutes en ce qui concerne le passage de la Vie de S. Euthyme, que nous avons cité comme une preuve pour notre thèse. « Antoine (le patriarche) est mort après la réconciliation du Pape et de Stylien, et l'union de toute l'Église ». Or, pour prévenir tous les doutes, nous déclarons que l'interprétation de ce passage que le savant Père donne comme également possible — c'est-à-dire « après la réconciliation du Pape et de Stylien, et l'union de toute l'Église (de l'Église romaine et byzantine) » — nous paraît absolument inadmissible. Nous ne pouvons pas comprendre la conception de l'Église à cet endroit dans le sens moderne auquel nous sommes habitués, c'est-à-dire l'Église universelle. Les Byzantins pensaient, en parlant de l'Église en général, principalement à leur Église. Justement le passage dont il est ici question doit être in-

(1) Voir *M.G.H.*, SS., I, pp. 460, 406, 476. E. PERELS, *Ein Berufungsschreiben Papsts Nicolaus I zur fränk. Reichssynode in Rom*, dans *Neues Archiv*, t. 32, 1907, pp. 135 et suiv.

terprété dans ce sens — la réconciliation de Stylien avec le pape, si cette lecture est exacte, — réconciliation dont résulta enfin l'union de toute l'Église byzantine. D'ailleurs, même l'emploi de termes différents — *συνέλευσις*, pour désigner l'arrangement entre le pape et Stylien et *ἕνωσις*, pour l'union de toute l'Église — semble désigner que le biographe distinguait bien entre les deux faits. On lit, d'ailleurs, plus loin, que le chef de cette Église — donc de l'Église byzantine — est devenu Nicolas le Mystique.

Nous trouvons un exemple classique d'une pareille méprise dans l'interprétation d'un autre passage grec concernant notre sujet et cité par M. Grumel, le passage de la lettre de Nicolas le Mystique (1). Ce passage était connu de nous quand nous écrivions notre étude sur le deuxième schisme de Photios. Nous avions été également troublé par la lecture *Πάπας*, qui se trouve maintenant, grâce à l'heureuse initiative de M. Grumel, corrigée en *Μάπας*, mais tout ce passage nous avait paru, après une lecture plus attentive, si suspect, que nous ne l'avions pas mentionné, en réservant sa discussion à plus tard.

En effet, Nicolas, en parlant de l'Église, n'a pas en vue l'Église entière, comme l'éditeur des lettres et d'autres l'ont pensé, mais l'Église de Constantinople, celle qui ne reconnaissait pas les quatrièmes noces de Léon VI. On peut s'en convaincre si on lit attentivement toute la lettre, et non pas seulement le passage en question. Nicolas est si loin de penser ici à l'entente avec l'Église romaine, qu'il considère le rétablissement de Photios sur le trône de Constantinople comme canonique dès la mort d'Ignace, sans attendre la confirmation de la part du pape et du concile de 879-880. Ignace est mort le 23 octobre 877 et Syracuse, dont la prise est mentionnée comme ayant eu lieu après le rétablissement de Photios, est tombée entre les mains des Sarrasins le 25 mai 878. Comment pourrait-on donc supposer que, tout d'un coup, dans la même lettre, la désignation de l'Église devrait être prise dans un autre sens, devant désigner l'Église universelle ?

Même chose quant à un autre passage cité par M. Gru-

(1) Ep. 75, *P.G.*, vol. 111, col. 277.

mel et qui nous était également connu quand nous écrivions notre étude, celui du biographe d'Antoine Cauléas sur l'union de l'Église effectuée sous le régne de son héros (1). Même dans ce passage, *τὸ παλαιὸν τῆς ἐκκλησίας ἕλκος*, qui a été guéri par Antoine, doit désigner le schisme à l'intérieur de l'Église byzantine auquel le patriarche avait mis fin après avoir réuni les représentants de l'Orient et de l'Occident.

La mention de Formose, dans les traités grecs tardifs sur le schisme, (2) comme ayant été le premier des papes qui ait enseigné en secret l'« hérésie latine » sur la procession du Saint-Esprit, ne peut pas non plus être citée à l'appui de l'hypothèse que Formose avait rompu avec Byzance à cause des Photianistes. D'abord, tous ces traités affirment que Formose n'avait pas inséré le *Filioque* dans le Symbole. Le premier traité dit même *expressis verbis* que Formose avait envoyé à tous les patriarches orientaux une lettre synodique sans *Filioque*, ce qui peut être cité comme preuve que Formose, après avoir pris possession du siège de Rome, voulait suivre la politique de conciliation avec Byzance. Si l'affirmation de l'auteur de ce traité est exacte —et pourquoi ne devrait-elle pas l'être ?— elle est en contradiction apparente avec la teneur de la fameuse lettre du même pape à Stylien, conservée dans le recueil antiphotianiste. S'il est vrai que Formose a laissé un mauvais souvenir aux Grecs, il n'est pas nécessaire, pour l'expliquer, d'inventer une rupture entre les deux Églises par sa faute. Pourquoi ne pas vouloir s'en tenir exactement aux rapports des susdits traités sur le schisme, qui indiquent pourtant assez clairement la raison de cette antipathie des Grecs contre la mémoire de Formose, c'est-à-dire que ce pape, tout en n'osant pas ajouter le *Filioque* dans le Symbole, ne s'opposait pas aussi énergiquement que son prédécesseur Léon par exemple, à ce que cet usage se répandît dans l'Église latine. N'oublions, d'ailleurs, pas que c'est Formose qui, sous Nicolas Ier, avait chassé de la Bulgarie les prêtres grecs, un fait que les Grecs n'ont certainement pas vite oublié.

(1) PAPADOPOULOS-KERAMEUS, *Monumenta... ad histor. Photii patr. pertinentia*, Petropoli, 1899, I, 14.

(2) HERGENRÖTHER, *Monumenta graeca ad Photium... pertinentia*, Ratisbonne, 1869, pp. 160, 179.

Il est d'ailleurs possible que ce fût l'activité de Formose en Bulgarie qui ait occasionné ces bruits sur sa doctrine « hérétique » concernant la procession du Saint-Esprit.

Les choses étant telles, on ne peut plus interpréter dans ce sens la lettre du pape Jean IX qui a été conservée à la fin du recueil antiphotianiste. Notre savant critique (1) veut conclure du fait que le pape Jean IX a omis de nommer Formose dans sa réplique à Stylien, que Formose avait rompu avec l'Église byzantine qui ne voulait pas accepter son compromis en ce qui concernait la reconnaissance des ordinations photianistes. Jean IX dit en effet : « Nous voulons donc que les décrets des très saints pontifes qui nous ont précédé, restent intacts et conservent le même rang qu'ils leur ont donné. Nous aussi, nous acceptons donc et reconnaissons Ignace, Photios, Étienne et Antoine dans le même rang où les ont reçus les très saints papes Nicolas, Jean et le sixième (2), Étienne, et toute l'Église romaine jusqu'à notre époque ».

Nous avons autrefois émis l'hypothèse que le nom de Formose est omis, dans ce passage, par une erreur de copiste. C'est une explication qui peut se défendre, mais qui a ses points faibles et nous ne nous étonnons pas du tout que M. Grumel ne veuille pas l'accepter. D'ailleurs elle nous paraît aujourd'hui même tout à fait inutile. Cette omission s'explique, en effet, d'une façon beaucoup plus naturelle. Si on juge extraordinaire qu'aucun pape ne soit nommé comme ayant reconnu le patriarche Antoine, il n'est pas du tout nécessaire d'en conclure à une rupture entre Rome et le patriarche, rupture que le pape Jean IX aurait voulu masquer dans sa lettre par les mots « et toute l'Église romaine » comme s'il voulait dire que l'Église n'approuvait pas cette attitude de Formose.

N'oublions pas que pendant le court règne du patriarche Antoine Cauléas il n'y eut pas moins de six papes qui se succé-

(1) *L. c.*, pp. 270, 287.

(2) Nous acceptons bien volontiers ici la correction apportée par M. Grumel. En effet, ce n'est pas Étienne VI, mais le sixième pape depuis Nicolas. Le commentaire que le compilateur donne de ce passage et que nous citons plus loin, exclut, d'ailleurs, une autre interprétation, ce qui a échappé à M. Grumel.

dèrent au siège de Rome, Formose, Étienne VII, Boniface VI, Romanos, Théodore II et Jean IX. Tous reconnurent Antoine, mais au lieu d'énumérer toute cette longue série — on comprend que Jean IX n'aime pas à évoquer, dans une lettre à un évêque oriental, le souvenir de cette triste période de l'histoire pontificale — Jean IX se contente de dire « et toute l'Église romaine, jusqu'à notre époque ».

Le copiste du recueil antiphotianiste qui y a ajouté cette lettre a aussi compris dans ce sens-là ces mots du pape, tout en les tournant, bien entendu, en faveur de sa thèse, c'est-à-dire que tous les prédécesseurs de Jean IX avaient condamné Photios. Voici ce qu'il dit : « Le sixième depuis Nicolas qui avait condamné Photios et réhabilité Ignace. — (En effet), le deuxième était Adrien, puis Jean, ensuite Marin, et après Marin, un autre Adrien, et le sixième, Étienne ; ensuite, Formose, et après lui il y en eut quatre autres, Boniface, Étienne, Romanos et Théodore, et après ceux-ci, Jean, qui avait écrit ceci (cette lettre). Et en disant que, comme tenait toute l'Église romaine jusqu'à notre époque, il a compris tous les pontifes qui l'avaient précédé et qui l'avaient suivi — c'est-à-dire Étienne, le dernier pape mentionné dans la lettre — les décrets desquels il voulait, lui aussi — c'est-à-dire Jean IX — suivre. »

D'ailleurs nous répétons ce que nous avons déjà dit dans notre dernière étude, que le silence de ce recueil sur une excommunication d'une partie des Photianistes par Formose nous paraît la preuve la plus évidente qu'une pareille excommunication n'a jamais eu lieu. M. Grumel veut échapper à cette conclusion en disant que la décision de Formose signifiait au fond un échec pour les Ignatiens dont il ne satisfaisait les demandes qu'en partie. Mais n'oublions pas que toutes les décisions des papes provoquées par les Ignatiens signifiaient un échec pour ceux-ci, et ils nous en ont quand même conservé la copie tout en les tournant en leur faveur. Un pareil fait — l'excommunication d'une partie des Photianistes par Formose — aurait fourni un excellent argument aux Ignatiens schismatiques. Étant donnée la mentalité du copiste — un des Ignatiens les plus acharnés — nous ne comprenons vraiment pas pourquoi il n'aurait pas plutôt insisté sur ce fait au lieu de vouloir tirer de la lettre de Jean IX dont la teneur est pourtant toute contraire à ses intentions, un médiocre argument en faveur de sa thèse. Non, il vaut mieux en revenir à nos premières conclusions. Rien ne nous autorise à admettre une nouvelle brouille entre Byzance et Rome, survenue par la faute de Formose et par son manque de clairvoyance. Formose a fait, il est vrai, une tentative pour liquider le schisme à l'intérieur de l'Église byzantine et pour concilier les Ignatiens avec l'Église officielle de Byzance, mais cette tentative n'a pas abouti.

Nous n'avons qu'un fragment d'une lettre de Formose à Stylien, qui nous donne quelques détails sur la démarche infructueuse de ce pape à Constantinople. Malheureusement, ce fragment est conservé dans un recueil tendancieux, dont le compilateur a donné maintes preuves de sa mauvaise volonté. Or, si nous voulons accepter tout ce qu'il y dit sur les instructions données par Formose aux légats, envoyés à Constantinople, nous devons en conclure que les légats, s'étant aperçus que l'exécution du mandat pontifical n'aboutirait qu'à une brouille avec l'Église de Constantinople, s'étaient abstenus de prononcer le jugement et en avaient référé au pape. Formose, se rendant à la raison, serait revenu sur sa décision et aurait abandonné les Ignatiens à leur sort, pour ne pas aggraver la situation.

Pouvons nous, pourtant, sans scrupules, accorder une créance entière à tout ce que le compilateur nous dit sur les conditions posées, d'après lui, par Formose au clergé ordonné par Photios, pour la reconnaissance de ses ordinations de la part du Saint-Siège? N'oublions pas que cette lettre est très incomplète. Le compilateur confesse lui-même qu'il avait omis de citer une grande partie de la missive pontificale. Ce qu'il a omis n'était certainement pas en faveur de sa thèse. Cette considération diminue sensiblement la valeur du fragment cité par lui. Ce qu'il y dit, diffère tellement de la ligne droite, suivie par le Saint-Siège dans sa politique à l'égard de l'Orient dans les dernières années. Nous serions donc enclin à croire que les interpolations du compilateur à cet endroit, étaient plus importantes que nous ne l'admettions dans notre première étude. Nous aurons encore l'occasion de trouver plus d'une preuve de mauvaise foi dans ce recueil dicté par la haine contre Photios.

En tout cas, nous devons prendre, ici encore, la défense de la mémoire du pape Formose. Non, il n'est pas responsable d'une nouvelle brouille entre l'Orient et l'Occident. Comme dans d'autres événements survenus pendant son règne, même à cette occasion cet infortuné pape a fait preuve de la meilleure volonté, et l'échec de sa tentative ne doit pas lui être reproché.

Prague.

III

THE PATRIARCH PHOTIUS: FATHER OF SCHISM – OR PATRON OF REUNION?

I HOPE you will excuse me if you find that the subject I have chosen is a little unusual even for a lecture during a Church Unity Octave. I quite agree that my title appears at first sight rather provocative. Yet I dare say that at the end it will seem quite suitable and natural. We always get something of a shock when a subject is presented to us in a new light, different from that in which we have been used to see it. I think, however, that we shall have to put up with more than one such shock if we really mean to arrive at a true understanding between the Christian Churches.

Many of the differences dividing the Christian Churches in general, and the Eastern and Western Churches in particular, are not of a doctrinal nature, but originated in a different historical evolution. We have, therefore, to approach every problem that divides us with the best will to examine it without prejudice, and to study it against its real historical background, not for apologetical purposes, but simply to find out the bare historical truth.

These were my intentions when I started, some years ago, to re-examine the history of Photius. Some of the results of my researches were a shock to me also, because they were sometimes absolutely contrary to what we have been taught on this subject for centuries. I intend to throw new light on one aspect in particular of the Photian schism, and I hope you will excuse me if you find this light rather strong. Any historical problem must be enlightened by a strong, penetrating light if we are to arrive at its solution.

I think that the Photian question and the differing views which the Eastern and Western world have expressed upon it constitute the greatest obstacle to a real *rapprochement* between the Eastern and Western churches. For the Orthodox, Photius is one of the greatest Eastern Fathers, the last great doctor of the Greek Church, a saint officially canonised by all Eastern churches, the valiant defender of the freedom and autonomy of his church against all encroachment from the Papacy, a great teacher, and a great Prince of the Church.

Catholics are used to regard Photius as the first great schismatic, the Father of Schism between East and West, the inventor of a heresy concerning the *Filioque*, an usurper of the patriarchal See, a man full of vanity and deceit, the falsifier of papal letters and the acts of a Council, excommunicated by the Western and Eastern church, a man whose memory is rightly detested by all Christendom. Naturally, there is not much room for such a man in the heavenly kingdom. How can we reconcile such diametrically opposed opinions ? How can we hope for a real *rapprochement*, so long as both churches persist in their differing judgments on a man whose name has for centuries been connected with the oriental schism ?

Fortunately, in recent years, new light has been thrown on the history of the unfortunate Patriarch. Let us recapitulate only those discoveries which have been so far accepted by the scientific world.

First of all, it has been proved that the second Photian schism never existed. The Patriarch Photius was duly and sincerely reconciled with Pope John VIII, and the Council of 879—880 officially sanctioned this reconciliation. Photius was never re-excommunicated by the Pope. On the contrary, when he was deposed by the Emperor Leo VI for political reasons, the Pope, Stephen VI, rose in his defence, and only entered into relations with his successor, the emperor's young brother Stephen, when the emperor sent him the copy of Photius' free resignation of the patriarchal see. Then when Photius died he was in communion with the Church of Rome.[1]

It has also been established that the Church of Rome was well aware of this reconciliation and that, to the end of the eleventh century, the papal Chancellery officially recognised only seven oecumenical councils, thus refusing to accept the so-called eighth council which publicly condemned Photius in 869—870. The Roman Curia has not forgotten that the decisions of this council were cancelled in 879—880 when Photius was reconciled with Rome, that this decision was confirmed by John VIII, and that it was never afterwards revoked by the Papacy.

The council which condemned Photius and whose decisions concerning the Patriarch were cancelled ten years later by another synod approved by the Pope, has never since been counted amongst the oecumenical councils in the Eastern Church. Nor can any official decision of the Western Church be found ordering this council to be counted again amongst the oecumenical councils. This synod owes the undeserved honour of being counted as the eighth oecumenical council to a singular mistake on the part of Roman canonists of the

[1] I think I have given sufficient evidence for these new theses in my study published in *Byzantion*, Vol. VIII, in 1933 (Le second schisme de Photius—une mystification historique, pp. 425—474). Almost simultaneously, the Assumptionist Father V. Grumel came independently to some similar conclusions (Y-eut-il un second schisme de Photius ? *Revue des sciences philosophiques et theologiques*, Vol. XII, 1933, pp. 432—457). I have answered some of his hesitations and objections in my article *Etudes sur Photios, Byzantion*, 1936, Vol. XI, pp. 1—19. I have since found other evidence for this thesis, and I shall resume the whole problem once more in my book on the Photian schism. *Cf.* also a small paper on this subject which I published in *The Eastern Church Quarterly*, Vol. III, 1939 (Rome and Constantinople in the ninth century).

eleventh century,[2] who found the Acts of this council in the Lateran archives and were delighted to read amongst them a decision forbidding the laity to interfere with the election of bishops. They were so delighted with this discovery that they not only forgot that this synod had been cancelled, but promoted it to be one of the greatest councils of Christianity.[3] Naturally, when this happened the whole history of the Patriarch Photius was bound to be misunderstood. A Photian legend was born in Western Christianity, a legend supported by the Acts of an oecumenical council, and which had accordingly to be believed without hesitation. This legend developed during the Middle Ages, and was codified by the first modern Church historian, Cardinal Baronius, in the seventeenth century.

These are the new discoveries concerning the history of the Patriarch Photius which have been so far in some degree accepted by the specialists. These new views are naturally destroying all that the Middle Ages built up. If we look at the history of " the Father of Schism " from this point of view, then naturally the imposing building which Cardinal Baronius erected in the seventeenth century and Cardinal Hergenrother so magnificently renovated in the nineteenth is cracking and collapsing before our eyes. The history of the great Greek has to be rewritten.

But what about the position of this great Patriarch with regard to the Church of Rome ? If the conclusions of the most modern researches are correct, then even this must be re-examined. Fortunately, beneath the imposing building erected by the two Cardinals we can see solid ground, which those two great Church historians failed to see, and which is revealed on closer examination as solid rock, which they neglected, but upon which we can construct a new building, different from the former, but simpler, stronger and more closely resembling historical truth.

Let us examine to-day how we could reconstruct the real Photius's ideas concerning the Papacy. Was he really the greatest enemy of the Bishops of Rome ? Did he really intend to start a campaign against Rome which would continue all through the Middle Ages until now ? Is he really the Father of Schism and enemy of every kind of reunion ?

In order to find the historical truth on this special and difficult

[2] *Cf.* my lecture on this special subject given to the members of the International Congress on Byzantine Studies, (Rome 1937), and to the members of the Royal Belgian Academy in Brussels (1938) on the occasion of my reception as an Associated Member, and published in the *Bulletins* of the Royal Academy of Belgium in 1938, Vol. XXIV, *Classes des Lettres*, under the title: " L'Œcuménicité du huitième concile (869—870) dans la tradition occidentale du Moyen Age."

[3] We can better understand the jubilation of the canonists at this discovery if we bear in mind that such a decision was lacking in Western canonical legislation. The Western writers from the tenth to the middle of the eleventh century generally recognised that some place belonged to the Emperors in the election of the Pope. The approval of the Prince in the appointment of bishops was regarded as in conformity with tradition in the Western Church even by some reformists up to 1075. This has been very clearly demonstrated by R. W. Carlyle in *A history of mediaeval political theory in the West*, Vol. IV, *The theories of the relation of the Empire and the Papacy from the tenth to the twelfth centuries*, London, 1922, pp. 11—40.

ground, I ask you to examine with me some particular details of the Photian history. We must first bear in mind that the crisis which brought about the dismissal of Patriarch Ignatius from the see of Constantinople and the appointment of Photius in his place was caused not by the ambition of Photius, but by the struggle of two political parties in Byzantium, the conservatives and the liberals. We can trace the existence of these two parties very far back in Byzantine history. Their predecessors were the factions of the Greens and Blues in the hippodrome, and they had always struggled for power over the state and even over the Church. Their animosity had already produced one schism in the ninth century under Ignatius's predecessor, the Patriarch Methodius. St. Methodius (842—847) advocated liberal tendencies in ecclesiastical policy, and the monks of the famous monastery of Studion, who were in favour of stricter methods, rose against him and were excommunicated.[4] The situation was so tense at that moment in the Byzantine church that the Empress Theodora dared not convoke a local synod to elect a new Patriarch after Methodius's death. In order to prevent any possible trouble she simply appointed Ignatius head of the Byzantine church.

A similar situation arose in Byzantium some years later, in 858. Ignatius was more inclined to a strict ecclesiastical policy. His personality and acts were misused by the conservative party for their own political purposes. When the leader of the conservative party—the empress Theodora—was overthrown by the liberals, led by the empress's brother Bardas and her son the young emperor Michael III, Ignatius's position was seriously compromised. Ignatius was not illegally deposed, as we are told by some historians; he presented his resignation in order to prevent another schism in the church.

The new government intended to imitate Theodora and appoint a new Patriarch. But the former followers of Ignatius having protested against so arbitrary a measure, a synod of the Byzantine church was convoked and Photius, director of the Emperor's Chancellery, lawfully elected Patriarch. This election was a compromise accepted by the two ecclesiastico-political parties. For two months the new Patriarch was recognised as legitimate successor by the whole Byzantine Church, and even by Ignatius. We can find absolute evidence for this fact in the documents of the Ignatian party, hitherto misinterpreted by all scholars who have studied them.[5]

If we follow the lead of the same sources we find that the compromise resulting in the election of a neutral, of a man who had no direct part in the struggles of either party and had not only the confidence of the new government as a relation of the imperial family, but was used to handling delicate matters as director of the Imperial Chancellery, proved unsuccessful. The struggle started again, provoked by the

[4] The details of this schism and its consequences have been discussed at length in my books: *Les Slaves, Byzance et Rome au IXe siècle*, Paris, 1926; and *Les Légendes de Constantin et de Méthode vues de Byzance*, Prague, 1933.

[5] I presented these discoveries to the specialists in Byzantine history in 1934 on the occasion of an international Congress of Byzantine Studies in Sofia. A resumé was published in the *Bulletin de l'Institut archéologique bulgare*, v. IX, 1935, in Sofia, under the title *Le premier schisme de Photios*.

ecclesiastical supporters of the Conservative party, who alleged that the new Patriarch was in no wise neutral but sympathised with the government and the Liberals. The leaders of the opposition declared that they did not regard themselves as bound by the stipulations of the compromise which they had accepted, and after assembling a kind of synod they declared Photius deposed and Ignatius the legitimate Patriarch. There must have been some political complications which provoked and accompanied this clerical pronouncement, because the new government immediately took the matter up and inflicted severe punishment on certain leaders of the opposition. The regent Bardas must have gone a bit too far, for Photius energetically protested against the persecution and threatened to resign if he continued to persecute the clergy. Only when this agitation started was Ignatius put in a safe place under lock and key, and in order to prevent the agitators having any communication with him the imperial police changed the place of his detention several times.

The great majority of the clergy of high rank condemned this revolution and continued to recognise Photius as legitimate Patriarch. A synod was assembled in the church of the Twelve Apostles and the principal agitators were deposed and excommunicated. In order to prevent recognition of Ignatius as legitimate Patriarch the synod declared his reappointment illegal. It seems that the opportunity was taken to point out that even his first accession to the patriarchal throne had not been legal because he had not been elected by a synod —as Photius had been—but simply appointed by the Empress, which was contrary to the canons of the Byzantine Church. His followers had therefore absolutely no right to call him Patriarch. This declaration was naturally equal to a deposition.

It is difficult to say if this agitation was started with the consent of Ignatius. One detail in the so-called *Vita Ignatii* written by Nicetas of Paphlagonia, which is in reality not a biography but an ecclesiastico-political pamphlet, seems to suggest that Ignatius was not responsible for these troubles and that his prestige and personality had been misused by some fanatics who were posing as his admirers. On this, as on other occasions, Ignatius did not show enough comprehension of the real situation and let things take their course.

These agitations lasted several months. Not until the end of the summer of 859 were the troubles suppressed and was peace restored. Only then could Photius send his synodal letter to the Pope according to custom. This was done not before the spring of 860. The young emperor Michael, in a special message, explained to the Pope the events of the past year and the abdication of Ignatius, and invited him to send legates to a synod which was to be held in Constantinople and was to deal with the final liquidation of the iconoclast heresy. It was the first time that Photius had been in touch with the Papacy.

Some historians have reproached Photius because his synodal letter was written in very vague terms, he made only slight allusion to Ignatius's case and to the convocation of a new council, and he abstained from asking the Pope to recognise him as the legitimate Patriarch. All these reproaches are, however, without foundation. Photius simply conformed to the centuries-old custom of the Eastern Church. Never did a Patriarch ask a Pope in his synodal letter for confirmation of his election. The election of the Patriarch and bishops was regarded as a matter concerning the internal affairs of the Eastern Church and the Emperor. The Eastern Church was always very jealous in defence of its absolute independence in disciplinary matters. Because the troubles which accompanied the resignation and deposition of Ignatius also had a political character, it was all the more the business of the Emperor and not of Photius to explain them to the Pope. The convocation of a council especially was a prerogative of the Emperor from the time of Constantine the Great. Neither the Patriarch nor the Pope had anything to do with the convocation of a council. We must not judge the matter from our modern point of view, but from the point of view of the Byzantines in the ninth century.[6]

We know well enough the ideas of Pope Nicholas I concerning the papacy. He is without doubt one of the greatest Popes of the early Middle Ages, and the increase of papal authority throughout the following centuries is for ever connected with the acts of that great Pope whose writings on the sublimity of the institution of the papacy had an unprecedented influence over the canonists and theologians of the Western Church during the Middle Ages. Nicholas was a great and noble figure on the papal throne. He succeeded in bringing the whole Western hierarchy under absolute obedience to him and he crushed all tendencies towards independence in the powerful Frankish Church. It is not surprising that he intended to handle the affairs of the Eastern Church in the same way.

In his reply to the Emperor Michael III, Nicholas first very vigorously asserted his Petrine claims. He claimed that Rome should first have been consulted before Ignatius was deposed because, as he said, the Fathers had decided that without the consent of the Roman See and the Roman Pontiff no final decision might be given in any controversy that arose. This assertion sounds too vague, and one would prefer more concrete facts about such a decision[7]; but the words well express the claims of the vigorous Pope. His objection to the elevation of Photius, that he was a simple layman when elevated, is not very grave. He refused, however, to recognise the new Patriarch until his legates had been to investigate and had made their report.

This letter and the Pope's answer to Photius's synodal letter did not close the door to an understanding. We can even see a hint of the price which the Pope was expecting for his recognition of Photius. The Pope was asking the Emperor to restore the province of Illyricum

[6] I have treated this subject in detail in a special lecture: *De auctoritate civili in conciliis oecumenicis* in the Acta VI Congressus Vilebradensis, Olomucii, 1933. An English translation of this paper appeared in *The Christian East*, Vol. XIV (The Authority of the State in the Oecumenical Councils). This problem was the subject of my lectures at the Sorbonne in Paris in 1940. I hope to treat this and other problems concerning the first oecumenical councils in a special study. Let us point out that these historical facts bear no prejudice to the rights of the Roman See.

[7] *Cf.* what E. Perels, the editor of Nicholas's letters, says on this quotation in *Monumenta Germaniae Historica*, Epistolae, Vol. VI, p. 434.

and Sicily to the Roman patriarchate. Constantinople was disappointed by the Pope's answer. To the Eastern Church the case of Ignatius was definitely settled. The Emperor and the Patriarch could neither cede Illyricum and Sicily, nor simply and calmly accept the Pope's interference in matters which they regarded as belonging to the internal discipline of their Church. On the other hand, they did not want a new complication with the Western Church. Besides, a new complication would stir up fresh political difficulties in Byzantium. They were, therefore, eager to arrive at a compromise.

On the other hand, the papal legates, once in Constantinople, could see clearly that the situation was more complicated than when seen from the Roman point of view, and that the opposition to the government and the new Patriarch was of no numerical importance. They were well aware that it would be best for the Papacy simply to accept the new situation and get as many concessions as possible from the new Patriarch. But they also knew their master, and were unwilling to disobey his orders.

When we examine the rare documents that illustrate this complex situation, we gather that several months were spent in negotiations between the legates and the Byzantines. The Emperor and his uncle Bardas had decided to make a concession to the Pope. The Byzantines could not regard the Pope's intention to re-examine the case of Ignatius as conforming to the practice and rights of their Church. They were, however, prepared to concede this, but asked the legates for another concession. The government and the Church were willing that the Pope's representatives should re-examine and judge the affair of Ignatius, but on condition that they gave judgment on the spot without reference to the Pope. The legates justly pointed out that Nicholas had reserved the final decision to himself, and they were not prepared to disobey his orders.

At this stage of the negotiations the Emperor announced emphatically: If you do not make this concession, there will be no judgment and no council, and you will have to return to Rome empty-handed. The two legates, Zacharias and Rodoald, were good canonists, and they were well aware that it would be a mistake to miss such an opportunity of judging and condemning, in the Pope's name, a Patriarch of the Byzantine Church. Faced with this alternative they yielded to the Emperor and announced that they were willing to pronounce judgment during the council, hoping that the Pope would approve their transgression of his orders when he learnt that they were bringing him a great concession, the submission of the Byzantine Church to the judgment of his representatives.

According to the custom of the Byzantime patriarchal chancellery, when this compromise had been reached, the letters from the Pope could not be read in the council in the version brought from Rome by the legates. All passages contrary to the spirit of the compromise had to be changed. The patriarchal chancellery therefore produced a new edition of these letters, and it was this new edition which was read to the Fathers of the council. Pope Nicholas complained later that changes had been made in his letters without his permission.

In the eyes of the Byzantines such changes were logical and were in no way intended to prejudice the sender's authority. The legates and the Byzantine authorities had to explain to the Pope how it came about that some passages of his letters had been read before the council in a different version.

I do not think that there was any kind of fraud on the part of the legates. They were not won over by any threats or gifts from the Emperor and Patriarch. Nicholas's collaborators were neither corrupt nor cowards. Historians who so regard them forget that they are insulting the Roman clergy of that time. They have no absolute evidence for it, and all they can quote is gossip spread about by the enemies of Photius. Even the Pope, when later he condemned them, did not accuse them of corruption or cowardice. They simply saw the situation as it was and thought they were doing their best in the interests of the Papacy.

The council met in Constantinople before Easter 861. The acts of this council were destroyed in 869 by order of the so-called eighth oecumenical council. From the Greek side we have only vague accounts of what happened at it. Fortunately an extract from the first sessions which dealt with Ignatius has been preserved for posterity in the collection of canon law written by Cardinal Deusdedit in the eleventh century. We can prove that this extract was compiled from the genuine acts, the official copy of which was brought to Rome either by the two legates or by a special ambassador from the Emperor, and was deposited in the Lateran archives. Their genuineness cannot be doubted. Unfortunately, Cardinal Deusdedit's collection has not been widely known in the Western Church, and its influence on other collections of canon law has been very small. This explains why this important document—the extract from the acts of the council—has so long escaped the attention of specialists. This collection was published for the first time by Martinucci, just before the Vatican council assembled. Nobody then grasped the great importance of that collection not only from the point of view of the evolution of canon law, but as an historical document. The Cardinal had copied many documents straight from the Lateran archives, documents which have since perished.[8] The second edition of this collection, published in 1905 by Wolf von Glanvell in Paderborn, has met the same fate. The Photian legend was, at that time, so firmly believed that it seemed dangerous to touch Acts which appeared to be in direct contradiction to the general belief.

Let us recapitulate the principal declarations of this council as recorded by the extract from the Acts. The Emperor was present at

[8] I have discussed this problem in the study: *L'affaire de Photios dans la littérature latine du Moyen Age* (Annales de l'Institut Kondakov, Vol. X, Prague, 1938, pp. 83 sq.) I shall discuss medieval literature on canon law in my book dealing with the Photian schism. The collections of canon law before Gratian are mostly unpublished, but it is interesting to study them and follow the mutual dependence of the authors and their copyists on some collections of the tenth and eleventh centuries. The extract of the synod of 861 appears at the end of Deusdedit's collection. It is followed by an important extract from the acts of the Photian council of 879—880.

the opening of the council. He said textually: "There is no need to discuss again the case of Ignatius, who has been deposed for his manifest transgressions. But in order to honour the holy Church of Rome and the very holy Pope Nicholas in the persons of his legates, we give permission for his case to be reopened." The speaker for the Byzantine Church, Paul, bishop of Cappadocia, said: "The sentence of the synod has been pronounced against Ignatius. So far as our Church is concerned Ignatius's case is closed and need not be discussed again. But in order to give due honour to Saint Peter and to the holy and universal Pope Nicholas, we readily give our consent to his case being again discussed and judged." The papal legates said: "We, representing our Lord the Pope Nicholas, declare that, in accordance with the authority of the holy Fathers assembled at the Synod of Sardica, we wish Ignatius to come into our presence and his case to be heard again." The speaker for the Byzantine Church again said: "There is no need for our Church to reopen the case of Ignatius. But in order to honour the Princes of the Apostles and the Lord Pope Nicholas, our Church wishes you to proceed as you like." The papal legates said: "What we are doing, we do by authority of the canons."

It is true that these words were very carefully weighed by the Emperor and by the speaker for the Byzantine Church. Evidently the Byzantines were taking every precaution to defend the rights and liberty of their Church. It cannot, however, be denied that the concession given to the Pope and his legates did constitute a breach with former practice and an important precedent, which could be exploited for the profit of the Papacy by any adroit canonist and theologian. The legates very well knew the importance of this concession, and they were endeavouring by their declarations to obtain from the Byzantines an official recognition of the right of appeal to the Pope as voted by the Synod of Sardica. During the same session they once again pointed out the juridical basis of the Pope's claim to reopen the process of Ignatius: "You know that all condemned persons can appeal, and bring their case before the Pope. The Pope has to send someone to act as judge in their case. If they have been justly condemned, the sentence has to be confirmed; if not, they must be absolved."

More important declarations were made during the second session. Let us quote them in a literal translation:—Paul, bishop of Caesarea in Cappadocia said: "Our Church gives its consent because of its devotion to the holy Apostles and the most holy Pope Nicholas that Ignatius may be judged again." Again . . . the legates said: "Even though you have already pronounced judgment, we are bringing his case before our tribunal by authority of canon law and as representing the Pope." The Bishop of Laodicaea said: "The Synod has no objection to the reopening of this case. On the contrary, the Church and the citizens greatly rejoice that you have these powers and are re-examining his case." The legates said: "Believe us, Brethren, it is because the Fathers in the Council of Sardica decided that the Bishop of Rome has power to reopen the cause of any bishop that we desire, with the authority we have mentioned, to re-examine the case." Theodore, Bishop of Laodicaea, said: "Our Church rejoices at it and has no objection to it and is not offended by it (*et ecclesia nostra gaudet in hoc et nullam habet contradictionem aut tristitiam*)."

It is difficult to deny the importance of these declarations. Even if we are reluctant to take at face value protestations of obedience to Rome made by Eastern prelates, we cannot refuse credit to declarations made during a synod and in the presence of papal legates. Rome here obtained what she had been asking for centuries. We have to recognise that this concession was given by a synod which was to proclaim the rights of Photius, hitherto regarded as the greatest opponent of the Papacy and its claims.

It is also very important to point out that this right of appeal was really exercised by the supporters of Photius. When the principal opponent of Ignatius, the Archbishop of Syracuse, Asbestas, was deposed by Ignatius and his local synod about the year 854 with some other bishops, he sent bishop Zacharias of Taormina to Pope Leo IV and appealed with his friends to the Pope against the Patriarch's judgment. The Pope saw that Ignatius had made too hasty a decision and that there were reasons other than ecclesiastical for the Patriarch's action. He asked Ignatius for an explanation, and the Patriarch had to send his envoy to Rome. The matter was re-examined by Leo IV's successor, Benedict III, and had not been settled when Ignatius lost his see. Even this appeal was reconsidered by the legates during the synod of 861 and it was decided that the deposition of the bishop was not canonically justified.

This incident is proof that even Ignatius and his party recognised the right of appeal. During the same synod Ignatius did not deny the right of the legates to judge the case—the appeal of his opponents against his judgment. He did, however, refuse to accept the legates as judges in his own case, because he had not appealed to the Pope: "*Ego non appellavi Romam, nec appello. Quid vultis iudicare?*" It seems, however, that on the insistence of the Emperor and the Synod he did submit to be judged, for, according to the extract from the Acts, he consented to accept the oaths of the witnesses giving testimony in his case.

If we read the extract from the Acts and consider the situation in Byzantium, we cannot help realising that the legates acted with great wisdom and circumspection. In spite of all the historians have said on this particular subject, this seems to have been the opinion of Nicholas himself when he received the acts of the Synod and his legates' reports. We must not forget that this was the first time that the Eastern Church had allowed the intervention of Rome in its disciplinary affairs. We can find an example of similar papal intervention in Byzantium only in the sixth century. But when Pope Agapetus intervened against the patriarch Anthimos (535) it was for doctrinal, not disciplinary reasons. The patriarch had accepted the Henoticon, a decree of the Emperor Zenon dealing unlawfully with doctrinal matters. Even the liquidation of the so-called Acacian schism by Pope Hormisdas in 519 was prompted mostly by doctrinal reasons. The legates had therefore brought a great concession on the part of the Byzantine Church and it is no wonder that Nicholas appreciated its full value.

Things would probably have rested there had not the most prominent and active agitator of the intransigent party, the abbot Theognostos, escaped secretly from Constantinople and presented a protest against the legates' action. Even then the Pope would not have listened to his impassioned and often unjust accusation if the new patriarch had paid the price of his recognition and ceded Illyricum and Sicily to Rome.

Very probably the Pope and his counsellors thought that the other party would give them more concessions than Photius. We do not know what Theognostos was promising. He presented a protest and an appeal in the name of Ignatius. This appeal has been preserved, and it is clear that he presented the whole matter with much bias and injustice. Moreover we can find evidence to prove that this appeal had been fabricated by Theognostos in Rome, and that Ignatius, even after his condemnation in 861, had not appealed to the Pope. Unfortunately Theognostos was listened to, and Photius was deposed and excommunicated.

The Pope was probably convinced that he was defending the just cause of an unjustly deposed bishop. He had no idea of the real situation in Byzantium. What was Photius's answer ? The Emperor answered the Pope in a very hostile letter,[9] but the Patriarch's attitude was very dignified. There came no answer to Rome. The Patriarch deeply regretted that he had not been believed, but the life of his Church went on as usual. The Pope was surprised at this silence, and there are some indications that he was considering a compromise, despite the strong expressions used by Rome and the Emperor. The defection of the Bulgarians from Constantinople to Rome (866) definitely spoilt everything and made a conciliation impossible. It was a terrible blow to the Byzantines: their national pride was offended, and the security of the Empire seemed to be endangered. Here it seems that Photius went too far, when in a new synod (867) he publicly accused Pope Nicholas and broke off relations with him.

This council is always quoted as irrefutable proof that Photius attacked the institution of the Papacy and condemned the whole Western Church. We must not, however, be too hasty to judge. First of all, let us not forget that we do not possess the Acts of this synod and that we have almost no information as to what was said and decided. We possess only the encyclical letter addressed by Photius to the Eastern patriarchs. If we compare this letter with other documents mentioning the council of 867, we come to the conclusion that Photius was speaking not of the Western Church as a whole, but only

[9] Unfortunately the letter has not been preserved for posterity. We can, however, reconstruct its most important features from the Pope's long answer to the Emperor's missive. There we can read a very important passage which has completely escaped the attention of specialists. The Pope says to the Emperor: " You may say that as regards the case of Ignatius it was not necessary to address the Apostolic See because Ignatius had not been involved in any kind of heretical error " (*Mon. Germaniae Hist.*, Epist. VI, p. 469: *Sed dicitis fortasse non fuisse in causa Ignatii sedem apostolicam convocare necesse, quia non hunc ullus hereseos error involverat*). If the Pope is here quoting a passage from the Emperor's letter—which is not absolutely evident—we read here a ninth century Byzantine definition of the Primacy.

of the Frankish missionaries preaching in Bulgaria who were suspected by the Greeks of holding heretical opinions.

I have the impression that the council and all the noisy demonstrations were designed to frighten the Bulgarian ruler—the Khagan Boris—and warn him against missionaries who were preaching heresy or at least very strange and suspect doctrines.

Even when he condemned Pope Nicholas, Photius was attacking only the person of the Pope and not the institution of the Papacy itself. Even if we consider that Photius went too far and here made his first great mistake, we must confess that there is some difference between the actual facts as they happened in Constantinople and the interpretation that has been put upon them.

I cannot dwell here on other details of Photius's history, important for our subject. I am discussing them fully and at length in my book dealing with the History and Legend of the Photian schism, which has been finished since 1939 and is only awaiting the opportunity to be published. In it I am adducing absolute evidence of the genuineness of the Acts of the so-called Photian Council held in Constantinople in 879—880, which confirmed the reconciliation of Photius with Rome and cancelled the council of 869—870. Photius has falsified nothing, and even the last two sessions of the Photian Council—whose authenticity has frequently been questioned—are genuine. I have been fortunate enough to find in London a Greek manuscript containing an unknown writing of an author of the early tenth century who, when quoting the last two sessions, uses the same text as has been preserved to us. Photius cannot even be accused of falsifying the Pope's letters, which were read to the Fathers of the 879—880 council in another edition, as we can read them in Pope John VIII's register. I hope I have found a plausible explanation of this difference. In any case, it can be proved that the Pope knew that his letters had been altered and, in the end, accepted, however reluctantly, those changes. Photius, then, was not such an impostor and falsifier as he has been represented as being by some scholars.

All I wanted to do to-day was to show you that even the attitude of Photius and his followers towards the Papacy has been misinterpreted in modern times. Photius accepted the institution of the Papacy as his Church accepted it. Although he defended the rights of his Church and its independence in disciplinary matters, he recognised the *ius appellationis*, the right of appeal to the Roman See, and his followers made use of it.

Ignatius was as fierce a defender of his Church's rights as Photius. We must not forget that the council of 869—870, called the eighth oecumenical, was in many ways a failure for the Papacy. Only thirteen bishops were present at the beginning, and the so-called "*libelli*", declarations on the Roman supremacy signed by the bishops, were so unpopular that the new Emperor Basil had first to order the legates' Greek butler to steal them, and when he had to give them back he very cleverly made an arrangement with the Slavonic pirates of Dalmatia, who robbed the legates on their way to Rome and destroyed the acts of the council and the *libelli*. Only the pontificial librarian,

Anastasius, who acted as ambassador of the Western Emperor in Constantinople in 870 saved his copy of the acts and the text of the *libelli*. So it came about that these acts have been preserved until now.

Ignatius had the same ideas about Bulgaria as Photius. When the Bulgarians came over from Rome to Constantinople (870), Ignatius ordained an archbishop and bishops for them and sent Greek missionaries to Bulgaria who expelled the Latin priests. He was on the point of being excommunicated by the Pope when he died. He had a very narrow escape.

No, the Byzantine Church was not willing to surrender its liberty and give the Popes more concessions than were officially given by Photius during the council of 861. These concessions are, I think, very important and fully acknowledge the essence of the Primacy. It is high time to take them into fuller consideration.

We can conclude that the Photian episode offers us very valuable material which has been neglected so far by theologians and historians. It is very significant that in the ninth century when the first big clash occurred between the West and the East and when the first important claims of the medieval Papacy were formulated, we find in the documents relating to this clash, the very basis on which not only the Eastern and the Roman Church, but also all Christian churches could meet and reaffirm their unity.

Thus why could not Photius, canonised by the Eastern Church in the tenth century[10] when East and West were united and canonisations were not reserved to the Popes, be regarded, not as the Father of all schism, but as the future Patron of Reunion ?

[10] *Cf.* what the Assumptionist Father M. Jugie says on the cult of Photius in the tenth century in his *Theologia dogmatica* of the Eastern Churches (Paris, 1926, Vol. I, p. 684).

IV

PHOTIUS ET LA RÉORGANISATION DE L'ACADÉMIE PATRIARCALE

I. L'École théologique de Constantinople avant Photius.

L'histoire des écoles byzantines d'enseignement supérieur, négligée et restée obscure pendant longtemps, a bénéficié des recherches faites en ces dernières années par des hommes compétents [1]. Un des résultats les plus importants de ces études a été de fournir la preuve de l'existence à Constantinople de deux institutions d'éducation supérieure : une école officielle destinée à l'instruction des fonctionnaires impériaux et une faculté de théologie pour la formation du clergé.

Les deux institutions reprenaient une vieille tradition remontant à la période hellénistique. Elle avait été inaugurée par Ptolémée Sôter (323-285 avant J.-C.). Celui-ci, sous l'inspiration du rhéteur et philosophe athénien Démétrius de Phalère, créa à Alexandrie une grande bibliothèque et groupa autour de lui des écrivains et des philosophes venus de tous les points de la Grèce. Le musée qu'il leur fit construire ressemblait à beaucoup d'égards à une Académie ou à une Université moderne. Cette fondation fut enrichie par les soins des successeurs de Ptolémée Sôter, Ptolémée Philadelphe (285-247) et Ptolémée Évergète (247-222). Des centres analogues surgirent plus tard à Rhodes et en Syrie. Quand Alexandrie fut tombée au pouvoir de Rome, l'exemple donné par les Ptolémées

[1] A consulter surtout : F. Fuchs, *Die höheren Schulen von Konstantinopel im Mittelalter* (= *Byzantinisches Archiv*, Heft 8, Leipzig, 1926), où l'on trouvera une bibliographie un peu périmée. Des études plus récentes ont été publiées par L. Bréhier : *Notes sur l'histoire de l'enseignement supérieur à Constantinople*, dans *Byzantion*, t. III (1926), p. 73-94 ; t. IV (1927-1928), p. 13-28 ; *L'enseignement classique et l'enseignement religieux à Byzance*, dans *Revue d'Histoire et de Philosophie religieuses*, t. XXI (1941), p. 34-69.

exerça un attrait sur plusieurs des nouveaux souverains : César accorda droit de cité romaine aux professeurs des arts libéraux ; Vespasien fonda à Rome des chaires de latin et de grec ; Antonin le Pieux s'intéressa aux bourses dans les provinces et Marc-Aurèle fonda l'École supérieure d'Athènes.

Cet exemple fut également suivi par les municipalités. Au moment de l'accession de Constantinople au rang de résidence impériale, toutes les grandes villes de l'Empire pouvaient se vanter de posséder une école supérieure, entretenue aux frais de la cité. Évidemment, la capitale ne pouvait pas rester sans la sienne, qui fut fondée par Constantin le Grand, puis enrichie et agrandie par son fils Constance. Thémistius, dans un de ses discours [1], ne ménageait pas les louanges à l'empereur pour ce qu'il avait fait en vue de promouvoir la vie intellectuelle de la nouvelle Rome. Ses paroles ne peuvent guère s'entendre que de la création d'une bibliothèque et des encouragements prodigués à la science. Cette bibliothèque et ces savants devaient faire partie d'une institution centrale qui serait la nouvelle Université impériale de Constantinople. De fait, son existence à Byzance vers 360 est confirmée par S. Jérôme [2], ainsi que par le Code Théodosien, qui nous apprend comment l'École fut réorganisée par Théodose II en 425 [3].

La fondation de l'École théologique prend, elle aussi, la suite d'une ancienne tradition, établie par le premier grand centre d'études chrétiennes d'Alexandrie. Il fallait s'attendre à voir chaque siège épiscopal de quelque renom s'intéresser à l'éducation du clergé et à l'instruction des catéchumènes possédant une certaine culture païenne. Ce fut le rôle important joué par l'Orient hellénistique dans le domaine des connaissances qui permit aux écoles théologiques nées de l'enseignement du catéchisme à Alexandrie, Antioche, Édesse et Nisibe, d'éclipser les institutions de l'Occident. Ici, Rome venait en tête, grâce entre autres au prestige de S. Justin, qui y avait donné son enseignement vers l'an 165.

Le premier, Clément, chef de l'École théologique d'Alexandrie, entreprit de mettre toute la sagesse grecque au service de la pensée

[1] *Oratio IV*, 59 D - 61 B, éd. DINDORF, p. 71-73.

[2] *Chronica*, dans *P. L.*, t. XXVII, col. 503 ; dans le Corpus de Berlin (*G. C. S.*), *Eusebius Werke*, t. VII, 1, p. 241.

[3] *Theodosiani Libri XVI...*, éd. Th. MOMMSEN, t. I, 2 (Berlin, 1905), p. 787.

théologique chrétienne. Cette tradition alexandrine survécut et fut imitée par d'autres centres de connaissances chrétiennes. Voilà pourquoi, pendant la période qui suit, une si grande part fut faite, dans l'enseignement théologique oriental, aux connaissances philosophiques grecques et à l'étude de la grammaire et de la rhétorique.

Quand les évêques de Byzance se rendirent indépendants d'Héraclée, ils reprirent la tradition, et une école théologique s'ouvrit à Constantinople ; mais le rôle principal resta, pendant un temps considérable, entre les mains d'Alexandrie, suivie de près par Antioche, Édesse et Nisibe. Byzance ne put se flatter de rivaliser avec ces centres de théologie, et Nestorius se plaignait du manque d'instruction parmi le clergé de Constantinople [1]. L'École romaine elle aussi semble avoir passé par des difficultés. Lorsqu'en 535 Cassiodore discuta avec le pape Agapet de la nécessité, à Rome, d'une école pour l'interprétation de l'Écriture sainte, il proposa l'exemple d'Alexandrie et celui de l'École de Nisibe, qui florissait encore à cette époque-là [2]. Il ne semble pas, d'après cela, que l'École patriarcale de Constantinople ait joui d'une grande réputation : Cassiodore n'aurait pas manqué d'en parler, s'il en avait su quelque chose. D'ailleurs, il n'y a pas un mot au sujet de l'École patriarcale dans la législation de Justinien, lequel portait cependant un vif intérêt à l'Université impériale et encourageait surtout les études juridiques à Constantinople [3]. Ce qui ne veut pas dire qu'il n'existât pas encore d'École patriarcale. Nous pouvons seulement conclure, d'après la tradition de l'Église, que l'éducation du clergé était l'affaire des évêques et que l'empereur ne pouvait légiférer en une matière qui ne le regardait qu'indirectement. Cette tradition fut soulignée au concile dit Quinisexte (692), dont le canon 64 interdisait aux laïques d'enseigner officiellement la théologie, cet enseignement étant réservé au clergé [4]. Ce canon peut servir de preuve indirecte de l'existence d'une École patriarcale indépendante à Constantinople. Nous apprenons d'une part par les Con-

[1] Cf. Fuchs, op. c., p. 39.

[2] *De Institutione Divinarum Litterarum*, *P. L.*, t. LXX, col. 1105.

[3] Constitution « Omnem », *Corpus Iuris civilis*, t. I (1928), p. 10-12. Cf. Kübler, dans Pauly-Wissowa, *Real-Encycklopädie*, Zweite Reihe, t. I, 1, col. 400-404, i. v. Rechtsunterricht.

[4] Cf. *P. G.*, t. CXXXVII, col. 736, avec l'explication de Balsamon.

stitutions de Théodose II et de Justinien que l'Université impériale ne comportait pas de chaire de théologie; ce n'était pas d'usage dans l'Église. Mais, le canon précité déclarant que l'enseignement de la théologie était réservé au clergé, il doit y avoir eu à Constantinople une autre École où cette instruction était donnée.

Il est naturel de penser que peu à peu, et surtout après la conquête de l'Égypte par les Perses et les Arabes, Constantinople aura fini par détrôner Alexandrie de sa préséance dans la chrétienté orientale et que l'École théologique de la capitale se sera relevée en conséquence. Mais le manque de sources nous empêche de suivre cette évolution. Il faut attendre la première moitié du VIIe siècle pour trouver les premières indications du rôle joué par le patriarche dans l'éducation byzantine.

Théophylacte Simocattès nous a laissé un passage intéressant dans le prologue de son travail historique. D'après lui, le patriarche Serge (610-638) se distingua dans le renouveau que connurent les sciences philosophiques et historiques à Constantinople. Jusqu'ici, le passage a été interprété comme si le patriarche avait réorganisé l'Université [1]. Mais ceci n'est pas admissible, si on examine le texte d'un peu près.

Dans sa préface, Simocattès introduit la Philosophie dialoguant avec l'Histoire. La Philosophie parle [2] : « Je voudrais vous demander, ma fille, par où et comment vous êtes naguère revenue à la vie... Vous étiez morte depuis longtemps, mon enfant, depuis qu'avait fait irruption dans le palais impérial le tyran Calydonius, bardé de fer, un homme à moitié barbare et descendant des Cyclopes... Moi-même, j'étais exilée du portique impérial, ma fille, et je ne pouvais aller en Attique, puisque Anytus de Thrace avait tué mon roi Socrate. Plus tard, des Héraclides me sauvèrent, me rendirent ma souveraineté et purifièrent le palais de toute souillure; en plus, ils rétablirent ma demeure dans l'enceinte sacrée des empereurs. Mes paroles résonnent dans le palais et j'y chante de nouveau les mêmes chants attiques anciens. Voilà comment tout s'est arrangé pour moi. Mais vous, ma fille, qui donc vous a délivrée et comment?» L'Histoire : « Ne connaissez-vous donc pas, ô Reine,

[1] Fuchs, op. c., p. 9.
[2] Theophylacti Simocattae *Historiae*, éd. de Boor, p. 20-21.

le grand archiprêtre qui préside à toute l'Oikouménè ? » La Philosophie : « Mais oui, je le connais. Il est mon très vieil ami et mon trésor le plus cher. » L'Histoire : « Eh bien ! ô Reine, voilà précisément la bonne aubaine dont vous vous enquériez. C'est lui qui m'a ranimée, me faisant pour ainsi dire sortir de la tombe de l'*ἀλογία* et me remettant sur pied avec la force d'un Hercule, libérateur du mal. Il m'a adoptée avec magnanimité, revêtue d'une robe magnifique et ornée d'un collier en or. Cet homme vénérable a aussi paré d'une cigale d'or et fait resplendir de la manière que vous voyez mes cheveux noués au sommet de ma tête. Il m'a gentiment offert une tribune dressée et la liberté de parler sans crainte. » La Philosophie : « J'admire, ma fille, l'esprit sublime de cet évêque et la hauteur à laquelle ses grandes actions l'ont élevé. Il s'est installé tout au sommet de la connaissance théologique, il est monté jusqu'au faîte des vertus pour y établir sa demeure. »

Cela ne signifie pas que Simocattès attribuait au patriarche Serge la restauration de l'Université impériale sous Héraclius (610-641). Au contraire, nonobstant son langage fleuri, l'historien l'attribue clairement à l'empereur [1]. Et ce qu'il dit ne peut s'entendre que de l'Université. Cette institution paraît avoir connu des revers sous Phocas (602-610), sans toutefois que nous puissions parler d'une suppression complète. L'historien marque surtout le bannissement de la Philosophie de la résidence impériale — la Basilica —, où l'École semble avoir été transférée en quittant le Capitole [2].

On comprend que Phocas, homme sans instruction et que beaucoup considéraient comme un intrus et un tyran, n'ait pas été populaire parmi les intellectuels byzantins et que lui-même ne se soit pas fié trop aux professeurs de l'Université chargés de former les fonctionnaires impériaux. Il les exclut de son entourage et ne leur prodigua pas ses faveurs. Mais la suppression totale d'une institution aussi importante pour l'administration aurait par trop renié le passé. Même pour un homme de son caractère, une telle mesure eût été inconcevable, et il ne se serait pas exposé ainsi au danger de perdre sa position. Théophylacte Simocattès, comme on en peut juger d'après sa description, n'aimait pas Phocas, et il faut faire la part de l'exagération.

[1] Qu'on se rappelle le mot *Ἡρακλεῖδαι* employé par la Philosophie pour désigner ses sauveteurs.

[2] Cf. Fuchs, op. c., p. 8.

Quand Héraclius eut mis fin au régime désastreux de Phocas, une de ses premières réformes fut la rénovation totale de l'Université, qui se vit alors logée dans la Basilica. A l'empereur seul en revient tout l'honneur ; le patriarche n'y fut pour rien [1].

A proprement parler, on ne peut tirer du dialogue de Simocattès aucune conclusion quant à la prétendue part prise par Serge dans le rétablissement des études à Constantinople au VIIe siècle. Tout ce qui est certain, c'est que Serge encouragea Théophylacte à écrire l'histoire de Maurice, prédécesseur de Phocas, et qu'il l'aida matériellement et moralement dans son travail. Il eût été impossible d'écrire un livre de ce genre sous le règne de Phocas. L'Histoire était morte, selon le langage pittoresque de Théophylacte, et elle fut ressuscitée par les encouragements du patriarche.

L'Histoire le loue de lui avoir assuré une tribune stable. Ceci veut-il dire que Simocattès obtint, par l'intermédiaire de Serge, une place à l'Université ou à l'École patriarcale? Le passage est trop vague pour qu'on puisse en décider. La carrière de Simocattès à l'administration avait été, sinon brillante, du moins honorable ; mais, n'étant pas clerc, il pouvait difficilement briguer un poste à l'École patriarcale. Il est plus probable que l'auteur n'a présente à l'esprit que l'aide matérielle qu'il reçut du patriarche.

Il est possible que le nom du recteur de l'Académie patriarcale au temps de Serge nous soit parvenu. Sous Héraclius vivait à Alexandrie un fameux professeur de philosophie et commentateur d'Aristote, du nom d'Étienne [2]. Dans les manuscrits de ses travaux il est appelé, non seulement *μέγας διδάσκαλος* et *καθολικὸς διδάσκαλος*, mais encore *οἰκουμενικὸς διδάσκαλος*. Comme nous verrons plus loin, ce dernier titre fut réservé, depuis le IXe siècle, au recteur de l'Académie patriarcale. Il est vrai aussi que certains professeurs de l'École de Droit à Beyrouth étaient appelés, au IXe siècle, *τῆς οἰκουμένης διδάσκαλοι* [3], et dans ce cas, le titre n'aurait aucune signification ecclésiastique, ne marquant que l'universalité de leur enseignement. Ce qui s'appliquerait également à *οἰκουμενικὸς διδάσκαλος*. Le philosophe Étienne ne serait dès lors qu'un professeur à Alexandrie renommé pour son savoir.

[1] Contrairement à ce que prétend Fuchs, op. c., p. 9.

[2] Cf. la monographie de H. Usener, *De Stephano Alexandrino*, Bonn, 1880.

[3] Cf. COLLINET, *Histoire de l'École de Droit de Beyrouth* (Paris, 1925), pp. 124 et suiv., 167-175.

D'un autre côté, le titre de « maître œcuménique » a une saveur ecclésiastique, et il fut souvent octroyé à S. Basile, que Théodoret de Cyr appelait *διδάσκαλος* et *φωστὴρ τῆς οἰκουμένης* [1], à S. Grégoire de Nazianze et à S. Jean Chrysostome [2]. Au début du IXe siècle, Naucratius [3] l'applique à son maître, S. Théodore Studite. Cela montre que le titre était décerné aux « docteurs de l'Église ». Et celui qui était responsable à Byzance de l'enseignement de la bonne doctrine devait être le recteur de l'Académie patriarcale. Dès la seconde moitié du Ve siècle, le patriarche de Constantinople se faisait appeler « patriarche œcuménique » (Simocattès en témoigne), et cet exemple peut avoir contribué à faire réserver le titre de « maître œcuménique », qui voulait dire d'abord maître de connaissances universelles, au recteur de l'École patriarcale. Cette évolution aurait été achevée au commencement du VIIe siècle, lorsque le patriarche Serge appela Étienne et lui confia la direction de l'École.

Si l'exemple d'Étienne n'est pas suffisamment probant, il en est un autre, de date postérieure. Georges Choiroboskos, commentateur des Psaumes, avant la première moitié du VIIIe siècle, diacre, grammairien et chartophylax, et qui donnait des cours sur des problèmes grammaticaux, s'appelait *οἰκουμενικὸς διδάσκαλος*. Il s'occupait aussi de matières philologiques, ce pourquoi on crut qu'il professait à l'Université impériale ; et parce qu'il portait le titre de chartophylax, il passait pour avoir été en charge des archives et de la bibliothèque [4].

Mais ces raisons ne sont pas valables. L'office de chartophylax, pour autant que nous le sachions, était purement ecclésiastique et ne pouvait être rempli que par un diacre, comme l'était Georges Choiroboskos. Rien ne prouve que le bibliothécaire de l'Université fût appelé chartophylax ; mais il est certain que plus tard le titre appartenait à un haut fonctionnaire du patriarcat [5], qui représentait le patriarche à certaines grandes solennités. Le fait que Georges était chargé d'un cours de grammaire ne s'opposait pas à ce qu'il

[1] *Hist. Eccl.*, l. IV, c. 16, *P. G.*, t. LXXXII, col. 1160 et suiv.

[2] Cf. *Ὡρολόγιον τὸ μέγα*, éd. B. Kutlumusianos (Venise, 1895), p. 277.

[3] *De obitu Theodori Studitae* (*BHG.* 1756), *P. G.*, t. XCIX, col. 97.

[4] K. Krumbacher, *Geschichte der byzantinischen Litteratur*, p. 583.

[5] Voyez, sur l'évolution de cet office, mon livre *Les légendes de Constantin et de Méthode vues de Byzance* (Prague, 1933), pp. 49-57, 61-67.

fût en même temps membre de l'Académie patriarcale. Les cours à cet institut n'étaient pas exclusivement d'ordre théologique, comme nous le verrons plus en détail ; ils comprenaient la philosophie, la grammaire et la rhétorique. Les commentaires grammaticaux de Choiroboskos sur les Psaumes sont un exemple unique de la littérature exégétique de Byzance. D'après cela, rien ne l'empêchait de donner des cours d'Écriture sainte. Plus tard, ce fut le privilège du recteur de l'Académie patriarcale, l'*οἰκουμενικὸς διδάσκαλος*. On peut donc conclure que dans la seconde moitié du VIIe siècle, l'époque la plus probable de Georges Choiroboskos, Constantinople était en possession d'une Académie patriarcale dirigée par un professeur œcuménique.

Ce qui confirme ma conclusion, c'est que, vers 1080, Nicétas d'Héraclée [1] obtint le titre de professeur œcuménique, lui qui professait la grammaire et l'exégèse tout comme Georges Choiroboskos. C'est donc que le recteur de l'Académie patriarcale avait la chaire d'interprétation de l'Écriture sainte, surtout des Évangiles, la partie la plus importante de l'enseignement théologique [2].

Ensuite, il y a de nouveau manque d'indications sur l'Académie jusqu'au VIIIe siècle. Nous lisons dans la Vie du patriarche S. Germain (715-730) [3] et dans la Chronique de Georges le Moine [4] qu'il existait alors à Constantinople une École supérieure avec douze professeurs sous un « professeur œcuménique » (*οἰκουμενικὸς διδάσκαλος*). Le biographe de Germain est prodigue de détails au sujet de cette école. D'après lui, les professeurs étaient souvent consultés par l'empereur à propos d'affaires d'état. Leurs élèves occupaientdes postes élevés dans l'Église et l'administration. Quand

[1] Cf. J. Sickenberger, *Die Lukaskatene des Niketas von Heraklea*, dans *Texte und Untersuchungen*, N. F., t. VII, 4 (1902), p. 6.

[2] D'autres preuves sont données par Fuchs, op. c., p. 36 : un professeur œcuménique se trouve parmi les correspondants de Tzetzès. Dans le ms. de l'Escurial y - π - 10 sont conservés les noms de trois professeurs œcuméniques : Michel de Thessalonique, Schizénos et Léon Balianitès, tous appartenant à la seconde moitié du XIIe siècle.

[3] *BHG*. 697, éd. Papadopoulos-Kerameus, dans *Anecdota Hellenica* (Constantinople, 1884), p. 3-17 ; rééditée par F. Fuchs, *Die oekumenische Akademie von Konstantinopel im frühen Mittelalter*, dans *Bayerische Blätter für das Gymnasialschulwesen*, t. LIX (1923), p. 177-192.

[4] *Georgii Monachi Chronicon*, éd. de Boor, t. II, p. 742.

Léon l'Isaurien décida de supprimer le culte des images, il tâcha de gagner à ses vues les professeurs ; n'y réussissant pas, il donna ordre de brûler les bâtiments de l'école, avec les professeurs et la riche bibliothèque.

L'analyse de ces rapports faite par L. Bréhier [1] a relégué parmi les légendes cette histoire, qui avait obtenu quelque crédit. Georges le Moine était un de ces *zelanti* qui se plaisaient à exagérer les accusations contre le premier empereur iconoclaste, et ses renseignements doivent être pris avec un grain de sel. Il écrivait un siècle après les événements et, si les chroniques postérieures lui ont emprunté leurs informations, celles-ci n'en deviennent pas plus véridiques. L'autre source, la Vie de Germain, est une compilation basée sur des chroniques précédentes, dont celle de Georges le Moine.

On peut cependant en dégager une conclusion. Le premier empereur iconoclaste, Léon III, s'occupa sans aucun doute, jusqu'à un certain point, des écoles supérieures de Constantinople. Ceci peut s'induire du rapport laconique de S. Théophane le Chronographe, qui fait preuve de plus de sens critique que le zélé Georges le Moine. Il dit simplement que Léon III « éteignit les écoles et l'enseignement pieux qui y avait prévalu depuis le temps de S. Constantin le Grand jusqu'à nos jours » [2]. Ces paroles manquent de précision, mais elles sont assez claires.

Le chroniqueur parle de suppression d'écoles. Probablement entend-il dire par là, songeant aux deux genres d'instruction donnée à l'Université et à l'Académie, que l'intervention de l'empereur se borna à écarter les éléments anti-iconoclastes et à réformer dans ce sens les deux institutions. « L'enseignement pieux » ne peut être que l'instruction dans la doctrine orthodoxe sur le culte des images, qui de fait fut supprimée. En rapportant cela, le chroniqueur n'exagérait pas.

[1] *La Légende de Léon l'Isaurien*, dans *Byzantion*, t. IV (1927-1928), p. 13-28. Cf. aussi son étude plus récente : *L'enseignement classique*, l. c., p. 47.

[2] *Theophanis Chronographia*, éd. C. de Boor, t. I, p. 405 : *ὥστε καὶ τὰ παιδευτήρια σβεσθῆναι καὶ τὴν εὐσεβῆ παίδευσιν τὴν ἀπὸ τοῦ ἐν ἁγίοις Κωνσταντίνου τοῦ Μεγάλου καὶ μέχρι νῦν κρατήσασαν, ἧς ... καθαιρέτης ... Λέων γέγονεν*. Cf. la traduction d'Anastase, ibid., t. II, p. 261 : ... *ut etiam eruditionum scholas et piam eruditionem a sanctae memoriae Constantino magno hucusque servatam extingueret.*

Il n'exagérait guère plus en accusant l'empereur d'avoir supprimé les écoles. L'éloignement du corps professoral équivaut à une suppression, bien qu'il ne s'agisse pas d'une extinction complète : les iconoclastes n'auraient pu se passer de ces deux institutions nécessaires à la formation de leurs employés, n'eût-ce été que pour s'assurer des adhérents à leur politique religieuse et un clergé d'opinion iconoclaste.

De fait, le Continuateur de Théophane [1] semble partager cette opinion sur l'interprétation de Théophane. Il dit que, sous le règne de Théophile (829-842), le dernier empereur iconoclaste, le nom de l'*οἰκουμενικὸς διδάσκαλος* Ignace fut gravé sur le portique du Sigma, une partie du palais construite par Théophile. Au IXᵉ siècle, quand la chronique fut écrite, pareil titre ne convenait qu'au recteur de l'Académie patriarcale. Georges le Moine et le biographe de S. Germain parlent aussi d'un « professeur œcuméniqne », qui dirigeait le collège des douze professeurs de sciences profanes et religieuses. Évidemment, les deux auteurs confondent l'Université impériale avec l'Académie patriarcale, mais leur « professeur œcuménique » ne peut s'appliquer qu'à l'institution ecclésiastique. Donc, d'après le Continuateur, cette Académie existait sous Théophile, mais elle était iconoclaste. Fut-elle restaurée par Théophile seul ? Il n'y a aucune raison de le croire, bien que cet empereur soit connu pour avoir favorisé les sciences. S'il a trouvé l'Académie utile à sa politique religieuse, pourquoi n'en irait-il pas de même pour les autres empereurs iconoclastes et pour Léon III qu'on accuse d'avoir exterminé toute science à Constantinople ?

Ce qui peut avoir induit en erreur Georges le Moine et le biographe de S. Germain et les aura amenés à confondre les deux écoles, c'est le fait que l'École patriarcale ne se bornait pas à l'enseignement théologique. Toutes les sciences philosophiques y étaient en honneur, à titre de préparation à la théologie, bien que moins peut-être qu'à l'Université. Georges le Moine n'était certainement pas favorable à ce système d'instruction, et c'est sans doute pourquoi son rapport, outre sa légende des professeurs brûlés vifs, est si vague à propos de l'organisation de l'École. Il admet cependant que les douze professeurs de l'École œcuménique enseignaient « la science théologique et profane ».

[1] Éd. de Bonn, p. 143 ; *P. G.*, t. CIX, col. 157.

Le caractère universel de l'enseignement à l'Académie patriarcale peut donc être considéré comme établi, ne fût-ce que sur la base de ce rapport. Il est difficile de savoir si les professeurs étaient toujours limités au nombre de douze, comme le disent Georges le Moine et ses continuateurs. L'auteur des *Patria Constantinopoleos* [1], qui écrivait en 955 et usait de sources largement dépendantes de Georges le Moine, comptait seize professeurs à l'École œcuménique, tous moines. Ici, un nouveau fléchissement dans la tradition : l'École patriarcale est confondue avec l'Université impériale et avec les écoles monastiques. Or, ni l'Académie ni l'Université n'admettaient des moines dans leur corps professoral.

La tradition au sujet des douze professeurs a cependant quelque fondement. Elle reparaît au XIIe siècle sous la plume de l'archevêque d'Havelberg, Anselme [2] ; celui-ci, dans l'introduction de son dialogue avec Nicétas, métropolitain de Nicomédie, note que son adversaire dans les discussions sur la réunion des Églises était le premier des douze professeurs qui, d'après la coutume grecque, dirigent les études des arts libéraux et de l'Écriture. On connaît la prédilection des Byzantins pour le nombre douze, celui des Apôtres [3]. Nous n'avons pas d'autres preuves à l'appui de cette tradition des douze professeurs, mais nous ne pouvons pas l'éliminer complètement.

Après la restauration du culte des images, l'Académie fut certainement débarrassée de ses éléments iconoclastes pour redevenir l'établissement où « le pieux enseignement avait prévalu depuis le temps de S. Constantin le Grand » jusqu'aux jours de Léon III. Le nouveau patriarche, S. Méthode, ne pouvait manquer de s'intéresser à l'École, car lui-même était fort instruit et pour cette raison fort estimé du dernier empereur iconoclaste. Méthode pouvait compter sur l'influence du premier ministre de Théodora, le logothète Théoctiste, un homme cultivé, qui tenait à ce que l'Université se maintînt au niveau que Théophile lui avait assuré [4]. A preuve,

[1] Éd. PREGER, *Scriptores originum CP.* (Leipzig, 1901-1907), p. 226.

[2] *P. L.*, t. CLXXXVIII, col. 1141.

[3] Cf. FUCHS, op. c., p. 17.

[4] Sur le rôle de Théoctiste dans la réorganisation de l'enseignement byzantin, voir mon étude : *La carrière universitaire de Constantin le Philosophe*, dans *Byzantinoslavica*, t. III (1931), p. 59-67. Voir aussi mes *Légendes de Constantin et de Méthode...*, p. 39 et suiv.

ce qui arriva au métropolitain de Thessalonique, Léon le Mathématicien. Celui-ci dut quitter son siège, mais, étant réputé pour sa science, fut nommé professeur à l'Université, en dépit du parti des zélés qui réclamaient des mesures plus sévères contre les iconoclastes. On peut ajouter que Méthode reconnaissait l'importance de la philosophie, de la grammaire et de la rhétorique et que ces branches étaient enseignées à l'Académie en préparation à la prêtrise.

Mais son successeur S. Ignace fut peut-être d'une autre opinion. D'après Anastase, bibliothécaire du Siège Romain, Ignace ne croyait pas aux sciences profanes [1]. Les *zelanti* son tsans doute excusables d'avoir méprisé le caractère profane de ces sciences, surtout à cause de la faveur que leur avait témoignée le dernier empereur iconoclaste [2]. Leurs écrits sont pleins de remarques peu flatteuses pour les grammairiens qui se bernent de mots, la verbosité d'Homère, les mensonges des rhéteurs, les dangers de la doctrine des philosophes païens et la vanité des sciences profanes [3]. Toute notre information montre que, sous Ignace, le parti des zélés gagnait du terrain au patriarcat et que, même avant que Bardas se fût débarrassé de Théoctiste en 856, Ignace et Théodora tombèrent sous l'influence des extrémistes [4].

Il en résulta que l'enseignement profane à l'École patriarcale subit une éclipse sous le premier patriarcat d'Ignace, surtout pendant sa seconde moitié, quand les extrémistes prirent le dessus au palais et à l'archevêché. C'était inévitable. Il suffit de parcourir les écrits des zélés de l'époque pour se convaincre qu'une fois maîtres au patriarcheion, ils devaient réclamer la suppression des études profanes comme préparation à la théologie. On peut donc conclure que, sous le patriarcat d'Ignace, l'enseignement de la philosophie, de la grammaire et de la rhétorique fut, sinon supprimé, du moins fortement réduit, à l'Académie patriarcale.

[1] Voir l'introduction d'Anastase à sa traduction des Actes du concile ignatien de 869-870, dans Mansi, t. XVI, col. 5.

[2] Comparer mon livre récent : *The Photian Schism. History and Legend* (Cambridge, 1949), p. 18 et suiv.

[3] Pour le détail, voir mon livre : *Les Légendes de Constantin et de Méthode...*, p. 27 et suiv.

[4] Voir le premier chapitre de mon livre sur *The Photian Schism.*

II. Le rôle de Photius.

Sous Photius, le parti modéré, dirigé par le régent Bardas et l'évêque de Syracuse, Asbestas, reconquit son influence au patriarcheion. Ses meilleurs représentants encourageaient l'enseignement profane. Bardas le montra en réorganisant, probablement après 863, l'Université impériale, qu'il enrichit et installa dans de meilleurs quartiers, au palais de Magnaura. Photius, lui, précédemment professeur à l'Université, inspira aux deux rivaux, Théoctiste et Bardas, de rétablir les études et l'enseignement à Byzance. Il fallait donc s'attendre à ce qu'il s'intéressât à l'Académie patriarcale, surtout à l'enseignement de la philosophie et aux études préparatoires à la théologie.

L'incident de 859 lui manifesta la nécessité d'une réforme radicale parmi le clergé et les moines. Les zélés se révoltèrent contre lui et tâchèrent de mêler le nom du vénérable Ignace à leur querelle. Il ne fallut pas moins d'un an pour déjouer leurs intrigues et les rendre inoffensifs. Mais le gouvernement et le patriarche s'aperçurent bien que le mal était sérieux. Dans l'entretemps, le radicalisme des zélés, violemment opposé aux vieux iconoclastes, était fortement critiqué et se faisait taxer d'étroitesse par les intellectuels. Puis les anciens abus qui avaient contribué à l'explosion de l'iconoclasme s'insinuèrent de nouveau dans la vie monastique à la faveur de la protection dont jouissaient les zélés au patriarcheion ; Byzance était menacée d'un retour de l'hérésie, qui était loin d'avoir été anéantie. Il n'y avait qu'un remède : la condamnation de l'erreur, la réforme monastique et l'extirpation du zélotisme parmi les rangs du clergé ; ce pourrait être l'œuvre d'un concile général [1].

Malheureusement, le pape Nicolas Ier se méprit sur la situation à Constantinople ; il ne s'intéressait qu'aux circonstances de la démission d'Ignace. Grâce à l'habileté des Byzantins à trouver un compromis, les légats pontificaux, satisfaits d'avoir obtenu la concession de juger un patriarche au nom du pape, consentirent à juger le patriarche sur place sans en référer au pontife. L'incident une fois clos, le concile qui se réunit en l'église des Saints-Apôtres pro-

[1] On trouvera les détails dans mon *Photian Schism*, p. 67 et suiv.

céda à la condamnation de l'iconoclasme et à la réforme du monachisme. Le concile tint sa première séance en janvier 861. Ce ne fut qu'après le concile que Photius s'appliqua à exécuter ses plans de réforme, en commençant par l'Académie patriarcale.

Sur ces entrefaites, un nouveau champ d'expansion s'ouvrit à l'Église byzantine. En 860, l'attaque des Russes contre Constantinople força les Byzantins à se mettre en bons termes avec les Khazars, qui régnaient alors sur le sud de la Russie moderne et étaient voisins de nations peu connues. L'ambassade khazare, dirigée par un élève de Photius, Constantin-Cyrille, et par son frère Méthode, ouvrit les yeux des Byzantins sur les possibilités politiques, culturelles et religieuses, parmi toutes ces nations gouvernées par les Khazars. Il suffit de lire le compte rendu de cette mission dans la Vie de S. Constantin-Cyrille pour s'en convaincre [1]. Le patriarche Photius, non plus que Bardas ni le jeune Michel III, n'était homme à laisser échapper cette chance. Et cette expansion n'eût jamais été possible sans une bonne réserve de missionnaires dûment instruits.

En même temps, il fallait un clergé bien averti pour résister à la propagande des zélés, et Photius eut à s'occuper de son Académie patriarcale. Un bref passage de la Vie de Constantin-Cyrille implique que Photius effectua la réforme de l'École. Dans le chapitre XIV nous lisons que « quand le philosophe (Constantin) retourna (en 861) à la cité impériale, il se reposa tranquillement après avoir vu l'empereur, priant Dieu, assis dans l'église des Saints-Apôtres [2] ». Pour se rendre compte de l'importance de ce passage, il faut se rappeler que Constantin-Cyrille était un des personnages les plus en vue de la renaissance culturelle à Byzance, au IXe siècle. Il fut d'abord le favori de Théoctiste, qui lui offrit sa fille adoptive en mariage. Comme le philosophe refusait de se faire une carrière administrative et mondaine, Théoctiste le persuada d'accepter le poste de chartophylax au patriarcheion. Bientôt Constantin, voyant que cette charge ne lui convenait pas, prit la place de Photius à l'Université, où il donna des cours de philosophie.

Quand son protecteur et ami fut assassiné par Bardas, Constantin-Cyrille, par crainte de représailles contre lui-même et ses amis,

[1] Voir la traduction française de la vieille légende slavonne dans l'Appendice de mon livre *Les Légendes de Constantin...*, p. 359-371.

[2] Texte dans *Fontes Rerum Bohemicarum*, t. I (Prague, 1865), p. 26 : *v tsrkvi svętikh apostolov siedę*.

abandonna son poste et rejoignit son frère Méthode pour se réfugier dans un monastère du mont Olympe en Asie Mineure. Mais les deux frères se réconcilièrent avec le régime, probablement sur l'intervention de Photius, et acceptèrent une mission importante chez les Khazars.

Au retour de cette mission, il eût été naturel que Cyrille reprît son poste à l'Université au lieu d'aller s'asseoir dans une église qui ne se trouvait même pas à proximité du palais où l'Université était abritée. Avait-il accepté un poste à l'église? Il n'était que diacre et avait été chartophylax à l'église patriarcale. Il aurait donc dû occuper un emploi semblable à Sainte-Sophie. Mais, d'après le biographe, il était « assis dans l'église des Saints-Apôtres », ce qui, dans la langue des documents byzantins, signifie toujours la fonction de l'enseignement.

Il enseignait donc en l'église des Saints-Apôtres, un office qui ne peut avoir été institué que par le patriarche comme partie de l'École patriarcale. Car l'Université, après la restauration de Bardas, obtint de nouveaux quartiers au Magnaura, non pas dans l'église des Apôtres. Allons plus loin, et voyons dans cette institution une des réformes entreprises par Photius en vue de la formation du clergé.

Ce n'est pas tout. Comme Constantin-Cyrille, appelé le philosophe, avait conquis ce titre à l'Université impériale et y donnait des cours dans sa matière avant 856, il est probable qu'il donna les mêmes cours à l'École de Photius. D'ailleurs, le patriarche désirait introduire dans son programme théologique la discipline philosophique que son prédécesseur avait négligée.

Nous trouvons à une époque postérieure des analogies qui peuvent étayer notre conclusion. Après la fin du XIe siècle et depuis le XIIe, on rencontre pour la première fois dans les sources la distinction stricte entre le recteur de l'Université, l'*ὕπατος τῶν φιλοσόφων*, et le recteur de l'Académie patriarcale, l'*οἰκουμενικὸς διδάσκαλος*, ainsi qu'entre les deux institutions [1]. On y apprend aussi que l'Académie possédait, outre son quartier général à l'église Sainte-Sophie [2], plusieurs sections éparpillées dans différentes églises de la

[1] Voir les preuves dans Fuchs, op. c., p. 47. Il s'agit d'un document de 1084-1111, mentionné par B. de Montfaucon dans sa *Bibliotheca Coisliniana*, p. 103.

[2] Mentionné par Constantin Porphyrogénète dans le *De Cerimoniis*, éd. de Bonn, t. I, p. 157.

ville. Les données les plus amples visent l'école près de l'église Sainte-Marie à Chalkopratia, au nord de Sainte-Sophie. Nous connaissons plusieurs grammairiens de cette école : Pierre le *πρώξιμος* (XIe siècle), Nicétas d'Héraclée, de la même époque, et Eustathe, du XIIIe siècle. Nous connaissons aussi, au XIe siècle, un *μαΐστωρ* de cette école, auquel Christophe de Mytilène fit la dédicace d'un poème ; un autre figure dans la correspondance de Psellos [1]. Cet établissement doit avoir existé dès le Xe siècle, mais probablement pas plus tôt, puisque Constantin Porphyrogénète ne le signale pas dans cette église [2]. Les termes *μαΐστωρ* et *πρώξιμος* désignent le recteur et le vice-recteur de l'école.

Un autre genre de collège faisant partie de l'Académie patriarcale est attesté comme ayant existé dans l'église Saint-Pierre, très près de Sainte-Sophie, et dans l'église Saint-Théodore, fondée par Sphorakios. Son *πρώξιμος* Eustrate prit part au procès contre Jean l'Italien en 1082. Dans le *Forum Tauri*, il y avait un autre collège près de l'église Sainte-Marie Diaconissa.

Toutes ces écoles dépendaient du patriarche et les professeurs étaient promus de l'une à l'autre. On sait que Nicétas d'Héraclée enseigna d'abord la grammaire à l'école de Chalkopratia. Il semble donc que cette dernière était affectée à l'enseignement de la grammaire, de la rhétorique et de la philosophie, ou à l'*ἐγκύκλιος παιδεία*, l'instruction générale. De là Nicétas reçut sa promotion pour l'école Saint-Pierre, qui faisait probablement partie du quartier général de l'Académie. Ce fut là qu'il rédigea ses commentaires sur S. Luc, ce qui prouve bien qu'il interprétait les Évangiles. Cela veut dire qu'une partie de la théologie se donnait à Saint-Pierre, dépendance de Sainte-Sophie. La correspondance de Psellos [3] nous apprend également que le recteur (*μαΐστωρ*) du collège Sainte-Marie Diaconissa demanda au patriarche de le nommer professeur à Saint-Pierre. Ceci confirme notre supposition que cette école était plus en vue comme faisant partie de la section centrale de l'Aca-

1 Pour les preuves, voir FUCHS, op. c., p. 48 et suiv. Il n'y a rien dans les sources citées par Fuchs qui indique que l'école patriarcale changeât souvent de quartier. L. Bréhier, *L'enseignement classique*, p. 48, a raison de corriger Fuchs sur ce point. Il ne peut être question que de différents collèges ou filiales de la même École patriarcale.

2 *De Cerimoniis*, éd. de Bonn, t. I, p. 167.

3 SATHAS, *Bibliotheca Medii Aevi*, t. V, p. 420.

démie où s'enseignait la théologie. On comprend ainsi pourquoi Nicétas, une fois promu au professorat à Saint-Pierre, devint du coup *οἰκουμενικὸς διδάσκαλος* ou recteur de l'Académie patriarcale.

Cette analogie avec le XIe et le XIIe siècle rend probable qu'en 861 Photius établit une branche de l'Académie dans l'église des Saints-Apôtres et qu'il y installa les chaires de philosophie, de grammaire et de rhétorique. Il n'est pas même nécessaire de supposer que Photius inaugura quelque chose de neuf et qu'il créa une tradition qui n'existait pas avant lui et ne se développa que durant les siècles suivants, comme nous l'avons vu. Une tradition semblable doit avoir existé plus tôt. Rappelons la suppression de l'école de Chalkopratia par Léon III. Si les documents sont étudiés sous cet angle, notre supposition que le premier empereur iconoclaste ne supprima ni l'Université ni l'Académie devient plus logique, et leurs termes, tout confus qu'ils soient, deviennent plus compréhensibles. Il est possible que Léon III supprima une des branches de l'Académie, et que ce fait fut généralisé par ses adversaires. Une autre preuve de l'existence, pendant la période iconoclaste, d'une branche de l'Académie dans l'église Saint-Théodore fondée par Sphorakios nous est fournie par l'auteur anonyme de la Vie de Léon l'Arménien. Il dit qu'Antoine-Kasymatas, le théologien le plus éminent de l'iconoclasme, fut professeur à cette école avant de devenir évêque de Syléon [1].

Mais l'analogie la plus probante en faveur de la fondation par Photius d'une école patriarcale aux Saints-Apôtres provient du rapport de Mésaritès [2] sur une école qui existait dans cette église au XIIe siècle. Le premier éditeur de Mésaritès, Heisenberg, a mal compris ce document. Son opinion au sujet de cette école, qu'il identifie avec l'Université impériale, laquelle était sous l'influence du patriarche Jean Camatéros et du clergé, opinion partagée par F. Fuchs [3], manque de fondement. En réalité, c'était une école patriarcale, une branche de l'Académie, où se donnait l'enseignement supérieur, l'*ἐγκύκλιος παιδεία*.

[1] *Incerti auctoris Vita Leonis Armeni*, dans Leo Grammaticus, éd. de Bonn, p. 350. Il semble avoir donné des cours de droit.

[2] Une seconde édition de Mésaritès avec commentaires sera publiée bientôt par G. Downey, professeur à Harvard University (Dumbarton Oaks).

[3] Bréhier, *L'enseignement classique*, p. 55, fait bien de corriger cette opinion qu'il avait acceptée précédemment dans *Byzantion*, t. III (1926), p. 77.

Nous ne savons pas si cette école constitue une nouvelle fondation ou une simple réorganisation de l'école fondée par Photius. Nous n'avons pas de renseignement sur son existence aux xe et xie siècles, mais ceci se comprendrait, puisque les informations sur l'évolution de l'École patriarcale à d'autres époques sont très restreintes. Il paraît probable que la tradition commencée par Photius en 861 avait survécu pendant la période suivante et fut ressuscitée par le patriarche Camatéros.

Nous pouvons donc attribuer à Photius une place considérable dans la réforme de l'Académie patriarcale et de la formation du clergé byzantin en général. Nous pouvons aussi ajouter un détail important à la carrière de S. Constantin-Cyrille, le futur apôtre des Slaves et une des figures les plus intéressantes de la renaissance culturelle de Byzance au ixe siècle. Ses relations avec son maître et ami Photius ont été longtemps présentées dans une fausse lumière, étant donné qu'il était impossible de supposer qu'un si saint homme pût être l'ami de Photius, que la légende avait dénigré. Maintenant que la tradition légendaire de Photius a été démasquée, il est possible de se faire une idée plus exacte de la grandeur de ces deux hommes. Ce détail complète aussi notre connaissance de l'histoire de l'église des Saints-Apôtres, la seconde, par ordre d'importance, de Constantinople. On ne s'étonnera plus que Photius ait fait de cette École la dépendance principale de l'Académie ecclésiastique et y ait installé le centre de l'enseignement des sciences profanes, pour réserver la théologie à l'École de Sainte-Sophie.

Washington.

V

THE PATRIARCH PHOTIUS AND ICONOCLASM

SO far it has been generally believed that the iconoclastic heresy was slowly dying out during the reign of Theophilus and that it was definitely liquidated in 843 when the Empress Theodora restored image worship. The fact that the Byzantine Church had instituted the feast of orthodoxy commemorating this event contributed to the spread of this belief.

When, however, we study in a more detailed way the circumstances in which image worship was restored, we find some occurrences which make us hesitate to accept the established opinion that iconoclasm was in evident decline when Theodora restored icon worship and that there was no further danger of a new iconoclastic outburst in Byzantium.

There is first the attitude of Theodora. We are surprised to learn from some accounts that she hesitated for more than a year to take the decisive step. This information comes from reports of the event found in all three historians – Simeon the Logothete, Genesius, and the Continuator of Theophanes.[1] Simeon the Logothete ascribes all the merit for the reëstablishment of orthodoxy to Theoctistos, whom the dying Emperor appointed co-regent with Theodora, and who occupied the high post of the logothete of the drome – the title of the Byzantine minister of intelligence and of foreign affairs. The two other historians praise the Magister Manuel, Theodora's uncle, as the true restorer of the images. The Continuator of Theophanes lists also Theoctistos and Bardas among Theodora's advisers. According to this author, Manuel held the title of Magister. He was an Armenian by birth and uncle of the Empress. Genesius calls Manuel proto-Magister and mentions only Theoctistos in addition to him.

The reports concerning the role played by Manuel are not clear. Simeon the Logothete mentions a Magister Manuel who served under the last two iconoclastic emperors, Michael II and Theophilus, and who died in 838.[2] If this Manuel was promoted by the Continuator of Theophanes and by Genesius to a restorer of icon worship, then their information is incorrect.

Another important source – the biography of Saint David and his companions Saints Simeon and George[3] – does not mention Manuel among Theodora's advisers. Instead of Magister Manuel, he speaks of Sergius of Niketia. This information seems more reliable than that given by the Con-

[1] Simeon the Logothete, Bonn, p. 647; the Continuator of Theophanes, Bonn, p. 148; Genesius, Bonn, p. 77.

[2] Bonn, p. 636.

[3] Van den Gheyn, "Acta Graeca SS. Davidis, Symeonis et Georgii Mytilenae in insula Lesbo," *Analecta Bollandiana*, XVIII (1899), 243 sq.

tinuator of Theophanes and by Genesius. According to the Synaxary of Constantinople,[4] the memory of a Magister Sergius, founder of a monastery in the Gulf of Nicomedia, was celebrated on June 28. Unfortunately, there is no direct evidence that the Sergius of the Synaxary should be identified with the Sergius mentioned in the biography. On the other hand, it should be stressed that Sergius of the Synaxary was also a native from Niketia and that he is called Theodora's relative.

H. Grégoire,[5] who studied this problem quite thoroughly, proposed an ingenious explanation of the puzzle. He identified the Sergius mentioned by the biographer with the Magister Sergius listed in the Synaxary. Sergius' place in the restoration of image worship – so he argued – seems to have been taken in the later tradition by the iconoclast Magister Manuel, who was also the founder of a monastery in Constantinople. The monks of this monastery promoted their iconoclastic founder who died in 838 to a champion of image worship. This adjusted tradition was picked up by later writers – Genesius and the Continuator of Theophanes.

There is again no direct evidence supporting this daring explanation. We should, however, point out that, according to the Continuator of Theophanes, his hero Manuel was an iconoclast and was converted to the true faith by the monks of Studion who promised him recovery from a dangerous malady should he abandon his error. Manuel recovered and became a fervent defender of image worship. This story bears a legendary trait, a circumstance which weakens the author's reliability in this particular case and which strengthens the probability of H. Grégoire's thesis. Grégoire's explanation, in spite of lack of direct evidence, can thus be accepted as a reasonable hypothesis.

H. Grégoire volunteered further the opinion that this Sergius is no other than Photius' brother. This seems, a priori, not impossible. We know that Photius' family was related to the imperial house and that Photius had addressed several letters to "his brother Sergius." It is true that the Synaxary does not mention Sergius' relationship to Photius. This difficulty could be perhaps waved away by the assertion that the Synaxary was composed under Leo the Wise and that Photius was not in great favor with Leo, who had forced him to abdicate the patriarchal dignity.

There is, however, another objection to the identification of the Synaxary's Sergius with Photius' brother. We know from Photius' letter to the

[4] A. S. (*Propylaeum ad A. S. Novembris*), p. 777.

[5] "Études sur le neuvième siècle," *Byzantion*, VIII (1933), 517 sq., 530 sq. Cf. also H. Grégoire's remark in A. A. Vasiliev, H. Grégoire, H. Canard, *Byzance et les Arabes*, I (Bruxelles, 1935), 191 sq.

deacon George [6] that he himself, his father, and his uncle were anathematized by the iconoclasts. The circumstance that Photius does not mention his brother in this connection militates strongly against the above supposition. Moreover, if Photius' brother had played an important role in the reëstablishment of orthodoxy, he would have been much older than Photius. This does not seem to have been the case.

Then there is another difficulty. The Synaxary discloses that the Magister Sergius was chosen by the Emperor Michael to lead an expedition against Crete, which was then in Arab hands. He died there and was buried in a church on the coast. His body was transferred later to the monastery he had founded. Michael III made an expedition against Crete in 866. We do not know, however, whether the story given by the Synaxary could be reconciled with the events which had taken place in 866. H. Grégoire was well aware of this difficulty, and on another occasion [7] he dated the expedition against Crete, mentioned in the Synaxary, from the year 843. It was Theoctistos who was the initiator of this expedition. This, however, does not contradict the version we read in the Synaxary. Michael, although a boy six or seven years old, was the rightful emperor and Theoctistos was acting in his stead. This new dating seems to be the correct one.

If this is so, then the person mentioned in the biography and in the Synaxary cannot be Photius' brother Sergius. Could he, however, be Photius' "uncle," mentioned by him in his letter to the monk George? Such a supposition is quite plausible, although we again cannot produce any direct evidence for this identification.[8] If this interpretation is true, then the merits of Photius' family in the restoration of image worship were considerable.

One thing is established from all the above statements, namely, that Theodora had to be encouraged by her advisers not to fear to make the decisive step. The biographer of Saint David and his companions Saints Simeon and George gives the most details in this respect. He enumerates, besides Sergius, Theodora's brothers Bardas and Petronas and the Logothete Theoctistos as particularly active in favor of the reëstablishment of orthodoxy. These men are said to have convinced the Empress that it would be safe enough to take the big plunge and to change the religious policy of her husband. It was a kind of family council. The preoccupation of Theodora and her relatives was to secure the interests of the dynasty. Because the Empress could count on the sympathies of the worshippers of images, Theo-

[6] *Photii Epistolae, II, epist.* LXIV, *P.G.*, vol. 102, col. 877.

[7] See H. Grégoire's footnote in *Byzance et les Arabes*, p. 195.

[8] It should be pointed out that Simeon the Logothete says that Photius' father's name was Sergius (Bonn, p. 668). This does not exclude the possibility that another relative of Photius whom he calls "uncle" bore the same name as his father.

dora's hesitations can be explained only by her fear of a new iconoclastic reaction which could become fatal to her and her young son Michael III. The influence of the iconoclasts was still great and their strength was far from broken. The regency knew it and therefore proceeded with the utmost caution.

This is also demonstrated by the way in which the Empress treated the iconoclastic Patriarch John (called also Ἰαννής). The same historical document – the life of Saints Simeon, David, and George [9] – gives us some interesting details concerning the iconoclastic patriarch, details which illustrate the situation in Byzantium before the proclamation of Orthodoxy. We learn from the biographer that the heretical patriarch continued to be in office for more than a year after Theodora had assumed the regency. He is said also to have distributed money among the clergy in order to secure their support for himself and for his religious teaching. On his proposition, a religious discussion on image worship was held in the imperial palace. The representative of the orthodox party in this discussion was the monk Methodius, the future patriarch. Of course, he was proclaimed victorious over the heretic John. The Patriarch is said to have asked also for a private discussion with the monk Simeon in the presence of the Empress. There are some legendary traits in the biographer's account. But one thing is clear: that the Patriarch John was in office for all this time and that he did all he could for the defense of his iconoclastic views.

We learn further from this source that when Theodora had made the decision to establish orthodoxy, everything was done according to canonical prescriptions. After the public discussion, a local council was convoked, and we are authorized to suppose that, before its convocation, the Patriarch was invited to attend it. He refused to abandon his religious opinion. He was therefore deposed by the council, and the monk Methodius elected in his stead. Instead of banishing the iconoclastic ex-patriarch to an island or to Asia Minor, Theodora let him live quietly, probably in his own property, called Psicha,[10] near the monastery in Kleidion not far from Constantinople, on the European side of the Bosporus.

Then there is the condition laid down by Theodora before she gave her consent to the reëstablishment of orthodoxy: that the memory of her husband would not be condemned. It is true that Theodora was a pious lady

[9] Van den Gheyn, *op. cit.*, pp. 245 sq. Cf. J. B. Bury, *A History of the Eastern Roman Empire* (London, 1912), pp. 143 sq.

[10] This information is given by the Continuator of Theophanes (Bonn, p. 151), and it should be preferred to that given by Simeon the Logothete and by the Continuator of George the Monk (Bonn, pp. 649, 811). Cf. Bury, *op. cit.*, pp. 151 sq. and my book, *Les Légendes de Constantin et de Méthode vues de Byzance* (Prague, 1933), pp. 71 sq.

who had loved her husband dearly. This reason could be regarded as sufficient and satisfactory to explain her attitude. But there may have been other considerations. Theodora and her councilors might have feared that a public anathematization of the memory of the late Emperor Theophilus, who was worshipped by the iconoclasts and was in great esteem also among the orthodox, would exasperate his followers, who were still numerous and could endanger the position of the Empress. We know that there was a party of intransigent monks who insisted on the anathematization of Theophilus' memory. The Continuator of Theophanes [11] depicts in vivid colors a very dramatic incident which happened during the banquet the Empress had organized in honor of the monks who had suffered persecution during the iconoclastic controversy. Two of the heroes – Theodorus and Theophanes – stood up and declared that they would call Theodora's husband before the tribunal of God for the wounds he had inflicted on them. Their confrère Simeon [12] is said to have particularly opposed Theodora's plea for her husband's memory, and to have thrown the money offered to him by the Empress, allegedly as the Emperor's legacy, into the face of the Empress with the angry words: "To perdition with him and his money." The intervention of Sergius and all the other most important men of the government – Theoctistos, Bardas, and Petronas – was necessary to break the zealot's opposition. Mollified by the insistence of so many important personages and by the intercession of some of his confrères, Simeon yielded, and then he remembered that the late Emperor had appeared to him, in a dream, of course, and begged humbly, "Good monk, have pity upon me." [13]

In order to calm the orthodox zealots, rumors were spread among the people that the late Emperor had repented before his death. Later a legend developed that Theophilus' name miraculously was erased from the list of iconoclastic heretics laid on an altar by the Patriarch Methodius.[14] All these stories show that Theodora must have had very serious reasons when making such conditions for the reëstablishment of orthodoxy. It was not only her love for her husband but also her desire not to hurt unnecessarily the feelings of the iconoclasts which induced her to do so.

The policy of the regency was to lessen the danger of a new iconoclastic reaction by lenient treatment of the iconoclasts and to bring back to orthodoxy at least the moderate heretics. Because of that policy, Methodius, who had found protection at the court of Theophilus, thanks to his erudition,

[11] Theoph. Contin., IV, ch. 11, Bonn, pp. 160 sq. Cf. my book, *Les Slaves, Byzance et Rome au IXe siècle* (Paris, 1926), p. 127.

[12] Van den Gheyn, *op. cit.*, p. 245.

[13] Van den Gheyn, *op. cit.*, pp. 246 sq.

[14] See, for details, Bury, *op. cit.*, pp. 149 sq.

was selected for the patriarchal office, although there were many candidates for the honor among the extremists who thought that they had greater merit and had fought better against iconoclasm than had Methodius.[15] The bishops and the clergy who professed their repentance of the heresy and who had not been ordained by an iconoclastic bishop were simply left in their posts. A particularly striking example of this liberal policy was the case of Leo the Mathematician, Archbishop of Thessalonica. As Leo had naturally been ordained by iconoclast prelates, he was replaced by an orthodox bishop, but because he was one of the most prominent scholars of the period, he got the important post of professor of philosophy at the Imperial University. It seems that Leo rather welcomed the change he was making, because he was, at heart, a scholar and preferred scholarly work to the episcopal office.

I have shown in my book on the Photian schism [16] that the new Patriarch Methodius studiously avoided appointing as bishops men of extremist views, knowing well that the radical measures against the heretics, advocated by the zealots, would only strengthen their resistance and increase the danger of a new iconoclastic reaction. The regency and the Patriarch wanted to bring about a peaceful liquidation of the heresy because they knew that iconoclastic sympathizers were still many.

The main inspirer of this policy was most probably the Logothete Theoctistos, who himself had been an iconoclast. He had faithfully served the late Emperor Theophilus, and belonged most probably to the moderate party among the iconoclasts. Since he was intimately associated with the Emperor, he must have known the real strength of the iconoclasts. His example was certainly followed by many moderate iconoclasts, and he knew that only a liberal policy towards the heretics could avoid new complications.

But this policy was severely criticized by the extremists, who found leaders among the monks of the famous monastery of Studion. In spite of this, Methodius persisted in his policy, and, when his opponents became too noisy in their criticism of the regularly established hierarchy, he refused to give them any concession but, on the contrary, went so far as to excommunicate them. This again seems to be rather puzzling. It would not have been difficult to appease this opposition by appointing some of its members to higher ecclesiastical posts. Some of them had manifested great courage during the iconoclastic persecution, and deserved a promotion after the reëstablishment of orthodoxy. If Methodius preferred the danger of a schism among the orthodox to the change of his ecclesiastical policy concerning the iconoclasts, he must have had very serious reasons for his attitude. He was

[15] I discussed it in detail in my book, *Les Slaves*, pp. 128 sq.
[16] *The Photian Schism, History and Legend* (London, 1949), pp. 13 sq.

not a petty man who would take offense at some criticism, nor was he an autocratic and harsh man; on the contrary, he is known for his mildness and liberal views. I see only one reason for his surprising decision in the affair of the monks of Studion – his fear of a new iconoclastic reaction, should the advocates of strong measures against the heretics win their cause. He could read the lesson of history. He knew what happened during the reign of Michael I, who left too much influence to the zealous monks of Studion and was not discreet enough in his orthodox propaganda.[17] A violent iconoclastic reaction followed, Michael was dethroned, and Leo V the Armenian was proclaimed Emperor. Methodius was determined to preclude the possibility of a new iconoclastic reaction.

It is probable that Methodius would have been fully successful and would have broken the opposition of the extremist monks, had he lived longer. But he died June 14, 847, after having been Patriarch for only four years. His death placed the regency in a very difficult situation. There was a schism in the Church, the most ardent defenders of image worship, the monks of Studion and their supporters having been excommunicated. The extremists were agitating among clergy and people, and the moderates were insisting on the necessity of continuing Methodius' religious policy. Theodora did not dare convoke the local synod, which, according to the eastern custom, should elect a patriarch and recommend him to the regency for confirmation. She was afraid of new agitations and complications. She therefore made use of the right of the emperors to appoint bishops, a right which was always basically recognized, although the canonical procedure of election by a local synod was preferred and mostly in use. She elevated to the patriarchal throne the son of the orthodox Emperor Michael I, Nicetas – now the monk Ignatius.[18] This choice was evidently meant as a concession to the extremists, but because Ignatius had not been involved in the controversy between Methodius and the Studites, it was hoped that he would be acceptable also to the defenders of the moderate policy.

The new Patriarch proved, however, that he was, basically, a partisan of the extremists' views, and the latter soon became masters of church affairs. The moderates, led by Asbestas, bishop of Syracuse, being disappointed, called Ignatius a parricide,[19] thus signifying that he had abandoned the tactics of his predecessor Methodius whom he should have venerated as his father. We know the sad result of this controversy. Ignatius, who after his

[17] Cf. my book *Les Slaves*, pp. 37 sq. Cf. my book, *The Photian Schism*, pp. 12, 68.

[18] For details on Ignatius' nomination without the usual canonical procedure, see my book, *The Photian Schism*, p. 81.

[19] Anastasius' introduction to his translation of the Acts of the Ignatian synod of 869–870 (Mansi, XVI, cols. 2, 3). Cf. my book, *The Photian Schism*, pp. 23 sq.

enthronization had recalled into the Church the excommunicated extremists, launched, at their instigation, a sentence of excommunication against the leaders of the moderates.

The position of the extremists in the Church and in the State was strengthened further by the political evolution. Theoctistos soon got a dangerous rival in the person of Theodora's brother Bardas. The latter was, so it seems, afraid that Theoctistos might become another Staurakios, the main adviser of the Empress Irene, who had also restored image worship. Bardas was apprehensive lest Theoctistos induce Theodora to put aside the young Emperor Michael III just as Irene had deposed her son Constantine VI.[20] Since Bardas and Michael had most of their sympathizers among the moderates, Theoctistos was forced, for political reasons, to look for support among the extremists. The latter thus became the dominant party in the Church and in the State. Theodora herself, by her natural inclination, was fond of the pious, extremist monks, and so it came about that a situation arose in Byzantium similar to that which had existed under the reign of the orthodox Emperor Michael I. Many open-minded men looked at this evolution with apprehensions, fearing new complications with the iconoclasts, more or less sincerely converted, who disliked the growing influence of the monks and the unrelenting policy of the new Patriarch.

Unfortunately, we have no direct indications concerning the former iconoclasts and the reactions which the new policy provoked among them. All contemporary writers were interested only in the conflict between Bardas and Theoctistos and the consequences which resulted from it: the assassination of Theoctistos, the relegation of Theodora to a convent, the assumption of the government by Michael III and Bardas, the abdication of Ignatius, and the election of Photius as Patriarch.

It would be pointless to go into details and to describe how the extremists, although they had also recognized Photius as the legitimate Patriarch, had revolted against him and had declared Ignatius again as the legitimate head of the Byzantine Church. A detailed discussion of all those upheavals will be found in my book on the Photian schism.[21] There is, however, one thing which should be particularly stressed and which is directly connected with the problem we are studying here. The rebellious attitude of the extremists had been condemned by Photius in two local synods in 859. The first of these assembled in the Church of the Holy Apostles and, when this assembly had been dissolved because of an open revolt of the zealots, the second met

[20] Cf. J. B. Bury, *A History of the Later Roman Empire*, II (London, 1889), 480 sq. Also Bury, *A History of the Eastern Roman Empire*, pp. 1 sq.

[21] Pages 39 sq.

in the Church of Blachernae. The Emperor Michael III then sent a solemn embassy to Rome, asking the Pope to dispatch legates to Constantinople to a council which should once more publicly condemn the iconoclastic heresy. Unfortunately, the imperial letter sent to the Pope is lost. We are in possession only of the synodical letter of the Patriarch which was forwarded to the Pope by the same embassy, and which naturally does not mention the convocation of the synod, because this was strictly a matter which concerned the emperor alone.[22] We can reconstruct, however, the main points of Michael's letter from the answer to the Emperor's missive sent by the Pope.[23] The Pope outlined in his letter the Catholic doctrine on images which indicates that this matter must have been stressed particularly in the Emperor's message.

The fact that the Emperor really requested the Pope to send legates to the council which should be convoked in Constantinople for the purpose of a final condemnation of the iconoclastic heresy is furthermore attested by the *Synodicum Vetus*,[24] a treatise on councils composed by a contemporary Ignatian supporter. It is also attested by the Papal Librarian Anastasius in the part of the *Liber Pontificalis* [25] describing the life of the Pope Nicolas.

Of course, both authors claim that this was only a pretext and that the real purpose of the Emperor and of Photius was to get, by this subterfuge, a new condemnation of Ignatius with the connivance of the papal legates. This interpretation was accepted by most of the historians. I think I have succeeded in showing in my book on the Photian schism [26] that this interpretation is biased, and that for the Byzantines the case of Ignatius was definitely settled in the two local synods mentioned above. The Emperor never thought of a new, more solemn condemnation of Ignatius. The affair of Ignatius was discussed and judged during the new council only because the Pope wanted it, and, as a concession to the Byzantine point of view, the legates had to pronounce the definite judgment in Constantinople before reporting to the Pope.

Why then did Michael III want to have a new condemnation of iconoclasm in 861? Only because the heresy was still rampant in Byzantium and because the regime of the zealot monks during the patriarchate of Ignatius made a new iconoclastic reaction a possibility. It is a pity that the Acts of the Council of 861 were destroyed by the order of the Ignatian synod of

[22] *Photii Epistolae*, I, *ep.* 1, *P.G.*, vol. 102, cols. 585 sq.

[23] *Mon. German. Hist.*, *Epistolae*, VI, pp. 433 sq.

[24] Published by J. Pappe in J. A. Fabricius and G. C. Harles, *Bibliotheca Graeca*, XII (Hamburg, 1809), 417, 418.

[25] Ed. L. Duchesne (Paris, 1886, 1892), II, 154 sq.

[26] Pages 70 sq.

869–870. We have only a Latin extract of the first part of the Acts containing the minutes of the process made against Ignatius. It is preserved in the Collection of Canon Law written by Cardinal Deusdedit in the eleventh century.[27] Unfortunately, the copyist who made these extracts from the Latin translation of the Acts kept in the Archives of the Lateran was not at all interested in the iconoclastic controversy, and, therefore, he did not copy a single sentence from the second part of the Acts.

We have only the text of seventeen canons, voted by the Council at the end of its sessions, which have been preserved because of their importance in Byzantine canon law.[28] This is our only directive if we want to guess, at least in most general lines, what was the subject of conciliar discussions or what were the main reasons for the fears that an iconoclastic reaction was not impossible.

It is a remarkable thing that the first seven canons voted by the synod deal with various problems which concern the monastic life. This can be taken as an indication of the main subject of the conciliar deliberations. Some wordings of the canons betray, moreover, that the Council was trying to remove abuses which must have crept into monastic institutions only recently.

For example, the first canon starts with the words: "The building of monasteries which is such a sublime and honorable practice and which was, in the old days, so well regulated by our holy and blessed fathers, is done wrongly in our days." Then the canon describes how rich people transform their houses into monasteries, declaring that they dedicate their property to God, but that, in spite of this dedication, they dispose of the property as if it were still theirs, selling it and giving it to whom they please. Therefore, the Council decreed that in the future a monastic foundation could be made only with the permission of a bishop. The property given to a monastery was to be surrendered to him, and a detailed record of it was to be deposited in the episcopal archives.

The second canon deals with an abuse which is a logical consequence of the practice condemned in the first canon. Some people become monks only to share the honors and privileges of the monastic vocation. After they have been invested with the monastic garb, they continue to live in their own houses, without submitting to any monastic discipline and without any monastic superior. This practice was strictly forbidden in the future. The consecration of a monk was allowed only when he consented to be placed under the authority of an abbot legitimately established.

[27] Cf. my book, *The Photian Schism*, pp. 28 sq.
[28] Text in Mansi, *Concil. Ampliss. Collectio*, XVI, cols. 536–49.

These two canons show clearly that, during Ignatius' tenure, the monks had regained the esteem and influence they used to have before the outbreak of the iconoclastic heresy. It was regarded as the greatest honor for a believer to be associated in some way with the monachism and to participate in its honor and privileges. And so the abuses described in the canons crept into the ninth century's monasticism, and spread to a wide extent.

This practice not only discredited this venerable institution in the eyes of many, but it was dangerous also in another respect. Let us remember that the first iconoclastic emperors were trying to reduce the influence of monasticism, not only because monks were the most zealous propagators of image worship, but also for economic reasons. There is enough evidence to show that during the iconoclastic period monastery lands were ruthlessly confiscated. It is also known that Constantine V, especially, discouraged rich people from retiring to monasteries at the end of their careers or from bequeathing their properties to ecclesiastical institutions.[29] The abuses which the Photian Council of 861 tried to extirpate existed in pre-iconoclastic days, and gave the iconoclastic emperors welcome pretexts to eradicate such excesses by forceful means.[30] We can imagine that this action of iconoclastic emperors found much applause among the population. It was apparent that many foundations of this kind were made, not so much for religious motives as to get exemptions from various state obligations. The emperors could not tolerate such practices in the interest of the State.

The establishment of orthodoxy in 843 was, of course, a great victory of Byzantine monachism. It was thus to be expected that monasteries would flourish once more. There was a danger that some zealous believers and monks might be tempted to go too far in their enthusiasm for monastic ideals. During the patriarchate of Methodius this danger was lessened by his prudent policy. The monks did not relish this restraint, as we have seen, and they regained their influence under Ignatius. Soon the abuses against which the iconoclastic emperors had fought appeared again. The iconoclasts and the more or less sincere converts viewed the spread of such practices with growing resentment and distaste. Iconoclastic propaganda was finding its best arguments there. Should such a situation continue, the danger of a new iconoclastic reaction would increase. Photius and his supporters saw it and tried to reform monasticism by canonical means.

[29] See, for details, Bury, *A History of the Later Roman Empire*, II, 460 sq. A. A. Vasiliev, "On the Question of Byzantine Feudalism," *Byzantion*, VIII (1933), 598 sq.

[30] It should be remembered that the Seventh Oecumenical Council also paid special attention to the reform of monasticism (Mansi, XIII, cols. 417 sq.; canons XIII, XVIII, XIX, XX, XXI, XXII).

The five following canons voted by the Council of 861 reveal the same tendency. In the third canon the abbots are reminded that their duty is to take good care of the religious progress of their subordinates. The fourth censures those monks who leave their monasteries without permission or take up residence in lay people's houses. The latter practice, the canon states, was allowed in the period of persecution but cannot be tolerated now when the Church lives in peace. The wording of the canon again permits the interpretation that this practice had increased recently and that it may be considered in connection with the abuses censured in the first and second canons. It was natural that the laymen who were transforming their houses into monasteries were anxious to have in their houses a real monk in order to give their new "institutions" a more monastic character.

In order to enforce the first two canons, the Council's fifth canon orders that everyone who has the intention of embracing the monastic life must live under the guidance of an experienced religious man for three years. The sixth canon enforces the obligation of poverty for every monk; candidates must dispose of their property before entering a monastery. The last forbids bishops to found new monasteries and to endow them with revenue from the bishopric.

This is all that was saved from the anti-iconoclastic decrees voted by the Council of 861. It is not much, but it is sufficient to show that eighteen years after the reëstablishment of orthodoxy iconoclasm was not yet completely eradicated and that monastic abuses which had increased during Ignatius' patriarchate had made the danger of an iconoclastic reaction a possibility.

Photius seems to have tried to diminish this danger also in other ways. We have to view the reorganization of the patriarchal academy by Photius [31] in connection with his endeavor to reform the monks. The philosophical training of the future clergy apparently was neglected during Ignatius' patriarchate. Extremist monks were always hostile to the teaching of philosophy. And again this attitude was not relished by the former iconoclasts who still remembered the interest which their last emperor Theophilus used to show in learning. Photius saw it, and the reorganization of the patriarchal academy was his first preoccupation after the conclusion of the conciliar debates. He chose the Church of the Holy Apostles as the seat of the Faculty of Philosophy of his reorganized academy. The dean of the faculty – if such a title may be used – was one of Photius' best disciples, Constantine-Cyril, the future Apostle of the Slavs. The learned Patriarch knew well that only

[31] For details see my study, "Photius et la réorganisation de l'Académie Patriarchal," *Analecta Bollandiana*, LXVIII (1951), 108–125.

a clergy well trained in theology and philosophy would be able to avoid the shallow waters of zealotism and fanaticism which always led to narrow-mindedness and provoked a strong reaction from the opponents.

Let us recall, in this connection, a story which we read in the biography of the same Constantine. In chapter five [32] a charming scene is depicted – a discussion which the young Constantine is said to have had on icon worship about the year 850 with the iconoclastic ex-Patriarch, John the Grammarian. The discussion is presented as a kind of examination. The Emperor is supposed to have said to Constantine, "If you can defeat him, young man, you will get your chair" (of philosophy at the university).

There are, of course, legendary traits in this account. It should be stressed, however, that the biographer was a Slav brought up in Byzantium and that he wrote the Life under the direction of Constantine's brother Methodius. He left Byzantium with the two brothers for Moravia in 862, thus soon after the Council of 861. His interest in the ex-Patriarch John and in iconoclasm shows clearly that this problem was still of lively importance in Byzantium at that period. The Life was written in old Slavonic in Moravia between 873 and 880 most probably. It is characteristic to note how anxious the biographer is to present Constantine as victorious in his disputation with John. He uses this opportunity to refute the main objections of the iconoclasts against the worship of images and of the cross. There was little danger of iconoclasm in Moravia, and the new Slavic converts were not much interested in the Byzantine heresiarch. The biographer sensed, however, although far from his homeland, the tense atmosphere he had breathed in the sixties when he lived in Byzantium. He was, therefore, very anxious to preserve his new converts from any iconoclastic danger because he knew how real this danger was in his time in Byzantium.

A similar attitude was taken by Photius himself when he wrote, about the year 865, his famous long letter to the other Byzantine convert, the Khagan Boris of Bulgaria.[33] The Patriarch reviews for the new Christian ruler, among other things, the decisions of the seven Oecumenical Councils, because they are the basis of the orthodox faith. His account of the Seventh Oecumenical Council, which had condemned iconoclasm, is the longest. The Patriarch takes great care to refute all the objections of the iconoclasts against the pictorial representation of Christ, and against the worship of images and of the cross. His account betrays how much he was preoccupied with the iconoclastic problem in the time when he wrote the letter. Because

[32] See my French translation of the Life in my book, *Les Légendes de Constantin et de Méthode*, pp. 353 sq. It is possible that the Life was composed by Methodius himself.

[33] *Photii Epistolae*, I, *epis.* 8, *P.G.*, vol. 102, cols. 649–56.

the danger of iconoclasm had not yet disappeared in Byzantium, Photius took great pains to preserve his new converts from any such taint.

Only when the main program of Photius' countermeasures against the iconoclastic danger was well on the way could the Patriarch engage in the final stage of the anti-iconoclastic reaction – the decoration of the main churches with mosaics and pictures of the saints. It seems that, in this respect, the Patriarchs Methodius and Ignatius both remained faithful to the policy of discretion. It is surprising to learn from one homily of Photius, pronounced on the occasion of the inauguration of an icon of Our Lady in Hagia Sophia,[34] that this mosaic was the first one solemnly inaugurated in 867, in the presence of the Emperor Michael III and his associate Basil. This fact is rather astonishing. Photius' declaration completely shatters the belief, so far generally accepted, that icons appeared everywhere in Byzantium after the reëstablishment of orthodoxy. It seems that in reality the authorities were rather anxious to go slowly in this matter for fear of provoking a reaction from the iconoclasts.

It appears that not even the measures advocated by Photius had succeeded in countering the iconoclastic danger. In any case, it is surprising to learn that even the Ignatian Council of 869–870, so far called the Eighth Oecumenical Council, found it necessary to condemn iconoclasm once more and to pronounce a new anathema over the heads of some notorious iconoclasts. We find most interesting details illustrating the survival of iconoclasm to that time in the Acts of the eighth conciliar session.[35] The head of the iconoclasts was Theodore Crithinus. He was summoned to appear before the Council, and the order was presented to him by the representative of the Emperor at the Council's meetings, Baanes himself. Theodore ignored the summons, and when he was asked by Baanes why he was ready to venerate the Emperor's picture on coins but refused to venerate Christ's image, the heretical leader said: "You see without any doubt that the coin you showed me reproduces the picture of the Emperor. You ask me to accept and to venerate also the picture of Christ. But I know not if such is Christ's order, and if it would be agreeable to him."

The Latin translation of the Acts made by Anastasius Bibliothecarius is even more explicit on the subject. When the assembly learned that Crithinus had refused to abjure the heresy, the Emperor himself intervened, asking the Council to admit three followers of Crithinus, the cleric Nicetas and two laymen, Theophilus and Theophanes, who evidently had shown their inten-

[34] See my "Lettre à M. H. Grégoire à propos de Michel III," *Byzantion*, X (1935), 5–9.
[35] Mansi, XVI, cols. 139 sq., 388 sq.

tion to abandon the heresy. They were introduced before the assembly, and after they had abjured the heresy and anathematized all heretical patriarchs and Crithinus, the Emperor himself embraced each of them and expressed his satisfaction at their conversion.[36]

One has the impression, when reading this passage of the Acts, that the whole scene was prearranged in order to impress other iconoclasts and to invite them to follow the example of the three converts. Such a public display of imperial favors towards three insignificant men was certainly something exceptional. It shows again that there were still many iconoclasts, and that the Emperor Basil was anxious to win them over to orthodoxy.

But, in spite of the efforts of the Emperor, there were still many who continued to display more or less publicly their hostility to image worship, as is indicated by the wording of the anathemas pronounced by the fathers against the iconoclasts at the end of the eighth session. The anathemas were directed first against the iconoclastic council – "which is still fighting against the holy images" – and against all iconoclastic patriarchs. Then the list continued: "To Paul, who was converted into Saul, and Theodore who was called Gastas, Stephen Molatas and men similar to him, anathema. To Theodore, the unreasonable who pretends to talk reasonably and who is called Crithinus, anathema. To them who still are in doubt [about the cult of images] and are losing their reasoning in their ambiguity and who, engulfed in the darkness of their iniquity, are suspected by some to have reverted [to the heresy], anathema. To Laludius, Leo and to all who think as them, whether they are numbered among bishops, priests, or monks and whatever degree of holy orders they had attained, anathema."

The list of notorious iconoclasts is here considerably longer than in the anathemas of the Seventh Oecumenical Council. One has the impression that Paul "who became a Saul," Theodore Gastas, and Stephen Molatas (Moltes) were prominent heretics who sided with the last iconoclast, the former Patriarch John, and who followed him also in the refusal to abandon the heresy. Since Theodore Crithinus is regarded in 870 as the leader of the iconoclasts, it appears that John the Grammarian was already dead at that time. Laludius and Leo are new names, two prominent partisans of Crithinus. The rest of the wording shows clearly that many conversions were not sincere and that the heresy had still numerous sympathizers among bishops, priests, monks, and laymen. Therefore the Council thought it necessary to renew in the third canon voted at the end an emphatic condemnation of the iconoclastic heresy; to repeat, in the solemn synodical decree, the

[36] *Op. cit.*, col. 142.

main anathemas; and to refute some subtle arguments of the iconoclasts. The Acts of the Ignatian Council make it thus evident that in 870 the heresy was far from suppressed.

The Council of 869–870 was a triumph of the zealous extremists over Photius and the moderates. One could thus expect that now, after a new and energetic condemnation of the heresy, the Ignatians would do everything to decorate the churches with sacred images and mosaics. But again the progress of the redecoration was not as rapid as could have been expected. The fathers of the Ignatian Council were responsible for the delay. Archaeologists and historians interested in this period have overlooked a canon voted by the Council which is of considerable importance for our study. This is what was decreed in the Greek version of canon seven: "It is most useful to create holy and venerable images and to teach men the disciplines of divine and human wisdom. But this should not be done by unworthy men. Therefore we decree that the men who are condemned and separated from the Church by an anathema should neither paint holy images in the churches nor should they teach in any place as long as they do not abandon their error. Therefore if anyone, after the publication of this our decree, would admit them to the painting of holy images in the churches or would give them any opportunity to teach, if he is a cleric, he should be suspended, and if he is a layman, he should be excluded from the Church and deprived of the use of the holy sacraments." [37]

This canon confirms first of all, as we have already indicated, that Photius and his supporters displayed, during his first patriarchate, a remarkable activity in the redecorating of churches with icons. It is thus suggested that Photius had succeeded in gathering around him a number of good artists and that the redecoration of the churches was well on its way, thanks to his initiative. The continuation of this artistic activity was now forbidden to the Photianists. When we remember that Photianists had an overwhelming majority in Byzantium, that Photius' supporters remained for the most part faithful to the exiled Patriarch, and, further, that the Council, because of the attitude of the papal legates, was on the whole unpopular and disappointed even the expectation of Basil I, we are justified in concluding that artistic activity in Byzantium suffered a considerable setback because of the decree forbidding Photianists to participate in the redecoration of churches.[38]

[37] *Ibid.*, cols. 402 sq., 164 (Latin version).

[38] This does not mean that Ignatius did nothing for the decoration of churches with mosaics and icons. One manuscript of George Cedrenus' *Compendium of History* (Bonn, p. 238) attributes the decoration of the Church of Sergius and Bacchus by Basil I to the exhortations of the Patriarch Ignatius.

As I have shown in my book on the Photian schism,[39] the rapprochement between Photius and the Emperor, who was disillusioned by the rigorist attitude of the extremists, started soon. It may be that Basil I had another reason for trying to appease the Photianists and their leader. We have seen that Basil was anxious to promote the liquidation of the iconoclastic heresy. His attitude during the eighth session of the Ignatian Council shows this clearly. It was to be expected that the troubles among the defenders of orthodoxy, now split into two parties – the extremist and the moderate – did not promote the liquidation of iconoclasm. On the contrary, the victory of the extremists over the moderates made their resistance more stubborn. We have to remember that the converts from iconoclasm sided rather with the moderates for reasons which are easy to grasp. All this made the situation more tense and Basil's position more difficult. He could not allow the split among the orthodox to be complicated by a new iconoclastic recrudescence.

It is remarkable that in one of his letters to Photius, then still in exile, but under better conditions, Basil asked the former Patriarch to give him some explanation of theological problems. One of the problems on which Basil wanted to have thorough information was that concerning the main arguments used by the iconoclasts against representing God or Christ by pictures. No one so far had seen God. Therefore, since God is invisible, he cannot be represented in pictures and images. Photius' answer to this question is published in his *Amphilochia*.[40] We know, however, that many pieces of this collection are simply Photius' letters, copied verbally, but without the name of the addressees. B. Laourdas, who is working on a new edition of Photius' letters, to be published by Dumbarton Oaks, Harvard University, found Photius' discussion on this problem in the Manuscript *Iveron* 684, which is a collection of the Patriarchal letters, among the letters addressed to the Emperor Basil, under the following title: "To the great Emperor Basil, when he started writing and when he asked for the solution of some problems."

Photius explains to his imperial correspondent the correct orthodox doctrine in this matter, and demonstrates it by quotations from the Holy Writ and from the Fathers, the guardians of catholic tradition. It is true that Photius does not mention iconoclasm in his exposé, but nevertheless the connection of this problem with iconoclasm is clear. We can deduce from this letter that iconoclastic argumentation preoccupied the Emperor even after the Council of 869–870, and that he missed, in the fight against rampant

[39] Pages 159 sq., 170 sq. (reconciliation with Ignatius).
[40] *Ad Amphilochiam Quaestio CXIX*, *P.G.*, vol. 101, cols. 696 sq.

iconoclasm, the help which the brilliant mind of the former Patriarch could give.

This letter to Basil is posterior to the other two letters which Photius had addressed to him at the beginning of his exile. It might have been written in 872. If so, it shows that Basil started soon to change his mind about Photius. In any case, from 873 on, the former Patriarch was back in Constantinople, in the imperial palace, directing the education of the Emperor's children and, probably, teaching again at Magnaura University. A complete reconciliation between Photius and Ignatius took place not later than 876. From that time on, if not from 873 when Photius was recalled from exile, we may suggest, the decree of the Ignatian Council concerning the artistic activity of the Photianists might have been applied less rigorously. But it was only during the second patriarchate of Photius, from the end of 877 on, that the new Byzantine religious art witnessed a period of flourishing renascence.

Photius remained very much alive to the theological and philosophical problems which were raised by the iconoclasts. We can read in his *Amphilochia* eight other discussions of problems connected with iconoclasm. The fact that Photius comes back so often to those problems is significant in itself and shows how much the Patriarch was preoccupied with the iconoclastic danger. But there is more. As B. Laourdas will show in his edition of Photius' letters, most of those "answers" were written first by Photius to friends who had asked him for advice. Later he included them, without the names of the addressees, in his collection of *Amphilochia*. A comparison of the *Amphilochia* with the oldest manuscript of Photius' letters – the *Baroccianus Graecus* 217, of the first half of the tenth century, a copy of an older manuscript written by one of Arethas' pupils – shows that the letters were addressed to the following men: one letter (*Amph.* 87) to Eyschymon, Archbishop of Caesarea in Cappadocia; three letters (*Amph.* 196, 197, 217) to John Chrysocheris, spatharios and protospatharios; one (*Amph.* 111) to Stephen, probably a convert; one (*Amph.* 205) to the Abbot Theodore; and one (*Amph.* 221) to Constantine the Patrician.

These findings show how much the iconoclastic problem was debated in Byzantium during the patriarchates of Photius. Men in high rank and ecclesiastics, mostly Photius' friends, asked the learned Patriarch for explanation of some difficult problems posed by the iconoclasts. The fact that Photius included these answers in his collection, *Amphilochia*, demonstrates once more his anxiety to provide every one who might in the future be in difficulties with the necessary material – both profound and popular – against iconoclastic propaganda.

We detect a strong echo of this anxiety also in Photius' homilies. There are two homilies which are of a special interest in this respect. They were both delivered, as the titles indicate, from the ambo of Hagia Sophia, and were parts of a series of homilies having for their object the historical account of the origin, spread, and refutation of Arianism. In the first homily Photius explains the attitude of the Church towards Arius, who was first accepted, in spite of his deposition, because he pretended to repent, but later rejected because his repentance proved to be insincere. Then Photius compares the attitude of Alexander of Constantinople, and of his namesake of Alexandria, towards Arius with that of the Patriarch Nicephorus towards the iconoclastic Patriarch John the Grammarian. The passage is of some importance, as Photius gives some detailed information on John which has been hitherto overlooked.

"The Church, which prescribes pardon, gladly received Arius when he abandoned his former error; but when he had drifted many times into the same madness, although he simulated a recantation by a repentance tract, yet, foreseeing his deceitful and sly character, and providing in advance that piety should not be held in contempt, it did not consent in any wise to open to him the gates of mercy, which he had wretchedly shut in his own face. This [attitude] our contemporary also, the fitly-named Nicephorus, has imitated with divine wisdom: for as the blessed Alexander received Arius, so Nicephorus received John (who was awarded this throne as a prize for his impiety), who formerly had clung to piety (for he too was a worshipper of the venerable images, and actually used the art of the painter as the profession of his life), but later because of times and tribulations had stepped over to impiety and fallen into that disease, and offered a tract of repentance. But when he went astray again and aspired to be proclaimed the leader of a heresy – just as neither Alexander nor God's Church shed a single drop of mercy on Arius feigning repentance – so the wondrous Nicephorus with a prophetic eye barred the entrance of the Church to John and his fellow-leaders of the heresy who had committed the same folly against the Church, even if they would assume the mask of repentance – asserting that their conversion would be unacceptable both to God and to the Church. But to what extent the heresy of the iconoclasts resembles the Arian craze will be expounded, with God's help, in proper time." [41]

This Photius did in the second homily. After enumerating the errors of

[41] S. Aristarchis, *Photii Orationes et Homiliae*, II (Constantinopoli, 1900), 256 seq. I quote the passages of this and the following homilies from the new edition of Photius' homilies which will be published by Dumbarton Oaks, Harvard University. The new Greek text was prepared by B. Laourdas and the Translation which I am using here was done by C. Mango. In the new edition this homily is numbered as the thirteenth.

Arian leaders and exposing their tactics in defending and spreading them, Photius compared the Arians with the Iconoclasts:

"Such are the tactics of heretics; for they have the serpent for teacher, who, having mixed the poison of death with disobedience, under the pretext of solicitude and kindness, filled our common ancestors with pollution, and drove them away from life in paradise. These men too first simulate piety, then little by little disclose their irreverence, while dissembling the insolence of blasphemy with newfangled and ambiguous words; when they accustom the audience to the disguised irreverence, then they spew out into the midst the pure poison of impiety, having prepared disaster for themselves and those that obey them.

"One may observe the Iconoclasts using the same device and base artifice as the Arians; for they too do not reveal at once or all together the goal of their intention, but devise grades of impiety, until they reach the very summit of evil. It is fitting to consider here the similarity between the [two] heresies. The Arians alleged that the word *Homoousios* [of the same nature] was a cause of offense to most people; the Iconoclasts started by saying that the depicting of images down below, near the ground, was a cause of error to the simple-minded. The Arians: because, instead of *Homoousios*, this corporeal and lowly word, it is proper to say *Homoeousios* [of like nature] of the Father and the Son, this being somehow elevated and more fitting for the incorporeal, and avoiding the division of substance; the Iconoclasts: because, instead of depicting images down below, near the ground, they should stand in an elevated position, for this is more fitting for images, and avoids the reproach of deceit. The Arians: *Homoeousios* is not proper either, but instead of it we must say *homoion* [like], having altogether cut off *ousia* [nature]. The Iconoclasts: It is not proper to revere even pictures which are high up, but to let them stand only on account of the depicted narrative, reverence being altogether spewed out. The Arians: the word *Homoousios* is unattested. The Iconoclasts: The worship of images is unattested. The Arians: the Son should be called 'unlike' a creation and a work, while the words *Homoousios*, *ousia*, and *Homoeousios* should be altogether banished from the Church. The Iconoclasts: images should be called vain idols, and their making, representation and worship should be altogether banished from the Church. The Arians: neither the Lord's words in the Gospels, nor the divine apostles, nor the Old Testament give any authority at all to say *Homoousios*, *Homoeousios* or *ousia* about the Father and the Son. The Iconoclasts: neither the Lord's words in the Gospels, nor the divine apostles, nor the Old Testament give authority for the making, representation or worship of images.

"Is it small, the resemblance and imitation which the sons have of the fathers, the successors of the leaders, the pupils of the teachers? The former raged against Christ; the latter have arrayed themselves against His image. The former set at nought the men with whom they had ratified the first Nicene Council, as well as the Council itself. The latter have scoffed at the men with whom they had held the second Nicene Council, as well as the Council itself. The former charged with impiety the men who had baptized them, and had ordained them priests by imposition of hands, and whom they called their fathers; the latter likewise spread the monstrous tale that the men who had ordained them, and celebrated holy baptism over them, were idolaters. The former, progressing by degrees of blasphemy, fell into ultimate godlessness, having deprived the Son of the Father's substance. The latter, having distributed their blasphemy according to the degree of their wickedness, slipped into the ultimate impiety, having, in their folly against the images, banished from the Church the honor and reverence due to Christ."

It is remarkable that the Patriarch makes iconoclasm parallel to Arianism, the first and most abhorred heresy, and that he compares the Second Council of Nicaea, which defined the cult of images, with the First Council of Nicaea which was regarded as the most important and most venerable of the Eastern Church. This indicates how much he was preoccupied with the suppression of the last vestiges of iconoclasm.

This and the preceding homily most probably date from the first patriarchate of Photius. This seems to be indicated by the invitation addressed by Photius at the end of the homily to all dissidents: "Thinking and believing in this wise, let us spew out every heretical conspiracy, and abominate every schismatic wickedness. Let us hate mutual dissension, remembering the aforesaid, and how great a harvest of evils internal seditions begat. Let none among you say, 'I am of Paul, and I am of Cephas,' [I Cor. 1:12] and I am of so and so, or so and so; 'Christ hath redeemed us from the curse of the law' [Gal. 3:13] by his own blood: of Christ we both are and bear the name. Christ was crucified for us, and suffered death, was buried and arose, that He may unite them that stand wide and far apart, having divinely established one baptism, one faith, and one Catholic and Apostolic Church. This is the core of Christ's residence among men. This is the achievement of that extreme and ineffable renovation. He who attempts to tear down or cut away any of these things, either by the love of a most impious heresy, or the pride of schismatic madness, such a man arrays himself against Christ's incarnation, arms himself against the common salvation, opposes His achievements, and, broken off from union with Him and torn away from the Lord's body, the Church, he is enrolled with the opposite side, and, having rent his members from the Bride Church, he makes them members of the harlot conventicle." [42]

The schismatics whom Photius calls back to the Church, are the fanatic Ignatians who refused to acknowledge Photius as legitimate Patriarch. They were condemned and branded as schismatics by the Council of 861, and this homily may have been pronounced soon after this year. The heretics who are also invited to return to the Church can be only the iconoclasts who were also condemned by the same Council.

In the homily mentioned above, delivered in the presence of the Emperor Michael III and the co-Emperor Basil, at the unveiling of the image of the Holy Virgin with Child in the church of Hagia Sophia, Photius also attacked the iconoclasts and their doctrine. It will not be amiss to quote the relevant passages:

"The cause of this celebration . . . is the following. Splendid piety erecting trophies against belief hostile to Christ; impiety lying low, stripped of her very last hopes; and the ungodly ideas of those half-barbarous and bastard clans, which have crept on to the Roman throne (who were an insult and a disgrace to the imperial line) – that hateful abomination being branded for all to see."

After describing the artistic representation of the Holy Virgin, the Patriarch strikes again at the hatred of images displayed by the iconoclastic emperors of the Isaurian dynasty:

"They have stripped the Church, Christ's bride, of her own ornaments, and have wantonly inflicted bitter wounds on her, wherewith her face was scarred, and she was naked, as it were, and unsightly, and afflicted by those many wounds, – seeking in their rage to submerge her in oblivion, in this too simulating Jewish folly. Still bearing on her body the scars of these wounds, in testimony of the Isaurian and godless purpose, and wiping them off, and in their stead putting on the splendor of her own glory, she now regains her ancient dignity, and sheds off the flat mockery of those who have raged against her, pitying their truly absurd madness. . . . And so, as the eye of the universe, this celebrated and sacred church, looked sullen, as it were, with the visual mysteries scraped off (for it had not yet received the privilege of pictorial restoration), it shed but faint rays from its face to visitors, and in this respect the countenance of Orthodoxy appeared gloomy. . ."

Now, thanks to the intervention of the Emperor Michael III, the Church

[42] S. Aristarchis, *op. cit.*, II, 283–286. Homily fourteen in the forthcoming edition.

"has escaped the blows, has been freed of her wounds, has cast off all blemish, has precipitated her detractors into Hell, has raised those who had sung her praises. And there is no spot in her [cf. Song of Songs 4:7]. She has overcome the blemishes wherewith a foul hand has maimed and spotted her whole body."

It should be stressed that Photius describes iconoclasm here as a barbarous idea invented by foreigners – the Isaurian dynasty. The logical conclusion from his statement is that pictorial art is congenial to the Greek soul which is now, after the victories over the Iconoclasts, coming to itself. After depicting the beauty of the unveiled image of the Holy Virgin with Child, Photius shows the importance of pictorial representation in Christian instruction:

"Christ has come to us in the flesh and was borne in the arms of His mother: This is seen and confirmed and proclaimed on pictures, the teaching made clear through seeing it with our own eyes, and impelling the spectator to unhesitating assent. Does a man hate the teaching through pictures? Then how has he not previously rejected and hated the message of the Gospels? Just as speech is transmitted by hearing, so a form by the faculty of sight is imprinted upon the tablets of the soul, giving to those whose apprehension is not soiled by wicked doctrines, a representation of knowledge concordant with piety. Martyrs have fought for the love of God, and have shown with their blood the dearest of their zeal, and their memory is contained in books. These things are seen enacted on pictures, also, which make the martyrdom of these blessed men more vivid to learn than from the written word. Others still alive have had their flesh burnt, making propitious their sacrifice of prayer and fasting and other labors. These things are conveyed by speech and by pictures, but it is the spectators rather than the bearers who are drawn to imitation. The Virgin is holding the Creator in her arms as an infant. Who is it that upon seeing this or hearing it, will not be astonished by the magnitude of the mystery and will not rise up to laud the ineffable condescension which surpasses all words? For even if the one introduces the other, yet, rather than the learning which penetrates through the ears, the apprehension through sight is shown in very fact to be far superior. Has a man lent his ear to a story? Has the intelligence visualized it and drawn to itself what has been heard? Then, judged with sober care, it is deposited in the memory. No less – yea, much greater, is the power of sight. For surely, it somehow, through the outpouring and effluence of optical rays, touches the object, and encompasses the essence of the thing seen and sends it on to the mind, to be forwarded thence to the memory for the unfailing concentration of knowledge. Has the mind seen? Has it grasped? Has it visualized? Then it has easily transmitted the forms to the memory."

These words are certainly a very able apology for pictorial representations of Christian doctrine, for its better understanding and grasping by the faithful. The Patriarch's words carried the more conviction, for he could demonstrate what he was saying by pointing to the beautiful work of art – the image of the Holy Virgin with Child – which was being unveiled.

Then, Photius went on to link the written word in the Gospels with its pictorial representation in images:

"Is there one who disregards the holy writings on these matters (whereby all lies are dispelled), and considers them not above dispute? This man went astray in his veneration long before he insulted the holy images. On the contrary, does he reverence them and honour them with the proper respect? Then such also is his disposition towards the writings. Whether one treats the one with reverence or with contempt, one necessarily confers the same on the other, unless, in addition to being impious, one has also abandoned reason, and preaches things contradictory to oneself. Therefore, those who have slipped into clashing against the holy images are proved not to have kept the correctness of doctrine but with the one they abjure the other. . . . Abominable in their misdeeds, they are more abominable in their impiety." [43]

All this reveals the lively interest of the Patriarch Photius in iconoclasm and in the eradication of the last traces of this heresy. It is not surprising, then, that Photius was anxious to have the oecumenicity of the Seventh Council recognized by the whole Church. He expressed his desire in this respect most urgently in his letter to the eastern patriarchs, dispatched in 867, with the invitation to send representatives to a council which should deal with doctrines spread by Frankish missionaries in Bulgaria. Photius says:

"I deemed it necessary also to include this in my letter in order that all the Churches under your authority be advised to add to and to enumerate with the six holy and oecumenical councils [this] seventh holy and oecumenical council. For the rumor reached my ears that several Churches, which are under the authority of your apostolic throne, count the oecumenical councils as far as the sixth, but do not recognize the seventh. But they put into effect, with zeal and reverence, if anything else, its de-

[43] S. Aristarchis, *op. cit.*, II, 294–308. Number fifteen in the new edition. See also above n. 34.

crees . . . It destroyed a very grave heresy, and had among its voting members men who came from the four archiepiscopal thrones . . .

"And when they all had assembled together with my father's brother, a most holy and thrice-blessed man, Tarasius, the Archbishop of Constantinople, the great Seventh Oecumenical Council was organized, which triumphed over the iconoclasts or [rather] the enemies of Christ, and destroyed their heresy . . .

"It is therefore necessary, as I said before, to proclaim publicly with the six, which preceded it, also this great, holy and oecumenical council. For not to comply with it and not to act thus would, in the first place, be a wrong done to the Church of Christ [by those] who overlook so important a council and break up and destroy to such an extent the bond of union and the connection [brought on by it]; in the second place, it would mean widening the mouths of the iconoclasts, whose godless doctrine, as I well know, you loath no less than [the teachings] of [all] the other heretics; [in that case] their godlessness would not be condemned by an oecumenical council, but would be punished by the decision of one see [only], and so [these heretics] would have a pretext for going on with their monstrous teaching." [44]

These words indicate clearly how well Photius, when he wrote these lines, was aware that iconoclasm was still rampant in Byzantium and how anxious he was to eradicate it. A solemn recognition by the Patriarchs of the Second Council of Nicea as the Seventh Oecumenical was most desirable, and would be of great help to the Patriarch in his endeavor.

The Council of 867 is supposed to have been convoked mainly to condemn the Latin addition to the Nicene Creed – the Filioque – and Pope Nicolas I, but it should be stressed that it also dealt with iconoclasm and reiterated the condemnation of all previous heresies, iconoclasm included. This can be deduced from the homily of Photius which – so it has been often assumed – was pronounced at the Feast of Orthodoxy which the Emperor Michael III and the co-Emperor Basil I attended. The homily is entitled: "Of the same [Patriarch Photius] sermon spoken from the Ambo of St. Sophia, when the triumph over all the heresies was proclaimed by our great and orthodox Emperors, Michael and Basil." A more careful study of the homily shows, however, that it was delivered, not at the celebration of the Feast of Orthodoxy in 866, or rather 867, but at another, more fitting, occasion, which could only have been after the Council of 867, perhaps at

[44] *Photii Epistolae*, I, *epist.* XIII, *P.G.* 102, cols. 740 sq., nos. 40–43. I follow the Greek text of Photius' Letters, edited by B. Laourdas for publication by Dumbarton Oaks, Harvard University. The English translation of this and the other letters is the work of F. W. Schehl.

the very close of the Council. A few quotations from the sermon will show that this was the case.

It is evident from the introductory words that the Patriarch had in mind, not a yearly celebration of the feast of orthodoxy, but a recent event, a deed the merit of which should be ascribed to Michael III. The young Emperor performed many deeds and has shown many excellent qualities for which he deserved praise. But, continues the Patriarch: "It is not my intention to enumerate any of these . . . Nay, not the capture and depopulation of hostile cities and the construction and rebuilding of friendly ones, nor the fact that he converses with those he meets with a joyful and smiling countenance, and has removed all dejection from every face by changing the fear of tyranny into a spontaneous love, eager to be called the father rather than the master of the country . . . not that he has extended to the citizens a hand flowing with gold, having driven poverty out of the body politic as no man has driven it out of his own home; and that the queenly city, which reigns in wealth, has spread the gifts of prosperity to all the subjects thanks to one imperial gesture, . . . not even because thanks to him this Church and the holy cares of holy buildings have reached an unhoped-for attainment and matchless beauty . . ."

There is another deed just performed by the Emperor, which Photius will celebrate — the victory over all heresies. In apostrophizing the Church which should rejoice over such a victory, the Patriarch continues:

"Seest thou thy beloved son, whom thou hast adopted from the very cradle and made emperor, whom thou hast bred in piety, and reared to manhood in reverence, and advanced to the same age as Christ? Seest thou him, what rewards he has offered thee for his rearing, with great interest, bearing thee novel and gay [gifts], and with how many and how great trophies he has filled this holy and august church? He does not bring thee Arius in chains, nor Macedonius a captive, nor Nestorius a prisoner and the children of Dioscorus, who barbarized the whole universe with a multitude of unnatural offspring, nor this or that enemy and foe of the Church, nor the leader of one or several heresies, but he has brought forward all the contingents of the enemy together, with their leaders, their devices, and their plans, dead and stripped bare, by one and the same blow of his imperial right hand. 'Lift up thine eyes round about, and behold thy children gathered' [Isa. 60:4], whom the bacchantes and harpies of the heresies and schisms had formerly snatched away, and, filling them with much corybantic frenzy, and goading them on, scattered on the mountains and cliffs of perdition. 'Rejoice and delight thyself with all thine heart' [Zeph. 3:14]: the Son is proclaimed consubstantial with the Father; the Ghost is included in the same Godhead with them; the Word which has taken on flesh from a virgin for the common salvation and renovation of our kind is not separated from the Godhead; the natures in Him remain unmingled, and are seen to act in concert each according to its energy; every error and trumpery is driven far away, no transmigration of souls is vainly imagined, nor does a throng of demons, riding on myths, leap into the sphere whence they have wilfully fallen. Nay, nor is Christ himself under the pretext of due reverence bitterly insulted and taunted: this is a new invention, and a strange kind of contumely devised by the Evil one, to rage against the image while monstrously pretending to be tearing it apart in honour of the one represented, thus raging a double frenzy. No manner of impiety will henceforth speak freely. For our victorious protagonist, using the writing pen like a spear forged by God, has struck the plague right through the bowels."

The last words suggest only one occasion which the Patriarch could have in mind: the signing by the Emperor of conciliar decrees by which all heresies, iconoclasm included, were condemned once more. The same idea is suggested when, after comparing Michael III with Moses who ordered the execution of idolaters in order to save the rest of the people, Photius continues:

"But Christ's disciple has not freed the remnant from the plague by the destruction of fellow-countrymen, nay he delivers the sum total of [his] subjects by defeating evil itself and, while thrusting against it the spear of the pen, he shows all his dependents free from stain therefrom."

At the end of the homily Photius addresses also the "choir of patricians, honorable and reverend old men who along with such great generals and commanders were picked to be joint generals and commanders against so great and so many heresies, and have joined in bearing these holy labours." [45] He seems to have in mind the imperial dignitaries, who accompanied the emperors and were present at the last meeting of the Council during which the condemnation of all heresies was proclaimed in a conciliar decree, which was signed by the emperors and then by the bishops.

The homily is the more important because it gives us some additional information on the Council of 867 about which we know very little. It should be stressed that we read there no attack against the Pope or the Western Church. This seems rather puzzling in view of the treatment this Council has so far received. Of course, when Photius speaks about heresies and schisms, he may have in mind also the teachings which the Frankish missionaries were spreading in Bulgaria or the attitude of Pope Nicolas

[45] S. Aristarchis, *op. cit.*, II, 314–326. In the new edition, number sixteen.

toward himself and the Byzantine Church. It is, however, important to note that he did not single out these "heresies" and "schisms" in his sermon for a special attack. This same reserved attitude is observed by Photius in his encyclical letter to the Eastern Patriarchs, quoted above, from which it is evident that Photius put the blame for the addition of the "Filioque" and other western customs, branded as alien to synodical decrees, on the Frankish missionaries in Bulgaria. All this raises the question, in which manner and to what extent Pope Nicolas' ecclesiastical policy was criticized or condemned by the Council of 867. Since the acts of the Council have been destroyed, we shall never be able to give a straightforward answer to these questions.

One can surmize that the Council of 867 solemnly added the Second Council of Nicaea to the six oecumenical councils and that, from that time on, the eastern patriarchs regarded it as the Seventh Oecumenical Council. The oecumenicity of this Council was stressed once more by the Ignatian council of 869–870,[46] but, in spite of that, the Roman Church still continued to count officially only six oecumenical councils, even after 870.[47] It was again Photius who endeavored to bring the Roman Church into line with other churches in this respect. During the fifth session of the Photian Council of 879–880 [48] Photius proposed that the Council should officially confer on the second synod of Nicaea the title of Seventh Oecumenical Council. Cardinal Paul, the papal legate, rose and, accepting the proposal, threatened to excommunicate any who should refuse to number that synod among the oecumenical councils. The legates of other patriarchal sees concurred and, from that time on, all churches counted, in official documents, seven oecumenical councils, although in the West, the old custom, to count only six councils lingered, in unofficial documents, for a considerable time.[49]

It should be noted in this connection that Arethas, one of the most devoted disciples of Patriarch Photius, manifested, at least on two occasions, a lively interest in the refutation of iconoclastic ideas. In his letter to the asecretis Nicolas, son of Gabriel, which is preserved in the Synodical Library in Moscow (no. 315, folios 52–54 recto), Arethas says that, although the iconoclastic heresy is defeated, there are still some "weaklings and simple-minded people" who are confused by the iconoclastic argumentation and who need a good instruction on the matter of image worship. Arethas gives then to his addressee a short review of the main arguments

[46] Mansi, XVI, col. 181.

[47] Cf. my book, *Les Légendes de Const. et de Méthode*, pp. 305–308, especially n. 5, p. 308.

[48] Mansi, XVIII, cols. 493 sq.

[49] See my book, *The Photian Schism*, pp. 309 sq.

used by the defenders of the image worship. He insists mostly on passages taken from the Old Testament, stressing especially the vision of Ezekiel.[50] The letter may have been written at the very end of the ninth century. Moreover, in one of his Scholia to Dio Chrysostom (Codex Urbinatus 124, fol. 12) Arethas marked a passage with the following words: "useful against the iconoclasts."[51]

The interest shown by Photius' disciple in the refutation of iconoclastic ideas is characteristic. As one of Photius' best disciples, Arethas shared, also in this respect, his master's main preoccupation.

The few facts studied above show that the danger of an iconoclastic revival in Byzantium after the reëstablishment of orthodoxy in 843 was still considerable for more than one generation and that the liquidation of the aftermath of iconoclasm was not as easy as it is sometimes thought. The merits due the Patriarch Photius for the final extirpation of the heresy are more considerable than has so far been acknowledged. He saw clearly what was needed in order to dispel the danger, and he knew how to combine solid theological knowledge with a moderate and conciliatory attitude towards the heretics in order to win them for orthodoxy.

Moreover, everything seems to indicate that Photius provided also the main inspiration for the artists who were engaged in redecorating the churches with pictures. The renaissance of the Byzantine art of the ninth century started thus under the patriarchate of Photius. His insight and his activity were well-remembered by his Church, and for his fight against heresy Photius was rewarded with the halo of a saint.

[50] An edition of Arethas' works contained in this MS. is being planned by B. Laourdas from the apograph made by Oskar von Gebhardt.

[51] See S. Kougeas, *Arethas of Caesarea* (in Greek) (Athens, 1913), pp. 42, 51, n. 2.

VI

THE PATRIARCH PHOTIUS IN THE LIGHT OF RECENT RESEARCH

The history of the Patriarch Photius appears now in a new light, thanks to the research of several scholars who, in recent years, have studied some problems connected especially with the so-called Photian schism. In spite of considerable progress made in the Photian studies, there still remain in the complicated tangle of facts some details that should be studied further. Unfortunately, because of the dearth of sources, we shall probably never be able to find adequate answers to some questions; answers that could eliminate all other explanations. Most of the documentation at our disposal comes from the side of Photius' adversaries, and its reliability is highly questionable.

In spite of that, it is generally felt that the evidence revealed in recent studies, calls for a new appreciation of Photius as a churchman and scholar, and that Photius' relations with the papacy especially must be viewed in a different light than has heretofore been done.

It should be stressed, however, that the great work on Photius written by Cardinal J. Hergenröther[1] is in no way completely superseded by the new findings. It should serve as a necessary point of departure for all scholars dealing with the history of the Patriarch and of the Eastern Schism.

I

Concerning Photius' origin, his youth, and his education, little can be added to what Hergenröther had said. The date of Photius' birth should be put at about the year 820. The recent research on the intrigues of Photius' enemies make us even more suspicious and cautious than was Hergenröther in accepting Pseudo-Symeon's phantasies on Photius' father Sergius, who, he says, was of pagan origin and had married a nun, Irene.[2] Also, the prophecies of St. Michael of Synnada, of the Abbot Hilarion of Dalmatos, and of St. Joannikios of Mount Olympus on the evil career of the child, reported by the same author, are inventions of Photius' adversaries. They reveal, however, to what extreme his enemies were able to go in their venomous propaganda against their adversary, a circumstance that we should keep in mind when re-examining the religious and political situation in Byzantium in Photius' time.

---

[1] Photius, Patriarch von Constantinopel. Sein Leben, seine Schriften und das griechische Schisma (Regensburg, 1867), 3 vols.

[2] Ed. Bekker, Bonn, pp. 668 seq. Cf. Hergenröther, op. cit., vol. I, pp. 317 seq.

What Photius says of his parents contradicts Symeon. In his enthronistical letter to the Patriarch of Antioch, Photius affirms that his father had suffered persecution from the iconoclasts because of his orthodox faith.[3] His words seem to indicate that Photius' father and mother had died before the Empress Theodora had recalled from exile the faithful iconodules (842) banned by her husband. Thus the crown of matyrdom which had adorned the heads of his father and his mother – Photius used such an expression in his letter to his brother Tarasius[4] – was the exile which they had both suffered. In reality, Photius' father has a commemorative notice in the Greek Synaxarion of the thirteenth of March, where he is recorded as confessor (ὁμολογητής).[5]

From a passage of Photius' letter to the deacon Gregory[6] it appears that the whole family was anathematized by the iconoclasts, together with the memory of Photius' uncle, the Patriarch Tarasius. This could have happened between the years 815 and 842, or about 830, after the birth of Photius and his brothers, Tarasius and Sergius. It is probable that the family's property was not confiscated and that only his parents were deprived of its use, for Photius and his brothers do not seem to have suffered any setback in their higher education, which they could have got only in Constantinople where they were born.[7] Such seems to have been the policy of the iconoclasts who hoped that the children, separated from their parents and forced to follow the instruction given in the schools by iconoclastic teachers, would become hostile to the worship of images.[8]

The words in which Photius describes the exile of his father and mother reveal, at the same time, that he had never forgotten the injustice done by the iconoclasts to his family, an injustice which had deeply impressed the adolescent, and considerably darkened the memories of the adult. This psychological observation helps us to explain Photius' zeal in the extermination of the last vestiges of iconoclasm, when he became head of the Byzantine Church. This sad experience of his youth might have promted in him a vague desire to become a monk, as he confesses in his letter to the Patriarch of Antioch;[9] a desire which was only the fruit of the youthful mood

[3] Epistola ad ecclesiam Antiochenam, P. G., vol. 102, col. 1020: "First of all [my] father invited me to a virtuous life, he who, because of orthodox teaching and the true faith, had renounced riches and all wordly honors, and, after having much suffered – let me not mention all details – had ended banned, in martyrdom, and [my] mother, lover of God and of virtue, [was] rivalling with her husband not to be left behind in anything of this."

[4] Ibid., col. 972.

[5] H. Delehaye, Synaxarium Constantinopolitanum (Brussels, 1902), A. S. Nov., col. 682.

[6] Ibid., col. 877.

[7] Cf. Photius' letter to his brother Tarasius (ibid., col. 972C) which might contain an allusion to the separation of Photius' parents from their children.

[8] It is quite possible that the children of Photius' exiled parents were taken care of by Theoctistus who was a favorite of the Emperor Theophilus and who, at that time, may already have exercised the high function of the logothete of the course (Genesios, Bonn, p. 23; Theophanes Cont., Bonn, p. 148). We know, at least that Theoctistus had later shown special favor to Photius, appreciating his scholarly talents.

[9] P. G., vol. 102, col. 1020A. Cf. also his first letter to Pope Nicholas, ibid., col. 585B.

created by circumstances and which was soon drowned in the more real and more ardent love for learning that dominated the young man.

Thanks to several recent studies we are now better informed on Byzantine education in the ninth century, and can thus follow in greater detail Photius' progress in his studies. We learn from the Lives of some Saints written during the ninth century[10] interesting details on elementary instruction in Byzantium, often called ἐγκύκλιος παιδεία, although the meaning of this word changed at different periods. It comprised the basic notions of grammar, dialectic, rhetoric, and the quadrivium: arithmetic, music, geometry, and astronomy.[11] This lower degree of instruction could be obtained in any Byzantine city as we learn from the Lives of the Saints. Higher education, however, could be obtained only in Constantinople. Even Thessalonica could not satisfy Constantine the Philosopher who was to become St. Cyril, Apostle of the Slavs, as we learn from his biography. He obtained what he desired only in Constantinople.[12]

We are now also better informed on the kind of higher education one could obtain in Constantinople in the ninth century. The existence of a school for higher education of the clergy under the reign of Theophilus (829–842) seems to be attested by the Continuator of Theophanes.[13] He mentions an Ignatius called the oecumenical teacher (οἰκουμενικὸς διδάσκαλος). This title used to be given to the rector of the patriarchal Academy destined for the higher education of the clergy. This kind of divinity school is said to have been supressed by the iconoclast Emperor Leo III in 726, according to George the Monk.[14] However, this appears to be an exaggeration. It is more probable that the school existed during the iconoclastic period also, and that Theophilus did not need to revive it, as has been suggested by F. Fuchs.[15]

However, Photius did not study at the patriarchal Academy which was then in the hands of iconoclastic theologians, but at the Imperial University which had existed in Constantinople from the time of Constantine the Great. The University had its reverses, but it was not suppressed by Leo III as had often been thought on the basis of George the Monk's exaggerated report.[16]

---

[10] Especially from that of St. Stephen the Younger, of St.Michael the Syncellus, of St.Stephen of Sugdaea, of St. Anthony Cauleas, of St. George of Amastris, of St. Theodore of Studios, of St. Nicephorus, the Patriarch, of St. Jean of Psicha. See for details and bibliographical indications F. Dvornik, Les Légendes de Constantin et de Methode vues de Byzance (Prague, 1933), pp. 25–31.

[11] See especially the Life of St. Nicephorus, ed. by C. de Boor, Nicephori archiep. Constant. opuscula historica (Leipzig, Teubner, 1880) pp. 144, 149 seq.

[12] See chaps. 3 and 4 of the Old Slavonic Vita Constantini, translated into French by F. Dvornik, Les Légendes, op. cit., pp. 350–352.

[13] Ed. Bonn, p. 143. P. G., vol. 109, col. 157 B.

[14] Georgii monachi Chronicon, ed. de Boor, p. 742.

[15] F. Fuchs, Die höheren Schulen in Konstantinopel im Mittelalter (Leipzig, 1928, Byzant. Archiv, vol. 8), p. 17. For details see F. Dvornik, "Photius et la réorganisation de l'académie patriarcale," Analecta Bollandiana, vol. 68 (1950), pp. 116 seq.

[16] L. Bréhier had shown clearly the unreliability of this report in his paper, "Notes sur l'histoire de l'enseignement supérieur à Constantinople" in Byzantion, vol. 3 (1926), pp. 73–94, vol. 4

We have thus to discard the opinion that Photius was ever an autodidact[17] or that he was educated at the school of the monastery of Studios.[18]

Photius' enemy Nicetas David, in his biography of Ignatius,[19] gives us a clear picture of the disciplines taught at the University, in which Photius had excelled: grammar, poetry, rhetoric, philosophy, medicine, and all wordly science.[20] Although Photius does not speak of his teachers, it seems almost certain that one of them was the famous Leo the Philosopher, who was discovered by Theophilus, thanks to the interest in learning of an Arab emir, and who had entrusted to Leo the direction of, and the teaching of philosophy at, the University of Constantinople. Leo taught at the University until about 839 when he was appointed Archbishop of Thessalonica by the iconoclastic Patriarch John Grammaticus. Leo was officially, of course, an iconoclast, although he does not seem to have been a very zealous believer in heretical doctrine.[21] So also were other professors who were teaching at the University under Theophilus when Photius studied there. This may be the most logical explanation of why Photius never mentioned the names of his teachers. He would, thereby, have offered to his adversaries another weapon with which they could have attacked him. Is it therefore necessary to ascribe Photius' silence on this score to his great pride which forbade him to mention anybody to whom he owed his initiation into scholarship?[22]

More light has been shed also on the teaching career of Photius. After the death of Theophilus and the establishment of orthodoxy, it was Theophilus' Prime Minister Theoctistus who seems to have shown a lively interest in the reorganization of the University. Leo the Philosopher, deprived of his see in Thessalonica, was appointed rector of the University, and Photius, his former disciple, became professor of dialectic and philosophy there.

Our principal source for information on the University after 842 is the *Vita*

(1927–1928), p. 13–28. Cf. what F. Dvornik says on the confusion of both high schools of Constantinople in the reports by Theophanes (ed. C. de Boor, p. 405) and by George the Monk. ("Photius et la réorganisation," op. cit., pp. 116 seq.).

[17] Dositheus Hieros., Τόμος Χαρᾶς (Jassy, 1705), fol. γ' b. Cf. J. Hergenröther, op. cit., vol. I, p. 322.

[18] E. Orth, Photiana (Leipzig, 1920), vol. I, p. 22.

[19] P. G., vol. 105, col. 509 B.

[20] The biographer of Constantine the Philosopher (Dvornik, Les Légendes, op. cit., p. 352) enumerates the following disciplines which were taught at the University: grammar, dialectic, philosophical disciplines, rhetoric, arithmetic, astronomy, music, and "other hellenic arts."

[21] On Leo's teaching career see F. Dvornik, Les Légendes, pp. 40–45, 80 seq. Cf. also F. Dvornik, Les Slaves, Byzance et Rome au IXe siècle (Paris, 1926), pp. 117 seq.

[22] C. Ziegler, "Photios" in Pauly Real-Encyklopädie (Stuttgart, 1941), vol. 20, col. 671, 30. Hergenröther, Patr. Photius, vol. I. p. 323 is less outspoken on this subject ("vielleicht... sein großer Stolz..."). Hergenröther (ibid., pp. 323, 324) ventures that perhaps the future Patriarch Methodius who, although a fervent iconodule, was highly esteemed by Theophilus, and Gregory Asbestas, future bishop of Syracuse, were Photius' teachers. This however, is improbable. It is hardly conceivable that Theophilus would have appointed fervent iconodules as teachers at the high school.

Constantini Philosophi.[23] We have thus to reject former opinions imagining the existence of a kind of private academy in Photius' house where he gave instruction to younger men and where he gathered his friends for scholarly discussions and reading of classical and theological books. Photius was a public teacher, professor of philosophy at the Imperial University which was forming officers for the Imperial service.

Photius occupied his chair of philosophy until about the year 850 or 851 when he was appointed by Theoctistus, Prime Minister of the Empress Theodora, director of the Imperial chancery. His successor at the University was his former student Constantine the Philosopher.[24] At that time Photius' family had already entered into a more intimate relationship with the Imperial house because Photius' brother Sergius had married Theodora's youngest sister Irene.[25] This illustrates the high position of Photius' family in Byzantine society.

Even in his new official function Photius continued to be in frequent contact with his former students, receiving them in his drawing room for scholarly discussions, as he reveals in his second letter to Pope Nicholas, wherein he describes his teaching activity before he was elected Patriarch. The passage is important because it reveals also the great success of Photius' teaching career.[26]

II

Two of his literary documents make it possible for us to measure the depth and breadth of Photius' learning acquired during this first period of his life – his *Myriobiblos* and his *Amphilochia.* The most exhaustive commentary on these works is still that of Hergenröther,[27] but we are now able to

---

[23] Dvornik, Les Légendes, pp. 43 seq., chap. 4 of the Vita: p. 352: "When he [Constantine] arrived at Constantinople, he was entrusted to teachers in order to be instructed. After having learned the grammar in three months, he devoted himself to other sciences. He studied Homer and geometry and also – with Leo and Photius – dialectic and other philosophical disciplines. In addition, he learned rhetoric, arithmetic, astronomy, music, and the other hellenic arts."

[24] F. Dvornik, Les Légendes, pp. 353 (chap. 4 of the Vita Constantini), pp. 79 seq. Cf. also idem, "La carrière universitaire de Constantin le Philosophe," Byzantinoslavica, vol. 3 (1931), pp. 59–67.

[25] Theophanes Cont., Bonn, p. 175, Georgius Cedrenus, Bonn, II, p. 161.

[26] P. G., vol. 102, col. 597.

[27] Photius, vol. 3, pp. 13–70. This volume, devoted to Photius' literary activity will long remain indispensable to all students of Photius. A considerable progress in studies on Photius' literary activity was made by K. Staab who published Photius' commentaries to St. Paul in his work: Pauluskommentare aus der griechischen Kirche aus Katenenhandschriften gesammelt (Neutestam. Abhandl., vol. XV, Münster i. W., 1933), pp. 470–652. See on pp. XL–XLVII Staab's appreciation of Photius' originality: "Es ist im ganzen eine Leistung, wie sie Jahrhunderte vor und nach ihm ihresgleichen nicht findet (p. XLIV)." The best Ms. containing Photius' text (Cod. Marc. 33) is from the tenth century. See also J. Reuss' remarks on Photius' commentary to Matthew ("Die Matthäus-Erklärung des Photius von Konstantinopel," Ostkirchliche Studien, vol. I, 1952, pp. 132–134). New material on Photius' homilies will be found in the introduction to the English edition of Photius' homilies, published by C. Mango in Dumbarton Oaks Studies, vol. III (Cambridge, Mass. 1958). Photius' authorship of the four treatises against the Manichaeans, attributed

determine with greater accuracy precisely when the material for the compo-sition of such exhaustive works had been gathered by their author.

Regarding the *Myriobiblos*, we have to discard the opinion that the w had been composed in the few weeks before Photius started on his emb to the Arabs for the exchange of prisoners in 855, or that the works descri by Photius were read and studied by him and his friends who accompan him during his journey through Asia Minor to the Arab frontier.[28] K. Zie ler[29] is right when he sees in this work the results of Photius' private stu and reading from his young years to 855. Photius read the works he de scribes with a pen in his hand, making numerous notes and critical remark and copying excerpts, sometimes long pages of passages which had awaken his interest. In the few weeks before his departure from the capital Photi simply completed and corrected his notes, adding sometimes remarks fro his memory or from the works he had still at hand. In this light the compo sition of such an enormous volume in a few weeks becomes comprehensible although it still represents an incredible amount of work.

Although the *Amphilochia* was written by Photius during his first exile, the three hundred chapters in which he answers different questions reflect also his teaching activity and scholarly research, made mostly before he became Patriarch.[30] The work is a kind of a supplement to his *Bibliotheca*. Naturally the author continued his research also during his first patriarchate and while in exile, but the main body of it is the fruit of studies undertaken before he was elected Patriarch. These two works do not, of course, exhaust all the literature studied by Photius. Indeed, he seems to have concentrated in his account to his brother Tarasius on lesser known classics and writers, regarding the study of the great writers as a matter-of-course for every Byzantine intellectual. Moreover, as he says in the introductory address to his brother, he intended to write another part of the *Bibliotheca* after his return from the embassy, but events had prevented his doing so.

These two principal works also give us an insight into Photius' main

---

to him (P. G., vol. 102, cols. 16–264) is still debated. H. Grégoire ("Les Sources de l'Histoire des Pauliciens," Acad. Royale de Belgique, Bulletins de la Classe des Lettres, 5e serie, f. XXII [Bruxelles, 1936], pp. 95–114) attributes only book four to Photius, doubting his authorship for the third and second books, and regarding the first book as a tenth-century forgery. F. Scheidweiler ("Paulikianerprobleme," B. Z. 43 [1950], pp. 10–39, 366–384) questioned the convincing value of some of Grégoire's arguments. J. Scharf, ("Zur Echtheitsfrage der Manichäerbücher des Photios," B. Z. 44 [1951], pp. 487–494), came to the conclusion that the three last books of the treatise reflect Photius' style and spirit to such a degree that we must attribute their composition to Photius. He admitted that the first book might have been subjected to changes, but he believed that he found even there traces of Photius' way of writing and thinking.

[28] E. Orth, Photiana (Leipzig, 1928) pp. 4 seq., idem., Die Stilkritik des Photios (Leipzig, 1929), pp. 134 seq. Cf. Richtsteig in the revue of Orth's book in Byzant. neugriech. Jahrbücher, 6 (1928), pp. 572 seq. and G. Inmisch, "Wirklichkeit und Literaturform," Rheinisches Museum, 78 (1929), pp. 113–123. Orth's thesis was also rejected by Güngerich in B. Z., 29 (1929/30), pp. 293 seq.

[29] Ziegler, op. cit., col. 684–693.

[30] Ziegler, ibid., col. 729.

in[illegible]est in scholarly research, and are useful indications as to his personal [illegible]acter and inclinations. They reveal, too, what the scholarly world owes [illegible]n to him and to his disciples. First of all, his *Bibliotheca* gives us a clear [illegible] of the importance and intensity of the rebirth of classical studies in [illegible]antium in the ninth century, a rebirth which was due in great part to [illegible]otius' initiative. On the other hand, in his choice of classical lore Photius [illegible]eals himself a realist, interested more in prose works and in exact science [illegible]an in poetry and in fiction. In his criticism of some historical writings, [illegible]otius regards a direct approach to historical problems and a clear exposé [illegible] the most valuable and distinctive attributes of a good historian (Codex 60, [illegible], 72, 92). He rejects any mythological speculation which he relegates to [illegible]e field of poetical imagination. A good historian should avoid unnecessary [illegible]igressions; his speech should be clear and to the point. The Christian [illegible]hetor or homilist must not neglect his style, of course, but first of all he [illegible]nust have his listeners in mind, and must give them some instruction in an [illegible]asily understandable way. John Chrysostom was such an ideal rhetor-homilist (Codex 172).

We owe to Photius the preservation of many classical literary treasures, but he himself was not a Synesius or Psellus or western humanist, all of whom were so completely pervaded by classical lore that their Christian character seems drowned by the use of classical pagan conceptions and expressions. Photius' main intention was to make the Hellenic and Hellenistic inheritance useful once more in the dissemination and understanding of Christian ideas. In spite of his enthusiasm for the classics, their works, and the purity of their language, he warned against a too-indiscreet love of the pagan classics. Most telling in this respect are three letters which he wrote to his friend George, Metropolitan of Nicomedia.[31] Here Photius reprimands his friend for his criticism of the language used by St. Peter and Paul in their epistles, which according to George, differed too much from the language of the old classics.

In this instance Photius seems prejudiced by bis Christian upbringing and by his respect for the founders of Christianity and for the first Christian writers. He gives vent to his Christian orthodox sentiments in many other chapters of his *Bibliotheca* also. Theological works discussed by Photius in this work are surprisingly numerous, a fact which shows that from his earliest years he had a lively interest in theology, and was well versed in all theological problems. This is, of course, quite natural in Byzantium where theology was always held in great honor, permeating both lower and higher education.[32] But this is not all. When we read Photius' commentaries on

---

31 Letters 156, 165, 166 in R. Montacutius' edition (Photii Epistolae [London, 1651], pp. 210, 224, seq., 235 seq.). *Amphilochia*, P. G., vol. 101, qu. 86. 92. 93, cols. 557. 575. 592.

32 We find in the *Amphilochia* several passages indicating clearly that Photius had treated in his lectures theological problems also: first in the introductory letter (P. G. vol. 101, col. 48), in quaestio 1, 15, col. 68 A, quaestio 24, 10, col. 189 (here there is a particularly clear allusion to lectures on theological questions).

theological works, we feel the author's sincere, even exaggerated, zeal for the orthodox faith. The heroes of the Eastern Orthodox Church, Athanasius, Basil, Cyril of Alexandria, and John Chrysostom, are highly praised and their argumentation against heretic doctrines warmly applauded. The numerous heretical authors read by Photius, are subjected by him to very sharp criticism, for example, Origen (Codex 8, 117), Philostorgius (Codex 40), John Aegeates (Codex 41), Theodore of Mopsuestia (Codex 177), Eunomius (Codex 137, 138), Agapius (Codex 179). Even John Philoponus, whose works seem to have been favorites of Photius, is sharply blamed for his doctrine on the resurrection, for his attack against the Council of Chalcedon, and for his doctrine on the Trinity (Codex 21, 55, 75). In the Pseudo-Clementine writings, too, Photius finds heretical ideas (Codex 112, 113), and the Apocryphal Acts of the Apostles are also rejected (Codex 114). Photius never failed to point out a heretical doctrine, and, when rejecting and criticizing its author, used a very sharp language.

His zeal for orthodox teaching influenced also his judgment of the literary merits of the authors he had read. The orthodox Fathers were usually praised for their excellent style and diction. The heretical writers were, in general, severely criticized, and their style and language often blamed, not always justifiably.[33]

Photius' propensity for utilizing once again the inheritance of the classical age in theological thinking is to be found also in his philosophical speculation. It is to his credit that he turned the attention of the Byzantines once more to Aristotle. Aristotelianism laid hold of Christian scholars after the third century, and became firmly entrenched in Alexandria where Aristotelian commentators rendered good service against the dangerous doctrines of the Pergamene school of Neoplatonism and against the paganism of the Athenian school. The many commentaries on Aristotle's works published in Alexandria and in Byzantium from the end of the third to the beginning of the seventh century testify to the intensity of interest in Aristotelian studies in the Christian East.

From the seventh century on, however, all commentary on Aristotle's works ceased in Byzantium, and this hiatus seems to extend to the eleventh century, when Michael of Ephesus renewed this kind of philosophical study.

After a long interruption in Aristotelian studies, Photius – an avowed Aristotelian – brought Byzantine philosophical and theological speculation back to the basis laid by this great philosopher. It was more Aristotle's logic than Plato's ideology that attracted Photius' realistic mind, and, although he lectured to his students on Plato's ideas as well,[34] he was very critical of the latter's system.[35] We find in Photius' *Amphilochia* not only many passages alluding to Aristotle's teaching, but also a long explanation of the ten cate-

---

[33] Cf. G. Hartmann, Photius' Literarästhetik (Borna-Leipzig, 1929), pp. 46 seq. See also Ziegler, op. cit., cols. 719 seq.

[34] Amphilochia, quaestio 77, P.G., vol. 101, col. 480C.

[35] For example, ibid., quaestio 92, col. 585A; quaestio 101, col. 625A.

gories of Aristotle.[36] Thus Photius filled to some extent the gap in the writing of commentaries on Aristotle's works. But even in his admiration for Aristotle Photius did not forget his own Christian background. He did not agree with all of Aristotle's philosophical system, and in the teaching of substance,[37] for example, he followed the doctrine of the Church. This treatise on the ten categories seems again to reflect Photius' teaching at the Imperial University. It is quite possible that he intended to publish his lectures on this subject for the use of his students, as he did his lectures on dialectical problems.[38] However, events prevented his realizing his intention and he incorporated his notes on the subject in his *Amphilochia*.[39]

III

While Photius was finishing the composition of his *Bibliotheca* he could not foresee that the happiest part of his career was coming to an abrupt end. During his absence from the capital events were to happen which would soon change his whole life. The embassy to the Arabs mentioned in the introduction of the *Bibliotheca* can be connected only with the exchange of prisoners initiated, according to Arab writers, by Theodora and Theoctistus in 855.[40] Photius does not seem to have been the person of the embassy principally entrusted with the negotiations with the Arab Khalif Mutawakkil. The head of the Embassy was a certain dignitary called George. He is most probably to be identified with the palatine (?) George mentioned by the *Vita Constantini*.[41] It could be, therefore, that Constantine-Cyril accompanied his former professor on this occasion.[42]

---

[36] Quaestiones 137–147, cols. 757–811.

[37] Ibid., col. 773 C–776 A.

[38] Quaestio 78, col. 501 B.

[39] K. Ziegler is right in denying that Photius had written several works, now lost, on other philosophical questions, as Hergenröther (op. cit., vol. III, p. 330) seems to suppose. Photius' position in the history of Byzantine philosophy has not yet been properly studied and appreciated. B. Tatakis, in his book, La philosophie byzantine (Paris, 1949), devotes to Photius only two very inadequate pages (pp. 131–133). A short philosophical treatise on time by Photius' disciple Zacharias of Chalcedon was published by K. Oehler, "Zacharias von Chalkedon über die Zeit," B. Z. vol. 50 (1957), pp. 31–38. It reflects the activity of Photius' philisophical school.

[40] See F. Dölger, Corpus der griechischen Urkunden, Regesten, vol. I (München, Berlin, 1924), p. 54. A. A. Vasiliev, H. Grégoire, M. Canard, Byzance et les Arabes (Bruxelles, 1935), vol. 1. pp. 225 seq. See ibidem pp. 276, 277 the short account on this exchange given by Yacqūbī and on pp. 317, 318 the more detailed report in Tabarī's historical work.

[41] Vita Constantini, ch. 6, ed. Dvornik, Les Légendes, p. 355. See ibidem pp. 93 seq. the variants in old Slavonic manuscripts of the Legend. The manuscript of Rylle and Lwów speak of an *asecretos* and George Polaša (palatine?). The *asecretos* could be Photius, but the manuscript tradition is rather confused.

[42] The *Vita Constantini* says that its hero was twenty-four years old when he started on the embassy. Because of that Constantine-Cyril's embassy used to be dated from 851, for he died in 869 when he was forty-two years old. On the other hand, however, we do not know of another embassy to the Arabs at this time. The last exchange of prisoners before 856 was made only in 845–846 which would be too early a date for Constantine. Constantine's embassy is described as

The embassy probably started in the late fall of 855. The exchange of prisoners on the river Lamus took place on February the twelfth or twenty-third, according to Arab sources. The members of the embassy could have returned to Constantinople only in the early spring. In the meantime, however, important events were happening in the capital between January and March 856. A palace revolution took place against the powerful logothete Theoctistus, protégé of Theodora, which had far-reaching consequences: not only the death of Theoctistus, but also the end of Theodora's regentship and her ousting from the imperial palace.

This political reversal can, in some ways, be compared to what happened when the Empress Irene, with her faithful minister Staurakios, was struggling for power that she should have yielded to her son Constantine III, the heir to the throne. She almost succeeded in 790 when her son became of age, but a military revolution spoiled her plans. She was victorious seven years later after having used all kinds of intrigues against her unreasonable son.[43] It is easy to imagine that many of Theodora's enemies were making this comparison and were fearful for Michael's future. There was, of course, Bardas who had, so far, been held in the background by his sister, and who did not mean to leave the most influential post to a eunuch. It seems that Bardas would have been satisfied with a simple banishment of Theoctistus by Michael who, in 855 had come of age, but other advisers of the young Emperor thought that only Theoctistus' death could avert the danger threatening him if the all-powerful minister were allowed to live; so he was murdered by the guards on the young Emperor's order.[44]

But, like Irene, Theodora had many supporters among the *dévots* in Byzantium because of her restoration of image-worship. It is now established that she sympathized with the intransigent *dévots* advocating strong measures against all enemies of the true faith, especially against the former iconoclasts, although Theoctistus himself had tried, at least in the beginning, to maintain a balance between the intransigents and the moderates.[45] The latter found in Bardas a political leader against whom all the venomous propaganda of Theodora's supporters was concentrated.

---

having as its main object a religious disputation at the Khalif's court. This is a legendary trait and it is quite possible that the author of the Legend made a mistake when speaking of Constantine's age on that occasion. The description given by the Arab writers is not clear, but we can conclude from Tabarī's report that the Greek embassy led by George reached Muttawakkil's capital. According to Tabarī, George's embassy consisted of about fifty dignitaries and servants.

[43] For details see J. B. Bury, A History of the Later Roman Empire (London, 1889), vol. 2, pp. 483 seq.

[44] See J. B. Bury, A History of the Eastern Roman Empire (London, 1912), pp. 157 seq. Cf. F. Dvornik, The Photian Schism, History and Legend (London, 1948), pp. 36 seq.

[45] The rivalry of these two politico-religious parties in Byzantium is the main feature of Byzantine political and religious life. They are, in some way, the heirs of the circus parties of Blues and Greens of the earlier period. This rivalry gives new meaning also to the conflict between Ignatius and Photius. On the parties see F. Dvornik, "The Circus Parties in Byzantium," Byzantina-Metabyzantina (New York, 1947), vol. I, pp. 119–133. Idem, The Photian Schism, pp. 1–38.

If the struggle had been limited to bickering for political power only, not much harm would have come from the conflict between the members of the imperial family. Unfortunately, in Byzantium struggles for political power often spread also to the religious field. But this time even this could have been, if not avoided, at least mitigated, if the Church had been led by a Tarasius, a Nicephorus, or a Methodius, all of whom experienced great difficulty with intransigent elements among the *dévots* although only Methodius considered himself forced to use ecclesiastical weapons against the Studites, the leaders of the opposition. The Patriarch Ignatius, certainly a saintly man, was appointed by Theodora without being first elected by a synod,[46] in the hope that he would be able to hold the balance between the moderates and the intransigents whose leaders, the Studites, had been, since the death of Methodius, under the ban of excommunication. However, Ignatius failed to show the circumspection that had characterized the administration of his great predecessors. He was loyal to Theodora and it was easy for the intransigents to use his prestige for their intrigues against Bardas, the strong man of the new government and their most dangerous opponent. Ignatius gave full credit to rumors, spread by the extremists, of the supposed incestuous behavior of Bardas, and publicly refused him holy communion.[47]

In spite of this moral blow to his person, Bardas did not then take any measures against the Patriarch. In order to deprive the extremists of all hope that Theodora, still living in the palace, would soon return to power, he and Michael decided to send her and her daughter to a convent. Ignatius, asked to bless their veils, refused, but even his refusal was not at once fully exploited by the new government against him. Only when the Patriarch had protested against the execution of a certain Gebeon who, posing as Theodora's son, had started a revolutionary movement against Michael and Bardas, did the government, tired of all the intrigues – there had been another similar attempt made by Theodora's supporters before Gebeon's revolt – arraign Ignatius for high treason and, on the twenty-third of November, 858, banish him to the Isle of Terebinthos.[48]

Thus, for over two years Ignatius was allowed by the new government to remain in office, which indicates the government's embarrassment over his attitude, and the unwillingness of Bardas, the responsible man, to complicate the situation by an attack against the Patriarch. If Ignatius had shown a little more circumspection he would, most probably, have been left unmolested, despite his intimate relationship with the intransigents. When we consider Ignatius' blundering behavior during his last two years in office, we can

---

[46] This fact is now firmly established. See for details F. Dvornik, The Photian Schism, pp. 17 seq.

[47] J. B. Bury, A History of the East. Rom Emp., p. 188, was the first to expose the unwarranted character of the gossip spread against Bardas and to criticize Ignatius' attitude. Cf. F. Dvornik, Les Légendes, pp. 139 seq., idem. The Photian Schism, pp. 36 seq.

[48] See J. B. Bury, *A History of the East. Rom. Emp.*, pp. 189, 469–471. This date seems preferable to that given by V. Grumel, Les Regestes des actes du patriarcat de Constantinople, (Kadiköy, 1936) p. 68 (July, August).

more readily credit Nicetas' report[49] that prelates, high functionaries, and senators – he mentions two deputations – insisted that the Patriarch resign in view of the difficulties of the time.

IV

There can be no doubt now about the fact that Ignatius did resign. It was a voluntary resignation, although, imposed by the circumstances, but the juridical value of Ignatius' abdication cannot be questioned.[50] The way was thus free for the election of a successor.

However, the situation remained delicate because of the growing tension between the two parties in the clergy – the intransigents and the moderates. The government, therefore, was looking for a man outside the rival ecclesiastical parties who would be acceptable to both factions and whose loyalty could be depended upon. Photius seemed to be the most suitable and competent man. In order to prevent any new complications, the government manifested its intention simply to follow the example of Theodora in the case of Ignatius and to appoint Photius as new Patriarch. But Bardas had to yield to the clergy assembled in a synod, which claimed its right to choose three candidates and to present them to the Emperor for nomination. It seems almost certain that the leader of the moderates – Gregory Asbestas, Bishop of Syracuse, was one of them. The instransigents had their own candidates whose names are not known. The choice of Photius by the bishops was the result of a compromise between the two factions and the government.

Why did the bishops accept Photius as Ignatius' successor? He seemed acceptable to both parties. As an intellectual he naturally sympathized with the moderates, but, up to then, he owed all his promotions, the professorship at the University, the post of First Secretary of the Chancery and the membership in the Senate, to Theoctistus and to Theodora. His last public function, the embassy to the Arabs, had been entrusted to him by Theoctistus and Theodora. The marriage of his brother to Theodora's sister seemed also to have tightened the relationship of Photius' family with Theodora. Moreover, he could not be blamed for any partisanship in the overthrow of Theoctistus and Theodora, for it had happened while he was on his mission to the Arabs. As head of Imperial Chancery, Photius must have shown an extraordinary talent for practical administration, because Nicetas stressed this ability especially in his characteristic of Photius.[51] It was certainly common

---

[49] Vita Ignatii, P. G., vol. 105, col. 505. See F. Dvornik, The Photian Schism, pp. 39 seq.

[50] See F. Dvornik, "Le premier schism de Photius," Actes du IVe congrès internat. des études byzantines (Sofia, 1935), pp. 319 seq. Idem, The Photian Schism, pp. 39–50. V. Grumel, "La genèse du schisme photien," Atti de V Congresso internaz. di studi bizantini (Rome, 1939), pp. 177, 179. Cf. also E. Amann, L'époque carolingienne, in A. Fliche, V. Martin, Histoire de l'Eglise, vol. 6 (Paris, 1947), p. 469.

[51] P. G., vol. 105, col. 509: ... σοφίᾳ τε κοσμικῇ καὶ συνέσει τῶν ἐν τῇ πολιτείᾳ στρεφομένων εὐδοκιμώτατος πάντων ἐνομίζετο.

knowledge that Photius was not only a fervent iconodule, but also well versed in theological lore, as has been shown by the study of the content of his *Bibliotheca*.

What was Photius' attitude to the proposed promotion? Is it true that he craved the patriarchal dignity and that he was himself furthering his nomination?[52] All that we know now of the circumstances in which Ignatius had to leave the patriarchal throne makes us hesitant to believe this. We have seen that the new government had, at first, no intention of depriving Ignatius of his post. He was left in the patriarchate for two years, in spite of serious political complications provoked by his attitude.[53] If Photius ever thought of the possibility of one day becoming Patriarch, he certainly did not expect it to happen as soon and under such circumstances as it did. All that interested him, in 855, when he was composing his *Bibliotheca*, was to continue his scholarly activity after his return from the embassy.

In his inthronistical letter to Pope Nicholas, Photius[54] confesses that he had, in his boyhood, a desire to become a monk but, he continues, "although the fact that I accepted government positions forced me to change my impulses directed towards other pursuits, never indeed did an idea enter my mind, bold [enough] to make bearable the thought that I might succeed to the dignity of the episcopate." Can we not catch in these words an echo of Photius' true sentiments? It was not a common practice in Byzantium to promote laymen to the patriarchal dignity. Such things happened only in special circumstances when the Church was in danger and needed the hand of an able diplomat and administrator. This was the case when Tarasius and Nicephorus were chosen for this dignity, but normally whoever accepted a government post, manifested thereby that he had no intention of entering Holy Orders. Why should we not apply this rule to Photius?

In the same letter Photius explains to the Pope the circumstances in which he had ascended to the patriarchal dignity.[55] His words have, so far, been

---

[52] This opinion is repeated by K. Ziegler (Photius, op. cit., col. 678) in very strong terms, although he fails to put forward any substantiating evidence.

[53] Theoctistus was murdered between January and March, 856. Theodora's regency was ended, and its end approved by the Senate, probably in March 856. She was expelled from the palace in August-September 858. Ignatius was sent to Terebinthos in November 858. See Bury, op. cit. pp. 469–471.

[54] P. G., vol. 102, col. 585.

[55] P. G., vol. 102, col. 588C, D.: "When my predecessor in the episcopal dignity had quietly left this high office, I was set upon vehemently, I do not know from what motives, by the whole clergy, the assembly of the bishops and metropolitans, and before them and with them by the Emperor. He did not yield even slightly in his attempt jointly (undertaken) with the aforementioned assembly of the clergy. [And] he put forward the unanimous wish and zeal of the clergy as an excuse for his not abandoning [the attempt], and [also] the fact that, even if he wanted to, he was unable to comply with my request. And the words of my [counter] appeal could not be clearly heard by [the clergy], for a great multitude had convened. And those who heard my words did not accept them, since they had one thing only in their minds, and kept saying that under all circumstances would I have to accept the burden of [wielding] authority over them, even against my wishes."

treated generally as empty oratory concealing the writer's true attitude in Ignatius' affair. The new findings concerning the circumstances in which the change in the patriarchal throne was effected, however, enhance the credibility of Photius' confession. He must certainly have become increasingly aware of the great difficulties of the situation, and it would not have been extraordinary for anyone in such circumstances to try every means of evading the burden. He yielded to the insistence of many who thought that extraordinary measures should be used to deal with such an emergency.

It seems that Photius finally accepted the offer on the condition that his election and acceptance by the synod be unanimous. This is indicated by the letter addressed by Metrophanes, Metropolitan of Smyrna, to Manuel, Logothete of the course, in which he describes the situation at the Synod.[56] It is clear from the statement made by this most faithful Ignatian that, in order to obtain the unanimity of votes, Photius was willing to make important concessions to Ignatius and his followers.

Why then did the peace which seemed so firmly established by Photius' election not last? It has been suggested[57] that the reason why the intransigents left the obedience of the new Patriarch, declaring Ignatius' abdication null and void, was that Photius chose as his consecrator Gregory Asbestas, who had been deposed by Ignatius. This, it has been said, was Photius' greatest mistake. Ignatius, when he learned of it, instructed his followers that it was unacceptable to him because it violated the condition under which he had abdicated. He regarded the ordination of Photius by a deposed prelate as invalid. The leaders of the intransigents, upon learning of Ignatius' attitude, declared Photius' election invalid and proclaimed Ignatius the legitimate Patriarch. After this, Photius had only one choice – to declare Ignatius' elevation to the patriarchate illegitimate. Because Ignatius was never a legitimate Patriarch, his deposition of Gregory Asbestas was invalid. Photius' ordination by Gregory was, therefore, valid and legitimate.

At first sight, this solution of the puzzling attitude of the Ignatians soon after Photius' consecration appears quite logical. When we study it in detail, however, we discover so many difficulties that we are forced to look for another solution. It is true that Gregory, with some of his followers, was deposed by Ignatius for reasons which do not seem to have warranted such treatment. Such seems to have been the impression in Rome also where the

---

[56] Mansi, vol. 16, col. 416: "Eventually, they [the bishops] were outwitted and all gave in, except five, including myself. When we realized that all the bishops were corrupt, we considered that we should demand that he should sign an official declaration in which he professed to be a son of the Church in Christ and bound himself to remain in communion with our very saintly Patriarch. We preferred doing this rather than disobeying our Patriarch, who had expressed a desire that we should elect as Patriarch one belonging to our Church in Christ. It was then that he signed in our presence a declaration affirming his wish to regard Ignatius as a Patriarch above suspicion and guiltless of the charges made against him; that he would never say a word against him nor allow anyone to do so. On those conditions we accepted Photius..." See also Theognostos' declaration, ibid., col. 300. For details Dvornik, The Photian Schism, pp. 43 seq.

[57] By V. Grumel, La genèse du schisme photien, op. cit., pp. 179–185.

Chancery of two Popes – of Leo IV (847–855) and of Benedict III (855–858) – had examined Gregory's and his friends' appeal to the tribunal of the first Patriarch. In 858 the appeal was still pending and no decision had yet been made by Rome. The prelates concerned were asked only to abstain from the execution of their functions until the decision was made.

This was well known in ecclesiastical circles in Constantinople, and Gregory's case was one of the items of synodal deliberations. The synod was regarded during a vacancy of the see as the sole religious authority in the Byzantine Church, and we have sufficient documentary evidence to show that the synod rehabilitated Gregory and his friends.[58] Again, their rehabilitation seems to have been approved also by Ignatius' followers who had obtained from Gregory and his partisans a kind of satisfaction concerning their former attitude towards Ignatius.[59] Actually, none of Ignatius' followers is known to have protested, at that time, against the ordination by Gregory. There is no mention of Gregory in the conditions under which the five Ignatian bishops were ready to recognize Photius. They were probably present at the consecration. Moreover, all points out that the bishops of both parties shared in the function of consecration. Gregory, the head of the moderates was delegated as the first consecrator, but two other consecrators were chosen among bishops who were not partisans of Gregory. This can be concluded from the declaration of Elias, representing the Patriarch of Jerusalem at the synod of 869–70, as well as from that of Metrophanes made at the same session of the synod.[60]

Ignatius must have been aware of it, and it would be preposterous to suppose that news of it had reached him only forty days after Photius' ordination. After all Terebinthos is one of the Princes' Islands which could be reached in a few hours from Constantinople. The surveillance of the imperial police was hardly as strict as to prevent any communications between

---

[58] See the letter by Pope Nicholas I to Michael III. M.G.H. Ep. VI, pp. 498–9. Cf. F. Dvornik, The Photian Schism, pp. 48 seq.

[59] This is indicated by Zachary of Chalcedon in his declaration in the course of the sixth session of the Council of 869–70. Mansi, vol. XVI, col. 87: .... *Uniti autem rursus et apostasiam illam reprobantes suscipiendi consistunt* .... It is still not clear what were the reasons that had prompted Ignatius to his harsh behavior against Asbestas on the day of his enthronement. Cf. the discussion by V. Grumel, "Le schisme de Grégoire de Syracuse," Echos d'Orient, vol. 39 (1940–42), pp. 257–267. The most plausible explanation seems to be Gregory's role in the conflict between Methodius and the Studites. He may have been accused by the Studites as the man responsible for Methodius' excommunication of them. They may have criticized Gregory's moderate ecclesiastical policy as they criticized that of his friend and countryman Methodius. Ignatius wanted to investigate these accusations after the admission of the Studites to the Church. Cf. Dvornik, The Photian Schism, pp. 16–35.

[60] Mansi, vol. XVI, cols. 85 E, 86 A, 90 C. Cf. also col. 92 A. In the same passage Metrophanes reprimands Photius for having willingly consented to be consecrated by Gregory: *volens consecrari a Gregorio proposuerit, nulla in hoc necessitate impulsus.* Unfortunately Zachary, who wanted to answer Metrophanes' accusations, was not permitted to speak. Such may have been the interpretation of the Ignatians, *post factum.* But if Photius had refused to be ordained by Gregory, he would have risked the opposition of the moderates who could have accused him of partisanship toward the intransigents.

Ignatius and his partisans in the capital. After Ignatius' abdication there was no reason for such restrictive measures.

If we accept the above-proposed explanation, we have to put all the responsibility for the schism which was to follow on Ignatius. It is true that he had shown more than once a particular stubborness in his conduct, but he was honest, and we are not entitled to launch such an accusation against him without very serious and reliable evidence. It would mean that Ignatius, although he abdicated and thus ceased to exercise jurisdiction over his Church, ignored the decision of the synod invested with supreme power during the vacancy of the see, and encouraged his followers to do the same, sacrificing the interest of his Church which needed peace, to his own offended self-righteousness.

Nor are we entitled to conclude, from the fact that it was Gregory who ordained Photius, that Photius himself had made this choice because he had been from the beginning in intimate relationship with Gregory, being one of the most devoted members of his party. There is no reliable evidence regarding the special relationship between Gregory and Photius during the latter's secular career. We have seen that Gregory could hardly have been Photius' teacher as has been suggested. The accusations of Photius' enemies, are, in this respect, vague and cannot be taken at their face value.[61] Photius himself did not show a special veneration and respect for Gregory during his patriarchate. In his correspondence Gregory has no prominent place.[62] Photius did not himself choose Gregory as his consecrator. This was imposed on him by the synod as a result of a compromise between the two factions. Let us not forget that Gregory's faction was victorious, and after it had acceded to government pressure not to insist on the candidature of one of its members, it wanted satisfaction and compensation for its resignation.

It was, of course, unfortunate that Photius had to accept such a compromise. There was somebody who could voice a protest against it – the papal curia. The synod ignored the fact that Gregory's and his friend's appeal to Rome from the judgment of Ignatius was still pending, and that the Roman chancery had asked the appellants to obstain from exercizing ecclesiastical functions before the Pope's decision. This omission was cleverly exploited by Theognostos who, in the name of Ignatius, had presented an appeal in Rome after the synod of 861. The omission by the synod of 858 and the consecration of Photius by Gregory were used as the most powerful weapons against Photius by Nicholas I, but only in his letters addressed to the Byzantines beginning with the year 863, after the intervention of Theognostos in

[61] They are quoted by Hergenröther, Photius, vol. I, pp. 363, 364. The good relationship of Photius with Theodora and Theoctistus, supporters of Ignatius in his strife with Gregory, should warn us to be cautious in evaluating these accusations.

[62] There is only one known letter from Photius to Gregory (P. G., vol. 102, cols 832, 833). It was written during Photius' first exile, and in it he lauds the fervor of his adherent and exhorts him to continue his religious activity. (Cf. Hergenröther, Photius, vol. II, p. 208). In 878, after Photius' rehabilitation, Gregory became metropolitan of Nicaea, when his metropole of Syracuse had been completely destroyed by the Saracens (Hergenröther, ibid., p. 313).

Rome. It should be stressed that in his previous letters to Michael III and to Photius, dating from 860, and even in his letters of 862 announcing the condemnation of the legates to the Church, to Michael III and to Photius,[63] he does not mention Gregory or Photius' ordination by him, although the legates must have reported to Nicholas all details concerning Photius' ordination.

This indicates that some fanatics – especially Theognostos – of Ignatius' party were, from the beginning, dissatisfied that their bishops had accepted the verdict of the synod of 858 rehabilitating Gregory and his friends. The protest against the ordination of Photius by Gregory had come from this group.

It is true that the acceptance of Photius by the Ignatians was conditional. Yet the conditions were dictated to Photius not by Ignatius, but by Metrophanes and his four colleagues. This is clear also from Theognostos' appeal made in the name of Ignatius in Rome[64] and from Nicetas' report in his Life of Ignatius.[65] The conditions concerned Ignatius' person and his good name. Metrophanes seemed especially anxious to obtain Photius' promise to stop all accusations attributing to Ignatius participation in political intrigue.

V

The discord was started by the difference in the explanation and practical application of the compromise's stipulations. Photius could see in them only a promise of respect to the retired Patriarch who should continue to live with full episcopal honors in revered retirement and whose name should not be misused in connection with political intrigues.

The intransigent Ignatians interpreted the conditions in their own way. In their view Photius pledged himself to "do everything in accordance with Ignatius' wishes," as Nicetas reported it, and they expected him to embrace completely theirs and Ignatius' ecclesiastical policy. This is indicated by Metrophanes' confession that Ignatius had exhorted them to elect as Patriarch someone "belonging to our Church of Christ." These words mean that they expected Photius to become a member of their faction or to behave as such. It remains to be proved that Ignatius himself had used these words – we have no authentic declaration of his in this respect – but one thing is certain, namely, that the five bishops and their followers interpreted them and the compromise in this way. Theognostos, in his appeal, put the following words into Ignatius' mouth:[66] "If the adulterer were a member of the Church, I would voluntarily consent with him. But how can I constitute an

[63] M. G. H., Ep. VI, pp. 433–451.

[64] Mansi, vol. XIII, col. 300.

[65] P. G., vol. 105, col. 513.

[66] Mansi, vol. XVI, col. 300B: εἰ ἐκ τῆς ἐκκλησίας ἦν ὁ μοιχός, συνένευσα ἂν καὶ ἑκὼν αὐτῷ· νῦν δὲ ἀλλότριον πῶς καταστήσω ποιμένα τῶν τοῦ Χριστοῦ προβάτων, ... ἓν μέν, ὅτι ἐκ τῶν ἀκοινωνήτων καὶ ἀναθεματισμένων ἐστίν.

alien shepherd of Christ's sheep? Many things are against it. The first, that he is of them who have been excommunicated and are struck by anathemas."

Let us, moreover, not forget that among the Ignatians there were some fanatics who were more intransigent than the five bishops who had accepted the compromise. The future was to show that even after Photius' death when Stylianos, the leader of the Ignatians, reconciled himself with Photius' successor, a small faction of fanatics continued their opposition. This is clearly shown by the anti-Photianist collection. We can presume that these fanatics did not approve of the compromise and were particularly shocked by the fact that the synod had rehabilitated Gregory and that Photius had accepted him as his main consecrator.

In these circumstances it was easy to provoke an incident which could be exploited against Photius. If the five bishops and the fanatics expected Photius to work for the return of Theodora, they were mistaken. Photius had to be loyal to the new government in his own and the Church's interest. He could not embrace their intransigent policy because he did not approve of it. He meant to rule, not to be a suffragan or assistant of the former Patriarch. A few admonitions addressed to the fanatics, a few acts which did not please the intransigents, some changes in the ecclesiastical body, planned or effected,[67] were subject to exploitation by the fanatics who convinced the five bishops that the conditions of their acceptance of Photius were being trampled upon by him. This was enough to cause an open schism. Gathered at the church of St. Irene in February 859, the Ignatians deposed Photius and proclaimed Ignatius to be the continuing legitimate Patriarch.

We can now follow with more precision Photius' reaction to the schismatics. He gathered a special synod of bishops at the Church of the Holy Apostles. The acts of the synod are not preserved. Only Zonaras gives us some important indications of the procedure of this synod. In explaining why the synod of 861 was called "first and second," he says:[68] "We learn that it met in the above-mentioned church of the Holy Apostles [in 859]; that a discussion arose between the orthodox and their opponents, and that when the orthodox had clearly won their point, all that had been said had to be put in writing. [We further learn] that the heretics objected to the

[67] It could have been, for example, the rehabilitation of Bishop Peter of Miletus who had been deposed by Methodius and who was a partisan of Gregory Asbestas (see V. Grumel, Regestes, vol. I, p. 73, no. 457). This rehabilitation might have been imposed on Photius by the victorious clerical party, and it seems to have been effected very soon after Photius' consecration. The Ignatians probably interpreted the compromise in the sense that all decisions made by Ignatius during his patriarchate should be respected and maintained. The rehabilitation of Peter, whose deposition by Methodius was confirmed by Ignatius, could have been regarded as a violation of the compromise. We have no evidence of other similar acts, but the victorious clerical party might have had some other demands concerning the appointments made by Ignatius which could be interpreted as a violation of the compromise. This would explain why, at the end, when Ignatius had refused to re-affirm his resignation, the synod had to declare his tenure illegitimate in order to prove all his acts invalid.

[68] J. Zonaras, Commentaria in Canones ..., P. G., vol. 137, cols. 1004 seq., Cf. Dvornik, The Photian Schism, p. 58.

decisions being put on record lest it should emphasize their defeat and their ejection from the community of the faithful, and this was why they fomented a revolt, which ended in fighting and bloodshed. That is how the first assembly suspended its deliberations and its meetings, and how some time later [in 861] another synod was summoned in the same church to discuss the same subjects...."

It is clear from this evidence that Photius proceeded against the revolutionaries according to the rules of Byzantine canon law. We learn further that the opposition was invited to present its case at the assembly.[69] When it was evident that the men responsible for the schism would be outvoted, convicted, and excommunicated, their fanatic followers organized a riot to bring the synod to an abrupt end before the Fathers had made their final decisions, and in this they were successful.

The fighting and bloodshed mentioned by Zonaras indicates that the riot had also a political background. The attempts made by the intransigents in 858 to bring about the downfall of Bardas were still fresh in the memory, and it is not surprising, if the government saw in the riot a new attempt to return Theodora to the palace and to the government. Only then did Bardas intervene and brutally put an end to the riot. All this is omitted in Ignatian sources which unanimously accused Photius of having broken his promises and of having started the persecution of Ignatius' followers. From this time also must be dated the four letters addressed to Bardas by Photius,[70] in which he protested against the abuse of physical force against the recalcitrants and pleaded in behalf of two prominent insurgents.

Nicetas does not mention the synod, but his report confirms our suspicion that the riot mentioned by Zonaras had a political background. After describing how Photius had broken his pledge and started to persecute the Ignatians, he says: "Then he overwhelmed them with promises of presents and honors in return for a signed document,[71] trying by every possible means to bring about Ignatius' ruin. Baffled in this, he suggested to the unscrupulous Bardas, and through Bardas to the lightheaded Michael, to send agents to enquire into Ignatius' activities, as though he had been secretly conspiring against the Emperor. A cruel and brutal band of prefects and soldiers immediately left for Terebinthos to make enquiries... at the end of their search they had found no plausible pretext for proceeding against him...."

---

[69] Cf. also what Metrophanes says about this synod: "Then it was that we personally upbraided him for his crime, with the result that we were subjected to violence, arrested without warning and imprisoned for days in the evil smelling gaol of the Numera." Metrophanes was one of the five bishops who had obtained a copy of the document containing the stipulations of the compromise, and his intervention indicates that the interpretation of the compromise was one of the subjects discussed at the synod. If his words, in this respect, are not clear, they at least confirm the fact, that he and his friends were present at the synod.

[70] P. G., vol. 102, cols. 617 seq.

[71] There are two possible interpretations of the χειρόγραφα for which Photius had asked. Does Nicetas mean the copies of the documents given to the five bishops, or declarations of recognition of Photius as the legitimate Patriarch? Both meanings imply that the action was taken at a synod.

Nicetas confirms by his words that Ignatius was not present at the synod convoked by Photius, although the rebellious prelates were there. This may mean that Ignatius was not held responsible for the start of the revolt against the new Patriarch; also that he was not involved in the riot, mentioned by Zonaras, which had turned into a political demonstration against the government. Because the rioters were demonstrating their fidelity to Ignatius, an enquiry was ordered at Terebinthos. In order to prevent the leaders of the demonstrators' getting in touch with Ignatius, he was deported to the Isle of Hiera, then sent to Prometon, and, at least according to Nicetas, brought back to Constantinople and incarcerated in the Numera gaol.

There he met Metrophanes and others of his supporters. This must have happened towards the end of the disturbances, when the government had the situation well in hand. In order to put an end also to the claims of the Ignatian fanatics, Photius convoked a synod in the Church of Our Lady in Blachernae, as we learn from the Ignatian document, the *Synodicon Vetus*.[72] There we read that Ignatius was not present at the synod and that he was deposed.[73] This synod also pronounced ecclesiastical sentences against the high and low clergy responsible for the schism and the disorders. This probably happened in August 859. At that time, according to Nicetas, Ignatius was already on the Island of Mytilene, where he stayed for six months, and was then allowed to return to Terebinthos. This seems to be the most acceptable reconstruction of the events based on Ignatian sources.

The fact that Ignatius was allowed to return to Terebinthos, nearer the capital, indicates that the government was at last satisfied that he had not been responsible for the outbreak of the troubles, and that there was no danger in letting him live in the proximity of Constantinople. Ignatius could have been spared the harsh treatment if he had made a public declaration that he did not approve of the initiative of his radical followers. It is probable that this or, at least, a reiteration of his abdication had been asked of him, and that he had refused to do either. He was loyal not only to Theodora, but also to his friends and followers, and the way in which they were treated by the government certainly did not encourage him to make such a declaration and perhaps to aggravate their fate. He never liked Bardas. Why should he assist him in his troubles and help him in the liquidation of his political opponents?

---

[72] J. Pappe in J. A. Fabricius and G. C. Harles, Bibliotheca Graeca (Hamburg, 1809), vol. XII, p. 417. Nicetas (loc. cit., col. 513) also speaks about a synod which had condemned Ignatius. He placed it in the Church of the Holy Apostles and dated it from the time when Ignatius was in Mytilene. Did he mean the synod of the Blachernae by which the synod of the Holy Apostles was closed? The information given by the *Synodicon Vetus* is more reliable. Cf. also another more complete version of this *Synodicon* in *Sinaiticus Graecus* 482 (1117), fol. 364^{v}, line 5 seq. On this newly-discovered document see infra p. 35 and the additional remark on p. 56.

[73] Nicetas (loc. cit.) mentions efforts made by officials to obtain from Ignatius a formal declaration that he did not consider himself to be the Patriarch. Ignatius' refusal to cooperate made a formal synodical declaration necessary. Nicetas' account of Ignatius, imprisonment in the Numera, although repeated by Metrophanes, seems rather dubious.

VI

For the Byzantines the case of Ignatius and of his followers was definitely settled by the synod of the Holy Apostles which was concluded in August 859 in the Church of Blachernae. Neither the Emperor nor Photius thought of a new condemnation of Ignatius by another more solemn assembly, as the author of the *Synodicon Vetus*[74] and Anastasius[75] falsely pretend when reporting that Michael III had dispatched, in the spring of 859, an embassy to Rome asking the Pope to send legates to Constantinople where a new council was about to be gathered for a new condemnation of the iconoclastic heresy.

The embassy brought also the inthronistical letter of the new Patriarch. The circumstances of Ignatius' abdication and of his deposition by a local council were explained to the Pope in the Imperial letter. Two of the bishops, rehabilitated by the synod which had elected Photius – Zachary and Theophilus – were among the members of the Imperial embassy. This was certainly arranged deliberately. Because they had appealed Ignatius' judgment to Rome and the appeal was still pending, they came to report their rehabilitation by a local synod which, they expected, would be confirmed by the new Pope. It was a sign of deference from the Byzantine Church to the first patriarchal see, a gesture which should be remembered.

Nicholas' attitude was not wholy unfavorable to Photius. Of course he was shocked by the circumstance that promoted Photius suddenly from lay status to the episcopacy and by the fact that the deposition of Ignatius by the local council was made without the knowledge of the Roman see.[76] He, therefore, sent two legates to Constantinople and ordered that "Ignatius who... has spontaneously and of his own free will relinquished the government of the... see and has been deposed by the general council of all [your] people, should appear before our legates and the general council in accordance with your Imperial custom, so that they may enquire why he abandoned the flock entrusted to him and why he made so little of, and treated with such contempt, the wishes of our predecessors and holy Pontiffs, Leo IV and Benedict."[77]

The last intimation indicates that the Pope had considered, too, the case of Gregory Asbestas and his followers. Their case was also to be re-examined by the synod, and the tenor of the Pope's words concerning Ignatius seemed to promise a favorable decision by Rome. It is thus important to stress that the new enquiry into the abdication and deposition of Ignatius in the presence of a local council was ordered by the Pope himself, and was not

---

[74] Ed. Fabricius, op. cit., pp. 417, 418. Cf. also *Sinait. Graec.* no. 482 (1117), fol. 364^{v}, line 10.

[75] Liber Pontificalis, vol. II, p. 155.

[76] Cf. Dvornik, The Photian Schism, p. 75. This is duly stressed by P. Stephanou, "Les débuts de la querelle photienne vus de Rome et de Byzance," Orient. Christ. Period., vol. 18 (1952), p. 271: "Plus que l'abdication d'Ignace, c'est la condamnation qui attira l'attention de Nicolas; elle heurtait un des principes fondamentaux de son gourvernement."

[77] Nicholas' letter to Michael III, M. G. H., Ep. VI, p. 436.

requested by the Emperor or the new Patriarch. The Pope reserved for himself only the final decision.

As for the Emperor's request for legates to a council which should condemn the inconoclastic heresy, recent research[78] has shown that there was in Byzantium, after Ignatius' resignation, sufficient reason for such a measure. The Patriarch Methodius had already complained, in 846 or 847, to the Patriarch of Jerusalem[79] about the obstinacy with which the iconoclastic clerics were resisting all his exhortations to abandon the heresy, although a sort of "amnesty" was promised the repentants, and all this in spite of the moderate religious policy that he followed. The rigorist policy embraced by Ignatius could hardly have had better results, and some spreading, abuses among the victorious monastic world, created naturally a reaction among the newly converted iconoclasts, for these abuses were particularly objectionable to the iconoclastic emperors. Even the Ignatian Council of 869–70 had to deal with iconoclastic dangers and condemned several prominent iconoclasts and their leader Crithinus.[80] This indicates that in 860 their number was even greater. Moreover, let us not forget that the restoration of image-worship by Theodora was made without a synodal decree which was quite unusual in Byzantine religious practice. The new Patriarch and the Emperor wanted to remedy this by the convocation of a special council at which Roman legates would be present.

The Byzantine government and the Patriarch were dismayed to learn of Nicholas' decision. A new enquiry into Ignatius' case and the long delay before the papal decision would reach Constantinople could only cause new complications in Byzantium. The Emperor and the Patriarch could simply have rejected such a demand on the grounds that it infringed upon the autonomous status of the Byzantine Church. When we look upon their decision to yield to the Pope's request and to reopen the investigation in a general council, from the Byzantine point of view, we have to confess that it was a very important concession, revealing in what high regard the position of the Roman Patriarch in the Church was held in ninth-century Byzantium. However, Byzantine political and religious authorities asked the legates,

[78] F. Dvornik, "The Patriarch Photius and Iconoclasm," *Dumbarton Oaks Papers*, vol. 7 (1955) pp. 69–97. The first image of Christ, after the final triumph of Orthodoxy was placed again by Theodora over the Brazen Gate. This must have happened before June 847, because Methodius who died that year, composed a lengthy epigram on it, published by Leo Sternbach in *Eos*, vol. 4, (Lwów, 1897) pp. 150, 151 and by S. G. Mercati in Bessarione, vol. 24 (1920), pp. 192–195, 198, 199. On the slow progress toward the restoration of images, see my study and the instructive remarks by Sirarpie Der Nersessian, "Le décor des églises du IXe siècle," Actes du VIe congrès international d'études byzantines (Paris, 1951), pp. 315–320.

[79] See Grumel, Les Regestes, no. 435. Grumel's dating is not clear.

[80] Mansi, XVI, col. 142. F. Halkin, in his review of F. Dvornik's study quoted above, when stating that in Photius' time the heresy was probably extinct, since no mention is made of prominent heretics, had overlooked this passage of the Acts. We would have learned more about the survival of the heresy if the second part of the Acts of the Council of 861 had been preserved. Moreover, John the Grammarian seems to have still been alive in 860. His excommunication is confirmed by Nicholas in his letter to the Byzantine bishops of 866 (M. G. H., Ep. VI, p. 522).

after informing them of the true state of affairs, to pronounce at the council a definite judgment in the name of the Pope.

It would be unjust calumny to accuse the legates of having been bribed by the Byzantines. They were honest prelates who knew well the high concept of the primacy of their master, and they were intelligent enough to appreciate the situation. Moreover, Rodoald (Radwald) of Porto was, during the first five years of Nicholas' reign, one of his most trusted and influential councillors. The idea of judging a Patriarch in Constantinople in the name of the Pope – such an event had never before occurred – appealed to them, and they were confident that Nicholas would be satisfied with such a striking confirmation of the supreme position of the Pope in the Church and of his right to act as supreme judge over other patriarchs.

The Acts of the Council of 861, partly preserved in the Collection of Canon Law of Cardinal Deusdedit,[81] the only canonist of the Gregorian period who saw their great importance for the documentation of the papal primacy, have been, so far, almost completely neglected by Church historians, as they were entirely overshadowed by the Acts of the Ignatian Council of 869–70, which ordered their destruction. They deserve a better treatment. From the declarations of the Greek Fathers and from the whole procedure itself, it can be deduced that the Byzantine Church for the first time recognized the canons of the Council of Sardica confirming the right of the Bishop of Rome to act as the supreme judge of the Church.

The case of Asbestas and his associates was examined again according to the wishes of the Pope, and the legates annulled the judgment by Ignatius, who objected to the whole procedure. We learn from Theognostus and Nicetas[82] that the intransigents had organized a public demonstration while accompanying Ignatius to the Church of the Holy Apostles where the Council was taking place; a detail which illustrates the dangerous and tense situation in Byzantium caused by the re-opening of Ignatius' trial on the order from Rome. The sentence of deposition of Ignatius was proclaimed by the legates on the grounds that he had not been canonically elected but simply appointed by the Empress Theodora. It was the same sentence which had been pronounced at the closing of the synod of the Holy Apostles in 859 at Blachernae. A formal deposition seemed necessary because the intransigents regarded Ignatius as the legitimate Patriarch and because Ignatius had refused to reaffirm his abdication.[83]

The Pope's reaction to what had happened in Constantinople is puzzling. On the one hand he did not reprimand his legates, although it was clear that they acted against his instructions – Rodoald was entrusted with even another confidential mission in the affair of King Lothaire – but on the other

---

81 Ed. by V. Wolf von Glanvell, Die Kanonensammlung des Kardinals Deusdedit (Paderborn, 1905), pp. 603–610.

82 Mansi, vol. XVI, col. 296; P. G., vol. 105, col. 517 C.

83 The recognition of Photius as legitimate Patriarch was not pronounced by the legates at the synod. They apparently reserved this for the Pope.

hand he refused to sanction his legates' decision. It is evident from his letters (from March 18, 862) to Photius and to the Emperor[84] that Nicholas did not want to break with them; rather, in asking for new proofs of Ignatius' guilt, he desired new negotiations. Besides the matter of principle – the neglect of the rights of a Roman Pontiff, as he conceived them – there was one important point which was not yet settled. The Pope's demand, this was expressed very clearly in his letter to Michael of 860, for the return of Illyricum and Sicily to Roman jurisdiction. It was a subject that had been very important in papal policy since 787 when Hadrian I made his demand for the return of provinces detached by Leo III from the Roman patriarchate. The popes continued to follow closely what was happening in those provinces and did not miss any opportunity to secure their supremacy over them. Rome had succeeded already in winning an important part of the former Illyricum. From the first half of the ninth century the Croats had their own bishopric at Nin, ancient Nona, directly subject to Rome, although the missionary work among the Croats was done mostly by the Frankish clergy from Aquileja and from the Dalmatian coastal cities.[85] This interest had later prompted Nicholas to invite Constantine-Cyril and Methodius, the apostles of Moravia who were on their way through ancient Pannonia to Venice, to visit Rome, directed his successor Hadrian II to revive the old metropolis of Sirmium with Methodius as Archbishop, with jurisdiction over Pannonia and Moravia, and inspired John VIII to ask the Serbian ruler Mutimir, although converted by the Byzantines, to place his lands under the metropolis of Sirmium.[86]

The Illyrian question occupies an important place in pontifical policy in the ninth century,[87] and the interest in that was logically extended later to Bulgaria, part of which had also sometimes belonged to Illyricum. Nicholas could not neglect this vital matter. He was determined to defend the rights of his see everywhere and in every particular, and when he determined to continue the negotiations with the Byzantines, it was not so much because he hoped for a bargain, as because he regarded it his duty to vindicate all the rights of his see. There was some hope for success. Photius' letter disclosed the Patriarch's willingness to make some concessions in this respect – at least his words could be so interpreted. In any case he seemed most anxious to obtain Rome's acknowledgment, for, in order to comply with the Pope's

---

[84] M. G. H., Ep. VI, pp. 440–446.

[85] On Roman and Frankish missions in Croatia see the resumé given by F. Dvornik, The Slavs, Their Early History and Civilization (Boston, 1956), pp. 76 seq. For more details see the chapter on Illyricum in Dvornik, Les Légendes de Const. et de Methode, op. cit., pp. 248–283.

[86] Cf. Dvornik, The Slavs, pp. 88 seq.

[87] This was overlooked by P. Stephanou in his paper Les débuts de la querelle photienn loc. cit., p. 273. If there was not much hope of winning back jurisdiction over the Greek provinces of former Illyricum, there was at least that part of southern Italy where Roman and Byzantine interests were continuously clashing. Later, under similar circumstances, John VIII obtained the promise of jurisdiction over Bulgaria and Stephen V some important concessions in Southern Italy (Dvornik, The Photian Schism, pp. 211 seq., 229 seq.).

wishes, he induced the council to vote a canon prohibiting, in the future, promotions of laymen to high ecclesiastical dignity.

It is regrettable that the Byzantines had not renewed the negotiations. Here, their conception of Rome's position in Church affairs and the Pope's conception were too far apart. What the Byzantines had regarded as an enormous concession to Rome – having a Patriarch judged by the Pope's legates – was for Nicholas a matter of course. He had a much higher conception of Rome's primacy and did not understand the lack of comprehension of Rome's rights on the part of the Byzantines. In spite of this he seems to have been very anxious to reopen negotiations, and he waited until August 863 for a Byzantine embassy before he took his fatal step.

VII

In the meantime, Nicholas was given other explanations of the Ignatian and Photian conflict from Greek refugees, determined foes of the new Patriarch, who had reached Rome. Their leader was the Abbot Theognostus[88] who pretended to represent the person of Ignatius. Offended by the negative attitude of the new Patriarch and the Emperor, Nicholas listened to Theognostus' exaggerated reports of the strong opposition to the new Patriarch and of the unstable position of Bardas and the young Emperor, and Nicholas was moved by the vivid description of persecutions of which Ignatius and his followers had reportedly been the objects. Seeing no hope of obtaining full recognition of the papal rights, as he had defined them, from the new ecclesiastical and political government in Byzantium, Nicholas put all his hope in the victory of the opposition, whose leaders in Rome appeared much more devoted to the Pope, who were willing to go much further in the recognition of his primacy, and who were promising to restore to the Pope his rights.[89]

Did Ignatius really appeal to Rome as Theognostus pretended? There is no evidence that he did except the declaration of Theognostus who presented

[88] Theognostus most probably left for Rome only after learning that the Pope was dissatisfied with the decisions of the Council of 861. It would have been pointless to seek Roman support as long as the Pope's reaction was unknown. He could have reached Rome at the end of 862 or in the spring of 863.

[89] A passage in the letter of John VIII to Boris-Michael of 874 (M. G. H., Ep. VII, pp. 294 seq.) indicates that some promises concerning Illyricum and Bulgaria had been made by Theognostus in the name of Ignatius under Hadrian II. P. Stephanou (op. cit., pp. 276, 277) tries, albeit unsuccessfully, to explain this passage. In view of the importance of the Bulgarian question for Rome, there must have been some negotiations in Rome, with Theognostus under Hadrian, to insure Bulgaria against any attempt from the Byzantines. Of course, in 863, as Stephanou points out, Theognostus could not give any promises concerning Bulgaria, which was not yet converted. In 860, when Nicholas asked Michael III for the return of Illyricum to Roman jurisdiction, there was little hope of an early conversion of Bulgaria, which comprised, at any rate, a great part of Thrace under Byzantine jurisdiction and only a small part of former Illyricum. This suggests that Nicholas had in mind the provinces of Illyricum proper and the papal patrimony in Southern Italy and Sicily, all of which are – together with the jurisdiction over Syracuse – explicitly mentioned in the Pope's letter (M. G. H., vol. VI, pp. 438, 439).

an appeal in Ignatius' name at the Roman synod of 863. However, no Byzantine Patriarch would have used expressions of deference and submission such as we read in the address of the appeal. Ignatius himself declared categorically during the synod of 861: *Ego non appellavi Romam, nec appello.* The experiences he had had with Nicholas' two precursors and with the papal legates did not encourage him to such action. He seems to have been, at any rate, rather a poor canonist. The embarrassed account by Nicetas of a document which Ignatius was "forced" to sign[90] seems to indicate that the ex-Patriarch submitted to the judgment of the synod of 861 and was, therefore, left to live unmolested in a monastery. Theognostus, however, thought that such a *pia fraus* was perfectly motivated and permissible, the more so as there was nobody in Rome on Photius' side who could contradict his passionate accusations.

The decisions of the Roman synod of 863 were thus a signal victory for Theognostus. In the canons of the synod preserved in papal letters from 866, addressed to the Byzantine Church and to the oriental patriarchs,[91] we can detect easily how much the Pope was influenced by Theognostus. For the first time in Nicholas' documents the name of Asbestas plays a prominent role. The investigation of his case made by the chanceries of Leo IV and Benedict III, which were not unfavorable to Asbestas, and the fact of Ignatius' abdication, are completely ignored. In these documents we discover the same *epitheta* that are given to Photius in the so-called anti-Photian collection.[92] Naturally, Photius was deposed with all those ordained by him, and Ignatius was reinstated Patriarch.[93]

---

[90] P. G. vol. 105, col. 521.

[91] M. G. H., Ep. VI, pp. 511 seq., 557 seq.

[92] See the comparison in Dvornik, The Photian Schism, pp. 98 seq.

[93] E. Amann (Photius, op. cit., col. 1518) comments on the synod as follows: "On n'accusera pas le synode romain de 863 d'avoir sous-estimé le pouvoir du Siège romain. Peut-être même donnait-il aux droits traditionnels reconnus à la première Eglise une extension un peu imprévue. Surtout l'usage qu'il en faisant était de nature à froisser l'Eglise de Constantinople. ... Un tel deploiment de force était-il nécessaire, alors que ... la question du conflit entre Ignace et Photius n'était pas encore definitivement ventilée?" It is regrettable that Rodoald of Porto, one of the legates at the Synod of 861, was not in Rome in 862 and 863 when Theognostos started to spread his pro-Ignatian propaganda. Until then Rodoald had been principal adviser to Nicholas, who had, therefore, entrusted him with an important embassy in the matter of Lothaire's marriage, which he had fulfilled, though not to the Pope's satisfaction. The pontifical librarian Anastasius took advantage of Rodoald's absence to undermine his influence in the Pope's entourage. Rodoald would have defended his attitude in Constantinople with more vigor and perhaps with more success than did his colleague Zacharias of Anagni. The latter accepted humbly his condemnation by the Pope, being satisfied with the income from a rich Abbey of St. Gregory the Great which seems to have been left to him. Although he was deposed, it is possible that his see was not given to another occupant; in any case, when re-established, he was reappointed Bishop of Anagni. Rodoald apparently always maintained his conviction that the Pope should not have listened to the refugees from Constantinople. His position at the Pope's court was taken by Anastasius, who, from that time on, became the Pope's chief adviser in eastern policy and author of this letter addressed to the Easterners. P. Stephanou (op. cit., p. 275) denies the version, so-far generally accepted, concerning Zacharias and the Abbey of St. Gregory the Great. His argument is, how-

In this manner the rupture between the official heads of the two Churches was consummated. Nicholas remaines faithful to his principles which he believed to be the only truth, and the upholding of which he regarded as his most sacred duty. One is entitled to admire this steadfastness and fidelity to principles that forced Nicholas to do his duty as he saw it, and that prevented his being swayed by the fact that 350 bishops – Michael III stressed the number in his letter – had accepted Photius and had agreed to the deposition of Ignatius. After all, this comprised the whole Byzantine Church, together with the Emperor, who held such a high position in the Eastern Christian commonwealth. But no such assemblage could influence Nicholas, nor could even the prospect of a possible schism.[94]

However, this was not the view of the Byzantines. They had no reason to admire the rigorous application of a principle of which they had had no knowledge before Nicholas, which was too bewildering even to many Westerners, as Nicholas' application of it in the West had shown, and which was the more alien to the Byzantine mentality as it seemed to encroach upon the autonomous status of their Church. They knew the weaknesses of their position. They knew that Ignatius, although "illegally" appointed had been regarded by all without protest for so many years as the legitimate Patriarch. They knew that promotion from the lay status to the bishopric was not regular, and they knew that political questions and the pressure exercised by the government were responsible for much of the trouble in their Church.[95] All they wanted in the new entanglement that was threatening the peace of their Church, was a more charitable understanding from the side of the more fortunate see of Rome and the application of their cherished system of οἰκονομία. This is the real meaning of Photius' praises of Christian charity in his second letter to Nicholas and of his regret that the Pope had not shown a sufficient appreciation of this principle in his judgment of the situation in the Byzantine Church.[96] Nicholas, with his high concept of the primacy and of all moral principles, had no comprehension of the Byzantine practice of οἰκονομία and continued to perform what he regarded as his

---

ever, not conclusive. The two quotations from *Vita Gregorii M.* by John the Deacon (P. L., vol. 75, chaps. 93, 97, cols. 236, 239) show only that Zacharias was administrator of the Abbey under Nicholas and John VIII. There is no evidence that he was reinstated by John after he had been removed by Nicholas. The context seems rather to suggest an uninterrupted administration by Zacharias up to the reign of John VIII. Not even the fact that John calls him bishop when he was given the administration of the Abbey by Nicholas, can be accepted as absolute proof that he had been so appointed before his condemnation. John the Deacon who knew about the rehabilitation of Zacharias and was favorable to him, could simply have suppressed any allusion to his humiliation. More secure appears Stephanou's thesis that the bishopric of Anagni was given to Alboinus, who had signed the Acts of the Roman Synod of 869 (Mansi, XVI, col. 130). There is still, however, some doubt about reading the name of his see: Anianensis or Anagnianensis.

[94] Nicholas' fidelity to his principles regarding the position of Rome in the Church is well illustrated by P. Stephanou, op. cit., pp. 271 seq.

[95] P. Stephanou is rightly not unaware of all this, loc. cit., pp. 278 seq.

[96] P. G., vol. 102, cols. 593 seq.

sacred duty.[97] This mutual misunderstanding illustrates also how far the estrangement between East and West had already progressed in the ninth century. It was difficult for Nicholas, if not impossible, to understand amid the changed western atmosphere, the mentality of the Byzantines.

It would have been better if the Byzantines had not taken any notice of Nicholas' action. They kept silent for a long time, but Michael's letter of 865 revealed all the bitter disappointment that the Pope's offensive action had left in Constantinople. Some of the Emperor's biting remarks about Rome and the Westerners, refuted in the Pope's passionate answers, were to contribute for centuries to the growth of unfriendly feeling towards the East by the West, for they were copied and recopied by western canonists. The Pope did not expect such violent repercussions and, in spite of the apparent confidence with which he answered, he was frightened and ready to reverse his policy. Both parties were asked, at the end of the long missive, to send their representatives to Rome for a definite decision by the Pope. This lack of consistency in the Pope's attitude is surprising.

It is apparent that the tone of Michael's letter and of the Pope's reply sounded the echo of events which had taken place in Bulgaria, a country coveted until then by both East and West. The Byzantines after concluding a politico-religious alliance with Great Moravia, directed against the Franks and the Bulgars, succeeded in 864 in detaching Boris of Bulgaria from the Franks and in inducing him to open his country to Byzantine missionaries. There went Nicholas' hope of winning this new nation to Roman obedience; the Byzantines had triumphed. The Pope, reading Michael's letter saw that he was in danger of losing too the achievements of his legates at the Council of 861: – the recognition by the Byzantine Church of Roman supremacy – and one can trace his fear and worry in the terms, often violent, that he used in answering the Emperor. In this fear can be found also the motive for his concession, granting re-examination of the affair of Ignatius and Photius in Rome. Only Asbestas and his friends were to be sacrificed.[98] Unfortunately the new arguments for the papal primacy accumulated from western practice and documents by Anastasius, the composer of this letter, could hardly have impressed the Byzantines.[99]

---

[97] J. Haller, Das Papsttum, Idee und Wirklichkeit (Stuttgart, 1951), pp. 113 seq., voiced, of course, a quite different appreciation of Nicholas' person and policy, and though his is a biased interpretation, it appears that the last word on Nicholas has not yet been spoken. A modern orthodox scholar's view on Nicholas is revealed by J. N. Karmiris in his study, "The Schism of the Roman Church," Θεολογία, vol. ΚΑ' (1950), pp. 408 seq.

[98] Nicholas must have been very worried by the long delay in hearing from the Emperor in answer to his letter of 863. He seems to have written again to the Emperor in the summer of 865 before receiving the Emperor's letter (M. G. H., Ep. VI, p. 454), but this second letter was not sent and is not preserved in the Papal Register. In it the Pope probably reiterated his demand to both parties to send their representatives to Rome for a final decision.

[99] It was unfortunate that when he received the Emperor's letter the Pope was seriously ill and could give to Anastasius only general directions for the composition of the answer. The Byzantines must have found very strange the Pope's contention that no synod could be summoned without the Pope's consent, and that the councils were not the concern of the Emperor. This, in

VIII

In spite of their violent clash, there was still a slight hope of reopening negotiations. However a new development in the Illyrian and Bulgarian affair brought the conflict to a tragic climax. The Pope's hopes of regaining jurisdiction over Illyricum were suddenly revived by the request for a patriarch presented to him by the newly-converted Khagan Boris-Michael of Bulgaria. Nicholas learned at the same time that the Khagan had also requested Louis the German to send him Frankish missionaries. Nicholas seized the occasion with both hands and, as is known, succeeded with the help of his legates, especially with that of the good psychologist Formosus, Bishop of Porto, not only in convincing Boris that he really did not need a patriarch, but also in eliminating the Frankish missionaries from Bulgaria. The newly converted land was once again under the direct jurisdiction of Rome.

It was a splendid victory which the Pope hoped to complete with a victory over Photius. The numerous letters that his legates were carrying to Constantinople through Bulgaria, addressed to many important personalities in Byzantium, and echoing his new triumphant mood, were to strengthen the opposition of the Ignatians and to induce the government to cease its support of Photius. The letters never reached their destination. The legates were stopped at the Byzantine frontier, and, after refusing to accept Photius as the legitimate patriarch, were sent back to the Bulgarian Khagan. Thus these long missives failed to influence any further development in the Photian affair. They remained in the papal register to be used by Roman canonists who were finding there new arguments for the papal primacy, some of them supplied by the famous Pseudo-Isidorian Decretals.[100]

In order to evaluate what happened afterwards in Constantinople, let us try to look at the situation from the Byzantine point of view. We understand the efforts of the Popes to recover the jurisdiction over Illyricum exercised by Rome before 732. Bulgaria, however, comprised a great part of Thrace which had never been under Roman jurisdiction, but always under that of Byzantium.

the Byzantine view, curtailed a right of the emperors that they had always exercised before. Cf. F. Dvornik, "The Emperors, Popes, and General Councils," Dumbarton Oaks Papers, vol. 6 (1951), pp. 1–23. The use of the "Petrine principle" to lower the prestige of Constantinople in the Church must also have considerably offended the Byzantines. There is, however, a passage in Nicholas' answer (M. G. H., vol. VI, p. 469) which seems to admit, on the part of the Emperor, the need for the Pope's cooperation in all doctrinal definitions. At the same time, in this passage the Emperor seems to defend the right of the Byzantine Church to be autonomous in disciplinary matters. The Byzantine and the Pope's ideas on primacy clashed again, although the Byzantine Church was ready to accept Rome's basic principle.

[100] Especially in the letter addressed to Michael III. M. G. H. Ep. VI, p. 493, no. 12, p. 495, nos. 3, 4 (according to Perels, editor of the letters). Cf. also Perels' remarks on the use of the Decretals in other letters, ibid., p. 381, no. 1, p. 383, no. 6, p. 388, no. 1, p. 389, no. 3, p. 393, no. 5, p. 397, no. 6, p. 405, no. 1, p. 407, no. 1. Cf. also Amann, Epoque carolingienne, p. 480. On Nicholas' use of the Decretals, see J. Haller, Nikolaus I. und Pseudoisidor (Stuttgart, 1936), pp. 175–190. In Nicholas' letters to the Easterners little use is made of the Decretals, and it remains to be more clearly shown how much they influenced his ideas on the primacy.

Moreover, the Council of Chalcedon had stipulated that the newly converted lands in the Eastern part of the Empire were to be subject to the jurisdiction of New Rome. Thus, the Byzantines regarded Rome's seizure of Bulgaria as a direct and unjust attack on the rights of the Byzantine patriarchate. In Rome they could not see how vital it was for the Byzantines to keep Bulgaria in their cultural sphere. This explains the violent reaction that Nicholas' success had provoked in Byzantium.

It would have been better if Photius had maintained his reserved attitude and left to the Emperor the defense of Byzantine interests in Bulgaria. Unfortunately, Boris was well established in his country, and any such military intervention as that of 864 was impossible.[101] Perhaps the murder of Bardas by Basil, the new favorite of Michael (on April 21st, 866) was partly responsible. To impress Boris, Photius tried ecclesiastical measures. First a local council condemned the intrusion of the Latins into Bulgaria, and Boris was so notified. He was, however, so little impressed that he transmitted the Imperial letter announcing this condemnation to the papal legates who brought it to the Pope.[102]

But Nicholas was so alarmed by the letter and by some pamphlets in which Greek missionaries were discrediting Latin customs in Bulgaria that he mobilized the whole Frankish Church, with Hincmar of Reims, to defend the Latin Church against the Greeks. So the first polemic writings against the Greeks were composed in the West.

Photius, on his side, mobilized, in his famous *Encyclica* the whole East, convoking a synod in Constantinople to condemn the false doctrines spread by the Latin missionaries in Bulgaria. His epistle had a more profound influence on the deepening of the tension between East and West than the writings of the Frankish polemics. The *Encyclica* became an armory for Greek polemics in the later period. More fateful for the future relations between East and West was the condemnation and deposition of Nicholas by the four Eastern patriarchs gathered at a synod in 867. Here Photius made the greatest mistake of his life, which the Westerners never forgave.

We can, however, not see in this action a condemnation of the Western Church or of the primacy of the Roman patriarch in the Church. Let us not forget that the target of the anathemas were the Latin missionaries in Bulgaria who were said to despise Greek customs and were preaching false doctrines. How could Photius, who counted on the help of western prelates and of the Emperor Louis II in the execution of the synodal sentence against Nicholas, make a frontal attack on the whole Latin Church and the papacy as such?

The anti-Photian reports of the council can now be confronted with the only official part of the Acts of this Council that has been preserved. It is the homily of Photius delivered at the end of the conciliar deliberations after the Emperor had signed the Acts and the confession of faith. This sole

---

[101] The army was away on an expedition to Crete. Cf. H. Grégoire, "Etudes sur le IXe siècle," Byzantion, vol. VIII (1933), pp. 524 seq.

[102] See Nicholas' letter to Hincmar, M. G. H., Ep. VI, p. 603.

genuine document[103] gives the lie to all Ignatian tales about the nonexistence of this synod, the falsification of the Emperor's and bishops' signatures by Photius, etc. Both Emperors, Michael III, and Basil, are addressed in a most solemn way by Photius, the presence of the senate, of high functionaries, and of numerous clergy is attested. What is striking, however, is the absence of any polemical topic. No mention is made of the Pope, of the Filioque, or of the Frankish missionaries in Bulgaria and their false doctrines. The main emphasis is laid on the "triumph over all the heresies," condemned by the previous general Councils, especially by that of 787, a triumph proclaimed anew by the council of 867 and confirmed by the signature of the Emperor whose pen, like a sword, had pierced them so that "no manner of impiety shall henceforth speak freely."

One gathers from Photius' words that the condemnation of the Pope was not the only, or even the main, subject of the deliberations. It is evident that the Council was meant to be oecumenical and, therefore, it had to rule on doctrinal matters. The preservation of the faith in all its purity is especially stressed. This had been achieved by the final victory of the Church over the last heresy – iconoclasm. The stressing of the importance of this victory is the main preoccupation of Photius from the beginning of his ecclesiastical career. In redefining the decisions of the seventh oecumenical Council, the Council of 867 had made – in his view – a final definition of orthodoxy. It is interesting to note that similar ideas on the victory over the heresies and especially over iconoclasm, are expressed by Photius in his letter to Boris-Michael.[104]

This homily was delivered at the last session of the Council, probably at the beginning of September 867. The confident tone which permeates it reveals that Photius was not prepared for the sudden change that was about to take place two or three weeks after the close of the Synod. Having assassinated his adoptive father Michael,[105] Basil thought it necessary to look for support among the intransigents and in Rome. Photius had to cede his place to Ignatius, and Louis II probably never learned that he was about to be recognized as basileus for helping to depose Nicholas,[106] who had died on November 13th, 867, before learning what had happened in Constantinople.

---

[103] It is the homily published first by P. Uspenskij (Četyre besedy Fotija [St. Petersburg, 1864], pp. 81 seq.) and by Aristarchis, Photii Homiliae (Constantinople, 1900), vol. II, p. 309. A commentary and a translation of this homily will be published by C. Mango in Dumbarton Oaks Studies (The Homilies of Photius, hom. 18).

[104] Cf. A. Grabar, "L'art religieux et l'empire byzantin à l'époque des Macédoniens," Annuaire 1939–40 de l'Ecole pratique des Hautes Etudes. (Melun, 1939), pp. 10 seq.

[105] An interesting and new appraisal of Michael and of his war with the Arabs was published by A. A. Vasiliev, "The Emperor Michael III in Apocryphal Literature," Byzantina-Metabyzantina, vol. I, New York, 1946, pp. 237–248.

[106] Cf. F. Dölger, Byzanz und die Europäische Staatenwelt (Ettal, 1953), pp. 314 seq. It is, however, going too far to construe the recognition of the imperial title for Louis II as the main reason for Basil's change of policy, and it is important to emphasize that in 867 in Byzantium there was still hope of unifying the Roman Empire, with an emperor in Constantinople and co-emperor in the West.

IX

Basil sent an embassy to Rome in order to announce the restoration of Ignatius to the patriarchal throne. He seems, however, to have been unaware of the change on the papal throne, as late as December 868, acting in accordance with the 865 directive of Nicholas, he sent representatives of both rivals to the Pope for final judgment.[107] Had the Emperor known that Nicholas had disappeared from the scene he would probably have written and acted differently. He could not know, of course, that the new Pope, Hadrian II, had in the first months of his reign shown, some inclination to change his predecessor's oriental policy. The partial rehabilitation of the condemned former legate Zachary was symptomatic in this respect. Basil would certainly have tried to profit from this change if he had known of it, because, even in his letter, while submitting to Nicholas' judgment, he recommended mercy. In asking for the attendance of papal legates at a new council to be held in Constantinople, Basil hoped that, after a new examination of the Ignatian and Photian controversy, a compromise would be found which would give the Ignatians satisfaction without hurting too much the feelings of the moderates who had followed Photius. Although he could not count on the support of the moderates after the assassination of Bardas and Michael, he could not exasperate them by the exercise of greater severity which might provoke their open opposition.

In Rome, however, the coup d'état in Constantinople had provoked quite a different reaction. If there were in some minds any doubts about the justice of Nicholas' stern eastern policy, all such doubts vanished when the news of the coup reached Rome. All that Nicholas had done and written in the Photian affair seemed confirmed in the clearest way by the Byzantines themselves. It was a new triumph for Theognostus. Everything he had said about the strength of the Ignatian party and the political weakness of Bardas' and Michael's regime appeared to have been well founded, and Nicholas was praised for having followed his advice. It was also the triumph of Nicholas, party in Rome which saw in the overthrow of Photius proof that the Byzantines had accepted Nicholas' definitions of the Roman primacy and were submitting completely and in every respect to the Pope's rule over the Church.

Basil would have been better advised not to have sent to Rome the Acts of the Synod of 867 which he had taken from Michael's ambassadors, recalled by him while on their way to Louis II. He would probably have had them destroyed in Constantinople, if he had known that Nicholas, deposed and excommunicated by the Council, was not living, and if he could have foreseen the kind of reaction that the knowledge of such an act would

---

[107] We must accept the sending of two letters by Basil. The one brought by the spathar Euthymius must have been sent in the spring of 868. The Pope's answer dated in August of the same year did not reach Constantinople before December 11th of that year. See Dvornik, The Photian Schism, pp. 138 seq. The dates of the imperial letter in Dölger's Regesten, no. 474, and of Ignatius' letter in Grumel's Actes des Patriarches, Les Regestes no. 499 must, therefore, be changed accordingly.

provoke in Rome. Thus came about the solemn condemnation of Photius at a Roman Council, the suspension of all those ordained by him, and the prescription that all bishops ordained before 858 who had followed him must sign a *libellus satisfactionis* expressing the papal primacy in a way very unpalatable to the Byzantines. Contrary to Basil's wishes, the new Council in Constantinople had to execute and confirm the decisions of the Pope and of the Roman Council.

It has already been related in detail[108] how disappointing for Basil and the Byzantines was the Council of 869–870. The papal legates, especially the deacon Marinus, were adamant in the execution of the Pope's orders, and Basil and his representative Baanes tried in vain to give a better turn to the agenda. Even the Ignatian bishops were reluctant to sign the *Libellus*. The Council opened with only twelve bishops and ended with 103. Photius kept a dignified silence and, in spite of the apparent reunion, the two Churches were more estranged than ever, and the Byzantine Church more divided than before.

The defection of the Bulgars from Rome and the decision of the three Eastern patriarchs on the submission of the Bulgarian Church to New Rome was the sad climax on which the Council ended, and if Anastasius, who happened to be in Constantinople as envoy of Louis II, had not saved and translated the Acts of the Council, we would not even have learned of the whole procedure – only an extract of the Greek text of the Acts is preserved – for the legates were robbed by Slavic pirates on their homeward journey and thus deprived of most of the documents, perhaps at Basil's instigation.

The initiative that Ignatius took in Bulgaria was welcomed by all – intransigents and moderates – and there are some indications that the Patriarch, contrary to the stipulations of the Council, used the services of the Photian clergy in missionary work.[109] Inasmuch as the great majority of the clergy remained faithful to Photius, and inasmuch as Rome had refused Ignatius' and the Emperor's requests[110] for a mitigation of the sentence against those ordained by Photius, the task of the Patriarch was very difficult. It was impossible to replace all Photian clergy, and in some places the Photian bishops remained in their posts. Photius continued to rule his Church with letters from his exile.[111] Such a situation could not last and Basil was quick to realize it. The radicalism of the die-hards among the intransigents seemed dangerous, and the Photian clergy's steadfastness revealed the moderate party's enormous strength. Photius and his bishops adopted a very shrewd

[108] See especially the pertinent remarks by Ammann, Photios, op. cit., cols. 1577–1582. Cf. also Dvornik, The Photian Schism, pp. 141 seq. The Photianists were justified in complaining that they were condemned in Rome and at the Council without a hearing. Their representative sent to Rome by Basil had perished on the way, and the legates curtailed the hearing at the Council, although Basil wanted to give them an opportunity to speak.

[109] Photius' letter to Arsenius, P. G., vol. 102, cols. 904, 905; John VIII's letter to Boris, M. G. H. Ep. VII, p. 277 (written between December 872 and May 873).

[110] Dölger, Regesten, no. 488; Grumel, Les Regestes, no. 504.

[111] See for details Dvornik, The Photian Schism, pp. 159–166.

policy, making a great show of loyalty to the new regime, all of which led to a rapprochement first between Photius and the Emperor, and then also between Photius and Ignatius.

We can now quote a new document illustrating Basil's changed attitude towards Photius. B. Laourdas discovered in the Manuscript Iveron 684 a letter of Photius' under the title: "To the great Emperor Basil, when he started writing and when he asked for the solution of some problems." The contents of this letter were known until then as *Quaestio CXIX ad Amphilochium*; they discussed one of the main arguments used by the iconoclasts against representing the invisible God or Christ.[112] The letter to Basil is posterior to the other two letters in which Photius asked, and then expressed thanks, for a certain relief in his exile.[113] This letter might have been written in 872, and it presupposes a friendly letter of the Emperor to Photius. It shows that Basil started soon to change his mind about Photius. In any case, from 873 on, Photius was back in Constantinople, in the Imperial palace, directing the education of the Emperor's children and, probably, teaching again at the Magnaura University, which had been reorganized by Bardas.

On the other hand the rapprochement between Photius and Ignatius was being slowly prepared by by Rome itself. Ignatius' activity in Bulgaria had provoked great indignation in Rome. Hadrian protested to the Emperor[114] menacing Ignatius with the threat of letting him taste "the vengeance of the canons" should he not withdraw from Bulgaria. His successor John VIII was even more adamant. In his letter to Boris he threatened to depose Ignatius, because he was restored to his see only on condition that he did not tresspass on the rights of Rome in Bulgaria. In 874–5 in his letter to Basil John protested anew against Ignatius' interference, asking the Patriarch to come to Rome to justify his action.[115] The depth to which Ignatius' stock in Rome had sunk is illustrated by the letter of 878 that menaced him with excommunication and deposition.[116] His loss of Rome's support made Ignatius readier for a reconciliation with his adversary, and this reconciliation was fully effected certainly in 876, if not earlier.

This is attested by Photius' affirmation during the Council of 879–880,[117] the sincerity of which we have no right to contest. It is also confirmed by Leo VI in the funeral oration for his father,[118] and by the newly-discovered, more complete version of the *Synodicon Vetus*.[119] Moreover, the letter of

[112] See Dvornik, The Patriarch Photius and Iconoclasm, pp. 85, 86. Edited by B. Laourdas, Ἐπιστολὴ τοῦ πατριάρχου Φωτίου πρὸς τὸν αὐτοκράτορα Βασίλειον, Ὀρθοδοξία, vol. 25 (1950), pp. 472–474. Ad Amphilochium, P. G., vol. 101, cols. 696 seq.

[113] P. G., vol. 101, cols. 765–72.

[114] M. G. H., Ep., vol. VI, pp. 759 seq. and p. 762.

[115] M. G. H. VII, p. 296.

[116] Ibid., pp. 62 seq.

[117] Mansi, XVII, col. 424.

[118] A. Vogt-I. Hausherr, "L'Oraison funèbre de Basil Ier," in Orientalia Christiana, vol. 26, 1932, pp. 62–9.

[119] It is contained in Sinaiticus Graecus no. 482 (1117), fols. 357v–365v. The manuscript is from the fourteenth century. See V. I. Beneševič Opisanie grečeskich rukopisej monastyrja

John VIII, dated April 878 discloses that in the previous year Basil had asked the Pope to send legates to Constantinople for a pacification of the Church. This can only mean that Basil, Ignatius, and Photius had decided to make a definite end to the schism between the Ignatians and Photianists by the convocation of a new council which would give satisfaction to Photius and to his followers. It was to this council that the Papal legates, Paul and Eugene, were sent, bearing letters to Boris of Bulgaria and the threatening letter to Ignatius mentioned above.

It is a pity that Ignatius died (October 23rd, 877) before the legates reached Constantinople. If the proposed council could have met during Ignatius' lifetime, the Photian "legend" which still worries Church historians would not have developed, and we would have a clearer insight into the complicated embroilment of political and religious parties in Byzantium at this period.

X

The stubborn attitude of Ignatius in the Bulgarian affair inclined John VIII more eagerly toward settlement of his differences with Photius, which explains the cordial, almost joyful tenor of the letters to the Emperor, to Photius, and to the Byzantine clergy[120] in which the Pope announced his decision to recognize Photius as legitimate Patriarch of whose ascension to

---

Svjatoj Ekateriny na Sinaje (St. Petersburg, 1911), vol. I, pp. 266–293. The manuscript is entitled Θεοδόρου τοῦ Βαλσαμὼν [νομικὸν] ὁραῖον and contains, in addition to the *Syntagma* of fourteen titles with *scholias*, various canonical documentation, and two Ignatian documents, the letter of Stephen V to Basil I in defense of the Pope Marinus (fols. 324r–326r) which will be discussed later, and a better version of the *Synodicon Vetus* published by Fabricius. This document is entitled: Συνοδικὸν περιέχον ἐν ἐπιτομῇ ἁπάσας ἀπὸ τῶν ἁγίων καὶ πανευφήμων τοῦ Χριστοῦ ἀποστόλων γεγονυίας ὀρθοδόξους τε καὶ αἱρετικὰς συνόδους μέχρι τῆς ὀγδόης οἰκουμενικῆς μεγάλης ἁγίας συνόδου. On f 364v, line 32, one reads ρξγ'. Μετὰ ταῦτα Φωτίου πρὸς τὸ φιλι(άσειν) 'Ιγνατίῳ πάντα λίθον κινήσαντος, 'Ιγνάτιος τὴν μὲν ἀγάπην αὐτοῦ ἀπεδέξατο, τὴν ἱερωσύν(ην) δὲ αὐτῷ οὐ μετέδωκε, λέγων "εἰ μὴ αὐτὸν οἱ 'Ρωμαῖοι προσδέξονται, πρὸς οὓς ἐποίησε τὴν παροινίαν, (..) ἐγὼ ἐξουσίαν οὐκ ἔχω δοῦναι τὴν ἄφεσιν (.....) τὰ γὰρ εἰς ἐμὲ αὐτοῦ πταίσματα συγχωρήσεται ὁ αἴρων τὴν ἁμαρτίαν τοῦ κόσμου Χριστὸς ὁ Θεὸς ἡμῶν. Πάντως γὰρ ἐὰν οἱ 'Ρωμαῖοι φιλ(αν)θρωπεύσονται εἰς αὐτόν, μετ' ἐκείνων συμπαθὴς κἀγὼ ἔσομαι." This page of the Manuscript is very difficult to read, some parts being illegible. I wish to thank Mr. John Parker, Fellow at Dumbarton Oaks, who is preparing the editions of some twelfth-century texts, for having deciphered the most difficult passages. The passage from λέγων to ἔσομαι is copied out in another hand at the foot of the page, but the copyist reproduced neither the parts of the text that are illegible, nor the character after παροινίαν which looks like δὲ. The original of this part of the *Synodicon* must certainly have been composed at the end of the ninth century, after the abdication of Photius. Another Ignatian source, the anti-Photian Collection (Mansi, vol. XVI, cols. 452, 453) speaks of pourparlers held with a view toward bringing about a reconciliation, but denies that they were successful, and blames Photius for it.

See Dvornik, The Photian Schism, p. 168. This source speaks also of ordinations made by Photius while Ignatius was still alive, and this contradicts the information of the newly-discovered version of the *Synodicon Vetus*, which denies that Ignatius had recognized Photius' sacerdotal status. The author here reveals himself as an intransigeant Ignatian.

[120] M. G. H., Ep. VII, pp. 166 seq.

the patriarchal throne he had learned through a Byzantine embassy[121] and in a letter from his irresolute legates. The conditions were that Photius should give certain satisfaction and ask for mercy at the synod. Here the Pontiff had most probably in mind Photius' attack on Nicholas at the Synod of 867. Of course, another condition was the respect of Rome's rights in Bulgaria.

The Pope sent the legates in Constantinople, through the cardinal priest Peter, a *commonitorium* with instructions how to proceed at the synod. Unfortunately this document is preserved only in a Greek translation as it was read at the fourth session of the synod.[122] The tenth clause of it orders the legates to proclaim the suppression of the Council of 869–70 and of the synods held against Photius. Because we do not have its Latin original, this clause of the document is generally regarded as interpolated by Photius.

It is true that in the letter to Basil John speaks only of an absolution of Photius from all censures, but in the letter to the Ignatians, issued at the same time and preserved only in its Latin original,[123] the Pope is much more outspoken concerning the decisions against Photius. The letter has almost a harsh tone. The Pope reproaches the Ignatian leaders for having already lived *multis iam annis usque ad praesens in discordiae divisione et in scandalorum perturbatione*.[124] After exhorting them to union with Photius, he exclaims: "Let none of you on turning back find excuses in writings on the subject, since all fetters are unfastened by the divine power which the Church of Christ has received, whenever what is bound is undone by our pastoral authority, for, as the saintly Pope Gelasius says, there is no tie that cannot be unfastened, except for those who persist in their error." If they persisted in their error and refused communion with Photius, the legates had the power to excommunicate them.

In this passage only the Roman and the Constantinopolitan anti-Photian synods can be meant. All the anti-Photian decisions being abrogated by the Pope, the synods remain valueless. This indicates that the clause concerning the abrogation of these synods was in the Latin original of the *commonitorium*. It was perhaps not as outspoken in the original as we read it in the present version, but the proclamation of the annulment of the anti-Photian decisions must have been ordered by the Pope, and it could not have differed substantially from the original. Even if we should accept a modification of this clause in the Greek translation, it must be only slight, and the legates could have accepted it in good faith for they knew that such was their master's intention.[125]

---

121 Dölger, Regesten, no. 497.

122 Mansi, vol. XVII, col. 472, M. G. H., Ep. VII, p. 189.

123 M. G. H., Ep. VII, pp. 186, 187.

124 V. Grumel, "Lettres de Jean VIII pour le rétablissement de Photius," Echos d'Orient, vol. 39 (1940–42), p. 154, explains these enigmatic words as follows: „Le pontif veut sans doute simplement dire que depuis bien longtemps la paix religieuse ne fleurit plus à Constantinople." This interpretation seems most probable.

125 See Dvornik, The Photian Schism, pp. 175 seq. I stress here once more how strange it appears that the account of the suppression of the Councils is preceded by the words ἀπὸ τοῦ

If the Pope's decision concerning the anti-Photian synod met Photius' *desiderata* almost in full, he could not accept the Pope's invitation to demand pardon for his past behavior before the council because he and his followers were convinced that the measures taken against them by Nicholas, Hadrian II, and the Council of 869–70 were utterly unfair and canonically unjustifiable. If the Pope had mainly in mind Photius' unfortunate initiative of 867, the Patriarch was ready to forget all about that council, to forget also Nicholas' encroachments into the autonomous status of the Byzantine Church, and not to ask for a rehabilitation or justification of that synod, but that was all.[126]

The legates who had been blamed by the Pope for lack of initiative in the face of an unforeseen situation and who were able to learn more in Byzantium about the true state of things in the whole affair than was known in Rome, where actions were necessarily appraised only on the basis of Theognostus' biased information, finally yielded and consented to change not only the last clause in the *commonitorium* that contained the invitation to Photius to apologize before the Council, but also to modify accordingly the content of the pontifical letters.

We must reject all other attempts thus far proposed to explain the existence of the two versions of the papal documents: redaction of the second version in Rome before the departure of the priest Peter to Constantinople,[127] falsification of the Acts in the thirteenth or fourteenth century,[128] or simply

παρόντος (from this very moment, from now on). Such words must certainly have been in the Latin version because they express the Pope's view, which he still held in 879, namely, that these synods had retained their full value up to the moment they were abrogated, for in both the Pope's and the West's opinion the synods' decisions concerning Photius were well justified. This opinion was, of course, completely contrary to that of Photius. The fact that these words were left in the Greek version shows that it does not differ substantially from the Latin original. It was well, in the judgement of John, that the anti-Photian synods, from that time on, should not be counted "among other holy synods." This appears more logical when we take into account the fact that the envoys had certainly informed the Pope about the sincere reconciliation between Photius and Ignatius before the latter's death.

[126] There seems to be only one slight reminder of the Council of 867 in the title introducing the Canons voted by the Council of 879–80 (Mansi, XVI, col. 549): "Canons formulated by the Holy Synod that convened in the Renowned Church named after the Wisdom of God, the Logos, that confirmed the Seventh Oecumenical Synod and *repulsed every schismatic and heretical error*." The last words are an echo of Photius' homily pronounced at the end of the last session of the Synod of 867, which also proclaimed the oecumenicity of the Anti-Iconoclastic Synod. Cf. the commentary to the homily by C. Mango.

[127] Amann, Jean VIII, in Dict. de Theol. Cath., vol. VIII, cols. 605 seq. It was rejected also by V. Grumel, "Lettres de Jean VIII pour le rétablissement de Photius," op. cit. pp. 144 seq. Cf. also G. Hofmann, "Ivo von Chartres über Photius," Orient. Christ. Period., vol. 14 (1948), p. 118.

[128] Cf. V. Laurent, "Le cas de Photius dans l'apologétique du Patriarche Jean XI Beccos au lendemain du deuxième Concile de Lyon," *Echos d'Orient*, vol. 29 (1930), pp. 396–415; idem, "Les Actes du Synode photien et Georges le Metochite," ibid., vol. 37 (1938), pp. 100–106; V. Grumel, "Le Filioque au concile photien de 879–880 et le témoignage de Michel d'Anchialos," ibid., vol. 29 (1930), pp. 257–264. Cf. the refutation by M. Jugie, "Les Actes du synode photien de Sainte-Sophie," ibid., vol. 37 (1938), pp. 89–99. Idem, Le Schisme byzantin (Paris, 1941), pp. 124 seq. Cf. also A. Michel, B. Z. vol. 38 (1938), p. 454.

as Photius' own version drawn up without the knowledge of the legates. The practice of reading papal letters at the councils in versions changed according to circumstances unknown in Rome, was an old one in Byzantium. The papal letters had been changed and adapted to the new situation in 787 and in 861, and a vain attempt at a change of orders from Rome was made by Basil in 869–70. In the first two cases the legates consented to the changes, in the third they were adamant in executing the rigid orders they had been given. Their victory was of short duration.

The legates could consent to the changes, although they were quite numerous, more willingly because, on Photius' instructions, the patriarchal chancellary had retained in the Greek version some passages from the Latin which expressed very clearly the Pope's ideas on the Roman primacy.[129] This is a point of first importance, and it should not be overlooked. Photius was even ready to give the legates the further satisfaction of excusing Nicholas and Hadrian for what they had decided against him. He paraphrased John's letter as follows: "Let no one, as many simple people think they may, appeal to the decrees of our blessed predecessors Nicholas and Hadrian, for they never credited what was alleged against the very saintly Photius."[130]

Thus, the Acts of the Photian Council must be regarded as genuine, and there is no reason to cast doubt on the two last sessions which had approved the *horos* of the Nicene Creed and had forbidden any deletion or additions to it.[131] The fact that Basil and the court were in mourning is sufficient to

[129] See for details Dvornik, The Photian Schism, pp. 182 seq. See ibid., pp. 198 seq. on the legates' effort to stress the papal primacy in their interventions at the Council.

[130] See ibid., pp. 186, 187. Mansi, XVII, col. 401.

[131] Dvornik, op. cit., pp. 194–198; 398 seq., 403 seq. On the controversy concerning the interpolation of the words forbidding any addition or deletion, see M. Jugie, "Origine de la controverse sur l'addition du Filioque au Symbole," Revue des sciences philosoph. et théolog. vol. 38 (1939), pp. 369–385. Idem, Le Schism byzantin, pp. 124 seq., V. Grumel, "Photius et l'addition du Filioque au Symbole de Nicée – Constantinople," Revue des études byzantines, vol. 5 (1947), pp. 218–234. The arguments of the two controversialists for or against Photius' knowledge of the Latin practice of addition of Filioque to the Creed are not conclusive. The matter should be investigated further, although, so far, M. Jugie's arguments for his thesis seem the more convincing. It is important to note that the Fathers had accepted the possibility of an addition in case "the Evil one brought forth, through his machinations, a new heresy." One has almost the impression that these words were added on the instigation of the papal legates. On the slow evolution of the custom of singing the Creed at the Mass in the West, see J. A. Jungmann, *Missarum Sollemnia* (Wien, 1948), pp. 578 seq. It was introduced in Rome only after 1014. Photius mentions the procession of the Holy Spirit in only one of his homilies, all of which seem to have been pronounced during his first patriarchate. In S. Aristarchis' edition (Photii orationes et homiliae, Constantinople 1908), I, p. 295. In C. Mango's edition it is homily sixteen. This homily should be dated most probably from 867. It might have been delivered as an introduction to the planned Council. See C. Mango's commentary on the homily in the introduction to his edition. In the treatise on the Councils by the Patriarch Euthymius (Dvornik, op. cit., pp. 383–385, 456, 457), there is clear awareness of the Acts of the Photian Council in the version known to us, with the words forbidding any addition to the Creed. V. Grumel, in reviewing my book on the Photian Schism (Revue des études byzantines, vol. 10, 1952, p. 283) implied that this treatise could have been written by Euthymius II (1410–1416) because the Ms. containing it is from the fifteenth century. If this were so, we would expect to read in the text ὁ Νέος, an indication that the author had Euthymius II in mind, especially since Euthymius I (907–912) was a well-known personage

explain the absence of the Emperor at the preceding sessions and the holding of the sixth session in the Imperial palace.[132]

The Acts were also brought to Rome by the legates, translated into Latin and deposited in the archives.[133] John had thus full knowledge of the Acts when writing his famous letter to Photius in which he expressed his astonishment about changes in his writings made at the Council, but, in spite of that, approving what was mercifully "done at the assembly" for Photius' reinstatement.[134] It is evident from this letter that Photius had explained to John that he could not ask pardon before the synod because he regarded all synodical decisions made against him as a grave injustice. The Pope preferred to pass over all this, although with some regret, in the interest of peace among the Churches and because he obtained considerable concessions from the Byzantines: return of Bulgaria to Roman jurisdiction, military help for "the land of St. Peter," and the return of the monastery of St. Sergius in Constantinople.

XI

John's decision to annul the decrees of the anti-Photian councils was courageous because not all of the Roman clergy approved of it. The most prominent and most energetic and dangerous of the opponents was Marinus, the former legate at the Council of 869–870, who had insisted with such stubborness on the exact execution of Hadrian's orders that he profoundly

and a Saint. The recent date of the Ms. is a very poor argument against its authenticity, as everyone knows. Besides, the text ascribed to Euthymius presents a much purer version than that of Neilos of Rhodes and other two Ms. I quoted. It seems evident that the treatise of Euthymius has been re-edited several times, at different periods, with additions of other Councils (that against Barlaam, for example) and with some changes.

132 It is also possible that Basil was rather pleased to use this pretext. The Synod of 869 was assembled on his initiative and he had signed the decrees of the Synod of 867, and both Synods were now abrogated. He must have been tired of synods and clerical controversies.

133 The extracts in Deusdedit's canonical collection are made from the original Acts. Ivo of Chartres used one of the so-called intermediary Collections – one of them, the Britannica, is still preserved at the British Museum, Addit. Ms. 8873 – containing extracts from the archives which could be useful for the canonists. These extracts are often abridged by copyists, or even shortened (see Dvornik, The Photian Schism, pp. 324 seq.); therefore no conclusions can be drawn on the basis of the few differences these versions contain. Cf. the thorough study by G. Hofmann, "Ivo von Chartres über Photios," Orient. Christ. period., vol. 14 (1948), pp. 105–137.

134 M. G. H., Ep. VII, pp. 227, 228. The newly discovered, more complete version of the *Synodicon Vetus* gives only a very short account of Photius' reconciliation with Rome. (Sinait. Graec. 482 [1117], fol. 364^{v}, lines 38–40): ρξε'. 'Αδριανοῦ δὲ τοῦ πάπα 'Ρώμης θανόντος, καὶ 'Ιω(άννου) τὸν θρόνον αὐτοῦ (εὐτυχή)σαντος,(?) τοποτηρηταὶ αὐτοῦκατ (ἦλθον) (εἰς) τὸ Βυζάντιον, Εὐγένιος καὶ Παῦλος ἐπίσκοποι καὶ Πέτρος (πρεσβύτερος), οἳ καὶ συνάρσει Βασιλείου τοῦ φιλοχρίστου βασιλέως τὰ δι(εστῶτα) συνάψαντες, Φώτιον κατ(έλιπον) εἰρηνεύον(τες), κἂν ἀψευδής ἐστι ὁ εἰπὼν δὲ καθὼς ἐποίησας, ἔσται σοι . . . . . It is characteristic of the author that he omits any mention of the synod that confirmed Photius' rehabilitation. His anti-Photian bias is even more evident in the ironical allusion, probably to Math. 7:2 ("the measure you give will be the measure you get"), the fulfillment of which he sees in what was to happen after Basil's death, when Photius was induced by Leo VI to abdicate. The connection of his account of Photius' abdication which follows after this paragraph, quoted here on p. 41 footnote 141, with this passage is clearly indicated by the word γάρ.

offended the sentiments of the Byzantine clergy and ruined Basil's plans. We learn from a newly discovered document that Marinus opposed John's decision so vehemently that the Pope had to intern him for a month, probably for the duration of the stay in Rome of the 879 Byzantine embassy. This new document is the more complete version of the letter of Stephen V to Basil,[135] and in it we read: "Because he thought and felt in the same way as his predecessor, the blessed Pope Nicholas, and because he endeavored to carry out his decision, the godly-minded Marinus had encountered your greatest disfavor. Because he refused, as is said, to join those who thought differently and to dissolve and to make void (καταλῦσαι καὶ ἀκυρῶσαι) what was synodically enacted by him in the presence of your Imperial Majesty, this same Marinus who because of that was retained in custody for thirty days, suffering this for nothing else except for the truth. He endured it with thanksgiving and remained steadfast to the end, regarding it rather as a glory than as an insult."[136]

This new evidence confirms also that there was no new legacy to Constantinople entrusted to Marinus, and that, contrary to what was originally supposed, no second schism followed it. John VIII remained united and at peace with Photius.[137]

The anti-Byzantine party in Rome must still, however, have been very strong. This is confirmed by the election of Marinus after John's death, which must also have been a very unpleasant surprise for Photius and Basil. Did it provoke a new break between Rome and Constantinople? One thing is certain, namely, that Marinus did not send an inthronistical letter to Photius. However, this could perhaps be explained by the short reign of the new Pope (December 882 – April 884), who also retained Zachary of Anagni in the important office of Librarian of the Roman see. Photius tried to make peace with him and sent him a cordial letter along with relics of the Holy

---

[135] Published by V. Grumel, "La lettre du pape Etienne V à Basile Ier," Revue des études byzantines, vol. 10 (1953), pp. 129–155. I readily accept the editor's interpretation of this passage (p. 145). This new evidence solves the problem of Marinus' internment which was mentioned in the anti-Photian Collection (M.G.H. Ep. VII, p. 374), and which occurred, therefore, not in Constantinople in 869 or after 880, but in Rome, in 879. Some corrections to Grumel's reading of the text were made by B. Laourdas in Ἑλληνικά, vol. 14 (1955), p. 172.

[136] Incidentally, this passage shows that the Roman council assembled in Rome in 879, after the arrival of the Byzantine embassy, had decided to dissolve and to cancel what was synodically enacted in 869–70. The words used here are the same as in the shorter version of the letter, and these expressions are very similar to those used in the Greek version of the *Commonitorium*: ἄκυρος καὶ ἀβέβαιος. This, and the opposition of Marinus, indicate that the Pope, when writing his *Commonitorium*, had really in mind the annulment of the Synod of 869–870. Marinus would hardly have been so adamant if the Pope had wanted only to grant a misericordious pardon without touching the Synods. The annulment was certainly requested by the Imperial embassy, and John probably thought that the conditions under which he granted the request would silence the Roman opposition as well.

[137] The fact that Bulgaria, in the end, did not return to Rome does not mean that the Pope had been deceived by the Byzantines. See Dvornik, op. cit., pp. 210 seq. Boris, cleverly discerning an opportunity to profit from the situation, founded the first autonomous national Church in this part of Europe.

Cross in 880.[138] Was the Roman Pope less noble and less generous than a Patriarch of Constantinople? The reply of Stephen to Basil's letter indicates clearly that, in spite of Marinus' reticence, there was no official break between the two sees.[139] Would it have come to a break if Marinus had reigned longer? That is difficult to say, because an attack against Marinus could have come from the Byzantines also, who must have disliked him intensely. We are probably not far from the truth in thinking that Marinus held to his conviction that the full force of the anti-Photian synods endured, and that, acquiescing to the *fait accompli* in Constantinople and to the acceptance of Photius by John VIII, he dared not initiate a new break, but awaited further developments.

The pro-Byzantine party in Rome succeeded in electing Hadrian III (884–885), who immediately sent his inthronistica to Photius, and thus renewed friendly relations. It is a pity that Photius' answer and Basil's letter, which came into the hands of Hadrian's successor Stephen V (885–891), are not preserved. Stephen's missive to the Emperor, of which we have now a longer version, gives us fuller information on Marinus and on Stephen's attitude. Judging from Stephen's passionate defense of Marinus, the Emperor was offended by the election of Marinus, and saw in it an indication that Rome was resuming Nicholas' anti-Byzantine attitude. That the inthronistical letter was not sent seemed to confirm this supposition. Basil was pleased to remind the Romans that they did not observe their own rules in transferring a bishop from one see to another,[140] and that his promotion was thus illegal. The validity of his episcopal functions seems to have been questioned when the Emperor declared him not to be a bishop.

From Stephen's answer we learn that Marinus, although ordained bishop by John VIII,[141] had never exercised episcopal functions, and that therefore his promotion to the Roman see could not be regarded as a transfer from one see to another, although such transfers had been practiced lawfully in the past. Apparently the Byzantines had received very biased information about Marinus from Roman refugees in Constantinople, for Stephen asks the Emperor, towards the end of his letter, not to listen to those "who escape like mice" from Rome to Constantinople, but to send them back to

---

138 Published by A. Papadopoulos-Kerameus, Photiaca (St. Petersburg, 1897), p. 5. English translation in Dvornik, op. cit., p. 203.

139 On Marinus and the Anti-Photian Collection, see Dvornik, op. cit., pp. 219 seq.

140 Translations were forbidden by the first canon of Sardica, the same council that forbade the precipitate elevation of laymen to the episcopate. When we consider that violation of this canon was one of the main objections raised by Nicholas against Photius, we see that the Byzantines tried here to take their vengeance.

141 This new information about Marinus, which we find in the fuller version of Stephen's letter, reopens the question of relations between John and Marinus. Did John, impelled by Marinus' impetuous opposition against his eastern policy, ordain Marinus bishop in order to prevent his election to the Roman see and thus to safeguard, in this way, good relations between Rome and Constantinople? Whatever the case, from all of this we learn that there was in Rome a strong party of intransigent adherents to Nicholas' policy, hostile to Byzantium, and that it was opposed by a moderate party determined to continue John's benevolent eastern policy.

Rome. The Pope seems to have those refugees principally in mind when he writes of "filthy and odorous flies which had touched the Emperor's ears, which filled with sweet odors of myrrh."

This indicates that some byzantinophile elements in Rome must have expected a break in relations between the two Churches when Marinus became Pope and, fearing for their safety, fled to Constantinople. We have here, then, another case where biased information spread by refugees – this time in Constantinople – endangered the peace between the Churches.

Stephen V himself was certainly a Nicholaite, as can be judged from his passionate defense of Marinus.[142] In spite of that, however, he recognized Photius as legitimate Patriarch. This is clear from the following (no. 25 in the new edition): "You believe perhaps, that it is permitted to a priest to offend, if he is eager to do so, another priest. Certainly not, because they are rather offering to God their prayers for each other. And if nobody dares to examine and to slender him who has been judged by us worthy of vengeance and by you has been dishonored, now, when he is priest, how much punishment do you think he deserves who dares to inflict dishonor and wounds on the priest of God and oecumenical pope and the successor of the blessed Peter?"

The Pope has in mind here the Council of 869–70, and he seems to think that its decisions were then justified. In another passage, however, he makes quite a clear allusion to the Photian synod (no. 48): "Where is the sin of the holy Roman Church that wicked people had urged you to turn and use your tongue against her? Did she not send her legates to Constantinople under your reign according to ancient synodal usage? Did she not take defense of this synod? She who takes defense of all of them? [No. 49] You are asking to whom the Roman Church sent her legates. To none but Photius, the layman." The context suggests that the Pope has in mind the Photian Council, the decision of which the Roman Church defends along with the decisions of other councils.

There is, of course, a direct contradiction in this passage with that quoted above. There the Pope calls Photius "priest" against whom no-one dares now to say a word, and here he is called a "layman." This word could not have been in the Latin original of the letter, nor could the following passage in which the Pope is said to regret that Constantinople had no patriarch.[143] We would be doing a great injustice to the Roman chancellery in imputing to it such contradictory practices. The words λαϊκός, παραβάτης, ἐπιβήτωρ

[142] The Nicholaites did not favor the policy of John VIII, and diverged from it in many points. Stephen V's interdiction of the use of the Slavonic liturgy in Moravia, a privilege given to the Archbishop Methodius by John VIII, can be explained by this hostile attitude on the part of the Nicholaites. See for details F. Dvornik, Les Slaves, Byzance et Rome au IXe siècle (Paris, 1926), pp. 286–296.

[143] The editor of the longer version (op. cit., p. 153) added to this word *digne de ce nom* in the French translation, but this is not warranted. The intransigeant Ignatians simply did not recognize Photius as priest and patriarch, and the whole passage indicates that the translator of the letter was one of them.

were the epitheta with which the die-hard Ignatians liked to honor Photius. There is a nice array of them in the anti-Photian collection. We must not forget that we do not have the original Latin version of Stephen's letter in hand. We have only a Greek translation made, evidently – as the Photianists were not at all interested in a letter defending Marinus – by an Ignatian who could not abstain from making a few slight additions, very few actually, and only in those passages that could – by the addition of a few words – be turned against Photius.[144] He was convinced that he was merely interpreting and clarifying the Pope's attitude towards Photius, which, in the minds of the Ignatians, could have been only unfavorable.

It would, therefore, be going too far to read in another passage of the same letter the Emperor's and Photius' attempt to induce Rome to declare publicly the abrogation of the Council of 869–70, silencing thereby the opposition of die-hard Ignatians who had refused to join Photius after his rehabilitation. The following passage is explained in this way:[145] (no. 56) "Thus let this new reckless action cease. Let nobody hope to achieve things which are not allowed. Let nobody strive to dissolve what has been decided by the holy fathers, my predecessors, in synods against the intruder, and what has been observed manifestly in the whole world."

This passage has to be interpreted in connection with the preceding paragraph. There the Pope admonishes the Emperor once more to cease the attacks against the memory of Marinus. The phrases quoted above are simply a continuation of these admonitions which are followed by other similar admonitions. The word "intruder" (ἐπιβήτωρ) again looks very suspicious,

---

[144] In the original letter the Pope probably regretted the troubles that had beset the Church of Constantinople. The following passage (no. 50) reveals this. In it the Pope returns again to the injury suffered by the Roman Church through the attack against Marinus: "And if our very special affection for you would not oblige us to support this injury inflicted on our Church, to suffer its presence and to appease it, certainly would we not be forced to rage against the apostate who had unsheathed against us the sword of impious words, or better it is not we who would do so but the most blessed Peter...." The word "apostate" παραβάτης in the translation is highly suspect here, and the whole phrase would be perfectly intelligible without it. The author of the anti-Photian Collection apparently realized against whom the translator wished to turn the Pope's words; so he paraphrased the passage as follows (Mansi, XVI, col. 424D): κατὰ τοῦ παραβάτου Φωτίου, τοῦ καθ' ἡμῶν τοὺς ἀθεμίτους λόγους ἐξερευξαμένου τιμωρίας πλείονας τῶν πρὸ ἡμῶν ὁρίσασθαι. These are the *epitheta* given to Photius in the various documents of the anti-Photian collection. Mansi XVI, col. 416A, E: μοιχός, λαϊκός, 425B: τύραννος καὶ ἐπιβήτωρ, 425C: παράνομος, 429E: μοιχὸς καὶ ἐπιβάτης' 429D: μοιχικῶς ἐπιβάντος, 436D: λαϊκός, 437D: ἀπόβλητος, 440E: παραβάτης, 444E: μοιχός, 448C: δὶς ἐπιβήτωρ, παραβάτης, 445E: μοιχός, 448C, D: νεόφυτος, ἐπιβήτωρ, μοιχός, 453E: παραβάτης, σταυροπάτης, κοσμικός, μοιχός, 457C: τύραννος, διώκτης πορνοβοσκός; Nicetas' Vita Ignatii, 245B: ἐπιβήτωρ καὶ μοιχός; Thegnostos' appeal, 297D: ἐπιβήτωρ, 300B, D: μοιχός; *Synodicon Vetus* (ed. J. A. Fabricius, Bibliotheca graeca, Hamburg, 1809, vol. 12), p. 418: Φώτιον ὡς μοιχὸν ἀναθεματίζει καὶ ἐπιβήτορα. In the other, slightly different, and more complete version of the *Synodicon Vetus*, preserved in the same manuscript that contains the interpolated translation of Pope Stephen's letter, one finds the "titles" mentioned above on fol. 369v, lines 18, 19. It is very significant to find in the same manuscript two Ignatian documents.

[145] V. Grumel, La lettre du pape Etienne, p. 135.

and clearly indicates an interpolation by the translator. Actually, the Pope mentions in the beginning of his letter numerous decisions of the holy Fathers in defense of Marinus' elevation to another see. Without the addition "my predecessors in synods against the intruder" the passage sounds more logical and fits better into the whole context.

It is very doubtful that Photius and the Emperor had asked for a more outspoken condemnation of the synod of 869–70. Photius regarded that Council as abolished, and was convinced that John VIII, too, regarded it so. Otherwise, he would hardly have praised the Pope so warmly in his *Mystagogy*.[146] The opposition was negligible during his second patriarchate, and the attitude of the die-hards was more embarrassing for the Roman Popes whose decrees they pretended to obey than for the Patriarch.

XII

Stephen V had soon to learn about the stubborness of the die-hards when Stylianos, recalled from exile by Leo VI after Photius' abdication, asked the Pope to give a special dispensation to all those who had under Photius' patriarchate acknowledged him as the legitimate pastor. From Stephen's letters it can be deduced with certainly that the Pope not only recognized Photius as legitimate Patriarch – he wanted even to investigate the circumstances under which he left the patriarchal throne – but that he also regarded Photius' ordination as valid.[147]

Photius' new reversal should be explained by the change in the attitude towards the two religious-political parties, effected by Leo VI. The misunderstandings which Leo had with his father who had even forced him to marry Theophano and to abandon Zoe, whom he loved, embittered Leo and inclined him to reverse his father's policy. He approached the intransigents, the consequence of which was the elevation of his young brother Stephen to the patriarchal throne, and hoped that the exiled leaders of the intransi-

---

[146] P. G., vol. 102, cols. 380, 381.

[147] See Mansi, XVI, cols. 420–5, 436, 437, M.G.H., Ep. VII, pp. 375 seq.; fragment from Stephen's Register, ibid., p. 348.Cf.V. Grumel, "La liquidation de la querelle Photienne," Echos d'Orient, vol. 33 (1939); F. Dvornik, The Photian Schism, pp. 227–236. We are able now to quote a new document on the abdication of Photius, the short account of the Synod to which the Patriarch had handed his written abdication, contained in Ms. 482 (1117) of Mount Sinai, fol. 364^{v}, 365, partly published by V. N. Beneševič. Opisanie, op. cit., vol. I, p. 292: Βασιλείου γὰρ τὴν πρόσκαιρον καταλιπόντος βασιλείαν Λέων τε καὶ Ἀλέξανδρος τῆς βασιλείας ἐγένοντο κάτοχοι, ἀληθῶς αἰώνιοι αὔγουστοι. Φωτίου δὲ χάριν ([Θεοδώρου τοῦ σανα? . . .] ἐν τῷ [αὐτοκράτορ . . .], προσ[ερω . . . τητος?] Θεόδωρος μὲν θυμῷ Θεοῦ καὶ ὀργῇ τοῦ βασιλέως ἀπ' ὀμμάτων ἐγένετο). Φώτιος δὲ τῇ ἐν Κωνσταντινουπόλει ἐνδημούσῃ μερικῇ συνόδῳ παραιτήσεως ἐπιδέδωκε λίβελλον διὰ βαθύτατον γῆρας καὶ σωματικὴν ἀσθένειαν τὰς αἰτίας ἀπαριθμούμενος. Ἡ εὐμαρῶς δεξαμένη αὐτοῦ τὴν παραίτησιν, ὃ ᾐτήσατο ἀπεπλήρωσε καὶ Στέφανον τῶν αὐτοκρατόρων ὁμοπάτριον καὶ ὁμομήτριον ἀδελφὸν ἐψηφίσατο καὶ τοῦ Βυζαντίου ἱεράρχην [. . . .] Κυρίῳ ἡμῶν ᾧ ἡ δόξα εἰς τοὺς αἰῶνας ἀμήν. Some of the words in the passage marked in brackets ( ) are almost illegible, and were left out by Beneševič.

gents whom he had recalled would recognize Stephen as the legitimate Patriarch, although he had been ordained deacon by Photius. The victims of this change were Photius, his protégé Santabarenos who seems to have been leader of the moderates, and Photius' relative Nicholas Mysticos, the future patriarch.

This change in Leo's policy, however, did not last. Leo seems to have had experiences with the intransigents similar to those of his father. The démarche of Stylianos in Rome which gave the Pope a pretext to interfere anew in the affairs of the Byzantine Church was, probably, one of the reasons why he decided to lean upon the support of the moderates. This new change is mirrored in Leo's funeral oration delivered in honor of his father in August 888.[148] It was in the interest of the dynasty to make a hero of its founder. The young monarch was quick to understand this, and, abandoning his attitude of petulance, he poured rhetorical approval on Basil's policy. Photius, with Santabarenos and Nicholas, profited from this new change in the young Emperor's mood, and their personal situations improved.[149] Photius lived, after that, in retirement in the monastery of Hieria, devoting himself again to scholarly activity. The enlarged edition of his treatise on the *Mystagogy*[150] of the Holy Spirit was the fruit of that period. He died there, most probably, on February 6th, 891.

---

[148] A. Vogt -I. Hausherr, "L'Oraison funèbre de Basile I," Orientalia Christiana, vol. 26 (1932).

[149] Basil learned by his own experience how important the office of the patriarch was, not only in the Church, but also in State affairs, and, in order to prevent any new complications that could endanger the safety of the new dynasty founded by him, he decided to reserve the patriarchal dignity to one of its members. The change in policy effected by Leo precipitated the implementation of Basil's plan. One can understand Leo's irritation when he learned that Stylianos had presented to the Pope the change in the patriarchal throne in a different way, as if Photius had been deposed by the Emperor. A new examination of the charge by Rome was particularly undesirable because the promotion of Stephen violated the canonical prescriptions concerning the age of a priest. Stephen was only sixteen years old.

[150] The origin and spread of the controversy about the *Filioque* deserves, in spite of numerous works dealing with it (M. Jugie's treatise in his Theologia dogmatica Christ. orient. [Paris, 1926 seq.], vol. I, pp. 167–223, deals especially with Photius' standpoint regarding it), a more thorough treatment. See also A. v. Harnack, Lehrbuch der Dogmengeschichte (Tübingen, 1934, 5th ed.) vol. II, pp. 302 seq. E. Hermann (Orientalia Christ. period. vol. XV, 1949, pp. 221, 222) in his review of F. Dvornik's book on the Photian Schism rightly pointed out: "Nel rispondere a tal quesito, non si potrà però ignorare che i teologi ammettono oggi che il domma latino facilmente doveva suonar falso agli orecchi dei Greci: 'l'ἐκ' greco non risponde del tutto al 'ex' latino." In this connection let me call attention to what Anastasius Bibliothecarius says in the introduction to his translation of a passage in Maximus' letter on the procession of the Holy Ghost: a translation (P. L., vol. 129, col. 577) dedicated to the Deacon John Hymmonides (M.G.H., Ep. VII, p. 425): *Interpretati sumus ex epistola eiusdem sancti Maximi ad Marinum scripta presbiterum circumstantiam de Spiritus sancti processione, ubi frustra causari contra nos innuit Graecos, cum nos non causam vel principium Filium dicamus Spiritus sancti, ut autumant, sed unitatem substantiae Patris et Filii non nescientes, sicut procedit ex Patre, ita eum procedere fateamur ex Filio, missionem nimirum processionem intelligentes, pie interpretans utriusque linguae gnaros ad pacem erudiens, dum scilicet, et nos et Grecos edocet secundum quiddam procedere et secundum quiddam non procedere Spiritum sanctum ex Filio, difficultatem exprimendi de alterius in alterius linguae proprietatem significans.* Anastasius wrote his commentary at the end of 874 and he certainly had in mind the controversy between the Greeks and the Latins, reopened in 867. His interpretation is of great interest as it might help us to understand John VIII's

The second letter in which Stylianus explained to the Pope that he could not speak of Photius' abdication because he regarded him as deprived of all priestly dignity seems to have been sent at the beginning of 891, most probably after the death of Photius. This may have been a favorable occasion for Stylianus to renew his request, made three years earlier, for a dispensation for the priests who had accepted Photius.

The reply to this letter, sent by Stephen's successor Formosus (891–896), very likely at the beginning of 892, presents more difficulties than the interpretation of Stephen's missives. If we take the fragment of Formosus' reply preserved in the anti-Photian collection at its face value,[151] we can conclude that Formosus disregarded the benevolent attitude towards Photius' second patriarchate manifested by his predecessors, declared all Photius' ordinations invalid, and sent legates to Constantinople to receive the penitent Photianists into the Church as laymen. The Byzantines, of course, could not accept such a decision, and the consequence of this severe attitude of the Pope was a schism between the two Churches, although Photius was already dead, a schism which was healed only at a quasi-general council that took place in Constantinople in 899.[152]

There are, however, most serious objections against such an interpretation of the events during Formosus' pontificate. First of all the examination of numerous Latin writings concerning Formosus' ordination reveals that there must have been a profound peace between Rome and Constantinople during Formosus' pontificate,[153] and that the Byzantines ignored the passionate controversy over the validity of Formosus' ordination, although it would have given them a welcome weapon against the Pope who had dared to interfere so glaringly in the affairs of their Church.

---

position in the question of *Filioque*, and the attitude of John's legates at the sixth session of the Council of 879–880. Cf. also Hergenröther, Photius, vol. II, pp. 22 seq. and E. Perels, Papst Nikolaus I. und Anastasius Bibliothecarius (Berlin, 1920), p. 258. Photius also seems to have been aware, to some degree, of the linguistic problem involved in the Latin doctrine on the procession (Mystagogia, P.G., vol. 102, col. 376, A, B). See the interesting remarks of J. Meyendorff in his paper "U istokov spora o Filioque" (Pravoslavnaja Mysl', IX, Paris, 1953, pp. 114–137). Cf. also the articles by catholic and orthodox scholars (Mgr. Cassien, J. Meyendorff, Th. Camelot, S. Verkhovsky, H. F. Dondaine, A. M. Dubarle) on *Filioque*, published in *Russie et Chrétienté*, fourth series, second year (1950, nos. 3–4), pp. 123–244.

[151] Mansi, XVI, cols. 440, 441; M. G. H. Ep. VII, pp. 382 seq. This is the most controversial passage: "If you mean a layman, he deserves pardon, as he received a dignity from a layman; but if you mean a priest, you overlook the fact that one who has no dignity cannot impart any to others. Photius could not give anything except the condemnation he incurred by the imposition of an impious hand, and this condemnation he gave."

[152] Cf. V. Grumel, "La liquidation de la querelle photienne," Echos d'Orient, vol. 33 (1934), pp. 257–288; idem, "Chronique des événements du règne de Léon VI," ibid., vol. 35 (1936), pp. 5–42. In his paper, "Formose ou Nicolas Ier," ibid., vol. 33 (1934), pp. 194 seq. Grumel has rightly shown that the Pope whom Photius had in mind in his *Mystagogy* (P. G., vol. 102, col. 377) is Nicholas, not Formosus.

[153] F. Dvornik, op. cit., pp. 256 seq. See also idem, "Etudes sur Photios," Byzantion, vol. XI (1936), p. 1–15.

If Formosus had acted as the writer of the anti-Photianist collection claimed he did, Stylianus, seven years later, need not have petitioned Rome again for permission to enter into communion with the Photianists.[154] This indicates clearly that, in 892, the ultra-Ignatians had not made peace with the official Church and that if the order given by Formosus to the legates is genuine, the legates did not execute it. Discovering that the situation in Byzantium differed greatly from what in Rome it was thought to be, the legates abstained from any action, and Formosus, now better informed by them, changed his attitude and took no further part in the controversy.

It is, however, possible, nay probable, that Formosus' letter was more interpolated by the copyist of the anti-Photian collection than it appears to be at first sight. We have seen, upon examination of Stephen's letter to Basil, that the Pope's missive had already sustained a few interpolations when translated from the Latin original, and that these were slightly "improved" by the author of the collection who made an extract of it. One passage in the fragment of Formosus' letter[155] indicates that the Pope's change in pontifical eastern policy was not as radical as is suggested by the interpolator, but followed rather the policy of his predecessor, regarding the decisions of the Council of 869–870 as justified, while, at the same time, recognizing Photius' rehabilitation by the Council of 879–880. If he ever thought of giving some concession to the Stylianists, he could have had in mind only the legitimacy of Photius' ordinations and the censure of his followers during his first patriarchate. Informed by the legates that even this concession could not be accepted by the official Church, he reversed his order. Stylianus' reconciliation with the official Church was made in 899, at a local synod, because the two Churches were not in schism.[156]

Upon the reconciliation of Stylianos and his followers with the official Church, an event welcomed by the Pope John IX in his answer to Stylianus,[157] the affair of Photius disappeared from the Roman scene. It seems that the few die-hards who had seen in Stylianus' reconciliation a "straying from the path of truth" and who had tried to read even in John IX's letter a confirmation of their intransigeant attitude, made no new intervention in Rome. The Romans continued to count, as did the Byzantines, only seven Oecumenical Councils[158] to the end of the eleventh century. The translated Acts

[154] Mansi, XVI, col. 456.

[155] Loc. cit.: "Take care above all that the sentence synodically passed on Photius, violator and transgressor of the law, by our predecessors, the oecumenical pontiffs, and besides confirmed by our humble self, remain forever valid and unchanged." The words "violator and transgressor of the law" (τῷ καὶ παραβάτῃ καὶ ἀθεμίτῳ) are an evident interpolation.

[156] I treated the controversy concerning this problem fully in my Photian Schism, pp. 265 seq. It is a serious thing to accuse a Pope of having caused a schism by his uncompromising attitude in a disciplinary matter that has been sanctified by other Popes. The documents at our disposal do not warrant such an accusation against Formosus.

[157] Mansi, XVI, col. 456, M.G.H. Ep. VII, pp. 383, 384.

[158] The second Council of Nicaea was added to the six Oecumenical Councils, counted so far by Rome, by John VIII after 880, on the demand of Photius and the Photian Council. This is a clear indication that John VIII did not want to count the so-called eighth Oecumenical Council

of the Photian and Ignatian Councils reposed forgotten in the Lateran archives; forgotten too was the affair of Photius. The Acts were discovered, however, by the canonists of the Gregorian period who were looking for new documentation on the plenitude of the papal primacy, and who found it in Nicholas' letters on the Photian affair and in the Acts of the Ignatian Council of 869–870, which the canonists repromoted to the eighth Oecumenical Council.[159] Thus was born the so-called Photian legend which grew from the Middle Ages to our time.[160] So it came about that the papal and conciliar documents concerning Photius contributed most to the birth and spread of the mediaeval conception on the superiority of the spiritual power over the temporal, a theory which inspired the papacy during the Investiture Contest and which, at the end, was to a great extent responsible for the split in Western Christianity during the Reformation.

XIII

When, retrospectively, we cast an eye on the relations between Rome and Constantinople in the second half of the ninth century, we see that they were not as disastrous as is usually believed. In spite of the estrangement caused primarily by the different political evolution in East and West, the belief in the necessity of Church unity was still very much alive in Byzantium. Even Photius' attitude testifies to it, notably his anxiety to obtain Rome's recognition of his election and of his restitution to the patriarchal see. On the other hand, Nicholas' attempt to bring the Eastern Church into the same dependence on the Roman see as he had brought the whole West, ended in failure and provoked a most violent reaction at the Synod of 867. Ignatius was as adamant as Photius in the defense of the autonomous status of his Church, disregarding the fact that he was reinstated with the help of Rome. Nevertheless, the desire, manifested so clearly by the two rival groups in Byzantium, to have Rome on their side shows that they were fully aware of the prominent role assigned to Rome in the Christian commonwealth. This is evident not only in the frantic declarations of the intransigents that they were following the decisions of the Roman see, but also in the attitude of the moderates who had a strong following among Byzantine intellectuals who were well versed in ecclesiastical law. The appeal to the Patriarch in

---

of 869–870 and the Photian Council of 879–880 among official Oecumenical Councils. He regarded the Council of 869–870 as cancelled by the Photian Synod of 879–880, which was a Council of Reconciliation and did not deal with questions of doctrine. On the number of Oecumenical Councils recognized by Rome up to the eleventh century, see the Appendices I and II in my book on the Photian Schism, pp. 435–451. See also pp. 309–330. My conclusions remain unchanged.

[159] It was Canon XXII of this Council forbidding the intervention of laymen in episcopal elections that was most welcome to the canonists during the Investiture contest. Their discovery prompted them to attribute great value to the Council of 869–870. Cf. F. Dvornik, "L'œcuménicité du huitième concil," Bulletin de la Classe des Lettres de l'Acad. R. de Belgique, vol. 29 (1938), pp. 468 seq.

[160] See the detailed history of the evolution of Photius' "legend" in the second part of my book, The Photian Schism (pp. 331 seq.). I have nothing substantial to add to this exposé.

Rome by Gregory Asbestas and his followers when they were censured by their own Patriarch is most revealing.[161] It is of even greater importance that this right of appeal was officially acknowledged by the Byzantine Church, under Photius' first patriarchate, at the Council of 861.

It is thus very significant that in the ninth century when the first major claims of the mediaeval Papacy were formulated and opposed by the Byzantine Church we find in a document relating to this clash some indications that a basis could be built on which the Eastern and Roman Church, and perhaps also all Christian Churches of good will, could meet and re-affirm their unity.

Photius himself seems to have considerably improved his attitude during his second patriarchate. The bitter disappointment with which his first patriarchate had ended taught him a lesson which he did not forget. He extended his hand in reconciliation to Marinus and Gauderich of Velletri, his most dangerous opponents in Rome, he tried to win over the leader of the opposition Metrophanes, and, to ease the tension and somewhat, to excuse, Rome or at least to attenuate the bad impression that Rome's intervention against him had produced on certain minds in Byzantium, he wrote his *Collationes*[162] quoting historical instances of bishops being deposed and reinstated. It should also be stressed once more that in the Greek "re-edition" of John's letters he retained important passages on the Roman primacy.

Often it has been argued, in order to show Photius' hostility to Rome, that he was the author of the pamphlet, "Against those who say that Rome is the first see,"[163] but it has already been demonstrated that this treatise could not have been written by Photius,[164] and to the arguments previously presented we can add a new one, concerning the mention of Andrew, the Apostle, as founder of the see of Byzantium. I show elsewhere[165] that the legendary tradition on Andrew and on Stachys, whom the Apostle is said to have ordained Bishop of Byzantium, appeared only in the eight century, and was not yet officially accepted in Byzantium in the ninth. The apostolicity

---

161 That they had really made an appeal to Rome is confirmed by Stylianus in his letter to Stephen (Mansi, XVI, col. 428B, M. G. H., Ep. VII, p. 376): ἐκεῖνοι δὲ γράμματά τε ἀπέστειλαν καὶ πρέσβεις πρὸς τὸν τηνικαῦτα ἁγιώτατον πάπαν 'Ρώμης τὸν μακάριον Λέοντα, ζητοῦντες τὴν παρ' αὐτοῦ ἐκδίκησιν, ὡς δῆθεν ἠδικημένοι. Grumel's hesitations to admit an appeal from the side of the condemned (Le schisme de Grégoire de Syracuse, loc. cit., p. 259) are not substantiated.

162 *Collationes accurataeque demonstrationes de episcopis et metropolitis*, P. G., vol. 104, cols. 1220–32.

163 See the latest edition by M. Gordillo, "Photius et primatus Romanus," in Orientalia Christ. period., vol. 6 (1940), pp. 5 seq. Latin interpretation in M. Jugie, Theologia dogmatica christ. orient. (Paris, 1926), vol. I, pp. 131 seq.

164 By M. Gordillo in the edit. cited above; cf. F. Dvornik, The Photian Schism, pp. 126 seq. Cf. the objections against Gordillo's thesis made by F. Dölger, Byz. Zeitschr., vol. 40 (1940), pp. 523 seq., and by M. Jugie, "L'opuscule contre la primauté romaine attribué à Photius," Mélanges L. Vaganay, Etudes de critique et d'histoire religieuse, vol. 2 (Lyon, 1938), pp. 43–66.

165 In my forthcoming book *The Idea of Apostolicity in Byzantium and the Legend of the Apostle Andrew* (Dumbarton Oaks Studies, IV, Cambridge, Mass., 1958), chap. 6. There I deal more thoroughly with the problem of Photius' authorship of the pamphlet.

of the Byzantine see was derived rather from the fact that Byzantium became the heir of the see of Ephesus, founded by John the Apostle. The Patriarch Ignatius combined the two traditions; the first claiming apostolicity from John, and the new one regarding Andrew as founder of the see of Byzantium.[166] Photius, however, seems to have been more critical. In the *Typicon* of Hagia Sophia, which was revised during his second patriarchate, no mention is made of Andrew's activity in Byzantium,[167] and the feast of Stachys, allegedly its first Bishop, is not yet listed. It is listed only in the Synaxaries of the tenth century and of later periods, and was to be celebrated on October 30th. No trace is found in Photius' writings of any special veneration of Andrew that could lead to the belief that he ever had accepted this new legendary tradition. Such a prominent role could hardly have been given to the Apostle Andrew by any polemist of the ninth century. The ideas expressed by the anonymous author of the treatise presuppose a much more advanced period in the relationship between Constantinople and Rome – perhaps the end of the twelfth and the beginning of the thirteenth century – but not earlier.

All of which, of course, demonstrates that it is presumptuous to attribute to Photius the intention of transferring the primacy from Rome to Constantinople.[168] It is, however, possible that the idea of dividing the rule of the Church between Rome and Constantinople had already appeared in Byzantium during the second patriarchate of Photius. Such a conception is to be found in the Life of the Apostle Andrew, called *Laudatio* and composed probably by a monk of the monastery of Callistratos, in which we read:[169] "The coryphaeus of all, Peter, obtained by lot, through the decision of the divine love, the western lands of the setting sun, that were without light to lighten them, and his companion, his brother Andrew, the eastern part, to illuminate them with the word of God, fearing preaching." No less interesting in this respect are some other passages in the *Laudatio* in which the author stresses the perfect unity and fraternal love between the two brothers, always, however, giving precedence to Peter, calling him[170] "the rock of the truly unbroken faith, who also carries on himself the newly founded Church that had been established, and who preserves it unconquerable by the gates of hell." All this seems in line with the mentality which prevailed in Byzantium, especially among the Photianists, after the reconciliation with Rome in 880. The monastery of Callistratos was apparently a Photianist stronghold.

[166] During the Council of 861. Wolf von Glanvell, Die Kanonensammlung des Kardinals Deusdedit (Paderborn, 1905), p. 603. Cf. Dvornik, The Photian Schism, p. 80 and chap. 6 of my book The Iden of Apostolicity.

[167] A. Dmitrievskij, Opisanie liturgičeskich rukopisei (Kiev, St. Petersburg, 1901–1917), vol. 1, p. 27.

[168] Cf. F. Dölger, "Rom in der Gedankenwelt der Byzantiner," Zeitschr. für Kirchengesch., vol. 56 (1937), p. 32, reprinted in Byzanz und die Europäische Staatenwelt (Ettal Verlag, 1953), p. 103; Idem in the review of Gordillo's study, in Byz. Zeitschr. vol. 90 (1940), p. 524.

[169] Ed. by M. Bonnet, Supplementum codicis apocryphi II (Paris, 1895), p. 7. Published first in Analecta Bollandiana, vol. 13 (1894), p. 315.

[170] Ibid., Supplementum, p. 6, Anal. Bol., p. 314. For details see chap. 6 of The Idea of Apostolicity.

This idea might have prompted Basil II (976–1025) to approach Pope John XIX (1024–1033) to ask, according to the enigmatic report by Raoul Glaber,[171] "whether, with the Roman Pontiff's consent, the Church of Constantinople might be entitled, within its own limits, to be called and treated as universal, just as Rome was universal throughout the world." If we are justified in so interpreting Raoul's only report of this incident, it would be interesting to trace the origins of this idea back to the ninth century.

Did Photius himself cherish such hopes? If he did, he could hardly have expected them to be realized after his tragic mistake of 867, or when, after the death of John VIII, the Roman see was again in the hands of Nicholaites.

It has been suggested that Photius had other politico-religious ambitions.[172] Is it true that, as has been supposed, his greatest ambition was to establish in Byzantium the principle of ecclesiastical power independent of secular power, and to become an eastern Pope?[173] The main argument for these pretensions is seen in the definition of the patriarch's and emperor's duties in the introductory titles of the *Epanagoge*, a proposed new legislative handbook, the introduction to which is rightly supposed to have been composed on Photius' initiative.[174] The importance of this document in the evolution of the relations between Church and State in Byzantium is often exaggerated, for traces of many of the definitions can be found earlier in Justinian's Novels. However, a new tone is apparent in one chapter on the definition of the patriarch's duties: "The patriarch alone is entitled to interpret the rules of the old patriarchs, the prescriptions of the Holy Fathers and the decisions of the Holy Synods." The duties of the Emperor in religious matters are defined as follows: "The Emperors must defend and enforce first, all that is written in Holy Writ, then all the dogmas approved by the seven Holy Councils, and also and in addition, the received Roman Laws."[175]

It would be an exaggeration to see in these definitions an attempt to emancipate the Church from the tutelage of the State. However, they demonstrate the tendency to limit imperial intervention in religious matters purely to the defense of accepted definitions of faith, and they stress more forcefully the exclusive right of the Church to define and to interpret the Christian doctrine. We see in them a bold attempt to terminate victoriously for the

---

171 Rodulphus Glaber, Historiarum libri quinque, P. L., vol. 142, book IV, chap. 1, col. 671 A.

172 F. Dölger, A. M. Schneider, Byzanz (Bern, 1952), pp. 135, 137.

173 F. Dölger, "Europas Gestaltung im Spiegel der fränkisch-byzant. Auseinandersetzung des 9. Jht." (Vertrag von Verdun 843, ed. by Th. Mayer, Leipzig, 1943, pp. 228 seq. and reprinted in F. Dölger, Byzanz und die europäische Staatenwelt, Speyer a. Rh. 1953, pp. 315 seq. Idem, "Rom in der Gedankenwelt der Byzantiner" (Zeitschr. f. Kirchengesch., vol. 56, 1937), p. 32, reprinted in Byzanz u. die Europ. Staatenwelt, p. 103.

174 See the recent study by J. Scharf, "Photios und die Epanagoge," Byz. Zeitschr., vol. 49 (1956), pp. 385–400.

175 Ed. K. E. Zachariae von Lingenthal, in J. Zepos and P. Zepos, Jus Graecoromanum (Athens, 1931), vol. II, p. 242. An English translation of the titles, II, III, VIII, IX, XI is to be found in E. Barker's book Social and Political Thought in Byzantium from Justinian I to the Last Palaeologus (Oxford, 1957), pp. 89–96.

Church the struggle which endured for centuries in the East for the rights of the Church in doctrinal matters and against imperial backing of heretical creeds. The defeat of the last glaring imperial intervention in matters of faith in the iconoclastic controversy gave Photius the courage to make this daring interpretation which, he hoped, would put a definite end to such interference.

But here again Photius went too far and spoiled his chances of success. In reserving the interpretation of the decisions of the Fathers and the synods to the patriarch alone, he was ignoring the general practice in Byzantium of giving to all bishops assembled in council the right to interpret the true doctrine. It is probable that this stipulation provoked opposition among the bishops who protested against the curtailment of their rights to the profit of the patriarch, and it might also have been one reason why Basil did not choose the *Epanagoge* as an official handbook of law. In any case, it is noteworthy that the above-mentioned definition of the patriarch's right was never quoted in other later law books, although their compilers had incorporated into them many other titles of this part of the *Epanagoge*.[176]

XIV

In this respect Photius outdistanced his contemporaries, but he was more successful with his canonical legislation, especially with the canons sanctioned by the councils of 861 and of 879–880.[177] Although the Acts of the Council of 861 were destroyed, the canons dealing principally with reforms of monastic life retained their validity for centuries to come. These canons give us an insight into Photius' program of Church reform which seemed necessary after some old abuses, especially in monastic life, had reappeared when the intransigents secured for themselves the direction of Church affairs during Ignatius' patriarchate. A better training of the secular clergy seems to have been another part of Photius' plan of reform. He appears to have been particularly anxious to reintroduce into the teaching schedule at the patriarchal Academy lectures on philosophy, as the best preparation for theological studies. This discipline was apparently neglected during Ignatius' patriarchate when the instransigents, especially the monks, who always showed hostility to the profane sciences,[178] were dominant in the administration of Church affairs. In reorganizing the Academy Photius established a chair of philosophy at the church of the Holy Apostles, and persuaded his friend and former pupil Constantine the Philosopher, the future Apostle of

---

[176] See for detailed quotations chap. 7 of my book *The Idea of Apostolicity*.

[177] They are listed by G. H. Rhalis and M. Potlis in vol. II of the Σύνταγμα (Athens 1852–1855), immediately after the canons of the seven Oecumenical Councils. Also, Photius' Decretals, issued mostly during his first patriarchate are important sources of Byzantine canonical legislation. They are printed in Valetta's edition of Photius' letters and described by Hergenröther (Photius, vol. III, pp. 128–143).

[178] Cf. on this opposition Dvornik, Les Légendes, pp. 27 seq.

the Slavs, to accept it.[179] This was probably effected at the end of 861 when Constantine had returned from his mission to the Khazars.

This mission, which had been undertaken to strengthen the Byzantine-Khazar alliance against the Russians, who, in 860 had attacked Constantinople, must have revealed to the Byzantines new possibilities for political, cultural, and religious expansion among the many races living under Khazar rule, and it was quite natural to entrust the training of missionaries for this new and promising field of activities to the very man who had discovered it.

The conclusion of the Khazar-Byzantine alliance hastened the decision of the Russians to become Christians, and, around 864, Photius was able to send a bishop to Kiev. This was not, however, a permanent success, for, about 885, Oleg, coming from Novgorod, overpowered Ascold and Dir, masters of Kiev, and brought this first phase of Christianization of Russia to an abrupt end.[180]

A very lively missionary activity characterizes the first patriarchate of Photius. The conversion of the Slavs settled in the middle of the Byzantine Empire in Thrace and Macedonia was completed, and during his second patriarchate the Serbs also were entirely won over to Christianity.[181] Photius included even Armenia also[182] in his plans for Byzantine religious expansion, as can be judged from his letters.

The spread of Byzantine religious influence among the Slavs, which started under the first patriarchate of Photius, yielded, as is known, permanent results, and this was due principally to two very bold and ingenious steps taken by Constantine-Cyril and his brother Methodius, who had been sent to Moravia[183] under the patronage of Photius; namely their invention of a special Slavonic alphabet and their translation of the Holy Writ and

---

179 See the detailed study by Dvornik, "Photius et la réorganisation de l'Académie patriarcale," Analecta Bollandiana, vol. 68 (1950), pp. 120 seq. The appointment of Constantine to the chair is based on the report of his biographer that "he sat in the Church of the Holy Apostles" (Fontes rerum bohemicarum, vol. I [Prague, 1865], p. 26: v tsrkvi svetich apostolov siede). In Byzantium this phrase usually designated a teaching function. We have a detailed description of this patriarchal school written in the twelfth century by Mesarites.

180 See for details on the Khazarian mission and on Russia, Dvornik, Les Légendes, pp. 148–180. On the Russian attack on Byzantium in 860 and on Photius' attitude during the siege, see the commentary on the two Photius' homilies dealing with this episode in the English edition of Photius' homilies by C. Mango.

181 Cf. Dvornik, Les Slaves, Byz. et Rome, pp. 132 seq., 233–258.

182 Photius' efforts to win the Armenians to orthodoxy will be better known when his letters to the Armenians, recently discovered by J. Darrouzès in Athens (Ms. Athen. B. N. 2756, fols. 169 seq.), are published. Cf. J. Darrouzès, "Notes d'épistolographie et d'histoire des textes," Revue des études byzantines, vol. 12 (1954), p. 185.

183 Archaelogical discoveries made in Moravia after the year 1948 show clearly that this country was under a strong Byzantine cultural influence. The discovery of foundations of stone churches built in the ninth century testify to a higher level of civilization. See a summary of information about these discoveries in my book, The Slavs, their Early History and Civilization (Boston, 1956), pp. 150 seq.

liturgical books into Slavonic.[184] Such measures could not have been accomplished without the consent of the head of the Byzantine Church. Recent research has shown that the Moravian mission apparently established, too, a solid basis for the further evolution of civil legislation among the Slavs. Constantine-Cyril appears to have composed the oldest Slavic legal work, based on the Greek handbook, the *Ecloga* of the Emperor Leo the Isaurian, which was still in use in Byzantium during Photius' first patriarchate.[185]

It has been alleged that the dispute between Ignatius and Photius found a strong echo as far as Moravia where Ignatius ordained a new bishop for the Moravians to replace the Photianist Methodius, but this statement does not appear to be justified.[186] Photius continued to be interested in Slavonic letters for missionary purposes. When, about 882, Methodius, who had been ordained Metropolitan of Sirmium and Moravia by Pope Hadrian II, visited Photius in Constantinople, the Patriarch retained in the capital some of Methodius' clerics as well as some Slavonic books, and founded thereby an important center in Constantinople which could provide the new converts with Greek books for translation.[187] We learn later from the Slavonic Life

---

[184] According to the results of Vašica's research, published in Byzantinoslavica, vol. 8 (1939–46), pp. 1–45, the Greek missionaries translated into Slavonic a Greek version of the Roman Mass formulary called the Liturgy of St. Peter, which seems to have been used in some places in Byzantium, perhaps also in Thessalonica, the native city of the two brothers. Cf. Dvornik, The Slavs, p. 166.

[185] See for details J. Vašica, "Origine Cyrillo-Méthodienne du plus ancien code slave dit 'Zakon sudnyj Ljudem'," Byzantinoslavica, vol. 12 (1951), pp. 153–174. F. Dvornik, "Byzantine Political Ideas in Kievan Russia," Dumbarton Oaks Papers, vol. 9–10 (1956), pp. 77 seq.

[186] E. Honigmann in his "Studies in Slavic Church History," Byzantion, vol. 17 (1945), pp. 163–182, thought that Agathon of Moravia mentioned in the Acts of the Council of 879–880 was identical with Archbishop Agathon, member of a Byzantine embassy to Germany in 873, and that he was ordained by Ignatius after 870 to replace Methodius. However, this Agathon was most probably bishop or archbishop of Moravia in modern Serbia. See Dvornik, The Slavs, pp. 97, 164. In any case, even if Ignatius had ordained another bishop for Moravia he would not have done so because Methodius was a Photianist – he had used Photian missionaries in Bulgaria – but because Methodius, although sent to Moravia by the Byzantine Patriarch, was working for the aggrandizement of the rival Patriarchate of Rome. Ignatius was adamant in the defense of the right of his Patriarchate.

[187] Cf. Dvornik, Les Légendes, pp. 275 seq. On Methodius' visit in Constantinople see the recent study of R. Jakobson, "Minor Native Sources for the Early History of the Slavic Church," in Harvard Slavic Studies, 2 (1954), pp. 64–68, and Dvornik, The Slavs, pp. 124 seq. It is possible that Methodius, who was in Rome in 880, had visited Croatia on his return from Rome, at the request of John VIII, who was anxious to attach this country more closely to his See and that the Slavonic liturgy, approved by the Pope, had started to spread in this country from that time on. Croatia was about to be lost by Rome when the pro-Byzantine Prince Zdeslav became ruler of that country in 878. It is perhaps not a coincidence that when a national revolution led by the Bishop-elect Theodosius, broke out against Zdeslav in 879, the Byzantines abstained from giving him substantial help. Zdeslav was defeated and killed. Anxious to restore good relationship with Rome, the Byzantines abandoned their plans of further expansion in the West and left this part of Illyricum under the jurisdiction of the Roman patriarchate. The part Methodius seems to have taken in attaching the Croats to Rome helps us to understand better what his biographer says concerning rumors which circulated in Moravia claiming that the Emperor was angry with Methodius. The latter's journey to Constantinople had thus a politico-religious background, and

of St. Naum, one of Methodius' disciples, that when, after the death of the Moravian archbishop, his disciples who were of Greek origin, were dispersed or even sold into slavery by the Franks, a high Byzantine official bought some of them in Venice and sent them to Constantinople.[188] Thus the Slavonic center in Byzantium was strengthened. Specialists in Slavonic philology are now inclined to believe that this center, founded in Constantinople by Photius, played a major role in the dissemination of Slavonic liturgy and Byzantine civilization throughout Bulgaria and Kievan Russia.

All of this reveals Photius as an able and intelligent organizer, eager to spread the Gospel to the pagans. New vistas and great possibilities for Byzantium and its Church were opened during his patriarchate. It is, therefore, the more regrettable that political intrigues, often of the lowest nature, marred his plans and slowed down the spread of Christianity and of Byzantine civilization. To what extent was Photius responsible for the troubles that engulfed many of his hopes? He seems to have defended his right with stubbornness and energy. Did he over-reach himself? It would have been only human to do so in such desperate circumstances. Certainly it was a mistake not to continue the negotiations with Nicholas I after 862. Was it Bardas who was the decisive factor in this, and was he also particularly hostile to the West? Possibly. Photius himself apparently always believed in the old idea of a universal Roman Empire embracing all Christian nations under the Basileus of Constantinople and a co-Emperor in the West. At least, he persuaded Michael III, after Bardas' death, to offer the Imperial title to Louis II, and, although this gesture was intended to win Louis' alliance against the Roman Pope, the fact by itself is noteworthy.

It would be interesting to know more about Photius' relationship with Ignatius. The reconciliation between the two rivals was sincere, and during his second patriarchate Photius seems to have tried to restore the good name of Ignatius. In the newly discovered version of the Synodicon Vetus there is a passage which clearly indicates that "Photius canonized Ignatius placing his name in the diptychs among the saints".[189] In reality in the *Typicon* of Hagia Sophia, revised most probably in the second patriarchate of Photius, we find a commemoration of Ignatius on October 22nd.[190] Moreover, in

---

the success he is said to have scored there – the biographer mentions a cordial reception by the Emperor (Basil) and the Patriarch (Photius) – reflects the good relationship which existed between Rome and Byzantium after the reconciliation.

188 Cf. Dvornik, Les Slaves, Byz. et Rome, pp. 298 seq.

189 Sinait. Gr. 482 (1117), fol. 364v, lines 36–38. ρξδ'. πρὸς Κύριον δὲ τοῦ μακαρίου Ἰγνατίου ἀπάροντος Φώτιος τῆς Κωνσταντινουπόλεως ἐκκλησίας τὸν θρόνον παρέλαβε, καὶ πρὸς αὐτὸν πᾶς ἐπίσκοπος αὐτῆς ἐστασίασε, [καί]περ αὐτοῦ Ἰγνάτιον τὸν μακάριον ἐν τοῖς ἱεροῖς διπτύχοις ἐπ' ἄμβωνος μετὰ πάντων ἁγίων ἀνακηρύττοντος καὶ τοῦ [πολέμου] τὴν ὀργὴν καταπαύοντος. The entire passage betrays the biased attitude of the author against Photius. Although he claims that the whole episcopate had turned against Photius, he nevertheless speaks of the canonization of Ignatius by Photius. This gesture throws a very favorable light on Photius' character.

190 Dmitrijevskij, Opisanie, vol. I, 15: κγ' . . . . τῇ αὐτῇ ἡμέρᾳ τοῦ ἁγίου Ἰγνατίου, ἀρχιεπισκόπου Κωνσταντινουπόλεως.

the recently-discovered series of standing Church Fathers reproduced in mosaics, on the north wall of the nave in Hagia Sophia, is a portrait of the Patriarch Ignatius.[191] The style of these mosaics is said to be that of the end of the ninth century.[192] They could thus have been executed, or at least planned, under the second patriarchate of Photius which ended in 887. If this homage to Ignatius could also be attributed to Photius' initiative we would perhaps be justified in seeing in it another act of restitution for past mistakes and misunderstandings.

Perhaps the uncovering of new evidence will some day help us to see more clearly into this imbroglio, and to ascertain and evaluate with greater precision the events and persons responsible for the politico-religious troubles that darkened a period of Byzantine development which had started with a promising cultural and political renaissance, and which could have become one of the most brilliant in the history of all Byzantium.

---

[191] Th. Whittemore, "The Unveiling of the Byzantine Mosaics in Hagia Sophia in Istanbul," Amer. Journal of Archeology, vol. 46 (1942), pp. 169 seq. The portrait of the Patriarch Ignatius has not yet been reproduced.

[192] K. Weitzmann, The Fresco Cycle of S. Maria di Castelseprio (Princeton, 1951), pp. 27, 96.

Additional note to p. 20

The correct reading of the passage of the *Synodicon Vetus* dealing with the deposition of Ignatius in 859 is as follows. Φώτιος . . . . . . συναθροίσας πονηρευομένων ἐν Βλαχέρναις συνέδριον, καθαιρεῖ μὴ π α ρ ό ν τ α τὸν ἀδικούμενον . . . .

The reading μὲν παρόντα found in the edition of Pappus (Fabricius Harles, XII p. 417) is a sixteenth-century corruption. The original version is to be found both in *Sinaiticus Greacus 482*, fol. 364[v] and in a manuscript copy of the document made by Leo Allatius in the seventeenth century, now in the Vallicelliana library in Rome. A critical edition of the *Synodicon* will shortly be published by John Parker.

VII

PATRIARCH PHOTIUS

Scholar and Statesman

The ninth century is one of the most momentous and brilliant periods in Byzantine records. Byzantium then stood at the close of a transformation inaugurated at the beginning of the eighth century by the Isaurian dynasty and characterized by the influx of oriental ideas. Of this transformation, iconoclasm was the most notorious symptom. The final restoration of icon veneration which took place in 843, embodied the vigorous reaction of the Greek spirit against the introduction of novelties, and the reaction achieved its object: the two elements that had been at variance for over a century, the Eastern and the Hellenic, at length brought together into common action the two main and equally important factors of Byzantine civilization. From that moment onward their harmonious combination led to the happiest results. Byzantium knew a renaissance that spread from the intellectual to the political arena, and national sentiment sufficiently arrested itself to claim preponderance in Byzantium's relations with other powers—the Mussulman and Latin worlds.

This is the background on which all intellectual and religious life of ninth century Byzantium is reflected. It is still clouded with many controversies—echoes of the violent clashes between iconoclasts and iconodules. There is a tinge of religious fanaticism provoked by the persecutions of the iconoclastic period and it is coloured with political partisanship which prevents students from gaining a deeper insight into this intricate picture. We must bear all this in mind if we wish to discover the main currents of thought which influenced ninth century political leaders, churchmen, and scholars.[1]

Fortunately, this period produced a man in whose life and work are faithfully reflected the main trends—the Patriarch Photius—and if we wish to understand the secrets of this period, it will suffice to concentrate on the study of this central personality of the ninth century. Let us first of all, portray this man at least with a few broad strokes.

Photius is without question the leading figure in the Byzan-

---

[1] Cf. what I wrote on the ninth century literary renaissance in Byzantium in my book *Les Slaves, Byzance et Rome au IXe siècle* (Paris, 1926), pp. 106 ff.

tine intellectual renaissance of the ninth century. The extent of his learning amazed his contemporaries and commanded the respect of his bitterest enemies.[2] He was the scion of a noble Byzantine family of ancient Greek stock and related to the Macedonian dynasty. His father had suffered persecution because of his fidelity to the cult of images.[3] A favourite of the imperial court, Photius commanded, if not the love, certainly the esteem of many rival personalities—the Empress Theodora, the Logothete Theoktistos, the young Emperor Michael and of his uncle, Bardas. He began his brilliant career at the University of Constantinople as a professor of philosophy; he became director of the imperial chancellory and a most prominent member of the Senate. His unselfish life, tact, diplomatic sense and the outstanding qualities which he showed in the execution of his office, attracted the attention of the court and of prominent churchmen. When the Church of Constantinople was in the throes of dangerous agitation provoked by the struggle of two rival parties—the Extremists and the Moderates—Photius, although a layman, was unanimously elected Patriarch after his predecessor Ignatius resigned his office.

From then on the name of Photius was dragged into the party struggle for control of political and religious life in Byzantium. He bravely opposed the extremist tendencies and became the target on which their bitterest attacks were concentrated. Unfortunately only the pamphlets of his enemies have survived the centuries, and this is the main reason why in the Middle Ages and in our day the name of Photius was quoted as the symbol of pride and of lust for ecclesiastical domination. His enemies succeeded, for some time at least, in obtaining a hearing even in Rome, and provoked by their intrigues a grave schism between East and West. The blame for this rupture was laid at the feet

---

2 Even Photius' most passionate adversary Nicetas the Paphlagonian could not refuse his enemy eloquent praise for his scholarship. He describes Photius' learning in the following words (Vita Ignatii, *P.G.* vol. 105, col. 509): "(Photius was) a not unknown and ignoble man, but a scion of a renowned and illustrious family, regarded as most famous in worldly wisdom and political science. He excelled so much in knowledge of grammar and literature, in rhetoric and philosophy, nay, also in medicine and in all worldly liberal arts, that he was not only considered first by his contemporaries, but could even compete with the ancients."

3 Photius' father has a commemorative notice in the Greek Synaxarion of the thirteenth of March, where he is commemorated as a confessor. H. Delehaye, *Synaxarium Constantinopolitanum* (Brussels, 1902), Acta Sanctorum Novembris, col. 682.

of Photius. The fact that he, himself, contributed to the healing of this rupture and never departed from his conciliatory attitude, was promptly forgotten, and even today his name is still regarded in the West as the badge of disruption and as an element destructive to Christian universality. Because the Eastern Church remained faithful to his memory, the name of Photius became one of the main stumbling blocks in the way of a better understanding between Eastern and Western Christianity.

Such is the man, at least in the so-called "historical" tradition, who dominated the intellectual and religious field in ninth century Byzantium. The circumstances which led him, rightly or wrongly, to become the main stumbling block in the way of an understanding between the East and West, shows us how important the ninth century was in Byzantine religious and political evolution.

It is not easy to disentangle the truth from the contradictory tradition which has evolved round the name of Photius. It is impossible to do so in a short paper. There is, however, one field of Photius' activity which has not yet been sufficiently clarified—his scholarly activity and his contribution to the preservation of classical lore and its perpetuation in Christian tradition. This aspect is mostly overshadowed by the religious controversies connected with his name, and the biased attitude by which Photius' activity has been judged, so far, has not allowed Church historians to appreciate justly his merits in this respect. It is, however, important to see Photius in his true light as a scholar, and when we have his correct measure in this field, we shall then see his other actions in a different light, and many prejudices should disappear.

The scholarly reputation of Photius is, first of all, established through his *Bibliotheca,* giving criticisms of and extracts from two hundred and eighty works which Photius had studied during his youth and with his friends in his drawing room.[4] It is an immense achievement which still arouses the admiration of classical scholars and historians of literature. In this work Photius reviews for the use of his brother Tarasius only some of the works which were systematically studied by him. Historians of Greek literature cannot abstain from praising Photius'

[4] Republished in Migne's *Patrologia Graeca,* vols. 103, 104.

sharp sense, acute judgement and critical understanding. Thanks to him, our knowledge of many Greek writers, whose works have since perished, has been saved.

This work has yet to be studied in all its aspects.[5] It is not written in systematic order and Photius himself, aware of this, asked his brother in the preface to excuse the hasty work. Because of this, the book has often been regarded by literary historians as an immense wastebasket into which it is pleasant to dip from time to time, and to pull out an interesting story. But it is much more than this, as a thorough and systematic study would undoubtedly show.

Although the work presents only a fragment of what the Byzantines knew and read in the ninth century, it does give us a clear idea of the high level of culture during this period. Thanks to Photius we are able to determine the main cultural currents which permeated Byzantium in his time. Above all, there is a definite tendency to return to the classical period of ancient Greece. This does not mean that it was only during this period that Byzantium turned with predilection to classical Greece. The literary treasures of the Great Age were on the tables of the learned Byzantine at all times and were avidly studied. However, when we stress the fact, there is reason for doing so. Byzantium was in danger, if not of losing, at least of putting in the background, her literary inheritance from the classical period. There were the difficult years of the seventh century when Byzantium was fighting for her very survival against the combined hordes of Persians, Avars and Slavs. "Inter arma silent Musae." It is the most barren period in Byzantine literary output when all cultural life seemed to stop, when even the soil of classical Greece was invaded, and when the Slavonic tongue could be

5 The most exhaustive commentary on Photius' *Bibliotheca* and his *Amphilochia,* which completes it in many ways, is still that of J. Hergenröther, *Photius, Patriarch von Constantinopel* (Regensburg, 1867), vol. 3, pp. 13-70. More recently Photius' literary activity was assessed by C. Ziegler in his study "Photios" in Pauly-Wissowa *Real-Encyclopädie* (Stuttgart, 1941). J. H. Freese translated into English 165 codices of Photius' Bibliotheca (*The Library of Photius,* 1920, vol. I, all published). R. Henry is publishing a new edition with a French translation and commentary: *Bibliothèque de Photius,* Tome I (codices 1-84) (Paris 1959). The work was composed before Photius' official embassy to Baghdad in 855. It is now generally accepted that it contains reviews of works read by Photius, beginning from his early years to 855. He incorporated the notes into a large work, at the request of his brother Tarasius, before his trip, as Photius indicates in the introduction to his work.

heard near Athens, Corinth and under the heights of Taygetos in the Peloponnese.[6] This danger was hardly averted when a new invasion came from Asia Minor, the half-hellenized Isaurians and other tribes establishing themselves in important posts in the capital. Oriental ideas triumphed over the Greek love of artistic beauty and this triumph manifested itself in iconoclasm.

But not even the Isaurian dynasty could resist the attraction of classical Greece. The last iconoclastic emperor, Theophilus, headed a strong move back to the classical tradition. This circumstance, however, opened the door to another danger. The monks, heroes of the struggle in favour of the cult of images, never completely reconciled with the literary inheritance from the pagan era, now had a new reason for their hostility to the classics in the fact that these studies were encouraged by the iconoclasts. This hostility became one of the battle cries of the extremist zealots, who accused the moderates of lacking true Christian piety. An echo of this struggle is still to be found in the lives of many saints of the period.[7]

It would have been a great pity, had the victory of the Greek genius over the influx of oriental ideas been limited to a revival of religious art and if Byzantium had had to pay for this victory by the loss of her classical inheritance. But the strong words with which some of the hagiographers condemned the classical, pagan culture,[8] indicate, at the same time, that there existed vigorous defenders of the classics, men who were determined not only to keep the literary treasures of the past, but also to

---

[6] See on the Slavic establishment in the Balkans and in Greece my book *The Slavs, their Early History and Civilization* (Boston, 1956), pp. 40 ff.

[7] For details see my books *Byzance et les Slaves au IXe siècle,* pp. 120 ff. and *Les Légendes de Constantin et de Méthode vues de Byzance* (Prague, 1933), pp. 25 ff.

[8] The most outspoken condemnation of classical studies can be read in the Life of St. John of Psacum, published by Van den Ven ("La vie grecque de St. Jean le Psichaïte," *Le Muséon,* N.S., vol. 3, pp. 97-125). In chapter four (p. 109) can be read the attack against profane and classical scholarship. The Saint "did not need to know how to coordinate words and phrases, nor to get lost in grammatical trifles, nor to read the prattle of Homer, his golden chain (Homer, Iliad, VIII, 19) . . . . Really what kind of profit can the men who are so proud of them obtain from the knowledge of such myths, fiction and diabolical inventions . . . . He did not need the lies of the rhetors . . . . He regarded astronomy, geometry and arithmetic as things which have no real existence . . . . And how can Plato, who knows all that, be elevated to intellectual heights, he, who like a serpent trails in the mud of passion, with a full stomach, like a parasite?"

increase and propagate their knowledge. Two influential men supported these defenders of the classics: Theoktistos, the Prime Minister of the Empress Theodora and his rival Bardas, Theodora's brother. The main inspiration of both men was Photius. And so it came about that all that the last iconoclast Emperor had done for the revival of classical letters was saved. On this basis was begun the greatest revival of classical studies which Byzantium had ever experienced.[9] It is largely to this ninth century revival we owe the fact that most of the literary treasures of the Greek classical age have been preserved up to our days.

Photius gives us a clear idea of the importance and the intensity of this rebirth. When he omits to mention in his *Bibliotheca* the works of famous Greek poets, of Plato, Xenophon or Aristotle, of Thucydides, Polybius, Pausanias, Hippocrates or Plutarch, this does not mean that he and his friends neglected these great classical writers. We find numerous allusions to the works of these great classics in his account of other works. It seems that, in the account destined for his brother, Photius concentrated rather on less well known classics, regarding the study of the great writers as a matter of course for every Byzantine intellectual.

In this way, we learn that in the ninth century the Byzantines knew many more works of the classical period, in different fields, that we know today, because many of the works quoted by Photius have since been lost. In some cases the extracts given by Photius are all that have been preserved. In classical history, for example, Photius had extensive knowledge of the works composed by Ctesias of Cnidus in the fourth century B.C. (Cod. 72), works dedicated to the history of Persia and containing information which Ctesias was able to gather about India while in Persia. Photius liked Ctesias' simple and pleasant style of writing. He read also the works of Theopompus of Chios of the third century B.C. which today are preserved only in fragments (Cod. 176).

The third historian of the classical period mentioned by Photius is Herodotus. He gives only a short indication of the content of his historical work (Cod. 60) but he calls this work

[9] The best history of this period was written by J. B. Bury, *A History of the Later Roman Empire* (London, 1912).

"a model of Ionic dialect." Thucydides and Xenophon are thought of by him as models for the Attic dialect, but he does not give any extracts from their works. Ephorus is mentioned (Cod. 176, 260), but Photius does not appear to have read his works.

Of the historians of the early Hellenistic period only Agatharchides attracted his attention. In Codex 213 he mentions his ten books *On Asia* and his forty-nine books *On Europe*. Photius also read his five books *On the Erythrean Sea* and he gives extracts from books one and five.

More numerous are the works of historians of the Imperial period, read, criticized, and excerpted by Photius. Many of them are completely or partially lost. He read all forty books of Diodorus Siculus, contemporary of Augustus (Cod. 70). Only the first five books and books eleven to twenty are preserved. The excerpts given in Codex 244 are all we know of the last ten books of Diodorus' historical work.

He read all twenty of the *Roman History* written by another contemporary of Augustus, Dionysius of Halicarnassus (Cod. 83) whose work is important in the study of ancient literary criticism.[10] Only the first eleven books have been preserved. Photius was also familiar with the abridgement of the *Roman History* made by the author himself (Cod. 84) but which is lost.

He was naturally interested in Josephus Flavius' *Jewish War* and *Jewish Antiquities* (Cod. 47, 76),[11] and found the work rich in argument and full of pathos. *On the Universe* (Cod. 48) another work attributed to Josephus, was actually written not by the priest Gaius as Photius read on the marginal note of his own copy, but by Hippolytus of Rome (second or third century).[12] He read also the work of Justus of Tiberias, adversary of Josephus, entitled *Chronicle of Jewish Kings* (Codex 33), which is completely lost.

From the works of later historians, Photius gives excerpts from Plutarch's *Biographies* (Cod. 245). He had read all twenty-four books of Appianus' *Roman History* (Cod. 57) of which only eleven books are preserved. He gives a summary

---

10 Cf. S. F. Bonner, *The Literary Treatise of Dionysius of Halicarnassus. A Study in the Development of Critical Method* (Cambridge, 1939).

11 Cf. A. J. Bouet, "The References to Josephus in the Bibliotheca of Photius," *Journal of Theological Studies*, vol. 36 (1935), pp. 289-293.

12 See the edition of the Bibliotheca by R. Heury, *op. cit.*, p. 35.

of all the books, both preserved and lost, and characterizes the style as plain and terse. Arrianus' *History of the Parthians* (second century A.D.) is known to us only through Photius' references. Only a few fragments of this work are preserved. He gives us also (Cod. 91, 92, 93) a long description of Arrianus' *History of the Reign of Alexander,* and of the ten books of the *History after Alexander,* and of the *Bithynica* by the same author. Photius praises the author's succinct narrative style.

The works of Cephalion, Phlegon and Amyntianus are known to us again because of references made to them by Photius. Cod. 68, 97, 131). So also is the local history of the City of Heraclea in Pontus, of which Photius was only able to read from books eight to sixteen (Cod. 224).

He also read the eighty books of a *History* by Dion of the third century A.D. (Cod. 71), whose work was also excerpted by Constantine Porphyrogenetus. Only books thirty-seven to sixty are preserved. Fragments survive of the three works by Dexippus (Cod. 82), *History, Historical Epitome* and *Scythica.* Photius especially praises the *Scythica* for the clarity of the style calling the author "a second Thucydides." The *History* of Julius Africanus, a Christian writer of the third century, mentioned in Cod. 34, is lost as is also his *Cesti* (embroideries). Photius speaks of Julius' correspondence with Origenes.

Some fragments of the *Chronicle* of Eunapius, continuator of Dexippus, were saved by Constantine Porphyrogenetus. This Photius read in its second edition (Cod. 77). Eunapius was a pagan and very hostile to Constantine the Great. It is especially regretted that the *History of Constantine the Great* written by the Athenian Praxagoras, is lost. In his review of the work Photius says (Cod. 62) that Praxagoras, although a pagan, praised Constantine and said that "in virtue, goodness, and in all his successes he excelled all his predecessors on the throne."

Olympiodorus' *History* covering the period from 407 to 425 and that of Candidus (from 457 to 491) are known to us only from Photius' description (Cod. 80, 79). Malchus' *Byzantine History* starting from the reign of Constantine up to 480 and a continuation of Priscus' *History* are known only from Photius' review (Cod. 78). Suidas and Constantine Porphyrogenetus saved only a few fragments of it.

A few fragments have survived from the *History of Christianity* written by Philip of Side described in Cod. 35. The historians of the sixth century, Nonnosus, Theophanes and Hesychius Illustrius, are known only from what Photius has said of them (Cod. 3, 64, 69). Of the historians of later periods—Photius describes the works of Zosimus, Procopius, Theophylactus Simocatta and the works of the Patriarch Nicephorus which are known to us. Sergius' *History,* starting from Constantine the Great up to 825, is lost and known only from Photius' description (Cod. 67).

From the description and criticism of these historical writings we see that Photius had a very well developed historical sense. He is inspired by the classical concepts of historiography which can be traced back to the fourth century B.C. and he applies them to Christian historiography. Photius believed that according to these ancient concepts history should be of use in daily life, should set forth examples from the past and should aim at the acquisition of truth.[13]

Besides history, classical rhetoric must have been particularly prized by the Byzantines, as Photius' account of works in this field is very complete like that of the historical writings. He gives many details of the orations of all ten of the most celebrated classical rhetors,[14] namely, Aeschines, Andocides, Antiphon, Isocrates, Lysias, Demosthenes, Dinarchus, Isaeus, Lycurgus, Hyperides (Cod. 259-268, 61, 159). From the later period he quotes the declamations of the Emperor Hadrian (Cod. 100) now lost, Dion of Prusa (Cod. 209), the works of Aristides (second century A.D.) (Cod. 246-248), Themistius (Cod. 74), Libanius (Cod. 90), Apthonius of Antioch (about 400 A.D.), of Maximus and of Eusebius (Cod. 133-135). The latter's name was preserved only by Photius.

This interest in classical and Hellenistic rhetoric is easily explained by practical reasons. There existed in Byzantium an official "graduate" school, of which we shall have more to say, for the training of imperial officials.[15] It was on those ancient

13 A thesis on *Photius' Idea of History* was written at Harvard by Custas, former Fellow at Dumbarton Oaks.

14 Cf. the dissertation by R. Ballheimer, *De Photii vitis decem Oratorum* (Bonn, 1877).

15 For the history of this "University" see my study "Photius et la réorganisation de l'académie patriarcale" *Analecta Bollandiana,* vol. 68, pp. 108 ff.

patterns that the candidates for imperial chancellery were trained to compose official documents and letters. Learned clerks, on the other hand, were trying to mature their oratorical talent by the study of classical orators. When reading some of the homilies delivered by Photius on different occasions, we notice to what degree Byzantine eloquence in the ninth century was influenced by the revived study of classical rhetoric.[16]

In his *Bibliotheca* Photius does not analyze the works of the great philosophers of the classical age. We can gather, however, from another work, addressed to his disciple Amphilochius, Metropolitan of Cyzicus, how well Photius had mastered the great Greek philosophers. Although well acquainted with the writings of Plato, he shows himself a determined opponent of Platonism, in particular the doctrine concerning the divine ideas which is regarded by Photius as useless in philosophical and theological speculation and contrary to the Christian idea of God.[17]

We touch here an important problem, which is not yet cleared up—that of Byzantine philosophy. There is no good general study on this subject and no agreement among specialists in their evaluation of Byzantine philosophical thought.[18] Great confusion is still prevalent in this kind of research, many modern writers expressing opinions which are directly contradictory. We know that in the whole history of Byzantine thought two currents can be clearly distinguished: Aristotelianism and Platonism. Aristotelianism won over Christian scholars after the third century. It was then firmly entrenched in Alexandria and Aristotelian commentators rendered good service against the dangerous doctrines of the Pergamene school of Neoplatonism and against the paganism of the Athenian school. Since then the logic of Aristotle was put to the service of theological thinking and was most useful to Byzantine theologians. The many commentaries on Aristotle's works, which were published in Alexandria and in Byzantium from the end

16 The eighteen homilies which have been preserved were published in an English translation with a scholarly commentary by C. Mango, *The Homilies of Photius, Patriarch of Constantinople* (Cambridge, Mass., 1958).

17 *Ad Amphilochium*, Migne, *P.G.*, vol. 101, col. 252, quaestio 87.

18 The study by B. Tatakis, *La philosophie byzantine* (Paris, 1949) is disappointing. The author devotes to Photius only two very inadequate pages (pp. 131-133).

of the third century to the beginning of the seventh, testify to the intensity of Aristotelian studies in the Christian East.

On the other hand, Platonism also had its attraction. Origen and Clement of Alexandria were able to make full use of all that seemed attractive in Greek philosophy, and fell under the spell of Plato, but pure Platonism soon appeared as a subtle danger to orthodoxy. This is illustrated by the long controversies over Origen and his his doctrine which ended in the sixth century with the condemnation of Origenism.

Pure Platonism, although still dominant here and there in Byzantine philosophical speculation, lost its hold on the Byzantine mind. It appeared, however, in a new form, the Neoplatonic and took hold of Byzantine mysticism through the work attributed to Dionysius the Areopagite.[19] The authority of St. Maximus Confessor,[20] the greatest theologian of the seventh century, dispelled the apprehensions which the Neoplatonic ideas had provoked, and due to his interpretation, the work of Dionysius was made freely accessible to all Byzantine theologians.

Scholars who are interested in the history of Byzantine philosophy are aware of the fact that from the seventh century on, all commentary on the work of Aristotle had ceased in Byzantium. There seems to be a gap which extends to the eleventh century when Michael of Ephesus renewed the interest in this kind of philosophical work. So far no explanation has been forthcoming to account for this sudden cessation of Aristotelian studies. Does it mean that Platonism was gaining new ground in Byzantine thinking? We cannot say, although John of Damascus would seem to have had recourse to Plato when defining the relation of the Icon to its Prototype.[21] Let us hope that some one will be attracted by this problem and will give us an adequate reply to the question. Bearing this in mind the attitude of Photius towards Platonism should not be overlooked.

19 His works are reprinted in Migne, *P.G.*, vols. 3, 4. New edition with a French translation by G. Heil and M. de Gandillac (Paris, 1958, Sources chrétiennes, vol. 58). English translation by C. E. Rolt (London, 1920). Cf. H. F. Müller, *Dionysios, Proklos, Plotinos, Ein historischer Beitrag zur neuplatonischen Philosophie,* 2d edit. (Münster i.W., 1926).

20 His works in Migne, *P.G.*, vols. 90, 91.

21 Oratio tertia de Imaginibus, ch. 19, Migne, *P.G.*, vol. 94, col. 1340. Cf. Oratio prima, ch. 10, col. 1240.

After a long interruption in Aristotelian studies, Photius brought philosophical and theological speculation back to the foundations established by Aristotle on which Byzantine religious thinkers of the early period had been building their theological systems. Photius is an avowed Aristotelian and, a fact which is often forgotten, he even fills the gap in the writing of Aristotelian commentaries, a gap which, as we have said above, stretched from the beginning of the seventh to the eleventh century. In his *Amphilolochia* we find, not only many passages alluding to the philosopher's writings, but a long explanation of the categories of Aristotle.[22]

Photius' interest in philosophy did not stop with Aristotle, although the latter attracted him most. He was also interested in Pyrrho, a contemporary of Alexander the Great, whose philosophical system was explained by Aenesidemus, a contemporary of Cicero. Photius gives a long review of his work in Cod. 212.

The spread of Neoplatonism in the fifth century of our era also received his attention. He gives extracts from the lost works of Hierocles on *Providence* and *Fate* (Cod. 214, 251), together with long selections and a description of the *Life of the Philosopher Isidorus,* described by Damascius, the last teacher of Neo-Platonism in Athens (Cod. 171, 242). In Cod. 74 Photius mentions Themistius' commentary on Aristotle's and Plato's works. His interest in political philosophy is revealed in Cod. 37 where he discusses an anonymous treatise on politics, in which the author recommends a political system with not only monarchic, but also aristocratic and democratic features. His own political ideas were expounded by Photius in his letter to Michael-Boris of Bulgaria.[23] In this letter it is easy to detect Hellenistic ideas of kingship, as disclosed by Isocrates in *Nicocles,* and which Photius adapts to Christian teaching. In the same context should be noted Photius' comments on the philosophical and political treatises of Philo (Cod. 103-105).

---

[22] Migne, *P.G.*, vol. 101, cols. 760-811. On several occasions Photius manifested his predilection for Aristotle and his dislike of Plato. For ex. *P.G.*, vol. 101, cols. 480, 488, vol. 103, Bibliotheca, cod. 37, cols. 69, cod. 242, cols. 1257-1260. Ad Amphilochium, quaestio 92, *P.G.*, vol. 101, col. 585. Photius' disciple Arethas of Caesarea composed also a treatise on Aristotle's categories, so far unpublished. He was, however, interested also in Plato.

[23] Migne, *P.G.*, vol. 102, cols. 628 ff. Cf. on the treatise mentioned by Photius and on his letter E. Barker, *Social and Political Thought in Byzantium* (Oxford), pp. 64, 109 ff.

Besides philosophical topics Photius also studied works on natural history, pure science, physics and medicine. Cod. 188, 189, 170 contain descriptions of the works of Alexander of Myndos on geography and natural history, of the geographer Protagoras, of Sotion, Nicholas of Damascus, Acestorides and Ptolemy Chennus. Incidentally, Nicholas dedicated his work to King Herod of Judea.

Photius' interest in medicine was evidently quite lively judging from the excerpts he made in his *Bibliotheca* from works on this subject. Theophrastus' zoological and medicinal works referred to in Cod. 278 are all lost. The surgical methods described by the famous Galen (second century A.D.) are analysed in Cod. 164. The work of the physician Dioscurides (fifth century A.D.) is reviewed in Cod. 178. The physiological and medicinal treatise of Dionysius of Aegae are discussed twice (Cod. 185, 211). The four works on medicine by Oribasius, adviser and personal physician to Julian the Apostate, are analysed in detail in Cod. 216-219. These are partly preserved, but the anthropological work by Archiatros Theon of Alexandria (Cod. 220) is known only from the short note by Photius. Precious are the indications given by Photius on the medical treatise written by the sixth century imperial physician Aetius of Amida (Cod. 221).

The history of Byzantine medicine, its dependence on the traditions and practices of the classical age, its development and the transmission of classical and Byzantine experience to a later age, has not yet been sufficiently explored. The student of this history will find it necessary to bear in mind the excerpts made by Photius from writings now lost.

In Codex 163 we see that Photius was interested also in works on agriculture. He read the twelve books on this subject written in the fourth century by Vindanius Anatolius of Beirut. The *Geoponica,* compiled on the order of Constantine Porphyrogenetus, contains excerpts from this work.

Students of the Hellenistic period generally complain that the Byzantines showed little understanding of the literary products of the early Hellenistic age covering the last three centuries B.C. and of the later period from Augustus to Constantine the Great. It is regrettable—they say—that in the eyes of the

Byzantines, this age was considered a deplorable interlude in the history of Greece, when no care was taken to preserve its literary works so that the attention of later generations was concentrated on the masterpieces of the classical great age. There is much truth in these complaints. The study of the Hellenistic period, so long neglected, is hampered by the fact that so few works, especially those written during the three centuries after the death of Alexander, have survived. But we must not generalize. The neglect of these works by the Byzantines was neither systematic nor complete. In the sixth century Hellenistic literature was known and read in Byzantium almost in its entirety. About 500 A.D. John Stobeaus published his famous anthology containing the most interesting passages from the numerous works he had read.[24] He was a man of extensive reading and among the five hundred fragments from poetic and prose writings which he quotes are many from the early Hellenistic period. It is possible that the troubles of the seventh century and the occupation of the Middle East by the Arabs, are mainly responsible for the loss of a great number of these works. But not all were lost and many were still read in Photius' time and were preserved for us, mainly as a result of the renaissance in Greek letters instigated by Photius. In his *Bibliotheca* (Cod. 213) he gives an account of the now lost *Narrationes,* a work on Greek gods and heroes by Conon, who dedicated it to King Archelaus Philopatris (reigned in Cappadocia from 36 B.C. to 17 A.D.). He found this work in the manuscript which also contained the famous *Bibliotheca,* falsely attributed to Apollodorus, an Athenian grammarian and historian who (about 140 B.C.) was studied under Aristarchus and the Stoic Panaetius. It is a veritable storehouse of material important for the study of Greek mythology. Although Apollodorus is the author of a work entitled *On the Gods* in twenty-four books, the attribution to him of the *Bibliotheca* should be rejected.

It is a pity that Photius was unable to write the second part of his own *Bibliotheca* as he intended to do, for in it we would most probably have found his critique of many other works of the Hellenistic age. But even so we are entitled to correct the

[24] *Joannis Stobaei Anthologium,* ed. by C. Wachsmuth, O. Heuse (Berlin, 1884-1912).

general judgment pronounced on the Byzantines of neglecting Hellenistic literature.

On one particular point the Byzantines of Photius' time appear to have been especially attracted to their Hellenistic inheritance. We know that this literature showed originality most of all in the composition of love romances and adventure stories. The leader in this field is undoubtedly not a native Greek but a hellenized Semite, Lucian of Samosata (second century A.D.). He should be regarded as the founder of a new literary form, the light, popular manner, which has only reached its full development in our time. He revealed the extraordinary talent which the Semites have for such literary activity, and it is here that we should look for the explanation as to why writers of Semitic origin are so prominent in modern journalism. If one has read the works of Lucian, full of biting criticism of second century society, sparkling with irony and wit, at times over-realistic in revealing the vices of pagan society, but far from the crude realism of a Zola, one cannot but agree with Photius in his lavish praise (Cod. 128) of the brilliant style of this first *feuilletoniste*.

Besides the works of Lucian, Photius also read with his friends the *Metamorphoses* of Lucius of Patras (Cod. 129) whom he compared to Lucian. The adventurous fiction of Antonius Diogenes (Cod. 166), the *Babyloniaca* of Jamblichus (second century A.D.) now completely lost and the *Aethiopica* of Heliodorus (third century A.D.). However, the *love stories* of Achilles Tatius (sixth century A.D.) are very sharply criticized for their licentiousness (Cod. 94). In this respect Photius considers Heliodorus more serious and restrained, Jamblichus less so. This judgment deserves more attention on the part of Byzantine students, for Photius here opens up a new and interesting vista, giving a better insight into the more intimate life of ninth century society and his interest in Hellenistic romance partly fills another gap in the evolution of Greek literary history. There is no link between the last pagan writer of romance Chariton (probably of the second century A.D.),[25] and the new era in this kind of literature which starts with Prodromos,

25 His romance entitled *The Love Adventures of Chaereas and Callirrhoé* was translated into English by E. Blake (Ann Arbor, Oxford, 1939). Edited by the same author (Oxford, 1938).

Manasses, Nicetas Eugemianos and Eustathius in the eleventh century.[26] It was assumed that the new Christian spirit eliminated all interest in pagan romances and had replaced them with legends of the Saints. Only recently have traces of the existence of popular *tragoúdia,* or recitals of the exploits of heroes, been found by Professor H. Grégoire, in the ninth century. The discovery is not as surprising as it appears, for Photius shows us that the Byzantines had not forgotten Hellenistic romance and that the revival of this literature, which culminated in the tenth or eleventh century in the great romance of Digenis Akritas,[27] may have been spurred on by the study and reading of Hellenistic romance.

We cannot go into more detail, but even from these few generalities, it is clear how important the role of Photius was in transmitting to later ages the inheritance of the Classical and Hellenistic age. I insist on the Hellenistic aspect quite intentionally as, so far, it has been mainly neglected. As a result of all this it is clear that Photius must be credited with the great merit of having made the bridge which, after the iconoclastic interruption, once more linked Byzantium firmly with the Greek past, namely, the Hellenistic and Classical periods. This is an important factor also in the study of the revival of religious art in this period. We are entitled to suppose that even Byzantine artists, guided by the leading figure in the new renaissance, endeavoured to return to the traditions of the ancients.

---

[26] See K. Krumbacher, *Geschichte der byzantinischen litteratur* 2d edit. (Munich, 1897), pp. 641 ff. E. Rhode, *Griechischer Roman und seine Vorläufer* (Leipzig, 1914), 3rd edit. pp. 521 ff. on Byzantine novels.

[27] The most recent edition by J. Mavrogordato, *Digenis Akritas* (Oxford, 1956) gives all bibliographical data on this important romance. He is inclined to date its composition from the eleventh century, H. Grégoire from the tenth. Cf. Grégoire's studies in *Byzantion,* especially vols. 4 (1929), and 9 (1934).

II

One more service rendered by the Patriarch to Greek scholarship should be pointed out. During his extensive reading of the classical, Hellenistic and early Christian literature, Photius experienced all the difficulties which such a study presents to the reader not familiar with the evolution of the language and with Greek archaeology through the ages. To facilitate such reading, he conceived the idea of composing an extensive dictionary of the Greek language. He must have made a thorough study of old grammarians and lexicographers, for in his *Bibliotheca* (Cod. 94-108) he speaks of the many works of this kind which have since, for the most part, perished: The work of Helladius of Alexandria (fifth century A.D.), of Diogenianus (time of Hadrian), of Valerius Pollio and his son Diodorus; also the glossaries compiled by Julian, Philostratus of Tyre, Pausanias, Boethus, Dorotheus of Ascalon, by Dionysius of Halicarnassus the Younger, and by three anonymous writers. He also used the *Atticist* of Moeris and the Lexicon to Plato's works composed by the sophist Timaeus. He speaks at length of the *Rhetorical Equipment* of Phrynichus, the Arabian, and praises the excellence of the linguistic material collected by him, but thinks that it could have been reduced to one fifth of its size. He regrets that the author did not himself make use of "the elegance and beauty of style" given as examples to others. The work which Photius himself composed was only partly preserved, but recently a new manuscript has been found containing the missing parts of Photius' Lexicon.[28] It was his desire to continue this sort of work, and, although he never had leisure to return to this kind of study, the work as it stands represents a great achievement. His collection of old Attic words and phrases is especially complete and represents a serious advance over the research

28 *Photii partriarchae Lexicon,* ed. by S. A. Naber (Leyden, 1864-65) *Lexicon Vindobonense,* ed. A. Nauck (St. Petersburg, 1867). The new manuscript containing the whole of the Lexicon was found recently by Linos Politis in the Monastery of Zabora. It dates back to the thirteenth century and will be published by a group of professors of the University of Thessalonica. Cf. *Byzant. Zeitschr.,* vol. 52 (1959), p. 503.

made in this field by his predecessor Moeris. It also contains much archaeological data and merits study by historians of Greek literature. A more profound study of his dictionary will be possible only when the newly discovered manuscript is published. It will considerably increase our knowledge of the number of classical and Hellenistic writers known in the time of Photius, whose works have since been lost.

It seems that Photius was an initiator in the composition of etymological dictionaries, for we find five passages in the still unpublished *Etymologicum genuinum* which contains statements made by Photius himself.[29] Thus, in the *Ampilochian Questions*[30] he describes a magnet, and his description is identical—although not verbally—with what we read in *Etymologicum*. It is probable that Photius participated in the final stage of the composition of this *Etymologicum* which was begun by an anonymous scholar, perhaps in the service of Photius, who in one passage laments his poverty. The *Etymologicum parvum,* posterior to the first, was also composed under Photius' direction. It was completed on May 13th, 882, the day on which the Church of Hagia Sophia was reopened after the completion of repairs ordered by the Emperor Basil I.

In order to complete our picture of Photius as a scholar we must consider his theological erudition. However, this is too great a task and a brief enumeration of some of the most important theological works discussed in his *Bibliotheca* will have to suffice. Even in this field we are indebted to him for the preservation of information and the contents of many works which have never reached us.

It is interesting to note that the critical mind of Photius

---

29 On the *Etymologica* see the general study by Reitzenstein in Pauly-Wissowa's *Realenzyklopädie,* vol. 6. (Stuttgart, 1909), cols. 807-817.

30 *Ad Amphilochium,* quaestio 131, col. 725. Photius seems to have taken this description of the magnet from Helladius' *Chrestomathia* from which he gives a very long excerpt with his own remarks in the *Bibliotheca* (Cod. 279). On Photius' initiating the composition of the *Etymologicum genuinum* and his authorship of the *Etymologicum parvum,* see R. Reitzenstein, *Geschichte der griechischen Etymologika* (Leipzig, 1897), pp. 56-69, 144 ff., 156, 190 ff. Cf. the *Etymologicum magnum,* of the twelfth century, in the edition by F. Sylburgius (Leipzig, 1816), col. 519, ed. by Th. Gaisford (Oxford, 1848), col. 573. It is interesting to read how the Patriarch, in the second chapter of the *Quaestio,* applies the function of the magnet to the spiritual life of a Christian, who should be attracted by God and His works as the iron is attracted by the magnet.

rejected the authenticity of the second letter of St. Clement, an object of long controversey in modern times. The Pseudo-Clementine writings were sharply criticized by him, although he thought them to be genuine. Several writings of Justin Martyr, no longer extant (Cod. 125) were read by him. The lost *Syntagma* of Hippolytus (Cod. 121) was also known to him. Origen was not his favorite Father (Cod. 8) although he did read several writings in defence of Origen which have not been preserved. In his day there still existed certain works of Apollinarius and of Julius Africanus of which we have only fragments.

He read some of the works of Athanasius (Cod. 32, 139, 140) but was more interested in Basil (Cod. 141-144, 191) and, above all, in John Chrysostom (Cod. 25, 86, 172-174, 270, 274, 277). His acquaintance with the works of Gregory of Nyssa (Cod. 6, 7) is manifest, and he praised Cyril of Alexandria (Cod. 49, 54, 136, 169) for the prose style.

Two prominent heretics of the fifth and sixth centuries, whose works are only partially preserved, attracted Photius' special attention—Theodore of Mopsuestia (Cod. 4, 38, 81, 177) and John Philoponus. The latter would seem to have been his favourite author, mainly because of his style whose clarity he praises, although he is severely critical of his teaching (Cod. 21-24, 43, 50, 55, 75, 215, 240). Perhaps Philoponus' predilection for Aristotle, Photius' favourite philosopher, incited him to a more thorough study of Philoponus' works and those of his opponents.

He studied the discourses of Ephrem the Syrian (Cod. 195), of Ephrem the Younger (Cod. 228, 229), the writings of Eusebius of Caesarea (Cod. 9-13, 39, 118, 127) whom he criticizes not always with reason, the lost theological works of Eulogius of Alexandria (Cod. 182, 208, 280) and of Eusebius of Thessalonica (Cod. 162). He also had in his library the dogmatic works of the monk Job which are now lost (Cod. 222).

His interest in biblical studies is attested by extracts from the anonymous commentary on the Octateuch (Cod. 36), and from another work by the sophist Procopius (Cod. 206, 207) and from the lost treatise of Hesychius of Constantinople on Moses' bronze serpent. He read also twenty-one homilies on the Old or New Testament and various other subjects.

Photius was, of course, also interested in the ascetico-mystical writings of Pseudo-Dionysius, since he quotes (Cod. 1) the now lost defence of the authenticity of this work, written by the priest Theodore, probably in the sixth century. It is, however, difficult to say whether Photius himself believed in its authenticity, although he quotes it elsewhere in his writings. In Cod. 197-201 Photius discusses ascetical works read by him. These are the writings of Cassian, the lives of holy hermits, the famous *Spiritual Meadow* by John Moschus, the ascetic treatises of the monk Mark, Diadochus and Nilus, and the letter of consolation and encouragement written by John Carpathius to the monks who were sent to India.

Church history was another subject studied by Photius, who was familiar with the works of all the early Church historians, Eusebius, Socrates, Sozomen, Theodoret and Euagrius (Cod. 27-31) as well as with the lost works of Philostorgius, John of Aegea (Cod. 40, 41), Basil of Cilicia (Cod. 43), Philip Sidetes (Cod. 35) and the ninth century confessor Sergius (Cod. 67). He preferred Theodoret to all of them because of the sober, clear and elevated style, which Photius regarded as best suited to historical writing, although he did find Theodoret's use of metaphors rather excessive. He read also all the other works by this author (Cod. 46, 56, 203-205, 273). In twelve codices Photius discusses the Acts of different Councils. Although his remarks are brief the student of early Church history must take them into account. Among the hagiographical works quoted by Photius is an extract from an anonymous biography of Pope Gregory the Great (Cod. 252); of the first bishops of Constantinople Metrophanes and Alexander (Cod. 256) now, unfortunately, lost; of Paul, Patriach of Constantinople (Cod. 257) and of Athanasius (Cod. 258), and certain *martyria* (Cod. 253-255).

It would be interesting to show how Photius applied the stylistic and grammatical principles he admired so much in the works of classical authors, to his own writing. However, it is not possible to do this in a short paper. Both the homilies and the letters show a very elaborate style in which the influence of classical writers can easily be detected. This is less perceptible in his writings against the Paulicians of which, at least the second and third books seem authentic. His work on the procession of the Holy Ghost is also written in elaborate, sometimes passionate language. His *Amphilochia* is a collection of answers to different dogmatic, ecclesiastical, practical and philological questions put to him mostly by his disciples and followers. The style is less elaborate, but many of the answers belong rather among the collection of his letters.

Photius' theological writings are not considered the best works of the Patriarch. However, one point must be stressed. The most recent research into Photius' literary activities concentrates mainly on his exegetical works. He is credited with commentaries on the Psalms, on the four Gospels, and on the epistles of St. Paul. It seems that his commentary on the Matthew Gospel is most extensive. Recently J. Reuss[31] discovered over one hundred Photian scholia on St. Matthew which may have been derived from the homilies which were not preserved. Another scholar, having studied the commentaries on St. Paul, praises Photius' originality in the following words: "This is an achievement the like of which cannot be found for centuries either before or after." It is a pity that the turbulent years of Photius' career did not allow the Patriarch to devote more of his time to literary activity, for which he yearned.

Even this short exposé shows how important the role of Photius was in the transmission of classical and Hellenistic lore to later generations. We also see from the study of his *Bibliotheca* and other writings how clearly the heritage of the ancients was once more made useful to the Christian world and this without creating many marked disturbances in Byzantine minds. On the contrary, from the manner in which Photius speaks of the classics, history, rhetoric and other disciplines, we see that the ninth century Byzantine had achieved a well balanced attitude in the study of the classical and Hellenistic inheritance, using both the technique and terminology of the classical disciplines and adjusting them to their Christian environment.

Thus Photius does not engage in polemics with pagan authors nor does he display an apologetic attitude towards them. He is

---

[31] J. Reuss, "Die Matthaeus-Erklaerung des Photius von Konstantinopel," *Ostkirchliche Studien,* vol. 1 (1952), pp. 132-34.

[32] K. Staab. *Pauluskommentare aus der griechischen Kirche aus Katenenhandschriften gesammelt* (Neutestam. Abhandl., vol. 15, Münster i.W., 1933), pp. 470-652. The quotation is on p. XLIV of the introduction.

aware of the superiority of Christian ideas unknown to the classics and therefore the works of early Christian authors are given an important place in his studies. These he appraises in the classical tradition and looks upon them as the continuators of the classical and Hellenistic era.

This harmony between pagan literary antecedents and the new Christian spirit which is a common feature of Byzantium, all along a self-evident necessity to the Byzantine intellectual, rather puzzles us when we consider what a religious and moral revolution was caused during the Western renaissance of the fifteenth century when the Western nations came into possession of the literary treasures of the classical and Hellenistic age.

Photius appears to have been well aware of the danger which an unbalanced estimate of the classical literary revival could create for certain enthusiasts. We read in his ninth Homily, preached on the birthday of the Virgin (September 30th),[33] a passionate denunciation of the absurdity of Greek mythological fables. He addresses his attack at those sceptics who, invoking the natural law criticized the tradition which held that the Virgin was born from a barren woman, St. Anne, but yet gave credence to the absurd myths on creation and the gods which they read in Greek mythology.

There are no traces of the survival of paganism in Byzantine society in the ninth century. The interest in classical mythology could only have been awakened by the general renaissance of classical and Hellenistic literary tradition during this period of Byzantium's history. Photius himself was well acquainted with Greek mythology, and he commented in his *Bibliotheca* (Cod. 186, 129) on the most valuable handbooks on classical mythology, those by Apollodorus and Lucius of Patras.

Photius' rebuke must, thus, be addressed to those admirers of the classics who were inclined to go too far in their enthusiasm, taking pagan classical tradition too seriously and becoming too rationalistic when comparing them with the Christian creed.

Photius was adamant in this respect, not allowing the classical examples to overshadow Christian writings. In one of his letters, he severely rebukes the philosopher Leo, probably his own former

33 C. Mango, *op. cit.*, pp. 166-171.

teacher, for having criticized certain grammatical solecisms in the Bible and calling them barbaric.[34] On another occasion, he reprimands his friend George, Metropolitan of Nicomedia, for his criticism of the language used by Sts. Peter and Paul in their epistles.[35] In the three letters addressed to George on this subject, Photius uses very severe language, although well aware of the fact that the idiom of the Apostles cannot be compared with the classics.

Modern critics[36] object to Photius, and not without reason, that his zeal for Christianity and Orthodox teaching often influenced his judgement on the literary merits of the authors whose works he had read. It has been pointed out that the defenders of Orthodox teaching were generally praised for the excellence of their style and diction, but that heretical writers were severely criticized for their style and language. There is some justification in this criticism, but it should not be generalized. We have seen, for example, that Photius praised the style of Philiponus' heretical writings.

If we bear in mind Photius' scholarly activities, his interest in the classics, and the role he played in the transmission of classical traditions to Christians of later generations, we will understand more clearly certain events which took place during his ecclesiastical career and which have, so far, been referred to as proofs of Photius' ambitions and his bad will.

It is now generally accepted that, contrary to what had been formerly believed, Photius was canonically elected to the patriarchal throne in December 857; this after Ignatius, his predecessor, had resigned because of his conflict with the regent Bardas.[37] However, it is not yet quite clear why part of the clergy revolted against him two months later, proclaiming Ignatius the only legitimate Patriarch, even though Ignatius' own supporters and all the bishops had previously recognized Photius as the legitimate Patriarch.

---

34 *Amphilochia,* quaestio 106, PG, vol. 101, cols. 640-41.

35 *Amphilochia,* quaestio 86, 92, 93, *PG., ibid.,* cols. 557, 575, 592.

36 Cf. G. Hartmann, *Photius' Literarästhetik* (Borna-Leipzig, 1929) pp. 46 ff. See also Ziegler, *op. cit.,* cols 719 ff.

37 See my book *The Photian Schism, History and Legend* (Cambridge, 1948) and my report to the Eleventh International Congress for Byzantine Studies in Munich, *The Patriarch Photius in the Light of Recent Research* (Munich, 1958).

All that has been said about the survival of classical and Hellenistic learning and the opposition which it provoked in some circles, will help us, perhaps, to gain greater insight into the situation which provoked a schism in the Byzantine Church. It seems certain that the revolt came from among the radical elements of Ignatius' followers including the monks, especially Abbott Theognostus, who were amongst the most vociferous opponents to the new Patriarch. As we have seen from the hagiographical literature of this period, many monks looked upon the classical revival with suspicion, if not with deep hostility, seeing in it a return to paganism.

An accusation of paganism was launched, for example, against Leo the Philosopher, a former iconoclast, by his disciple Constantine.[38]. From the verses in which the accusation is couched, we deduce that the basis of this accusation was Leo's enthusiasm for classical lore. Deep interest in mythology is interpreted as denial of the Trinity. Leo is also said to have made several predictions based on astrological practices and his interest in astrology is certainly documented.[39] While he taught at the imperial University Photius had been one of his students and later a colleague.

In fact a similar accusation was launched against Photius himself by one of his bitterest enemies, the monk Pseudo-Symeon, author of a Chronicle.[40] He charged that in his youth Photius had renounced Christ in exchange for having "every Hellenic writing on the tip of his tongue, and surpassing all men in wisdom." Here again "Hellenic wisdom" is interpreted by a radical devotee as renouncing Christ, or as paganism. Prominent scholars of the time, the iconoclast Patriarch John the Grammarian, Leo the Philosopher, Photius, were even accused of sorcery. The

---

[38] Matrangza, *Anecdota graeca* (Rome, 1850), vol. 2, pp. 555-559. Reprinted in *PG.*, vol. 107, cols. LXI ff., 660 ff. In the second passage Constantine justifies the accusations of his former teacher, and praises his new teacher, the old Patriarch Photius "who nourished him with the milk of divine streams." G. Kolias, in his study *Léon Choerospactès* (Athens, 1939), pp. 66-68 proved that the two texts refer to Leo the Mathematician. J. B. Bury, *A History of the Eastern Roman Empire* (London, 1912), pp. 440, 441 translated a part of Constantine's attack in English verses.

[39] For example, *Theophilus Contin.* (Bonn Corpus), pp. 189, 191, 197, 233. See what C. Mango, *l.c.*, p. 162 says about Leo.

[40] Pseudo-Symeon (Bonn Corpus), pp. 670, 672, 673.

accusations came from the same milieu and the basis was the revival of the classical "pagan" studies favoured by them.

When we consider the mentality of these radical devotees, we can well understand their dislike of Photius and their horror at seeing a successor to Ignatius, who had no such "pagan" inclinations, a man who had "every Hellenic writing on the tip of his tongue." They feared that Orthodoxy was in danger as long as such a man was head of the Church and they won over to their way of thinking certain Ignatian bishops who had previously supported Photius. This was one of the causes of the schism and for the violent opposition to Photius from reactionaries, bigots, supporters of the deposed Empress Theodora, besides other causes of a political or an unknown nature. The fact that the classical renaissance had already begun under Theophilus, the last Iconoclast Emperor, aggravated the danger in their eyes.[41]

In his inthronistical letter to Pope Nicholas I[42] after the suppression of the revolt, Photius insisted that he had accepted the election very unwillingly. An historian of classical scholarship characterizes this letter in the following terms: "One of the most beautiful passages of his longer letters is that in the first letter to Pope Nicholas (861), in which he describes the loss of a life of peaceful calm which was his lot when he ceased being a layman, and regretfully dwells on the happiness of his home in the days when he was surrounded by eager enquirers after learning by whom he was always welcomed on his return from court."[43] Every true scholar will sympathise with a colleague who has had to abandon the scholarly life knowing that he will become the object of controversies and vilification from people to whom scholarship appeared to be a danger to Orthodoxy. It is a pity

---

41 The role of the Iconoclast emperors, especially of Theophilus, in the classical renaissance is not yet sufficiently known. It is certain that it started, at least at the beginning of the ninth century and that it was favored by he Iconoclasts. Cf. what L. Bréhier says on the opposition of the conservative monks against classical studies in his paper "L'enseignement classique et l'enseignement religieux à Byzance," in *Revue d'histoire de philos. relig.*, vol. 21(1941), pp. 59 ff.

42 *PG.*, vol. 102, col. 597.

43 J. E. Sandys, *A History of Classical Scholarship* (Cambridge 1903), p. 393. Card. Hergenröther, *Photius,* vol. I, p. 441, sees in this declaration of Photius "the old lie" (die alte Lüge). Cf. what I said about this in my book *The Photian Schism,* p. 95.

that Pope Nicholas was not a scholar. He would have composed his reply to Photius' letter in more indulgent terms.

Had Roman ecclesiastical circles known that Photius' scholarship was not limited to profane things and that a Byzantine-trained layman was better versed in theology than most clerics in the West, perhaps they would have been less horrified at the knowledge that a director of the imperial chancellery had become head of the Byzantine Church.

In this light we understand much better the importance of an action of great value in the education of the Byzantine clergy which was initiated by Photius during his first patriarchate. Photius had begun his career as a professor at the University of Constantinople. We learn this from the biography of his disciple and young friend, St. Constantine-Cyril, apostle of the Slavs, written in Moravia in the ninth century.[44] This university was an old institution which had existed in Byzantium uninterruptedly since its foundation by Constantine the Great. As already mentioned, its first aim was the training of good imperial officials and administrators.

Besides the University, there had always existed in Byzantium another advanced school — the patriarchal academy — for the training of the clergy. This institution had also had its difficulties, and for a long time it was believed that its rich library had been burned down, together with its twelve professors, by the first Iconoclast Emperor Leo III. Modern research has proved that this is a legend.[45] The patriarchal academy was not destroyed but only "reformed" in the iconoclast sense, the professors recalcitrant to the Emperor's theological ideas being replaced by Iconoclasts. We find in the *Chronicle* of the monk George a mention of the deacon Ignatius, who was "the ecumenical or universal teacher," a title reserved to the director of the patriarchal Academy.[46] This Ignatius lived in the reign of the last Iconoclast Emperor, Theophilus.

It seems, however, that the institution was thoroughly reformed

---

[44] See the French translation from Old Slavonic of this legend in my book *Les Légendes de Const. et de Méthode,* p. 352.

[45] See the bibliographical references on this problem in my paper "Photius et la réorganisation de l'académie patriarcale," *Analecta Bollandiana,* vol. 48(1950), pp. 108 ff.

[46] Bonn *Corpus,* vol. II, p. 742.

by Photius when he became Patriarch of Constantinople. We learn from the life of Constantine-Cyril that this disciple of Photius was most probably his successor at the University. He abandoned his post when the Prime Minister Theoctistus, who until then had been his benefactor, was assassinated by Bardas; but when his teacher Photius was elected Patriarch, Constantine-Cyril was reconciled to the new régime and with his brother Methodius accepted an important diplomatic and religious mission to the Khazars, of Turkish race, who at that time dominated the territory of what is now Southern Russia. When he returned from this mission in 861, he is pictured by his biographer as "sitting in the church of the Holy Apostles and enjoying his conversation with God."[47]

This was the first year in which Photius could devote all his attention to the reorganization of religious life in Constantinople, the two previous years having been occupied in surmounting the opposition of the zealots. It is thus quite reasonable to assume that when Constantine-Cyril returned from his mission, he was asked by Photius to assist him in the reorganization of the Academy. The fact that in a later period of Byzantine history the Patriarchal Academy had its quarters in the Church of the Holy Apostles allows us to interpret the information given by the *Vita Constantini* in the sense that the future apostle of the Slavs had accepted a chair, probably that of philosophy, at the Patriarchal Academy, newly reorganized by Photius, in the second most important church in Constantinople, the Church of the Holy Apostles.

It is easy to understand why Photius was so interested in the reorganization of the Academy. He had need of a well educated clergy in order to weaken the opposition of the zealots to profane science, and especially to the teaching of philosophy regarded by Photius as essential to the study of theology. According to the meagre sources at our disposal concerning the history and aims of the Patriarchal Academy, we are told that there were twelve professors who instructed the clergy in "theological and profane lore." We are entitled to suppose that during the patri-

---

47 See my paper *Photius et la réorganisation,* p. 121. According to Byzantine terminology the word "sitting" in this context should mean sitting in the chair of the master, i.e. teaching.

archate of Ignatius the teaching of profane sciences, grammar, rhetoric, and philosophy was, if not suppressed, at least curtailed. Anastasius, the Librarian, the translator of the Acts of the Ignatian Council of 869-70, admits that Ignatius treated profane learning with the utmost contempt, thus sharing the feelings of the zealous bigots.[48] By reintroducing classical scholarship as the basis of education for the secular clergy in Byzantium, Photius made still another signal contribution to the Christian perpetuation of the Classics.

There may still be another reason which spurred Photius to increase the numbers of educated clergy at his disposal. The Khazar embassy must have opened up new possibilities to the Byzantines for political, cultural and religious expansion and the many races living under Khazar rule surely attracted them. We have only to read the lively account of this mission in the *Life of Constantine-Cyril* to realize this very clearly.[49] The Patriarch Photius was not a man to miss such an opportunity, nor was Bardas, who governed in the name of Michael III. Such an expansion would be successful only if numerous well instructed missionaries were available. It was natural to entrust the training of such missionaries to the very man who had discovered, on his successful embassy to the Khazars, this new and promising field of missionary activity for the Byzantine Church. And the Church of the Holy Apostles would be the most appropriate place for such training.

In this connection we should emphasize that during the first patriarchate of Photius the Byzantine Church was at the height of its greatest missionary expansion. For the first time Greek culture penetrated beyond the middle Danube into the valley of Moravia, and the messengers were the same two brothers, Constantine-Cyril and Methodius, sent to Moravia by the Emperor and by Photius. Because of this politico-religious alliance between Byzantium and Moravia, the Bulgars, who were about to be converted by the Franks, had to abandon their Frankish allies and their Khazan, Boris was baptized by Photius. The Patriarch succeeded in sending a bishop to the Russians in Kiev,

---

48 Mansi, *Concilia,* vol. XII, col. 6 "qui (Ignatius) scilicet viros exterioris sapientiae repulisset."

49 See my book *Les Légendes,* pp. 148 ff. 358 ff.

and due to his efforts, even the Serbs were won definitely for Christianity. Byzantine influence spread as far as Dalmatia where the Croats founded an independent realm.[50] Photius, who had Armenian blood in his veins, included Armenia in his plans for Byzantine expansion, as can be judged from his embassies and letters.

The spread of Byzantine influence among the Slavs which began under Photius yielded, as we well know, a permanent result. This happened mainly as the result of a bold and ingenious step undertaken by Constantine-Cyril, a disciple of Photius, and his brother Methodius, under the patronage of the same Photius: namely, the invention of a special Slavonic alphabet and the translation of Holy Writ and liturgical books into Slavonic. Such an action could not have been accomplished without the consent of the head of the Byzantine Church. When we read carefully the *Life of Constantine-Cyril,* we see that this was done not only with his consent but, most probably, on his initiative.

Photius continued to be interested in Slavonic letters. When, about 882, Methodius, after being consecrated Metropolitan of Sirmium and Moravia by Pope Hadrian II, visited Photius in Constantinople, possibly bringing with him a message from Pope John VIII whom he had visited in Rome in 880, the Patriarch kept in the capital some of Methodius' clerics as well as Slavonic books and founded, in this way, an important centre from which to provide the new converts with Greek books for translation. Later, we learn from the Slavonic life of one of Methodius' disciples, St. Naum, that when, after the death of the Moravian archbishop, his disciples who were of Greek origin, were dispersed by the Franks and some even sold into slavery, a high Byzantine official bought some of them in Venice and sent them to Constantinople.[51] In this way the Slavonic centre in Byzantium was strengthened. Specialists in Slavonic philology are now inclined to believe that this centre, founded in Con-

---

50 See *ibidem,* pp. 212 ff.

51 See for details my book *Les Slaves, Byzance et Rome,* pp. 266 ff., 297-300 (Naum) and *Les Légendes,* pp. 334, 344 ff., 390 ff. (*Vita Methodii*). On Methodius' visit to Constantinople see also R. Jakobson "Minor Slavic Sources" in *Harvard Slavic Studies,* vol. 2 (1954) pp. 64 ff. and my remarks in my book *The Slavs,* pp. 124 ff.

stantinople by Photius, had a lion's share in the spreading of Slavonic liturgy and Byzantine civilization in Bulgaria and in Kievan Russia. With his talent for organization the Patriarch might have foreseen the use to which this centre could be put for Byzantine religious propaganda. However, in this instance he followed the old Greek and Byzantine tradition of a liberal attitude toward the language of those to be converted to Christianity. Perhaps he also shared, as a scholar, the philological interest of his disciple Constantine-Cyril, one of the finest philological scholars Byzantium has produced.[52]

The vital interest which Photius had shown in the preservation of classical and Hellenistic traditions in Byzantium will help us to gain greater insight into his relations with Rome, the ancient capital of the Empire. So far, in this respect, he has been regarded as the sworn enemy of the primacy of the Roman bishop and as generally hostile to Rome and to the West. As the main argument for this point of view, reference is made to the Council of 867, convoked by Photius in order to condemn Pope Nicholas I, who refused to recognize Photius as legitimate Patriarch. It appears that this judgment is too severe. The Acts of this Council were destroyed both in Rome and Constantinople. We learn, however, from another source that the Emperor Michael had sent (a copy of) its Acts to the Emperor of the West, Louis II, with an offer to recognize his imperial title if he would depose Nicholas—using as a basis for this act the condemnable material contained in the Acts.[53]

Until recently this was regarded as a definite proof of Photius' denial of the Roman primacy. But when we look at it from a different point of view the whole problem takes on quite another

---

52 The review of the scholarly activity of Photius helps us also to understand a weak point in Photius' character. He is blamed in the Acts of the Ignatian Council (Mansi, *Concilia,* XVI, canons 8, 9. cols. 164, 165) for having asked from his students and later from priests, signed declarations that they would always remain faithful to his views. Although according to the wording of the two canons this was done also before Photius by other Patriarchs, it is likely that Photius indulged in this practice more than was customary. This reveals the pedantic side of the teacher, and it is also confirmed by the many admonitions addressed to his students and friends to observe grammatical rules better in their writings. (see Hergenröther, *Photius,* vol. I, p. 602.)

53 *Vita Ignatii* by Nicetas, Migne, *PG.,* vol. 105, col. 537. Antiphotian Collection, Mansi, vol. XVI, col. 417. Cf. Dölger, *Byzanz und die europäische Staatenwelt* (Ettal, 1953), pp. 313 ff.

aspect. It is true that the Byzantines were wary of accepting the Roman arguments for the primacy of the Pope, namely, the scriptural declaration in St. Matthew 16: 18, 19. But, on the other hand, they did not reject the Roman bishop's claim to primacy. They based this claim not on the principle of Apostolicity but on that of the conformity of the ecclesiastical organization with that of the division of the Empire. This principle already adopted by the Apostles, who were able to start preaching the Gospel only in the major cities, the capitals of the civil provinces, was sanctioned by the First Ecumenical Council, that of Nicaea in 325.[54]

In this connection we must not forget that the Byzantines regarded their Empire as the continuation of the Roman Empire and that they called themselves not Greeks, but Romans. This is important and should not be overlooked when studying the relations between Byzantium and Rome. Because the Byzantines thought of themselves as Romans and their Emperors as Roman Emperors they could not give second place to Rome and her bishop in the Empire, nor would they have transferred the primacy of her bishop to Constantinople, as has been sometimes thought. It is known how anxious the Byzantines were to keep alive the idea of one Roman Empire with one Roman Emperor residing in the city called New Rome. The coronation of Charlemagne by Pope Leo III on Christmas Day 800 was looked upon as an expression of revolt against the lawful Emperor, and Charlemagne was an usurper in Byzantine eyes. The war which followed this "usurpation" ended in 812 when Byzantine envoys, sent by Emperor Michael I to sign the peace treaty, solemnly saluted Charlemagne at Aix-la-Chapelle as Emperor. The Byzantine interpretation of this compromise meant that Charlemagne was accepted as co-Emperor reigning over the Western part of the Roman Empire. The idea of unity in one Christian Roman Empire with the supreme Emperor in New Rome was thus saved.[55]

It is extremely important to realise that this idea of the unity of the Roman Empire was still alive in Byzantium in 867,

---

54 For details, see my book, *The Idea of Apostolicity in Byzantium and the Legend of the Apostle Andrew* (Cambridge, Mass. 1958), pp. 3 ff.
55 See F. Dölger, *op. cit.*, pp. 282 ff.

and that a further attempt at sealing this unity was made by offering to Louis II recognition of his imperial title. We may well think of the learned Patriarch as the chief initiator of this attempt, guardian of the ancient traditions in literary and political fields. This enables us to go further and to reject the belief that the Acts, a copy of which was being sent to Louis II, contained the negation of the Roman primacy as such and condemnation of the usages of the Western Church. This would have been the worst way for Photius to win the sympathy of Louis II and to induce him to take the bold action of deposing Pope Nicholas I.

It is not without interest to note that the homily which Photius delivered at the end of this Synod of 867, probably the only official record of this Council that has survived, contains no attack against Rome, the papacy, or the person of Nicholas.[56] One may, therefore, conclude that the Acts contained a condemnation of the "errors" preached by the missionaries sent by Nicholas to Bulgaria ("errors" enumerated in Photius' encyclical letter to the Eastern Patriarchs)[57] and an accusation against the Pope of having "invaded" a territory claimed by the Byzantine

56 C. Mango, *Homilies,* pp. 296 ff.
57 Migne, *PG.*, vol. 102, cols. 732 ff.

Church, and of having shown disrespect to the autonomous status of the Byzantine Church by having condemned her Patriarch who had been canonically elected according to the customs of this Church.

Thus, it would appear that Photius the guardian and defender of classical and Hellenistic traditions, was also a supporter of the ancient Roman tradition of the unity of the Roman Empire with the old capital in Rome and the new capital and residential city in Constantinople. If he and his followers wished to be faithful to this basic principle of Byzantine political philosophy, it was necessary to respect the special position held by Rome and her bishop. In this light, therefore, the appeal made to the Pope by Bishop Gregory Asbestas and his friends after they were condemned by the Patriarch Ignatius, is much more understandable. Also, the declarations made by Photius' followers during the Synod of 861 were tantamount to a quasi-official acceptance of the Canons of Sardica (343) which declared the see of Rome the final tribunal in Church affairs to which all who were not satisfied with the decisions of their bishops could appeal, an attitude much less surprising.[58]

In the eyes of the Byzantines, the basis of this prerogative was that of the old principle of the political division of the Empire. But in Photius' time the Byzantines seemed to have come to a fuller appreciation of the scriptural argument contained in (St. Matthew 16: 18, 19) and invoked by Rome in favour of her primacy. When we compare the Acts of the Seventh Ecumenical Council (787) with the Latin text of the letters sent to the Council by Hadrian I, we see that the Greeks made significant changes in their translations, which were read at the Council. The papal primacy is recognized, but the most expressive scriptural argument in its favour invoked by the Pope in his letter to the Empress, is omitted, and wherever the Pope speaks of Peter as founder of the bishopric, the Greeks have added the name of St. Paul. On this point, authoritative circles in Byzantium in the eighth century, still clung to the old tradition which attributed the foundation of Roman Christianity to both Apostles, who had both preached and died in the capital.

58 On this synod see my book, *The Photian Schism,* pp. 70-90.

This belief was also observed in Rome in the primitive Church, but from the fourth century on it was St. Peter who was named as founder of the Roman Church and as her first bishop.[59]

When we compare the changes made in the papal letters of the Acts of the Seventh Ecumenical Council with those made by Photius' chancellery in the Acts of the Council of 879-80, which restored him, we are surprised to see an interesting difference. The changes are more extensive in the letters of Hadrian I, but the scriptural arguments in favour of Roman primacy are left in the Greek version. The most telling passage is found in the letter of John VIII to the Emperor Basil I:[60] "After receiving the Keys of the Kingdom of Heaven from the first great Pontiff Jesus Christ, through the intermediary of the first of the Apostles, Peter, to whom He said: 'I will give thee the keys of the kingdom of heaven (St. Matthew 16: 19) and whatsoever thou shalt bind on earth shall be bound in heaven, and whatsoever thou shalt loose on earth shall be loosed in heaven,' this Apostolic throne has the power to bind and loose all, and in the words of Jeremiah (Jerem. 1:10) 'to uproot and plant.' For this very reason, we also, by the authority of the Prince of the Apostles, Peter, announce to you with our entire Holy Church, and through you, to our dear brothers and co-ministers, the Patriarchs . . . bishops and priests . . . that we agree and consent with you, or rather with God, to your request" . . . namely to accept Photius as legitimate Patriarch. The quotation from St. Matthew 16: 19, can be read in the Latin original as well, but that from Jeremiah was added by the Greek interpolators.

This passage, wholly overlooked by modern Church historians, was quoted by Ivo of Chartres,[61] the foremost twelfth century canonist. It was copied from his collection by others who recognized its significance and used it as proof that the Pope, because he is in possession of the plenitude of power, can annul any sentence.

Two other quotations used as scriptural argument for the

---

59 The Acts of the Council, Mansi, XII, cols. 1056 ff. (Second Session of the Council).

60 Cf. the new edition in the *Monumenta Germaniae historica,* Epistolae, vol. VII, pp. 166 ff. See for details and translation my book, *The Photian Schism,* pp. 182 ff.

61 Ivo of Chartres, Decretum, Migne, *PL.,* vol. 161, cols. 56 ff.

papal primacy are also left in the Greek version of the papal letters: St. John 21: 17 and St. Luke 22: 23. Moreover, not only is St. Peter called the *coryphaeus* of the Apostles in the Greek version, but the name of St. Paul is never added to his name, as had been done in 787. Thus Photius accepted the Roman tradition which attributed the foundation of the Roman see to Peter alone.

Nor can the opinion be any longer accepted that Photius, in order to weaken the Petrine arguments of the Roman primacy, invented the legend that the see of Byzantium had been founded by St. Andrew, Peter's brother, "the first called" by the Lord. It has been shown elsewhere that the story of Andrew's stay in Byzantium was recorded in the apocryphal *Travels of Andrew,* which were composed probably at the end of the third century. Photius had read this apocryphal writing (*Bibliotheca,* Co. 14) and attributes it to a certain Leucius whom he does not spare in his biting criticism of the stupid stories and heretical teachings in which the book abounds. Surely, it is unjust to think that Photius would make use of this miserable work to concoct a legend that would exalt the prestige of his own see. We have seen from the review of his *Bibliotheca* that the Patriarch had a well developed critical sense, and although this legendary tradition had been circulating in Byzantium from the eighth century onward, Photius does not refer to it in the *Typicon* of Hagia Sophia, which he revised during his second patriarchate.[62] It would appear, therefore, that he did not accept it. It was not until the tenth century that this story was incorporated in the official *Synaxaria.*

These are only a few of the conclusions which come to mind when we reflect on Photius in this new light. The review of his scholarly career not only shows the great worth of this extraordinary man in reviving the study of the classics and making possible their transmission to later generations, but it also makes it possible to judge his ecclesiastical career more fairly. He courageously defended the autonomous position of his Church, but he did not forget the ancient tradition of one Church in one Christian Empire, with Old Rome as its foundation. He was one of the last churchmen to revive the idea of one Christian

---

[62] See for details my book *The Idea of Apostolicity,* pp. 245 ff. 254 ff.

Empire, which idea in Photius' time, was already dead in the West and slowly dying in the East. It is the irony of fate that his good intentions were blackened by the calumnies of his ad-adversaries and that he is still regarded by many as the initiator of the rupture between East and West, whereas it became definitive so much later.

Dumbarton Oaks Research Library
Washington, D. C.

VIII

THE EMBASSIES OF CONSTANTINE-CYRIL AND PHOTIUS TO THE ARABS

AMONG the problems concerning the career of Constantine-Cyril in Byzantium, the question of his participation in an embassy to the Arabs has not yet been answered satisfactorily. It is related in chapter six of the *Vita Constantini*,[1] in which the author speaks of an invitation being sent by the Arabs to Constantinople to hold a religious disputation, with particular reference to the Holy Trinity and belief in one God. The emperor thereupon is said to have convoked the Senate in order to deliberate as to what should be done. He asked Constantine, at that time only twenty-four years old, to go to the Arabs and to take part in the religious discussion.

What are we to think of this? Is this a story invented by the biographer anxious to extol the scholarship of his hero as being superior to that of his opponents? There are so many details which cannot be substantiated. First of all, it is unlikely that the Arabs would have requested the Emperor to arrange a dispute on the subjects of Islam and Christianity. Also, the biographer's affirmation that Constantine headed the embassy sent to the Khalif is unacceptable, and his pretention that the Arabs intended to poison Constantine when the council ended, during which he had shown his superiority over the Arab theologians, is hardly tenable.

These are all inventions of the author for the glorification of his hero.[2] On the other hand, they correspond to the spirit of Byzantine hagiographical writings. Nevertheless, the story does have an historical background. We do not know of an embassy sent to the Arabs in 851, when Constantine was twenty-four years old. However, it is not absolutely impossible that there was a series of *pourparlers* between Byzantium and the Arab Khalif Mutawakkil (847-861) in that year.

[1] P. A. Lavrov, *Materialy po istorii vozniknovenija drevnejšej slavjanskoj pismennosti* (Leningrad, 1930), 7 seq., 45 seq.

[2] H. H. Schaeder, "Geschichte und Legende im Werk der Slavenmissionare Konstantin und Method", *Historische Zeitschrift*, CLII (1935), 232 seq., thinks that the whole story was invented by the hagiographer who wanted to ascribe three disputations to the hero, because of his predilection for the sacred number three. This, however, cannot be the case. Not three, but four disputations are attributed to Constantine, one with the ex-Patriarch John, the second with the Arabs, the third with the Khazars, and the fourth with the Venetians, as described in chapter 14 of the *Vita*.

The most recent exchange of prisoners made between Byzantium and the Arabs took place in the year 845-846.[3] From this time on we do not hear of any military action taking place on the Arab frontier up to the year 851, for during this period the Byzantines were heavily engaged in fighting the Arabs in Sicily.[4] It is possible that in 851 the Byzantines attempted to renew the truce with the Khalif so as to leave their hands free for their operations in Sicily, which were not going well.

There are details in the account of the disputation which favor the assumption that such an event as a religious discussion really did take place in 851. First, the biographer's description of the city in which the conference was held corresponds to what was known at the time of the residence of the Khalifs, which, from 836 to 889, was in Samarra, near Bagdad. Another point mentioned in the recital could be regarded as confirmation of the hypothesis that some kind of *pourparlers* had taken place between the Arabs and the Byzantines in 851, for Constantine was asked by them why it was that the Byzantines refused to pay tribute to them.

Constantine replied that Christ had paid tribute only to the Roman Empire, and that therefore tribute should be paid only to the Romans. It could be deduced from this that the Arab request for tribute was a condition for continuance of the truce, and that the ambassadors had refused. Another detail referred to by the author of the *Vita* points out that such an incident could have taken place in the first years of the reign of the Khalif Mutawakkil. The Khalif manifested a keen interest in religious matters, and showed his hostility to the Christians by promulgating, in 849-850, several edicts restricting the free movement of his Christian subjects. One of these anti-Christian measures is mentioned in the *Vita*. The Arabs are said to have pointed out that a figure of the devil 'adorned' the doors of all Christian houses, and to have asked Constantine what this meant. He is said to have answered cleverly that the devil, being expelled from the interior of the houses of Christians, was hanging onto their doors, while he was not to be seen on the doors of the Mussulmans because he was inside their houses. It was to be expected that the religious disputes would take place at the court, and therefore the philosopher Constantine was asked to accompany the ambassador.

Constantine's replies to certain objections made by the Arabs, preserved or imagined, by the biographer, disclose a clever mind. Christian doctrine is compared to a large, deep sea. Only strong souls are able to penetrate its depths and sail to its coasts. The feeble spirits fail and become heretics, because they master only a small part of the sea. The doctrine of Mohammed is a small, shallow lake which anyone can subdue. In defending Christian doctrine on the Trinity, Constantine is said to have quoted Sura 19, 17 of the Koran, where the incarnation of the Word through the Spirit of God is described. This passage was often quoted in Byzantine polemic literature.

If such an embassy took place in 851, Constantine certainly did not lead it. We

[3] A. A. Vasiliev, H. Grégoire, M. Canard, *Byzance et les Arabes* (Bruxelles, 1935), I, 198 seq.
[4] *Ibid.*, 204seq.

are told by the hagiographer that the Emperor sent with him the *asecrete* George, who was probably the senior envoy. Since it was expected that religious problems would be discussed at the Khalif's court in view of Muttawakkil's great interest in these matters, Constantine, as a young cleric and scholar, was present.

If this embassy did take place, it did not fulfil the hopes of the Byzantines. This would seem to be indicated by the biographer's report of the Arabs wanting to poison Constantine. According to Tabari, the Arab historian, hostilities between the Byzantines and the Khalif were initiated in the summer of 851, by an incursion into Byzantine territory, a move which was repeated in 852, and again in 853.[5] It is thus quite possible that diplomatic negotiations were opened between the Byzantines and the Khalif in 851, and that a religious dispute did take place at the Khalif's court, during which Constantine defended the Christian faith.

Because Constantine was a disciple of Photius, one is tempted to associate him with an embassy to the Arabs in which Photius participated. Unfortunately, the manuscript tradition of the passage in the *Vita* referring to his participation in such an embassy is rather confused. I was tempted to follow another manuscript which seems to suggest that a personage with the title of *palata* (*palatine*) who was perhaps Photius, took part in this embassy. Such a reading, however, is problematic. It is safer to read simply: "They attached to him the asecrete George and sent them" (*asikrita Georgia i poslaše ja*).[6]

It is an established fact that Photius was a member of a Byzantine embassy sent to the Arabs. He himself says so in the introductory letter addressed to his brother Tarasius, to whom he dedicated his *Bibliotheca*, composed at his brother's request before his departure on a mission to the 'Assyrians'.[7] Photius excuses himself from not describing in more exhaustive fashion the books read by the members of his circle, during Tarasius' absence, and he promises to continue the work after his return. It is evident from the contents of the *Bibliotheca* that the work is incomplete. If the embassy, of which Photius was a member, did occur in 851, he would have had enough time to finish his promised continuation before his elevation to the

[5] *Ibid.*, 214seq.

[6] F. Dvornik, *Les Légendes de Constantin et de Méthode vues de Byzance* (Prague, 1933), 93, 94. See *ibid.*, 104-111, on theological controversies between the Arabs and the Byzantines. Cf. also A. Abel, "La lettre polémique d'Aréthas à l'émir de Damas", *Byzantion*, XXIV (1954), 344-370; J. Meyendorff, "Byzantine views of Islam", *Dumberton Oaks Papers*, XVIII (1964), 115-132.

[7] The letter is written as an introduction and conclusion of the *Bibliotheca*, *PG* 103, cols. 41, 44; 104, cols. 353, 356. Cf. J. Hergenröther, *Photius, Patriarch von Konstantinopel* (Regensburg, 1867-69), III, p. 14. The latter is not to be found in the manuscripts used by the modern edition. Hergenröther found it in Codex Vallicellanus graecus 125 (R 2 6) which contains only the letter to Tarasius on folio 50. It is known that the letter is found only in a few manuscripts of the *Bibliotheca*. It is quite possible that the manuscript of the Vallicellanus contains an authentic version which was abridged in other manuscripts. On the manuscripts of the *Bibliotheca*, see E. Martini, *Textgeschichte der Bibliotheke* (= *Abhandlungen der sächsischen Akademie*, phil. hist. Cl., vol. 28, no. 6) (Leipzig, 1911). On the Vallicellanus, see *ibid.*, 46. A new edition with a German translation is to be found in K. Ziegler, "Photios", *Paulys Real Encyclopädie*, XXXIX (Stuttgart, 1941), cols. 685-688; R. Henry, *Photius Bibliothèque* (Paris, 1959). (Collection byzantine de l'Association Guillaume Budé), vol. I, XIXseq., 1seq.

patriarchate in 858. If we accept Photius' testimony as genuine, then the embassy to which he was attached must have taken place between the years 851 and 858.

However, because to some scholars it seems impossible that he could have accomplished such a literary achievement in the short time before leaving Constantinople on a diplomatic mission, they have advanced the hypothesis that the letter to Tarasius, which opens and closes the *Bibliotheca*, is fictitious. Krumbacher[8] himself was of such an opinion. A similar view was ventured recently by F. Halkin in his paper, "La date de composition de la '*Bibliothèque*' de Photius remise en question".[9] He bases his conclusions on the Greek *Life* of St. Gregory the Great, from which Photius quotes certain passages in his *Bibliotheca* (codex 252). Since it has been shown that the Greek *Life* of St. Gregory was based on the Latin *Life* of the saint, composed between 873 and 875 by the Roman deacon John Hymnonides, at the invitation of Pope John VIII,[10] Photius could not have known of the Greek *Life* before 877, and therefore the composition of the *Bibliotheca* should be dated somewhere between 877 and 886.

This argument, however, is unconvincing. We are not certain that the passages quoted by Photius are extracted from the Βίος ἐνσυντόμῳ which a Greek monk had taken in shorter form from the Latin *Life* which contained four books. St. Gregory the Great was popular also in Byzantium, and it is not improbable that the authors of both the Greek *Life* (known to Photius) and the Latin *Life* used an older source which has not been preserved.[11]

The author affirms that Photius added the fictitious letter to his work, written during his second patriarchate (877-886), in order to escape the criticism of his enemies[12] who would attack him because, as patriarch, he was reading and propagating works of a profane, and even heretical, nature. In order to protect himself from this accusation, Photius is said to have fabricated a letter to his brother, Tarasius, in which he gives the impression that it was in his youth, and before he entered holy orders, that he read the books about which he was writing.

Such an interpretation is preposterous. On the other hand, it has been shown that Photius' opponents were not numerous, consisting mostly of intransigent monks and bishops.[13] After his reconciliation with Ignatius, which took place before the death of the latter,[14] and after his rehabilitation by the synod of 879-880, Photius

[8] *Geschichte der byzantinischen Literatur* (Munich, 1896), 519.

[9] *Analecta Bollandiana*, LXXXIII (1963), 414-417.

[10] *PL*, 75, cols. 59-242; H. Delehaye, "S. Grégoire le Grand dans l'hagiographie grecque", *Analecta Bollandiana*, XXIII (1904), 449-454.

[11] This was rightly pointed out by H. Ahrweiler, "Sur la carrière de Photios avant son Patriarcat", *Byzantinische Zeitschrift*, LVIII (1965), 538.

[12] F. Halkin, *op. cit.*, 417.

[13] See my book *The Photian Schism. History and Legend* (Cambridge, 1948), 39seq., 159seq.

[14] See F. Dvornik, "The Patriarch Photius in the Light of Recent Research", in *Berichte zum XI. Internat. Byzantinisten-Kongress* (Munich, 1958), 34, 35. According to the *Sinaiticus graecus*, no. 482 (1117) fols. 357^r–365^v, Photius did not only reconcile himself with Ignatius, but even canonized him after the latter's death. The manuscript contains another version of the *Synodicon Vetus* pub-

was almost unanimously reinstated. He was therefore able to ignore the small number of fanatics whose attitude continued hostile.

The fact that Photius had reviewed the writings of certain heretics induced M. Hemmerdinger[15] to state that it would have been impossible for Photius to have found such books in Constantinople, since the works of heretics were condemned. But such books could have been found in Bagdad, where, in the ninth century, lived many Greeks, famous scribes and translators. These works were kept in the Khalif's library (which was destroyed in 1258) and Photius had access to what he could not find in Constantinople, while staying in Bagdad during the negotiations with the Khalif. This explanation may be ingenious, but cannot be accepted. The writings of heretics were obtainable in Constantinople, and from 836 to 889 the residence of the Khalifs was not in Bagdad, but in Samarra, which is some distance from Bagdad. It is difficult to understand how members of the embassy, who were there to negotiate with the Arab authorities, could absent themselves for so many days in Bagdad.

The theory that Photius had taken his library with him and that he finished his *Bibliotheca* while travelling to Samarra, or that he took some of his students with him, cannot be accepted.[16] Ziegler, in his study on Photius, has already rejected this fantastic explanation.[17] All these difficulties can be explained if we suppose that Photius, after reading or studying a work with his friends, made notes as to the content, author and style, to which he added his own criticism. It would then be easy to assemble his notes in a reasonably short time before his departure with the embassy.

Thus it remains established that Photius wrote his *Bibliotheca* before leaving with the embassy to the Arabs, and that both parts of his letter to his brother Tarasius, the introduction and the postscript, are genuine.

However, we still have the problem of when the embassy, to which he was attached, took place. H. Ahrweiler, in her recently published paper, thinks that it occurred in 838, before the capture of Amorion by the Arabs, during the first half of August, or soon after the disastrous defeat of the Byzantine army. Her main argument is to be found in her interpretation of Photius' letter to Tarasius. She quotes Photius' words describing to Tarasius the difficulty of such an enterprise, and she deduces from them that Photius was afraid, even for his survival. This would, so she thinks, fit in very well with the embassy sent by Emperor Theophilus to the Khalif after the loss of Amorion.[18] In reality, this embassy was badly received, and suffered mis-

---

lished by J. Pappe in J. A. Fabricius and G. C. Harles, *Bibliotheca graeca*, XII (Hamburg, 1809). Another manuscript containing the same information as the manuscript of Sinai has been found. The document will be published by Dumbarton Oaks.

15 "Les 'notices et extraits' des bibliothèques grecques de Bagdad par Photius", *Révue des études grecques*, LXIX (1956), 101-103. Cf. H. Henry, *op. cit.*, LI, LII.

16 Put forward especially by E. Orth, *Photiana* (Leipzig, 1929).

17 *Op. cit.*, cols. 689, 690.

18 *Op. cit.*, 360.

treatment from the victorious Arab ruler.[19] On the other hand the fact that Photius does not give his brother the title of *patricius*, which he had done in previous letters, indicates, according to H. Ahrweiler, that Tarasius was too young at that time, and that Photius was not very far along in his career in the imperial service. But she thinks that he was already an *asecretos*, or, perhaps, *decanos* in the imperial chancellery. In this function he would accompany the emperor on military expeditions, and he would be in charge of the official papers which were transported in a special vehicle. The young Photius would thus be able to hide his own notes on the books he had read among the official documents, and he would be able to find time during the expedition to finish the work he sent to his brother in Constantinople. This interpretation is believed to explain why it was so difficult for Photius to find a scribe to whom he could dictate his comments. Although there would be no difficulty in finding one in Constantinople, it was not easy to do so in a military camp in Asia Minor.

Although very plausible, this interpretation cannot be accepted. Photius may have had difficulty in finding a good scribe even in Constantinople. He may have tried out several, and, at last, found one who was qualified for the task for which he was hired. Photius was in a hurry and wanted to finish up his domestic affairs while he was still in Constantinople, and he was anxious to send his composition to his 'dear' brother as early as possible. It si not easy to find a good secretary for an urgent task.

The fact that Photius does not give his brother the title of *patricius*, should not be exaggerated. It was his last letter to Tarasius; it could have been his very last, since travelling to an enemy country, at that time, was dangerous and might have ended tragically. Photius was well aware of this and preferred to write to his brother quite simply as "my beloved brother". There is a tenderness in this address felt by all of us when leaving our families for some time, and when the future is uncertain. Photius writes to Tarasius, "You who are dearest to me of all who were born from the womb of the same mother as myself". These words are very indicative.

But again, H. Ahrweiler is faced with the difficulty of explaining how a work of such dimensions as the *Bibliotheca* could have been written in the tents of military camps. The supposition that Photius was only twenty-five years old at that time, and that neither he nor his brother held a prominent place in Byzantine society, is unwarranted and hangs in the air. However, the author is right when she affirms that Photius was not at the head of that embassy. She is also correct in saying that it is necessary to distinguish between simple exchanges of prisoners between the Arabs and the Byzantines on the frontier, on the one hand, and between embassies which represented the emperors at the Arab court, on the other.

Because of this, she rejects the possibility that Photius was attached to an embassy

[19] The Byzantine sources are unanimous in describing the humiliating reception of the embassy by the Khalif. See Genesios, Bonn, 64, 65; Cedrenus, Bonn, II, 531, 532; Theophanes continuatus, Bonn, 129, 130.

in 855-856, since the Byzantine authors speak only of an exchange of prisoners during that time. However, may we not suppose that such exchanges were sometimes prepared by negotiations conducted by an embassy? Such seems to be the case in 855. Photius says, when speaking of his participation in the embassy, that not only was he encouraged to join it by the members already selected, but that the emperor himself chose him, as he had chosen the others. Such ceremonial practice was unnecessary when an exchange of prisoners took place, as this function was carried out by the *strategos* and the officers of the Asiatic theme. In reality, the exchange of prisoners which took place on the River Lamos was directed — according to Tabari — by one such officer called George, but it was effected after the embassy had finished its negotiations with the Arabs in Samarra. Arab sources, in particular Tabari and Yaqūbī,[20] speak of embassies sent by Theodora to the Khalif, and of the Arab envoy Ibn Farag whose task it was to discover how many Arab prisoners were held captive by the Byzantines. Both sources — especially that of Yaqūbī[21] — mention an exchange of gifts by the embassies to both courts. It is thus established that an exchange of prisoners in 855-856 was arranged by a solemn embassy sent by the Empress Theodora and her prime minister, Theoctistos, to the Khalif Muttawakil. It was to this embassy that Photius was attached.

There is yet one more fact which supports the dating of Photius' embassy in 855-856. At this time an important political upheaval occurred in the capital in 856. The logothete Theoctistos, Theodora's prime minister, was murdered by the supporters of Theodora's brother, the ambitious Bardas, with the consent of the young Emperor Michael III, who was distrustful both of his mother and of Theoctistos. Other events followed. The Senate put an end to the regency of Theodora in the same year and, to prevent a counter-revolution by her partisans, she was expelled from the palace at the end of the summer of 857. Patriarch Ignatius, a supporter of Theodora, became embroiled with the new regent, Bardas, and, in order to avoid an open clash between the Church and the new government, the bishops advised Ignatius to resign his patriarchate. This he did in 858. The local synod elected as his successor, Photius, the chancellor of the Empire.[22] The consent of all the bishops was given to the election of the new patriarch, even by those who most fervently supported Ignatius, their attitude having been influenced by the fact that Photius was not involved in any way in the upheaval of 856, since he was absent from the city and on his way back from the embassy to the Arabs. He may not have returned until the early part of 857, thus giving the followers of Theodora time to become reconciled to the idea of Photius as the successor of Ignatius. Had he been present in Constantinople at the time of the disturbance, it is possible that the reactionary

[20] A. A. Vasiliev, H. Grégoire, M. Canard, *op. cit.*, I, 224. It is not sure whether this George is the same person as the official mentioned in the *Life of Constantine*, but it is possible.

[21] See *ibid.*, 224seq., 276, 277. An exchange of prisoners during the regin of Leo the Wise was also prepared by solemn embassies, as is described by George the Monk (Bonn), 868.

[22] For details, see F. Dvornik, *The Photian Schism*, 39seq. Cf. also, idem, "Patriarch Ignatius and Caesar Bardas", *Byzantinoslavica*, XXVII (1966), 7-22.

members of the clergy would have refused to accept Bardas' proposal to elevate him to the patriarchate, for it was Bardas who was responsible for the changes in the government, and who was favorably inclined to the intellectual circle of which Photius was the center.

DUMBARTON OAKS, WASHINGTON, D. C.

IX

Photius, Nicholas I and Hadrian II

Many of the problems relating to the Photian schism and the attitude of Photius to Rome have recently been clarified. The Patriarch himself now appears in a more favorable light to most scholars and ecclesiastical specialists than he did in the Latin Middle Ages and from the seventeenth century onwards, in particular. His second excommunication by Rome after 879—880 is now definitely rejected as legend. Several profound studies of ninth century Byzantium, published lately, have helped us to understand better the circumstances which led to the first formal schism between the papacy and the Eastern Church. However, when we review the latest bibliography dealing with Photius, we become aware of how hard it was, and still is, for western church historians to abandon centuries old-prejudices and to study objectively the fateful events of the ninth century. Such a review was recently undertaken by H. GROTZ;[1] he there discusses the results of his preparatory research made in connection with a biography of Pope Hadrian II[2] whose person and political activities, as he rightly says, have so far been neglected by church historians, even though Hadrian's short reign can be looked upon as a turning point in church history.

While studying the problems with which Hadrian II was faced — especially the Photian Schism — H. Grotz frequently chose a new point of view, different from the many writers whose works he had before him. He has come to conclusions which confirm the rehabilitation of this Patriarch, proposed in my book,[3] adding some observations which show how much the Romans of the ninth century had misunderstood the situation in the Byzantine Church. Because he is the first German church historian not to have been influenced by J. Hergenröther's prejudiced judgement of Photius, his work deserves special attention. When analyzing his new ideas, I limited myself only to some observations based on my own research.

First, he insists that the conflict between Photius and Ignatius must be more thoroughly reconsidered by the specialists of Eastern and Western Churches canonical rules. A deeper understanding of these canonical complications will help us to assess the reasons which led to the conflict and enable us to measure the extent to which the men involved were responsible for its tragic consequences.

Let us first consider the manner in which Ignatius was elevated to the patriarchal throne. When, after some hesitation, but at the urgency of her first minister

---

1 H. Grotz, *Die Zeit Papst Hadrians II. (867—872) und der Anfang des Photianischen Schismas im Spiegel der Geschichtsliteratur (1880—1966)*, Zeitschr. f. kathol. Theologie 90 (1968) 40—60, 177—194. This is a very detailed and well-balanced review of the works dealing with all those authors who had touched on many of the matters which occupied Hadrian II during his reign, starting with J. Hergenröther and continuing with Hefele's *History of Councils* up to the year 1968. He pays special attention to my book, *The Photian Schism: History and Legend*, Cambridge, 1948; reprint 1970, and to my paper, *The Patriarch Photius in the Light of Recent Research* given at the XIth International Congress of Byzantine Studies at Munich in 1958. He comments upon all the objections voiced by my critics. It is a great pleasure when a scholar finds another researcher who, on his own, comes to the same conclusions.

2 Published in the meantime under the title *Erbe wider Willen. Hadrian II. (862—872) und seine Zeit*. Wien—Köln—Graz: Hermann Böhlaus Nachf. 1970, 356 pp.

3 F. Dvornik, *The Photian Schism, op. cit.*

Theoctistus, Theodora condemned the iconoclastic practices, the atmosphere in Constantinople was very heavy. The victorious workshippers of icons, mostly monks who had suffered for their religious convictions, demanded the application of rigorous measures against the condemned heretics. More liberal minded bishops and clergy were inclined to follow the less rigid policy of the late Patriarch Methodius. They were led by Gregory Asbestas, metropolitan of Syracuse, compatriot of Methodius, who seems to have been in Constantinople at that time (847), not as a refugee as was once thought, but as envoy of the Sicilian Greeks requesting help against the Arabs who were threatening Syracuse. The city fell into Arab hands only in 878.

Fearing a conflict between the two clerical parties during the synod which used to be called to elect a new patriarch, Theodora appointed the *hegumenos* Ignatius as successor to Methodius, who was regarded as a great hero by the zealous monks. Ignatius was the son of the orthodox Emperor Michael I, and had been castrated by the iconoclastic Emperor Leo V who succeeded his father.

Theodora's decision was a mistake, for without a synodal election Ignatius' appointment could be considered as uncanonical by the liberals, and in the case of a conflict as invalid. Moreover, the attitude of Gregory Asbestas following Theodora's choice reveals that the liberals would have accepted the imperial candidate, had the Empress assembled a synod to elect a new patriarch. Although rejected by the Empress as successor to Methodius, Gregory Asbestas appeared in Hagia Sophia with his followers, wearing episcopal dress and with a candle in his hand, prepared to participate in the consecration and inauguration of Ignatius.

Here the new patriarch committed a frightful blunder. He made it clear to Asbestas that his presence at his consecration was unwelcome. Thereupon Asbestas threw down the candle and with his followers left the church. By this unreasonable gesture Ignatius lost the opportunity of mediating between the two parties, and declared war upon those inclined to a more conciliatory ecclesiastical policy. Nicetas, the author of an antiphotianist pamphlet called Ignatius' biography, himself admits that Ignatius' negative behavior to Asbestas created bitterness among the clergy.[4] It is interesting to note that he gives no explanation for the unyielding attitude of his hero.

This situation was aggravated when Ignatius, at a local synod, deposed and excommunicated Gregory Asbestas and his chief followers, Peter, bishop of Sardis, and Eulampius, bishop of Apamea. At this synod Ignatius annulled the sentence handed down by his predecessor by which Methodius excommunicated the over-zealous monks of Studios who opposed his conciliatory ecclesiastical policy. It is probable, I think, that the condemnation of the three bishops was connected with this act, the bishops having upheld the policy of Methodius.

The condemned bishops' reply probably surprized Ignatius, for they declared their condemnation to be uncanonical and appealed for judgement to the first Patriarch, the Bishop of Rome. This was an important act. Unfortunately, the events of the following years overshadowed this action, and even those defenders in the West of the supreme rights of the Popes overlooked its importance, even though it was a clear acknowledgement of the right of appeal to the Pope as supreme judge. Pope Nicholas I, although hostile to them was aware of the legitimacy of such an appeal, declaring that it had been made because of a definition of the synod of Sardica (343) authorizing such an appeal.[5] I have stressed on another occasion how rare were the appeals to Rome from the clergy of the Eastern Church in disciplinary matters.[6]

---

[4] Nicetas Paphlago, *Vita Ignatii*, PG 105, col. 512.

[5] MGH Ep. VI, p. 537. Cf. F. Dvorník, *The Photian Schism*, p. 26.

[6] F. Dvorník, *Byzantium and the Roman Primacy*, New York 1966, pp. 108—109 (*Byzance et la Primauté Romaine*, Paris 1964, p. 97). H. Grotz, *op. cit.*, p. 54, quotes the case of Dionysius of Alexandria in order to show that the Popes used to intervene against bishops. But, in this case, the Pope's intervention concerns a dogmatic question, not a disciplinary one. What H. Grotz says about the Popes intervention against bishops during the Donatist struggle, is that in those cases the Popes were acting in their Roman patriarchate.

Ignatius appears to have been very ignorant of canonical practices because, in his letter to Pope Leo IV, he asked firstly, for confirmation of his appointment, and secondly, for the condemnation of the three bishops.[7] The Patriarchs did not ask for confirmation by the Pope, but simply announced their elevation, and added their confession of faith in order to show that their belief was the same as that of the First Patriarchal see. Similar declarations were sent to the other Patriarchs. Ignatius' ignorance of canonical practice was especially revealed by his offering of a pallium to the Pope. It was a blunder and almost an offence to the Pope, for the Popes had worn the pallium from the fourth century on and were accustomed from the sixth century on to bestowing it on metropolitans as a symbol of their prerogatives.

Pope Leo IV sent back his present to Ignatius and refused to confirm the condemnation of Gregory Asbestas and his friends, stating that such an action was contrary to canonical rules, as no bishop may be condemned without the confirmation of the Pope. The Patriarchs, said the Pope, had referred all such cases in the past to the First Patriarch asking him both for advice and a decision.

There is evident exaggeration in Leo's declaration. In general, the Patriarchs acted independently in the disciplinary affairs of their patriarchates. So far, no canonical rule existed which obliged the Patriarchs to present all such cases to the supreme tribunal in Rome. In making general the exceptional practice, Leo introduced a new element into Canon Law. Thus it must be stressed that he was the first to declare that any condemnation of a bishop without the cooperation of the Pope was invalid.

This also reveals that about the middle of the ninth century, the claim of supreme jurisdiction of the Roman See over all bishops was already very much advanced in Rome. However, such a claim was clearly formulated outside Rome, by the anonymous author of the Pseudo-Isidorian Decretals.[8] The document is based on a known collection of Canon Law, the so-called *Hispana Gallica,* but the falsifier added about one hundred spurious documents, quoted as letters of the Popes from the first to the eighth centuries, together with synodical decisions. It was composed during the first half of the ninth century and some of its "canons" were quoted as authentic documents during the imperial synod in Quierzy in 857. The Pseudo-Isidorian decretals appear to have reached Rome only in 864.[9] Leo IV's declaration thus ante-dated the false collection. Its author, of course, was unaware of Leo's letter which he would certainly have quoted as an authentic document in support of his false thesis. This is a new discovery the importance of which should have been emphasized more by H. Grotz.

Although the letter of Leo IV (as it is preserved today) does not contain the instruction that Ignatius should send an envoy to the Pope to reply to the accusations voiced against the Patriarch by Asbestas' envoy, bishop Zachary, such a command was addressed to Ignatius by the Pope. We learn this fact from the letter of Nicholas I to Michael III.[10] In this letter we are given to understand that Ignatius paid no attention to the Pope's request, which is surprising as he seems to have been very anxious to obtain a favorable decision from him.

The suspended bishops approached Leo's successor Benedict III, who refused Ignatius' demand and insisted on the sending of an envoy to Rome within a fixed time. In the meantime, the bishops condemned by Ignatius were asked to abstain from exercising their episcopal functions. The Pope thus made it clear to Ignatius that he was determined to give a just decision in this controversy that would respect

---

7 MGH V, pp. 589, 607.

8 P. Hinschius, *Decretales pseudoisidorianae et capitula Angilramni,* Leipzig 1863, pp. 456 ff.; cf. also W. Schafer, *The Pseudo-Isidorian Problem Today,* Speculum 29 (1954).

9 The Decretals were probably brought to Rome by Bishop Rothad of Soissons who protested against Hincmar, the archbishop of Reims who had deposed him. When reinstating him to his see, Nicholas quoted the passage from the Decretals reserving the right of the judging of a bishop to the Pope. H. Grotz, *op. cit.,* p. 84, also rightly shows that in his letter to the bishops of Gaul Nicholas speaks of the Decretals as a genuine document; MGH Ep. VI, 393 ff.

10 MGH Ep. VI, p. 527.

not only the prerogatives of the Patriarch, but also the rights of the bishops. After this second summons from the Pope, Ignatius yielded and sent the monk Lazarus to Rome with the Acts of the synod which condemned Asbestas who, however, did not arrive in Rome until the end of 855, or early in 856, after Ignatius had already been deposed.

From the Roman point of view, Ignatius was not recognized as legitimate Patriarch either by Leo IV or by Benedict III, and as both had been prevented from examining the case of the deposed bishops, the latter continued to be regarded as possessing their episcopal rank, because the decision of the Patriarch, made without the consent of Rome, was invalid. This declaration is very important and it is rightly stressed by H. Grotz.[11]

As patriarch Ignatius was not successful. He was devoted to the Empress Theodora who had promoted him to the patriarchal see, and could not adapt himself to the new situation which developed when Theoctistus was killed and Michael III proclaimed reigning Emperor, and when Theodora's brother, Bardas became the most important factor in Byzantine affairs.

This political reversal signified at the same time that the partisans of a more liberal policy in religious matters had gained influence at the court. The zealots, however, did not intend to surrender.[12] The downfall of Theodora spelled to them the danger that iconoclasm might be restored, and many of them felt that only the restoration of Theodora could prevent such a danger. They concentrated their attacks against Bardas whose good name had been discredited by rumors of misbehavior with his own daughter-in-law. A re-examination of Bardas' case, based on evidence so far neglected, has convinced me that Ignatius, because of his hostile attitude to Bardas, was the victim of intrigues hatched by the political enemies of the new régime.[13] It was also unwise on the part of the Patriarch to intervene in favor of the leader of an unsuccessful conspiracy against the Emperor. One wonders why Ignatius did not follow the example of his predecessors who, in similar cases, acted in the spirit of οἰκονομία or compromise, in conflicts with the civil government when doctrinal matters were not involved, though he acted in this spirit later when he acknowledged Basil, the murderer of Bardas and Michael III as legitimate emperor.

There can be no doubt about the resignation of Ignatius. In such cases, the emperors followed canonical practice: a successor could only be elected after his resignation of the office had been signed by the occupant and presented to the synod. To what extent the resignation was voluntary is another question, but such a document had to be presented, and Ignatius' case was not an exception. It was also necessary for him to consent to the election of his successor. The synod, after first considering three candidates, unanimously consented to elect Photius who was recommended by the government. H. Grotz rightly remarks that the accusation later made against Photius by the followers of Ignatius that he had deceived them and had pretended to favor Ignatius, may have been invented by them so as to excuse their having voted for Photius at the synod.[14]

It is also true that Photius accepted the election only after constant urging from both the bishops and the Emperor. Once he had accepted, it was his duty to keep the office, fulfill its obligations, and maintain his position against pressure from his unlawful opponents. H. Grotz very significantly quotes the example of St. Athanasius who continued to hold his high office in spite of the appointment of anti-bishops, of exile and persecution, and even when the Pope for a time had abandoned him.[15] It is unjust to accuse Photius of holding stubbornly to his high rank because of avidity.

It is regrettable that Ignatius after his resignation and the acceptance of his successor, had not the wisdom to dissociate himself from the radical dissenters who again declared him legitimate Patriarch. It would have been unnecessary for his successor to convoke a synod of more than 170 bishops who would declare that not

---

11 Grotz, *op. cit.*, pp. 54, 55.

12 For details, see my book *The Photian Schism*, pp. 39—69.

13 See my paper *Patriarch Ignatius and Caesar Bardas*, ByzSlav 27 (1966) 7—22.

14 Grotz, *op. cit.*, p. 60.

15 *Op. cit.*, p. 61.

only was reappointment by the dissenters nul and void, but, also, that his first elevation to the patriarchal throne was invalid, having been made uncanonically by the Empress without the convocation of a synod.

It was invalid not only according to the declaration of the synod, but also according to Rome, at least, in so far as none of the Popes during his first patriarchate had accepted him as legitimate Patriarch, neither Leo IV, nor Benedict III, and not even Nicholas I. This was because the accusation launched against him by the bishops whom he had deposed and excommunicated, had not yet been examined nor judgement given by the supreme court of the First Patriarch.

With regard to the attitude of Nicholas towards Photius' and Michael III's letters announcing the election of Photius to the patriarchal throne, Grotz rightly remarks that Canon Ten of the Synod of Sardica which prohibits the elevation of laymen to episcopal rank without the canonical intervals was not accepted in the Eastern Church.[16] He quotes passages from Anastasius' introduction to the Acts of the Ignatian Council (869—870),[17] and from several similar cases which show clearly that the strict Roman practice was not followed in the East.

The Pope's declaration that the synod which had elected Photius was invalid because it was convoked without the consent of Rome was unjustified. Synods convoked for the election of new patriarchs were a privileged custom of the eastern patriarchates and used to be held without any intervention from Rome. The Pope was probably unaware that the dissenters had summoned a synod at the Church of St. Irene for the deposition of Photius and the reintegration of Ignatius, otherwise he should have declared as invalid even this synod convoked without authorization from Rome.

However, when charging Photius that he had been ordained uncanonically by Gregory Asbestas, the Pope had some reason for doing so. Gregory had been confirmed in his rank by that synod, but, from the Roman point of view, his case was still pending because Rome had not yet had an opportunity of making a decision.

But H. Grotz has discovered an inconsistency in this accusation.[18] From the Roman point of view Ignatius should also be accused of acting as Patriarch and of condemning Asbestas and two other bishops, without having been acknowledged by Rome as legitimate Patriach. Even when Nicholas sent his letter to Photius, Ignatius had not yet been accepted by him as legitimate head of the Byzantine Church. In the same letter, Nicholas expressed his intention of continuing the investigation of the dispute by sending two legates to Constantinople. It was only in 863, after the break with Photius, that Ignatius was accepted as legitimate Patriarch.

Nicholas I went even further than did Leo IV when he affirmed that a synod convoked without the consent of the papacy was invalid. Such privilege was attributed to the popes by the compiler of the Pseudo-Isidorian Decretals. One cannot say, however, that Nicholas was inspired in this respect by this false document. In 860, when the Pope addressed his refusal to Photius and to Michael III, the Decretals were scarcely known in Rome. Nicholas' declaration thus shows how far the idea of the papal primacy had developed in the West during the eighth and the ninth centuries. H. Grotz sees in this the main reason for the misunderstandings which had developed between East and West. He describes it very fittingly:[19] "While in the West the extraordinary position of the Pope had relatively rapidly crystallized owing to the progress made by theological speculation, owing to the Germanic devotional piety towards Rome, thanks also to the political development which promoted the Pope almost to a guardian of the imperial crown, but also thanks to the legend of Pope Silvester, to the legendary Donation of Constantine and to the appearance of the Pseudo-Decretals, in the East the ecclesiastical consciousness was developing much more slowly." He attributes this to the different ideas prevailing in the East as to the position of the Emperor in the Church and to the doctrine of the pentarchy, that is, the belief that the Church is governed by the five Patriarchs amongst whom

---

16 *Op. cit.*, p. 68.
17 Mansi XVI, col. 16.
18 Grotz, *op. cit.*, p. 69.
19 *Op. cit.*, pp. 69—70.

the Patriarch of Rome was first, but whose privileged position had never been clearly defined in the East, although often recognized.

Such an explanation corresponds to reality. I once defined the political Byzantine ideas as Christian Hellenism.[20] As a matter of fact, the Eastern Church never developed an ecclesiology, and even its greatest thinkers had rather vague ideas about the structure of the Church. The idea of the pentarchy was the highest point reached by Byzantine ecclesiastical speculation,[21] and it represented progress because, in some way, it limited the role of the Emperors in the development of Christianity.

The first two letters sent to Byzantium in Photius' case express almost a promise that Photius would be accepted by the Pope if certain conditions were fulfilled. The first being a satisfactory report of the investigators and the second, the return to Roman jurisdiction, at least, of the Latin provinces of Illyricum placed under the patriarchate of Constantinople by the Emperor Leo III. Nicholas I thus had renewed the old struggle for Illyricum. He must have seen that this was a demand which the Byzantines would not be overzealous to fulfill. The difficult position into which the imperial governement was thrown by the patriarchal crisis may have given him some hope for success. None of the pretenders to the patriarchate was yet accepted by Rome. If Photius was unable to exercise an influence on the Emperor in this respect, there seemed to be a possibility that Ignatius would be more willing and perhaps successful.

The Acts of the synod of 861 of Constantinople[22] show clearly how anxious the Byzantines were to remain on good terms with Rome. The two legates, Rodoald of Porto and Zacharias of Anagni directed the whole investigation, according to Roman not Byzantine procedure, and were even invited to act as judges in the name of St. Peter. Although the Pope reserved the final word to himself, the legates, acting in good faith, and seeing how events had developed in Byzantium, proclaimed not only Ignatius guilty, but, and here trespassing on the Pope's preserve, deposed him. They hoped that Nicholas would acept their decision, because they saw in it important substantiation of his claim for supreme rights over all bishops in the West and in the East. However, they left the acceptance of Photius as legitimate patriarch to the Pope's judgement. After their return they certainly explained to the Pope all that had taken place in Constantinople, trying to justify their attitude, for they saw in the condemnation of a patriarch in the name of St. Peter, the triumph of Rome over Constantinople. Unfortunately they did not bring with them a favorable response to the request that Illyricum be returned to Roman jurisdiction. This seemed not to have even been discussed at the synod. Photius, in his letter, expressed his willingness to accede to this demand had it depended only on him. But in such matters the will of the Emperor was decisive.

This failure to obtain the return of Illyricum to his patriarchate also changed the Pope's attitude. Perhaps Ignatius — the other antagonist — would be more devoted to Rome if accepted as the legitimate Patriarch, and would be able to obtain the desired concession from the Emperor. This change in the Pope's policy became known in March 862 when he presented the envoy with letters to the Emperor and to Photius.[23] He refused to accept Photius, declared as invalid the actions of his legates at the synod of 861, and pronounced the deposition of Ignatius as invalid, although, from the Roman point of view, Ignatius was considered as accused for deposing illegally three bishops, and the process was still pending.

In spite of the firmness with which the Pope's decision against Photius was expressed, the door was not yet closed to a possible further explanation and understanding between Constantinople and Rome. One has the impression that the Pope

20 F. Dvorník, *Early Christiàn and Byzantine Political Philosophy. Origins and Background.* (= Dumbarton Oaks Studies, IX) Washington 1966, vol. 2, pp. 611—658.

21 See for details, F. Dvorník, *Byzantium and the Roman Primacy,* pp. 27 ff., 102 ff.

22 Only a Latin extract of the "Ignatius" part of the synod is preserved in Cardinal Deusdedit's canonical collection, ed. by Wolf von Glanvel, *Die Kanonensammlung des Kardinals Deusdedit,* Paderborn 1905; see my *The Photian Schism,* pp. 70 ff.

23 MGH Ep. VI, 440 ff.

wished to exercise more pressure on Photius realizing from the Patriarch's letters how much he desired to be accepted by Rome.

Nicholas' hope that Ignatius would be more favorable to Rome and fulfill his demand for the return of Illyricum increased when, at the end of the year 862, Theognostus the representative of the anti-Photian opposition, together with a few monks, appeared in Rome and presented himself as Ignatius' envoy, assuring the Pope of Ignatius' fidelity to the Roman see. It seems unbelievable that Nicholas would have pinned all his hopes on Ignatius and have believed the stories of his fidelity to the papacy, as described by the rebellious refugees. He must have known of the experiences his predecessors Leo IV and Benedict III had had with Ignatius. The whole Acts of the synod of 861 were in the Lateran archives and he should have read them. We have at our disposal only an extract from these Acts, and from this it is clear that Ignatius was far from showing any respect for the legates representing the Pope. He questioned their authority and conscious of the dignity of his patriarchate, declared himself against the Petrine claim of the legates as successors of the Apostles Andrew and John. In the end, he stated contemptuously, "I did not appeal to Rome, neither do I appeal now (*Ego non appelavi Romam, nec appello*)."

In spite of all this Nicholas accepted the "appeal" to his see devised by Theognostus in Rome, and broke definitely with Photius at the synod convoked during the summer of 863. When commenting on the Pope's decision, H. Grotz writes:[26] "The imminent danger of a schism was hardly outweighed by the avaricious hope of the Pope to obtain the return of territories lost a long time ago. So, today, we have to admit that wisdom was not every time the lodestar illuminating the *patriarcheion* in Rome, when Nicholas one-sidedly and obstinately had in mind only his own legal point of view, even if it was justified. The general welfare of the Church required rather cooperation with Photius than with Ignatius. If it was thought in Rome that Ignatius would be more receptive to Rome's desires and that, in general, he was a friend to the West, they were mistaken. On the contrary, Photius without doubt would have fully appreciated the support of Rome in such a difficult situation for him. When we read the first letters addressed to the Pope by Photius, we are deeply impressed by the warm cordiality and open respect of the man who looked to find a friend in Rome. Only men who are profoundly prejudiced can put aside these letters as hypocritical and misleading. Alas, that Rome has made of this remarkable man an enemy. History has shown how disastrous this enmity had become for the whole Church. We are still suffering from it today. How valuable the friendship between the great Nicholas and the great Photius could have become. Regrettably, this can only be left to the imagination."

If the Pope expected that the Easterners would make new overtures to continue the negotiations, he was wrong. The East remained silent. It was only towards the end of the summer of 865 that an imperial envoy brought a letter to the Pope. The letter was written in a haughty tone implying that the Pope did not appreciate the concession made by the Byzantine Church to Rome in permitting the papal legates to judge a patriarch. Only then did Nicholas seem to be aware of the danger of the approach of a definite rupture between Rome and the East, and it was a shock to him. With the baptism of the Bulgarians by the Byzantines in 864, it appears that all his hopes for the return of Illyricum vanished. Alarmed by these dangers he tried to re-open negotiations in a letter composed by his right hand and scribe, Anastasius, under papal supervision. In spite of the passionate polemic with which the rights of the Pope in the patriarchal affair are defended, and the position of the Byzantine patriarchate abased, the Pope declared his willingness to re-examine in Rome the dispute between Ignatius and Photius, in the presence of the disputants, or their representatives. This "concession" clearly shows that Nicholas finally realized that he might have gone too far and that he was ready to reconsider his verdict in order to avert an open rupture between Constantinople and Rome.

I have analysed this letter in my book on the Photian schism,[25] but one of the arguments by which the Pope justified the need for papal intervention in such disputes,

[24] Grotz, *op. cit.*, p. 87.
[25] F. Dvornik, *The Photian Schism*, pp. 106 ff.

was by reference to Canon Nine voted by the Council of Chalcedon, and it escaped my attention. The canon indicates that "if a cleric has a complaint against his, or another bishop, this should be judged by the synod of the province. When, however, a cleric or a bishop has a dispute with the metropolitan of the province, let him approach the *exarch* of the diocese, or the see of Constantinople before whom the dispute should be judged."[26]

Only the see of Constantinople is mentioned in the canon and no allusion is made to the Romen see. The Pope interpreted this canon as follows:[27] "When the synod said, let him address himself to the primate of the diocese, the same synod expressed a precept and a rule. When it had, however, disjunctively added, or the see of the imperial city of Constantinople, this was permitted by indulgence... Whom, however, the synod had meant when speaking of the primate of the diocese, than the vicar of the first apostle, should be clear to everybody. He is namely the first and the supreme... One should know that when he says the primate of one diocese it means as if he said of dioceses..."

Nicholas interprets Canon Nine of the Council of Chalcedon in favor of Rome, as if all metropolitans should be judged by the first primate — the Pope. This is called a precept, a rule pronounced by the Council. H. Grotz, who was the first to attract attention to this explanation of Canon Nine of Chalcedon, calls it a "Gesetzverdrehung", that is, a distortion of the law.[28] He adds, "das Wort ist hart aber angebracht"; it is a harsh word, but appropriate.

In reality there is a very serious misinterpretation of the canon which can be explained only by the translation of the Greek word *exarchos* by *primas*. This was done already by the first canonist, Dionysius Exiguus, the author of the famous *Collectio Dionysiana*,[29] who died before the year 556. The Pope, or Anastasius seems to have misinterpreted here the system of accommodation of Church organization to the division of the Empire into provinces and dioceses (composed of several provinces). The head of the diocese was called *exarchos* and so was the bishop residing in the capital of the diocese. The incorrect Latin translation of *exarchos* as *primas* was here applied to the Bishops of Rome. Although the canon refers to only one diocese, the author of the letter pretends that this means more, or, rather, all dioceses. Thus, all metropolitans should be judged by the Pope.

I found that this misinterpretation of this canon was used by Nicholas also in a letter sent about January 865 to Charles the Bald, announcing the restitution of Rothad, bishop of Soissons. We read there:[30] "Let nobody wonder why we have ordered the Bishop Rothad to come to Rome, or to be heard and judged by us. Let it be known that in this case we have followed faithfully a paternal tradition and a special prerogative of the apostolic see." Then, selecting one example from many, he writes: "If a cleric or bishop has a complaint against his metropolitan, let him approach, according to the rule given in Chalcedon, the primate of the diocese or the bishop of the royal city of Constantinople before whom the dispute should be judged. Nobody will doubt that this should be much more observed as concerns the see of Rome than that of Constantinople." Anastasius Bibliothecarius, one of the few in Rome who knew Greek, should have spotted this misinterpretation and should have known what the Greeks meant by the word *exarchos*, and that the interpretation of the function of an *exarchos* with the Latin word *primas* was misleading.

In spite of the Pope's willingness to re-examine the case of Photius and Ignatius, expressed in this letter, the East remained silent. Disappointed by the negative attitude of Constantinople, Nicholas I not only saw that his hopes for regaining jurisdiction over Illyricum appeared to be definitely lost, but that the dispute might end in an open schism.

---

26 Mansi VII, col. 376; Aberig — P. Joannon — C. Leonard — P. Prod — H. Jedin, *Conciliorum œcumenicorum decreta*, Freiburg 1962, p. 67. The Greek text is clearer than the Latin translation.

27 MGH VI, 471.

28 Grotz, *op. cit.*, p. 86.

29 PL 67, col. 173.

30 MGH Ep. VI, 385.

We can imagine with what joyful sentiments he received the embassy of the Bulgarian Khagan Boris in August 866 asking for a patriarch, and presenting him with a number of questions on which he sought the Pope's advice. Knowing that the Franks were also anxious to bring Bulgaria under their influence — they had started missionary work there before the intervention of Byzantium — the Pope, losing no time, dispatched in the autumn of the same year a special embassy to Bulgaria, led by two bishops, Formosus and Paul. They carried a long letter from the Pope in which he replied to all the questions raised by Boris. In his desire to put Bulgaria, which occupied a great part of Illyricum and Thrace, under his direct jurisdiction, Nichols did not see the psychological background of Boris' request. The astute Khagan intended to keep his land independent from the Byzantines and the Franks in both political and eclesiastical fields. Dissatisfied with Photius who had sent him only priests, a long letter, but no bishops, he hoped to obtain a bishop of patriarchal rank from the Pope.

This famous letter called by Western canonists *Responsa ad consulta Bulgarorum* is praised by them as a masterpiece of pastoral wisdom, but, in his efforts to win over the Bulgars to the Roman Church, the Pope exaggerated when criticizing certain rituals introduced into Bulgaria by the Greek priests, and in declaring that Byzantium was not a true patriarchate, as it had not been founded by an Apostle.

Unfortunately, the letter fell into the hands of the Byzantines, and the sharp criticism of Eastern rites and the debasement of their patriarchate offended the Greeks and Easterners alike, provoking anti-Latin sentiments. An attempt has recently been made by G. T. Dennis to show that the content of the letter is not anti-Greek and anti-Eastern,[31] but his defense is not convincing.

H.-G. Beck is of another opinion when rightly stating:[32] *"The Responsa ad consulta Bulgarorum* are praised as a masterly piece of pastoral wisdom, but one forgets too easily the very ponderous fact that it was Pope Nicholas I who, in this letter without regard to the duties of his office, attacked the rites of the Greek Church, presenting them in a ridiculous way." Refuting Dennis' defense, he adds: "I do not think that the *Responsa* can be so easily exculpated. Anyhow, Photius and his Church saw in them a general attack against their rite."

Unfortunately, H.-G. Beck is right. It does not matter if the Pope really intended to attack openly the Eastern rites. The important point is what the Greeks thought about it. In reality, the Pope's letter added fuel to the fire. Nicholas, wishing to keep Bulgaria in his hands, tried to show Boris the superiority of the Latin rites over the Greek and in doing so went too far. H. Grotz comments on this new development as follows:[33] "Actually Nicholas I by his letter to Boris has challenged and provoked the whole East against himself. Neither the Westerners nor the Easterners had the generosity of mind to overlook trifles. Both sides lacked the good will to accept another's Church organization as equal to its own, even though the other's rite was based on an equally good tradition. In the West there was no man who — as in days past Irenaeus had warned Pope Victor — able to warn Pope Nicholas not to take such a fatal step. The essential fact was forgotten, namely, unity in love and the consciousness of belonging together."

The Pope's letter to Boris provoked great indignation in Byzantium which swelled even more when the Greek missionaries, expelled by Boris, appeared in the capital and described the missionary methods of their rivals in Bulgaria. In their eagerness to win over the Bulgarians to the Western Church the Latins appear to have criticized Greek rites even more sharply than did the Pope in his letter. The addition of *Filioque* to the Creed by Franks would have become known in Constantinople only after the return of the Greek missionaries. All this forced Photius to abandon his negative attitude and to come forward in defense of the Eastern rites and of the Eastern Church. This he did in a letter to the Easterners which expresses all the bitterness and disappointment he experienced during his dealings with the Western Church. He blamed

---

[31] G. T. Dennis, *The "anti-Greek" character of the Responsa ad Bulgaros of Nicholas I?* Or. chr. per. 24 (1958) 165—174.

[32] In: *Handbuch der Kirchengeschichte,* ed. by H. Jedin, vol. III, Freiburg 1966, p. 203.

[33] Grotz, *op. cit.,* p. 104.

the Latins for having introduced many changes into the old discipline of the Church. The greater part of his letter is devoted to the *Filioque*.

It is a pity that this problem could not have been discussed in common by both the East and West at this time. H. Grotz[34] rightly states that the *Filioque* does not contradict the teaching of the Fathers, and not even of the Greek thinkers. Both Greek and Latin versions of the Creed present reasonable philosophical arguments for themselves. The Greeks, of course, mostly objected to its addition to the Creed without a conciliar decision. Without exception the Eastern Church was against the *Filioque*, but in the Western Church there was not yet full agreement. H. Grotz quotes the example of Scotus Eriugena (died in 877), whom even J. Hergenröther suspected of being against the addition of *Filioque*, who would have declared himself for Photius if the general atmosphere in the West had permitted him to do so.[35] I have quoted a curious passage from a work of Anastasius Bibliothecarius himself, namely, the introduction to the translation of a letter of St. Maximus the Confessor (580—662), saying that "the Greeks have in this matter become needlessly opposed to us", trying to explain that both the Greek and Latin versions can be easily reconciled with the doctrine on the Holy Trinity.[36]

H.-G. Beck stressed rightly that the anti-Photian Council of 869—870 did not touch on the question of *Filioque*, perhaps because the Latins feared strong opposition from the whole Eastern Church. They even made a great concession to the Easterners when adding to their Profession of Faith that any addition to the symbol of Nicaea and Constantinople was forbidden under threat of excommunication.[37]

All this would seem to indicate that a reasonable solution of this problem might have been reached in the ninth century if conciliar discussion without prejudice could have taken place. But sharp conflict between Constantinople and Rome made any such discussion impossible, and the *Filioque* became a war cry and a bone of contention throughout the following centuries in the conflict between East and West.

Photius' letter provoked a sharp reaction in the whole East. All Easterners saw in the Latin intrusion into Bulgaria and the Pope's criticism of Eastern usages, an attack on their rites and on the privileges of their churches. The Greek clergy and all the eastern patriarchs were represented at the synod convoked by Photius in the summer of 867, which was presided over by the Emperor Michael III and Basil I. Only the sermon given by Photius at the end of this synod is preserved and it is curious to find that there is no mention of the Pope, although we know that the synod condemned and deposed him. All we learn from it is that the Fathers once more condemned all the heresies which had been censured by the previous Councils, the condemnation of iconoclasm by the Seventh Council being particularly stressed. The Emperor's true faith is praised because it was suggested to him — as Photius says — "by the key bearer of the heavenly gates, proclaimed by Truth to be the rock and foundation of the faith, Peter, the chief of the disciples, who whispered some such inspired and holy words in the ears of thy heart."[38]

This homily should be quoted as another argument against those who pretend that this Photian synod attacked the Latin Church and denied the primacy of Rome. The

---

34 *Op. cit.*, p. 108.

35 J. Hergenröther, *Photius Patriarch von Konstantinopel*, Regensburg 1867—1869, vol. I, p. 673.

36 MGH Ep. VII, 425 (PL 129, col. 560): "We do not say, as they pretend we do, that the Son is the cause and the principle of the Holy Spirit. On the contrary, in our preoccupation to assert the unity of substance of the Father and the Son, we say that the Holy Spirit, while He proceeds from the Father, also proceeds from the Son, understanding this procession as a mission . . ." Maximus says that both we and the Greeks understand that the Holy Spirit proceeds, in one sense from the Son, but that in another sense he does not proceed from the Son. Cf. F. Dvornik, *Byzantium and the Roman Primacy*, *op. cit.*, p. 12.

37 In: *Handbuch der Kirchengeschichte*, *op. cit.*, vol. III, p. 214.

38 Cf. the English translation of the homily by C. Mango, *The Homilies of Photius Patriarch of Constantinople* (= Dumbarton Oaks Studies, III) Cambridge, Mass. 1958, pp. 306—314; the quoted passage, p. 312.

reverend praise of "Peter the key bearer of the heavenly gates" in this homily closing the Acts of the synod is very eloquent. The Acts were directed only against the person of Nicholas I.

It should be stressed that the examination of all of Photius' genuine writings lead to the conclusion that in none of them had the Patriarch denied the Roman primacy. H.-G. Beck expressed the suspicion that perhaps the anonymous work "Against them who pretend that Rome is the First See" may have been written by Photius himself.[39] M. Cordillo, who re-edited it, attributes it to an anonymous writer of the thirteenth century,[40] and I agreed with his conclusion.[41] But because some scholars still refuse to be convinced, Beck thought it necessary to decide *in dubiis pro reo.* H. Grotz remarks to this: "It seems to one that this Latin phrase is out of place here. In none of the genuine writings of Photius can be found anything which can be explained as the negation of the Roman Primacy, it is up to them who attribute this work to Photius to prove it, not up to them who deny it. The presumption is in favor of Photius, not against him."[42]

The condemnation of Nicholas I was a *faux pas,* a mistake considered in the West as a great misdemeanor because it violated the principle accepted in the West that the Pope is judgeless. However, let me add to it that this principle was not as intangible in the East as in the West. In this respect there existed one precedent in the East. The Sixth Ecumenical Council in 681 during its tenth session condemned Pope Honorius, suspected of favoring Monothelitism.[43] This condemnation of a Pope was repeated again at the synod in Trullo in 692,[44] and also by the Seventh Ecumenical Council.[45] What is more pertinent is that this condemnation of Pope Honorius was reiterated by the Ignatian Council which assembled to condemn Photius who had dared to censure Pope Nicholas I.[46] In the West this condemnation of Honorius was repeated by every Pope when making his *Confessio fidei* following his election. The tetx is preserved in the *Liber Diurnus,*[47] but appears to have been forgotten during the high Middle Ages when the principle that the Pope should never be judged became general belief. Later Latin canonists tried to do away with this condemnation as being a falsification of the conciliar Acts by the Easterners.

The Eastern prelates agreed unanimously with Photius in the condemnation of Nicholas, because they interpreted the Pope's letter and his missionary activities in Bulgaria as attacks on their ritual which violated the rights of the whole Eastern Church. It was only later, when Photius was deposed by Basil I that his enemies declared the signatures of the Acts by the bishops and Basil I as having been falsified by Photius. In order to prevent the Romans from discovering their lies the imperial ambassador in Rome declared that the synod did not exist and permitted the Acts which he had brought to Rome, to be destroyed.[48]

Let us see how H. Grotz explains this fateful act of Photius:[49] "It cannot be denied that Photius saw a deep personal offence in the fact that he was denounced by Nicholas I in an official document as an irregular Patriarch, nay, an intruder, without having been given an opportunity of being heard although he was willing to remain in communion with Rome, only on the grounds of calumnies spread by a malevolent opposition. Can one wonder that Photius, after this, did not regard Nicholas as the representative of Christ and that he broke ecclesiastical relations with him? But one cannot break off relations with a pope as one can with a bishop, for when one

---

39 In: *Handbuch der Kirchengeschichte, op. cit.,* vol. III, p. 215.

40 M. Gordillo, *Photius et Primatus Romanus,* Or. Chr. Per. 6 (1940) 1—39.

41 F. Dvornik, *The Photian Schism,* p. 126.

42 H. Grotz, *Die Zeit Papst Hadrians II., op. cit.,* p. 193.

43 Mansi XI, 580.

44 Mansi XI, 937.

45 Mansi XIII, 377.

46 Mansi XVI, 181.

47 H. Foerster, *Liber Diurnus,* Bern 1958, p. 155. See what I wrote on *Liber Diurnus* in *The Photian Schism, op. cit.,* pp. 435—447.

48 Read the description of his masquerading in the *Liber Pontificalis,* ed. L. Duchesne, Paris 1886—1892, vol. II, 178 ff.

49 H. Grotz, *Die Zeit Papst Hadrians II., op. cit.,* pp. 192—193.

recognizes a pope as legitimate, one recognizes him as the cornerstone and central point of Church unity. Thus, a person who regards the pope as legitimate and then breaks with him, [he] consciously puts himself outside the Church. If, therefore, Photius did not wish to exclude himself from communion with the Church and, at the same time, did not consider Nicholas I as legitimate pope, he had logically to declare the pope as deposed." This is what he did, perhaps encouraged by complaints which had reached him in Constantinople of the harshness of Nicholas.

The behavior of Nicholas I in this oriental complication is characterized by H. Grotz in the following way:[50]"Nicholas I is indeed venerated in the Catholic Church as a saint. He embodied the Christian conscience in a decadent society and defended with firm and unrelenting courage the disciplinary order of the Church and the morality of public life. Nevertheless, one can hardly do him an injustice when one states that he sometimes omitted to act with moderation and with good will for mutual understanding."

It is also to be regretted that the polemics between the East and West were not started by Photius in spite of his encyclica, but by the West, at the invitation of Nicholas I. The later was frightened by the strong reaction of the Byzantines to the Bulgarian affair. The encyclic letter of the Patriarch warned him of the danger of a definite break with the East, and of the probability of fierce theological attacks on the Western Church. Therefore we are able to understand his cry of alarm and his invitation to Hincmar and the Western bishops to defend the Western Church against the Greeks. He was already almost on his death bed. In order to spur his bishops to sharp controversy with the Greeks, he pretended that the Byzantines has transferred the primacy of the Church from Rome to Constantinople, because Photius had called himself ecumenical patriarch. It was a false alarm. The Byzantines never had denied the primacy of the see of Rome in the Church.[51] Anastasius, who acted as Nicholas' scribe, could have explained to him the meaning of the title given to the Patriarchs of Constantinople; at least, he did so later in his presentation to John VIII of his translation of the Acts of the Council of 869—870.[52] The title expressed that the Patriarch of New Rome was as ecumenical as the Byzantine Empire. The ecumenicity of the Church was expressed by the Greeks as *katholikē ekklesia.*

Unfortunately, the appeal of the dying Pope produced a vehement reaction among the Frankish hierarch. At the imperial synod of Worms in May 868, the bishops expressed their indignation by inviting every scholar to defend the Church against Greek attacks. Hincmar of Reims himself wrote an anti-Greek treatise,[53] followed by Ratram of Corbia[54] and Aeneas of Paris.[55] Their writings survived, but that of Odo of Beauvais is lost. These writings produced a resounding echo among the Latin clergy and inaugurated the polemic literature which nourished the animosity between Greeks and Latins for centuries to come.

This appeal for a mobilization of the Westerners against the Greek Church was attributed by some to Anastasius who composed the Pope's letters. The Pope's letter dated October 867 containing this appeal and addresssed to Hincmar of Reims,[56] testifies, however, remarks H. Grotz, that this polemical discussion with the Eastern Church was a matter of personal interest to Nicholas and that he really intended to mobilize the whole West in the warfare with the East which he regarded as imminent.

The vigorous and self-confident reign of Nicholas I made a great impression in Rome and in the West. His authoritative dealings with Kings and Princes dramatized the pontifical power which appeared to reign over all worldly powers, and his treatment of the Easterners seemed to confirm the superiority of Rome over the whole Church. Many clerics were outspoken "Nicholaites" and hoped that the energetic, dynamic, vigorous, strong policy of the deceased pope would be continued by Nicholas' successor.

---

50 H. Grotz, *Erbe wider Willen, op. cit.,* p. 105.
51 I have shown this in my book *Byzantium and the Roman Primacy, op. cit.*
52 MGH Ep. VII, 417.
53 *Epistola ad Odonem episcopum:* PL 126, cols. 94 ff.
54 PL 121, 225 ff.
55 PL 121, 680 ff.
56 MGH Ep. VI, 601.

Hadrian II, consecrated Pope on December 14, 867 was confronted with a difficult choice. By character he was inclined to indulgence, but, at the same time, he was determined to defend the papal prerogatives.

Many "Nicholaites" were anxious fearing that the new Pope might take a more conciliatory attitude towards the Easterners, and panic seems to have spread among the Ignatian monks who were most responsible for Nicholas' antiphotianist policy. The *Liber pontificalis* even reports that some of them hanged themselves fearing repercussions from papal policy.[57] In fact, a few conciliatory gestures made by Hadrian II to some of the bishops and persons punished by Nicholas, seemed to give substance to this reverse.

On the other hand, the "Nicholaites" urged the new Pope to remain faithful to the memory of his holy predecessor and to continue his energetic policy in the West and the East. Hadrian II felt that his hands were tied by the policy of Nicholas which had found such approval in the West, and he saw himself forced to appease the "Nicholaites", and to assure the orientals in Rome that he did not wish to be unfaithful to the policy of Nicholas in the East. He did so in his proclamation made to the eastern monks who were invited to a banquet on February 12, 868.[58] At that time the reversal of the political and religious situation in Constantinople was as yet unknown in Rome.

In spite of his solemn declaration that he was determined to follow the policy of Nicholas, Hadrian II wished to do so in his own way. In his letter to Ado of Vienne, a stout „Nicholaite", he wrote on May 8, 868 that "he wanted to end with moderation the affairs which Nicholas had begun with harshness".[59]

The Bulgarian affair was the first cause which claimed Hadrian's attention in the East, and in searching for a solution to the Bulgarian problem, Hadrian thought it would be wise to follow in Nicholas' footsteps. Here, Hadrian, in following too faithfully the policy of Nicholas, made a mistake. Like his predecessor he probably ment to keep Bulgaria firmly in the hands of Rome and hesitated to approve the choice of candidates made by Boris. Boris was of another mind and did not intend to be as ready to serve Rome as did some Frankish rulers. Grotz rightly observes that the only two men who would have been able to save Bulgaria for Rome — Formosus or Marinus — were rejected by the Popes.[60] So it happened that in the end Rome lost Bulgaria, a prize for whose possession Rome had provoked the wrath of the whole Christian East.

There was yet another inheritance from the pontificate of Nicholas I, namely, the contest between Photius and Ignatius. If Hadrian II desired to solve this conflict, which had already ended in a schism, by using moderation and avoiding Nicholas' harsh attitude, he was spared such a decision by the events which had taken place in Constantinople.

At the beginnong of the summer of 868 the imperial envoy, Euthymius appeared in Rome with a letter from the new Emperor Basil I explaining the changes which had taken place in Constantinople. The news that Photius was exiled and that Ignatius was again on the patriarchal throne produced a great sensation in Rome. The "Nicolaites" saw in the change the confirmation that Nicholas' policy had been right because the Byzantines themselves had repudiated Photius and accepted Ignatius. No one in Rome in papal circles could know the real reasons for such unexpected changes. Basil, after murdering his benefactor Michael III in September 867 so as to become autocrator, could not rely on the support of the partisans of Michael and Photius. In order to win over the conservative monks and hierarchs it was necessary to replace Photius with their candidate Ignatius. When so doing he had hoped to gain

---

57 *Lib. pontif.* II, p. 176: *cum per dies aliquot quidam Graecorum et aliarum gentium servorum Dei per id tempus Romae morantium se clanculo suspendissent ...*

58 Liber pontif. II, pp. 176 ff.

59 Jaffé-Wattenbach, № 2907: *Addoni, archiepiscopo Viennensi, ad Nicolai decreta omnino servanda hortanti laudem tribuit. Sed addit, lenitate perficienda esse, quae ille severe inchoaverit.*

60 H. Grotz, *Erbe wider Willen, op. cit.,* p. 209.

favor with Rome to bolster his own prestige. Unfortunately, he was unaware that Nicholas I whose favor he tried to win, was dead.

Hadrian sent a letter of congratulation to the Emperor and to Ignatius. However, if he thought that Ignatius was entirely devoted to Rome, he was mistaken. He himself reproached Ignatius for not announcing his restoration to the Pope sooner. According to the Roman view, clearly expressed by Nicholas, each Patriarch must announce his appointment to the Roman See, which appointment must be acknowledged by the Pope. But this instruction had been overlooked in the case of Ignatius.

Basil had evidently accepted the last decision made by Nicholas, namely, that the controversy should be judged by Rome in the presence of the representatives of both parties. He sent a new embassy to Rome at the end of the winter of 869, headed by the Emperor's representative, the spatharius Basil, consisting of Bishop John of Sylaeon representing Ignatius, and Bishop Peter of Sardis representing Photius. Unfortunately, the ship bearing the representative of Photius perished at sea together with the envoy, and only one poor monk survived the catastrophe.

If Hadrian had wished to act as a just judge in this matter, he should have requested another representative of Photius to explain the deposed Patriarch's case. But Hadrian, under pressure from the "Nicholaites" was so convinced of the culpability of Photius that he pronounced judgement without even granting the defendants a hearing.

During this hearing of the Byzantine embassy held in the Church of St. Mary Major,[61] the Pope could have found a discrepancy ,between the statements of the delegates of Ignatius and of the Emperor. John of Sylaeon confessed that Photius had convoked a synod in 867 against Nicholas, but the spatharius Basil, throwing down the Acts of this synod before the assembly, declared that such a synod did not exist; the synod, the signatures of the bishops and of the Emperor having been falsified by Photius. The Pope permitted the Acts to be examined by a commission — which most probably was composed of only one man — Anastasius — who knew Greek. The Emperor's ambassador was satisfied when his wish was fulfilled, and the Acts, in theatrical gesture, were burnt. By this action independent examination was prevented, and the Roman synod once more condemned Photius and excommunicated him.

One has impression that Hadrian and the "Nicholaites" were now convinced that the Byzantines and their new Patriarch were feeling indebted to Rome for its decision and had sincerely accepted the supremacy of Rome over their Church. They were again mistaken, for they did not understand the true position of Basil nor his intentions. He asked for the convocation of a general council in Constantinople which would reexamine the whole question and leave the final judgement to him and the Fathers. He knew very well that the Photian party was very strong and that his political position was still rather shaky. He hoped that if the Photianists were given an occasion to defend their cause, and were treated with moderation, their opposition to his régime would be weakened.

This was not the intention of the legates — Bishop Donatus of Ostia, Stephen of Nepi and the Deacon Marinus, an especially tough "Nicholaite". All the bishops before being admitted to the council were asked to sign a *Libellus* containing a declaration of fidelity to Rome, condemnation of the Photian synods, and acceptance of all the decisions made by Nicholas and Hadrian during the Roman synods in the Photian affairs. Even the Ignatians were asked to sign. The Pope wished to make sure of their fidelity to papal decisions. All this was composed in a "Nicholaite" spirit, and one has the impression that in Rome there was a feeling of certainty that victory over Byzantium would be complete.

But again the Romans misunderstood the Byzantine mentality. First, the presentation of the *Libellus* provoked a protest from the Emperor and from Ignatius. The legates pretended that no further examination need be made as all was decided by the Pope. They did not succeed and suffered the humiliation to admit Photius and a few of his chief supporters to a hearing because they had not been present at their condemnation in Rome. The Emperor even threatened to refuse to sign the Acts if his demand was rejected. They had to witness to the reserved attitude of Photius declaring simply

[61] See the detailed account given in the *Liber Pontificalis* II, 178 ff.

that it was his silence that was speaking. All this did not change the conclusions prepared in Rome, but was intended to show the Romans the Byzantine independence of mind.

It became clear to the legates that Photius was in a very strong position because in spite of the Emperor's imperative invitation, only 103 bishops voted on the twenty-seven canons of the synod at the final session. All this was very painful to the legates and the Ignatianists. Instead of being a triumph for Rome and the Pope, the synod was almost a failure.

There were other matters over which the legates had to swallow their pride. It was during the debates at this synod, led mainly by the patrician Baanes, that the doctrine of the pentarchy was elaborated upon and clearly defined. It did not deny the primacy of Rome, but the concept was certainly not "Nicholaite". Even Anastasius became favorable to this doctrine, as he writes in his introduction to the translation of the Acts of this Council.[62] He made an effort to preserve the primacy of Rome when comparing the number of patriarchs to the number of man's senses. "And because among them the See of Rome has precedence, it can well be compared to the sense of sight which is certainly the first of the senses of the body since it is the most vigilant, and since it remains more than any of the other senses in communion with the whole body."

The most humiliating defeat awaited them at the end of the Council. A Bulgarian embassy appeared in Constantinople and presented to the Fathers the demand from Boris that it should decide to which patriarchate his realm should belong in ecclesiastical matters. After the closure of the Council a conference was summoned which included representatives of the four oriental patriarchates, the Bulgarian envoys, and the Emperor. The papal legates were not invited and their vehement protest against the procedure was overlooked. It was decided that the representatives of the Eastern patriarchates should arbitrate in the matter. They, of course, concluded that because the land of the Bulgarians had once belonged to the Eastern Empire, therefore their Church should be subject to the patriarchate of Constantinople.

Ignatius was presented with Hadrian's letter by the protesting legates in which the Pope reminded the Patriarch of Rome's benevolence to him and exhorted him to avoid intervention in the Bulgarian affair. The Patriarch accepted the letter, refused to read it, made an evasive answer and that was the end. Soon afterwards Ignatius ordained an archbishop and seven bishops for Bulgaria. Rome had lost its cause in a most outrageous way. The man for whose restoration Nicholas had used the prestige of the Roman See, and on whose fidelity Rome had built its hopes, had shown that he had first kept in mind the rights and prestige of his own patriarchate.

Having obtained what he wanted, Basil showed how little he appreciated the work done by the Pope's representatives in Byzantium. They were escorted as far as Dyrrhachium whence they embarked in a few days for Italy without an escort of the imperial navy. Soon their boat was taken by Slavic pirates who were mostly interested in the written documents the legates had with them — the Acts of the Council and the *Libellus* signed by the bishops.

It is probable that the incident was arranged by Basil's agents to whom the documents were very unpopular. If the legates had not permitted Anastasius, who was in Byzantium as envoy of Louis II, to copy the documents, we would have never learned what really took place in Constantinople in the years 869 to 870. Anastasius embarked for Brindisi and arrived safely in Rome with the Acts.

Hadrian protested against the Bulgarian verdict in a letter sent to the Emperor and to Ignatius, of course without result. Against the complaint that Latin priests had been invited to leave Bulgaria, Ignatius seems to have answered that the Latins had behaved in similar fashion to the Greek priests. Nicholas would have probably excommunicated Ignatius for his betrayal of the Roman see, but Hadrian saw that it was wiser not to break the ties with the Church of Constantinople because of a misdeed by its head. At the end of this conflict he acted with moderation. From what he had learned of the events in 869—870 in Constantinople, he may have come to the conclusion that it would have been more profitable for his Church had his predecessor sided with Ignatius' opponent.

62 Mansi XVI, col. 7.

The future was to show that such an attitude would have saved Rome and Byzantium a great amount of trouble and bitterness. Basil, meanwhile, recalled Photius from exile and entrusted to him the education of his son. Ignatius was wise enough to make his peace with Photius before his death. He asked Rome for a new synod for the peace of his Church. John VIII's legates found Photius already on the patriarchal throne. The Council of 869—870 mended the break after having given satisfaction to Photius who not only recognized the primacy of Rome, but also promised not to ordain priests for Bulgaria which was to be under the patriarchate of Rome. In reality, from this time on, Bulgaria did not appear in the list of Byzantine bishoprics. It was Boris who destroyed the last remaining hopes of the Romans. He kept the Greek bishops and refused to have any dealings with Rome, trying at the same time to keep his young Church independent from the Byzanine patriarchate as far as possible. The result of this controversy between Rome and Byzantium was the birth of the first national Church in the Balkans.

When following the path opened up by Nicholas I's oriental policy, Hadrian reached an *impasse*. He had to witness the betrayal of the prelate on whose questionable devotion to Rome his predecessor had gambled. The closing of the schism seemingly achieved by the Council of 869—870 was poor consolation, because the Byzantine Church continued to the divided, and anti-Roman sentiments revealed during the sessions had increased rather than diminished. The whole Eastern Church had disclosed its true attitude to Rome when it decided that Bulgaria should be placed under the jurisdiction of New Rome.

It was a disaster for which Hadrian, however, was only partially responsible. In his oriental policy his hands were tied because of the attitude of his predecessor, an attitude which had been applauded by all the leading prelates of the Western Church. But we would do an injustice to Hadrian if we judge his reign merely from this point of view. The true character of a man is revealed only by acts which he makes on his own, freely, and uninfluenced by circumstances for which he is not responsible.

In reality, Hadrian was offered such an occasion at the very beginning of his reign to make a decision which none of his predecessors had dared to make. Curiously enough even this opportunity had been prepared by his predecessor, Nicholas I. It was the latter who had been informed by Frankish clergy that in the neighborhood of their country, in Moravia, Greek missionaries were introducing an unheard of innnovation.

Moravia had already been christianized to a great extent by Frankish missionaries, and the bishop of Passau regarded the country almost as a part of his diocese. The Moravian ruler Rastislav, however, was anxious to keep his land independent from the Frankish Empire, and addressed himself to Byzantium asking for missionaries who would establish in his country a church organisation independent from the Frankish clergy.

The Byzantine mission was sent to Moravia in 863 by the Emperor Michael III and the Patriarch Photius. It was led by two brothers, Constantine and Methodius, who spoke the Slavic language and had had some experience in dealing with Slavs. Before accepting the Moravian mission the brothers invented a new Slavic alphabet and began to translate the Gospel into a Slavic Macedonian dialect. In Moravia they were translating also the liturgy into the Slavonic language and were even celebrating the Mass and saying the Office in that barbarian tongue.

The activities of the Greek missionaries was a great success in Moravia and the ruler entrusted a number of young men to them to learn the Slavic script. After three years the two brothers decided to return to Constantinople with their disciples so that some of them could be consecrated as bishops and priests for work in the new missionary territory.[63]

Nicholas I was alarmed at hearing of these events. The activities of Byzantine missionaries in a country which to a great extent had already been converted by Frankish priests must have aroused his suspicions. They could have been sent to Moravia only by Photius whom he had refused to accept as legitimate Patriarch. The accusations of the Frankish clergy looked very serious. Therefore, he decided to

[63] For details see my book *Byzantine Missions Among the Slavs*, New Brunswick 1970.

inquire himself into the accusations against the Greeks, and invited them to come to Rome in order to explain their activities.

This did not augur well for the reception of the brothers in Rome. They must have learned of the hostile attitude of Nicholas towards their own Patriarch to whom they intended to present their disciples for consecration. Nevertheless, they decided to accept the invitation and changed their plans accordingly and went to Rome. Their only hope was through the intercession of St. Clement, third successor to St. Peter, whose relics Constantine believed he had discovered in Cherson, and which they had brought to Moravia, and were now returning to Constantinople with them.[64]

Fortunately for the Greek brothers, it was not Nicholas I but his successor, Hadrian II, who was expecting them. He received them with great benevolence and listened with sympathy to their reasons for having invented a new alphabet for the Slavs, and for giving them the Holy Books in their own language. Hadrian approved their new missionary methods and manifested great sagacity in doing so. The brothers were sent to Moravia by Photius and were returning to their Patriarch to ask him to ordain their disciples. Why could their invention not be approved and used by the Roman Church for the conversion of the Slavs, especially the Bulgars? He saw that not only the Byzantines but also the Franks were interested in their conversion. On the other hand, the two brothers made a great impression in Roman circles because of their learning, intelligence, and piety. The fact that they accepted a papal invitation and had come to Rome evidenced their respect for the authority of the First Patriarch, successor to St. Peter.

After reflecting on all these possibilities, and after realizing that this new method introduced by the brothers was a great success, the Pope made a decision which no other Pope before him had made, and which was the weightiest of his reign. He approved the translation of Holy Writ and of the liturgy, accepted their Slavic books, blessed them, and deposited them on the altar in the church of Santa Maria Maggiore.

This decision of Hadrian II could have been an important break through in the history of the whole West. Other nations would have followed the example of the Slavs and a new era would have been introduced into the cultural development of Western Europe. It was, however, difficult to go against the old traditions. Hadrian's reign was short and his successors lacked his foresight and his open mind. John VIII was the only one who tried to keep alive Hadrian's grandiose ideals. He closed the schism with the Eastern Church giving full satisfaction to Photius by approving the Acts of the Council of 879—880, which suppressed the decisions of the Ignatian Council of 869—870. Faithful to the old tradition the Easterners, even to this day, count only Seven Ecumenical Councils, calling the Council which restored Photius the Union Council, and bewail the fact that the Western Church does not follow the old tradition.[65]

Stephen V, however, did not continue the policy of his predecessors and prohibited the use of the Slavic language in the liturgy. So it happened that the Catholics of Western nations have had to wait until the twentieth century until the reign of John XXIII and the Second Vatican Council to obtain he privileges which they could have enjoyed already in the ninth century had Hadrian's plan succeeded.

---

64 Cf. my book *Byzantine Missions,* op. cit., pp. 66, 343.

65 H. Grotz, *op. cit.*, p. 313, concludes his observations as follows: "The sharp conflict between Rome and Byzantium about the jurisdiction over Bulgaria which, in the end, has been lost to both of them, had for a consequence a very deep alienation between the Christian East and West which has lasted to our time. The efforts at reconciliation are wearisome. The first was the encounter of Pope Paul VI with Patriarch Athenagoras in Jerusadem. The second, the formal abrogation of the bull, composed by Cardinal Humbert of Silva Candida, containing the excommunication of Patriarch Cerularius (1954). We think that a much more important move would be to abstain officially from counting the Forth Council of Constantinople as ecumenical. This would not touch any dogma of the Catholic Church. On the contrary, we would do justice to some historical facts. At the Council of 879—880 in Constantinople which declared the decisions of the previous Council as invalid, Rome was anyhow also represented by its legates."

The intervention of the Frankish hierarchy also ruined another grandiose idea, namely that of creating an independent Slavic metropolis with Methodius as archbishop. So it came about that, in the end, Hadrian's approval of Slavic liturgy and letters benefitted not Rome, but Constantinople. In 882 Methodius, invited by both Basil I and Photius and with the blessing of John VIII, visited Constantinople, Photius immediately saw and understood the importance of his work, and asked him to leave behind a Slavic priest and deacon and the Slavic books. In this way, a kind of Slavic center was formed in Constantinople which was reinforced after Methodius' death (885) when most of his disciples were exiled from Moravia by the Frankish Bishop Wiching. A few of them found refuge in Bulgaria, but others were sold into slavery and brought to Venice to the slave market. A representative of Basil I found them, freed them and sent them to Constantinople. It was this center which continued the work of Methodius and provided Slavic priests in Bulgaria with Greek books for translation. It is possible that even Russian Christianity owes a debt to this nucleus of a Slavic school in Constantinople, although most of the Slavic literary treasures came to Russia from Bulgaria.

However, although Moravia had flourished as a state only for a few decades,[66] the Moravian mission of the two Byzantine brothers, sanctioned by Hadrian II and John VIII, albeit of sort duration, had a lasting importance for the whole of Christianity. This fact, generally overlooked, is stressed by Professor John Meyendorff in his review of my book *Byzantine Missions Among the Slavs* in these words:[67] "The remarkable missionary expansion of the Byzantine Church in the ninth and tenth centuries is one of the crucial events of European history. If this expansion had not taken place, the Greek Church, which was during the same period engaged in competing with Rome and which had lost control since the fifth century over the non-Greek speaking Christians of the Middle East, would have entered modern history as a purely ethnic Church. Thus, historically, the Slavic mission of Byzantium preserved the universality of Orthodoxy and secured its effectiveness as a world religious body."

---

[66] H. Grotz, *op. cit.*, gives a well balanced account of the history of Moravia, the fate of the Greek brothers and Methodius' conflict with the Frankish clergy on pp. 73 ff. and 149 ff.

[67] St. Vladimir Theological Quarterly 14 (1970) 233.

X

Photius' Career in Teaching and Diplomacy

On the teaching career of Photius there is only one piece of documentary evidence. It is the Old Slavonic *Life* of Constantine-Cyril in which one reads that the *logothete* Theoctistus brought the young orphan to the capital to give him a higher education.[1] "When he had reached Constantinople, he was entrusted to teachers in order to obtain an education. After having learned the grammar in three months, he attacked other sciences. He studied Homer and geometry, and also, with Leo and Photius, dialectic and all other philosophical disciplines. He even learned, after that, rhetoric, arithmetic, astronomy, music and all other Hellenic arts."

Further on in the *Life* we understand that Constantine was being educated for a career in the imperial administration. Theoctistus is said to have promised him rapid advancement in the imperial service by telling him that he could be appointed quite early on as *strategus,* or military and civil administrator of a province, called *thema.* The logical conclusion from this account should be that there existed, at that time, in the imperial residence a kind of high school, the main purpose of which was the instruction of young men for the imperial service. The second conclusion should be that Leo called the Mathematician, and Photius were the foremost teachers in this school.

The origin and development of the imperial university in Constantinople, the history of teaching and of the hellenic culture in the Empire has recently been studied by P. Lemerle in his brilliantly written book, *Le premier humanisme byzantin.*[2] His research has brought to light many obscure points in Byzantine cultural history, and he has discarded many theories which have been advanced by some of the specialists. He correctly emphasizes that it was not Constantine, but Constantius II who should be regarded as the true savior of hellenism in Byzantium, and as initiator of the new cultural expansion in the Empire. He also gives credit to Julian the Apostate for all that he did in furthering this development, and pays due attention to the reorganization of the instruction and the foundation of an imperial university by Theodosius II.

Justinian's intervention in the development of hellenism is rightly criticized, and in the description of the decadence in public teaching during the seventh century, the roles of Mauritius, Phocas and Heraclius appear in a better light. Having refuted the legend of the iconoclastic Emperors' hostility to higher education and the university, he has, however, had to conclude that this imperial institution during this period lost its usefulness and fell into a kind of oblivion. However, the organization and character of secular teaching remained intact and the literary and scholarly prospectus did not change.[3] Most interesting, however, is the information that the

---

[1] F. Grivec — F. Tomšič, *Constantinus et Methodius Thessalonicenses — Fontes,* Zagreb 1960, p. 99; *Magnae Moraviae fontes historici,* vol. II, Brno 1967, pp 65—66. See also the French translation of the *Life* in my book, *Les légendes de Constantin et de Méthode vues de Byzance,* Prague 1933, p. 352. An English translation with a commentary is being prepared by Professor Ihor Ševčenko.

[2] P. Lemerle, *Le premier humanisme byzantin. Notes et remarques sur enseignement et culture à Byzance des origines au X*e *siècle.* (= Bibliothèque byzantine — Études, 6) Paris 1971, pp. 43 ff.

[3] I studied the problem of secondary teaching in Byzantium in the eighth and ninth centuries in my book, *Les légendes de Constantin et de Méthode, op. cit.,* pp. 25 ff., using the information given by the contemporary hagiography. Lemerle, *op. cit.,* p. 78 followed the same method.

hagiographers of the Patriarchs Nicephorus, Tarasius and Methodius who, before taking holy orders, had occupied important post in the imperial administration, knew nothing of their instruction at an imperial institution before beginning their secular career. They seem only to have progressed through all the stages of secular education — the *paideia* — which appears to have been all that was necessary for a career in the administration.

This omission does not imply that such instruction was non-eixstent. Hagiographers are seldom interested in emphasizing the secular education of their heroes. On the other hand, even if it is true that the imperial university was no longer of first importance, it appears that candidates for the administration required some instruction before being appointed.

Unfortunately we know very little of how such appointments were made, or of what was required of the candidates. I have found only one document in the *Life* of the monophysite hero, Bishop John of Tella[4] which gives us a lead in this respect. John of Tella was born in the city of Callinicus, the son of wealthy parents. His father died when he was two and a half years old, but his mother and his relatives educated him "in all Greek letters and wisdom" which meant that he went to preparatory school, the *propaideia* and the *paideia*. When he was twenty years old "they made him serve in the praetorium of the *dux* of that city, that he may be trained and instructed". And he was wearing splendid vestments according to the grade of his service ... and they provided him with a pedagogue who had to instruct him. This pedagogue, a pious man — he recited with John the Psalms in Syriac — lived with John for five years and hid John's pious exercises from his mother who wanted him to live in the world, and who was delighted when the pedagogue assured her that her son looked tired only because he was reading many books. She thought that he was enlarging his knowledge of profane sciences.

The important city of Callinicus had been conquered in 542 by Chosroes following the violation by the Persians of the treaty of "eternal peace" concluded in 532 with Justinian. Having finished his secondary education, the young John at the age of twenty was admitted to the service of the municipal administration. He was instructed by other officers in the performance of his duties and advanced to higher posts according to the municipal program. We can say that this was the practice both in municipal and imperial administration. The fact that he was given a pedagogue to complete his hellenic education, as his mother wished, is interesting. It confirms Lemerle's thesis that a more profound education was to be obtained only by private study. One should also call attention to the fact that such studies were possible in a city near the Persian border.

We do not learn anything of the existence of a high school in Constantinople during the iconoclastic period, although the legendary accounts of the twelve professors under Leo V would indicate that the government may have kept some professionals at court in order to instruct candidates for the imperial service. More precise information is available in the reign of the Emperor Theophilus who discovered the existence of a great scholar, Leo the Mathematician, whose fame had reached the Arab Khalif Mamun from a prisoner who had been Leo's student in Constantinople.[5] Leo seems to have been self-taught as there was no high school in Constantinople.

He was therefore an autodidact visiting monastic and other libraries and readings works of hellenic scholars, many of whom had already been forgotten. He established a kind of private school in the capital and, thanks to his encyclopaedic knowledge, taught young men who were going through the *paideia* or who wished to increase their learning. When the Emperor had heard of him he generously decided to remunerate him for his teaching.

Lemerle thinks[6] that even after this appointment Leo continued to teach privately — "à titre personnel". It is true that we do not learn anything about the establishment of an official high school in the palace — Leo had to teach in the Church of the Forty

---

[4] *Corpus scriptorum christianorum orientalium,* ed. I, B. Chabot, Scriptores Syri, Series 3, vol. 24, Paris 1907, pp. 28 ff.

[5] All problems concerning Leo are discussed by P. Lemerle, *op. cit.,* 148—176.

[6] Lemerle, *op. cit.,* p. 154.

Martyrs — but as Lemerle himself accepts the fact that Leo was in the entourage of the Emperor for whom he had constructed the famous optic telegraph, we can see in his appointment the nucleus of a new imperial high school, a continuation of what had been left of the old school of higher teaching which had not completely disappeared during the seventh and eigth centuries. It should be pointed out that Theoctistus, the famous *logothete,* is mentioned for the first time as being interested in Leo's scholarship.

In order to honor him, Theophilus, possibly at the suggestion of his relative the iconoclast Patriarch John the Grammarian, promoted Leo to the archbishopric of Thessalonica where he worked to 843 when Theodora had condemned iconoclasm, deposing both the Patriarch and Leo. The latter was above all a scholar and, as we can judge from the only homily which has survived and given by him in 842, he was not a convinced iconoclast.[7] This fact helped Leo to return to Constantinople where he intended to continue his teaching which had been interrupted by his appointment to Thessalonica. We have seen that Theoctistus was interested in Leo and that he had introduced him to the Emperor Theophilus who had appointed him as public teacher in the Church of the Forty Martyrs.[8] Acting as *logothete* during the reign of Theodora, Theoctistus who appreciated teaching and scholarship, went further than Theophilus and revived the idea of public higher teaching, appointing the foremost scholars of that time, Leo the Mathematician and Photius as the leading teachers. This school of higher teaching, after the assassination of Theoctistus in 855, was reorganized by Bardas, uncle of Michael III. This reorganization is described in detail by the Continuator of Theophanes.[9]

Lemerle, accepting the fact that Leo was a professional teacher, rejects the thesis that Photius was associated with Leo in teaching at the reorganized public high school. He is of the opinion that if Photius had had even a short career in teaching, this would havė been confirmed by at least one witness.[10] There is no such witness. But we have seen that there is a witness, namely, the *Life* of Constantine-Cyril. The author denies this witness its credibility. His preconceived idea is that this witness is a hagiographer whose information about his hero must be taken "cum grano salis". Hagiographers have a general inclination to bring their heroes into contact with famous men of their time. This tendency explains why the hagiographer made Constantine a student of the two most learned men of the period, Leo and Photius.

Such an explanation could not be denied a certain credibility had the author of the *Life* been writing for a Greek public well aware of the importance of the two men. But the *Life* was not written in Greek — as Lemerle would like to say — but in Old Slavonic and not for a Greek public. It was written for the Moravian people who had never heard of Leo or Photius and were unable to understand the connection of these teachers with their holy man. Therefore, if the hagiographer mentioned that Constantine was a student of Leo and Photiüs, he did so because it was true, and there is no reason to deny him credibility. Mentioning Photius in a western land could even have been dangerous because of his conflict with Pope Nicholas. The Frankish clergy in Moravia may have had some vague knowledge of it, and could use it against Methodius. If, in spite of this, the hagiographer refers to Photius as Constantine's teacher, he did so because he knew it to be a fact.

P. Lemerle is determined to show that before Bardas' reform there was no public high school in Constantinople, and therefore is prejudiced against the report in the *Vita Constantini.* However, he admits that Theophilus had appointed Leo the Mathematician as teacher at the Church of the Forty Martyrs. We know that, in this respect, the Byzantines continued the old hellenic tradition of establishing schools in the churches, or in their vicinity. Leo was paid for this teaching by the Emperor, thus

---

7 Published by V. Laurent, *Une homélie inédite de l'archevêque de Thessalonique Léon le Philosophe sur l'Annonciation (25 Mars, 842).* In: Mélanges Eugène Tisserant (= Studi e Testi, 232) Vatican 1964, pp. 281—302. Cf. P. Lemerle, *op. cit.,* p. 157.

8 Kedrenos, II (Bonn, p. 168); cf. P. Lemerle, *op. cit.,* p. 151.

9 Theophanes Continuatus, IV, 126 (Bonn, p. 185); cf. P. Lemerle, *op. cit.,* p. 159.

10 P. Lemerle, *op. cit.,* p. 183.

why should the author be determined to call this teaching "private", "à titre personnel"?

Concerning Leo's career after 843, P. Lemerle hesitates to accept the fact that Theoctistus dared to appoint a former iconoclast to an official position in an imperial high school. This doubt is not warranted. I have shown in detail[11] the role of Theoctistus in the re-establishment of the cult of images. He was a good statesman and saw the necessity for a change in the religious policy and, although a former iconoclast, encouraged Theodora to take the necessary step. He also supported the moderate policy of the new Patriarch Methodius towards the former iconoclasts, and without his support Methodius would not have dared to excommunicate the monks of Studios, partisans of an uncompromising policy towards the former heretics. On the contrary, the mild treatment of Leo following his deposition from the episcopacy and his appointment to a post at the restored public high school in Constantinople, corresponds perfectly to the reconciliatory policy of Theoctistus, which was also the policy of the Patriarch Methodius.

In this respect the biographer of Constantine filled up the gap in the history of the reappearance of a public high school in the capital, and also gave us the names of the two scholars appointed as its first teachers. It is true that Bardas, continuing the policy of his rival, is celebrated as the founder of the imperial high school, probably after 855—856. The fact that Bardas came to power after his assassination of Theoctistus most probably contributed to the fact that Theoctistus' first step in this respect was not mentioned in the chronicles. Bardas also favored Leo, appointing him head of the University and grouping round him three scholars, Theodore, Theodegios and Cometas.

Also, there is no reason why the biographer's statement that his hero, Constantine was appointed professor at this University should be rejected. Constantine may have replaced Photius whose services were needed in the imperial chancery. One can dispute the date of this appointment. My theory that it took place in 851 may be questioned, but this theory has not yet been replaced by a better one.

When reporting Constantine's appointment, the biographer writes that he had to teach philosopy to the indigenous and to foreigners. Some critics[12] have suspected in these words a faulty translation of the Greek common definition of the εἴσω and the ἔξω σοφία. I do not think that such an interpretation should be accepted. In the public University there was no teaching of the εἴσω σοφία. The word meant a religious or rather monastic life, the true philosophy of a convinced Christian.

The University was public, accessible to the indigenous and to foreigners alike. In this respect we can quote Psellos who describes the many foreigners who, besides the indigenous, followed his courses of philosophy.[13] On the other hand, I do not believe that the author of the biography — and I suppose that it was Clement collaborating with Methodius — had such a poor knowledge of Greek as to translate εἴσω καὶ ἔξω σοφία by "teaching indigenous and foreigners".

The question about the εἴσω σοφία leads us to another problem which also concerns Constantine-Cyril and Photius, namely, did there exist in Constantinople a theological high school, or a kind of patriarchal academy? I discussed this problem in a paper "Photius et la réorganisation de l'Académie patriarcale",[14] but I must confess that after reexamining the whole question, I came to the conclusion that at least up to the tenth century, as far as we can judge, there did not exist in Byzantium any religious high school which could be called a patriarchal academy. Those who defended the existence of such a school were misled by the prejudice that such a school for the education of the clergy should have existed in Byzantium as it existed in the West during the Middle Ages, and also by legendary accounts in some chronicles concerning the destruction of the academy by the iconoclasts. The title of οἰκουμενικὸς διδάσκαλος

[11] F. Dvorník, *Les légendes de Constantine et de Méthode, op. cit.*, pp. 40 ff. Cf. also J. B. Bury, *A History of the Later Roman Empire,* London 1912, pp. 143 ff.

[12] A. Vaillant, *Textes vieux-slaves,* vol. 2, Paris 1968, p. 22 — translation of a note to the *Vita Constantini.*

[13] See C. N. Sathas, *Bibliotheca graeca medii aevi,* vol. 5, Paris 1876, p. 508.

[14] Anal. Boll. 68 (1950) 108—125.

given to some scholars seemed misleading and was wrongly attributed to teachers at the patriarchal academy.[15]

It is to the credit of Professor H.-G. Beck to have shown that such an institution did not exist in Byzantium, at least up to the tenth century.[16] From his description of the practice followed by teacher in the παιδεία it follows that a special thelogical school in Byzantium was unnecessary. Teachers did not confine themselves to classical authors in grammatical, rhetorical and philosophical lectures, but also examined the writings of Church Fathers and Holy Writ, of course, rather from the stylistic point of view. Men who went through the course of the paideía were enabled to acquaint themselves also with theological terminology and were able to analyze the dialectic of the orthodox doctrine. A deeper insight into orthodox theology could be obtained by listening to the many readings from Holy Writ and the Church Fathers in the liturgy, and by private study. In this way Byzantine teaching differed from the practices of mediaeval teaching in the West.

The instruction of priests was the responsibility of the bishops. But, then again, we know nothing of a kind of preparatory school at the residence of the bishops. The candidates were supposed to know how to read and write, to be acquainted with the Psalms — many learned them by heart — and with the liturgical readings.[17] Of course, candidates who went through the *paideia* were considered to be well prepared for the priesthood, and for the instructing of the faithful.

Again, the biographer of the monophysite Bishop John of Tella gives us an example of how the "examination of the candidates for the priesthood" went on: "I should describe with what kind of words and admonitions he instructed the candidates to priesthood who used to come to him, because the words are edifying and because the candidates used to listen to him with love." Then follows a long list of moral admonitions, how they were to behave as priests, to give a good example to their people by their lives according to rules which the Apostle Paul described especially in his letters to the Romans, to the Corinthians, and to Timothy.

There is still one problem to be discussed. Did Photius take the initiative in the founding of a kind of patriarchal school, and did his former student Constantine teach at this school? I interpreted in the positive sense the report in the *Vita Constantini* that, after his return from the Khazar embassy, Constantine was "sitting" in the Church of the Holy Apostles. Considering that in antiquity teachers were represented as "sitting" and that in the New Testament, Christ when preaching, is said to have sat down, and that in early Christian art, Christ as teacher was represented sitting, I concluded that Constantine was teaching in a new school founded by the Patriarch Photius. The fact that, according to Nicholas Mesarites' description, there existed a patriarchal school in this church in the twelfth century, induced me to outline the theory that this school might have been already founded by Photius in the ninth century. It should be regarded as a new foundation, not as a reorganization, because before that date the existence of a patriarchal school is not warranted. H.-G. Beck[18] and P. Lemerle[19] deny categorically the existence of such a school and the validity of my interpretation.

It is true that my interpretation of the word "sitting" as "teaching" may appear daring as I was unable to quote from any other contemporary document to confirm such an interpretation. However, I had in mind the old Greek practice of establishing schools in, or near churches.[20] The Sophists also often held their classes in the temples. Libanius, for example, was advised to establish his school in a temple.

---

[15] On this title, see Lemerle, *op. cit.*, pp. 81 ff.

[16] H.-G. Beck, *Bildung und Theologie im frühmittelalterlichen Byzanz.* In: Polychronion, Festschrift F. Dölger, ed. P. Wirth, Heidelberg 1966, pp. 69—81.

[17] In this respect I would like to draw attention to the numerous short and larger treatises on the Councils, containing their dogmatic and also the disciplinary canons. In my *The Schism of Photius,* Cambridge 1948, p. 553, I quoted 54 such treatises. The short ones were a kind of catechism for everybody; the larger and more detailed were probably handbooks for priests.

[18] Beck, *op. cit.*, p. 76.

[19] Lemerle, *op. cit.*, p. 87.

[20] Cf. H. W. H. Walden, *The Universities of Ancient Greece,* New York 1909, p. 366.

He was also counselled, when he complained that only a few students were visiting him at his house, to follow the example of those teachers who *sat* in public.[21] Libanius, following this advice, hired rooms in the city and *sat* down near the agora. We know that the Byzantines followed the old practice, establishing schools in churches, and it could be imagined that they were familiar also with the imaginary description of teachers as sitting in the chair.

There is another detail in this description of Constantine's biography which appeared to me indicative. If we accept the biographer's recital as to Constantine's teaching philosophy at the imperial high school, we are surprised that Constantine is not reported as having returned to his chair at the high school when he returned from the Khazar embassy. Why is he said to have been sitting in the Church of the Holy Apostles? Was the high school transferred there, or are we entitled to see there a new foundation which could have been established by Photius?

P. Lemerle thinks that Constantine was given by the Emperor a kind of pension, "une cellule et une place au réfectoire, un κάθισμα.[22] This word, however, signifies rather, according to Ducange, "une place de moine". But was there a monastery by this church? Anyhow, Constantine was not a monk, but a deacon. Such a "pension" would be rather poor compensation for a learned man who had just returned from an important embassy which he had successfully accomplished. He had to have a certain position after his return which corresponded to his previous occupation. The Moravian embassy described by the biographer did not follow immediately upon the Khazar mission, and one can hardly imagine that he rested in the church waiting about for a new embassy. Moreover, he required time to prepare the Moravian mission, arranged by Bardas and Photius, to invent the glagolitic alphabet, and to begin the translation of Holy Writ into Slavonic.

I quite agree that my theory is daring in many ways, but it is not unacceptable. Perhaps a more profound study of the Byzantine schools and of teaching in the tenth and eleventh centuries will shed more light even on this problem.

* * *

The diplomatic career of Photius is closely connected with the problems concerning the composition of his famous work called *Bibliotheca,* so brilliantly analysed by P. Lemerle.[23] Because Photius confesses that he prepared this book at the request of his brother Tarasius before leaving Constantinople on a diplomatic mission to the Arabs,[24] the date of the composition of this important work depends on the year in which Photius' embassy took place. I discussed the different theories proposed by several scholars,[25] and was pleased to note that P. Lemerle agreed with some of my criticisms. He rejected Mr. Hemmerdinger's theory that Photius obtained the Greek heretical books which he quotes only from the Arab library in Bagdad,[26] also the theory that Photius took his library with him and finished the *Bibliotheca* while travelling to Samara, perhaps with some of his students.[27] He rejected also Halkin's date of the composition (after 877—878).[28]

I am sorry that he refused to accept the year 855 as the date of the embassy proposed not only by me, but by other scholars as well. He accepts the date of 838

---

21 Libanius, *Oratio* 1, 102, ed. Foerster, Teubner 1903, vol. 1, pp. 132—133.

22 Lemerle, *op. cit.,* p. 184.

23 Lemerle, *op. cit.,* p. 189 ff.

24 *PG,* 103, cols. 41, 44; 104, cols. 353, 356.

25 See the Appendix I (The Embassies of Constantine-Cyril and Photius to the Arabs) to my book *Byzantine Missions Among the Slavs,* New Brunswick, N. J. 1970, pp. 285—296.

26 B. Hemmerdinger, *Les Notices et Extraits des bibliothèques grecques de Bagdad,* Rev. des Ét. Grecques 69 (1956) 101—103; idem, *La culture grecque classique du VIIe au IXe siècle,* Byzantion 34 (1964) 127—133; idem, *Photius à Bagdad,* Byz. Zeitschr 64 (1971) 37. Cf. P. Lemerle, *op. cit.,* pp. 40—41.

27 E. Orth, *Rhetorische Forschungen — I: Photiana,* Leipzig 1908; P. Lemerle, *op cit.,* p. 195.

28 F. Halkin, *La date de composition de la « Bibliothèque » de Photius remise en question,* Anal. Boll. 81 (1963) 414—417; P. Lemerle, *op. cit.,* p. 38, 190.

put forward by his disciple, H. Ahrweiler as most probable.[29] I have dealt with her paper in my book.[30] Although we cannot deny the remarkable originality of her ideas her dating cannot be accepted. I shall limit myself to adding a few remarks to my objections to the proposed date. I cannot believe that Photius was able to accumulate, read and appraise such a great number of books before this date, even if we accept that he was born about 810.[31] When discussing the career of Leo the Mathematician, P. Lemerle shows how difficult it was to find books of the hellenic age in Constantinople. Not only Leo, but also Photius had to search in different libraries and *scriptoria* in order to find new scholarly material. He could not have begun this activity as a young boy. On the other hand, according to P. Lemerle, Photius' first work was his *Lexicon,* and he is correct when referring to the *Lexicon* as the work of Photius' young years.[32] Well, the composition of such a work must have lasted a few years. It does not seem that there could have been a sufficient length of time for the supposition that both works were achieved before 838, unless we accept that Photius was a wonder child. The date of 855 seems much more appropriate.

H. Ahrweiler sees strong argument for her theory in Photius' words that the embassy may be dangerous and that he may not return. This remark would apply very well to the embassy sent by the Emperor Theophilus to the Caliph after the loss of Amorion in 838.

However, this should not be taken as proof. Travelling of any kind through Asia Minor at that time to the Arab frontier was dangerous. I think we must date this embassy to the winter of 855. It was not sent by Theodora — as I said in my book — but by Michael III and Bardas. Theoctistus was murdered on the twenty-fifth of November, 855 by Michael's uncle, Bardas and his conspirators. Theodora was forced to surrender control of the government and Michael III was proclaimed by the Senate as an independent ruler. According to diplomatic usage a change on the throne had to be announced to the Arab partner and *vice versa.* Michael III and Bardas were certainly anxious to inform Mutawakkil of this change as early as possible. An embassy was composed and sent to Bagdad during the winter. Travelling through Asia Minor through the Tarsus passes to the Arab court during this season surely presented many dangers. Photius was certainly not the head of this embassy, but it was in the diplomatic tradition of Byzantine protocol to choose their ambassadors carefully, many of them being related to the ruling families, and all occupying high positions at court. It appears, as I have remarked in my book, that the presence of Byzantine embassies at the Arabic courts very often led to the discussion of religious matters.[33] It is quite probable that the choice of Photius to take part in the embassy was motivated by the need to add to the embassy a high official who could impress the Arabs with his scholarship and theological knowledge. Let us not forget that the Caliph Mutawakkil was very much interested in religious matters.

P. Lemerle rejects the existence of a Byzantine embassy in 855 because the Arabic sources speak only about the exchange of prisoners in 856, "de négotiations banales, et en quelque sorte de routine" which could be achieved by the Arab and Byzantine generals.[34] This is an exaggeration. The exchanges of prisoners were prepared mostly by Byzantine or Arab embassies. Let us mention only two important embassies from this period sent to prepare such exchanges.

In 845 Theodora sent an embassy to the Caliph Watiq carrying with them many presents and charged with the negotiations for an exchange of prisoners. Byzantine sources do not mention this embassy, but Tabari gives us detailed information about

---

29 H. Ahrweiler, *Sur la carrière de Photius avant son patriarcat,* Byz. Zeitschr. 58 (1965) 348—363.

30 F. Dvorník, *Byzantine Missions, op. cit.,* Appendix I, pp. 290—291.

31 P. Lemerle, *op. cit.,* p. 40.

32 *Ibid.,* pp. 185 ff. Cf. also short remarks on the *Lexicon* in my paper, *Patriarch Photius, Scholar and Statesman,* Classical Folia 14 (1960) pp. 3 ff.

33 F. Dvorník, *Byzantine Missions, op. cit.,* pp. 292 ff. Cf. also my short paper *Constantine-Cyril's religious discussion with the Arabs,* in: Studia Palaeoslovenica, Prague 1971, pp. 77—78.

34 Lemerle, *op. cit.,* p. 39.

the exchange which is corroborated by some other Arab writers. The exchange prepared by this embassy took place on the usual territory, on the river Lamos, from September 7, 845 to August 27, 846.[35]

An Arab embassy was sent to Michael III in 860, again having as its purpose an exchange of prisoners. Tabari gives us a picturesque account of this embassy.[36] The Arab ambassador was Nasr-ibn al-Azhar. He presented himself for the imperial audience in a black dress, and bearing his sword, dagger and turban. This was against Byzantine diplomatic etiquette. The Byzantines at first refused to admit him to the audience hall, but when he threatened to leave, Petronas, the Emperor's uncle, intervened, and Nasr was admitted to the imperial presence. Tabari's description of the events during this audience corresponds perfectly to Byzantine protocol. The Emperor Michael III was sitting on his throne, but did not pronounce one word during the whole audience. All conversation was carried on by the Emperor's uncle, Petronas through interpreters, the Emperor manifesting his consent or refusal by nodding or shaking his head.

I do not see any reason for denying that the exchange of prisoners arranged in 856 on the river Lamos was not prepared by an embassy sent by Michael III to Muttawakkil in 855. The exchange of prisoners was, of course, directed by generals appointed by both rulers. Anyhow, Ja'qubi speaks of Byzantine embassies which "the tyrant Greek" had sent with many presents to the Khalif in 845 and 856 to propose exchanges of prisoners.[37] If we take into consideration the change of government in Byzantium, an embassy sent to Samara at the end of 855 was the more needed.

---

[35] A. A. Vasiliev, *Byzance et les Arabes,* ed. by H. Grégoire and M. Canard, vol. I, Bruxelles 1935, pp. 199, 311.

[36] A. A. Vasiliev, *op. cit.,* vol. I, pp. 320, 321. I speak about the diplomatic relations between Byzantium and the Arabs in my book, *Origins of Intelligence Services* (chapter IV), in preparation.

[37] A. A. Vasiliev, *op. cit.,* vol. I, pp. 276, 277. Ja'qubi died at the end of the ninth century. Tabari (died 923) calls the imperial ambassador George (*ibid.,* p. 317, 318). The latter was only in charge of the exchanges.

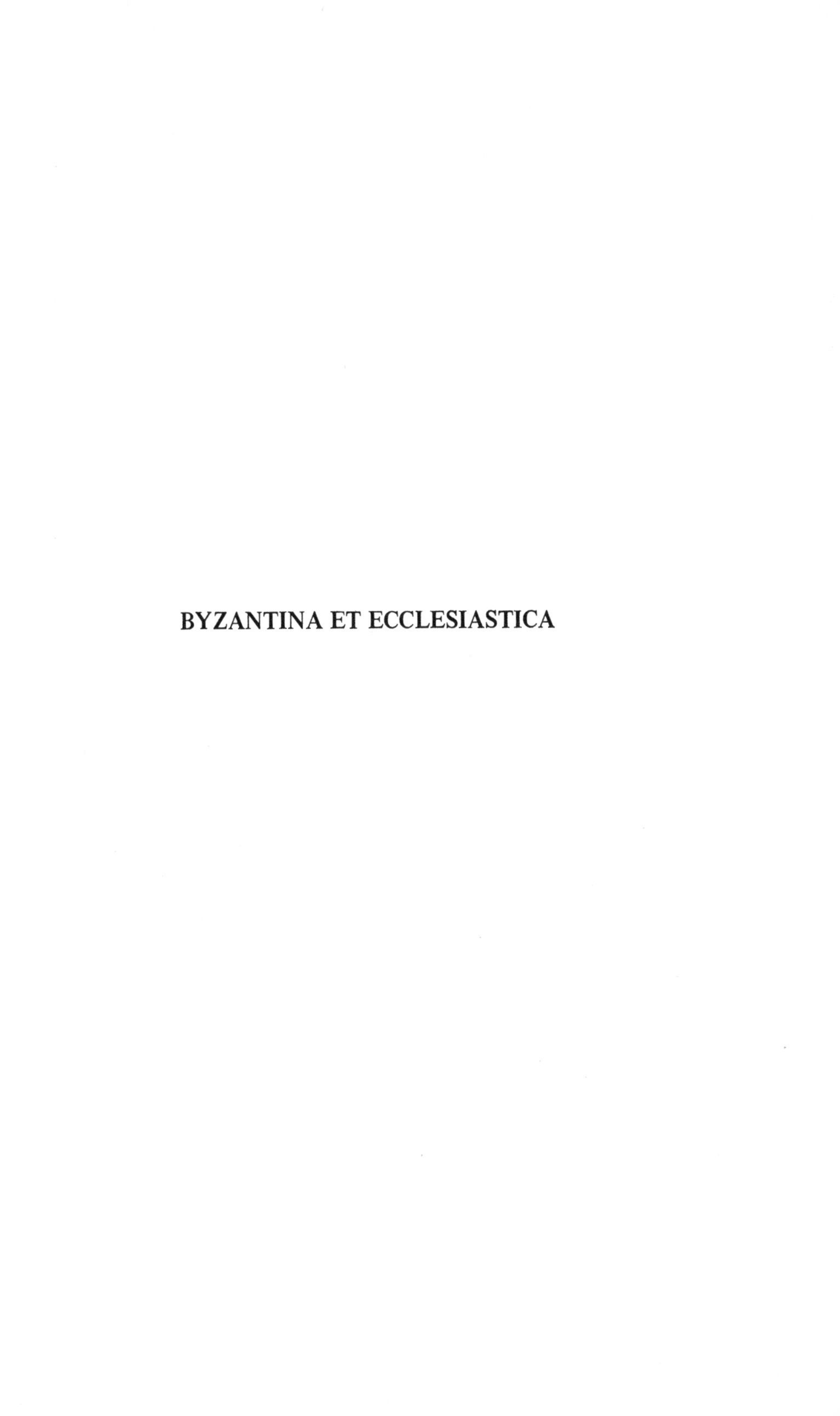

BYZANTINA ET ECCLESIASTICA

XI

QUOMODO INCREMENTUM INFLUXUS ORIENTALIS IN IMPERIO BYZANTINO S. VII.—IX. DISSENSIONEM INTER ECCLESIAM ROMANAM ET ORIENTALEM PROMOVERIT

Quaestionem unionis ecclesiarum orientalium cum Ecclesia Romana maximi esse momenti nemo est qui neget. Quam plurimi eruditi et pii christiani ad istum finem adlaborare hodierna die conantur. Non est dubium quin statum *actualem* ecclesiarum orientalium cognoscere necessarium sit, ut unio efficiatur; attamen studium *historiae et evolutionis* ecclesiarum orientalium non est negligendum. Nam omnes dissensiones inter Orientem et Occidentem in temporibus anterioribus radices habent, et solummodo justo studio historicae evolutionis Orientis christiani elucidari et removeri possunt.

Non est mirum, quod hucusque haud aliqui — praesertim catholici — ad has quaestiones animum eo modo, quo necesse fuit, adverterint. Studium Orientis christiani, speciali modo imperii byzantini nostris demum temporibus increvit. Sperandum est et catholicos eruditos viros postpositis aliquantulum quaestionibus litigiosis, quas protestantium invectiones in catholicos hucusque evocabant, omnes vires suas ad evolutionem primitivae Ecclesiae et ad historiam Orientis christiani investigandam consecraturos esse. Quo in studio etiam plurima invenienda sunt documenta, quibus apparebit, quam inanes sint assertiones theologorum protestantium quoad constitutionem Ecclesiae.

In evolutione Ecclesiae orientalis specialiter periodus, quae praecedit separationi, digna est, quae attentissime consideretur. Nonnisi hoc modo causas et originem separationis, quae eventibus posteriorum saeculorum definitiva evasit, cognoscere possumus. Quae cognitio prima conditio est in unione adlaboranda.

In lectione hac animos eruditorum ad unam quaestionem explorandam excitare in mente habemus, quae in schismatis evolutione magni nobis videtur esse momenti: Qualis nempe fuerit influxus orientalis in ecclesiam byzantinam saeculis septimo, octavo et nono. Quam orientalisationem e principalibus causis fuisse dissensionis inter Romam et Byzantium demonstrabimus.

I

Imperium byzantinum saeculis septimo, octavo et nono permultas calamitates perpessum est. Erant tempora illa turbulentissima et pro ulteriore evolutione imperii nec non totius ecclesiae maximi momenti. In sinu imperii fiebant permagnae mutationes, quas hisce verbis possumus exprimere: Antiquum imperium Romanum Orientale hisce temporibus factum est imperium Byzantinum. Centrum eius potestatis ex occidentalibus provinciis in orientales translatum est. Imperium non solum characterem latinum, quem Constantinus Magnus et successores eius usque ad Iustinianum imperatorem ei imponere volebant, definitive amisit, neque vero purum characterem graecum conservare poterat, quamvis maxima ex parte ex provinciis graecae linguae constabat. Elementis orientalibus tam profunde penetratum est, ut etiam culturam eius hoc tempore formatam et nono saeculo reflorescentem optimo iure non graecam, sed byzantinam dicere liceat.

Quaenam sunt causae tam magnae transformationis?

Causa primo-prima erat sic dicta *migratio populorum,* quae, uti notum est, antiquum imperium Romanum dislocavit. A saeculo quinto imperium Romanum Orientale quam maxime incursionibus barbarorum vexabatur. Post Hunnos Gothi, Langobardi, Avari et Slavi eius provincias invaserunt. Imperium Occidentale violentiis barbarorum non potuit resistere et periit. Imperium Orientale amisit quidem magnam partem provinciarum suarum, magnaque amaritudine affectum est, attamen existentiam suam retinuit.

Saeculum septimum certe difficillima periodus in historia imperii Orientalis appellari potest. Tempore enim hoc non multum abfuit, quin imperium interiret. Ex una parte Avari et Slavi omnes fere provincias Europae vastabant et ex altera parte Persae bellum Byzantio intulerunt imperium e medio tollere cupientes. Mirum est, quod imperium tot tantisque pugnis, quas cum barbaris gesserat, exhaustum periculum persicum avertere potuerit.

Persis ab imperatore Heraclio victis et Slavis Europae provincias adhuc occupantibus bellum cum Arabis exortum est. Periculum arabicum magis urgebat quam persicum. Erant enim Arabes praepotentes, in bello peritissimi, religioni suae musulmanicae addictissimi. Etiam intellectus cultura Arabes Byzantinis haud impares erant, nam artes et litterae apud eos tunc temporis florebant. Et revera, non tam facile erat Arabes vincere quam Persas. Quod supererat de provinciis africanis, Aegyptus, Palestina, Syria in manus Arabum inciderunt. In Asia Minore, in Syria in Sicilia et in Italia usque ad saeculum nonum Byzantini et Arabes sine intermissione bellis decertabant.

Frequens commercium cum populis orientalibus maximi factum est momenti pro ulteriore evolutione imperii. Prima consequentia eaque gravissima erat, quod populi orientales, praesertim Asiae Minoris, ab his temporibus in imperio praevalerent. Quanti momenti haec circumstantia fuerit, brevi tempore conspici potuit. Imperium in manus dynastiae Isaurianae sub Leone III. (a. 717) pervenit, quae usque ad saeculum nonum regnavit. Qua in periodo milites thematum orientalium, Asiae Minoris praepotentes permanebant. Saeculo nono ineunte eadem themata contra imperatores saepissime rebelantia efficiebant, ut Asia in imperio potentior fieret.[1] Etiam populatio constantinopolitana populis ex orientalibus provinciis venientibus miscebatur.

Scimus exempli gratia imperatorem Heraclium milites Armenos in Thraciam mittere consuevisse, Leonem III. ibidem a. 745 et 751 Syros misisse, Constantinum Copronymum a. 756 Syros et Armenos de urbe Melitenae Theodisiopolim transplantasse, Leonem Armenum Armenos in Thracia collocasse, Theophilum imperatorem 30.000 Persarum in diversis thematibus imperii sparsisse.[2] Etiam urbs Constantinopolis anno 747 peste vastata a Syris et Armenis repopulata erat. Toto hoc tempore permulti Asiatae et Armeni Constantinopolim emigrabant et saepe supremos magistratus non solum in rebus militaribus, sed etiam in rebus publicis et in Ecclesia occupaverunt. Ita Constantinopolis et provinciae urbi proximae purum characterem graecum amiserunt.

1 Quae praeponderantia thematum orientalium maxime in reorganisatione administrationis imperii videtur. Strategi thematum Asiae primum locum tenent. Themata Europae posteriori tempore oriuntur et minoris sunt momenti. Gelzer, Geschichte der byzant. Themenverfassung, Sitzungsbericht d. bayr. k. Ak. 1895, p. 64 sq. Bury, Administratory System of the byz. Empire, London, 1911, p. 64 sq.

2 Vide librum meum, Les Slaves, Byzance et Rome au IX. s., Paris, 1924, p. 68.

Iste influxus orientalis originem dedit controversiis de cultu imaginum. Origo istius orientalis haeresis non potest in dubium vocari. Nec dubitari potest, quin traditiones arabicae et semiticae progressum haeresis quam maxime foverint.[1]

Quanti momenti influxus Araborum in Byzantino imperio fuerit, saeculo nono in evolutione artis byzantinae lucidissime apparet. Imperator Theophilus ita admirabatur artes arabicas, ut novum palatium suum Brysae ad instar palatii chalifae bagdadensis construxerit.[2]

Etiam progressus scientiarum et litterarum hoc tempore Byzantii exemplo Bagdadi quam maxime promovebatur. Quod historia Leonis philosophi, Joannis Syncelli, necnon Photii et aliorum satis demonstrat.[3]

Hoc commercium cum Oriente maxime profuit imperio byzantino. Nullo alio modo explicari potest, quod artes et litterae Byzantii praesertim saeculo nono denuo florescere coeperint. Attamen in historia Byzantii elucidanda hi eventus historici non sunt negligendi. Nam influxus hic orientalis maioris erat momenti, quam primo visu intelligere possumus.

II

Illud incrementum influxus Orientis in imperio byzantino notissimum est. Necnon momentum istius evolutionis pro ulteriore imperii historia a rerum gestarum scriptoribus generaliter optime interpretatur. Attamen quomodo transformatio haec profundissima in Ecclesiam byzantinam penetraverit, non satis clare ab historicis usque in hodiernam diem dictum est. Quod quidem mirum est, nam omnibus patet res ecclesiasticas cum civilibus in imperio byzantino intime coniunctas fuisse.

Disputationes de cultu imaginum pugnam illam, quae gerebatur, ut statueretur, quinam animus in ecclesia byzantina praevaleret, orientalis an graecus, disertissime illustrant. Contra iconoclastas ex orientalibus provinciis provenientes populus graecus ex Europae provinciis cultum

1 Quoad historiam controversionis de cultu imaginum praesertim consulenda sunt opera: D. Schwartzlose, Der Bilderstreit, Gotha, 1890, et D. Brehier, La querelle des images, Paris, 1904, necnon D. G. Ostrogorski, Studien zur Geschichte des byzant. Bilderstreites, Breslau, 1929.

2 Ch. Diehl, Manuel d'art byzantin, Paris, 1927, I, p. 87 sq., 360 sq.

3 Bury, A history of the later Roman Empire, London, 1914, p. 434 sq. Confer quae Ostrogorski, l-c., p. 59 sq, de influxu orientali ss. VIII.—IX. dicit.

imaginum fortissime defendebat. Omnes revolutiones cultorum imaginum contra imperatores iconoclastas in provinciis graecis originem habuerunt. Graecia et Cyclades insulae contra Leonem III. insurgebant. Artavasdus, qui a. 741 contra Constantinum V. insurrexerat, in eisdem provinciis plurimos asseclas invenit, imperatrix Irena, restauratrix cultus imaginum post mortem Leonis IV. Chazaris, Atheniensis erat, Thomas Slavus, qui contra Michaelem II. rebellionem movit, etiam favorem iconodulorum praesertim e graecis provinciis provenientium quaerebat. Genius graecus quidem in pugna ista victor evasit, attamen victoria eius non tam perfecta erat, quam nonnulli dicunt. Ab hoc tempore vetitum est statuas sanctorum exculpere, quod concessionem indicat, quam genius graecus genio orientali facere coactus est. Quae concessio ab Ecclesia byzantina quasi consecrata ad oculos demonstrat, quam altus in Ecclesia fuerit influxus orientalis. Notandum est victoriam hanc Graecos non sine adiutorio Occidentis latini reportasse.

Altera consequentia incrementi influxus orientalis in Ecclesiam byzantinam a nobis nunc examinanda est. Ab initio imperator Byzantii summam potestatem non solum in rebus civilibus, sed etiam in rebus ecclesiasticis pro se exigebat. Nemo est, qui nesciat originem istius absolutae potestatis quam imperatores christiani ab imperatoribus paganis haereditaverunt, neque romanam neque graecam, sed orientalem esse. Qua de re plurimi et clarissimi viri sufficienter disseruerunt.[1]

Quae absolutae potestatis imperatoriae mens etiam in rebus theologicis saeculis septimo, nono et octavo profundiores radices jecit.

Tempora ista difficillima, in quibus patria maximis periculis jactabatur, exigebant, ut imperatores essent viri audaces, fortitudine eximii atque suprema auctoritate praediti. Nonnulli imperatores iconoclastici, imprimis Leo III. Isauricus et Constantinus V., maxima gloria militari excelluerunt, quod et eorum studium sese in res eclesiasticas ingerendi vehementissime augebat. Populus provinciarum orientalium facillime augmentum absolutae imperatorum potestatis, quos ad thronum provexerat, accipiebat. Ita evasit, ut ideologia ista, iam pridem generaliter accepta, tam firmiter mentibus Byzantinorum imprimeretur.

1 Vide imprimis librum, quem Gasquet scripsit: De l'autorité imperiale en matière religieuse à Byzance, Clermont-Ferrand, 1878; Buerlier, Les vestiges du culte impér. à Byzance et la querelle des iconoclastes (Congrès scient. inter. cath., Paris, 1891, p. 167 sq.); cf. Battifol-Brehier, Les survivances du culte imperiale romain, Paris, 1920.

Huic autem conceptioni Graeci orthodoxi magna ex parte inimici erant. Attamen eorum conatus Ecclesiae ab iugo imperatorum liberandae, ut quidam dicunt, non supra meritum sunt aestimandi. Nam omnes, etiam Studitae, maximi illi propugnatores libertatis ecclesiasticae, de facto interventionem imperatorum admittebant et reclamabant, si adiumento et saluti Ecclesiae inserviebat. Etiam hac in re videre possumus concessionem quandam, quam genius graecus genio orientali facere coactus erat. In hoc proelio neque imperatores neque regentes Ecclesiam tota victoria gloriari potuerunt. Post dissensiones iconoclasticas imperator quidem non ut ita dicamus iura Summi Pontificis appetit, sed etiam tacente Ecclesia quoddam „ius circa sacra" sibi reservat. Ab hoc tempore res publica et Ecclesia byzantina sibi amicitiores quam prioribus temporibus erant. Error est Ecclesiam perpetuam ancillam rei publicae byzantinae appellare. Ab hoc quidem tempore utraque in amicitia plerumque vivebat, iuvans altra alteram. Sed verum est imperatores numquam clero aliquam rem in administratione rei publicae gerere permisisse, ipsi autem in Ecclesia gerenda quaedam iura semper sibi usurpaverunt.[1] Ut posterius dicemus, evolutio relationum inter Ecclesiam romanam et principes occidentales haud eadem erat. Facillime ergo perspicitur quam grave momentum pro evolutione totius Ecclesiae haec res habuerit.

Liceat nobis unam consequentiam istius evolutionis Ecclesiae byzantinae adhuc ostendere. Victoria quam genius graecus in proelio cum iconoclastis orientalibus adeptus erat, incrementum ut ita dicamus nationalismi apud Byzantinos adiuvabat. Haec efferventia ita appellati nationalismi magni erat momenti in relationibus ulterioribus inter Latinos et Byzantinos.

Quod tertio sequitur ex illo augmento orientalis influxus in Ecclesia, longiore dignum est enarratione. Prouti dictum, evolutio illa provinciis orientalibus in imperio primatum dedit. Qui primatus etiam in rebus ecclesiasticis conspici potest. Nam provinciae occidentales, quae saeculis anterioribus tantopere desudaverant in vita Ecclesiae promovenda, a Slavis vastatae et occupatae his temporibus pro Ecclesia tam-

1 Qua de re doctissimus H. Gelzer optime scripsit. Vide praesertim quae de potestate imperatorum byzantinorum in scriptis suis *Byzantinische Kulturgeschichte,* Lipsiae, 1911 (caput „de re publica et monachis"), et Ausgewählte kleine Schriften, Tübingen, 1901 (caput „Kirche und Staat"), dixit.

quam mortuae erant. Plurimae sedes episcopales, quondam celeberrimae, episcopis orbatae erant. Et quae hierarchiam suam retinuerant, praeter maxima pericula et temporum pressuras quasi nullam partem in vita Ecclesiae habere potuerunt et per multos annos quasi absque commercio cum aliis Ecclesiis permanserunt. Quam tristis fuerit status religiosus harum provinciarum eo tempore, satis notum est. Hierarchia ecclesiastica latinarum Illyrici provinciarum, quae olim maximam partem in disputationibus arianisticis habebat, saeculo sexto et septimo totaliter evanuit. Ultimum vestigium religiosae harum provinciarum activitatis in actis synodi Gradensis, quae anno 579 ad quaestiones dogmaticas de Tribus Capitulis solvendas convocata est, invenimus. Nonnulli latini episcopi illyrici acta Synodae huius subscripserunt.[1]

Sed et graecae provinciae illyricae maiori ex parte sedium episcopalium orbatae evaserunt. *Dacia Ripensis* et *Dardania* omnes sedes episcopales amiserunt. *Moesia inferior* solummodo sedem odyssenam (Odyssos) usque ad saeculum nonum conservavisse videtur, attamen episcopus odyssenus nullibi in hac periodo nominatur. Eadem dici possunt de episcopo *Scythiae,* qui Tomis residebat. *Epirus Nova* de septem sedibus nonnisi duas retinuit et quidem Dyrrhachiensem et Aulonensem. *Epirus Vetus* etiam omnibus sedibus, duobus exceptis (Nicopolis et Corcyra) orbata erat. Neque usque ad saeculum nonum ullo loco fit mentio episcoporum *Thessaliae.* Provincia ecclesiastica *Macedoniae* - olim celeberrima his temporibus in ruinas redacta est, nam Slavi usque ad portas Thessalonicenses penetraverunt. Nec antiqua *Hellas* salva evasit. Slavi eam invadentes usque ad Pentedactylum pervenerunt et vitam religiosam tam in Achaia quam in Peloponneso magna ex parte decursu aliquot decenniorum extinxerunt. *Insula Crete vero,* quae etiam ad patriarchatum Romanum pertinebat, saeculo nono ineunte ditioni Arabum subiecta erat.

Rumor quidam earum tribulationum usque ad provincias pervenit, quae semper sub iurisdictione patriarchatus Constantinopolitani permanserant, et quidem in Thraciam, Haemimontum, Europam et Rhodopen.

Ita evenit, ut in vita Ecclesiae byzantinae hisce temporibus eparchiae asiaticae, sive orientales primatum tenerent. Quod maxime actibus conciliorum eo tempore in imperio byzantino habitorum illustratur.

1 Mansi, Concil. ampl. coll. X, 926.

Hac de causa laborem non parvum suscepimus acta conciliorum sexti (a. 680), quinisexti (a. 692), septimi (a. 787), octavi (870), photiani (879), examinandi, omnes episcopos ex Europae provinciis, qui illis conciliis intererant, invenire studentes. Ex provinciis graecis, illyricis, Dacia Ripensi, ex Dardania, Moesia inferiore et Scythia nullus episcopus illis conciliis interfuit. Ex *Epiro Nova* dyrrhachiensis episcopus ad concilium oecumenicum septimum anno 787 habitum, monachum Joannem, tamquam sui[1] locum tenentem misit. De Antonio Dyrrhachiensi etiam Theodorus Studita in una ex innumeris epistolis[2] suis loquitur. Episcopus Aulonae Soterus ad concilium oecumenicum septimum venisse videtur,[3] *Epirus Vetus* ad concilium VII. solummodo duos episcopos misit et quidem Anastasium Nicopolensem et Philippum Corcyrensem.[4]

Acta conciliorum saeculo septimo et octavo habitorum nullius episcopi provinciae *Thessaliae* mentionem faciunt. Saeculo nono Euthymius episcopus Larissae ad concilium octavum oecumenicum anno 870 apparuit.[5] Concilio Photiano (879) eius successor Basilius cum episcopis Dematriadeos, Scopelonis et Novar. Patrarum interfuit.[6]

In *Achaia* has sedes episcopales ante invasiones invenimus: Athenarum, Coroneae, Carysti, Naupacti, Orei in Euboea, Porthmi, Marathonis, Elateae, Megarae, Opuntis, Plataearum, Thebarum, Thespiarum, Tanagrae, Scarphiae, Chalcidis. In *Peloponneso*: Corinthii, quae metropolis erat totius Helladis, Patrarum Veterum, Argi, Megalopoleos, Lacedaemonis, Elidis, Tegeae, Messenensem, Aeginae, Methonensem, Boiarum et in insula Zacynthi. In conciliis a saeculo septimo usque ad saeculum nonum habitis hos solummodo praelatos Achaiae invenimus: In sexta synodo oecumenica Stephanum Corinthii, Joannem Athenarum, Joannem Argi, Theodosium Lacedaemonis.[7] Canones synodae quinisextae (Trullanae) anno 692 habitae nullus signavit. Acta synodi septimae (787) septem episcopi provinciae Helladis subscripserunt: Gabril Aeginae, Petrus Monembatiae, Antonius Troezenae, Leo Porthumi, Philetus Orei, pro episcopo Cephaloniae Gregorius presbyter, Leo Zacynthi.[8] Concilio generali octavo (870) sex solummodo: Niceta, metropolita Athenarum, Heraclius Corinthii, Marianus Thebarum,

1 Mansi, Conciliorum amplis. col. XII, 994; XIII, 936. 2 Theodori Stud. Epist. Libri II, Migne, P. G., vol. 99, col. 489 et sq. 3 Le Quien, Oriens Christianus, II, p. 253. 4 Mansi, XIII, 137; XIII, 145. 5 Mansi, XVI, 191. 6 Mansi, XVII, 373. 7 Mansi, XI, 641, 644, 645. 8 Mansi, XIII, 392.

Theoclitus Lacedaemonis, Nicephorus Zacynthi, nec non Theodorus Eurypi (Chalcidis).[1]

In synodo Photiana, anno 879 habita, Joannes Corinthii, Sabas Athenarum, Antonius Naupacti, Theophylactus Eurypi (Chalcidis), Sabas Patrarum, Leo Neopatrensis, Antonius Cephaloniae, Antonius Lacedaemonis, Damianus Ezeri (nova sedes pro Slavis).[2]

Etiam provincia *Macedoniae* his temporibus minimam partem in vita religiosa Byzantinae Ecclesiae habuit, nam a Slavis depopulata erat. De sexdecim episcopis (Thessalonica, Philippi, Berrhoea, Dios, Stobi, Parthicopolis, Doberus, Cassandria, Edessa, Heraclea, Amphipolis — Chrysopolis — Serrae, Bargala, Theorium, Lemnos, Thassos) solummodo sequentes in synodis saeculis septimo, octavo et nono habitis apparuerunt: In sexta synodo oecumenica (680) Joannes Thessalonicensis, Joannes Stobensium, Georgius Theorii.[3] In concilio quinisexto: Margarites Stoborum, Isidorus Edessae, Andreas Amphipoleos, Silvanus Lemni.[4] Inter subscriptiones canonum concilii septimi (787)[5] solummodo nomina Theophili Thessalonicensis et Joannis episcopi insulae Lemni legimus. Episcopi Amphipoleos Theodorus Studita in litteris suis una vice mentionem facit.[6] In synodo octava Theodorum Thessalonicensem, Josephum Berhaeae, Germanum Citri invenimus.[7] In photiana synodo[8] Theodorus Thessalonicensis, Nicolaus Philipporum, Joannes Chrysopolensis, Arsenius Lemnensis, Petrus Drugobitiae aderant. Sedes Drugobitiae nec non Moraviae, cuius episcopus Agathon etiam in Photiano concilio aderat, sunt novae fundationes pro populis slavicis in fidem christianam conversis.

Hoc de provinciis antiqui Illyrici, quod usque ad a. 732 ad patriarchatum Romanum pertinebat.

Videmus ex hoc schemate, quam minimus numerus praelatorum ex devastatis provinciis occidentalibus partem activam in evolutione Ecclesiae byzantinae hisce saeculis habuerit. Etiam praelati *ex Italia meridionali*, quae cum Sicilia ad imperium pertinebat, non valde numerosi erant in conciliis in hac periodo habitis. In sexto concilio Theodorus presbyter locum tenuit Theodori episcopi Ravennatis, Joannes Portuensis episcopus in persona aderat, Abundantius Tempsacae eccle-

1 Mansi, XVI, 191, 195. 2 Mansi, XVII, 373-377. 3 Mansi, XI, 645. 4 Mansi, XI, 993 sq. 5 Mansi, XIII, 133, 728. 6 S. Theodori Stud. Epistolae, Migne, P. G. vol. 99, col. 1073. 7 Mansi, XVI, 191, 199. 8 Mansi, XVII, 373.

siae et Joannes Rhegitanae ecclesiae tamquam legati romani signaverunt.[1]

Numerus praelatorum italicorum, praesertim ex Calabria et Siculorum concilio septimo (787) adstantium memorabilis est.[2] Haecce sunt nomina eorum: Epiphanius Catanae Siculorum, Constans Rhegii, Joannes Tauromenii, Galato presbyter, vicarius ep. Syracusarum, Gaudiosus Messinae, Theodorus Panorum, Stephanus Bibonis, Constans Leontinae, Theodorus Taurianae, Basilius Leparensium, Theotimus Crotonensium, Constans Carinae, Theophanes Silybaei, Theodorus Tropaeorum, Joannes Treocaleos, Sergius Nicoberensium. Quae circumstantia haud est parvi momenti: Scimus enim italicas provincias decreti imperatorum iconoclastium quam maxime restitisse. Quapropter tam numerosi praelati ex Italia Nicaeam venerunt, ut suis votis cultum imaginum defenderent.

Concilio octavo[3] solummodo Gregorium Messinae Demetrium Scyllatii, Leontinum Rhegii, Paulum Taurinae aderant. In photiana synodo[4] Leo Rhegii, Paulus Taurianae, Marcus Hydruntis, Demetrius Scylatii.

Insula Cretae, quae etiam ad patriarchatum occidentalem pertinebat, minoris mihi videtur esse momenti in nostra quaestione propter distantiam ab urbe Roma. Attamen etiam hic eamdem rem videmus sicut in participatione episcoporum italicorum in conciliis.

Synodae generali sextae solummodo duo episcopi astiterunt. Basilius Gortynae et Gregorius Cantani. Quinisextae quinque: Basilius Gortynae, Sisinnius Chersonesi Cretae, Joannes Lappae, Nicetas Cydoniae, Theopemptus[5] Cissami. Numerus praelatorum cretensium concilio septimo adstantium valde elevatus erat. Non minus quam undecim praelati cretenses accurrerunt, ut causam imaginum defenderent. Elias Gortynae, Anastasius Gnossi, Joannes Arcadiae, Epiphanius Lampae (Lappae), Theodorus Subritensium, Epiphanius Eleuthernae, Sisinnius Chersonesi, Leo Cissani, Photinus Cantani.[6]

Anastasius Gnossi a Theodoro Studita particulariter in una epistola propter zelum suum quoad cultum imaginum laudatur.[7] Notum est Cretam insulam circa a. 822 in manus Arabum incidisse. Synodae octa-

1 Mansi, XI, 641. 2 Mansi, XIII, 381, 384. 3 Mansi, XVI, 195. 4 Mansi, XVII, 373, 376. 5 Mansi XI, 642, 645, 989 sq. 6 Mansi, XIII, 381 sq. 7 Theodori Studitae Epistolae, Migne P. G., vol. 99, libr. I, ep. 11.

vae nemo ex insula Creta aderat et synodo Photianae solummodo Basilius Cretae, probabiliter episcopus Gortynensis. Haec observatio non est parvipendenda; testificatur enim, Irenam sollicitudinem summam adhibuisse in invitandis praelatis ad concilium Nicaenum II. idque esse prosecutam, ut praelati e provinciis occidentalibus, quae cultum imaginum magis fovebant, numerosissimi adparerent.

Quoad historiam iconoclasmi in Creta insula haec circumstantia magni est momenti. Quod etiam demonstrare videtur, traditiones occidentales in Creta insula longo tempore firmas permansisse. Basilius Gortynae in concilio sexto tamquam legatus apostolici throni Romae „Veteris", cum episcopo Thessalonicensi et Corinthio fungitur. In quinisexto concilio etiam functionem legati Romani — nescimus utrum iuste an iniuste — sibi usurpat. Notum est etiam ultimum actum iurisdictionis Papae Romani in antiquo Illyrico in insula Cretae locum habuisse. Papa Vitalianus a. 667 litem inter episcopum Lappae et Gortynae dirimit.[1]

Quaedam etiam de provinciis europaeis dicenda sunt, quae semper ad patriarchatum Constantinopolitanum pertinebant et quidem de provincia *Thraciae, Haemimontis, Europae et Rhodopeos.*

Ex *Thracia* et Europa conciliis, quae studio nostro submisimus, astiterunt sequentes praelati: Sexto concilio: Sisinnius Heracleae, Rheginus Panii, Sergius Salymbriae, Georgius Bizyae,[2] Leo Heracleae, Joannes Panii, Leonides Coeli, Melchisedech Galiopoleos, Joannes Afri, Sisinnius Chersonesi, Joannes Rhaedesti, Sisinnius Tzoruli, Cyriacus Dryziparae, Constans presbyter episcopi Lyzimachiae locum tenens, Benjaminus Lyzici, Theophylactus Chariopoleos, Michael Pamphyli, Thomas Daonii, Joannes Arcadiopoleos, Leonidas Madyti, Gregorius Euchaniae, Theodorus Byziae, Constantinus Metrensis, Sisinnius Chalcidis, Gregorius Delci, Constans Sebastopoleos, Joannes Nicopoleos, Sisinnius Garellensis, Joannes Decateri, Joannes Lithoprosopi, Theophanes Lebedi acta concilii septimi subscripserunt.[3]

Concilio octavo paucissimi praelati ex nostris provinciis aderant: Joannes Heracleae, Basilius Tzoruli, Michael Bizyae.[4] Synodo photia-

1 *Jaffé, Regesta pontificum Romanorum, I.* Confer, quae in Mélanges Ch. Diehl (Paris, 1930) de Illyrico dixit: La lutte entre Byzance et Rome autour de l'Illyricum au IXe siècle. 2 Mansi, XI, 673, 692. 3 Mansi, XIII, 141, 373 sq., 381 sq., 387 sq. 4 Mansi, XVI, 191 sq.

nae omnes fere astiterunt: Joannes Heraclea, Strategius Panii, Sabbas Apri, Nicolaus Rhaedesti, Methodius Lyzimachiae, Georgius Lizici, Cosmas Chariopoleos, Petrus Pamphyli, Clemens Daonii, Basilius Arcadiopoleos, Symeon Selymbriae, Constantinus Madyti, Joannes Euchaniae, Petrus Bizyae, Gregorius Metrensis, Nicolaus Philippopoleos, Neophytus Delci, Joannes Joannitzae, Symeon Leucae, Nicolaus Nicopoleos, Basilius Garellae.[1]

Eundem statum invenimus in provinciis ecclesiasticis Haemimontis et Rhodopeos. Etiam ex hisce provinciis perpauci episcopi synodae sextae et Trullanae aderant. In actis horum conciliorum solummodo nomina Petri et Mamali Mesembriae, Petri Sozopoleos et Georgii Aeni invenimus.[2] Ad cultum imaginum defendendum permulti Nicaeam venerunt: Emanuel Hadrianopoleos, Leo Mesembriae, Euthymius Sozopoleos cum oeconomo Leone, Eustratius Debelti, Georgius Plutinopoleos, Theodorus Bulgarophygi, Rubinus Scopeli, Joannes Brysensis, Gregorius, locum tenens episcopi Trajanopoleos, Theophylactus Cypseli, Eustathius Teni, Michael Pamphili.[3] Acta concilii octavi solummodo Cosmas Hadrianopoleos et Stephanus Cypseli subscripserunt.[4]

Photius tamen numerosissimos sectatores in eparchiis Haemimontis et Rhodopeos invenit: Philippum Hadrianopoleos, Timotheum Mesembriae, Ignatium Sozopoleos, Symeonem Debelti, Manuelem Probati, Constantinum Bulgarophygi, Bardanem Scopeli, Nicetam Brysensem, Joannem Bucelli, Nicolaum Anchiali, Nicephorum Trajanopoleos, Nicetam Maroneae, Tryphonem Topiri, Joannem Aeni, Marianum Anastasiopoleos, Nicephorum Pori.[5]

Subscriptiones horum conciliorum conferentes statuere possumus, numerum praelatorum orientalium in omnibus hisce conciliis multo maiorem fuisse numero episcoporum ex Europae provinciis provenientium. Quod ad oculos demonstrat, quantam partem provinciae orientales in evolutione Ecclesiae byzantinae hisce temporibus habuerint. Etiam ex sic dictis notitiis, quae sunt quaedam consignatio ecclesiarum

1 Mansi, XVII, 373 sq. 2 Mansi, XI, 673, 992. 3 Mansi, XIII, l. c. 4 Mansi, XVI, 673, 992. 5 Mansi, XVII, 373 sq. Vide, quae de fatis provinciarum ecclesiasticarum europeensium in libro meo, iam pridem citato (p. 74—99), dixi. Etiam ex hoc schemate, quod certe compleri posset, apparet, historiam organisationis ecclesiasticae imperii byzantini ad evolutionem Ecclesiae illustrandam maximi esse momenti.

Byzantio subditarum, videmus, eparchias orientales primum locum tenuisse.[1]

Acta concilii septimi sub Irena imperatrice (a. 787) habiti iterum atque iterum istam pugnam inter influxum orientalem et graecum in Ecclesia byzantina demonstrant. Maximus numerus episcoporum ex Europae regionibus provenientium, quorum nomina in sessionibus et subscriptionibus conciliorum saeculis septimo, octavo et nono habitis invenimus, leguntur in actis septimi concilii.

Maxime deplorandum est, quod pene omnes provinciae antiqui Illyrici, latinae et graecae a Slavis magna ex parte occupatae et vastatae, omnem suam hierarchiam amiserint et — quod praesertim de provinciis latinis illyricis dici potest — terrae missionum evaserint. Provinciae istae ad instar quorumdam mediatorum inter Occidentem Romanum et Byzantium fungi poterant. Revera Illyricum quasi quoddam medium inter Byzantium et Romam erat, quod et dissensionibus inter Romam et Byzantium oriundis mederi posset. In provinciis istis, quae olim ad patriarchatum Romanum pertinebant, quamquam a Byzantio attrahebantur, tamen certe traditiones occidentales fortiores erant, quam in aliis provinciis ecclesiasticis, quae semper ad Byzantium pertinebant. Haec provinciae nullam partem in vita Ecclesiae hisce temporibus gravissimis habere potuerunt. Nullus ergo mediator inter Romam et Byzantium aderat. Quod pro ulteriori evolutione totius Ecclesiae maximi erat momenti.

III

Quae cum in Oriente ita se haberent, historia Ecclesiae occidentalis latinae modo prorsus differenti evolvebatur. Romano imperio occidentali destructo Ecclesia cum Pontifice suo Romano sola tamquam haeres imperii populis barbaris terras imperii devastantibus sese opposuit. Quos et auctoritate sua morali sibi subiecit et ad fidem christianam convertit. Ast non solam fidem, sed etiam litteras et artes Romanas, quas a perditione servaverat, conversis populis tradidit. Papa Romanus omni iure igitur pater et protector istarum nationum appellabatur, quippe quae omnia ab eo acceperant. Ecclesia occidentalis autem in rebus sive intellectus sive litterarum et artium ab illis nationibus nihil accipere poterat.

1 Parthey, Hieroclis Synecdemus et notitiae episcopatuum, Berlin, 1866.

Genius latinus, quem Ecclesia Romana conservabat, in commercio intimo cum barbaris nonnisi aliquid de puritate sua amittere poterat. Cum tempora turbida commercium cum Oriente in rebus intellectus minime promoverant, genius Ecclesiae latinae magis magisque a graeco discedebat. Mutatio, quae in Byzantio efficiebatur, a Latinis non intelligebatur. Illyrico destructo nullus mediator inter Romam latinam et Byzantium graeco-orientale aderat. Neque Italia meridionalis sub ditione imperii byzantini officio mediatoris fungi poterat, nam brevi tempore sub Arabum potestatem ex parte redacta est. Saeculo nono Arabes usque ad portas Romae appropinquabant. Scimus, quam salutares evolutioni artium et litterarum tempore sic dictae regenerationis carolinae, impulsus quidam fuerint, quos monachi graeci tempore iconoclasticae haeresis apportaverant et qui ex Italia byzantina usque in Occidentem penetraverint. Quod tamen non sufficiebat, ut Occidentales genium byzantinum comprehenderent.

Romani Pontificem suum supremam auctoritatem non solum in rebus Ecclesiasticis exercentem, sed etiam saepissime regibus et principibus imperantem videre consueti, praesumptiones imperatorum byzantinorum maxima cum aversione perhorescere debebant. Brevi tempore Occidens latinus et Oriens graecus quasi penitus sibimet alieni exstiterunt.

Talibus sub auspiciis pacifica cooperatio utriusque Ecclesiae haud possibilis erat. Res ad schisma evolvebantur.

Ex iis, quae diximus patet, haud omnes quaestiones, quae cum origine schismatis connectuntur, sufficienter elucidatas esse. Schisma Ecclesiarum non solummodo duobus vel tribus personis imputari potest. Longa evolutione origo schismatis praeparabatur. Quanto profundius causas schismatis intelligere studemus, eo magis nobis persuasum erit, evolutionem Ecclesiae orientalis cum maximo amore christiano esse examinandam.

XII

National Churches
and
The Church Universal

TABLE OF CONTENTS

FOREWORD

I am indebted for the subject of the present study to the Anglican Society for Promoting Catholic Unity, whose President, the Rev. W. R. Corbould, did me the honour of asking me to read a paper on National Churches and the Church Universal to a meeting of the Society held on September 18th, 1943. As the lecture aroused a certain amount of interest, I considerably enlarged it when invited by the Newman Association to give its members and guests three lectures on the same subject in November of the same year.[1] It was not my first intention to issue the three lectures in pamphlet form and only the interest which the study aroused among Catholics, Anglicans and Orthodox induced me to act on the suggestion of my friends and make it accessible to a wider public. But it is not without hesitation that I am doing so, as I should know better than anybody how impossible it is to do justice in so short a survey to a subject that raises contiguous problems of the most complex nature. But adequate information is so difficult to find that perhaps even so short a study will be found to justify itself as an introduction to more careful and extensive research.

This dearth of information, however, does not mean that the question of the National Churches and of the universal element in Christianity has not attracted considerable attention, especially among religious thinkers. The rise of national feelings at the present period was bound to provoke a corresponding urge in the religious field, to which were due a number of recent attempts at co-ordinating the rising wave of nationalism with religious needs and founding new religious bodies on a purely national basis. To a certain extent they all failed, because those national movements were mostly initiated and often inspired by anti-Catholic motives or religious indifference from which the faithful reacted instinctively by stressing the bonds that unite the different Christian nations in common faith and leadership in defence of their menaced inheritance.

Although excesses to which the straining of the national idea has driven mankind at the present day and the common danger facing Christianity as a body in the spread of Godless and anti-Christian doctrines have intensified the desire for a

[1] These lectures were published in the *Eastern Churches Quarterly*, Vol. v, July-December, 1943, Nos. 7 and 8, pp. 172-219.

rapprochement between the various Christian bodies and revealed the strength which the notion of universality would lend the Christians in their stand against Godless materialism, national sentiment is not likely ever to be relegated to the background; so we may as well face the problem squarely and try to take its measure by sincerely studying the problem of universality in the evolution of Christianity.

It was the above consideration that decided us to study this vital problem and to place a few results of our research before the public. What we are presenting in this booklet is of course far from complete and is no more than an attempt to reveal but a few aspects of the problem. Unfortunately, present-day difficulties, war restrictions and the paper shortage have prevented us completing it to our own satisfaction and it was only for the purpose of showing the vitality and importance of these problems and of stimulating their study that we have re-issued unaltered, with the kind permission of the editor, the Rev. B. Winslow, O.S.B., the lectures as they were published in the *Eastern Churches Quarterly*. The bibliography inserted in the Appendix, far from being exhaustive, is only intended to furnish any reader who may wish to go into the matter more fully with an introduction to some of the work which has recently been done upon it by Continental scholars.

London, May 1944.

NATIONAL CHURCHES AND THE CHURCH UNIVERSAL

THE problem of the National Churches in their relation to the Church Universal has always bristled with many serious difficulties, not merely because so few students have dared to touch it, but also because the notion of a National Church too often evokes in the western mind the illusory picture of the multiplicity of churches, denominations and sects that spread over Western Europe and the New World as the result of the Protestant Reformation. Such an impression is only too apt to tempt one to look for a solution in and around the period of the Reformation or at later stages of Christianity, whilst the root of the matter lies much deeper beneath the surface and further back in time. It is a wrong scent that leads nowhere.

As a matter of fact, the problem of nationality and universality in the Church is as old as Christendom and the whole evolution of Christianity down to our own days is characterised by repeated attempts, more or less successful, at discovering the right balance between the national and the universal elements present in the Church founded by Jesus Christ. To reach the roots of the problem, we must go back to the early days of Christianity and follow its growth in the Christian East and throughout the medieval history of the Western Church, but with special emphasis on the Christian East, since it is the Eastern Churches that have best preserved some features of early Christianity. Along such lines lies the best method for understanding the growth of Western Christianity, and its great crisis at the Reformation period, as well as for discovering the secret that will straighten out the many misunderstandings, and bring about the rapprochement between the Churches.

The problem presents many aspects and can be approached from different angles. We intend to limit our short study to the historical aspect of our problem and to leave aside completely the dogmatic and theological issues involved. There is a growing conviction that we have far too often neglected the historical method and insisted too heavily on the dogmatic and theological side of the many problems that keep the Churches apart. Research into a number of questions that require an answer before any real rapprochement can be effected has so far vindicated the historical method. I tried it on a great problem which separates the Eastern and the Western Churches, the difficult case of the Patriarch Photius, and the result has been so encouraging, as will presently be explained, that there is good hope that the same issue will in the near future cease to form an obstacle to mutual understanding. Let us then try the method in the examination of the difficult subject of National Churches and the Church Universal and watch its results.

* *
*

I

National Churches of the East in Relation to the Church Universal

The Christian Mission of the Persian Empire—Expansion of Persian Christianity—Organization of the Persian National Church—The National Churches of Armenia and Abyssinia—General Synods—Bond with the Church Universal

It is not surprising that to many Catholics it sounds odd to-day to speak of National Churches. Centuries of evolution have so built up our mentality that we can only look at the Church of Christ from its universal angle, as an organism embodying the whole of humanity, and stress the necessity for unity and universality, to the point of often confusing universality with uniformity in every aspect whether essential or not. It is thus quite understandable that to people embarrassed with such a mentality the idea of a National Church should seem irreconcilable with the definition of an Universal Church.

Yet the truth is that the very same notion that sounds so shocking to many good Christians of our day had no terror for the early Christians. Christianity took its rise in an Eastern province of the Roman Empire, not far from its

Eastern frontier, whence it could not only spread to other Roman provinces, but also cross the *limes* towards the East and the South, a geographical advantage we generally overlook, wont as we are to look, with the early Fathers, upon the Roman Empire as a political formation chosen by Providence to spread the Christian faith over the civilised world at that time. This is true enough, but the world was a trifle bigger, even at that time, than the Roman Empire, and there were many great nations, with lofty cultural traditions, thriving outside the *limes Romanus* and destined, as things turned out, to remain outside for ever; and since the Saviour redeemed the whole world, these nations, too, from the Euphrates and the Persian Gulf to India, in the interior of Asia, in the Far East, and to the South as far as Africa, had to be converted. If we look at it from this angle, we must confess that not only did the formation of the Roman Empire prove a providential factor in the spread of Christianity, but also the circumstance that its cradle stood in Palestine, near the frontier, and faced the nations and the countries to the East.

And Christianity did spread from its Eastern birthplace to Eastern nations and empires outside the *limes*. We are apt to forget that there existed in the East another Empire, one destined to become in time a formidable rival of the Romans, Persia. Christianity penetrated into Persia or Iran *via* Edessa, which in the first century was still the capital of an autonomous State under Roman supremacy, though it was to be incorporated into the Empire two centuries later. As the same language—Syriac—was spoken on both sides of the Romano-Persian frontier, Christianity spread from Edessa first along the Tigris and thence into Chaldea and other parts of the Persian Empire. The Parthian kings did not interfere with its diffusion and their Persian successors after A.D. 226 spontaneously offered asylum to Christians seeking refuge in Persia from persecution in the Roman Empire. Not until war broke out between the Romans and the Persians in 340 did the Christians come under public suspicion, as was only to be expected, and a bloody persecution was let loose under Sapor II. It seems none the less true that the Christian religion was treated with tolerance throughout the period of the Sassanid kings and that, even when persecution was at its worst, Christian worship was freely carried on in some provinces. In Persia, persecutions never assumed the character of a general imperial policy as in the Roman Empire, being mostly directed against the leaders only, provoked by political incidents, or embittered by the Persian Christians' fellow-feeling for the Romans—who, from the days of Constantine the Great, had looked upon Christianity as the official State religion—and by the jealousies of the Mazdaite priests.[1]

Of special interest is the way the Persian authorities dealt with the Persian followers of the national religion of Zoroaster when they embraced Christianity. It is generally assumed that every sort of propaganda among the Persian Mazdaites was forbidden, apostasy from the national religion being punished by death ; that therefore the Christians in Persia were recruited only from among pagans, Jews, Manichaeans and other sects. But it appears that in practice, only priests ranking high in the Zoroastrian religion and members of the royal family or of the high aristocracy were liable to the death sentence on becoming Christians, while many cases are quoted of notable Persians leaving the Mazdaite religion and joining the Christian faith without any interference. In their case, the law was therefore not rigorously pressed.[2]. It thus came about that Christianity penetrated from the Syriac provinces of the Persian Empire into Persia proper and that many Christian communities existed in Media and Persis as early as the fourth century. These could only consist of Persian converts from Zoroastrianism. The position considerably improved in the following century when Persia made peace with Byzantium, the successor of Rome.

The Persian Church dug itself in and expanded its organisation by the erection of numerous episcopal sees. The bishop of Seleucia-Ctesiphon—the city that later became the royal residence—started early to claim a certain ascendancy over other sees, not without encountering vigorous opposition, as the primitive organisation of the Persian Church was very loose and could not, owing to geographical difficulties and to persecution, develop as fast as the Church in the Roman Empire.

Papa Bar Aggai was the first bishop of Seleucia-Ctesiphon to succeed, from 315 onward, in asserting his authority over all the bishops of Persia for all practical purposes. He must have been influenced by the example of the great patriarchal sees in the Roman Empire, since we find that the Greek

[1] Important and interesting details concerning persecution of Christians in Persia are given in the work of G. Hoffmann, *Auszuege aus Syrischen Akten Persischer Maertyrer*, Leipzig, 1880, Abhandlungen fuer die Kunde des Morgenlandes, VII, 3.

[2] For ampler details cfr. E. Sachau, *Von den Rechtlichen Verhältnissen der Christen im Sassanidenreich*, *Mitteilungen des Seminars für orientalische Sprachen zu Berlin*, 2 Abs. Westasiatische Studien, 1907, pp. 72 sq. Cfr. also E. Sachau, *Die Chronik von Arbela, Ein Beitrag für Kenntnis des ältesten Christentums im Orient.* Abhandlungen of the Prussian Academy, Berlin, 1915.

administrative organisation, as it had developed in the Roman Empire, had been introduced into Persia ; and what eventually stabilised the position of the bishop of Seleucia-Ctesiphon was the famous synod of the Persian Church which met at Seleucia in 410, when the Primate of Persia adopted the title of Katholikos.

From that moment the Persian Church entered upon a period of wide expansion ; not only did the Syriac countries of Assyria, Chaldea and Kurdistan become entirely Christian, but Christianity found itself at home in the most remote provinces, whence it spread to the south-east, the north-east and into Arabia. It is one of the most glorious chapters in the history of Christianity, which has remained closed to so many for no other reason but that its glories are so distant. At the beginning of the fifth century, Christianity had penetrated into the northernmost provinces of the Persian Empire, Gurzan and Arran, and Christian bishoprics were established on the south-east coast of the Caspian Sea. Parthia had its own bishops and the Merw Oasis sent prelates to every Persian Council held between 424 and 584. Later, in the seventh century, a bishop of Merw, Elias, made his reputation as a successful missionary among the Turkish tribes. In the fifth century, Christianity penetrated as far as north-western and western Afghanistan with the normal complement of bishops and in 544 we come across a bishop in the south-west of that country.

From the Persian Gulf the Gospel reached the Island of Socotra. The famous Cosmas Indikopleustes (520–525) who in the account of his travels gives us valuable information about distant countries, expressly states that the Christians of Socotra were getting their priests from Persis, i.e. from Persia proper, not from the Syriac provinces. References to the spread of Christianity to India can be traced in Persian chronicles as far back as A.D. 300 and one Persian chronicle records a lively intercourse between Persian and Indian Christians at the end of the fifth century. Traces of the Persian Church's early activities can also be found in Ceylon. The Arabian peninsula likewise came under the influence of the Persian Church as early as A.D. 420. From Afghanistan there ran a direct road through the interior of Asia into Mongolia and China, and there exists evidence of early Christian penetration into Baktra on the Oxus and of the later activities in Smarkan and China of Nestorian monks hailing from Persia.

This rapid survey should help us to visualise the immense possibilities that opened to the Persian Christians and of which we may assume they were fully aware at the period of their orthodoxy. Before the Persian Church adopted the Nestorian dogma at the Council of 486, it looked as though the Gospel would be broadcast over the whole East from the Persian Empire as it was about to be broadcast from the Roman Empire over the West, and this mission to the Eastern world was assigned to the lands lying between the Euphrates, the Persian Gulf, the Caspian Sea and the highlands of Afghanistan and Baluchistan as the main centre of radiation towards the interior of Asia, India and across the seas to the Far East. But the memory of this historical mission was obliterated by the Arab, and later, the Mongol and Turkish onslaught on what was once a flourishing Empire, which then sank back into the condition of a province and was put in the shade by the mighty Ottoman Empire. It is only recently, since the fall of the Ottoman Empire, that we have begun to realise the importance of the Iranian Plateau, as commanding the cross roads between the West and the East, to India, the Caspian Sea and to Mongolia. Christianity had realised it as early as the fifth century and was making ready to take full advantage of it.

* *
*

What were then the main features of Persian Christianity? Here it is important to note that the Persian Church formed in no way part of the Church as established on Roman territory. The hostility which for centuries divided the two Empires made it absolutely necessary for the Christians of the Persian Empire to build up their own independent ecclesiastical organisation and to foster as little contact as possible with the Christian Churches of the Roman Empire. This made the Persian Church a sort of National Church over which the bishop of Seleucia-Ctesiphon wielded well-nigh unlimited

[1] Cfr. L. Duchesne, *Autonomies Ecclésiastiques, Eglises Separées*, Paris, 1896, pp. 19 sq.; A. Harnack, *The Expansion of Christianity in the First Three Centuries* (translation by I. Moffat), London, 1905, pp. 292 sq.; I. Labourt, *Le Christianisme dans l'Empire Perse*, Paris, 1904, pp. 15 sq.; A. Fortescue, *The Lesser Eastern Churches*, London, 1913, pp. 38 sq. But the best information on the spread of Christianity in Persia and in Asia is to be found in an important study by E. Sachau, *Zur Ausbreitung des Christentums in Asien*, Abhandlungen der Preuss. Akademie der Wissenschaften, Berlin, 1919, pp. 62 sq. In the most recent publication on this period of Persian history—A. Christensen, *L'Iran sous les Sassanides*, Copenhague, 1936—a special chapter is reserved to the development of Christianity in Persia (pp. 253–310: "Les Chrétiens d'Iran"). Cf. also A. Mingana, *The Early Spread of Christianity in Central Asia and the Far East*, Manchester, 1925; *The Early Spread of Christianity in India*, Manchester, 1926 (The Bulletin of the John Rylands Library, vol. 9, 10).

authority. It adopted, none the less, the Church organisation as it had grown up in Roman Christianity, complete with patriarchs, metropolitans and bishops, ruling from definite sees over carefully delimited dioceses as the necessary framework to carry on its mission to the East. This organisation the Persian Church owed to the assistance of Marutha, bishop of Maiferkat, between the Tigris and Lake Van, who went to Persia as the ambassador of Theodosius II and represented the "Western Fathers" at the synod of 410. Seleucia-Ctesiphon had all the makings of a patriarchate for Persia and for the communities that were to spring from the Persian missions. It should be remembered that a similar development took place in the Roman Empire of the East, where the bishop of the capital, Constantinople, gradually gathered into his hands extraordinary powers and rose to be a Patriarch, to become in later centuries the head of the Christian Churches founded by his missionaries among neighbouring nations; and such he remained as long as those Churches—we have chiefly in mind Bulgarian, Serbian and Rumanian Christianity—remained without their own patriarchates. No doubt, the Persian Church and her foundations would have evolved along similar lines.

And yet the sense of unity was very much alive and more than once in the first period of Persian Church History found adequate expression. It was certainly conscious of its old connection with Edessa and Antioch, so much so that in 315 Papa Bar Aggai considered it necessary to reduce opposition to his authority by appealing to the "Western Fathers," the Patriarch of Antioch and the metropolitan of Edessa, and to their decision the Persian Church submitted. Letters from the "Western Fathers" were even read at the opening of the synod of 410, and Harnack[1] admits that a bishop of Persia attended the first Council of Nicaea, though there are serious doubts as to the identity of this bishop and his Persian origin is questionable[2]. But the Persian Church accepted the decisions of Nicaea in 410 and ten years later another synod of the Persian Church accepted the canons of some other Western synods. She even admitted into her legislation some decrees on religious matters issued by the Roman Emperors.

But in all other things, the Persian Church followed the

[1] L.c., pp. 297 sq. Harnack is of opinion that he was the bishop of Kerkuk or Arabela, but not of Seleucia.

[2] I. Labourt, l.c., p. 32, is of opinion that the name of "John of Beit-Parsaya," found in some Syriac lists of the Fathers of the Council, was incorrectly copied and should be read as John of Perrhae.

direction of her own growth. The works of her greatest Father, Afrahat, or Aphraates, written in the first half of the fourth century,[1] reveal a mentality all its own, Christian no doubt, yet Syriac and Persian for all that, and unaffected by the course of Greek Christianity. In 424 the Persian Church took an important step when a new Persian synod decreed that thereafter there would be no appeal from the judgement of the Katholikos to the Western Fathers, the metropolitan of Edessa and the Patriarch of Antioch: "Easterners shall not complain of their own Patriarch to the Western Patriarchs; any case that cannot be settled by him shall await the tribunal of Christ."[2]

The above decision has often been construed into an expression of the Persian Church's schism in disguise, but the verdict is rash; we should rather read the decision as the manifestation of the natural desire of every National Church to be independent of other Churches, which in its eyes are also national. There was a general tendency all over the East for every Church to be autocephalous: the Armenian Church was a second case in point, and even within the Roman Empire, the Church of Cyprus built up its own organisation and became independent of other Patriarchates. Such a tendency was on a fair way to grow into the common feature of Christianity outside the *limes Romanus*. At the same time, we should remember that the Persian decree was to a large extent influenced by the desire to allay the distrust with which the Persian kings watched their Christians' intercourse with their fellow-Christians of the Roman Empire and thereby to forestall any unpleasantness.

This development of the Persian Church has been so persistently neglected, because that institution fell to pieces before it reached maturity and left only ruins for remembrance, but in the fourth and fifth centuries the position in Persia was not as hopeless as it is to-day. That Church, on the contrary, bid fair to become the centre of a powerful and zealous Christianity and the Persian Empire to serve as the instrument of Providence for the spread of Christianity towards the East. One point merits special attention—the fact that the Persian kings were not Christians, but that, though the Churches in Persia never enjoyed the position and the privileges of a State religion, this in no way prejudiced the development of Persian Christianity and its spread to the East; on the contrary,

[1] Cfr. O. Bardenhewer, *Geschichte der Altkirchlichen Literatur*, Freiburg, i.B., 1924, v. IV, pp. 327–342.

[2] Chabot, *Synodicon Orientale*, Notices et Extraits des MSS. de la Bibl. Nationale et autres Bibliothèques, Paris, 1902, vol. 37, p. 51, 296.

such dissociation between Church and State would have benefited the whole of Christendom, as the Persian example could have shown that the Church needs no privileges to fulfil its mission. The Church in the Persian Empire would have had all the characteristics of a National Church without the dangerous entanglements which a State Church could scarcely avoid.

Christianity needed such an experience. Unfortunately, as, after Constantine the Great, Christianity blossomed into a State religion with unrivalled privileges, a pattern and a rule was set for all new Christian formations to follow in East and West, and we realise only too well to-day that the position was not an unmixed blessing for the Church. It is only in modern times that in many countries the Church has had to adapt herself to a situation with which the Christians in Persia were already familiar and has found the readjustment none too easy after acting for centuries as the State's associate in return for that hard taskmaster's support.

And Christianity would have triumphed even in Persia. From what we know of its position, we may presume that Mazdaism, Persia's national religion, would have shared, after a few centuries, the fate of Roman paganism. The royal house of Persia might also have had its Constantine, but not until the Church had gathered sufficient strength to maintain her independence in religious matters and felt safe against the dangers of "a Christ-loving King" who considered it his God-appointed task to propagate the true faith, as was the case in Byzantium during the reigns of Constantine's successors. Instead, the Church of Persia contented herself for the time being with a certain *modus vivendi* with the State authorities and, when persecution had ceased, she gladly left, as a tacit concession and an unwritten rule of practical procedure, the nomination of the Katholikos of Seleucia-Ctesiphon to the discretion of the Persian kings.

* *
*

Another National Church came into existence about the same time in the neighbourhood of the Persian and Roman Empires, the Church of Armenia. The evangelisation of Armenia is one of the most thrilling episodes in early Church history. Traces of Christianity are to be found west of the Euphrates dating from A.D. 200, the faith having come to the Armenians from Edessa and Caesarea in Cappadocia, when through the zeal of Armenia's greatest missionary and

Church founder, Gregory the Illuminator, the whole country east of the Euphrates, Armenia Major, with the king at its head, was Christianised. Armenia was thus the first country to have a Christian ruler, well before the conversion of Constantine the Great. Though in its initial stage the liturgical language was Syriac and Greek, Armenian Christianity developed from the start its own distinctive features. The dignity of Katholikos was hereditary and passed on to Gregory's descendants; the bishops were married, at any rate at the outset, and their functions were hereditary; the Katholikos was consecrated by the Metropolitan of Caesarea until in St. Basil's time (379) the tendency prevailed in Armenia to shake itself free of Caesarea, when the Katholikos was consecrated by his suffragans. The National Church of Armenia thus reached its manhood and the introduction of an Armenian liturgy by Sahak and Mesrob at the beginning of the fifth century brought it to final maturity.

When about 440 the Armenian State collapsed, the Armenian Church had a sufficient reserve of strength to survive and to protect its faithful, and whilst the Armenian kingdom was divided between the Empires of the Romans and the Persians, Armenian Christianity successfully withstood every effort to divide it between the jurisdictions of the Byzantine and Persian Churches. The Armenian bishops refused to join either the Patriarch of Constantinople or the Katholikos of Ctesiphon and remained grouped around their own Katholikos; and with a reasonable attitude of tolerance on the part of the other Churches, the Armenian Church continued to develop along strictly national lines.

It is somehow remarkable that the Greek colonies scattered over the Roman part of Armenia refused to mix with the native Church and were provided by the Mother Church with their own Greek bishoprics, as was the case with Theodosiopolis (Erzerum), which was made subject to the metropolitan of Caesarea, whereas in the Persian part of Armenia, Syriac bishoprics were made subject to the Katholikos of Persia[1]. The Armenian Church indeed grew to be so national that neither the Greeks nor the Arameans settled in the very

1 We find a Greek bishopric of Theodosiopolis under the metropolis of Caesarea in the oldest list of bishoprics attributed to St. Epiphanios and drawn up in the seventh century (H. Gelzer, *Texte der Notitiae Episcopatuum,* Abhandlungen of the Bavarian Academy, Classe Phil., Munich, 1901, Vol. 21, p. 536. Cfr. the List of Leo the Wise, *ibid.*, p. 551). The list only reveals a state of things of old standing. Armenia figures in 420 among the countries over which the Katholikos exercised his jurisdiction and bishops of Armenia attended the Persian synods of 424 and 486 (E. Sachau, *Zur Ausbreitung des Christentums in Asien,* l. c., p. 62).

midst of the Armenian population felt themselves at home in Armenian churches and had Greek and Syriac churches built for their own use. This is a curious case of particularism which so far has not been appreciated by Church historians at its full value.[1]

A third National Church came into existence, as we all know, in Abyssinia. Its first mission hailed from Constantinople, but later the Patriarchs of Alexandria, beginning with the great Athanasius, got the country under their complete control. Though the Syriacs kept jealous watch over their rights in Abyssinia and never allowed the Church to wriggle out of their tutelage, they still contributed to its nationalisation, when the Coptic monks translated the Bible into the national language. The national character of the Abyssinian Church became paramount at the beginning of the sixth century when the ruler of Abyssinia became a Christian and Christianity became the official religion of the State.[2]

* *
*

Now, there exists a general tendency to belittle the interest of this evolution by writing all those Churches off as heretical and by attributing their national character and their distinctiveness to heresy, forgetting that in those countries Christianity grew into national Churches long before Nestorianism and Monophysitism had swept over them. The Persians, the Armenians and the Abyssinians received a perfectly orthodox brand of Christianity and grew devotedly attached to it. Moreover, the bloodiest persecutions that stained early Christian history fell not upon Roman, but on Persian Christianity, the very same that had allotted such a place to the national element. This is important, for it proves that Christianity, for all its universal and supra-national character, is not averse to nationality and that even in the Church Universal, there is elbow room and scope for the national idiosyncracies of every nation.

One should also emphasise that in spite of their national character, the Churches outside the *limes Romanus* retained

[1] Cfr. on Armenian Christianity, L. Duchesne, l.c., pp. 26 sq. ; A. Harnack, l.c., pp. 342 sq. ; Fortescue, l.c., pp. 396 sq. ; F. Tournebize, *Histoire Politique et Religieuse de l'Arménie*, Paris, 1910 ; H. Gelzer, *Die Anfänge der Armenischen Kirche*, Berichte of the Saxon Royal Academy, Classe Phil. Hist., Vol. 47, 1895, pp. 109–174 ; T. Markwart, *Die Entstehung der Armenischen Bistümer*, *Orientalia Christiana*, No. 80, Rome, 1930.

[2] Cfr. E. A. Wallis Budge, *A History of Ethiopia, Nubia and Abyssinia*, London, 1928.

a vivid consciousness of a common interest with the rest of Christendom. All were united in the same faith and the ties of common origin with the Churches in the Roman Empire encouraged intercourse, as far as linguistic and political differences permitted.

From what we know about the organisation of these National Churches, especially of the Persian Church, we can just visualise how Christianity would have fared in the Far East, the interior of Asia and India, had the Church of Persia only been able to fulfil its mission. An indication of how the organisation of Christian Churches deriving their origin from Persia would have developed is found in a Syriac chronicle which records the activities of a Persian bishop at the end of the fifth century and tells us how bishop Ma'na translated the Syriac Christian literature into Persian, composed religious hymns in that language and sent his works to the Christians living in India and on the Isles of the Indian Ocean.[1] This shows that Syriac, or rather Aramaic, would not have remained the liturgical language of Persian Christianity but that the production of national religious literature would have kept abreast of the expansion of the Church over new fields.

It is patent from the foregoing that the Christian communities would have been organised on a national basis, one in faith, yet each organising its interior and domestic life and its relations with political powers according to its own standards and possibilities, without the slightest prejudice to the universality of the Church; for with the General Synods as embodying the Church Universal, a sufficiently firm bond would have united the various Churches and maintained among them the sense of their unity. It is true that the synods used to be summoned by the Roman Emperors,[2] but their work was directed by the presiding bishops, i.e. the Patriarchs, amongst whom the Patriarch of Rome, the successor of St. Peter, occupied not merely a first, but a dominant and unique position. Acceptance of the synodal decisions by the National Churches had to be their supreme and most significant act of submission to the Church Universal and, by implication, to the visible Head, the Bishop of Rome.

This bond may be considered loose and inadequate by present-day Catholics, but we should not project our modern standards and institutions into the fifth century. At that

1 *Chronique de Séert*, II, p. 117; *Histoire Nestorienne Inédite*, published by Addai Scher, Paris, 1907, 1911; *Patrologia Orientalis*, t. VII.

2 On this problem, see the Latin study "The Authority of the State in the Oecumenical Councils" (a translation of which appeared in the *Christian East*, Vol. XIV, 1934, pp. 95–108), by the author of this booklet.

period it had to suffice, since there was no other means available to make the supremacy of St. Peter's successor at all acceptable. The Papacy had not yet completed its organisation and formulated all its claims, leaving open quite a fair possibility that in later centuries they would have found readier acceptance in the Persian, Asiatic and Far Eastern communities than they found in Byzantium, since the distance between Rome and those far-flung countries would have precluded any fear in eastern minds of direct interference from a foreign patriarchate in their purely domestic and national affairs. What frequently made matters so difficult between Rome and Byzantium was the fact that the two cities were at the same time political rivals within the Roman Empire and that their interests were often interlocked, more especially in the province of Illyricum, which included the whole of Greece and Crete and was, until the eighth century, part of the Roman patriarchate.[1] The existence of a strong Christian body outside the Roman Empire would undoubtedly have acted as a brake and exercised a sobering effect on the religious reactions between East and West.

It is on these lines that the Church Universal would seemingly have developed outside the *limes Romanus*, as every new mission would have followed precedent and laid the foundation of a new National Church. As L. Duchesne has shown in an excellent study, published in 1896 and still the last word on the subject,[2] before the great heretical movement had started, i.e. at the period we are discussing, new Christian formations were in course of erection outside the Roman frontiers, in the Sahara, at Axum and Himyan amongst the Arabs, when unexpected events cut this line of development and diverted the Church from her original course into new channels of world history and Christian growth.

* *
*

1 We believe we have shown the importance of this problem for the development of the Schism in our study : *La lutte entre Byzance et Rome à propos de l'Illyricum au IXᵉs.*, in *Mélanges Ch. Diehl*, Paris, 1930, pp. 61–80, and in our work *Les Légendes de Constantin et de Méthode vues de Byzance*, Prague, 1933, pp. 248–283.

2 L.c., pp. 281–353 : *Les Missions Chrétiennes au Sud de l'Empire Romain.*

II

Islam and the Evolution of the National Churches

Arabs, Islam and Christianity—National Churches under Islam—Mongol and Persian Christianity—The Byzantine Church before and after the Turkish Conquest

It is generally admitted that, besides the spread of the great heresies of the early period, Monophysitism and Nestorianism, one of these unexpected events was the invasion of the Arabs. The readiness with which the national Churches of the East embraced heretical creeds illustrates the danger to the Church of over-stressing the national element: national jealousies and incompatibility with the Roman Empire certainly facilitated the spread of Nestorianism among the Persians, and of Monophysitism among the Armenians. We should however not forget that none of those heresies originated in those Churches, and that the centralising and intolerant policy of the Empire had not a little to do with the diffusion of heretical creeds over the Syrian countries and over Egypt; that therefore the blame cannot be put on the regard professed by early Eastern Christianity for national life and individuality.

More pregnant with consequences was the second factor—the invasion of the Arabs. The influence of the Arab invasions on the subsequent evolution of Christianity was enormous and far more important than is generally admitted in the handbooks of Church history. They were provoked by a phenomenon common in the West, the migration of nations; only this time not the Germanic tribes, but the Arabs were hammering at the eastern gates of the Roman Empire and the south-western gates of Persia. The Arabs had been on the move before Mohammed was born, but his new religion certainly lent the Arab migration a new impetus. It is quite possible that they would have followed lines similar to those followed by the Germanic tribes, which also broke through the defences of the Roman Empire, settled in its rich provinces, adopted the religion they found in the occupied territories, mostly Arianism, but eventually fused with the native population, adhered to the orthodox faith and proudly proclaimed themselves to be heirs of the Romans. Unfortunately, the Arabs, in starting out on their trek, had, unlike the Germans, their own religion, Islam, and their own great prophet, Mohammed. After conquering the countries where Hellenistic civilisation was flourishing, the Arabs also succumbed to the charm of its culture and readily adopted the inheritance of ancient Greece such as the Christian Churches and other religious bodies had treasured for centuries.

The first among the various bodies to initiate the barbarian conquerors into the secrets of Hellenistic culture were the Syriac and the Persian Christians, who at that moment were adherents of Nestorianism. The court of the Khalifs of Bagdad was filled with Christians occupying high posts and the Emirs in the provinces mostly selected Christians as their secretaries. In fact, the Nestorian Christians taught their masters, the uncultured Arabs, the principles of philosophy, astronomy, physics and medicine, treasures of the ancient Greeks that were unknown to the Arabs. The famous treatises of Aristotle, Euclid, Ptolemy, Hippocrates, Galienus and Dioscorides were translated into Arabic mostly by Syriac Christians, and their rugged pupils shaped and progressed so well in the study of Greek philosophy that the Aristotelian schools of Bagdad acquired world-wide fame; and when the Arabs had conquered Africa and Spain, two of the Arab commentators of Aristotle made names for themselves in the West—Avicenna (Ibn-Sina) who lived in the East and died in 1037 at Hamadan, and Averroes (Ibn-Roshd) who died in Cordova in 1198.

By a strange irony of fate, not uncommon in history, it was the Nestorian Christians, who by translating Aristotle from the Syriac into Arabic, benefited the West which in the thirteenth century gathered from their Arabic translations a more extensive knowledge of Aristotle and Greek philosophy. Arabic translations and commentaries imported into Europe between the years 1200 and 1270, often through the good services of the Emperor Frederick II and the cultural centre he had established at Palermo, found their way into the Universities of Paris, Oxford and Cambridge and paved the way to the great work of St. Thomas and the rise of Scholasticism in the West.

To return to the parallel between the Arab and German migrations, we note that when the Germanic tribes, after their conversion to Christianity, made contact with the remnants of Hellenistic culture which they had omitted to destroy in their first conquest of the Roman Empire, the court of Charlemagne, the founder of the Frankish Empire, also developed into a centre of learning of which the new converts were very proud. But there was no comparison between the Frankish performance and the Khalifs' achievement which rivalled the best of Greek scholarship in Byzantium.

So far, the Arabs proved to be excellent disciples of their

Christian teachers, but in the things that mattered most, unlike the Germanic and Slavonic tribes which destroyed the western part of the Roman Empire and considerably reduced its eastern half, the Arabs remained unimpressed by their new subjects; they had their own religion, a synthesis of pagan, Jewish, Christian and Mazdaite doctrines, which in spite of deficiencies and incoherence, could claim a certain superiority over polytheistic paganism and threatened, with the backing of political power, to become a dangerous rival of Christianity. The fact that the Nestorians of Syria and the Monophysites of Egypt were hostile to the Emperors who stood for orthodoxy considerably assisted the invaders in gaining control of the Eastern Byzantine provinces, whilst the decadent conditions of Christianity in Syria and Egypt induced Islam to keep aloof from Christendom and to adopt the pose, in the eyes of many, of being a superior religion, a sort of "reformed" and "modernised" Christianity. This explains the numerous conversions Islam made in Christian countries, though at the outset the Arabs discountenanced and forbade conversions to Islam, being only interested in seizing political power and levying tribute.

It so came about that the prospects of a rapid diffusion of Christianity towards the Far East, Central Asia and Africa collapsed before realisation. The disaster was worst in Persia, where Mazdaism, instead of being peacefully laid to rest by Christianity, was destroyed by Islam, and the country, instead of being the centre of Christian radiation towards the East, became the protagonist of Islam. Mohammedanism took advantage of the country's central position at the Asiatic cross roads to overrun, during the centuries that followed, the countries that had seemed predestined to be Christian: Afghanistan, Baluchistan, Ceylon, India and the lands of the Mongolian and Turkish tribes.

* * *

It is interesting to consider the effects of the Arab conquest on the further evolution of the National Churches. This conquest happened to be far too rapid for consolidation and the Arab State suddenly took such unwieldy proportions that it became next to impossible to deal at once with the administrative problems as they arose. The Arab Bedouins were culturally inferior to the conquered races and could not possibly administer those vast districts by themselves. The result was that since the heretical Churches had given the conquerors such a friendly welcome, the Arabs handed over the responsibility of administering the Christians to their bishops. This gave rise to an interesting position. The National Churches found themselves transformed into some kind of ecclesiastical States, whose bishops wielded political as well as religious authority and whose Patriarchs blossomed into the political leaders of their flocks, naturally under the supremacy of the Khalifs.

It thus happened that by sheer pressure of circumstances, the people identified themselves body and soul with their Churches, a situation that was ideal in some respects, as affecting the relations between the Church and the nation. No conflict of interests could be possible between them, since patriotism amounted at the same time to a profession of the Christian faith, fighting for a nation meant fighting for religion without the aid of propaganda, and every sacrifice for the nation implied a sacrifice for God. It must be admitted that the Oriental National Churches thus did good service to their nationals who, to a large extent, owed their political existence to the fatherly protection of their bishops and Patriarchs ; though it should also be added that by such a fusion of the political and the spiritual, the Church lost a good deal of her purity and strayed from the spiritual and supra-national aims imposed on her by Christ. The fact is that the Arab solution of the National Church problem brought about the degradation of Eastern Christianity, for it gradually lost its dominant position which was promptly seized by Islam after a period of construction, to sink to the status of a tolerated religion on a level with Judaism, paganism, Manichaeism and other local sects.

The most tenacious of all the Eastern National Churches that were overrun by the Arabs was the Persian Nestorian Church. As she had not been trained to being treated as a privileged body, the Arab conquest meant no more to her at first than a change of masters and, despite all the difficulties, she carried on her mission as best she could. But this time, she met in the religion of her conquerors an aggressive rival. The Persians had been content with maintaining Mazdaism as their national religion and protecting it against encroachments, but without the least desire to proselytise or impose their own creed on other nations. With Islam, things were different. However, the Nestorian Persian Church not only kept going from her new centre in Bagdad the missions which the Orthodox Church had founded from its Seleucia-Ctesiphon headquarters, but inaugurated a period of flourishing Nestorian missions, which lasted for some centuries and reached their zenith in the thirteenth century. It was then that China and Mongolia for the first time came under Christian influence.[1]

* *
*

The Mongol conquerors of Bagdad (1258), far from interfering with this magnificent effort, seemed to be more amenable to Christian influence than the Arabs, for whilst Christianity spread through the south of India, many princes in Turkestan accepted baptism, and prospects in China were very bright. Curiously enough, at the time when the works of Aristotle, as transmitted to the Arabs by the Syriac and Persian Christians, found their way to the West, the Nestorians of Persia again opened contact with the West and with the Papacy. In 1288, the Katholikos Yaballaha, of Chinese extraction, sent from Bagdad, at the request of the Prince of the Mongols, Argon Khan, an embassy to the Pope, the Emperor and the Western Princes, to arrange an alliance against Islam. The ambassador, also a Chinese born in Pekin, was the monk Rabban Sauma. There exists an interesting report of his long journey from Pekin to Gascony,[2] where he met Edward I, King of England. What is surprising is that this Nestorian availed himself of every chance to insist on his orthodoxy and that he was welcomed everywhere in the West as a perfectly orthodox Christian. The Cardinals he met in Rome before the election of Nicholas IV seem to have taken their foreign guest's orthodoxy for granted, and only grew suspicious on finding out that the Chinese from Bagdad had not the faintest notion of the "Filioque," the famous addition to the Nicene Creed over which the Romans had fallen out with the Greeks. So firmly convinced were the Romans that they were dealing with a correct Catholic that the Pope honoured the Nestorian monk by giving him Holy Communion on Palm Sunday with his own hands.

True to Chinese manners, the ambassador was extravagantly profuse in marks of respect and reverence for the Pope, greeting him as Lord Pope, Katholikos, Patriarch of Roman lands and of all Western nations, the Romans never suspecting for a moment that the Eastern Christian knew nothing about the universal claims which the Papacy had been trying so hard

1 On these activities, there is an excellent study written by the famous orientalist W. Bartold, *Zur Geschichte des Christentums in Mittelasien bis zur Mongolischen Eroberung* (enlarged translation from the Russian) Tübingen, 1901. Cf. also the studies of A. Mingana quoted above.

2 I. B. Chabot, *Histoire de Mar Yab-Alaha, Patriarche et de Raban-Sauma*, Paris, 1895, especially pp. 65 and 87. English translation by Sir E. A. Wallis Budge, *The Monks of Kublâi Khân, Emperor of China*, London, 1928, pp. 172–196.

to force on the schismatic Greeks. This was significant: it showed that when the Papacy of the thirteenth century had reached the last limits of its expansion, the Westerners had almost completely forgotten the early history of Christianity.

It is well known that the discovery of the Mongols and their Empire raised high hopes in Rome and in the West, and that numbers of Franciscans made ready to go out and convert the Mongols to the Christian faith. To a certain extent, these hopes were well founded and, given the mentality prevailing in Rome with regard to the Nestorians, collaboration between the Western and Eastern Churches came within the realm of possibilities, to the possible benefit of the Nestorians, by making them aware of their deviations from tradition, and to the benefit of the West and the missions themselves. But Islam shattered all those fine prospects, when the Mongol princes definitely accepted the faith of the Prophet—the first Prince to do so was Gazan who died in 1304—and when that part of the world had its doors closed to Christianity for centuries. Then started a period of bloody wars and devastation as Khan Timur swept over Asia with his wild hordes. For Asiatics had their own notions on war and on the privileges of victory, as when the brave monk Sauma, on arriving in Naples on his way to Rome, and hearing of the war between Charles II of Anjou—or rather his son Charles Martel, who was then regent during his father's captivity—and James II of Aragon, was amazed to learn that only actual combatants were killed in battle and that the population was to a great extent left unmolested.[1] The Asiatics already knew then the horrors of totalitarian wars, and so did Timur when he literally wiped out, amongst others, a number of Christian communities. Later aggressions by the Turks against the Persians who had broken away from the "Sunnis" or traditionalist Moslems, to become Shiahs or Separatists and heretics, completed the havoc operated by Timur and turned the regions of Persia, once the richest of the world, into a desert. Christian propaganda ceased with the destruction of the Christian base in Persia from where alone a drive towards Central Asia and the Far East had any chance, and to-day nothing but ruins are left of the once flourishing Orthodox and Nestorian Churches that did so well and so much for the spread of Christ's message.[2]

* *
*

1 I. B. Chabot, l.c., p. 61. E. A. Wallis Budge, l.c., p. 171.

2 About the present state of these Churches, see A. Fortescue, l.c., pp. 114 sq., 353 sq.

The Arab conquest also left its mark on the Byzantine Church. Religious conditions in the Roman Empire of the East, the Byzantine Empire, took shape on lines slightly different from those followed in States abroad. There the head of the State, on becoming a Christian, kept all the prerogatives over the new religion which he had previously possessed over the pagan creed; he claimed for one thing to be the Pontifex Maximus in the Church, and the Church, in her joy at feeling herself free, agreed to the claim. The Church became a State Church and adapted her organisation to the institutions of the State, while the Christian Emperors clung to the mission of the Romans and their pretence to be the only authority in the world, in the hope of extending their sway over all nations and converting them as a matter of course. In this they secured the support of the Church which prayed for the extension of the Roman Empire as the providential instrument for the propagation of the faith.

But the Emperors never realised their ambition. The Arabs hacked their way to the East; the Slavs overran the whole of the Balkans as far as Thrace and Greece; the Germans conquered the whole West and in the name of the Emperor occupied Rome. All these Slav and German conquests at the same time caused the territory of the Byzantine State and the jurisdiction of the Byzantine Church to shrink in proportion. With the loss of imperial and patriarchal supremacy over the provinces that went by the board in the process, the Byzantine Church, in converting new nations, had to content herself with rearing them for Christian life as she had been reared herself. Wherever the Byzantine missionaries found their way, new churches came into being with the local Princes at their head, as was the case in Byzantium. Every Church became a State Church, and as the new Slavonic States carved out of the Roman provinces, or rising on their north-eastern borders, consisted of distinct nations, the Church split up into National Churches in each of them, always after the fashion set by the first Christian missionaries of the early period, with their own liturgical language and literature.

But the process went further and presently the Byzantine Church, without losing her pre-eminent position in the whole East and amongst the new Slavonic Churches—the Patriarch of Constantinople has kept even to our days some vestiges of his former prestige—gradually awoke to the consciousness of her Greek tongue and her Greek past, dropped by force of circumstances her pretensions to be the heir of Rome, made her leadership representative of Greek national life and took up the defence of national and religious freedom. Thus the process which had started operating outside the *limes Romanus* in the early Christian period, reached its culmination throughout the territory of the former Eastern Roman Empire; and when another nation, the Turkish nation, took its inspiration from Islam to conquer and overrun the last remnants of this Eastern Empire with Constantinople as its choicest prize, the National Churches of the Greeks, the Serbians, the Bulgarians, the Rumanians and even, to some extent, of the Albanians, all daughters of the Church of Constantinople, stepped into the breach to console and to comfort their nationals during the trying period of Turkish domination. Something similar took place in Russia, too, which from the end of the thirteenth century to the end of the fifteenth, chafed under the Mongol yoke and found itself almost completely cut off from Western Europe and from the rest of Christendom.

Nobody will deny that these National Churches, in their darkest days, rendered their members services which the nations concerned should ever remember. Their position was indeed providential for the conquered nations, but only as long as these remained under the yoke of the Infidel and as long as their religious and political freedom could not be maintained without constant vigilance and readiness to fight. And the Balkan National Churches shared with their sisters of the East the same conditions and the same anomalies. But eventually the principle of universality in Christendom was bound to suffer in the process; once the nations felt able to breathe again in a new atmosphere of freedom, their National Churches would have to face another dangerous crisis. This is exactly what happened, and to-day the crisis is still on them.

* * *

III

The Western Church and the Idea of Universality

Germanic invasions and Rome—Dominant position of Latin in the West—Moravian Christianity and the Papacy—Franks, Latin language and Roman liturgy—Arabs isolate the West—New kind of National Church and the Reformers' Universality

Things proceeded differently in the Western portion of the Roman Empire. Rome also, at the beginning of its official Christian era, had to struggle through the same evolution as Constantinople. The bishops of Rome, however conscious they were of their pre-eminent position in the Church Universal, agreed with the other Patriarchs to the Emperors' claims over the Church and prayed with Tertullian for the prosperity of the Roman Empire as God's chosen channel for the propagation of the faith. This tradition still lingers in the Roman liturgy and in the prayers of the Good Friday Mass. In the West, too, the Church was evolving into a State Church, the process in Rome being slowed down only by the fact that the centre of the Empire had shifted to Constantinople.

Humanly speaking, the Church of Rome could not have escaped from the fate that befell Constantinople but for the intervention of Providence. We have only to read, for example, certain formulas of the *Liber Diurnus*,[1] the early medieval handbook of the Roman Chancellery, regulating papal elections at the Byzantine period of Roman history, to realise how imminent the danger was, and that, at the time, the Popes were not much better off than the Byzantine Patriarchs. But at the very moment when the danger was at its worst, the might of the Roman Empire in the West collapsed under the heavy blows of the Germanic tribes in search of living space. There is no doubt that the effects of the Germanic immigrations into the Western parts of the Roman Empire turned out to be more disastrous than those of the Arab immigration in the East, for the Germans broke the imperial power not only in the provinces, but also in its very centre, Rome.

The bishop of Rome, who had so far waged an uneven struggle against the all-pervading power of the Emperors, suddenly found himself not only free from imperial interference, but almost in the place of the Emperor, and his Church rose above the ruins of the Western Roman Empire as the one rock that promised security and peace. The Pope and his Church actually took over the succession from the Emperors and the Empire. Quick to grasp the situation and its implications, the Romans soon looked to the Pope as their *Dominus*, a title that had so far been reserved to the Emperor, and began regarding his person and all things connected with him as *sacer* and *sanctus*, two imperial prerogatives. Henceforth the Roman Church considered it to be her duty to carry on the universal mission of the Roman Empire, now combined with her own mission to preach the Gospel to all nations; and since none of the newcomers had any culture to offer nor any master to impose any; since the Church of Rome was the only cultural power left in the whole West embodying the traditions of the Roman Empire, the new nations expected

[1] M. von Sickel, *Liber Diurnus Romanorum Pontificum*, Wien, 1888 especially formulas 57–63.

from her nothing different from Christianity in the shape into which she had moulded it.

* *
*

Here we must touch on a problem which often complicates the major issue of Nationality and Universality in the Church we are discussing: How and why did it come about that Latin obtained such a monopoly in Western Christianity as to become the only liturgical language throughout the West? And why did Eastern Christianity follow a different practice in its divine worship? The question is important and a right answer would considerably help one in appreciating and solving the major problem of the right balance between nationality and universality in the Church.

Though Church historians and philologists are interested enough,[1] the question has not attracted the attention it deserves. And yet, to understand this particular evolution in Western Christianity, one has but to go further back along the line of research to the days when pagan Rome ruled supreme over East and West. Gaul and Spain, the two countries that were completely latinised, fell under the spell of Roman influence in every sphere, religion included. Their native pagan cults were too primitive and too poorly equipped to withstand the drive of their conquerors' more refined worship, so much so that scarcely any traces of the old Iberian creeds survived in Spain; the Celtic religion vanished and the Druidic priests in Gaul suspended their interminable recitations in the native tongue in deference to their faithful who preferred the more elaborate display of Roman paganism. Even the intricate ritual of the Punic pagan mysteries of North Africa only managed to survive in a Roman version and its gods under Latin names.

As Roman paganism imposed its liturgical language—Latin—as a matter of course, at the expense of the native speech, the Romanisation and Latinisation of Spain, Gaul and North Africa proceeded at a rapid pace, radiating from the forums, where the conquerors issued their legislation and planted their cultural institutions, as well as from the temples whence the Roman gods soon ousted the native divinities. Long

1 We may here recall the studies written by two Belgian scholars, as full of ideas as they are short: P. Fredericq, *Les Conséquences de l'Evangélisation par Rome et par Byzance sur le Développement de la Langue Maternelle des Peuples Convertis*, Bulletin de l'Académie Royale de Belgique, Classe des Lettres, 1903, 738–751; F. Cumont, *Pourquoi le Latin fut la seule Langue Liturgique de l'Occident*, Mélanges Paul Fredericq, Bruxelles, 1904, pp. 63–66.

before Christianity had reached the Western provinces of the Roman Empire, their inhabitants had learned to look upon Latin as the only respectable language in which priests could address the Deity enthroned in the Romans' gorgeous temples before their congregations of Romanised natives. The native tongue continued to survive in the homes, but it had lost its right of way into the temples.

Such was the position as the Christian missionaries found it in the West, and who would blame them for accepting and using the materials that lay at hand? Never for a moment could it occur to them to use in the official worship of the true God they were preaching, the native tongue they found relegated to the hovels of the humble and the poor.

Things developed quite differently in the East. There Hellenism, by nature far more tolerant than Latinism, never succeeded in imposing its cult and its language on the Eastern provinces, however ready the natives were to adopt its philosophy and its culture. The Semitic races, together with the Egyptians and the Iranians, never took to the Greek divinities, but stood by their own rites, which were better organised and more fully developed. It was rather the other way about, for the Syriac divinities gathered many believers both in Rome and in Greece, chiefly Isis and Mithra, whose popularity throughout the Roman Empire reached as far as Roman Britain. The Syriac, Egyptian, Iranian and other rites were carried on in the native tongue and successfully held their ground against the glamours of Greek. Evidence has come down to us that even Scythian and Thracian continued to be used in pagan worship, and similar conditions must have obtained in Asia Minor, which was never completely Hellenised. The Romans had no remedy for this state of things, except that of adding to the Babel of tongues current in the East their own Latin, the official language of administration and army.

This divergence sufficiently shows why Christianity in the East could never impose a foreign language on its faithful for the use of official worship, why its missionaries had to conform to existing usage and use the vernacular in the liturgy, why such centres of Hellenistic culture as Alexandria and Antioch never dreamed, after their Christianisation, of forcing Greek into their sanctuaries, and why the Patriarchs of those cities ordered the translation of the divine liturgies into Syriac, Armenian, Coptic and Arabic.

This is important, as it all goes to show that the exclusion of the vernacular as a medium for ritual purposes is not characteristic of the Christian spirit, and that the Latin monopoly of liturgical expression in the West was due to circumstances that preceded the advent of the new faith. The Western Church naturally took advantage of her opportunity to stress the notion of the universality of Christianity, when all her faithful were familiar with one single liturgical language, to maintain, for some centuries at any rate, doctrinal unity and orthodoxy throughout the West and to steer clear of the danger that afflicted the East, where differences in liturgical self-expression were soon often followed by differences in Creeds.

Bearing all this in mind, one need not wonder why the missionaries who were sent to the Germanic nations and settled in the Western provinces of the Roman Empire never considered it expedient or even advisable to translate the sacred books of Holy Scripture into the vernaculars of their flocks, and why, instead of making of the local dialects the common vehicle for a deeper instruction in Christian doctrine and theology, they preferred to encourage the use of Latin for its easier access to a knowledge of the faith. Nor should we forget that the men who instructed the missionaries and sent them out were Romans whose ancestors had been the conquerors and the rulers of the whole West. Even after the collapse of the Roman Empire, there were still Romans left in Rome to rally round the Pope and think *à la romaine* and these same men were there to organise and launch the new missions. Who could have expected them to have recourse in the religious field to methods other than those their ancestors had been used to and trained in, in the political, cultural and religious fields ? It was only in the East that the old Romans had to resort to compromise and adaptation, since there they were dealing with cultured nations that had something of their own to offer. But in the West !

* *
*

Well, the upshot of it was, whether we like it or not, that Roman Christianity in its Roman form and with its Latin liturgical language was readily accepted by the barbarians who in exchange could give the Church nothing but their youthful strength and good will. There was only one exception in the West, though a short-lived one, Christianity in Moravia. There the Popes accepted the innovation introduced by the Byzantine missionaries, SS. Cyril and Methodius, and blessed the liturgical books written in Slavonic and representing an interesting mixture of Byzantine and Roman rites.[1]

[1] The writer has dealt with this problem in his books : *Les Slaves, Byzance et Rome au IXe siècle*, Paris, 1926—and *Les Légendes de Constantin et de Méthode Vues de Byzance*, Prague, 1933.

The exception is all the more interesting as it occurred in the second half of the ninth century and as the Popes who confirmed the privilege of the Church of the Moravian Empire were Hadrian II and John VIII, immediate successors of Nicholas I, an outstanding figure on the throne of St. Peter, who did more than anybody else to formulate and press home the medieval claims of the Papacy. Here was evidence that in ninth-century Rome there was, on principle, no objection to the use of national languages in the liturgy and that a door was still left open to an alternative solution of the national problem, including the linguistic issue in the liturgy. Any bold innovation in this field could still meet with ready comprehension in Rome as long as it was likely to further the interests of the Church.

Curiously enough, the most stubborn opposition to the Popes' initiative in Moravia came from the Frankish Church. It was the Frankish bishops who, with the help of the Magyars, the new Asiatic invaders of Europe, assisted Lewis and Arnulf, Kings of East Francia or the future Germany, in crushing the first Slavonic political formation centring in the Valley of the Morava and other tributaries of the Middle Danube as far as the river Tisza. This hostility was due not only to the century-old antagonism between Slavs and Germans, or to the blind pressure of the Franks' eastward expansion, followed, a century later, by the German's *Drang nach Osten*, but to other motives as well. The newly converted Germanic tribes accepted Christianity in its Roman form and with its Latin liturgy so readily; they grew, in their first century of Christian life, so accustomed to it, and the tradition took such firm roots that throughout the West and especially among the Franks, Christianity in any form but Roman, and a liturgy in any other language than Latin, looked to the converted nations like something very akin to heresy.

The Romans of the period, to repeat it once more, did not go so far, as the Moravian instance proves; it was Frankish opposition that wrecked the Moravian Empire with its Moravian Christianity and Slavonic liturgy, and the Popes did not alter their Moravian policy until they realised that resistance to the Frankish clergy's opposition was hopeless. A few remnants of the Slavonic liturgy of the Roman rite in Dalmatia and Croatia are all that is left of Rome's frustrated effort.

* *
*

On top of all this, the newly converted Franks went much further than the Popes ever intended to go, when Charlemagne and his Frankish bishops originated the idea of introducing the Roman liturgy throughout the West. That the Popes had no intention of forcing all the Roman customs on the new Churches founded by their missionaries was best illustrated by the advice Gregory the Great gave St. Augustine for his work among the Anglo-Saxons of Britain, when Augustine was recommended to examine all the existing customs in the liturgical and disciplinary fields, to keep whatever he judged becoming and to frame rules of divine worship that would suit the converts best.[1] In the second half of the seventh century, Pope Vitalianus so little thought of imposing Rome's liturgical usage on the new Anglo-Saxon Church that he sent to Britain a Greek, Theodore of Tarsus, after consecrating him bishop; and we can still trace the many non-Roman customs which this Greek introduced into the Anglo-Saxon Church.

Charlemagne's initiative thus altered the whole course of religious evolution just when Rome seemed inclined to exchange its own liturgy for that of the Greeks and the orientals. It is therefore the Franks we have to thank for the survival of the genuine Roman liturgy, its monopoly of the whole West, and the suppression of all other local liturgies in Gaul, Spain, Britain and Northern Italy. They thus contributed most to the uniformity of Roman Christianity, when Rome, far from stressing it, contented itself at the outset with stressing the notion of universality. They also were primarily responsible in the period that followed for confusing the same uniformity with universality, often to the detriment of the reality for which Rome had always striven.

That is how, throughout the West, and with the assistance of the Germanic nations, a novel universal formation, resembling a theocratic monarchy and strongly steeped in the Roman tradition, came into existence. The close connection between the old ideals of the Roman Empire and the new Christian conquest of the world by Rome was pointed out by the great Roman and Christian, Leo I, who in one of his homilies drew an impressive parallel between the Roman and the Christian conquests of the world[2]. This notion took such possession of the Roman mind that the Church could not find a more suitable quotation for a nocturn of the feast of her apostolic Princes, St. Peter and St. Paul, than this eloquent extract from the great Roman's homily; and for centuries the tradition has prevailed in the West on the strength of this reading in the Roman breviary.

[1] Migne, *Patres Latini*, Vol. 77, col. 1187 (letter 64).
[2] Migne, *Patres Latini*, Vol. 54, col. 418 sq.

Thus, on the ruins of the old Roman Empire there rose a sort of Latin religious Empire in the West, ruled by the Pope and claiming supreme spiritual power over all the kings and chieftains of the newly converted nations. It was the environment that was needed for a further expansion of papal power, and to create the notion that all power, religious and political, in the world was, by the will of God, concentrated in the hands of the Pope, a notion that hardened into a principle and took hold of the western mind throughout the Middle Ages.

* * *

Such a development was, of course, poles apart from the line of progress in the East, and again Islam stepped in to seal up the position in the West. The Arabs, by occupying the whole of North Africa, settling in Spain, securing a foothold in Sicily and threatening the very shores of Italy, became the real masters of the Mediterranean and made, for a vital period, all intercourse between East and West impossible. The situation has been accurately summed up by the great Belgian historian, Professor H. Pirenne, in his masterly work on Mohammed and Charlemagne.[1] The first consequence was the political and economic decadence of South Francia, once the most cultured part of the ancient Roman provinces, through the loss of almost all its connections with the East. But the loss of South Francia was the gain of East Francia, a province less amenable to the influence of Roman culture, which stepped into the limelight under Charlemagne and, after the collapse of the Frankish Empire, became the German kingdom, heir to the Carolingian Empire.

From the cultural and religious point of view, the situation was equally disastrous, as the Western Church was almost completely cut off from the East, where Byzantium was still the only centre of civilisation; and as the Slavs had cut off access by land to Byzantium by their occupation of the Balkans, there remained for several centuries no easy way for the East to share with the West its cultural treasures and feed the Western stores with its own Hellenistic inheritance. The alternative channel between Byzantium and the West, that was being made by the Moravian princes, was cut and obliterated by the Franks and the invading Magyars before it was completed. This severance was fatal, as Rome was busy at the time transmitting the Christian faith to the new arrivals, and with the faith, the Popes were only able to hand over what they had saved of Hellenistic culture, which was not much. East and West

1 English translation by B. Miall, London, 1939.

could not therefore control each other's movements and progress so as to prevent the Church on either side from overbalancing by any excessive stress either on the national or on the universal element in the further shaping of Christian thought.

All this explains why it was so easy, at the time of the organisation of Christianity in the West, to overlook all but completely the national element, which was not yet conscious of itself, and to put the accent more heavily on the notion of universality, which Rome had cultivated more than any other Church.

* * *

However, subsequent events were to show that the national element had not been disposed of as completely as it seemed. The formula of *Rex-Sacerdos* (Priest-King) which was rather of Oriental origin, but had been adopted and developed by the Roman Emperors and which the Church had agreed to after Constantine's conversion, found its way into the West and into the primitive courts of the new Christian princes who accepted it the more readily as the old Germanic conception concerning the origin of the power of their kings (who were believed to be of sacred, divine stock) met the Constantinian conception half-way.[1] Charlemagne saw its implications, little as he was impressed by the notorious *Donatio Constantini*, the famous forgery which was meant to record Constantine's gift of the West to the Popes and was designed to impress the young nations, to help the Franks to be on their best behaviour and to teach them respect for the Pope. But instead of behaving like the legendary Constantine, Charlemagne preferred to follow the example of the historical Constantine by ruling his Church according to his whims, and setting an evil precedent for his German successors, the Ottos and their heirs. The danger was obvious: curtailment of the rights that the Popes claimed over their new converts and the rise of a new class of National Churches in the West.

What complicated matters was, that though the Germanic nations accepted the Roman and Latin culture without question, Roman influence was not strong enough to eliminate the less desirable German notions and customs and replace them by the Roman variants. On one point the Germans proved uncomfortably tenacious: in their own conception of ownership, which was more comprehensive than the

1 Cf. especially what H. von Schubert says on this German conception, in his illuminating study, *Der Kampf des Geistlichen und Weltlichen Rechts*, in Sitzungsberichte of the Academy of Heidelberg, 1927, pp. 25 sq.

Roman conception, they could never see why a Roman bishop should expect the builders of churches to surrender all their rights over church and land to the Church authorities ; instead, the lords not only continued to regard the churches they had erected on their property, or which happened to stand on land that came into their possession, as exclusively their own, but even claimed a share in the authority which so far bishops alone had exercised over them and over the priests in charge. This system of proprietary churches—*Eigenkirchen*[1]—spread over all the Western countries that had slowly emerged into political consciousness, Germany, France, England, Lombardy, Spain, and was extended even to the bishoprics themselves, with the result that the combination of Germanic ideology and Roman theocracy gave the princes almost absolute control over the churches. The Emperor Otto I and his successors succeeded thus in setting up a *Reichskirche* which in some respects was more loyal to them than to the Popes. The intervention of Henry III, who deposed three Popes and put a German bishop in their stead, almost amounted to the incorporation of Rome into the *Reichskirche*. The upshot was that in the eleventh century Western Christianity was gradually growing into an agglomerate of autonomous and National Churches, of which the princes, as " kings and priests " combined, claimed supreme leadership, nay ownership, whilst the central power, the Papacy, the real backbone of the Church, was condemned to a purely passive rôle, at the cost of the Church's unity and universality. It is really curious to watch the national element, which at the beginning of Western Christianity was almost non-existent, expanding and reacting against too strict an application of the principle of universality, without, however, ceasing to respect it.

It is at this particular point that we strike at the roots of the subsequent evolution of the Western Church. We all know how the Reformists of the eleventh century came to the final conclusion that the true source of all the abuses of the time was the theocratic system, and how Gregory VII made the first bold attempt to revive the old Roman notion of universality, and to set up in the West a new order by replacing the theocratic system by a kind of hierocracy, and declaring that all power, both secular and spiritual, lay by God's designs in the hands of the Pope.

To this day, Gregory's innovation has been violently

[1] The authority on this matter is the German scholar Ulrich Stutz. One of his studies, *The Proprietary Church as an element of Medieval German Ecclesiastical Law*, appeared in G. Barraclough's *Studies in Medieval Germany*, Oxford, 1938, Vol. II, pp. 35–70.

criticised by historians, but it is only right to say that his ideas were nothing but a deduction from the old theory of the two powers, the secular and the ecclesiastical, both of divine origin—a theory once formulated by Pope Gelasius I in the fifth century,[1] which served as a basis for all political thought in the Middle Ages. Gregory went but a step further by concluding that since the priest had the power of absolving even an emperor, therefore sacerdotal power stood above imperial power, and he was convinced that there lay the only means to free the Church from the many abuses that arose from the princes' interference in ecclesiastical affairs. Taking into consideration all the reasons that provoked the conflict, one is driven to the conclusion that the clash was one between the Germanic and the old Roman conception of canon law. The old Roman order thus rose against a Germanic order imposed on the Church by the conquerors of the Roman Empire of the West and the invaders of Roman Christendom, for the return to the bishops of powers they had exercised under Roman Christianity and which belonged to them in virtue of the responsibilities of their office ;—and to this extent the Reformists and Gregory were entitled to claim that they were only returning to conceptions essential to the Christian spirit, distinctive of the Roman period, though obscured since by practices that were incompatible with sound Christian principles.[2]

But in claiming greater powers for the bishops, or rather their independence of any sort of lay interference in ecclesiastical matters such as they had enjoyed in the early Christian period, the Reformists could not have meant to accept in all its details the old Roman order as embodied in the first Collections of the rudimentary Roman canon law. They could not, for instance, demand the restoration of the almost absolute powers the bishops had been exercising then, when they arrogated exclusive rights over church property, disposed of their clergy *ad nutum* by sending them wherever they pleased, or deprived them of their living, whenever they suspected their loyalty, whether personal or professional. In this particular matter, the Church had again to make concessions to the Germanic notion of canon law.

1 Cfr. what R. W. Carlyle, *A History of Medieval Political Theory in the West*, London, I, 1903, pp. 190 sq. says on this evolution.

2 We draw the reader's attention to the recent publication on this controversy by G. Tellenbach (Libertas, Leipzig, 1936), recently translated by R. F. Bennett and published in G. Barraclough's *Studies in Medieval History* in 1940. For a new and important aspect of this controversy see Z. N. Brooke's study, *Lay Investiture. . .* in *Proceedings of the British Academy*, XXV, 1939.

The system of proprietary churches had decentralised Church administration and placed in authority over the bishops numbers of laymen who claimed the right of disposing of church property, of nominating or deposing local parish priests. But, as the Papacy needed the support of the German aristocracy in its struggle against the Ghibelline Emperors, the Reformists could not ask the German nobles to give up all their claims to participation in Church administration, with the result that the bishops, while recovering in theory their exclusive powers of administration, had in practice to submit to further limitations by accepting legal control over their relations with the subordinate clergy and with the nobles who claimed to be the protectors of the Church. This was followed by a long and painful transformation of canon law to the great benefit of the subordinate clergy who, without the mitigations of Germanic custom, would probably have fared very hardly under a canon law shaped on the old principle of the bishops' diocesan omnipotence. The outcome of this protracted evolution, which started from the period of the "Investiture" contest, is the modern canon law on the status and the rights of the clergy, which confers on the parish priest a permanence of tenure amounting to almost inalienability. In the Church of England, the transformation produced the "freehold" of which the Anglican clergy are still so proud.

Nor could the Reformists of the eleventh century reintroduce into Western Christianity the quasi-federal principle prevailing in the early Roman period as embodied in the all but autonomous status of the different metropolitan sees and churches, no doubt under the supreme leadership of the Papacy, but a Papacy standing in all disciplinary matters discreetly aloof in the background, and patiently waiting to be asked for advice or for a decision in any particular controversial matter. They could not but emphasise the Papacy's supreme mission in the Church, aim at effacing the last vestige of the autonomy that had prevailed so far, and forestall similar dangers in the future by placing all bishops, regardless of metropolitan and other local rights, directly and immediately under the only supreme head, the Pope. Though they were logical in their inferences and lucky to find arguments in favour of their opinions in the writings of Pope Nicholas I (his productions obtained pride of place in medieval canon law), the principles they advocated must have sounded revolutionary in the ears of their contemporaries.

* *
*

IV

Reaction of the National Element in the West

Investiture Contest—Conflict between Nationalism and Universality ?—Renascence, its cult of individuality and the Church—Revolt of the National Languages against Latin—National tradition of Bohemia and England—Reformers' ignorance of the Eastern tradition

We know that this new concept of universality provoked a violent reaction in all the new Western States—in Germany, France, England and northern lands; but the struggle was after all not so much, as is generally held, one between the spiritual and the secular powers, but one between the supra-national element, represented and enforced by the spiritual power, the Church, and the national element represented by secular authority.

It would be futile to try and picture here the various phases of the conflict. It was tragic for the Papacy and the Church that the German king and Roman Emperor Henry IV refused to understand such high principles and, giving the Pope a German answer, gallantly drew the sword—the only one among Christian princes to do so—in defence of his royal theocracy. In the struggle that followed, the Papacy was forced to mobilise all its forces and to seize every scrap of material and political power it could lay its hands on to secure the triumph of its ideas; and if it eventually succeeded, at least temporarily, it was because the internal structure of the German kingdom could not hold out against the blows of the combined forces of the Papacy and the German aristocracy. The ideas of the eleventh century Reformists triumphed at last, but the supra-national principle, which had been their battle cry, was over-stressed and bolstered up with a mixture of spiritual power and worldly policies which, as a cure, seemed to many pious souls to be worse than the disease.

This gigantic struggle took many unexpected turns. At one time, when Henry VI started realising the plan of building an Empire stretching over Italy, Sicily, Germany and those countries which the Normans, whose heir he was, had planned to conquer, i.e. Greece and North Africa, there was a moment when it seemed that the Papacy was about to lose all its territorial possessions in Central Italy, and that the cool and astute statesman would impose on the Popes the solution that was only framed eight centuries later, in 1929, under the Lateran

Treaty. Neither papal excommunications nor any shrewd diplomacy, but just accident stopped him, for it was the unscrupulous Emperor's premature death that gave the Papacy under Innocent III the opportunity to rise to unprecedented heights, a retrieval that has given to many the impression that the Papacy then set the seal on its medieval claims. But the impression is erroneous, as the renewal of the struggle under Otto IV and Frederick II was to show. Not till imperial authority had ceased to exist were the Popes in a position to impose respect for the political ideology as it had come from the brains of the Reformists of the eleventh century.

In reality, the right solution of the problem has not yet been discovered, nor has the exact balance between the national principle as represented by the princes, and the principle of universality as defended by the Papacy, yet been held. The princes never completely gave in, and after Germany, France stepped into the breach under Philip the Fair with better luck than ever favoured the German Emperors. The pillars of the lofty edifice designed by the Reformists of the eleventh century and erected by Gregory VII and his successors, with the finishing touches added by that great theorician in canon law and practical statesman, Innocent III, cracked in many places under the blows of Frederick II, the half-German and half-Norman statesman and paganised Christian, forerunner of Voltaire, Frederick the Great and of all the grandees of the "Illumination" period, who for all his fluctuations in religious matters remained at bottom a staunch supporter of the old *Rex-Sacerdos* principle.

Boniface VIII tried in vain to stop the decay; his passionate encyclicals only provoked the irreverent laughter of Philip the Fair and his Chancellor Nogaret and their scorn followed the unfortunate Pope into his grave. The New Order, so brilliantly trumpeted in, ended in the unprecedented muddle of the Western Schism and the decadence of the Western Church, not exactly the result foreshadowed by the noble Gregory VII when he set out to purge the Church with the unquestionably sincere desire to raise her to the highest perfection. Although the Papacy's dominant position continued to be respected throughout the West, the national idea was not silenced by any means; the old German claims were revived under Lewis of Bavaria and their bitterness ran right through the *Gravamina Gentis Germanicae*, in protest against the unwarranted interference of the Curia in German national affairs on the pretext of universality. Their ominous rumble had not died out in Luther's days.

All this time, the Kings of England kept as much as they

could clear of the struggle with the Papacy, left the Emperors to fight their own battles, and the Popes to extricate themselves from their own troubles, but took their pickings as circumstances allowed. William the Conqueror never surrendered his claims over the Church, and took full advantage of the theocratic notion for which Henry IV was doing all the fighting; and though the Papacy rose to dominance in England under King John and during the minority of Henry III, William's successors never disclaimed the implications of the *Rex-Sacerdos*. In the reigns of the Edwards, English national consciousness, and the bringing of the Papacy under French influence, considerably tempered the attraction of universality as the Popes preached it, and encouraged national tendencies. For instance, the petition sent by the Commons to the Council in 1428 respecting Martin V's request, with the backing of the Archbishops of Canterbury and York, for the disposal of benefices in England set the pace in this evolution, for the petition stood for the national principle better than any other document when it implied that the Pope was asking for something that would prejudice "oure aller Moder ye Cherche of Canterbury." The position thus created and the Kings' success, due, amongst other reasons, to the insular isolation of their realm, in saving what could be saved of the theocratic theory, prepared the ground for Henry VIII's revolt against the Pope and for the final transformation of the Church of England into a State Church and a National Church.

* * *

Such was the position in Western Christianity when the Western nations reached their maturity at last and entered, at the Renascence period, into full possession, unfortunately too late, of the treasures of classical and Hellenistic culture. The puzzle was that this direct contact with the old world and the discoveries which Western minds made in its literary and cultural store house should have had such a secularising effect on the West, Churchmen not excluded, when we remember that the East had been drawing on it for centuries without losing its head, only a limited number of its "pious" people suspecting, in the study of old pagan writers and philosophers, a danger to orthodoxy. The vast majority of the Greek Christians adopted the attitude of the great Fathers of the Church and went on erecting the Christian edifice on these very foundations. Some of the Patriarchs of Constantinople, foremost among them the great Photius, are still held in veneration by all students of the classics for having contributed to the transmission of these treasures to posterity. Why then did the same studies raise such a storm in the West?

Though the problem deserves a fuller examination, the answer must be left over for some other occasion; it must suffice to inquire to what extent the new doctrines and theories borrowed from the ancient Greeks influenced the growth in the Church of the notions of nationality and universality. All that we can now venture to suggest as one of the main reasons for the extraordinary difference is that the Western nations waited too long before getting acquainted with the secrets of classical and Hellenistic culture. Unlike the Greeks and other Oriental Christian races, they had not been brought up in that vigorous atmosphere from their very childhood, and, as they emerged into manhood, came up with a start against intoxicating materials that promptly turned their heads. That the Church, their teacher and preceptor, should have failed to transmit to them this valuable inheritance was a disappointment, and disposed them to appreciate the new knowledge as a transcendent attainment that would usher in things better and nobler, as well as to depreciate what the Church had taught them so far, without taking into consideration the valid reasons why the Church had not been able to do more for them than she had done. They forgot that it was their own irruption into the Roman Empire that had been responsible for cutting off from her the only source that could have supplied her with the better knowledge. In any case, the surprise of coming upon the discovery of classical philosophy and Hellenistic culture without the direct intermediary of the Church undoubtedly coloured the attitude of the Western Renascence to the Church.

But the Renascence had other consequences, some of which indirectly affected the subsequent progress of the notions of nationality and universality as applied by and in the Church. The art historian, Jacob Burckhardt, whose influence left such deep marks on the Germany of the second half of the nineteenth century (Nietzsche was one of his greatest admirers), and whose ideas still leaven the modern mind,[1] described in his own charming way how the Renascence roused and cultivated the spirit of individuality, though it would be idle to claim that individualism was the discovery of the Renascence. Were the ancient Hellenes not in many respects the greatest individualists? And already St. Thomas Aquinas had allotted

[1] The fourth English edition of his work on *The Civilisation of the Renascence in Italy* was translated by S. G. C. Middlemore (Wien, London, 1937) from the fourteenth German edition. His *Reflections on History* were published in English in London, 1943.

to man's individuality a large place in his first systematic work on theology and philosophy. It is none the less true that the revival of the old Hellenistic culture produced a deeper appreciation of individuality; that Humanism and the Renascence came under its spell and that it was the sixteenth century, the century of the so-called Reforms, that brought the cultus of the individual to its climax.

In the religious field, however, the consequences proved disastrous to Western Christianity, which so far had succeeded in maintaining its unity of doctrine and organisation. The new individualistic craze raised evil "spirits" after their long period of repression by the Church under the principle of unity and universality which, however, continued to be honoured as fundamental characteristics of Christianity; but they had been over-stressed during the latter centuries and too often used as a cloak for policies and notions which had little in common with them. The memory of these extravagances and the search for individuality intoxicated the minds, inspired the Reformers and made their work easier than might have been expected. When the craze shifted to the religious field, it created disruption in the Universal Church and produced a spate of National Churches and denominations, all reflecting the individuality of their founders and their followers.

The walls erected by the Papacy to protect the Church against this very evil proved inadequate and the overgrowth of abuses made them anything but evident to the average faithful. Unrestricted individualism led straight to the denial of a central authority even in doctrinal matters and set up, among others, the principle of private interpretation. Thus a movement full of promise ruined the work of centuries.

There was of course a healthy element in this individualistic fever and some of the Reformers were right in appealing to our Lord's love, not only for humanity but for each individual soul, arguing that it is everybody's individual duty to come to a full knowledge of God. But this was no novelty in Western Christianity, though insistence on the fact would have done the Church no harm: but driven to extremes, the doctrine worked havoc and we see the results in the riot of antagonistic religious bodies, often jealous of each other, in Europe and in the New World. Surely, our Lord never intended the principle of individuality to be stretched to such length as to break up the universality of the Church. We repeat it again, though Eastern Christianity always enjoyed free access to the treasures of Greek and Hellenistic culture—it was part and parcel of its inheritance—and had been reared in its atmosphere (probably for that very reason), yet it never fell a prey to the intoxication of individualism.

And another point : is it not remarkable that the theocratic ideology, once believed to have been defeated by papal hierocracy, once more rose to the surface and was placed in the forefront of his platform by the greatest of the German Reformers, Luther ? For what else was the basis of his solution for the relations between Church and State but the old Order of *Rex-Sacerdos* for which the German Emperors had been fighting for centuries ? Even the obnoxious principle—*cujus regio illius et religio* (each country its own religion)—is only a deduction from this principle, an odd and erroneous deduction that would have shocked even Henry IV, but a deduction none the less. It all goes to show how hollow the victory of the hierocratic theory had been.

* *
*

Reaction against the principle of universality also invaded another field. So far, the universal supra-national character of the Western Church had found its outward expression in a common liturgy and a common liturgical language, Latin, which at the same time was adopted as the normal medium of communication by the cultured classes and diplomacy. The link of course provided immense facilities for the exchange of ideas, the progress of science and international intercourse ; but other consequences were not so satisfactory. That the Church and the intellectual élite should affect a language of their own, different from the common vernaculars, could only be defended as long as the national instincts of young nations remained dormant and their national language undeveloped ; but it was not likely to promote Christian knowledge amongst the simple faithful.

With the passing of years, the economic transformation of the West from primitive agrarianism to commerce and industry, and the rise of the middle classes in the new cities, this lingual separatism only deepened the estrangement between the intellectual classes and the people and threatened to leave the Church in dignified isolation as a foreign product. Charlemagne, responsible though he was—more than any other—for the unification, soon became aware of its difficulties, and his successor, Louis the Pious, endeavoured to bring round the unwilling converts of Saxony and teach them the new doctrines by giving his encouragement to the composition of a long poem, the famous *Heliand* which for the benefit of those rude Saxons explained in some 6,000 lines the life and doctrine of the Saviour, whilst a similar composition treated the history of the Old Testament; only a few hundred lines of this composition have survived. Charlemagne once intended to write a grammar of the Frankish language and instead encouraged the literature of the old heroic sagas.

Little was done in this direction among the Germans in the centuries that followed, as Latin seemed to be sufficient and more convenient to convey the mysteries of the faith to the nations and the prayers of the faithful to the Lord. Only a few prayers, some religious formulae, and short popular treatises were translated into the vernacular, but the German School of translators, which had its headquarters at the Abbey of St. Gallus in modern Switzerland, broke up with the death of its leader Notker (†1022). This Latin sufficiency enormously hampered the growth of literature in the West, and the Church lost the opportunity to play, in the national lives of the people, the part that was expected.

The loss to national letters among Western nations can best be measured by the progress made in the same field by nations that were evangelised by Greek or Syriac missionaries. There the Church enriched Syriac literature, created Coptic and Armenian literature, and inaugurated the golden age of Slavonic letters as early as the ninth and tenth centuries, when the Slav missionaries, SS. Cyril and Methodius, devised the Slav alphabet and translated into the vernacular the Bible and the liturgical books. The two Legends recording their lives and written in Old Slavonic in Moravia at the end of the ninth century are literary treasures that remained for centuries unsurpassed by any similar achievement in the West. Bulgaria had its golden age of Slavonic letters in the tenth century under the Tsar Simeon and the Russians had their national history already in the twelfth century, the Annals of Nestor, written in a mixture of old Slavonic and Russian and equal to the best Byzantine production in the same line. Before that date, scarcely a century after the conversion of Russia, Hilarion of Kiev wrote an original work, a treatise on the Old and the New Testaments, which is in the best tradition of the Greek Fathers. The twelfth century was productive of a number of such original works in Russian prose, written by churchmen.

The nations of the West did not begin to develop their prose till after the twelfth century, mostly in the fourteenth. The Goths provide a useful test case. They received as early as the fourth century the translation of the Bible by Wulfila, a disciple of the Greeks, but no sooner did they leave the sphere of Byzantium to settle in that of the Western Church in Spain and in Italy than their language and their literature were swamped by Latin and decayed.

* *
*

This illustrates best the danger which the privileged position of Latin spelled to the growth of national letters, and the danger was liable to turn into disaster the moment the Western nations, especially those of non-Latin stock, would begin to grow conscious of the inferiority to which their best national elements were condemned. It is surprising to note that a warning of what might happen came from the very nation that had succeeded in the ninth century in making sure of the foundations of its own national literature and liturgy—the Czechs. In the tenth century, Bohemia and Prague took the place of the Moravian Empire after its destruction and up to the beginning of the twelfth century preserved what could be saved of the old Slavonic letters. The decadent state of the German Empire gave the Czech kings the necessary respite to build a strong and influential cultural centre in Prague during the thirteenth and fourteenth centuries, till King Charles IV, Roman Emperor, founded, in 1348, the University of Prague, the first institution of its kind in Central Europe and one that was not long in taking rank next to the best Universities of the West: Bologna, Paris, Oxford and Cambridge.

Few scholars have so far paid attention to the influence this foundation had in Bohemia on the growth of Czech national sentiment, Czech literature and religious life. This intellectual revival was responsible for the first attempt to translate some works of St. Thomas Aquinas and of scholastic theology into the vernacular for the benefit of the rising middle classes, and the same revival inspired the literary activities of the Czech philosopher, Thomas of Shtitny, a Catholic of sound orthodoxy. Only recently has it been discovered that the inspiration of the so-called *devotio moderna* which produced the greatest and most popular Western mystical writer, Thomas à Kempis, is to be found in Prague, in the atmosphere of the University, the breeding ground of all this theological and literary activity.[1]

All this explains why the first Reformers of the Western Church, John Hus and his disciples, laid such stress on the use of the vernacular in divine worship and theological speculation. The pity is that this aspect of a movement that ended so tragically in heresy, has escaped the attention of scholars.

[1] Cf. E. Winter, *Tausend Jahre Geisteskampf im Sudetenraum*, Prague, 1938, pp. 57–97, 143 sq.

Those who dealt with this problem were mostly under the influence of the ideology that swept over Europe in the nineteenth century and at the beginning of the twentieth, and saw in the first Reformation no more than the negative side, i.e. the fight against Rome and the Papacy, forgetting that there were other aspects more interesting, though less spectacular, those national and social aspects which are still waiting for a scholar detached enough to see their value and bring them to light. Not until then shall we be able to view the whole movement in its proper setting and in its own place in the evolution of Western Christianity.

The endeavour of the so-called " Utraquists " to receive Communion under both kinds, to say Mass and the Office in Czech, without for that reason being heretics or ceasing to be good Catholics, is significant. In vain did they try to obtain from Rome the consecration of an archbishop of their own; the German Masters saw to it that what was an interesting development should pass for heresy and be crushed. The Bohemian lesson was lost—for Rome, but signs are not wanting that it was learnt by the German Reformer, Martin Luther.

And so it came about that the sense of inferiority in this respect and the growing desire of the middle classes to expand in influence throughout Western society was thoroughly understood by the Reformers who were often indebted to the use of the vernacular in religious propaganda and liturgy for the rapid spread of their doctrines. They precipitated the pace of the Western Church's slow progress, took full advantage of the initiative, and by their translations of the Bible not only promoted the knowledge of Scripture among large classes of the population, but also created the wrong impression that the Roman Church had done nothing for the promotion of Biblical studies. It thus happened that the admission of the vernacular into the official divine worship, instead of copying the marvellous results so familiar to the East, became an instrument of disruption. This is extraordinary, if we remember that this revolution originated among the Germanic people whose ancestors had, by their ready acceptance of Latin as a medium for religious and liturgical expression, contributed most to the state of things that drew such violent reactions in the sixteenth century.

And again, we should note that in this respect the insular kingdom of England slightly deviated from the general drift observable in Europe, especially in the Germanic parts, as the conversion of Anglo-Saxon England was brought about by methods in many cases different from those in vogue among the Germanic tribes. In England, Latin never succeeded in completely supplanting the national tongue and Anglo-Saxon maintained its right of existence, in subordination to Latin, in official communications throughout the kingdom. In the seventh century, the Anglo-Saxons hailed a great religious poet in the monk Caedmon who used his native tongue to sing the history of the Creation and of Israel, the Life of Christ, the Last Judgment, the torments of Hell and the joys of Paradise and sang better than the anonymous Saxon author of *Heliand*. It is still a matter of controversy how far Caedmon influenced *Heliand*. There were many other minor poets who, as Bede testifies, tried to versify the Christian mysteries in Anglo-Saxon; one of them—Cynewulf—was good enough to take rank next to Caedmon. Bede himself, the greatest Christian scholar of the eighth century, professed particular veneration for his native tongue, an example not always followed by contemporaries of Germanic origin : he was keenly interested in the national folk songs and on his death-bed finished an Anglo-Saxon translation of St. John's Gospel. This remarkable tradition, so uncommon in European history, was again revived in the days of King Alfred, found new inspiration after the Norman conquest, and endured till the advent of Humanism. Thomas More did not share the dislike for his native tongue of his friend, the great Humanist, Erasmus of Rotterdam, and he was at his best in English. It would be interesting to inquire in greater detail how far this regard for native speech, which was such a feature of medieval England, facilitated the introduction of the vernacular into the liturgy of the National Church established by Henry VIII.[1]

* *
*

But havoc was worst in the doctrinal field. The Reformation was a revolt against an old Order which had grown obsolete and failed to keep step with new developments, as well as against its representatives who had gone too far in enforcing some of their ideological claims without making an effort at the right moment to meet an intelligent opposition and to watch their steps. But the Reformist momentum rushed beyond its premisses. Instead of pulling up at the right door, where reasonable reforms were needed, the Reformers allowed their team to take the bit between their teeth and to damage

1 Cfr. some valuable indications in this direction in a study on *Milton und Caedmon*, published in 1911 by H. v. Gajsek in the *Wiener Beiträge zur Englischen Philologie*, Vol. XXXV.

the fences, knocking over such essential institutions as the Mass, the centre of every Christian liturgy, the sacraments and the solid hierarchical structure of the Church. Where they were wrong was in imagining that they were driving back to early Church history and restoring the Church's doctrine and liturgy as these had flourished in apostolic days, and many learned Protestant schools, whilst contributing immensely to a better knowledge of the Church's evolution, have tried in vain to prove that the Reformers were right.

The pity is that the Reformers knew so little about the Eastern Churches and their history. For centuries, Eastern Christianity had stood discredited in Western eyes, and all that the Reformers knew about it was derived from the Latins' polemical writings against the schismatic Greeks and from the venomous complaints made by French, Normans and Venetians about the duplicity of the Greeks, who stubbornly refused to see any blessing in the ruthless colonising methods applied by the foreign invaders of the once mighty Byzantine Empire. At the time of the Western Reformation, the whole Christian East was under a cloud and lay paralysed under the heel of the conquering Turks, all out to convince their subjects that Allah was the only God and Mohammed His greatest prophet. Had the Reformers' information in this respect been more adequate, it is quite possible that at least some of them would have paused to think before taking the plunge; for, after all, in doctrinal matters and in the principles of hierarchical structure, the Eastern Churches still remain in many ways, owing to their conservatism, the best witnesses to the doctrine and to the institutions of the primitive Christian age. Eastern dismay at the transformation of Western Christianity, and the Easterners' curt refusal to accept the Reformers' teaching, is a fair test of the distance the reforming movement had drifted from the common base of the Eastern and Western Churches, the *depositum fidei*.

And that is how it has come about that to-day Rome is left standing as the sole and last protagonist of the principle of universality and unity.

* * *

V

Balance Between the National and the Universal the Way to Reunion

A Byzantine solution of the problem—Responsibilities of modern Christianity and the Mission of the Church of England

To-day we stand disrupted and divided against the united forces of evil in league against the principles of Christianity and of all fundamental religion, and we feel our helplessness and the weight of our responsibility before history. Our race is facing perhaps the worst crisis in its evolution and looks to us for the right answer and correct guidance. There are millions of souls still waiting for the message which Christ delivered to His Church. The political might of Islam is broken, but its influence is still formidable in Africa and Asia. The Far East is not yet conquered to Christ: we have been marking time for fifteen centuries and find ourselves in exactly the same position as when Christianity was stopped by Islam in its eastward spread from the Persian Empire. Great, therefore, is our task, but how shall we face it? And how can our Lord's blessing be on our work, if we force our disunion on the nations that still await the message of Christ?

Is there then no way to save the principle of universality of Christ's Church, so sacred to the Christians of all ages from the beginning of the Christian era down to our days both in East and West, yet at the same time allow the national and racial element its rightful place in Christianity? For after all, racial and national identity cannot be fundamentally incompatible with Christianity: it is part of our nature and has never been silenced, not even at the time when Rome succeeded in applying the principle of universality, which it always gallantly defended, to its utmost stretch. The evolution of Christianity in the past has demonstrated with sufficient clarity that the problem of Christian unity ultimately reposes on the right application of these two principles and the right balancing of these two elements.

If my personal opinion counts for anything, it seems to me that there was one moment in Church history, long before the revolution of the Reformation tore the unity of the Western Church to pieces, when the right solution of these problems seemed to be on the verge of realisation, and the man who proposed this solution was no other than the Patriarch Photius, one of the greatest figures in the annals of the Eastern Churches, yet one who has so far been branded by the West as the Father of all schisms and the mortal enemy of the Roman Primacy.

It is true that he was the first of the Oriental Patriarchs to come into conflict with the Roman See at the very moment when the Papacy, after converting the Western nations, was riding the crest of the wave; when Nicholas I for the first time stressed the principle of the Church's universality and its unity under one head so strongly, made public what we call to-day the medieval claims of the Papacy and, worst of all, attempted to apply it to the East. It is my conviction, after studying the history of this first schism in all its details, that the traditional opinion about Photius has been led astray[1].

Photius never questioned the necessity for the Church's universality and for the union of his See with Rome, any more than did his predecessors and all the Eastern Patriarchs; but when faced with Nicholas' claim to rule the East with the same absolute power as he wielded in the West, Photius took an important step to do justice to some of the Pope's claims and to save the unity of the Church, yet at the same time to maintain the rights of his own Church as theyt had evolved in Eastern Christianity; his Church *de facto* re cognised the right of appeal to the Holy See of Rome as to he supreme court of the Church Universal, whose decisions had to be final and irrevocable. This happened at the synod of 861, which gave the pontifical legates the right to judge a Byzantine Patriarch—Ignatius. The Acts of this synod disappeared and only a Latin extract from a copy kept in the Lateran Archives has been preserved in Cardinal Deusdedit's Collection of canon law. This Collection was written at the end of the eleventh century and came to light in 1870 (edition by Martinucci), and again in 1905 (edition by Wolf von Glanvell). Though the extract is absolutely genuine, no expert has ever dared to touch it, because it gave the direct lie to what so far had been generally admitted as historical truth.

From this important document, we are now in a position to visualise how the Byzantines of the ninth century understood

[1] I have published some of the most important findings in the reviews, *Byzantion*, Vol. VIII, XI, 1933, 1936, in the *Bulletin of the Bulgarian Archaeclogical Institute*, Vol. IX, 1935, in the *Annals of Institut Kondakov*, Vol. X, Prague, 1938 and in the *Bulletin of R. Academy of Belgium*, Vol. XXIV, Bruxelles, 1938. A resumé in English appeared in the *Report of the Proceedings at the Unity Octave*, Oxford, 1942 (*The Patriarch Photius: Father of Schism, or Patron of Reunion?* pp. 19–31), and in *The Month*, Vol. 179, No. 934, 1943 (*East and West, The Photian Schism: A Re-Statement of Facts*, pp. 257–270). My work on the History and the Legend of the Photian Schism has been ready for publication since 1940 and is waiting for a publisher.

he organisation of the Universal Church. They defended the quasi-autonomous rights of the different Churches to manage their own affairs according to their own laws and customs without admitting the direct intervention of any other Church ; but in order to save the unity and universal character of Christ's Church, they acknowledged the necessity of a supreme Head, not only to be consulted in matters concerning faith and morals, but acting as a supreme court of appeal even in disciplinary matters. This Byzantine doctrine as contained in the Acts of the synod in Photius' reign does ample justice to the Roman Primacy and preserves the Church's unity without prejudicing the national element, which is part and parcel of our Christian evolution. And what is better still, the Byzantine Church of the ninth and tenth centuries made repeated use of its right of appeal.

We know that this solution of the problem has so far not been fully tried. The Westerners and the Reformists of the eleventh century inaugurated a new world order and even tried to improve on the claims of Pope Nicholas I ; but once we understand their mentality as we have tried to explain it, we need not wonder that the most representative of the reformist school, Cardinal Humbert, not only fell foul of the Patriarch Cerularius of Constantinople, but even completely failed to understand the different growth and the spirit of Eastern Christianity, when he excommunicated him. The schism that resulted from the clash has deepened ever since, the solution arrived at in the ninth century being completely forgotten by the East as well as by the West.

* *
*

And yet, the fact remains that the solution has been tried. To-day, when, after centuries of bitter experience we are again facing a great crisis and deploring the loss of our unity, we could do worse than go back to the ninth century when, for the first time, the Churches came upon the same problem ; and we could do worse than give consideration to the solution devised by the Byzantine Church and its great Patriarch. If we discover there an avenue leading to reconciliation, we have to follow it, should it even be overgrown with past misunderstandings and obliterated by centuries of oblivion. It is our sacred duty to clear it and re-open it to traffic, were it but to fulfil the last desire of the Divine Founder of the Church for one flock and one Shepherd.

The same applies to-day to British Christianity more than to any other. Providence has bestowed on the British nation exceptional facilities. There is again in the world an Empire uniting the West with Africa and the Far East, an Empire that has all the possibilities of a channel for the propagation of the faith to the farthest corners of the earth and with access to the Islamic world, and an Empire that has found a mighty partner in another Anglo-Saxon world, the United States. The Roman Empire was not more Christian than the British, even much less, and it certainly commanded no better opportunities. Will the British Empire and the Anglo-Saxon world fulfil the mission with which Providence has charged them, at any rate as much as He charged the Roman Empire? Or will history one day register their lost opportunities as it does for the Persian Empire and its unfulfilled mission in the Far East? We do not know the future; nor do we know if a new Islam will not be on the move to spoil our chances as it spoiled the chances of the Persian Empire. All we know is that we have to strain every nerve to help towards the realisation of a great task, which will not grow less if Providence gives the Anglo-Saxon nations and the Empire the world's leadership.

Great responsibilities are also facing the largest Christian body in the Anglo-Saxon world—the Church of England, the last stronghold of the medieval ideology of *Rex-Sacerdos*, carried to the further stage of a king sharing his powers and prerogatives in religious matters with his Parliament, but still holding the substance of the ideals for which the Emperor Henry IV fought and which William the Conqueror upheld and handed on to his successors. England, thanks to its kings' capacity to hold aloof from the conflict between the two rival theories that monopolised the continent during the Middle Ages, was able to elaborate its own workable solution, which, but for Henry VIII's unfortunate doings, would have allowed the British Isles to keep out of the tornado that swept over the continent at the time of the Reformation. Now the National Church of England, established by Henry VIII, was facing the danger that awaits every Church, as it tears itself away from the Church Universal and its visible Head; and yet, unable as she was to withstand every onslaught by the Reformers, she did contrive to save a goodly portion of the *depositum fidei* inherited from Rome.

Because of this and of her position, she may yet deserve well of Christianity by serving as a bridge to convey to more dissident bodies some truths and practices that were discarded by the Reformers. Such may be the part which Providence in His divine wisdom has destined her to play, provided she be not content with looking for some vague formula to federate denominations and make confusion worse confounded. Only one way lies open to the inspiration and strength necessary for such a task: by boldly stepping forward and giving the lead in the direction of Christian reunion and unity in doctrine and leadership, she may fulfil the first condition for God's blessing on the British Empire's Christian and spiritual mission. It may be the signal for the great crusade for the Christian conquest of distant continents to start, when a new Bede may rise, to record the deeds and recall the title which the French once gave to a history of their conquest of the Holy Land—*Gesta Dei per Anglos*.

This is not a vision : even a historian has the right, besides recording the past and deploring lost opportunities, to look ahead and open new vistas in the light of the past. If the consummation sounds impossible to-day (human insufficiency, lack of courage and good will have wrecked so many possibilities), a Christian need never despair, knowing that *omnia possibilia in Christo*—with Christ, nothing is impossible.

POSTSCRIPT

The survey, short as it is, of the evolution of the ideas of universality and nationalism in Christianity which the reader has just read must have shown him the complexity of the problem, since it touches on so many cognate questions and needs re-stating or qualifying at every new angle. A few bibliographical indications may introduce the reader to aspects that have lost none of their timeliness to this very day.

Recent developments in Germany have revealed, as we think, more clearly than elsewhere the growing vitality and urgency of this problem in the life of a nation. Was it not a desire, driven to its extreme limits, to discover a national expression for every form of human activity that prompted so many to look for the pattern of a national religion in the pre-Christian period of the nation and to complete the few elements found there with such scraps of Christianity as seemed to reflect German character and mentality best? The notion of a national Church as elaborated at the end of the nineteenth century by the famous Orientalist Paul de Lagarde (P. A. Bötticher) did not die with him, but lived to be in the twenties and thirties of our century the most popular and topical of his utterances. Nor was it mere coincidence that his name found its place of honour in A. Rosenberg's *Mythus des XX Jahrhunderts* (6th edition, Munich, 1933, p. 458) side by side with the mystic of the fourteenth century, Master Eckhart. De Lagarde's *Deutsche Schriften* (German Writings—Göttingen, 1886) in which he launched out into his new opinions and criticisms of Catholicism and Protestantism found its new editor in 1924 and 1934 and proved a lively topic of debate: suffice it to mention L. Schmid, *Paul de Lagardes Kritik an Kirche, Theologie und Christentum*, Stuttgart 1935 (Paul de Lagarde's Criticism of the Church, Theology and Christianity); H. Wiltig, *Die Geistige Welt Paul de Lagardes*, Hamburg, 1937 (Paul de Lagarde's Spiritual World), and two characteristic studies published in the *Zeitschrift für Theologie und Kirche*, 1934: H. E. Eisenhuth, "Die Idee der Nationalen Kirche bei Paul de Lagarde," pp. 145—166 (Paul de Lagarde's Notion of a National Church) and K. Heussi, "Die Germanisierung des Christentums als Historisches Problem," pp. 119—145 (The Germanisation of

Christianity as a Historical Problem). These indications are of course not complete and are only intended to show the importance and the actuality of the present subject and to help those who might intend to go further into it.

The anxiety to formulate the national spirit as it operated in the development of Christianity can be traced in recent historical and theological literature and here again Germany, the greatest western Christian nation of non-Latin stock, has evinced the liveliest interest. Good and useful ideas on nations and their relation to religion in general and their place in the evolution of Christianity in particular are to be found in Th. Grentrup's study—*Volk und Volkstum im Lichte der Religion*, Freiburg i.B., 1937 (Nations and Nationality in the Light of Religion) and in his book, disappointing though it is in many ways, *Religion und Muttersprache*, Münster i.W., 1932 (Religion and the Vernacular), published in the collection Deutschtum und Ausland, Heft 47—49. In many German quarters the Germanisation of Christianity has become quite a popular slogan, though not always felicitously formulated. There is also a problem of Germanisation still awaiting investigation in the early growth of the Western Church at its medieval period, for between the sixth and the tenth centuries the new converts of Germanic stock transformed Western Christianity in many ways and it was that same Germanisation of the Western Church which to a great extent brought about the deterioration of the mutual understanding between East and West and thereby schism and disruption. Here we have touched on only one aspect of the problem; a fuller treatment must be held over for another occasion. Complementary indications disclosing some interesting vistas may be found in H. Dausend, *Germanische Frömmigkeit in der kirchlichen Liturgie*, Wiesbaden, 1936 (German Piety in Church Liturgy), and in *Germanische Rechtssymbolik in der Römischen Liturgie* (Symbolism of German Law in the Roman Liturgy), written by the Abbot of Maria-Laach, I. Herwegen, Heidelberg, 1913 (Deutschrechtliche Beiträge, Band VIII). The same authority on the history of the Liturgy has tried in a short synthesis to place in its true setting the problem that has preoccupied so many historians and theologians—*Antike, Germanentum und Christentum*, Salzburg, 1932 (The Classical Age, Germans and Christianity), but the subject is far from exhausted and is still growing in interest and importance.

With this transformation of Western Christianity by the new converts of the early Middle Ages in mind, we considered it necessary to insist in our lectures on the evolution of Eastern

Christianity in the first centuries and to examine how the Christians of that early period faced the problem of nationalism and universality, a point of view that is often neglected; being naturally inclined to leave western problems in their western setting, we forget that the attitude to these same problems in early Christianity can only be traced along its eastern lineage. In this respect, the penetration of Christianity into the interior of Asia deserves special attention, and given the race between the great western and eastern powers for political and economic supremacy in that part of the world, its lesson is applicable to every age. Whoever wishes to go further into the question than was possible in these lectures, will find useful information in I. B. Aufhauser's book, *Christentum und Buddhismus im Ringen um Fernasien*, Leipzig, 1922, Bücherei der Kultur und Geschichte, Bd. 25 (Christianity and Buddhism in their contest for the Far East).

The study of this period would no doubt have gained in thoroughness and clarity by a survey of the evolution of papal power and a parallel between the conditions obtaining in East and West, showing the reasons for the growth of papal prestige during the invasions of the Roman Empire and the extent of the response from the East to the urgency of a central lead in religious matters. Such digressions would have had a bearing on the problem of universality, but needed more space; for this reason, we preferred to hold it over for easier days. There also exists a close affinity between this problem and the growth of political ideologies in East and West from the time of Constantine the Great till the separation of the Churches and many useful observations could be made in this connection, but we are reserving this comparative survey for a separate study.

This is a subject, as evidenced by the interest which these problems have aroused among English scholars, which has a special appeal to Anglo-Saxon genius. The ideas of the German pioneer in this field, O. F. von Gierke, found a quick response in the great historian of English Law, F. W. Maitland, who translated the most valuable part of Gierke's *Das Deutsche Genossenschaftsrecht* (Berlin, 1868—1913) and published it in 1900 (*Political Theories of the Middle Ages*, Cambridge, fifth impression in 1938) with a masterly introduction that should be read by every student of the evolution of political theories in England. The more recent book by F. Kern, *Gottesgnadentum und Widerstandsrecht im Früheren Mittelalter*, Leipzig, 1914 (The Divine Right of Kings and the Right of Resistance in the early Middle Ages) was made accessible to the British public in an English translation in T. Barraclough's *Medieval Studies* (vol. 4, *Kingship and Law in the Middle Ages*, Oxford, 1939).

The ecclesiastical aspect of the problem was more fully developed by J. N. Figgis (*The Political Aspects of St. Augustine's "City of God,"* London, 1921; *Studies of Political Thought. From Gerson to Grotius*, Cambridge, 1916; *Churches in the Modern State*, London, 1923) and by R. W. and A. J. Carlyle in the work quoted above. Very useful are also the works: C. H. McIlwain, *The Growth of Political Thought in the West*, London, 1932, and A. P. D'Entrèves, *The Mediaeval Contribution to Political Thought. Thomas Aquinas, Marsilius of Padua*, Oxford, 1939. The editor of Marsilius of Padua's *Defensor Pacis* (Cambridge, 1928), Ch. W. Previté Orton, published in 1935 a synthetical study on this curious political thinker (*Marsilius of Padua*, from the Proceedings of the British Academy).

Another problem that would deserve fuller treatment is, besides the Renascence, the progress of laicization at the close of the Middle Ages, of institutions which till then had been under the exclusive control of churchmen. Obviously, the transfer greatly contributed to the deterioration of the spirit of universality in the West. As the lay element of the middle classes, which took over the direction of affairs in the new national States, was jealous of the churchmen and felt more inclined, nay driven, to use the vernacular in its contact with the masses, its opposition often took the character of a struggle between nationalism and the notion of universality. The problem is interesting enough to call for expert examination and all we can do now is to draw the attention of those who wish for fuller information to the study by G. de Lagarde, *La Naissance de l'Esprit Laique au Déclin du Moyen Age* (3 vol., Paris, 1934—1937).

Fascinating as the story of Christianity's constructive metabolism in medieval Germany is and essential to the understanding of the problem of nationalism and universality in western Christendom, the religious growth of England is no less provocative, though many of its features, so different from the continental variety, are apt to be puzzling. We have touched on the growth of the Anglo-Saxon Church, but more information can now be found in F. M. Stenton's *Anglo-Saxon England* (Oxford, 1943, The Oxford History of England) issued after the publication of our paper. Especially interesting is what we find in this captivating book (pp. 101 sq.) on the proprietary sanctuaries in the pagan Anglo-Saxon period—Cusan weoh near Farnham in Surrey, and the weoh or shrine that belonged to a man named Paeccel, a name that still survives in the disguise of Patchway, near Stanmer in Sussex; on Gregory the Great's missionary work in England (pp. 103 sq.) and on Anglo-Saxon poetry (pp. 191 sq.).

Another field of interesting inquiry touched on in our survey is the growth of nationalism in England's religious history with its alternating stages of acceptance and repudiation of the universality as conceived by the reformed papacy from William the Conqueror's time till the reign of Henry VIII. The period covering the reigns of William I, William II, Stephen and Henry II has been treated very thoroughly by Z. N. Brooke, now professor of Medieval History in Cambridge, and his findings on the subject (*The English Church and the Papacy*, Cambridge, 1931), will for long remain classical. Different in many ways as the corresponding evolutions in England and Germany are, they still originate from the same source—the old *Rex-Sacerdos* theory. William I's reformatory zeal coupled with his firm attitude to the new claims recalls the emperor Henry III rather than Henry IV. England's atmosphere differed so much from the Empire's and the way to a fair solution, judging from the attitude of the rulers and the clergy, looked so easy, that it seems a puzzle how such radical views on the subject could ever find their way into England as we find them in the tracts of the so-called Anonymous of York. It is rather piquant that the most uncompromising defence of the *Rex-Sacerdos* theory, at its first clash with the hierocratic ideology, should have come, not from Germany, but from a Norman and a stout supporter of King Henry I.

An important step towards a possible compromise was taken by King Henry II, who, without renouncing all control on his Church and its officials, had, after Thomas Becket's murder, to authorize contact with Rome and canonical elections; yet, St. Anselm of Canterbury and Thomas Becket notwithstanding, and in spite of the Magna Carta and its famous clause on the liberty of the Church, this country remained the last refuge and sanctuary of the *Rex-Sacerdos* theory. It would be interesting to inquire how such a situation was brought about, altered in the thirteenth and fourteenth centuries and to what extent it was influenced by the Papacy's French captivity. As an exceptionally striking illustration of further developments, let us quote the incident of January 13th, 1428, when the Commons rejected Martin V's request, backed though it was by the archbishops of Canterbury and York. The solemn protocol of the archbishops' intervention before Parliament is to be found in D. Wilkins's *Concilia Magnae Britanniae et Hiberniae* (London, 1737, III, 483), and the petition by the Commons to the King requesting him to defend the archbishop of Canterbury against unjust accusations in Rome (that he schulde have been and procured ayens the Liberties of the Courte of Rome in this lond) is the only answer to the request for cancelling the prohibition of papal provisions in England. This petition clearly formulates, as far as we can see, the national principle, however humbly it refers to " oure holy Fader the Pope ": " Be cause whereof, oure holy Fader was mevyd to make certein proces ayens him, in prejudice of him and aure aller Moder ye Cherche of Canterbury, which we been alle holden to worship and susteyne in as muche as in us is. . . ." The royal answer to the Petition was: Le Roi le voet (Rolls of Parliament, IV, 322). The relations of Martin V with England were suggestive enough for the German historian J. Haller to devote to them a special monograph (*England und Rome unter Martin V*. Quellen und Forschungen aus Italianischen Archiven, Bd. 8, 1905). That Henry VIII's innovations should have met with such subservient acceptance would point to the existence in England of a peculiar mentality of several centuries' growth—which opens up another field for impartial inquiry with special reference to the evolution we are studying here.

No study of the genesis of English Christianity can afford to omit reference to the growth of Christianity in the sister island, for the Irish contribution to the early developments of western Christendom was important enough to find a place in any survey of the problem under consideration. Irish Christianity has generally been treated as the Cinderella of Church history and we know of only one study of western Christianity that almost does justice to the Irish contribution in the building of western Christendom—H. Schnürer, *Kirche und Kultur im Mittelalter*, Paderborn, 1935, vol. II (Church and Culture in the Middle Ages).

These are some of the aspects on which we should have liked to dwell in this study and we have mentioned them to make it clear that we are fully conscious of the fact that it could not be seriously meant to be exhaustive. Let these few words suffice as a lead to those who would feel inclined to go into further details.

XIII

THE CIRCUS PARTIES IN BYZANTIUM

THEIR EVOLUTION AND THEIR SUPPRESSION

The problems of the origin and evolution of the Circus parties in Byzantium have of recent years attracted increasing attention among specialists. This growing interest is only natural, as every student of the early period of Byzantine history is aware of the important rôle which the Circus parties often played in the political and religious life of Byzantium. The problems raised are many and some of them difficult. It is not always easy to give a clear picture of the growth of those parties, as the sources referring to them are not numerous and often lack precision. The present short study has no other object than to recapitulate the results of recent researches and to call the attention of experts to some details that might perhaps help them in solving the puzzle of the sudden disappearance of the Circus parties from political life.

As students of Byzantine history used to look at the world of Byzantium from a Roman angle, little was known until fairly recently of the people's share in public affairs in the Byzantine Empire. It is true, of course, that both people and Senate once participated very actively in the government of ancient Rome, but their rights and influence gradually dwindled to almost complete absorption into the emperor's divine and absolute power; and as the people thus surrendered its sovereignty to the emperor to make him the exclusive and autocratic source of law, the old legislative assemblies ceased to meet and the Senate degenerated into a purely ornamental body with little more than the shadow of its old powers and prerogatives.

The decline definitely began under the successors of Diocletian; and when Constantine the Great founded his dynasty, he could safely offer his administrative posts to senators as well as to knights, since the senators had long ceased to be the monarch's rivals. Since Constantine had transferred the whole organism of Roman institutions to the Bosphorus, it was assumed that things continued to evolve in Byzantium along the same lines as they had done in Rome under the Caesars, and that they were not affected by Christianity, however much it may have transformed some of the old Roman institutions. But it seemed difficult to accept the view that in a Christian empire the imperial sovereignty which the Church had accepted in its Roman form should tolerate any limitation from a body such as the Senate or the people, when the old formula "Senatus Populusque Romanus" was nothing but the empty shell of its old self.[1]

But this general conviction is open to correction, for Christianity did influence the growth of political ideas in Byzantium more than might have seemed possible at first sight. It is now established that when Constantine, compelled by the spread of the Arian heresy and the trouble it created in the Church and in the Empire, decided to summon a council in order to define the true Christian doctrine on the subject, he took his inspiration from the Roman Senate and modelled the convocation and the procedure of the council on the senatorial assemblies, which were to remain the pattern of all subsequent meetings of the same kind.[2]

The new ecclesiastical senate found it of course impossible to keep to the restrictive procedure to which the emperors had subjected the Roman Senate, since the topics on which the bishops, the new senators, had to give their decision, were of vital importance; nor could the emperor, who personally presided at the meetings, unless represented by his magistrates, expect the council merely to express their agreement by acclamation, as had been the general custom at the sessions of the Senate during the last period of the Roman Empire. The new senators were given full freedom of speech and in spite of the emperor's claim to be *summus ponti-*

---

[1] Cf. on the functions of the Roman people and the Senate under the Republic and the Patriciate, Th. Mommsen, *Römisches Staatsrecht,* III, (Leipzig, 1887, 1888), 1, 2. An exhaustive study on Roman Senate from the Roman Kingdom to the period of the Caesars was written by O'Brien Moore for Pauly's *Real-Enzyklopädie der Classischen Altertumswissenschaft,* Supplementband VI (Stuttgart, 1935), *s.v.* "Senatus," col. 660-800, where a full bibliography will be found.

[2] Cf. our study "De Potestate Civili in Conciliis Oecumenicis, Acta VI Congressus pro Unione Ecclesiarum"; *Academia Velehradensis* vol. X (Olomouc, 1930). An English translation of the lecture appeared in the Review *Christian East,* X (1932), 95-108. Constantine's initiative must have been accepted the more readily by his contemporaries since the bishops themselves had followed in their deliberative assemblies before the Nicean Council the agenda of the Senate. Cf. P. Batiffol, "Le Règlement des premiers Conciles Africains et le Règlement du Sénat Romain," *Bulletin de l'anc. Lit. et d'archéol. chrét.,* III (1913), 3-19; *Idem,* "Origine du Règlement des conciles," *Études de liturgie et d' archéol.* (Paris, 1919), 84-153.

fex, they actually restricted his authority in religious matters, since they were the only voters, to the exclusion of the emperor or his representatives, as by a special dispensation of Providence it had been the case in the Roman Senate. Their decisions were given force of law in ecclesiastical matters and were endorsed with the emperor's signature. The ecclesiastical senate therefore revived features which had been a credit to the Roman Senate under the Republic.

It is quite possible that this development acted as a stimulant on the further evolution of the Senate in Byzantium. In fact, the Byzantine Senate, contrary to what has been hitherto assumed, was anything but a dead institution, and many instances can be quoted to prove that although it never attained the freedom and importance of its ecclesiastical partner, it still did continue to exist and to perform some important functions for many centuries. In many ways, the Byzantine Senate differed from its Roman predecessor: it was composed of high administrative officials and acted as an imperial council advising the emperor in all matters of imperial concern, the custom gradually prevailing that some political questions should not be decided by the emperor without first being laid before the Senate for its opinion. In the VIIIth century we see that body opposing the emperor's wishes and the weak Michael I yielding to the Senate's will; and in the intervals between two succeeding reigns, the Senate used to function on its own authority.[3] It is then not improbable that the oecumenical councils, which after all were an offshoot of the senatorial institution, infused into the Byzantine Senate, by expanding their own powers, the will to recover some of the functions which had been the attribution of the early Senate.[4]

---

[3] This matter has so far not been adequately studied. Cf. J. B. Bury, *The Constitution of the Later Roman Empire* (Cambridge, 1910), 4, 7, 34, 48. J. B. Bury compares the functions of the Senate in Byzantium with those of the Synhedrion in the Hellenistic kingdoms. The resemblance deserves to be noted: was there in Byzantium a certain survival of the old Hellenistic traditions which rose again to the surface when the central government was transferred from West to East? Cf. on the interaction of Roman and Oriental law L. Mitteis's book *Reichsrecht und Volksrecht in den Östlichen Provinzen des Römischen Kaiserreichs* (Leipzig, 1891).

[4] On the Byzantine Senate in the VIIth and XIth centuries, cf. C. Diehl, "Le Sénat et le Peuple Byzantin aux VIIe et VIIIe siècles," *Byzantion,* 1 (1924), 201. On the evolution of the Senate in the western part of the Empire, cf. C. Lécrivain, *Le Sénat Romain depuis Dioclétien à Rome et â Con-*

The fact is that although the old Roman conception of the monarch's absolute sovereignty continued to hold the field in Byzantium, the people had apparently more to say in political affairs than they had in Rome under the Caesars. The people's share in the installation of a new emperor is well known: the emperor had first to be acclaimed by the crowds in the Hippodrome before his coronation. It is well known also that the people of Constantinople often had a voice in the autocrats' decisions; this voice, in the first centuries of the Empire, was pronounced by the two prominent parties in the Circus of the city, the Greens and the Blues. The introduction of this new public feature must somehow be linked with the religious status of the Empire. The great theological controversies which had started with the rise of Arianism were not limited to churchmen and intellectuals, but roused the interest of the middle classes in the cities as well. The special character of eastern Church organisation and of eastern mentality made this inevitable. The growth of eastern Christianity on a national basis had resulted in a lively participation by the ordinary faithful in the divine service and in the life of the Church, and since the champions of the new faith had always made it their policy to appeal to the crowds for support of their doctrines, it was impossible for the faithful to keep clear of controversies. As the agitators looked outside the churches for their base of attack, they could only find it in the existing popular organisations.

On the other hand, if the emperor happened to adhere to the decisions of a heretical assembly and, as executor of the bishops, imposed their decisions on the clergy and the faithful of the Empire, these were left but one way to redress and to restore the faith —to wait patiently for the advent of the next emperor and count on his orthodoxy to reverse the unorthodox acts of his predecessor. It was only natural that many of them did not limit themselves to prayers and pious wishes to attain their end, but cast about for some more tangible methods to get rid of the heretical emperor. Here again, the Byzantine constitution came to the rescue.[5] The

stantinople (Paris, 1888), *Bibliothèque des Ecoles Françaises d'Athènes et de Rome,* LII. We should especially mention two studies by H. Gelzer, *Das Verhältnis von Staat und Kirche in Byzanz,* and *Die Konzilien als Reichsparlamente,* republished in his *Ausgewählte Schriften* (Leipzig, 1907), 56-155.

[5] A work on the Byzantine constitution is still wanting. E. Stein has been preparing a study on the Byzantine State, but his preparatory study — "Untersuchungen zur Spätbyzantinischen Verfassung und Wirtschaftsgeschichte," published in *Mitteilungen zur Osmanischen Geschichte,* Bd. I (1922),

emperor was God's Anointed, chosen by the Lord to carry out His will. Only the Lord had the disposal of the throne. He alone could discard an emperor as He had discarded Saul, and select a better representative as He had selected David to replace Saul. But the only sign of an alteration in God's will was the success of a usurper in seizing the throne and ejecting the occupant, which made a successful revolution the only possible method, one that had the semblance of legality, of getting rid of a monarch who was not wanted. Malcontents could thus hardly think of a better expedient to turn out any emperor who failed to fall in with their political or religious views or to pander to their ambitions.

If any opposition party was to achieve success, it was essential that it should be organised and find a backing in the army as well as among a portion of the populace. Evidently there was in Byzantium no political organisation as such which could be used as a spearhead for any agitation, political or otherwise; but the necessity for giving some sort of expression to agreement or disagreement with imperial policy was so imperative that since such a spearhead did not exist, it had to be created. So it came about that in the early public life of Byzantium the Circus factions provided just the material for the purpose.

The Byzantines had inherited the Romans' passion for horse racing and the organisation which in Rome had grown round the Circus and public entertainments found its way into the new eastern capital. Here the Circus parties—Blues, Greens, Reds and Whites—were at the outset neither more nor less than sporting organisations to look after the numerous personnel employed in the Circus and to finance public sports. Dealing at the beginning only with horse racing, these Circus parties later took over control of al Circus entertainments and, as is the case with our modern foot-

I-26 — does not touch our problem. We call the reader's attention to the booklet, *The Byzantine Empire,* by N. Baynes (London, 1925), as it would be difficult to find a clearer and more illuminating *exposé* of Byzantine political ideology and one based on more solid knowledge of Roman institutions, especially on pp. 5ff,. 114 ff., 191 ff. Cf. also, H. Gelzer, *Byzantinische Kulturgeschichte* (Leipzig, 1909), the studies mentioned in the *Ausgewählte Schriften*. and J. B. Bury's *The Constitution of the Later Roman Empire* (London, 1910). Cf. the more recent papers: G. Ostrogorski, "Otnoshenye Cerkvi i Gosudarstva v Vizantii," *Seminarium Kondakovianum,* IV (1931), and P. Charanis, "Coronation and Its Constitutional Significance in the Later Roman Empire," *Byzantion,* XV (1940-1941), 48-66.

ball clubs, a certain amount of rivalry, which generated not a little heat, kept them interested and in good humour.[6]

In Rome, the Circus parties were probably never more than private organisations; but in Constantinople and in the great cities of the eastern Empire, their private character was soon lost and probably from the IVth century onwards the parties were charged with functions and duties that had little in common with their original purpose. The government formed around the main Circus parties, the Blues and the Greens, a special organisation of the urban population called the *demes (collegia popularia)* whose leaders were appointed, or at any rate, approved by the government. These *demes* constituted a sort of armed popular militia ready at any moment to be summoned to the defence of the cities or to take their share in official celebrations, their task being regulated by the numerous and minute prescriptions of the Byzantine ceremonial code.[7]

The *demes* grew in importance in the centuries that followed, especially at times of invasion when the popular militia had to stand by the imperial army to cooperate in the defence of the threatened cities, while their influence in political life grew apace and became a factor which emperors had to respect. Meanwhile, the Blues and the Greens developed their respective characteristic features as kinds of political parties: the Greens represented the truly popular elements, liberal, "democratic," and were recruited from among the lower classes of artisans, workers and peasants, a turbulent crowd and fond of novelties; the Blues or conservative elements, more stolid and steady, were recruited from among the higher classes, their clients and dependents. In many towns, the two parties often melted into local groups. It is thanks to G. Manojlovic's researches that we are better informed today about these divisions and the people's contribution to the growth of the Byzantine Empire.[8]

---

[6] Cf. E. Stein, *Geschichte des Spätrömischen Reiches,* I (Wien, 1928), 441 ff., which has a short account of the evolution of the Circus parties.

[7] It is a moot point whether this interesting and important growth of a popular element in the cities was not a survival under a Roman cloak of old Greek and Hellenistic influences.

[8] "Carigradski Narod," a study published in 1904 in *Nastavni Vjesnik* (Zagreb), XIIth fascicule, translated into French and corrected by M. H. Grégoire in *Byzantion,* XI (1936), 617-716, under the heading "Le Peuple de Constantinople." Cf. also G. I. Bratianu, "L'Empire et la Démocratie à By-

The Constantinople Hippodrome was in fact a sort of parliament, if it be allowable to use such a comparison, where the populace ventilated its opinion, wishes and grievances, and often took its share in the government's important moves. In order to secure the popular support they needed, emperors often found themselves driven to favour one or other of these parties, whose intervention more than once altered the course of the Empire's destiny.[9] They often counterbalanced the emperor's absolute power with happy results, and since religious and political questions had a way of getting inextricably mixed, the influence of either Blues or Greens, whichever happened to be in power, was equally decisive in religious quarrels.

In a few pages, G. Manojlovic[10] has told us of the part played by the Blues and the Greens in Byzantium and throughout the Empire in the Monophysite conflict; but a more detailed account comes from a Russian scholar of Syrian origin, the Hieromonachus Gerasim Yared.[11] Both works show that on religious issues the two factions usually adopted opposite points of view. Generally speaking, the turbulent and liberty-loving Greens were no more friendly to the established religion than they were to the established dynasty and they freely supplied every new heresy with its recruits;

---

zance," *Byz. Zeitschrift,* XXXVII (1937), 86-111. Cf. besides, some previous studies on this subject: Wilken, "Die Parteien der Rennbahn, vornehmlich im Byzantinischen Kaiserthum," *Abhandl. d. Phil. Hist. d. Preuss. Ak.* (Berlin, 1827), 217-243; A. Rambaud, *De Byzantino Hippodromo et Circensibus Factionibus* (Paris, 1870); "Le Monde Byzantin," *Revue de Deux Mondes,* Aug. 15, 1871; and Th. Uspenskij, "Partii cirka i Demy v Konstantinoplje," viz. *Vremennik,* I (1894), 1-16. Other indications are to be found in the following writings: E. Stein, *Geschichte des Spätrömischen Reiches,* I (Wien, 1928), 441 ff. Friedländer-Wissova, *Darstellungen aus der Sittengeschichte Roms,* II (1922), 1 ff. H. Gelzer, "Die Genesis der Byzantinischen Themenverfassung," *Abh. d. Sächs. Ges. d. Wissensch. Ph. Hist. Kl.* XVIII, 5 (1899), II, 13-15. The very last treatment of this important subject has just appeared in the *Vizantiiski Sbornik* (Moscow-Leningrad, 1945), pp. 144-227. It is a very scholarly article by A. P. Diakonov, *Vizantiiskie dimy i fakcii v V-VII vv.*

9 Cf. the study by Yvonne Janssens, "Les Bleus et les Verts sous Maurice Phocas et Heraclius," *Byzantion,* XI (1936), 499, 536.

10 "Le Peuple de Constantinople," *loc. cit.,* 655-665. This portion of his study lacks precision.

11 "Otzuivui sovremennikov o sv. Fotiye Patr. Konst. v svyazi s istorieyu politicheskikh Partii v imperii," *Khristianskoe Chtenie,* 1872-1873. This study has been overlooked by all those who dealt with the problem.

whereas the conservative Blues, who believed in order in State affairs and supported the dynasty, usually stood by the representatives of orthodoxy. That such were to a large extent their respective attitudes in the evolution of the Empire, at any rate till the rise of iconoclasm, will be evident to anyone who examines the religious policy of the Byzantine emperors as they succeeded each other from the Vth century onwards.

Theodosius II for instance, a very learned man according to Cedrenus,[12] first favoured the Greens,[13] then dropped them after they committed themselves to the spread of Monophysitism, to turn to the Blues who supported his sister Pulcheria; and as this lady was recalled from exile, Chrysaphius, the Green leader, as Theophanes the chronicler calls him, was banished in her stead.[14] Marcianus, unlettered and suspicious of all profane knowledge,[15] but naturally orthodox and reactionary, hated the Greens who supported Monophysitism, and he ordered Chrysaphius' execution.[16] Leo I, his successor, (457-474) described by Cedrenus as a man "without instruction or letters,"[17] who insisted on the strict observance of the decisions of the Council of Chalcedon,[18] followed Marcianus' policy and looked for his support among the orthodox Blues.

This policy was reversed by Zeno (474-491), who succeeded to the imperial throne after the second Leo's short reign and favoured the Monophysites,[19] though more discreetly than the usurper Basiliscus (475-476). The latter was eventually dethroned by Zeno with the Blues' assistance in return for his reluctant championship of orthodoxy; yet, no small share in his success was due to the Greens, who were aware of his secret sympathy with their cause and whose interest in the usurper Basiliscus[20] had been at best half-hearted. The edict of union that was to seal the reconciliation between the Orthodox and the Monophysites was the outcome

---

12 Cedren. (Bonn), I, 587.

13 Malalas, lib. XIV, (Bonn), 351 ff. Yared, *loc. cit.*, I, (1872), 95.

14 Theoph. 5942, (Bonn) I, 157 ff.; (de Boor) I, 101.

15 Cedren., (Bonn) I, 603.

16 Malal., lib. XIV, (Bonn) 368.

17 Cedren., (Bonn) I, 607.

18 Theoph. 5952, (Bonn) I, 173; (de Boor) I, 112.

19 On his attitude in the East before his accession to the throne cf. Cedrenus, (Bonn) I, 611 ff.; and Theoph., (Bonn) I, 176; (de Boor) I, 113.

20 As may be inferred from Malalas' account lib. XV, (Bonn) 379.

of Zeno's fluctuations, though his efforts in the matter remained all but fruitless.[21]

Zeno's successor, Anastasius (491-518) followed his predecessor's vacillating policy, which only encouraged the Greens' disorderly displays under his rule both in Constantinople and in Antioch.[22] Later, Anastasius somewhat turned against orthodoxy,[23] so that when Vitalianus revolted in 514-515, he could do so with the aid of the Blues.[24] The advent of Justin (518-527), another unlettered man, if we may credit Malalas,[25] and Procopius,[26] marked a complete turn of the tide in favour of the Orthodox and the Blues, though he had the good sense to stop their persecution of the Greens and to curb their violence.[27] Justinian carried on his uncle's policy;[28] and as his zeal for orthodoxy prompted him to rough treatment of all disseminators of heresy, the persecution of the Greens flared up again, engineered this time by Blues and Emperor in combination.[29] The notorious Nikè sedition, which all but cost Justinian his throne, had actually been fomented by the Greens with the aid of a number of Blues who resented certain measures taken by the Emperor's government.[30] In due time, the desire to bring about a settlement between the parties and their contradictory theologies inspired a more reasonable religious policy and explains the Emperor Justinian's attitude with regard to the Three Chapters, and his convocation of the Vth Oecumenical Council. At the outset, his wife Theodora befriended the Greens, her father's party, but later, when they failed her at a critical juncture, she transferred her favours to the Blues.[31] Peace was not restored

---

21 The main source of information for this period and Anastasius' religious policy is Theophanes, (Bonn) I, 202 ff.; (de Boor) I, 130 ff.

22 Malal., I, XVI, (Bonn), 394, 398.

23 Theoph., (Bonn) I, 246; (de Boor) I, 159, 160; Malal., I,XVI, (Bonn) 407.

24 Theoph., *loc. cit.* Cf. J. B. Bury, *A History of the Later Roman Empire from Arcadius to Irene* (London, 1899), I, 295 ff.; Yared, *loc. cit.* (1872), I, 101-105.

25 L. XVII (Bonn) 410.

26 *Historia Arcana.* (Bonn) 44.

27 Theoph., (Bonn) I, 256 ff.; (de Boor) I, 166.

28 Malal., lib. XVIII, 425; Proc., *Hist. Arc.*, (Bonn) 47.

29 Proc., *Hist. Arc.,* (Bonn) 76; *De Bello Persico,* (Bonn) II, 203.

30 Theoph., (Bonn) I, 278 ff.; (de Boor) I, 181 ff.

31 Proc., *Hist. Arc.,* (Bonn) 58 ff.

till the reign of Justin II (565-578), who whilst refusing to yield to the Blues' exaggerated pretensions, made the Greens realise that the sooner they dropped the truculent attitude they had paraded under Justinian, the better it would be for everyone.[32] Peace then seems to have lasted till the reign of Tiberius II (579-582).

Inter-party wrangles blazed up again under Mauricius (582-602) and Phocas (602-610). Which party Mauricius supported is still a matter of controversy, but contrary to what has been lately asserted, he seems to have patronised the Blues.[33] The Greens then fomented a rebellion against him, turned down the candidature of his son-in-law Germanus, whom they considered too "Blue" and appointed their own candidate Phocas.[34] But Phocas did not enjoy their favour much longer, for he had soon to fall back upon the Blues. Though all these affrays were mainly political in character, religious issues never ceased to hover in the background.

A new phase in the life of the two rival parties seems to have been ushered in by Heraclius (610-641). This great soldier, for all his pro-Green proclivities, apparently practised a policy of conciliation, rendered imperative by the constant threat from Persia looming over the Empire. It was under these circumstances that Heraclius published his *Ekthesis* on the singleness of the will in Christ after His Incarnation. Unfortunate as this publication turned out to be, it apparently revealed certain imperial sympathies for the Greens, invariably the less orthodox of the two parties. Here it is important to note that our information about the

---

[32] Theoph., (Bonn) I, 373; (de Boor) I, 243.

[33] For further details, cf. the studies of Yvonne Janssens, "Les Bleus et les Verts," *loc. cit.*, pp. 499 ff.; and by M. H. Grégoire, *"L'Empereur Maurice s'appuyait-il sur les Verts ou sur les Bleus?" Ann. de l'Institut Kondakov,* X (1938), 107-111; and "Maurice le Marcioniste, l'Empereur Arménien et Vert," *Byzantion,* XIII (1938), 395, 396. Cf. the judicious remarks by F. Dölger in *Byzant. Zeitschrift,* XXXVIII (1938), 525-528. Prof. Henri Grégoire, upholding Miss Yvonne Janssens' view, maintains, however, that Mauricius was in sympathy with the Greens, until the revolution which overthrew him — a revolution in which the Greens, betraying their protector, took a prominent part. Prof. H. Grégoire's opinion was effectively backed by Prof. A. A. Vasiliev, in *Byzantion,* XVI (1942-1943), 184-188. The late Diakonov (article quoted above on p. 125) clings to the older theory (the Greens were Mauricius' own party).

[34] Theoph. (Bonn) I, 446; (de Boor) I. 289. Still it is perfectly clear that Phocas's overthrow, and the conquest of Egypt by Heraclius' relatives and generals was made possible only by a mass rebellion of the Greens. On the religious policy of Heraclius and his successors, see Prof. H. Grégoire's article in the *Armenian Quarterly,* I (1946), fascicle 1 (January-March), p. 4-21.

two parties' activities under Heraclius is far scarcer than that covering the reigns of his predecessors. This is significant and is generally interpreted as an indication that the Emperor succeeded in his policy of appeasement and that the common danger had induced the factions to forget their grievances and rally round the Emperor. There is some justification for the inference, but is it adequate? Did this forceful soldier not discipline the parties more unconventionally? It is difficult to say; but before clearing up the puzzle, let us see what became of the factions in the years following Heraclius' reign.

The ephemeral reigns of Constantine III and Heracleonas (641) tell us little about the matter under consideration, for they do not seem to have affected the parties at all, though Martina and her family probably shared Heraclius' secret sympathies for the Greens. More important is the reign of Constans II. Under him (642-668), religious polemics flared up again and the Emperor issued the famous *Typos,* which heralded the outbreak of Monothelite hostilities, when the Orthodox were in their turn harrassed by persecution, and Pope Martin, with S. Maximus, paid so dearly for their gallant resistance to the Emperor. The murderous and fatal assault on Constans in Syracuse was attributed by Theophanes[35] to religious motives.

What was Constans' attitude to the parties? First of all, it seems that the revolution which made Constans II the sole ruler, had been fomented by the Blues and that therefore the Emperor must have lent support to that party in the first days of his reign. He must, however, have considerably revised his policy about the year 648, the date of the publication of his *Typos,* a writing which was certainly not appreciated by the Blues. The suppression of the name "Blues" from an inscription on the Great Wall of Constantinople, as deciphered and completed by M. Grégoire, [36] could be perhaps dated from that year. But are we entitled to infer from the foregoing that Constans II went so far as to eject the Blues and the Greens from political life altogether? We can in any case observe features in Constans II's policy towards the parties simi-

---

[35] Theoph. (Bonn) I, 537; (de Boor) I, 351.

[36] H. Grégoire, "Une Inscription au nom de Constantin III, ou la Liquilation des Partis à Byzance," *Byzantion,* XIII (1938), 165-175. We rather feel inclined to adopt a cautious attitude with regard to this inscription. But H. Grégoire's views are adopted by G. J. Bratianu, *La Fin du régime des Partis à Byzance et la crise antisémite du VIIe siècle,* Revue historique du Sud-Est européen, XVIII, 49-67.

lar to those of Heraclius. Though slightly partial to the Greens, both apparently were anxious to secure appeasement, and the parties seem to have lost their preponderating influence in Byzantine life ever since the reign of Heraclius and Constans II.

These observations would appear to be confirmed by developments in the second half of the VIIth century. Surprisingly few references to the parties are found at this period. Constantine IV (668-685), son of Constans II, profited by the lesson of his father's violent death, and the VIth Oecumenical Council assured the triumph of Orthodoxy over the Monothelite heresy; but however much this looked like a victory for the Blues' policy, no mention of the parties' stand for or against Orthodoxy can be found. The only reference to the Blues under Justinian II (685-695) has rather an athletic character: in order to enlarge the Circus on the emplacement reserved to the Blues, the Emperor was prevailed upon to remove the Church of Our Lady which stood in the vicinity of the Hippodrome [37] and was obviously in the way. May one infer from this that Justinian II, who certainly favoured Constantine IVth's religious policy, rather sided with the Blues? Nothing is said about the two parties under Leontios (695-698), under Tiberius III Apsimarus (698-705), nor under Justinian II's second reign (705-711); this is remarkable, since all these changes on the throne were brought about by revolutions, and in revolutions the two parties were generally prominent.

The Greens seem to have stepped into prominence only under Philippicus Bardanes (711-713) who revived Monothelism, the Greens' favourite tenet. Strangely enough, the usurper was blinded and dethroned the very day he celebrated the victory of the Greens in the Circus.[38] Though no emphasis is laid by the sources on the parties' contribution to these changes, the coincidence deserves some emphasis. Anastasius II (Artemius 713-716) restored Orthodoxy and was dethroned by Theodosius III (716-717). Again nothing is heard of the two parties. How to explain this? Something must have happened to lower the prestige of these politico-religious clans.

To all appearances, their decline was completed under Leo III the Isaurian. In fact, references to the two parties are few from the VIIIth century onwards and when their names occur in the

[37] Theoph. (Bonn) I, 563; (de Boor) I, 368.

[38] Theoph. (Bonn) I, 586, 587; (de Boor) I, 383.

documents, it is almost exclusively in connection with sports. This fact and the reputation which Leo III has so far enjoyed among historians as a great reformer of Byzantine political, legal and financial institutions seem to point to the iconoclastic Emperor as the man who confined the activities of the Blues and the Greens strictly to the field of sports.

On the suppression itself, we have, as already stated, no precise information. There is, however, one document which has been neglected so far, yet gives some interesting details on the parties' rôle before and after their suppression. It is found in Theodore Balsamon's *Commentary* on the XXIVth canon of the Council of Trullo, also called *Quinisextum*. The Greek canonist, who was writing at the end of the XIIth century, in commenting on the twenty-fourth canon of the Council forbidding clergy to attend circus exhibitions, gives some valuable information on the Circus and its parties, and as the passage might easily escape the attention of experts, we shall quote it in full. After stating that some canonists regarded the Council's canon as not binding in their days, he writes:

"In those days people abused their freedom and even grew unruly at the chariot races: they held them when and how they liked and organised them at their own expense; they owned buildings, horses and stables which still exist to-day and drew revenues from the entertainments for their upkeep. They insulted the emperor, but he was unable to check the abuses. As some belonged to the Blues and others to the Greens, clashes sometimes occurred between the opposite factions and insolent words were uttered even in the presence of the emperor, as we learn from various chronicles. Such things happened in the reign of Justinian and at the time of Anastasius, of the tyrant Phocas and other emperors. Though the parties were not forbidden to play for stakes, they used to try to make sure of their victory by divinations and incantations, which is strictly forbidden by the canons. Even fights between animals, with other disgraceful and shameless things, used to be permitted. . . . Yet, Christians have always been warned to keep away from places where there is evil and blasphemy. But to-day, since horse-racing is done in the presence of the emperor, there is nothing that need be shunned or condemned, nor is any suspicion of evil associated with the games. So it was said that however praiseworthy it may be not to find pleasure in horse-racing or other entertainments, yet clerics are allowed to attend them. For if races as they were practised then and as they are practised now were to be prohibited as well as all theatricals and hunting, then such things could not be done either by the emperor or by anybody else, which is absurd. For these reasons, races and spectacular entertainments must be divided into two classes, as stated before: those that ought to be avoided and shunned, which neither clerics nor laity should be allowed to attend under pain of excommunication; and those which are permitted, are in use to-day and should be open to clergy as well as to laity without any prejudice to themselves."[39]

The document is rather late, it is true and it does not possess the value of a contemporary witness. It warrants no conclusion as to the date of the suppression of the parties' supremacy; but there is no valid reason why we should not accept Balsamon's statement on their rôle before and after the reform as reliable. We may thus conclude that the re-organisation of those circus exhibitions must have been very thorough; that the Greens and the Blues must have lost their autonomous status and that the management of public entertainments in the Hippodrome must have been, to use a modern expression, secularised. The Imperial Chancellery took complete charge, even financially, of all public sports, while the factions of the Greens and the Blues were left with only executive powers. One can read in the *Book of Ceremonies* composed by the Emperor Constantine Porphyrogennetos what an insignificant part they were allowed to play: their leaders were only figure-heads whose main function was to greet the emperor according to a definite ritual whenever he presided at State ceremonies.

As to the authorship of this reorganisation, could it be attributed to Leo III? The reputation which this Emperor has had among historians for re-organising the Empire is not wholly deserved and the first iconoclastic Emperor has received the credit for reforms that should have gone to his great predecessor, the Emperor Heraclius, especially in relation to the division of the Empire into *themes* and the concentration of all civic and military powers into the hands of the *strategos* or leader of the *theme*.[40] It was Hera-

---

[39] *Theodori Balsamonis Comment. in Canones, P. G.*, 138, col. 592 ff.

[40] G. Ostrogorsky, "Uber die vermeintliche Reformtätigkeit der Isaurer," *Byz. Zeitschrift*, XXX (1929-30), 394-400. On the *themes*, cf. J. Bury, *A History of the Later Roman Empire from Arcadius to Irene* (London, 1889), II, 407-438. Cf. what we wrote on the evolution of the Byzantine *themes* in our

clius, not Leo, who overhauled the Byzantine administration and provided the Empire with the solid framework that enabled it for centuries to weather the worst storms. When the Empire was simultaneously threatened by Persians, Arabs and Slavs, Heraclius was not likely to overlook the urgency of keeping the two parties under strict control, and to him was probably due the suppression of that endless and dangerous rivalry between the two parties. His reforms in the administration of the State must have dealt the deathblow to the factions, as the new division of the Empire into *themes* left little room for the old *demes*.

Heraclius' successors, and especially Constans II, carried on his policy and the measures taken by these two Emperors must have clipped the wings of the factions for centuries to come and considerably reduced their contributions to the political and religious evolution of the Empire.

If this is correct, it is possible to explain why the parties—or at least the old party spirit—reasserted themselves, as was stated previously, even after Heraclius' reign, but without their accustomed virulence. They gradually faded away, as the new administrative and military reforms took roots, a process of dissolution that was finally completed in Leo's reign. If then Leo III did have any share in the suppression of the political parties, it was far more limited than would appear at first sight. Just as in the administrative reorganisation, Leo III only gave the final touch to Heraclius' schemes by further dividing the *themes* into smaller units, so in the matter of the Circus parties Leo III may at most be assumed to have set the seal on the process initiated by Heraclius and carried on by his immediate successors, especially Constans II.

Pound Hill - Crawley
Sussex, Great Britain.

book *Les Légendes de Constantin et de Méthode vues de Byzance* (Prague, 1933), 3 ff. Cf. also Ostrogorsky's review of E. J. Martin's book, *A History of the Iconoclastic Controversy* (London, 1930), in *Byz. Zeitschrift*, XXXI (1921), 383 ff.

XIV

POPE GELASIUS AND EMPEROR ANASTASIUS I

It is generally believed that Gelasius's letter to the Emperor Anastasius I in which he tried to define the limits of the imperial potestas and the ecclesiastical auctoritas represented a break with the current political theory concerning the prominent position of the emperors in the Church and was a starting point of a new era in the relationship between Church and State. The position of the emperors in religious and ecclesiastical affairs was defined – as I hope to show in detail in my forthcoming work on "The Origins of Christian Political Philosophy" – on the basis of Hellenistic political theories adapted to the Christian teaching, after a protracted evolution, by Clement of Alexandria and Eusebius of Caesarea. According to this Christian Hellenism the Emperor was the representative of God on earth. It was thus his foremost duty to lead his people to God and therefore to care not only for their material but also religious and spiritual welfare.

This belief gives us the key to the understanding of all the complications which arose from the practical application of this principle to the Trinitarian and christological controversies. When studied from this point of view, the history of the dogmatic controversies from Constantine the Great to Justinian I is even more fascinating and presents a clearer picture.

A kind of compromise between the imperial claims and the Church's rights in the definition of the true faith was worked out under Constantine the Great. It was not always observed by the emperors as the churchmen would have liked it. But in spite of the bad experiences which the bishops had with Constantius and some of his successors the principle outlined above continued to be generally accepted in the East and in the West. However, whenever a new crisis arose, caused by the emperors – conscious of their duty as leaders to God –, trying to impose on their subjects a doctrine which they regarded as the true one but which was in fact a heresy, attempts were made by prominent orthodox churchmen, to limit the imperial prerogatives so as to respect the Church's exclusive right in defining the true faith.

The Acacian schism was a crisis of this kind. It was caused by the Emperor Zeno's attempt at a compromise between orthodoxy and Monophysitism. Although Zeno published his Henoticon under the inspiration of the Patriarch Acacius, his initiative was, in fact, a dangerous break with ecclesiastical and imperial practice. It violated the compromise on the respective responsibilities of Emperors and bishops in a matter of faith which had proved such a blessing to the orthodox at Chalcedon. The Emperor, when publishing his Henoticon, acted on his own will, although under the inspiration of the Patriarch, without convoking a council or without inviting the bishops to a referendum on the matter.

This circumstance gave Felix III an additional reason for rejecting the Henoticon and strengthened considerably the opposition of the Western Church against this encroachment of the Emperor into the rights of the Church in defining the true faith. The Popes could become the bolder in their opposition as the Emperor's hold over Rome and the West was, at that time, rather more theoretic than real. No wonder then, that the controversy between Popes and Emperors during the so-called Acacian schism is given such a prominent place by Church historians in the evolution of relations between Church and State.

The most fateful episode of this new crisis was the encounter between Pope Gelasius, successor of Felix III, and Anastasius I, successor of Zeno. In order to evaluate how far the Romans were ready to go in their efforts to limit the Emperors to their own sphere of action, we should study in detail Felix's letters and the two treatises on the Acacian schism published by the member of Felix's chancery, the future Pope Gelasius. I intend to do this in the book now in preparation. Here I will simply state that Felix III, although opposing the intervention of the Emperor still adhered to the old political ideology as concerns the unique position of the emperor in the world and in the Church. Traces of the same belief can be found also in the two treatises written by Gelasius.

I have to limit myself here only to the analysis of the famous and fateful letter sent by Gelasius to Anastasius in order to show to what extent this letter can be regarded as a break, from the side of the Papacy, with the current imperial political theory.

What was the occasion of this missive? The Emperor Anastasius asked the Pope why he had neglected to inform Constantinople of his elevation to the Roman See, as it had been customary to do up to that time. Gelasius politely excused himself on the ground of the existing schism and made declarations[1] which betray that in spite of his disagreement with the Emperor in matters of faith, he still "respected, loved and welcomed the Roman Princeps." This outburst of patriotic feeling is of some importance for the right evaluation of other passages contained in the letter. It testifies that Gelasius was not yet ready to break with the current political ideas concerning the supreme position of the Emperor. Further on, in the same letter, he makes the following distinction between the imperial potestas and the ecclesiastical auctoritas: "There are mainly two things, August Emperor, by which this world is governed: the sacred authority (auctoritas) of the pontiffs and the royal power (potestas). Of these, priests carry

[1] Gelasii Papae Epistolae et Decreta Migne PL 59, 41; A. Thiel, Epistulae Romanorum Pontificum Genuinae I (Brunsbergae 1868) 350 seq. (ep. 12).

a weight all the greater, as they must render an account to the Lord even for kings before the divine Judgment. You know, most merciful son, that though you surpass the human race in dignity, yet you must bend a submissive head to the ministers of divine things and that it is from them that you must receive the conditions of your salvation. And you know that in receiving the heavenly sacraments which it is within their competence to dispense, you know that you must rather obey the ministry of religion than rule it. You know, therefore, that in these things, it is you who depend on their judgment, not they on yours. For when in things concerning the public weal religious leaders know that imperial power has been conferred on you from above, they will obey your laws, for fear that in worldly matters they should seem to thwart your will. Does it not then behoove you to obey those who have been set apart for the administration of the sacred mysteries?"

Such is the famous doctrine on the two authorities that govern the world, which has been a favourite topic of learned disquisitions ever since. It is generally assumed – as said before – that it amounted to a revolutionary innovation, a sudden break with the past. It was certainly ahead of its time, without however being out of tune with the principles of previous Christian political writers. It is often overlooked that Gelasius used the word potestas for the Emperor's competence, the auctoritas for the Church's particular province.[1] For a Roman, it was the potestas that mattered most, for it sprang from the sovereignty of the Roman people who, during the Republican period, delegated it to the magistrates for the length of their tenure of office. It was later surrendered to the Princeps as to the first executor of the people's sovereignty and he held it as an imperium. Auctoritas was founded on tradition and the social position of certain public bodies such as the Senate, the collegia of the Roman pagan clergy or the private capacity of the Princeps. The ethical prestige of auctoritas was higher than that of potestas, but effective power lay with the potestas.

This distinction was certainly known in Byzantium at the end of the fifth century, when Roman juridical tradition was still alive at the imperial chancery; so, there could be no objection to it. In Roman law, the holder of the potestas exercised the imperium, but in religious matters only on the advice of the holder of the auctoritas. In this light the Pope's statement was not startlingly new.

Moreover, the Pope wisely reminds the Emperor of the priests' exclusive right to administer the sacraments and to celebrate the liturgy. Anastasius,[2] well known for his personal piety, never missed an opportunity

---

[1] This was pointed out by E. Caspar, Geschichte des Papsttums II (Tübingen 1933) 65 seq.; 753 seq. E. Stein's criticism of Caspar's interpretation (The Catholic Historical Review 21 (1935) 134 seq.) is inadequate and not convincing.

[2] PL 59, 43; ed. A. Thiel I 352: "Nec me latet, imperator Auguste, quod pietatis tuae studium fuerit in privata vita."

to be present at a liturgical celebration. He knew then that certain functions were outside his province. So did the Byzantines, and the Pope's statement could hardly have surprised them. Chrysostom on the Christian priesthood, Theodoret on the Ambrose-Theodosius incident and on Theodosius II had been far more forcible than Pope Gelasius.

What was really new and an event in the history of Christian political thought was the contrast between the ecclesiastical auctoritas and the imperial potestas, with the proviso that the world was governed by both. This could easily lead to confusion, as the holders of the auctoritas claimed also the power to bind and to loose. In Gelasius' letter, this power was subordinate to the auctoritas and included in it, but it would be easy for a Westerner, living in another atmosphere, to go one step further, as it actually happened, and claim the potestas for the Church too.

Gelasius lent himself to the tendency in another treatise. Denying the secular power's right to judge in spiritual matters, he writes:[1] "Let it be that before the advent of Christ there existed men who were kings and priests all in one, in a prefigurative sense, yet in actual reality. Sacred History (Gen. XIV) records that such was Saint Melchisedech. But as the Devil, who always tyrannically arrogates to himself what is proper to divine worship, has copied this, the pagan Emperors had themselves called Supreme Pontiffs. But when the One had come who was truly king and Pontiff, then no Emperor adopted the name of Pontiff and no Pontiff claimed the supreme dignity of the king, although as His members, that is of the true King and Pontiff, they are said to have, in participation of His nature, obtained in a splendid way both, thanks to His sacred generosity, so that they are called kingly and priestly race. But He has remembered human frailty and by a marvellous dispensation has regulated what would serve the salvation of His own by keeping the offices of the two powers (officia utriusque potestatis) by distinctive functions and dignity. He has thus laid it down that His own should be saved by His curative humility, not carried away by human pride. Hence, Emperors are in need of Pontiffs for their eternal life, and Pontiffs must make use of imperial services for temporal necessities."

This was a dangerous attempt at equalizing the two potestates, and what was worse, a denial of the Emperor's priestly status. But in this, Gelasius was not lucky; for, to make his point, he had to ignore historical facts. It is simply not true that the Emperors, on becoming Christian, gave up the pagan title of Pontifex Maximus. Gratian was the first to do so. Emperors did claim the priestly character and the Christians let them have it. Gelasius also mishandled the Melchisedech precedent, as though it were an exception, only tolerated before the coming of Christ. Western medieval rulers were to appeal to Melchisedech as their main evidence against the champions of hierocracy.

---

[1] Gelasii Tomus De Anathematis Vinculo, PL 59, 108 seq., ed. A. Thiel I 567 seq.

But apart from the denial of the Emperor's priestly character, Gelasius' treatise is not fundamentally at variance with the current notions on kingship in the Roman empire of the fifth century. In no case did Gelasius attribute to the sacerdotium any prerogative of the imperium, not did his words imply that the secular power should be subordinate to the ecclesiastical: only as a man was the Emperor subject to the auctoritas of the Church which included the potestas ligandi et solvendi. The interdependence of the two powers left room for the Emperor's customary share in the execution of Church decisions.

The attitude of Gelasius' successor Anastasius II (496–498) shows clearly that Gelasius' ideas on the relations between Church and State were not interpreted by his contemporaries as the medieval canonists did it. In the letter sent by Anastasius II to the Emperor, we read the following words:[1] "The heart of your pious Majesty is the holy shrine of public welfare, so that through the intervention of yours whom God had ordered to govern, as His vicar, the world, the evangelical and apostolic precepts are not resisted in false pride, but that, in obedience, what is salutary be completed." The words are plain evidence that the basic principle of the Hellenistic political theory, namely that the Emperor was the vicar of God on earth, was still current in Rome. The tenor of the letter is very deferrent to the Emperor. In trying to win Anastasius' cooperation in the liquidation of the schism, the Pope implicitly recognizes the Emperor's function in the Church. He is anxious only to persuade the Emperor to embrace the decision of the Roman Church and to make it accepted by the whole Church.[2]

What happened in Rome after Pope Anastasius' death shows even more clearly that Gelasius' contemporaries were far from giving his words radical anti-imperial meaning. The Byzantinophile party in Rome and the followers of Gelasius' policy fell out, and a schism resulted. The Gelasianists asked the Arian king Theodoric for a decision in their favour, and when later the Pope Symmachus became the target of partisan accusations, Theodoric summoned an Italian synod which put the Gelasianists on their mettle to reconcile their appeal with papal prerogatives.[3] When a second synod, also summoned by Theodoric, failed to restore peace, the bishops decided to leave the decision to the Gothic king. They

---

[1] Mansi VIII 190; ed. A. Thiel I 620.

[2] Cf. especially (ibid.): „Hoc tamen praecipue insinuo serenitati tuae, gloriosissime et clementissime Auguste, ut cum causae Alexandrinorum patuerint piissimis auribus vestris, ad catholicam et sinceram fidem eos auctoritate, sapientia, divinisque (sic!) vestris monitis redire faciat" and at the end: „Unde . . . secundum preces nostras annisu et auctoritate imperiali offerte Deo nostro unam catholicam ecclesiam et apostolicam, quia hoc solum est, in quo non solum in terris, sed etiam in coelo triumphare possitis."

[3] For details see E. Caspar, Geschichte des Papsttums II 88 seq. Cf. also G. Schnürer, Die politische Stellung des Papsttums zur Zeit Theodorichs des Großen, Historisches Jahrbuch 9 (1888) 251–283; 10 (1889) 253–301.

addressed him as follows:[1] "It is therefore the concern of your Imperium to see, on God's invitation, to the rehabilitation of the Church, the peace of the city of Rome and of the provinces. So, we request you to come to the assistance, as a pious ruler, of our weakness and powerlessness, since the simplicity of the priests is not equal to the cunning of the laity, and we can no longer avert the danger to which our bodies and lives are exposed in Rome. Allow us then by your long awaited orders to return to our Churches."

None will say that western bishops, asking for the assistance of a heretical king in passing judgment on a Pope and craving for the king's permission to break up a synod summoned by him to judge the Pope, were averse to the Emperor's rights over Church affairs according to political theories current so far in the Church. In their final verdict, the bishops insisted that they returned to Pope Symmachus "by the authority (potestas) granted to them by orders of the ruler" all his priestly rights, and they appealed to all to return to communion with him.[2]

But not even the denial of priestly character to the Emperor by Gelasius found a general acceptance. This is illustrated by the following incident. To further his chances against Byzantium, Theodoric rallied to Symmachus, whereupon Ennodius, the champion of Symmachus, enthusiastically addressed Theodoric as the ideal ruler[3] "in strength, vigilance and fortune a prince, in mildness a priest." That is what the Romans thought at the beginning of the sixth century. One may see in this outburst a poetical exaggeration. Let us, however, not forget that Pope Vigilius speaks also of the "priestly soul" of the Emperor Justinian.[4]

These few lines may suffice to show that Gelasius' words[5] were not regarded by his contemporaries as a break with the current ideas on the role of the Emperor in religious matters. What is true is that Gelasius' words, apart from the historical and ideological background which was familiar to the Romans of the time, could be taken for a charter for the equality of the two powers, or even for the superiority of the ecclesiastical over the secular, and as a declaration of papal dominion over the whole world. Gelasius himself never dreamed of anything of this kind.

---

1 Acta Synhodorum Habitarum Romae (Relatio episcoporum), ed. Mommsen, MGH, Auct. Ant. XII 423.

2 Acta Synhodorum, loc. cit., p. 431.

3 M. Felicis Ennodii Opera, ed. F. Vogel, MGH, Auct. Ant. VII 213 (Panegyricus dictus Theodorico, c. XVII). I am treating the problem of priest-emperor more fully in my forthcoming book.

4 Epistolae Vigilii Papae, Mansi IX 35 (ep. IV). Collectio Avellana, ed. O. Günther (Corpus Script. Eccles. Lat. XXXV 1) p. 348 (ep. 92).

5 Cf. also his Commonitorium handed to Magister Faustus (PL 59, 30; ed. A.Thiel I 347) and his letter to the bishop of Dardania (PL 59, ep. 13; ed. A. Thiel I 399).

XV

EMPERORS, POPES, AND COUNCILS

THE role played by the emperors in the first ecumenical councils is a question of the greatest importance. All available documentary evidence shows that the convocation of the first ecumenical councils was made not by the popes or bishops, but by the emperors themselves. The emperors or their representatives presided at synods, directed the debates at meetings, and confirmed the decisions made by the assemblies. How can all this be reconciled with the Catholic doctrine concerning the exclusive right of the Church in matters of the faith?

This problem has occupied the minds of all leading theologians since the Reformation. Many theories have been proposed in order to solve this problem by Catholic scholars as well as by theologians rejecting the primacy of Rome, but none of them has been found satisfactory so far. I intend to study more thoroughly all problems concerning the relations between Church and State in the Roman and Byzantine Empire in a book on which I am now working. In this paper I shall try to show how this difficult problem of the imperial authority in general councils can be solved by a historian to the satisfaction of the theologians.

We have, first of all, to find out what method was adopted by the bishops in their meetings before the conversion of Constantine. Then we shall have to study in more detail the attitude of the first Christian emperor toward the bishops and the divine worship. This will help us to explain Constantine's initiative in convoking the first ecumenical council in Nicaea and the role he played during the meetings. Constantine set up a tradition which was followed by all his successors. It was accepted by churchmen and popes as we shall see when examining some of their declarations.

It is generally known that the young Christian Church modeled its external organization and its juridical procedure in disciplinary matters on the administrative and juridical system of the Roman Empire. This was a natural evolution and there is nothing objectionable in this adaptation of highly developed and experienced methods already existing. The bishops were Roman citizens familiar with Roman forms of government. When the need arose to discuss problems concerning Christians of a whole province, it was logical for the bishops to meet in the residence of the most prominent prelate in order to discuss the matters which touched the life in their dioceses. Such a necessity for common meetings arose in the Church of Africa when the controversy over the baptism of heretics started. Thanks to Saint Cyprian, Bishop of Carthage, the main city of Roman Africa, we can follow in all details how the meetings of the African bishops, the first local synods, were organized. Saint Cyprian described in his letters the whole process of such meetings and due to him the Acts of the first African synods came down to us. From this documentary evidence we are entitled to conclude with certainty that the gatherings of the bishops gradually modeled themselves on the meetings of the Roman senate. This was pointed out some time ago by Battifol,[1] but strangely enough, this finding was not carried to all its conclusions either by him or by other Catholic scholars.

We find in Cyprian's letters the same forms of convocation for the synods and also the same wordings as were used for the Roman senate: *cogere concilium; cogere senatum; convocare concilium; vocare, convocare senatum; habere concilium, senatum habere.* Like the senate under the emperors, the council was a deliberative assembly, and the bishops had equal rights like the senators. When Cyprian, as the bishop of the capital city, summoned a council, he followed the procedure once used in the senate. He read out his *relatio* or outline of the discussions, as the magistrate who represented the Emperor did in the senate, then added a few words of explanation – *verba facere.* Then followed the *interrogatio* of all the bishops present, who each gave their *sententia* without any display of rhetoric, as was customary in the senate, using the senatorial formula – *censeo, decerno, mea sententia est, existimo.* If we find no trace of any vote, it was because the *sententiae* were unanimous, probably as a result of preliminary discussions. The *sententia* was subsequently announced in a synodal letter to the parties concerned.[2]

It was, then, on this senatorial model that the ecclesiastical gatherings built up their procedure. The same was observed at the Roman council of 313 [3] in the house of Fausta, and although we have no other evidence, we can gather that this method was adopted also by the bishops in other Roman provinces. This procedure was the more familiar to them since the meetings of the local senates or municipal councils were also modeled on the procedure followed by the Roman senate. In this way a precedent was created which had to be respected also by the first Christian emperors.

But before we examine Constantine's initiative in the convocation of the

[1] "Les Règlements des premiers conciles Africains," *Bulletin d'Ancienne Littérature et d'Archéologie Chrétienne*, vol. III (1913), pp. 1–19.

[2] Cyprian's letters relevant to this subject are: Ep. 4, 17, 56, 59, 64, 67, 70, and 72, *Corp. Scr. Eccl. Lat.*, vol. III, pars 2, pp. 472, 523, 649, 678, 717, 735, 766, and 775. Cf. *ibid.*, pp. 432–461, minutes of the council of 256. On the senate's procedure see T. Mommsen, *Römisches Staatsrecht*, vol. III (Leipzig, 1888), pp. 905–1003.

[3] P. Monceaux, *Histoire Littéraire de l'Afrique Chrétienne*, vol. IV (Paris, 1912), pp. 338 ff.

first ecumenical council in Nicaea, we have first to answer one very important question. Did his conversion to the Christian faith proceed from conviction or from policy? Did he believe Christianity to be the true religion or did he think it would give his empire the cohesion and moral strength it needed, or both? All further judgments on the relations between Church and State will depend on the answer. So far, historians have favored the opinion that Constantine was a skeptical despot, whose only interest in spiritual power was to see it useful and subservient to his empire; that relations between Church and State for him meant only relations between a master and his willing tool. This opinion can no longer be held. After a careful study of all the documents and the literature bearing on Constantine's conversion, I have come to the conclusion that N. H. Baynes,[4] who almost single-handed and in the face of a mass attack of modern criticism, has defended the sincerity of Constantine's conversion, is right. Constantine was no agnostic, but a man of his time, a believer in the spiritual and the divine.

It is from this angle that Constantine's relations with the Church should be viewed. Fortunately, Eusebius, the first Church historian, whose reputation for veracity has risen with Constantine's reputation for sincerity, has left us most of the letters and decrees of Constantine relating to Church matters.[5] His political creed, his Church policy, and evidence of his sincerity will be found there.

How did Constantine appraise his role as a Christian emperor and his political duties to the Church? A relevant statement by him is found in a letter he wrote to his representative in Africa, the Christian Aelafus, in 314 on the subject of the convocation of a synod in Arles to settle the African schism of the Donatists. He writes: "Since I know that you also worship the Supreme, I advise Your Excellency that I do not consider it proper to make a secret of all these quarrels and wrangles. For they might well rouse God not only against the human race, but also against me, to whose rule and care His holy will has committed all earthly things, and provoke other measures. I shall never rest content nor expect prosperity and happiness from the Al-

[4] *Constantine the Great and the Christian Church* (London, 1931; *Proc. Brit. Acad.*, vol. XV). It is a fine piece of British scholarship, its most valuable part being its notes (pp. 30–95), where with due caution he deals with all the works on Constantine published before 1930. To judge from the studies by H. Lietzmann and H. v. Schoenebeck, Professor Baynes must have gained the day.

[5] See N. H. Baynes, *op. cit.*, pp. 40–50, for opinions on the authenticity of these documents. I fully agree with the author on their genuine character.

mighty's merciful power until I feel that all men offer to the All Holy the right worship of the Catholic religion in a common brotherhood." [6]

These words reveal clearly that Constantine was inspired even after becoming a Christian by the Hellenistic political ideas which I shall explain more thoroughly in my forthcoming book. Constantine believed in holding absolute royal power over all things material and spiritual as had the Hellenistic kings, including naturally the duty of enforcing the right sort of worship, together with the sincere conviction that it was addressed to the only true God. His letter to the synod of Arles,[7] in some respects Constantine's profession of faith, breathes the same sincerity.

In the so-called Donatist Dossier, there is Constantine's letter to Miltiades of Rome, written in 313 on the subject of the convocation of a Roman synod, where he states what he thinks of his powers: "What seems to me intolerable in those provinces which Divine Providence has spontaneously given me to rule and which are so thickly populated, is that the people should be split into two camps to their own damage, and that the bishops should not be able to agree among themselves." [8] And when in 316 he sent the Donatist bishops back to Africa, he announced to his Governor Celsus his intention of using his own authority to settle the controversy on the spot and to teach the Donatist clergy "which divine worship should be used and in what manner. I believe that I can in no way escape the heaviest guilt save by bringing wickedness to light. Is there anything more consonant with my fixed resolve and my imperial duty that I can do than to scatter errors, extirpate all vain opinions and to cause men to offer to the Almighty a genuine religion, a sincere concord and a worship that is His due?" [9]

We find the same earnestness in his letter to Bishop Alexander of Alexandria and to Arius, when he states that in marching to the east, he planned "to restore to health the body of the [Roman] world, so badly shaken by a severe illness," and chiefly "to gather what is sound in what all the nations think of God into one common creed and practice . . . For it seems to me that if I could establish the same concord between all the worshippers of God as it was my desire, the government of the Republic would receive the improvements which all so patriotically desire." Towards the end of the letter Constantine exclaims: "By the Providence and under the protection

[6] S. Optati Milevitani Libri VII, Appendix III, ed. C. Ziwsa, *Corp. Scr. Eccl. Lat.*, vol. XXVI, p. 206.

[7] *Ibid.*, vol. V, p. 208. See Baynes, *op. cit.*, pp. 75 ff., on the authenticity of the Donatist Dossier.

[8] *Historia Ecclesiastica*, X, ch. 5, *P.G.*, vol. 20, col. 888, ed. E. Schwartz, p. 888.

[9] Optatus, *op. cit.*, p. 212.

of the Saviour, grant to me, His servant and worshipper, that I may bring this work to the happy conclusion of seeing His people recalled to the unity of the faith by my words, my assistance and my urgent appeals." [10]

For Constantine, things divine and earthly were interlocked in human society. Thus, in a letter to Anulinus, Constantine grants the clergy immunity from public service and argues that the State will eventually benefit by it: "The Republic will derive the greatest benefit from the display of their wonderful respect for God." [11] In a letter to the bishops after the Council of Nicaea, he affirms it to be his duty to watch over spiritual interests and their bearing on the people's material welfare: "As I discovered from the prosperous state of the Republic how great the grace of the divine power has been, I thought it my primary duty to bring it about that the saintly multitudes of the Catholic Church shall preserve one faith, a sincere charity and a profound reverence for the Almighty." [12]

It is thus clear from these quotations that Constantine, in the spirit of the definition of Hellenistic royal competence, regarded himself as legally entitled to interfere in religious affairs. He represented the Divinity on earth and was given by God supreme power in things material and spiritual. He thought that it was his foremost duty to lead men to God. As he said himself, he had to teach his subjects *quae et qualis divinitati adhibenda veneratio* – "which divine worship should be used and in what manner."

Because the Christians, chiefly in the eastern parts of the empire, had long been familiar with Hellenistic thought, it had never occurred to them to contest such imperial claims. They even went out of their way to make the best of them, as when the Donatists and the schismatics of northern Africa petitioned Constantine to appoint independent judges from Gaul to examine their case. The emperor appointed five, including the Bishop of Rome, who made no objection: he only adapted the appointment to Church practice by transforming the court into a council to which he invited fourteen Italian bishops.

The pope's procedure in this case served as a useful precedent for future interventions. Constantine was apparently not acquainted with the ecclesiastical practice, and to the first case submitted to him he applied the Roman juridical procedure by setting up a court of investigation and judgment. Once he learned of the Church method – decision by bishops meeting in

[10] *Vita Constantini*, II, chs. 64–72, ed. Heikel, pp. 67–71, *P.G.*, vol. 20, cols. 1037–1048.

[11] Eusebius, *Hist. Eccl.* X, ch. 7, ed. Schwartz, p. 891; *P.G.*, vol. 20, col. 893.

[12] *Vita Const.*, III, ch. 17, ed. Heikel, p. 84; *P.G.*, vol. 20, col. 1073.

synods — he adopted it, and when the Donatists repudiated the decision of the Roman synod, he decided to summon another council at Arles.[13]

It is often said that Constantine treated the bishops only as his counselors in ecclesiastical affairs, reserving the final decision to himself. This opinion does not seem to be fully warranted. Apparently, the Emperor not only let the synods take over from his courts in ecclesiastical matters, but was ready to accept the ecclesiastical practice, so far followed by the Church, according to which the decision of the bishops should be regarded as final. This much can be inferred from the letter he wrote to the bishops at Arles on learning that the Donatists had again appealed from their decision to his arbitration: "They claim judgment from me, who am awaiting the judgment of Christ; for I declare, as is the truth, that the judgment of bishops ought to be looked upon as if the Lord himself were sitting in judgment . . . They have lodged an appeal, as is done in the lawsuits of pagans; for pagans are accustomed at times to avoid the lower courts where justice can be quickly discerned and through the intervention of the authorities to resort to an appeal to the higher courts. What is to be said of these defamers of the law, who, after rejecting the judgment of Heaven, have thought that they should demand judgment from me?" [14]

We can conclude from these words that Constantine would have been only too glad to let bishops settle the Donatist quarrel. Failing this, however, he could not let things drift without evading his imperial duty, since, as he said, the spread of the schism "would rouse the wrath of Providence in Heaven." He first detained the Donatist bishops at his court. Then in the last resort, he announced his intention of giving his own final decision at the actual scene of the controversy. His words expressed his sense of his imperial responsibility: "I believe that I can in no way escape the heaviest guilt, save by bringing wickedness to light. Is there anything more consonant with my fixed resolve and my imperial duty that I can do than to scatter errors, extirpate all vain opinions and to cause men to offer to the Almighty a genuine religion, a sincere concord and a worship that is His due?" He eventually did not go to Africa, but confirmed the decision of the council of Arles against the Donatists.

The way Constantine dealt with this controversy proved him to be alive to a clash between two authorities: that of the bishops in ecclesiastical matters and that of the emperor in his higher responsibility for the right way of

[13] See E. Caspar, *Geschichte des Papsttums* (Tübingen, 1930), pp. 109–117, 582, on the disparity between the Roman and Constantinian practices.

[14] Optatus, *op. cit.*, p. 209.

worshipping God. He saw the necessity of a compromise and this was first outlined at the council of Nicaea. In attempting to settle the Arian heresy, Constantine adopted, from the start, the current Church practice. No question this time of any imperial court. When the emperor's trusted adviser, Hosius, Bishop of Cordova, had failed in his mission, Constantine adopted the procedure followed by the bishops assembled at Antioch in order to define the true faith and summoned a synod at Nicaea.

The synod was thus the joint result of an episcopal and imperial decision. Its procedure was the usual one used by both Church and State, the senatorial procedure, which the Church in Rome and in Africa had made its own. Judging from the description of the first ecumenical council left us by the author of the *Vita Constantini*,[15] Nicaea proceeded in the same way. The emperor convoked the bishops as he convoked the senators, presided at the sessions of the council as he presided at the senate, and after making his *relatio*, called upon the members to state their point of view (*sententiam rogare*).[16] As with the Roman senate, the issue – in this case the *Homoousios* – had been put on the agenda at private consultations before the public meeting.

This part of the procedure suited both emperor and bishops; but there was one item which providentially saved the autonomy of the bishops in doctrinal matters: the emperor never had the right to vote in the senate. This was the senators' privilege, a survival of their independence under the Roman Republic, which suffered a setback under the Principate, but was actually saved in principle even under the most autocratic emperors. There is no trace in the accounts of the council of Nicaea of Constantine voting with the bishops: he only confirmed their decisions and made them legal. Applied to the ecclesiastical senate or the councils, this principle enabled the Church to safeguard her independence in all matters of doctrine. The compromise proved unobjectionable to the emperor, since it was justified by historical precedent.

It is possible that at the council of Nicaea the principle was not yet fully acted upon, but it was admitted and became the ruling of all future councils. Moreover, the representatives of the Roman See gave their opinion and signed the Acts before the other bishops as did the Princeps Senatus or the leader of the House. This guaranteed their privileged position. That Bishop

[15] *Vita Const.*, III, chs. 6–20, ed. Heikel, pp. 79–87; *P.G.*, vol. 20, cols. 1060–1080.

[16] *Ibid.*, III, ch. 13, ed. Heikel, p. 83; *P.G.*, vol. 20, col. 1069. According to this report, the proceedings were not as peaceful as might have been and seemed to justify the emperor's conviction that it needed his authority to direct the debate. Cf. Baynes, *Constantine*, p. 88.

Hosius happened to sign first[17] was due to his being the emperor's trusted counselor, the most conspicuous representative of the Western Church and the principal agent in the formulation of the Creed. He was, besides, a bishop, enough to account for his signing before the two priests who represented the Bishop of Rome. (This would explain why Hosius and the two Roman legates were classed together in the list of signatories and why a later tradition, starting in the fifth century with Gelasius of Cyzicus,[18] made Hosius a representative of the Holy See.) If only roughly applied, the principle was laid down at Nicaea and safeguarded the preëminence of the Roman See side by side with that of the emperor who convoked and directed the councils.[19]

Constantine's letter to the bishops who had been absent from the council of Nicaea, to inform them of its decision on the celebration of Easter, shows that he had improved his opinion of the function of bishops. He wrote: "Such being the case, be willing to accept this heavenly favour and an order so manifestly from God. For whatever is decided in the holy councils of the bishops must be attributed to the divine will."[20] These are more than empty words and recall Constantine's declaration after the synod of Arles — "the bishops' decision should be looked upon as though the Lord Himself had been sitting in judgment." Evidently, Constantine was trying to be fair to the bishops without prejudicing his own rights as Basileus in the Hellenistic tradition.

The danger of all such claims was obvious. Yet the feeling of relief experienced under the benign regime of the first Christian emperor after bitter years of persecution, coupled with the widespread notion of Hellenistic kingship among the Christians, encouraged the acceptance of the emperor's leadership even in spiritual things. The sincerity of Constantine's conversion could only help it. God's interests were safe in the hands of a ruler who could be so deferential to the rights of the bishops. And the danger of the new order passed unnoticed.

Yet the moment the bishops and the emperor agreed to it, they sowed the seed of endless abuses. The steps Constantine took against heretics and

[17] Cf. V. Grumel, "Le Siège de Rome et le Concile de Nicée," *Echos d'Orient*, vol. 28 (1925), pp. 411–423.

[18] Gelasius of Cyzicus, *Historia Conc. Nic.*, II, ch. 5, Mansi, II, col. 805.

[19] See my short study, "De Auctoritate Civili in Conciliis Oecumenicis," *Acta VI Congressus pro Unione Ecclesiarum* (Olomouc, 1930). English translation in *The Christian East* (1932), vol. X, pp. 95–108.

[20] *Vita Const.*, III, ch. 20, ed. Heikel, p. 87; *P.G.*, vol. 20, col. 1080. See Baynes' plea for the authenticity of this letter, *Constantine*, pp. 89 ff.

pagans were a first danger signal: he banned the writings of the greatest pagan opponent of Christianity, Porphyry, and to this index the works of Arius and other dissidents were added later.[21] This augured ill for the individual freedom which the Christians had been claiming for themselves in persecution days and foreshadowed the highhandedness with which Constantine's successors were to treat the freedom of both their Christian and their pagan subjects.

Another ominous precedent was his letter to the king of Persia,[22] in defense of the Persian Christians. This showed that the Christian emperor fancied himself as the Caesar of every Christian in the world, claiming a monopoly that could only rest on an identification of a universal Church and a universal empire. It was a deduction from the monarchic argument: since there was only one God in Heaven, only one emperor should represent Him on earth. The missionary role of the empire was thereby specified and the expansion of the kingdom of God linked with the expansion of the empire.

The danger of this conception was realized by orthodox bishops during the reign of Constantius. The latter was attracted by the doctrine of Arius denying the divine nature of the second person in the Trinity, because this Arian view of God's monarchy seemed to agree better with the current concept of the Roman empire as the reflection of one single divine empire. Any division in the Blessed Trinity seemed to endanger the conception of one empire on earth and of one emperor representing the one God. When Constantius declared openly for the Arians, he of course regarded it as his duty to bring his subjcts to his idea of the Trinity which, according to him, was the right one. But, contrary to what is often said concerning his religious policy, Constantius respected, in general, the leading principle laid down by Constantine, which amounted to a compromise between the old practice of the Church and the emperor's alleged duty to lead his people to the true God. He never pretended to dictate the acceptance of his own creed, but respected the function of the synods in defining the faith. That is why so many synods were held under his reign, all convoked by the emperor. Unfortunately the synods were filled with heretical bishops. In spite of this the right of the emperors to convoke a synod was generally accepted, as is shown by the controversy between Pope Julius I and the Arian sympathizers of Antioch. The pope convoked the synod of bishops in Rome in order to rehabilitate St. Athanasius, unjustly condemned by the synod of Tyre (335).

[21] Gelasius of Cyzicus, *Historia*, ch. 36, Mansi, vol. II, col. 920. *Vita Const.*, III, ch. 66, ed. Heikel, p. 113; *P.G.*, vol. 20, cols. 1141 ff.

[22] *Vita Const.*, IV, ch. 9–13, ed. Heikel, pp. 121 ff.; *P.G.*, vol. 20, cols. 1157–1161.

The Antiochians reminded the pope that convoking a synod without imperial orders was an innovation in the Church practice and that no decision by a council summoned by the emperor and meant to be a general council could be rescinded by an ordinary Roman synod. The pope, in his letter,[23] answering this charge, stood somewhat on the defensive. He argued, however, that it was not the emperor's convocation, but the recognition of the synodal decisions by the whole Church that gave a council its general and abiding character, as was the case of the council of Nicaea. The Roman synod was summoned in defense of Nicaea.

We can see that the pope's answer marks an important step in the progress of clarification of the function of synods, but the principle that a general synod should be convoked by the emperor is not denied by him. Julius I would have taken no such initiative if the synods convoked by the emperor had made a decision conforming to the right faith.

This first conflict between emperor and bishops in matters of faith led to interesting attempts at defining more clearly the position of the emperor in the Church. There are some indications that Constantius claimed for the emperor in Church affairs the authority of an apostle. The emperor's authority was thus superior to that of ordinary bishops. The Arians applauded but the orthodox protested. The latter did not deny the principle that the emperor's duty was to care for the definition of the true faith. But in the Church assemblies the emperor had no more authority than any bishop. He should therefore accept the decision of the orthodox majority. It might be that the famous declaration of Constantine reported by Eusebius in the *Vita Constantini*, "I am the bishop of those outside the Church," was not written by Eusebius but was added to the new edition of the *Vita* by an orthodox writer trying to lower the position of the emperor from that of representative of God on earth and claimant of the authority of an apostle to that of an ordinary bishop. This declaration seems also to exclude the emperor from all matters concerning the interior organization of the Church, and to limit his activity to those outside the church, whom he should help to convert to Christianity, and to the right faith.[24]

But not even Athanasius, the greatest opponent of Constantius' religious policy, denied the emperor the exclusive right to convoke an ecumenical council. In spite of the bitterness which this first conflict must have left in the minds of many bishops, there was no great change in the general appre-

[23] See the pope's letter in Athanasius' *Apologia contra Arianos, P.G.*, vol. 25, cols. 281–308.
[24] Cf. W. Seston, "Constantine as a 'Bishop,'" *Journal of Roman Studies*, vol. XXXVII (1947), pp. 127–131.

ciation of the emperor's leading role in the church. This is illustrated by the declaration of the Emperor Theodosius with whose help Arianism was definitely liquidated. By a decree issued in Milan in 379, Theodosius banned every heresy condemned by previous imperial decrees. The document was most probably inspired by St. Ambrose.

A second edict authorized no creed except the Nicaean: "We wish all the nations that are governed by our merciful and lenient rule to practice that faith which, as religion teaches, has been handed down by St. Peter to the Romans to this day and which is undoubtedly practiced by Pope Damasus and by Peter, Bishop of Alexandria, a man of apostolic holiness." [25] It was but a repetition of Constantine's intervention in the Donatist and Arian troubles: as the representative of God, the emperor must show his subjects which faith and which worship it is safe for them to follow. It is not the faith of the emperor, but that taught by the bishops, two of whom are singled out for special mention. Only, this was not exactly the freedom of conscience which the Lord upheld and which Christians had once claimed for themselves.

But the bishops at that time did not view the matter in that light. This is how the 150 bishops, gathered in 381 for the second ecumenical council, announced their decisions to Theodosius I: "Our first duty in writing to Your Piety is to thank God for having established your empire for the common peace of the Churches and for the confirmation of the true faith. Having rendered to God the thanks due to Him, we must lay before Your Piety what has been decided in this holy council . . . We therefore ask Your Clemency that a letter of Your Piety should ratify the decrees of this council. As you honored the Church by your letter of convocation, so also lend your authority to our decisions." [26]

In this respect, the western bishops differed little from their eastern confreres. One has only to read the letter addressed to the emperor by the synod of Aquileia which had been summoned by Gratian and was presided over by Ambrose; or the letter of the Roman synod under Pope Damasus in 382; or the Acts of the Synod of Carthage which was summoned by imperial decree to deal with the Donatists and was presided over by an imperial official.[27] All submitted to current imperialism without question. Theodosius II, in his letter to Cyril of Alexandria and the bishops summoned to define

[25] *Cod. Theod.*, XVI, 1, 2, ed. Mommsen, p. 833.
[26] Mansi, vol. III, col. 557.
[27] Mansi, vol. III, cols. 602 ff., 624 ff., vol. IV, cols. 51 ff.

the faith in the human nature of the Savior against the teachings of Nestorius, outlined the theory best. A few extracts will not be amiss.[28]

The letter starts with the theme dear to Constantine: "The stability of the Republic depends on the religion by which we honor God. There is a close link between the two. They depend on each other and each thrives on the progress of the other. So that true religion will reveal itself in just dealing and the Republic will flourish supported by both. Since, then, God has handed us the reins of government and made us the link of piety and rectitude for all our subjects, we shall always keep undivided association between them and watch over the interests of both God and men. For we must minister to the prosperity of the Republic, and keeping so to speak a watchful eye on our subjects, we must see to it that they believe piously, lead lives worthy of pious believers, doing their best in both ways as far as in them lies. It cannot be that those who watch over one thing should neglect others. Above all, we are anxious to bring about such ecclesiastical conditions as do credit to God and as befit our times, so that unanimity and concord produce peace and keep us free from Church controversies, riots and seditions; that our holy religion be kept safe from any criticism; and that the lives of those who are numbered among the clerics or are invested with the high dignity of the priesthood be without stain or blemish."

Such were the Basileus' responsibilities after the Hellenistic manner. Conscious of his imperial duties, Theodosius II proceeds to explain that the synod is the best way for clearing religious differences and summons all the bishops to attend it: "We also are keenly interested in these matters and shall not easily allow anyone to absent himself. Anyone who will not be punctually present at the proposed place at the appointed time will have no excuse before God or ourselves . . ." Theodosius then explains the role of the bishops and of the imperial representative in his "sacred letter" to the conciliar fathers, and summarizes the functions of his representative at the synod in the following words: "[He is sent] with this injunction and on this condition that he shall have nothing to do with problems and controversies regarding dogmas of faith, for it is not desirable that one who does not belong to the body of holy bishops should meddle with ecclesiastical questions and discussions. But he must use every means to remove from the city any monks or laymen who have gathered there for this council or will do so: those who are not required for the study of the sacred dogmas must not be allowed to create trouble or put obstacles in the way in matters which Your

[28] Mansi, vol. IV, cols. 1112 ff.

Holinesses are there to settle and define . . ."[29] In other words, the emperor's representative was there as a police officer, responsible for order and the synod's peaceful proceedings. Theodosius II therefore observed the compromise between synodal and imperial rights as laid down by the council of Nicaea.

Pope Celestine's reply to the emperor's summons shows agreement: "It is gratifying to hear with what eagerness Your Clemency hastens to the defense of the Catholic faith for the love of Christ who is the ruler of your empire, how you keep that faith pure and unsullied, condemning the errors of heresy. In this way, you are constantly strengthening your regime, knowing that the strength and the permanence of your empire rest on the observance of our holy religion. Every one of us, in virtue of our priestly functions, shall give all the help we can to such holy and glorious zeal and we shall be present through our legates at the synod which you have summoned." The Pope exhorts the emperor not to tolerate any decision that would run counter to the faith and the peace of the Church and proceeds: "Your Clemency should be more eager for the peace of the Churches than for the security of the whole world . . . If things dear to God are provided for first, every prosperity follows . . . Whatever is done for the peace of the Church and for the observance of our holy religion is done for the safety of the empire."[30] This was exactly what Constantine and Theodosius II had said before.

At Ephesus (*ca.* 431) things did not quite turn out as Cyril and Celestine had expected; yet, the Acts of the genuine synod and of the Nestorian meetings in opposition are there to show that both bodies acknowledged the emperor's right to convoke them and that they tried to run their meetings in accordance with his orders. Both parties made efforts to rally the emperor to their respective sides.[31] In the end he decided in favor of the orthodox and again appealed to his responsibilities in his condemnation of the Nestorians in the following words: "We believe it behoves our royal majesty to remind our subjects of their religious duties. For thereby do we hope to conciliate the favour and mercy of our Saviour Jesus Christ, if we also try to please Him and assist our subjects in doing the same."[32]

The same idea was expressed by pope, emperor, and fathers of the council in the Monophysite struggles which culminated in the Council of Chal-

[29] Mansi, vol. IV, col. 1120.

[30] Mansi, vol. IV, col. 1291.

[31] Mansi, vol. IV, cols. 1129, 1228, 1260 ff., 1301 ff., 1352 ff., 1372 ff., 1421 ff., 1433 ff., 1441 ff.

[32] Mansi, vol. V, col. 417.

cedon (451). Far from denying the emperor's right to care about divine things, Pope Leo the Great, in his letter 24 to Theodosius II before the convocation of a new council in Ephesus gives one to understand that the Christians of the fifth century still attributed to the emperor a semblance of sacerdotal character: "The letter you have sent me proves what comfort the Lord has prepared for His Church through the faith of Your Clemency. It gives us joy to find in you a soul that is not only royal, but priestly. For besides your imperial and public cares, you display such pious solicitude for the Christian religion that schism, heresy and scandal shall not grow among the people of God. Your empire prospers most when the eternal and immutable Trinity is served best in the profession of the one Divinity." [33]

This was by no means an isolated case. In a letter to Marcian written in 453, the pope wished God to give the emperor "besides the imperial, also the priestly palm." [34] On another occasion, he wrote of Marcian as one "in whom for the salvation of the world there flourish both royal power and priestly zeal." [35] In a message to Pulcheria, he praises "the priestly doctrine of the emperor and the empress." [36] Writing to Bishop Julian, the pope expresses satisfaction at Marcian's edict and Pulcheria's letter against some monks, as they demonstrated to all "the sublimity of their royal greatness and their sacerdotal holiness." [37] Elsewhere he extols the emperor's "priestly feelings." [38]

He uses the same language about the Emperor Leo I. This is the most telling passage from the pope's letter written in 457: "Addressing the most Christian Princeps, one deservedly numbered among the preachers of Christ, I confidently exhort you with the freedom of the Catholic faith to associate yourself with the Apostles and the Prophets by firmly putting down and repelling those who have renounced the Christian name . . . Since the Lord has enriched Your Clemency with the great light of His sacrament, you must unhesitatingly realize that royal power has been bestowed on you, not merely to rule the world, but chiefly to protect the Church . . . For the priestly and apostolic soul of Your Piety should be roused to the justice of retribution by the evil which so disastrously dims the purity of the Church of Constantinople, where some clerics are found to favour heretical tenets . . . If my brother Anatolius is found to be remiss and too indulgent

[33] Mansi, vol. V, col. 1241.
[34] Letter 111, ch. 3, Mansi, vol. VI, col. 219.
[35] Letter 115, ch. 1, *ibid.*, col. 229.
[36] Letter 116, ch. 1, *ibid.*, col. 233.
[37] Letter 117, ch. 2, *ibid.*, col. 235.
[38] Letter 134, ch. 1, *ibid.*, col. 288.

to restrain those men, be so good in virtue of your faith to administer to the Church even the remedy of removing such men not only from the clerical ranks but from the territory of the city, lest the holy people of God be further infected by the contagion of their perversion." [39]

This was going very far indeed: in some respects the pope placed the emperor above the bishops, giving him the right to make up for their neglect and to take disciplinary measures against the clergy. In another letter to Leo I (March 458) the pope used some phrases which caused a great deal of embarrassment to some theologians because they sounded as though the pontiff were foisting on the emperor a kind of infallibility in matters of faith: "The words of Your Piety make it undoubtedly clear to me that through your instrumentality the Holy Spirit works for the welfare of the whole Church . . . I expect much from the heart of Your Piety and see that you are sufficiently taught by the indwelling spirit of God and that no error could mislead your faith." [40]

In the light of the context there is no question of the pope's believing in the emperor's infallibility. The words illustrate, however, more clearly than anything else how deeply was imbedded in the Christian minds of the fifth century the theory that the emperor, as the representative of God on earth, was, with the collaboration of the bishops, responsible for the definition and spread of the true faith.

Pope Leo the Great, of course, also agreed with the emperor's claim to summon councils, for in his letter to Theodosius II dated 449 he promises to send his legates to the council: "Your Piety . . . has summoned a council at Ephesus." [41] However dissatisfied with the results of this "Robber Synod" of Ephesus, Pope Leo contented himself with a protest addressed to the emperor and a request for another council to be summoned in Italy.[42] The pope only gained his point when Marcian became emperor. The latter fully accepted the compromise between imperial and ecclesiastical rights in the definition of the faith. Definitions are the bishops' concern, but the emperor's part is to facilitate the definitions by convoking the synod. When inviting the pope to the council he intended to summon, Marcian wrote: "If the journey . . . should be difficult [for you], will Your Holiness inform us personally by letter, so that we may send our sacred letters to the whole East, . . . , inviting all the holy bishops to gather at a place we shall ap-

[39] Letter 156, ch. III, VI, *ibid.*, cols. 325 ff.
[40] Letter 162, ch. I, III, *ibid.*, cols. 338 ff.
[41] Mansi, vol. V, col. 1291 (letter 29).
[42] Mansi, vol. VI, cols. 8, 9, 23, 63, 85.

point in order that they may define as they think fit what concerns the peace of the Christians and the Catholic faith as laid down by Your Holiness in accordance with ecclesiastical regulations." [43]

In this respect, special value should be attached to the Acts of the Council of Chalcedon. At this Council, the function of General Councils was more accurately defined, and the important contribution made to the Monophysite controversy by Leo I brought about a fuller recognition of the position due to the Roman bishops. The declarations of the papal legates and of the Fathers [44] make it evident that the sort of presidency at the councils which popes and legates claimed and which emperors and council Fathers were ready to concede was none other than the function once exercised by the *princeps senatus* of the Roman senate. He was in a way the Speaker of the House, but the summoning of the meetings and the leading of the debates remained imperial prerogatives.

The Acts of the Council show also that the meetings were arranged as the sessions of the Roman senate used to be. The members attending the sitting were placed in the same order as the senators. The metropolitans, corresponding to the praetors, followed the princeps senatus; then came the bishops, corresponding to those of aedile rank; then the abbots, corresponding to the knights. The last were required to stand and did not possess the right to vote. The Gospel was set in the center of the Council as the Altar of Victory was set in the senate. The same analogy existed in the manner of voting. As in the sessions of the Councils, so also in the sessions of the Senate, the practice was to acclaim the emperors. This is how the Fathers acclaimed Marcian and Pulcheria at the end of the sixth session: "To Marcian, the new Constantine, the new Paul, the new David: [many] years to the emperor David . . . You are the peace of the world . . . May Christ, whom you honor, protect you. You have strengthened the orthodox faith; you have the faith of the Apostles . . . You are the light of the orthodox faith. That is why peace reigns everywhere. Lord, protect the lights of peace. Lord, protect the lights of the world . . . Many years to the priest-emperor. You have set the Churches right, O victor in battle, doctor of the faith . . . You have destroyed the heretics . . . Be your empire eternal." [45]

These are the favorite materials of the Hellenistic theorists: the king leads the people to God; he is a priest; he gives peace to his people; he is the light of the world and his empire is eternal; lastly, he is the most divine, a

[43] Letter 76, *ibid.*, col. 100.

[44] See especially Mansi, vol. VI, col. 985, 1097 ff.; VII, cols. 101, 135, 425.

[45] *Ibid.*, vol. VII, cols. 169 ff.; 177.

title constantly conferred in the Acts on the Christian emperor as the last vestige of the Hellenistic rulers' divinization.

But in spite of the divinity ascribed to him, the emperor knew quite well that definitions of faith lay outside his scope and were the exclusive right of the bishops. This is how Marcian announced the decisions of the council to the people of Constantinople. "Saintly priests came from various provinces to Chalcedon by our command and accurately defined what should be preserved. So, let there be an end to all vain controversy . . ."[46]

The compromise between the Imperium and the Sacerdotium expressed so well in the Acts of Chalcedon continued to be observed by both parties in the second half of the fifth century, although not always in favor of orthodoxy. The emperor Leo I, successor to Marcian, professed to be a supporter of the faith as defined at Chalcedon but considered summoning a council to give satisfaction to the Monophysites who had again risen to power in Alexandria.[47] Pope Leo the Great dissuaded him from making such a concession,[48] and the emperor adopted instead the new practice of the referendum. He asked the bishops to send him their opinion on Chalcedon in writing.[49] From their answers and the pope's we can see that, on the whole, East and West gave the Christian emperor the same functions: assisting the bishops in defining the faith, legalizing their definitions, removing reluctant bishops from their sees, and checking heretics.

Pope Simplicius (468–483), when learning that the usurper of the imperial throne Basiliscus (475–476) was thinking of repealing the decisions of the Council of Chalcedon, reminded him in a long letter of the emperor's duty to defend the faith defined by the orthodox council.[50] The emperor should not summon another council. This last clause meant, again, recognition of the emperor's right to summon councils.

When the emperor Zeno restored the authority of Chalcedon, he was congratulated by Pope Simplicius for having shown the priestly spirit as emperors should: "We rejoice to see in you the spirit of a very faithful priest and prince. This will make your imperial authority, as enhanced by your Christian devotion, more acceptable to God . . ."[51] But a dangerous break with the tradition was effected by the emperor Zeno when in an attempt at a compromise between orthodoxy and Monophysitism, he published his

[46] Mansi, vol. VII, col. 476.
[47] According to Facundus Hermianensis, *P.L.*, vol. 67, col. 834.
[48] Mansi, vol. VI, cols. 307–312 (letters 145, 146).
[49] *Ibid.*, cols. 323 ff.
[50] A. Thiel, *Epist. Roman. Pontificum* (Brumbergae, 1868), vol. I, p. 179.
[51] Mansi, vol. VII, col. 988.

Henoticon. The formula was apparently suggested by the patriarch Acacius, but when it was published without a conciliar decision and without a referendum to the bishops, Pope Felix III declared the formula to be a violation of the decision at Chalcedon and in a very outspoken manner defended the right of the priests to define the true doctrine. In spite of his courageous defense, he was so much under the spell of the traditional view on the emperor's right to care for the purity of the faith that he did not dare to accuse Zeno directly. He shifted the main responsibility to the patriarch Acacius. From the two missives the pope sent to the emperor it is clear that the pope was eager to make peace with the emperor.[52] In his opinion, although emperors do abuse their right, their office is still the highest in the world, they do have an ecclesiastical mission, and they can choose bishops. But they must leave them free to decide in matters of faith.

The Acacian schism which resulted from this break in tradition was bound to make the popes less enthusiastic about the emperors' prerogatives in Church matters. But in spite of the tenseness of the situation, the popes dealt with the Basileus with the utmost deference. It was during this schism that Pope Gelasius made the famous distinction, in his letter to Emperor Anastasius, between the imperial *potestas* and the ecclesiastical *auctoritas.* The pope's definition was to become the basis of political speculation throughout the Western medieval world. I hope to show in my forthcoming book that the pope's declaration was not as revolutionary as it is usually held to be.[53] Apart from the denial of the emperor's priestly character, Gelasius' letter is not fundamentally at variance with the current notions on kingship in the Roman Empire of the fifth century. In no case did Gelasius attribute to the sacerdotium any prerogative of the imperium, nor did his words imply that the secular power should be subordinated to the ecclesiastical: only as a man was the emperor subject to the *auctoritas* and to the *potestas ligandi et solvendi.* The interdependence of the two powers left room for the emperor's customary share in the execution of Church decisions.

As concerns the convocation of the councils by the emperor, nothing had changed. Pope Anastasius (496–498) addressed the emperor in the following way: "The heart of Your Pious Majesty is the holy shrine of public welfare, and . . . God has appointed you to rule, as His vicar, over the world. . ."[54] Moreover, when, after Anastasius' death, a schism broke out in Rome, the

[52] Mansi, vol. VII, col. 1066, 1097 ff.

[53] See also my paper on "Pope Gelasius and Emperor Anastasius," in Festschrift F. Dölger, *Byzantinische Zeitschrift*, 1951.

[54] Mansi, vol. VIII, col. 190.

followers of Gelasius asked the Arian king Theodoric for a decision and made no objection when he summoned a synod to pass judgment on the accusations launched against Pope Symmachus. When later Pope Hormisdas negotiated with the emperor for the liquidation of the schism, and when the question of a new council came up for discussion, the pope did not query the emperor's right to convoke it. He even declared his readiness to break with the established custom and to attend the council in person.[55]

In these circumstances it is not surprising that even the Emperor Justinian, who took his role as defender and propagator of the true faith most seriously, found no opposition to his theological edicts. Let us quote the response of Pope John II to Justinian's edict of 533 on the theological proposition: One of the Blessed Trinity has been crucified. "We hear," says the Pope, "that you have addressed to all the faithful an edict in which religious zeal for the right faith prompts you to support apostolic doctrine against heretical machinations, with the encouragement of our brethren and co-bishops. As your action is true to apostolic teaching, we confirm it with our authority."[56] Pope Vigilius, moreover, again credited Justinian with a priestly spirit.[57]

A storm of opposition broke out only when Justinian made his most glaring intrusion into theology, condemning the so-called Three Chapters. African bishops revolted and Pope Vigilius, although willing to coöperate, had to join the opposition. The real reason for all this was that the emperor issued the condemnation without convoking a synod and without a referendum to the bishops. It was a break with the traditional practice and, at the end, Justinian had to yield and convoke the sixth ecumenical council. In his letter of convocation,[58] he returned to the traditional practice and sensibly limited the emperor's share in discussions on matters of faith. Had he done it at the beginning, he would have saved himself a good deal of trouble. In fact, the incident made the Church more conscious of its rights and more determined than ever to defend them.

Even the iconoclastic emperors could not ignore the leading role of the bishops in defining the Christian doctrine. They forbade the worship of images on the advice of some Asiatic bishops and convoked a council of bishops — mostly from Asia Minor — in Hieria, with the injunction to define the Christian doctrine on images.

The same method was used by the Empress Irene in order to condemn

[55] Mansi, vol. VIII, cols. 393 ff.
[56] *P.L.*, vol. 66, cols. 17 ff.
[57] Mansi, vol. IX, col. 35.
[58] Mansi, vol. IX, cols. 178 ff.

iconoclasm. She stated herself in her letter to the Pope Hadrian I: "We have decreed that a universal Council shall take place. And we ask your paternal Beatitude . . . to acquiesce and to make no delay but to come hither to confirm and strengthen the ancient tradition as to the venerable images." [59] In her address to the Council Fathers, the Empress expressed very clearly the traditional doctrine on the role of the bishop: "By God's good pleasure and will, we have brought together you His sacred priests . . . in order that your decision may be in accordance with the definitions of the Councils which have given right dogmatic precisions and that the glorious Light of the Spirit may enlighten all." [60] The same principles were observed at the councils convoked by the emperor Michael III and Basil I in the affair of the patriarchs Photius and Ignatius.[61]

In summing up the main results of these investigations we have to confess that the Church was not despotically ruled by the emperors during the period which preceded the Eastern schism, as has very often been believed. The role which the emperors had played in the definition of the true faith, especially in convoking councils and directing their debates, looks less formidable and dangerous for the Church in the light of the Hellenistic ideas on kingship, ideas accepted by the Christians and ennobled by the Christian doctrine. There is something sublime in the idea that the emperor should be the image of God, imitating his generosity and clemency, and that the emperor's foremost duty was to lead his subjects to God. Because of this duty he could not be indifferent to the definition of the true faith. This is a high conception of rulership, a conception which our age of material statism will hardly understand and appreciate.

It is not true, either, that the bishops were willing instruments in the hands of the imperial despots. This period of Church history is filled with hard struggles of the hierarchy for the exclusive right of defining Christian doctrine. This right was recognized by Constantine the Great and, in spite of some setbacks, the hierarchy remained, at the end, victorious in the struggle.

Finally the analogy between the councils and the Roman senate explains many problems. First of all, the fact that the emperors claimed the exclusive privilege of convoking the councils ceases to threaten the independence of the Church in doctrinal matters, because only the bishops — the ecclesiastical senators — possessed the right to express their opinion at the meetings

[59] Mansi, vol. XII, col. 985.

[60] Mansi, vol. XII, col. 1003.

[61] See for details my book *The Photian Schism: History and Legend* (Cambridge 1948).

and to vote. On the other hand, when we look at the facts from this angle we must confess that the Catholic doctrine of papal supremacy was not at stake. The legates of the First See being given the place of the princeps senatus, they exercised a great authority at the councils. They were first to give their opinion, they voted first, and, as used to be the case in the senate, the opinion of the princeps was regarded as the most important.

XVI

The Byzantine Church and the Immaculate Conception

One of the characteristic features of eastern Christianity is a deep and warm devotion to Our Lady, the Mother of Christ. Innumerable examples of this devotion are to be found in Eastern liturgies, in literature, in art, and in the spiritual life of simple believers. The Byzantine Church is particularly renowned for its devotion to Mary. This love of the Mother of God inspired Greek poets to compose hymns in her honor, hymns which are still sung in the Divine Office. And who does not know the numerous artistic representations of Mary, many of which still adorn Greek churches. Greek artists of the Byzantine period produced some masterpieces representing Our Lady, which inspired the piety of the faithful for centuries, were imitated by western artists, and still provoke admiration for the artists' achievements, and our humble homage by reason of their personal piety. The Byzantine Church inculcated in all the people whom it converted to Christianity, a profound devotion to Our Lady; and it was the Russian Church which became its best disciple in this respect. There also, in Kiev, Novgorod and Moscow, the iconography of Our Lady reached its greatest heights from the eleventh to the eighteenth centuries.

I

THE EASTERN CHURCH AND THE IMMACULATE CONCEPTION

In spite of that, it was not the Eastern Church but the Western Church which succeeded in defining the more clearly the great prerogatives which God bestowed on the One who should become the Mother of His incarnate Son. From the scholastic period on, the best western theologians worked ceaselessly on Mariology, and the result of their theological research permitted the highest authority in the Catholic Church to proclaim solemnly the two dogmas of the Immaculate Conception of Our Lady and of her Assumption after her death. Both doctrines are intimately connected. If it is true that Our Lady was exempted by a special privilege and in virtue of the future merits of the divine Saviour, from inheriting original sin, then it is logical to believe that God, in anticipating for her the resurrection of the body—a belief which is so dear to all Christians—exempted her from the corruption of the body which, with death, is one of the consequences of original sin.

Modern Eastern Theologians

Eastern theologians of more recent times have not followed their western colleagues in their research into Mariology. Some of them have even expressed bewilderment over the proclamation of the two dogmas.[1] It seems, however, almost impossible to believe that the Church, which in the earlier stages of its development did so much for the spread of devotion to Our Lady, would have contributed nothing to a better understanding of Mary's prerogatives. The doctrine of the Immaculate Conception would seem to make a particular appeal to the genius of eastern Christianity. It appears fitting, therefore, to investigate the theology and liturgy of the Byzantine Church for any indications that some at least of its thinkers and theologians had envisaged the possibility, probability or certainty of God's granting this greatest privilege to Mary.

Such an investigation should be the more desirable, because the Byzantine Church was the heir and guardian of the patristic tradition to whose formation the greatest Greek thinkers of the first Christian centuries had contributed so much. It is in the patristic tradition that theologians have to find the necessary documentation for their doctrinal deductions.

The Patristic Period

It is generally known that in the patristic period, Mariology was not especially cultivated.[2] The first great theologians were preoccupied with the definition and defence of other vital Christian doctrines. The divinity

[1] A detailed account of the attitude of modern Greek and Russian theologians toward the dogma of the Immaculate Conception is given by M. Jugie in his book *L'Immaculée Conception dans l'Ecriture Sainte et dans la tradition orientale* (Rome, 1952), pp. 348-477. On the attitude of Serbian orthodox theologians see Ch. Balić "L'Immaculée Conception de Marie dans la théologie contemporaine serbo-orthodoxe," *Revue des Études Byzantines,* 11 (*Mélanges Martin Jugie,* 1953), pp. 36-46. Numerous criticisms by modern Protestant and Orthodox theologians of the proclamation of the dogma of the Assumption are collated by Friedrich Heiler in the symposium "Das neue Mariendogma im Lichte der Geschichte und im Urteil der Oekumene" (*Oekumenische Einheit,* 1951, Heft 2).

[2] Cf. P. Ortiz de Urbina, "Le sviluppo della mariologia nella patrologia orientale," in *Orientalia christiana periodica* 6 (1940).

of Our Lord, the nature of the Holy Trinity, the two natures and the two wills in One Lord were attacked and needed explanation and clear definition. The role which Our Lady was chosen to play in our salvation was naturally left very much in the background. Nevertheless, the theological struggle for the true definition of the doctrine of the Holy Trinity, the Incarnation of Our Lord and His two natures helped the Church to clarify and to defend some other prerogatives of Our Lady: her perpetual virginity, her great sanctity and her title "Mother of God". The decision made at the Council of Ephesus that the Blessed Virgin was truly and verily *Theotokos*—Mother of God—was received with enthusiasm by the faithful and contributed greatly to the spread of the cult of Our Lady.

There are many indications that some theologians of the patristic period, when meditating on the degree of sanctity of the Mother of God, came very near to a belief in her Immaculate Conception. It was the comparison of Mary with Eve which suggested to some of them that Mary—the new Eve—was as immaculate from the beginning of her existence as Eve was when she was created. This, of course, suggests the idea of the Immaculate Conception, because Eve was also without original sin when she was created by God.[3]

II

THE SIXTH TO THE NINTH CENTURIES

These were the premises on which Byzantine theologians were working from the end of the fifth century on. The most important period for the study of this subject is that from the sixth to the ninth centuries. It was the time when Byzantine thinkers, stimulated by the fight against the monophysites, the monothelites and the iconoclasts, made important contributions to dogmatic theology in general. It is a period of consolidation of dogmatic theology in the Orthodox Church which must still be regarded as the great period of Greek dogmatic theology. It produced some ecclesiastical writers of great renown: Leontios of Byzantium, Anastasius of Sinai, stout defenders of Catholic dogma against the monophysites; Sophronius of Jerusalem and Maximus the Confessor, who explained the teaching on two wills in the person of Christ; Germanus of Constantinople, John of Damascus, Theodore of Studios and Nicephorus of Constantinople, who led the theological campaign against iconoclasm. The most important

[3] For details, see chap. II of the present volume; also G. JOUASSARD, "Marie à travers la patristique" in H. DU MANOIR, *Maria, Etudes sur la Sainte Vierge* (Paris, 1949), I, pp. 69-157; and M. JUGIE, *L'Immaculée Conception dans l'Ecriture sainte et dans la tradition orientale* (Rome, 1952), pp. 55-94.

of them all was St. John of Damascus, who was also the most prominent among Greek mariologists.

New Marian Feasts

The cult of Our Lady and the theological speculation on the role she had played in our salvation, were greatly stimulated by the introduction of new Marian feasts into Byzantine liturgy. So far, the Eastern Church had recognised only one feast commemorating Mary in its liturgical calendar.[4] From the sixth century on, however, three other festive commemorations of the Blessed Virgin were introduced: The Annunciation (Εὐαγγελισμός) on March 25th, the Nativity of Our Lady on September 8th and the Κοίμησις or Dormitio, commemorating Our Lady's death, on August 15th. During the seventh century, the commemoration of St. Anne's conception was also introduced and celebrated on December 9th.[5]

For these new feasts, new offices had to be composed and new hymns were needed to celebrate the virtues and the merits of Mary. This period gave the Byzantine Church also one of the greatest Greek religious poets, the famous Romanos the Melodian. He composed the hymns for the feast of the Annunciation, and for the Nativity of Our Lady.

St. Anne's Conception

The fact that the Byzantine Church had introduced a special feast of the Conception of St. Anne has been interpreted by some western mariologists as a counterpart to the feast of the Immaculate Conception as the Western Church knows it. In reality the importance of this feast for the evolution of the doctrine of the Immaculate Conception should not be exaggerated. This feast was originally simply a counterpart to another similar commemoration—the feast of the Conception of St. John the Baptist. The introduction of the feast of St. Anne's Conception was inspired by the legendary account in the apocryphal Gospel of St. James[6] which described how the conception of Our Lady was announced to St. Anne and St. Joachim by an angel. Evidently this account is a reproduction of the narrative given in St. Luke when he speaks of the appearance of an angel to Zachary. The liturgies of the two feasts are very similar. It

[4] See M. Jugie, "La Premiere fête mariale en Orient," in *Echos d'Orient,* 22 (1923), pp. 129-151.

[5] For details, see chapter IV of the present volume, pp. 114-123; also H. Kellner, *Heortologie* (Freiburg in Br., 1911), 3d ed., pp. 182, 287, and S. Salaville, "Marie dans la Liturgie Byzantine ou Gréco-slave," in Hubert du Manoir, *Maria, études sur la sainte Vierge* (Paris, 1949), I, pp. 249-326. Cf. also P. de Meester, "La festa dell' Immacolata Concezione nella chiesa graeca," *Bessarione,* Ser. II, 7 (1904), pp. 89-102; A. Schultz, *Der liturgische Grad des Festes der Empfängnis Mariens im byzantischen Ritus vom 8. bis zum 13. Jahrhundert* (Rom, 1941).

[6] E. Amann, *Le Protoévangile de Jacques et ses remaniements latins* (Paris, 1910), p. 99 ff. Cf. chapter II of the present volume, pp. 58 f.; 81 f.; and especially the text cited on p. 513 ff.

should be pointed out here that the feast of Mary's Conception, which was introduced into England and Normandy during the eleventh century, also stressed the miraculous announcement of Mary's birth.[7] Eastern influences on the introduction of this feast are evident.

But besides the miraculous announcement of Mary's birth, the Byzantine Church also stressed, in the liturgy of this feast, the miraculous conception in the sterile womb of Anne and the beginning of life of the future Mother of God. In their poems and homilies Byzantine poets and orators insisted more and more on Our Lady's *passive* Conception, and on her holiness from the very beginning of her existence. So it happened that the introduction of this feast into the eastern liturgy contributed a great deal to the development of theological speculation on the greatest of Mary's prerogatives.

Features of Byzantine Theology

Before starting a more detailed study of the subject, certain particular features of Byzantine theological history, which differ considerably from the developments of dogmatic history in the West, must be recalled. First of all, the Eastern Church never witnessed among its theologians a struggle for the definition of Mary's prerogatives similar to that in the West. No Eastern theologian went so far as to deny explicitly Mary's prerogatives. Although the Eastern Church believed equally firmly in the existence of original sin, and in its consequences—concupiscence, death, the corruption of the body—its theologians were less interested than those of the West in the definition of the nature of original sin. The consequence of these facts was that the Eastern theologians never manifested such a lively interest in the Immaculate Conception of Our Lady as did their Latin colleagues. It would be wrong therefore to expect to find in the works of Byzantine theologians such clear declarations as are to be found in the treatises of western thinkers in favor of the solemn confirmation of this greatest privilege of Mary.

The starting point of Eastern theological speculation on Mary's prerogatives was different. The basis of this speculation on Mary's holiness was the dogmatic proclamation of the Council of Ephesus (431) that Mary was the Mother of God. This sublime fact presupposes a great degree of sanctity in the Blessed Virgin, and theological speculation in the Byzantine Church produced various estimates of this degree. Because all agree that God could not have chosen for His sojourn a body stained by sin, some of them at least, were induced quite logically to conclude that the Mother of God could not have been subject to original sin and its consequences. Because this speculation did not encounter any serious

[7] Cf. *infra,* p. 131; also F.-X. Le Bachelet, "Immaculée Conception dans l'Eglise Latine après le concile d'Éphèse," in *Dictionnaire de Théologie catholique* (Paris, 1923), VII, cols. 990-994; and M. Jugie on the character of this feast, *ibid.,* cols. 956-960.

opposition, Byzantine thinkers were often uncertain about the moment when the Mother of God became exempt from original sin, but some of them rightly supposed that it should have been from the very moment of her passive conception.

In appreciating some declarations in Byzantine mariological literature, care must be taken not to attribute too much value to some titles given to Mary by poets and by some enthusiastic preachers. These writers liked to use metaphors, similes, and epithets which seem, at first sight, to express clearly the doctrine of her Immaculate Conception. In reality, however, they can only be connected with Mary's other privileges and give general expression to the high degree of her sanctity.

It will, therefore, be advisable to limit our research to theologians, and to panegyrists who have a solid theological background. It should, of course, be understood that even the panegyrists with their generalisations and flowery expressions of Mary's praises contributed considerably to the spread of Our Lady's cult in Byzantium, and that they stimulated speculation on the degree of sanctity God had bestowed upon the Mother of His Son.[8]

The most important sources for investigation are the theological writings of the famous Byzantine saints of the eighth century: St. Andrew of Crete († 740), St. Germanus, Patriarch of Constantinople († about 733) and St. John of Damascus († 749). They are preceded by St. Sophronius, Patriarch of Jerusalem, who died in 638.

The last-named is famous among eastern theologians for his Synodal Letter sent, after a synod held in Jerusalem in 634, to the Patriarch Sergius of Constantinople and to other patriarchs, in which he gave a very clear exposition of the Catholic doctrine on original sin and on the Incarnation. When speaking of the Incarnation, Sophronius uses the following words:

> I believe . . . that God the Word, the only Son of the Father, . . . descended into our lowliness . . . and became incarnate, entering the inviolate womb, resplendent with virginal purity, of the holy and radiant Mary, who was full of divine wisdom, and free from all contamination of body, soul and spirit. . . . He willed to become man in order to purify like by like, to save brother by brother . . . For this purpose, a holy

[8] Byzantine Mariology has, so far, been undeservedly neglected. The work of Passaglia, *De immaculato Deiparae semper virginis conceptu Commentarius* (Roma, 1854-1855, 3 vols.), treats Byzantine Mariology very inadequately, and is lacking in critical sense. Th. Toscani and J. Cozza (*De Immaculatae Deiparae conceptione hymnologia graecorum*, Roma, 1862) limited themselves to Greek hymnology. The works of M. Jugie, which are included or resumed in his latest book *L'Immaculée Conception dans l'Ecriture Sainte et dans la tradition orientale* (Rome, *Bibl. Immac. Conc.*, 3, 1952) have opened new vistas in Byzantine Mariology. He made many unknown works accessible and he is certainly the most prominent specialist in Eastern Mariology. See also F. S. Müller, "Die Unbefleckte Empfängnis der Gottesmutter in der griechischen Ueberlieferung," *Gregorianum*, 16 (1935), pp. 74-96, 225-250, vol. 17 (1936), pp. 82-115. For a complete bibliography on Eastern Mariology, see M. Gordillo, *Mariologia Orientalis* (Roma, 1954), *Orientalia Christiana Analecta*, 141.

> Virgin is chosen and is sanctified in soul and body; and thus, because pure, chaste and immaculate, she is able to serve in the Incarnation of the Creator.[9]

One thing seems clear to Sophronius, namely, that Mary was holy before the Incarnation of Our Lord. The plenitude of holiness on which Sophronius insists could perhaps be interpreted as exemption from original sin also. He suggests the same idea in an interesting passage of one of his homilies. When exalting Mary's holiness, Sophronius exclaims:

> Many saints appeared before thee, but none was as filled with grace as thou . . . No one has been purified in advance as thou hast been . . . Thou dost surpass all that is most excellent in man, as well as all the gifts which have been bestowed by God upon all others . . .[10]

The most important part of this passage is formed by the words: "None has been purified in advance," because they express the idea of Mary's being purified before her birth. It is thus legitimate to conclude that Sophronius was very near to belief in the Immaculate Conception, although he is not clear enough in his expression and fails to indicate the very moment when Our Lady "was exempted from all contamination of the body" and "when she was purified in advance."

Speculation about the degree of Mary's sanctity must have been spreading considerably in Byzantium in the seventh century, and the prevailing tendency was to attribute to her a privileged position before her birth. This is illustrated by the diffusion among the faithful of two erroneous beliefs concerning Mary, namely, that her conception was virginal and that she remained only seven months in her mother's womb.

These details may be learned from the writings of St. Andrew of Crete,[11] a famous Greek orator and poet.[12] Eight of his numerous homilies and two of his poems celebrate Mary's sanctity and virtues.

[9] *Epistola synodica ad Sergium, P.G.*, 87³, cols. 3160C-3161A: Πιστεύω . . . ὡς ὁ Θεὸς Λόγος, ὁ τοῦ Πατρὸς μονογενὴς Υἱός . . . πρὸς τοὺς ταπεινοὺς ἡμᾶς καταβέβηκεν, . . . καὶ μήτραν εἰσδὺς ἀπειρόγαμον, παρθενίας ἀγλαιζομένην ἀγνότητι, Μαρίας τῆς ἁγίας καὶ φαιδρᾶς καὶ θεόφρονος καὶ παντὸς ἐλευθέρας μολύσματος τοῦ τε κατὰ σῶμα καὶ ψυχὴν καὶ διάνοιαν, σαρκοῦται ὁ ἄσαρκος . . . Ἄνθρωπος γὰρ χρηματίζειν ἐβούλετο, ἵνα τῷ ὁμοίῳ ἀνακαθάρῃ τὸ ὅμοιον, καὶ τῷ συγγενεῖ τὸ συγγενὲς ἀνασώσηται, καὶ τῷ συμφυεῖ τὸ συμφυὲς ἐκλαμπρύνῃ. Διὰ τοῦτο Παρθένος ἁγία λαμβάνεται, καὶ σῶμα καὶ ψυχὴν ἁγιάζεται, καὶ οὕτως ὑπουργεῖ τῇ σαρκώσει τοῦ κτίσαντος ὡς καθαρὰ καὶ ἁγνὴ καὶ ἀμόλυντος.

[10] *Oratio II in Ss. Deiparae Annuntiationem, ch. XXV, PG,* 87, col. 3248A. Cf. also ch. XLIII, *ibid.* col. 3273: "The Holy Spirit will descend upon thee, O Immaculate, in order to make thee more pure." Ch. XVIII (*ibid.* col. 3237D): "Thou art more radiant in purity than any other creature." There are similar eulogies in chs. XIX and XXXI (*ibid.* cols. 3240, 3241).

[11] *Canon in Beatae Annae conceptionem, PG,* 97, col. 1313A.

[12] For details on his work see S. Vailhé, "St. André de Crète," in *Echos d'Orient,* 5 (1901-1902), pp. 378-387. On Andrew's poetical works consult the important study by L. Petit, in *Dictionnaire d'archéol. Chrét. et de Liturgie* (Paris, 1907), I. cols. 2034-2041.

Andrew is clearer than Sophronius in stressing Mary's sanctity before her birth. In the hymn which Andrew had composed for the feast of St. Anne's conception, it can also be clearly seen that this feast was becoming more and more the commemoration of the passive conception of Our Lady. Andrew terms the conception of Mary "holy" and her birth "venerable" and "immaculate."[13]

Moreover, Andrew introduced into Byzantium a new title for Mary—*daughter of God, θεόπαις*—which became very popular among Byzantine mariologists. Andrew gave this title a broader meaning by speculating as to whether God intervened in a special manner at the moment of her conception.[14] In his homily in honor of Mary's birth, he says:

> Today, Adam presents Mary to God as the first fruits of our nature . . . Today, humanity recovers the gift it had received when first formed by divine hands, and returns immaculate to its original nobility. The shame of sin had cast a shadow upon the splendor and charm of human nature; but when the Mother of Him who is Beauty itself is born, this nature recovers in her person its ancient privileges, and is fashioned according to a perfect model, truly worthy of God. And this fashioning is a perfect restoration; this restoration is a divinization, and this divinization is an assimilation to the primitive state . . . In a word, the reformation of our nature begins today; the world, which had grown old, undergoes a transformation which is wholly divine, and receives the first-fruits of its second creation.[15]

These words are very eloquent and indicate clearly enough that Andrew regarded Our Lady as the first specimen, the beginning of our human nature recreated or brought back to its original status, when it was freed from the stain of original sin.[16a] Andrew often insists on this idea, calling Our Lady "the first fruit of our nature"[16b] or of our reformation, or "the first who was exempted (or freed) from the first transgression of our first parents."[16c] In another instance he designates the body of Mary as "the clay which was moulded by the hands of the divine artist."[17]

[13] *Ibid.* cols. 1309, 1313.

[14] Cf. M. Jugie, "Saint André de Crète et l'Immaculée Conception," *Echos d'Orient*, 13 (1910), pp. 129-133.

[15] *Hom. I in Nativ. B. Mariae, P.G.*, 97, cols. 809D-812: *Σήμερον ἐξ ἡμῶν ἀνθ' ἡμῶν ἀπαρχὴν ὁ 'Αδὰμ τῷ Θεῷ προσφέρων, τὴν Μαρίαν ἀπάρχεται . . . Σήμερον ἡ καθαρὰ τῶν ἀνθρώπων εὐγένεια, τῆς πρώτης θεοπλαστίας ἀπολαμβάνει τὸ χάρισμα, καὶ πρὸς ἑαυτὴν ἀντεπάνεισι· καὶ ἣν ἀπημαύρωσε τοῦ κάλους εὐπρέπειαν ἡ τῆς κακίας δυσγένεια, ταύτην ἡ φύσις τεχθείσῃ τῇ μητρὶ τοῦ ὡραίου προσέχουσα, πλάσιν ἀρίστην τε καὶ θεοπρεπεστάτην εἰσδέχεται. Και γίνεται κυρίως ἡ πλάσις ἀνάκλησις· καὶ ἡ ἀνάκλησις, θέωσις· . . . Καὶ συνελόντι φάναι· σήμερον ἡ τῆς φύσεως ἡμῶν ἀναμόρφωσις ἄρχεται, καὶ ὁ γηράσας κόσμος θεοειδεστάτην λαμβάνων στοιχείωσιν, δευτέρας θεοπλαστίας προοίμια δέχεται.*

[16a] *Homil. III in Nativ. B. Mariae, ibid.* col. 860B: *ταύτην δὴ λέγω τὴν βασιλίδα τὴν φύσεως, τὴν ἀπαρχὴν τοῦ ἡμετέρου φυράματος.*

[16b] *Homil. IV. Ibid.* col. 865A: *ἡ ἀπαρχὴ τῆς ἡμῶν ἀναπλάσεως.*

[16c] *Ibid.* col. 880C: *ἡ πρώτη τοῦ πρώτου πτώματος τῶν προγόνων ἀνάκλησις.*

[17] *Homil. I. in Dormitionem, B. Mariae, ibid*, col. 1068C: . . . *ἡ θεογεώργητος γῆ* . . .

Andrew is also one of the first Byzantine theologians to perceive that there is a logical connection between the Immaculate Conception and the Assumption of the body of Our Lady. On several occasions he ponders on the circumstances of the death of the Mother of God and comes to the conclusion that, if Mary had to die, it was because even Our Lord had to die, but that her death was different from the death of ordinary men. Death is the consequence of original sin. Andrew's words suggest the idea that because Mary was exempted from original sin, her death was also quite different. He does not go so far as to suggest the Assumption of her body, but he was well aware of the consequences to which his first supposition, namely that Mary was exempt from original sin, led.

St. Germanus of Constantinople was Andrew's contemporary, but it is improbable that he was influenced by the latter in his speculation on Mary's holiness. It is therefore all the more remarkable that St. Germanus insists in his writings, like St. Andrew, on the absolute holiness of Mary. One of his comparisons of Mary is particularly indicative. In his homily on the Presentation of Our Lady in the Temple, he lets Joachim and Anne apostrophize God as follows:

> Accept her whom you have chosen, predestined and sanctified, . . . her whom you have chosen as a lily among the thorns of our unworthiness.[18]

On another occasion, Germanus takes thorns as a symbol of our sins.[19] The comparison of Our Lady with a lily among thorns, suggests the idea that she alone was without sin. He also follows St. Andrew in his meditation on Mary's death and comes to the conclusion that Mary had to die like her Son, but that her body like that of her Son was exempt from corruption.[20] In his homilies St. Germanus also developed the idea of Mary's intermediary role in the distribution of supernatural gifts to men.[21]

τὸ πανόμοιον τῆς ἀρχικῆς ὡραιότητος ἴνδαλμα . . . ὁ θεοτελὴς τοῦ παντουργοῦ καὶ ἀριστοτέχνου πηλός.
A similar imagery is used by Andrew in his *Homil. I. in Nativ. B. Mariae,* ibid. cols. 813 sq. God chose an Immaculate Virgin for his Incarnation as he had formed the first Adam from an immaculate clay.

[18] *Homil. I. in Praesent. Ss. Deiparae P.G.,* 98, col. 300D: ἀπολάμβανε, ἣν ᾑρετίσω, καὶ προώρισας, καὶ ἡγίασας . . . ἣν ὡς κρίνον ἐξ ἀκανθῶν τῆς ἡμετέρας ἀναξιότητος ἐξελέξω.

[19] *Homil. in Dominici corporis sepulturam, ibid.* col. 253D: Ἁμαρτίας δὴ σύμβολον, ἄκανθα . . . .

[20] The most telling passage is in the *Homil. in Dormitionem Deiparae, ibid.,* col. 345.

[21] On the authenticity of Germanus' Marian homilies see F. Cayré's study, "St. Germain, patriarche de Constantinople" in *Diction. de Théol. cath.* (Paris, 1924), VI, 1, col. 1306. The lessons of the Office of the Immaculate Conception are taken from Germanus' homilies. "A bon droit," says Cayré, "car si on n'y trouve pas ce dogme signalé en propres termes, il y est enseigné, sans aucun doute possible, au moins d'une manière indirecte. Tant dans des affirmations positives que dans d'innombrables comparaisons, Marie y est exaltée pour sa pureté incomparable écartant

The Mariology of St. John of Damascus is very important, because he is the leading theologian of the Orthodox Church, and his works still constitute for Orthodox theologians the basis of theological speculation. St. John, in his systematic exposition of the true faith, explained first of all, very clearly, the two great prerogatives of Our Lady: her Divine Maternity and her perpetual virginity. But this does not represent the sum of the great theologian's beliefs concerning the Blessed Virgin. Numerous expressions are to be found in his writings testifying to John's belief in the highest degree of Mary's sanctity, some of them pointing to his conviction that her sanctity, which means exemption from any kind of sin, had its beginning before her natural birth.[22]

St. John of Damascus' utterances on the sanctity of the Blessed Virgin in his greatest work, *On Orthodox Faith,* the first systematic work of dogmatic theology, should first be examined. He speaks there of the "holy and immaculate flesh and blood" of the holy Virgin from which the body of Jesus was formed,[23] characterizes her conception as unaccompanied by any sensual pleasure and the birth of Jesus as having been without pain.[24] The most conspicuous description of Mary's sanctity is, however, the following:

> And then, transplanted into the temple of God, and enriched by the Spirit like a fruitful olive tree, (Mary) became the dwelling of every virtue. She banished all worldly and carnal desires from her mind, and thus preserved her soul virginal, like her body, as befitted her who was to conceive God in her womb. . . . Thus, therefore, she pursued sanctity, and became a holy and admirable temple, worthy of the Most High God.[25]

John's description of Mary as a Virgin, not only in body, but also in soul, suggests the idea that she was free from any sin, including original sin. This is, however, only an indirect indication that John regarded Mary as exempt from any kind of sin from the time of her conception.

More positive testimonies to Mary's initial sanctity can be found in John's homilies on Mary.[26] In the homily on the Virgin's nativity John's

---

toute souillure, sans moindre restriction ni pour une tache quelquonque, ni pour un moment de son existence. Le péchè originel est évidement exclu aussi."

[22] On St. John of Damascus and his Mariology see the following studies: M. Jugie, "Saint Jean Damascène," in *Dict. de Theol. Cath.* (Paris, 1924), VIII, 1, cols. 693-751; M. Gordillo, "Damascenica," in *Orient. Christ.,* 3 (Roma, 1926), pp. 45-103; V. A. Mitchel, *The Mariology of St. John Damascene* (Kirkwood, U.S.A., and Proost, Turnhut, 1930), C. Chevalier, "La Mariologie de St. Jean Damascène," *Orient. Christ. Anal.,* No. 109 (1936), reviewed by Grumel in *Echos d'Orient,* 36 (1937).

[23] *De Fide orth.* IV, 14. *PG,* 94, col. 1160C; cf. also *ibid.* III, 1, col. 985B.

[24] *De Fide orth.* IV, 14, *PG,* 94, col. 1160D. Cf. *II hom. in Dormit,* 3, *PG,* 96, col. 728B.

[25] *De Fide orth.* IV, 14, *PG,* 94, col. 1160A.

[26] On the authorship of the homilies ascribed to St. John of Damascus see M. Jugie, *Saint Jean Damascène, op. cit.,* cols. 703 sq. Among the nine homilies which

most eloquent statement on this matter is to be found. In describing why Mary was born of a sterile mother, John exclaims:

> Nature was defeated by grace and stopped, trembling, not daring to take precedence over it (grace). Since the Virgin Mother of God was to be born of Anne, nature did not dare to precede the product of grace; but remained sterile until grace had produced its fruit.[27]

Then addressing Joachim and Anne, St. John makes his most clear and most advanced statement:

> O happy loins of Joachim, which had produced a germ which is all immaculate. O wondrous womb of Anne in which an all-holy child slowly grew and took shape . . .

This is the most eloquent statement and a direct proof that John regarded Mary as exempt from all sin from the very moment of her passive conception. In other words, the Catholic doctrine of the Immaculate Conception is clearly expressed in this statement.

Some other expressions can also be quoted which show, at least indirectly, that this was John's belief. According to John, Mary is all beautiful, nearest to God. She is above the Cherubim and Seraphim.[28] She is the lily which grew in the middle of thorns.[29] Here St. John uses the familiar comparison already found in the writings of other Fathers. The thorns are sins, and thus Mary is the only one without any sin. In another passage of the same homily, St. John says that the flaming visage of the enemy could not reach her and that she never knew the attacks of concupiscence.[30] All this confirms our impression that St. John believed in the initial sanctity of Our Lady. He merely failed to express his belief in her Immaculate Conception with the same clarity as we do, because in his time such a thing was not yet possible.[31]

Yet another fact must be adduced. St. John is known to have defined most accurately the orthodox doctrine on original sin. Thus he knew that death was introduced into the world by original sin and was the most

---

should doubtless be attributed to the Damascene, four are dedicated to Our Lady: one on the Nativity of the Blessed Virgin (*PG,* 96, cols. 661-680) and three on the *Dormitio* or Assumption. On the authorship of the hymn attributed to St. John see J. M. Hussey, "The Authorship of the Six Hymns attributed to St. John of Damascus," in *Journal of Theological Studies,* 47 (1946) pp. 74-96.

[27] ***Homil. in Nativ. B. Mariae, P.G.***, **96, col. 664A, B:** *Ἡ γὰρ φύσις ἥττηται τῇ χάριτι, καὶ ἕστηκεν ὑπότρομος, προβαίνειν μὴ φέρουσα. Ἐπεὶ οὖν ἔμελλεν ἡ Θεοτόκος Παρθένος ἐκ τῆς Ἄννης τίκτεσθαι, οὐκ ἐτόλμησεν ἡ φύσις προλαβεῖν τὸ τῆς χάριτος βλάστημα· ἀλλ' ἔμεινεν ἄκαρπος, ἕως ἡ χάρις τὸν καρπὸν ἐβλάστησεν. . . . Ὦ ὀσφὺς τοῦ Ἰωακεὶμ παμμακάριστε, ἐξ ἧς κατεβλήθη σπέρμα πανάμωμον! Ὦ μήτρα τῆς Ἄννης ἀοίδιμε, ἐν ᾗ ταῖς κατὰ μικρὸν ἐξ αὐτῆς προσθήκαις ηὐξήθη, καὶ διαμορφωθὲν ἐτέχθη βρέφος πανάγιον! . . .*

[28] *Ibid.* col. 676C, 669A.

[29] ***Ibid.***, **col. 669AB:** *ὦ κρίνον ἀναμέσον τῶν ἀκανθῶν . . . Ὦ ῥόδον ἐξ ἀκανθῶν . . .*

[30] *Ibid.* col. 672B, 676A,C.

[31] **For more details see Chevalier, *op. cit.*, pp. 130-148.**

rigorous punishment for it. But, on the other hand, John believes in the initial sanctity of Mary, which includes exemption from original sin, so he was led to explain why Mary had to die. He did so in his three homilies on Mary's death. He resolves this dilemma by explaining that Mary, as a daughter of Adam had to pay this death penalty because her Son, who is Life itself did not refuse to do so.[32]

> What could death have meant for her in whom the "sting of death"—sin [1 Cor. 15:56]—was slain? It could only have been the beginning of a better and unending life.[33]

A little further on in the same homily, St. John expresses a very outspoken testimony to the Assumption of Our Lady.

Against this interpretation of John's doctrine on the Immaculate Conception, some theologians quote two passages, one from his main work, *On Orthodox Faith*,[34] and another from a homily[35] in which he says that the Holy Spirit descended on Mary in order to purify her. These passages should, however, be explained in connexion with other declarations. From this comparison it is permissible to conclude that St. John had in mind, not the beginning but only the increase of sanctity in Mary through the Holy Spirit at the moment of her conception.[36]

Of the other Byzantine theologians of this period some declarations may be quoted from John, Bishop of Euboea († about 750)[37] and St. Theodore of Studion († 826). In his homily on the Conception of Mary, the Bishop used some phrases which confirm, at least, that on the initial sanctity of Mary, he had a very high opinion approaching that of the present day. This is the most expressive passage apostrophising Joachim and Anne:

> You are Earth, but she is Heaven. You are earthly, but it is through her that the sons of the Earth become inhabitants of Heaven.[38]

[32] *Homil. II in Dormit. PG*, 96, col. 725C,D.

[33] *Homil. II in Dormit., P.G.*, 96, col. 728C: *ἐν ᾗ δὲ τὸ κέντρον τοῦ θανάτου ἡ ἁμαρτία νενέκρωτο, τί φήσομεν, ἢ ζωῆς ἀρχὴν ἀλήκτου καὶ κρείττονος;*

[34] *De fide orthod.* III, 2, *PG*, 94, col. 985B.

[35] *Homil. I in Dormit. B. Mariae, PG*, 96, col. 704A. Cf. on the controversy V. A. Mitchell, *op. cit.*, pp. 113-125 and M. Jugie *L'Immaculée Concept.*, pp. 120 seq., 126. Cf. also F. S. Müller, "Die Unbefleckte Empfängniss der Gottesmutter," *Gregorianum*, 16 (1935), pp. 232 seq.

[36] See M. Jugie, *L'Immaculée Conception*, pp. 120 seq. Chevalier *op. cit.*, pp. 49-58 enumerates all figurative comparisons of Mary taken from the Old Testament, and which suggest the great degree of holiness the Damascene attributed to Mary.

[37] On the Bishop of Euboea see the recent study by F. Dölger, "Johannes von Euboia," in *Analecta Bollandiana*, 68 (1949), *Mélanges P. Peeters*, II), pp. 5-26. The author characterizes John as "das Beispiel eines provinziellen Homiletentypus" and publishes a new homily of John on the resurrection of Lazarus which shows many stylistic affinities with the Homily on the Conception of Mary. John is often called in the manuscripts only "monk and priest," in others bishop, and he is often identified with John of Damascus.

[38] *P.G.*, 96, col. 1477B: *Ὑμεῖς γὰρ γῆ ἐστε, αὐτὴ δὲ οὐρανός. Ὑμεῖς χοϊκοί, δι' αὐτῆς δὲ οἱ χοϊκοὶ ἐπουράνιοι.*

> The Creator himself made from the old earth a new heaven and a throne which defies the flames. He transformed the old image of man in order to prepare a new, all-heavenly dwelling for the Word. . . Sing and rejoice because here the devil, the tyrant over our nature, was defeated.[39]

St. Theodore of Studion in one of his homilies on Mary's Nativity, which used to be ascribed to St. John of Damascus,[40] uses a comparison similar to that of the Bishop of Euboea. The most telling passage deserves quotation:

> Mary is the earth on which the thorns of sin did not grow. On the contrary, she brought forth a plant through which sin has been uprooted and taken away. She is an earth which was not cursed as was the first earth, fertile in thorns and thistles, but was blessed by the Lord; and her fruit also is blessed, as says the word of the Lord.[41] . . . She is the new dough that has been remade by God, the holy first-fruits of the human race, the root of that stem spoken of by the prophet.[42]

III

THE PHOTIAN PERIOD

With the second half of the ninth century a new period begins in Byzantine history and civilization. After the loss of the eastern provinces to the Arabs, the Byzantine Empire was at last able to stop their penetration further into the interior of Asia Minor and to take a stand in Sicily and southern Italy in order to block, at least temporarily, Arab penetration into Italy. Asia Minor became the backbone of Byzantine military, naval and economic power. Of its western provinces, Byzantium was able to keep only Greece, Thrace, a great part of Macedonia and the coastal cities on the Adriatic Sea, from Epirus to Zara and Venice. All the rest was engulfed by the Slavic masses which, during the period of migrations, had taken possession of what is now Jugoslavia and Bulgaria.

[39] *Ibid.*, col. 1485B, C: *Αὐτὸς ὁ Δημιουργὸς ἐκ τῆς παλαιωθείσης γῆς ἐποίησεν οὐρανὸν καινὸν καὶ θρόνον ἀκατάφλεκτον, καὶ τὸν παλαιωθέντα χοϊκὸν εἰς ἐπουράνιον παστάδα μετέβαλεν . . . Ἰδοὺ γὰρ νενίκηται ὁ τὴν ἡμετέραν φύσιν τυραννήσας διάβολος.*

[40] C. van de Vorst, "A propos d'un discours attribué à Jean Damascène," in *Byzantin. Zeitschrift,* 23 (1914-1920), pp. 128-132.

[41] *In Nativ. B. Mariae, 4, P.G.*, 96, col. 685A: *Γῆ ἐστιν, ἐφ' ἣν τῆς ἁμαρτίας ἄκανθα οὐκ ἀνέτειλε. Τουναντίον δὲ μᾶλλον διὰ τοῦ ταύτης ἔρνους πρόρριζος ἐκτέτιλται. Γῆ ἐστιν, οὐχ ὡς ἡ πρότερον κατηραμένη, καὶ ἧς καρποὶ πλήρεις ἀκανθῶν καὶ τριβόλων· ἀλλ' ἐφ' ἣν εὐλογία Κυρίου, καὶ ἧς εὐλογημένος ὁ καρπὸς τῆς κοιλίας, ὥς φησιν ὁ ἱερὸς λόγος.*

[42] Ibid. col. 685D: Τὸ *νέον φύραμα τῆς θείας ἀναπλάσεως, ἡ Παναγία ἀπαρχὴ τοῦ γένους, ἡ ῥίζα τοῦ θεοφράστου κλάδου.*

For some other less important testimonies of St. Tarasius, Patriarch of Constantinople, Theodore Abou Dourra, the Monk Epiphanius and some anonymous writers, see M. Jugie, *L'Immaculée Concept.* pp. 128-135.

Unable to reconquer the lost territories, the Byzantines started a religious offensive in order to win over the new nations to Christianity and to subject them to their spiritual domination. New bishoprics arose in Macedonia and Greece in place of others destroyed by the invaders; and the Slavs in these provinces were soon converted to Christianity. This was the beginning of their complete assimilation by the Greeks. About the middle of the ninth century, the Byzantines succeeded in establishing definitely their form of Christianity among the Bulgarians and the Serbs. Their missionaries penetrated as far as the middle Danube and Moravia, where two Greek brothers, St. Cyril and St. Methodius, founded a Slavic Church subject to Rome, but using the Roman rite in a Slavic version.

This wide-spread activity betrays the penetration of the Byzantine Church by a new and vigorous spirit. The victory won about the middle of the ninth century over the iconoclastic doctrine, gave the Byzantines a great self-consciousness and stimulated theological speculation. At the same time, however, Byzantium was becoming more and more estranged from the West and from Rome. The misunderstandings between Rome and Byzantium, which arose during the patriarchates of Ignatius and Photius, and which led to a short-lived schism, augured ill for the future and preceded the schism which broke out in the eleventh century.[43]

Because of the growing mistrust between the Christian East and the Christian West, it is all the more important to study the attitude of Byzantine theologians of this period to the question of the Immaculate Conception. The victory over iconoclasm was, at the same time, a victory for the worship of saints. In reality, Byzantine hagiography enjoyed one of its most flourishing ages in the ninth and tenth centuries. It is natural to expect that with the veneration of the saints, the veneration of Mary, the Queen of Saints should increase. And this is indeed what happened. The number of Our Lady's panegyrists increased considerably in this period. Because the whole tendency of Byzantine theologians from this period on was conservative, anxious to preserve intact the heritage of the past, venturing but rarely into new speculations, it can be presumed that their teaching on Mary's initial sanctity would tend to preserve inherited traditions.

The Byzantine cultural renaissance of the ninth century is dominated by the figure of the learned Patriarch Photius. For some centuries he was regarded by Westerners as the main inspiration of the anti-Roman and anti-Western tendencies which started to manifest themselves in his time and was believed to have been the initiator of the great schism. Recent researches have shown that this was not so. He was a great Churchman, a very learned scholar, and in spite of his misunderstanding with Rome,

[43] On these problems see F. Dvornik, *The Photian Schism. History and Legend* (Cambridge Univ. Press, 1948). Cf. also F. Dvornik, "The Photian Schism in Western and Eastern Tradition," *The Review of Politics*, 10 (1948), pp. 310-331.

he stretched out his hand in reconciliation and died in communion with Rome.

Most recent studies have shown that, contrary to previous statements, Photius was mainly responsible for the liquidation of the last vestiges of iconoclasm.[44] This would indicate that Photius was also a promoter of the veneration of the saints, and especially of Our Lady. In fact we find among his homilies one on Mary's Nativity and two on the Annunciation. All, especially the two on the Annunciation are important for the study of the Immaculate Conception. A long passage from the second homily on the Annunciation deserves quotation, first of all. It provides moreover an example of Byzantine rhetoric and of the elaborate and difficult style of the learned Patriarch:

> The archangel comes to Mary, that fragrant and never fading flower of the race of David, that admirable, great and divinely fashioned ornament of human kind. For the Virgin, having been nourished, so to speak, from the very swaddling clothes on the virtues, and having grown with them, gave an example of an immaterial life on earth, and having opened the gates of the road to virtue, she made it possible for those who have an inborn and unquenchable desire to wait on the heavenly bridal chamber to tread [this road] by emulating her. Who has been from very childhood so self-controlled in the face of pleasures? . . . . . . Nay, the Blessed Virgin did not permit her thoughts even to tend towards any of those [pleasures], but was entirely possessed by divine love, showing and proclaiming in these and all other respects that she had been truly designated as a bride for the Creator of all, even before her birth. For, moreover, having also fettered anger, like some uncouth beast, with her impassive mind as with indissoluble threads, she made her whole soul a holy shrine of meekness, having with stable judgment at no time appeared to lessen the force of her courage, and even at the Lord's Passion, at which she was present, having let fall no word of blasphemy and indignation, such as distressed mothers are wont to do at such great suffering of their children. Her strength in this respect is sufficient evidence of the fortitude and courage which she possessed from the very beginning, and the exaltation of her soul grew like a noble plant. Her inimitable gift of sagacity and a clear understanding blossoms out in deeds and works, by means of which she prudently composed and adapted herself in divers ways against all the storms of life's temptations, and those which were roused by the violent hurricane of evil spirits, never allowing any of her pliant [emotions] even to touch the brink of evil.
>
> Thus while the Virgin by surpassing human standards showed herself worthy of the heavenly chambers, and brightened with her own beauty

[44] F. Dvornik, "The Patriarch Photius and Iconoclasm," *Dumbarton Oaks Papers*, 6 (1953) pp. 67-97. Photius also provided the main inspiration for the artists who were engaged in redecorating the churches with ikons. One of his homilies was pronounced in the presence of the emperors in the Church of Santa Sophia when the first ikon of Our Lady was solemnly dedicated. Cf. F. Dvornik, "Lettre a M. H. Grégoire à propos de Michel III et des mosaiques de Sainte-Sophie," in *Byzantion*, 10 (1935), pp. 5-9.

our unsightly aspect, which the pollution of our ancestors had stained, there appeared Gabriel, ministering to the mystery of the King's coming, and cried out, with unrestrained voice and tongue "Hail, much graced one, the Lord is with thee, delivering through thee the whole race from the ancient sorrow and curse."[45]

In the same homily Photius calls Mary:

> . . . forever Virgin, the unblemished daughter of our race, chosen . . . among all others of the entire universe, alone as bride for the absolute King and Lord of all.

He apostrophizes Our Lady towards the end of this homily in the following way:

> Mayest thou rejoice, furnace forged by God, in which the Creator, having leavened anew our nature with the most pure and virginal dough, has cleansed us of that sour and distressing staleness, renovating man into a new creature.

This passage alone expresses most clearly Photius' ideas on Mary's privileged position. Photius believed that Mary had been chosen before she was born, by a special act of God's predestination, to become the Mother of the Lord. He does not see in her any stain of original sin, because he says that she is the immaculate daughter of our human race, the furnace forged by God, the most pure and virginal dough with which God had leavened anew our nature and cleansed it. When he says that she knew no movements of concupiscence, that she completely dominated all human inclinations, he presupposes that she was without original sin, because concupiscence is one of its consequences. He also believes that Mary never committed the least offence against God.

This quotation with its parallels in the other two Marian homilies[46] is sufficient to show that this Patriarch who has hitherto been regarded with suspicion by Westerners, was not only a fervent worshipper of Mary, but also believed in her initial sanctity long before the dogma of the Immaculate Conception was proclaimed.

Attention should next be turned to a disciple of Photius who even surpassed his master in this respect—GEORGE, METROPOLITAN OF NICOMEDIA, who died at the end of the ninth century. George of Nicomedia was a particularly prolific homiletist. He wrote about 170 homilies, of which

[45] S. ARISTARCHIS, *Photii sermones et Homiliae* (Constantinople, 1901), 2, pp. 372-374. An English translation of the homilies by C. Mango is about to be published by Dumbarton Oaks. This extract is taken from his translation.

[46] See *ibid.*, pp. 334, 343, 348 seq. (*Homil. in Nativ. Deiparae*), pp. 236, 244 (*Hom. I in Annuntiat.*) Even J. HERGENRÖTHER (*Photius von Constantinople* Regensburg, 1867-1869, III, pp. 555 seq.) who presented Photius in a very bad light, had to confess that Photius had expressed sufficiently clearly his belief in the Immaculate Conception, although he knew only his homily on Mary's Nativity.

only ten have been published.[47] All but one of them are devoted to Mary and the homily on the Presentation in the Temple is the most important for our research. First of all, it provides the two comparisons of Mary which are to be found in the writings of Andrew of Crete and which point directly to the belief in Mary's initial sanctity, namely, "Mary, the holy and desirable soil," and "Mary, the magnificent first fruit of human nature offered to the Creator."[48] In one passage he seems to sense that this great privilege of Mary is expressed by the salutation of the divine messenger "Hail, full of grace."[49] He also thought that Mary did not know concupiscence, and he asserts firmly that she had never committed the slightest sin. These are his words:

> She is beautiful by nature. There is no stain in her . . . She was a closed garden, inaccessible to sinful thoughts . . . One could not find in her glorified body the least vestige of the corrupt clay.[50] . . . She was purified of all human habits and human passions . . . and elevated above the requirements of our nature.[51] . . . The heavenly food which the Immaculate Virgin received enriched her with divine grace . . . , but it did not bring about a cleansing from sins in her, because she who partook of it had no sins; she was pure and free from any stain.[52]

It is probable that among the unpublished homilies there are still some devoted to Our Lady. It would be worth while if a mariologist anxious to investigate the progress of speculation on Mary's prerogatives in Byzantium at this period, would go through the unpublished material and select the passages which prove that the Byzantines of the ninth century believed, at least implicitly, in the Immaculate Conception.

There is another writer of this period who can also be regarded as a supporter of Photius, because he acknowledged him as the legitimate Patriarch after Ignatius' death, St. Joseph, called the Hymnographer, who died in 883. He was a poet, and many of his religious hymns were incorporated into the Byzantine liturgy and the offices of the Saints. St. Joseph was very devoted to Our Lady and numerous expressions could be quoted from his poems to indicate, at least indirectly, that he believed in the initial sanctity of Mary, or in her Immaculate Conception. One would not be justified, however, in taking all the poetical expressions of the

[47] K. Krumbacher, *Geschichte der byzant. Literatur* (München, 1894), p. 166.

[48] *Orat. VI, In Ss. Dei Genitricis Ingressum in Templum, PG,* 100, cols. 1424D, 1444B.

[49] *Oratio VII, ibid.,* col. 1453B.

[50] *Orat. VI, ibid.,* col. 1425B, D, C: *ἡ ὡραία τῇ φύσει, καὶ μώμου ἀνεπίδεκτος . . . τὸν κῆπον τὸν κεκλεισμένον τὸν λοχισμοῖς ἀνεπίβατον ἁμαρτίας . . . ἐν ᾗ τῆς ἐπιθολούσης ἰλύος οὐκ ἐφωράθη λείψανον.*

[51] *Orat. VII,* col. 1449A.

[52] *Ibid.,* col. 1448B: *Ἀλλ' ἐκείνη μὲν ἁμαρτημάτων κάθαρσιν οὐκ ἐνήργησεν ἡ τροφή· οὐδὲ γὰρ τούτοις ἡ μεταλαμβάνουσα ὑπέκειτο, καθαρά τε οὖσα, καὶ ῥύψεως ἁπάσης ἀνενδεής· . . .*

hymnographer as arguments, even of an indirect nature, for our thesis. The same should be said concerning the hymns of Romanos the Melodian from the sixth century who was mentioned above. Of course, the works of these poets have a certain documentary evidence because they show how profound was the veneration for Our Lady in Byzantium and how widely it had spread among the faithful. Their praises for the prerogatives of Our Lady also contributed considerably to the spread of veneration for her, and to a better and more profound understanding of her prerogatives, including her initial sanctity.

Two passages may be quoted as evidence that St. Joseph the Hymnographer believed in what we call the Immaculate Conception. In the first passage, he apostrophizes the Virgin as follows:

> Thy spiritual bridegroom found thee as a very pure lily among the thorns and chose his sojourn in Thee.[53]

In another passage[54] the poet exclaims:

> Thou art dying now in consequence of a law which was not made for thee, thou, who art the only pure one.

When the meaning which was given to such expressions by other Fathers is recalled, then their value for our thesis is undeniable, even if they are repeated by a poet. They are already regarded as standard prerogatives of Our Lady.

This study of the theological writers of the Photian period may be closed with a short extract from a homily whose author is the monk THEOGNOSTUS, one of the fiercest enemies of Photius. In spite of that, his belief in the initial sanctity of Our Lady seems to be identical with that of his opponent. He expressed it most clearly in the following passage:

> She who, from the very start, had been conceived in the womb of a holy mother, through a holy prayer, in virtue of a sanctifying act . . . could not but be granted a holy death. For if the beginning of her life is holy, so, too, is its continuation, so is its ending; and thus her whole existence is holy.[55]

This passage suggests strongly our idea of the Immaculate Conception because the author presupposes a direct sanctifying act by God at the moment of Mary's passive conception.

[53] *Canon in festo ss. Samonae, Guriae et Abibi, PG*, 105, col. 1244B. Cp. *Canon in Ss. Chrysanthum et Dariam, PG*, 105, col. 1080C.

[54] *In pervigilio Dormit., Canon III, ibid.*, cols. 1000C, 1001D: Νόμους τῆς φύσεως λαθοῦσα τῇ κυήσει σου, τῷ ἀνομίμῳ νόμῳ θνήσκεις, μόνη ἁγνή . . .

[55] *Homilia in Dormit. Mariae*, ed. M. JUGIE in *Patrologia Orientalis* (1922), 16, p. 457: . . . ἔπρεπεν ὄντως τὴν ἐξ ἀρχῆς δι' εὐχῆς ἁγίας εἰς μήτραν μητρὸς ἁγίας ἁγιαστικῶς ἐμβρυωθεῖσαν . . . τὴν κοίμησιν ἁγίαν κομίσασθαι. Ἧς γὰρ ἡ ἀρχὴ ἁγία, ταύτης καὶ τὰ μέσα ἅγια, καὶ τὸ τέλος ἅγιον, καὶ πᾶσα ἡ ἔντευξις ἁγία.

Cf. also M. JUGIE. "La vie et les oeuvres du moine Théognoste (IXe siècle). Son témoignage sur l'Immac. Concept.," in *Bessarione*, 35 (1918), pp. 162-174.

IV

THE TENTH TO THE FOURTEENTH CENTURIES

Numerous are the panegyrists from the tenth to the fourteenth centuries who glorified the Mother of God. Many of them used expressions which are highly suggestive, and which we have already analyzed in the writings of other Byzantine theologians and mariologists. For example, the figurative designation of Our Lady as the first fruit or ornament of the human race is used in panegyrics written by the Emperor Leo the Wise (886-912),[56] by John Mauropos,[57] by James the Monk,[58], by the hermit Neophytus († about 1220).[59] Leo the Wise,[60] Peter of Argos[61] (beginning of the tenth century) and the Patriarch Germanus II (1222-1240)[62] used the suggestive comparisons of Mary to the lily among thorns or to the fragrant rose. Of course, the contrast between Eve and Mary, the new Eve, is also used by John the Geometer[63] (end of the tenth century), by Psellos, the Archbishop Theophylactus[64] (end of the eleventh century) and Germanus II.[65] All this shows how popular these expressions, indirectly indicative of the original sanctity of Mary, were becoming in Byzantium.

Some passages from the writings of the above-mentioned authors deserve however to be quoted. It seems perhaps strange that the first author deserving of quotation should be not a theologian, but the famous Byzantine polygraph who was, at the same time, orator, philosopher, statesman, and panegyrist: MICHAEL PSELLOS (1018 to about 1079).[66] Among his numerous writings—over 200 in number—M. Jugie found a homily on the Annunciation[67] which he published, and which deserves the special attention

56 *Homil. in Praesentat., PG,* 107, col. 13A (also Mary, lily among thorns); col. 20C: Mary, root planted by God.

57 *Homil. in Dormit.*, chap. 10, *PG,* 120, col. 1085A,B. See also chap. 4, col. 1080A: ἡ τοῦ γένους εὐγένεια.

58 *Homil. in Nativit.*, 7, 15, P.G., 127, cols. 577D-588C: . . . ἐγκαλλώπισμα τῆς φύσεως . . . τῆς μόνης τοῦ ἀνθρωπείου γένους . . . κεκληρωμένης προεδρίαν. Cf. also chs. 17, 18.

59 *Homil. in Nativit., PO,* 16, p. 530: ἀπαρχὴ τῆς ἡμῶν σωτηρίας.

60 *Homil. in Praesent., PG,* 107, col. 12D.

61 *In concept. B. Annae, PG,* 104, col. 1352A; cf. also 1353A: ὁρῶντες τὴν τῆς ἡμετέρας εὐγένειαν φύσεως ἀρχομένην.

62 *Homil. in Deiparae Annunciationem,* 9 (BALLERINI, A., *Syllagoge monumentorum ad mysterium conceptionis immaculatae Virginis Deiparae illustrandum,* Rome, 1855, II, p. 310).

63 In the unpublished homily on the *Dormitio* (*Cod. Vatic. graecus* 504), quoted by M. JUGIE, *L'Immaculée Concept. op. cit.* p. 186 (folio 175). Cf. also his homily *In Annunt.* 8, *PG,* 106, col. 817B.

64 *Enarratio in Evang. Lucae,* chap. I, vers. 26-30, *PG* 123, col. 701C-D.

65 See below, p. 107.

66 On Psellos see E. RENAULT's introduction to his edition of Psellos' *Chronography* (Paris, Collection G. Budé, 1926) I, pp. I-XLVIII and M. JUGIE's study in *Dict. de Théol. Cathol.* XIII, 1, (1936), cols. 1149-1158.

of mariologists. When interpreting the words with which Gabriel had saluted the Blessed Virgin, Psellos writes:

> Full of grace . . . Verily, from long ago she was filled with grace, completely united with God and favored from above with (increase of) graces and illuminations . . . Before the Virgin, our race had inherited the malediction of the first mother. Then a dam was erected against the torrent, and the Virgin became the wall protecting and delivering us from evil. . . . You are blessed among women . . . because you have not violated the precept and after being first divinized yourself, you have divinized our race.[68]

This passage indicates quite clearly that Psellos regarded Our Lady as free from original sin.

Theophylactus, Archbishop of Ochrida, the Greek head of the Bulgarian Church, also commented on the Archangel's salutation, but he did not see its profound theological significance.[69] In his homily on the Presentation, however, some words merit our attention. This passage shows that the Byzantines of his time believed in a legendary tradition, namely that the high priest, having contemplated the child presented to him by the parents, did not hesitate to introduce the infant Mary into the Holy of Holies, the most sacred part of the Temple. Commenting on this legend, Theophylactus exclaims:

> She who surpassed all nature in purity and holiness, and who was justified from her mother's womb, had to be exempt from a law made not for the just but for sinners.[70]

John Phournes, who lived at the beginning of the twelfth century, is an important witness testifying that the Byzantines believed in the Assumption of Our Lady; and he rightly connects this privilege with the fact that Mary was preserved from what he calls the mortal virus of corruption,[71] which can only be original sin. Another author of the same period—Theodore Prodromus—declared:

> It is absolutely impossible to suppose or to imagine in Mary the slightest stain of sin.[72]

[67] M. Jugie, "L'homélie de Michel Psellos sur l'Annonciation," in *Echos d'Orient,* 18 (1916-1919), pp. 138-140.

[68] *Homil. in Annunt., 3, Patrologia Orientalis,* 16, p. 522: Τὸ *χαῖρε προσθεὶς . . . Κεχαρίτωτο γὰρ πάλαι, ὅλη προσανακειμένη Θεῷ καὶ τὰς ἄνωθεν δεχομένη ἐλλάμψεις καὶ χάριτας . . . καὶ μεμένηκε μέχρι τῆς Παρθένου τοῦτο δὴ τὸ γένος κληρονομοῦν τὴν ἀρὰν τῆς προμήτορος. Εἶτα ᾠκοδομήθη τὸ ἔρυμα τῆς ἐπιρροῆς, καὶ γέγονεν ἐπιτείχισμα ἡ Παρθένος τῆς τῶν κακῶν ἐπιλύσεως. Εὐλογημένη σὺ ἐν γυναιξίν, ὡς μήτε τοῦ ξύλου γευσαμένη τῆς γνώσεως, μήτε παραβᾶσα τὴν ἐντολήν, ἡ αὐτή τε θεωθεῖσα καὶ τὸ γένος θεώσασα.*

[69] *In Evangelium Lucae* I, *PG,* 123, col. 701C sqq. There he compares Mary with Eve.

[70] *Orat. in Praesentat.,* 6, *PG,* 126, col. 137A.

[71] Homily on the Assumption, published by G. Palamas (Jerusalem 1860), pp. 272 seq.

[72] *Theodori Prodromi Commentarii in carmina sacra . . . , ed.* H. M. Stevenson (Rome, 1882), p. 52.

Then there is the testimony of a very holy, but simple, almost illiterate monk—NEOPHYTUS—who spent many years of his life in strict isolation. In one of his simple homilies, Neophytus uses very adroitly the well-known designation of Mary as the first fruit of the human race. Inspired by the metaphor used by other Fathers—that of the clay from which God himself had fashioned Mary—he uses it in his own manner, imagining the divine Baker, choosing a piece of the dough, and sanctifying and transforming it.[73] The poor monk is certainly not a brilliant stylist and his comparison is expressed in a very awkward manner, but in spite of all these insufficiencies, his idea on the initial sanctity of Mary is clearly outlined, and deserves to be specially stressed.

GERMANUS II, the Greek Patriarch, who resided in Nicaea after the conquest of Constantinople by the Latins, also deserves special mention in a survey of Byzantine mariologists. He makes very original use of the traditional comparison of Mary with Eve, representing Eve as the bitter root and Mary as the fruit of this root which is sweeter than honey.[74] Then he repeats with great emphasis that the fruit of this bitter root received the gift of incorruptibility and, contrary to nature, communicated this quality to the root. In the same passage, Germanus also compares Mary to the lily among thorns, "whiter than snow, more fragrant than balm." These are only comparisons and figures of speech, but they are very illuminating.

FOURTEENTH AND FIFTEENTH CENTURIES

In his book on the Immaculate Conception in the Eastern tradition, M. Jugie[75] devotes more than eighty pages to the study of ideas on the degree of Mary's sanctity expressed by Byzantine theologians of the fourteenth and fifteenth centuries, the declining period of the Byzantine Empire. It is the period he knows best and one which is very often neglected by western scholars and theologians. I would, however, hesitate to attribute to this period such great importance concerning the subject of the Immaculate Conception as does the learned theologian. The two centuries are characterized by a very lively intercourse between the Greeks and the Latins. The attempts at union made at the Councils of Lyons (1274), Constance (1315) and Florence (1439), generated a mass of polemical literature, and hostility against the Latins was constantly growing among the Greeks. In spite of that, many of the Greek theologians became well acquainted with Latin works on theology, and some of them perhaps

[73] *Homilia in Nativ. B. Mariae,* 3, *Patrol. Orient.,* 16, p. 530. Cf. *ibid.* p. 534 (ed. M. JUGIE).

[74] In his homily *in Deiparae Annutiationem,* published by A. BALLERINI in *Sylloge monumentorum ad mysterium concept. immac. Virg. Deiparae illustrandum* (Rome 1851), II, chap. 8, 9, p. 307, reprinted in *PG,* 140, cols. 684 seq. Most of Germanus' works are still unpublished. See K. KRUMBACHER, *op. cit.* p. 174.

[75] *Op. cit.* pp. 217-307.

with the controversy between the Franciscans and Dominicans concerning the doctrine of the Immaculate Conception. Both orders had monasteries in or near Constantinople and even counted some native members from among the Greek Uniates.

One of the first Greek theologians of this period—NICEPHORUS CALLISTUS who died about the year 1335—although violently anti-Latin, expressed, in the discussion on the Immaculate Conception, ideas similar to those of the Dominicans. Although he wrote beautifully on Mary's virtues and prerogatives, he thought that she was delivered from original sin only at the moment of the Annunciation.[76]

The homilies of ISIDORE GLABAS, metropolitan of Thessalonica, contain many passages which could be quoted in favour of the doctrine of the Immaculate Conception. In his homily on the Annunciation,[77] Isidore places Mary between the angels and God himself, and makes her co-operate with God for our salvation. In another homily[78] he lets Mary declare:

> I was not conceived in iniquity; I am the only one whose mother did not conceive her in sin.

In the homily on Mary's death,[79] we read, however, a passage containing a very clear declaration that Mary had inherited original sin. The editors of the homily think that this passage is an interpolation. This is possible, but the arguments are not entirely convincing. It is possible that the prelate, who died about 1397, had learned about the controversy concerning the Immaculate Conception and he seems uncertain what position he should take. His testimony is thus inconclusive.

The Uniate DEMETRIUS CYDONES,[80] who died in 1397 or 1398 in Crete, was a great admirer of St. Thomas Aquinas and translated the first two parts of the *Summa*. It is, therefore, the more interesting to see that Demetrius, although greatly influenced by Thomas' theology, hesitated to follow his master all the way in his opposition to the doctrine of the Immaculate Conception. In his unpublished homily on the Annunciation, there are several passages indicating that Demetrius, although believing that Mary should have inherited original sin like any other human being, thought that God had in a mysterious way, exempted Mary from this general law.[81]

[76] See M. JUGIE, *op. cit.*, p. 218, quotation from an unpublished Ms. (Oxford, Bodleian Lib. *Cod. Miscellaneous* 79, f. 192 v, and *Cod. Roe* 3, f. 147 v).

[77] *In Annunt.* 16, 22, *PG*, 139, cols. 96C., 104 B,C.

[78] *In Praesent. B. Mariae,* 13, *ibid.*, col. 52C: Οὐκ ἐν ἀνομίαις συνελήφθην, οὐκ ἐν ἁμαρτίαις ἐκίσσησέ με μόνην ἡ μήτηρ μου . . .

[79] *In Dormit.,* 33, *ibid,* col. 161B: προῆλθε μὲν τῆς ἰδίας μητρὸς, ὥσπερ ἄνθρωπος, καὶ διὰ τοῦτο τὸ ἀρχαῖον πάχος, λέγω δὲ τὴν προγονικὴν ἁμαρτίαν, μεθ' ἧς ἐγεννήθη.

[80] On this interesting figure of fourteenth century Byzantium, see the work of Cardinal G. MERCATI, *Notizie di Procoro e Demetrio Cydone di Manuele Caleca e Teodoro Meliteniota, ed altri appunti per la storia della teologia e della letteratura byzantina del secolo XIV* (Roma, 1931).

[81] Cf. M. JUGIE's study, "Le discours de Demetrius Cydonès sur l'Annonciation et

The learned Emperor Manuel II Paleologus (1391-1425), who attended the Council of Florence (1439), seems also to have been influenced by western theologians, but, if this is so, he is inclined rather to follow the Franciscan school, although he does not express his view clearly about the moment when Mary became exempt from original sin.[82]

Among the representatives of the purely Byzantine tradition, Gregory Palamas, Nicholas Cabasilas and Joseph Bryennius deserve special mention. Palamas, who died in 1359, a mystic and a theologian of importance, was a defender and propagator of the *hesychast*[83] movement representing a kind of Byzantine mysticism, which preoccupied many Greek thinkers of this period.

It is to be expected that a mystic of Palamas' renown should have a profound devotion to Our Lady. He must often have meditated on the mystery of the Incarnation and on the purity of the Mother of God. Knowing that nobody is exempt from original sin and unable to imagine how the Word could take flesh from a body stained by sin, he imagined that God had chosen Mary from the beginning and had prepared her sanctity by purifying her ancestors and lastly Mary herself. He does not say exactly at what moment this last purification took place, but we can gather from his writings that he could not accept the idea of God taking his flesh from a body which had been even slightly stained with sin.[84] In another passage he expresses his idea even more clearly saying that the Lord needed for his Incarnation a flesh which was human, but was, at the same time, new. It was Mary who from her own substance gave him an immaculate nature.[85]

---

sa doctrine sur l'Immaculée Conception," *Echos d'Orient,* 17 (1913-1914), pp. 96-106. See the quotations from *Codex Parisinus graecus* 1213 in Jugie's *L'Immaculée Conception,* 277-281.

[82] Cf. the Emperor's homily *In Dormitionem* published by M. Jugie in *Patrol. Orient.,* 16. The most important passages are on pp. 552 seq., 555 seq., 559. A Latin translation of the homily was reprinted in *PG,* 156, cols. 91-108.

[83] For details see M. Jugie's studies, "Palamas," and, "Palamite (Controverse)," in *Dict. de Théol. Cath.* XI, cols. 1735-1818.

[84] *Homil. in Christi genealogiam,* 2, 3, ed. Sophoclis. Τοῦ ἐν ἁγίοις πατρὸς ἡμῶν Γρηγορίου τοῦ Παλαμᾶ ὁμιλίαι τεσσαράκοντα καὶ μία. (Athenes, 1861), pp. 213 seq. 216. Unfortunately the homilies which are most important for our subject are not reprinted in Migne's Patrology. It was a Czech Jesuit, Spaldák, who, in a study on the Greek Fathers and the Immaculate Conception, published in the Czech *Review of the Catholic Clergy* in 1905, first pointed out the importance of Palamas' Mariology.

[85] *Homil. in Praesent. Deiparae* 1 (ed. Sophoclis, p. 120): Ἐπεὶ σαρκὸς ἐδεῖτο προσλήμματος, καὶ σαρκὸς καινῆς ὁμοῦ τε καὶ ἡμετέρας . . . ὑπηρέτιν πρὸς πάντα πρεπωδεστάτην εὑρίσκει καὶ χορηγὸν ἀμολύντου φύσεως τὴν παρ' ἡμῶν ὑμνουμένην ἀειπαρθένον ταύτην. Cf. also *Homil. XIV. in Annuntiat., P.G.,* 151, col. 172A-C: Mary escaped the malediction of Eve. Free from the old servitude, she became the source of deliverance of men from it. In his homily XXXVII in Dormit. (*P.G.,* 151, col. 460 seq.), Palamas gives eloquent expression to his belief in Mary's Assumption. Palamas' Mariology impressed the modern Russian philosopher V. Lossky (*Essai sur la théologie mystique de l'Eglise d'Orient,* Paris, 1944, p. 136). He seems to accept Palamas' explana-

Nicholas Cabasilas († after 1396) seems to be an even more fitting representative of Byzantine tradition on Mary's initial sanctity than Palamas. His homilies were only published recently by M. Jugie, and that is the reason why Cabasilas was till then unknown, although he certainly deserves a prominent place among mariologists in general.

Considerations of space preclude more than a few short quotations from Cabasilas' writings, although his Mariological doctrine deserves more attention.[86] In one of his homilies Cabasilas describes the conception of Mary as a fruit of the fervent prayers of her parents. Many similar divine interventions happened in the past, but Mary's case supersedes all others.

> It was in consequence of this that nature was unable to contribute anything to the engendering of the all-holy (Virgin), and that God Himself did everything in her case, putting nature aside in order to form the Blessed Virgin Himself, without any intermediary, so to speak, just as He had created the first man. For, in a true and proper sense, it is the Virgin who is the first man, being the first and only one to exhibit what human nature really is.[87]

The passage praising Mary as the ideal type of humanity through the grace of God is very suggestive, but two others can be quoted which are even more clear. In another homily Cabasilas writes:

> The wall of separation, the barrier of enmity, did not exist for her, and everything which kept the human race away from God was removed in her. She alone made her peace (with God) before the general reconciliation; or rather she never needed reconciliation of any sort, because from the beginning she occupied the first place in the choir of the friends (of God).[88]

And the last quotation:

> Earth she is, because she is from the earth; but she is a new earth, since she derives in no way from her ancestors and has not inherited the old leaven. She is . . . a new dough and has originated a new race.[89]

---

tion of Mary's purification although he thinks erroneously that the dogma of the Immaculate Conception is alien to Oriental theology.

86 Cf. M. Jugie, "La doctrine mariale de Nicolas Cabasilas," *Echos d'Orient*, 18 (1916-1919), pp. 375-388.

87 *In Nativitatem*, 4, *Patrol. Orient.*, 19, 469.

88 *In Annuntiationem*, 3, *ibid.*, p. 486: Καὶ τὸ μεσότοιχον τῆς ἔχθρας καὶ ὁ φραγμὸς πρὸς ἐκείνην ἦσαν εὐδέν, ἀλλ' ἅπαν τὸ διεῖργον ἀπὸ τοῦ Θεοῦ τὸ γένος, τὸ ταύτης ἀνήρητο μέρος· καὶ πρὸ τῶν κοινῶν διαλλαγῶν ἐσπείσατο μόνη· μᾶλλον δὲ σπονδῶν ἐκείνη μὲν οὐδαμῶς οὐδεπώποτε ἐδεήθη, κορυφαῖος ἐξαρχῆς ἐν τῷ τῶν φίλων ἱσταμένη χορῷ.

89 *Homil. in Dormitionem B. Mariae*, 4, *ibid.*, p. 498: Γῆ μὲν, ὅτι ἐκεῖθεν· καινὴ δέ, ὅτι τοῖς προγόνοις οὐδαμόθεν προσῆκεν, οὐδὲ τῆς παλαιᾶς ἐκληρονόμησε ζύμης, ἀλλ' αὐτή, κατὰ τὸν τοῦ Παύλου λόγον (I Cor. 5:7) φύραμα νέον κατέστη, καὶ νέου τινὸς ἦρξατο γένους.

Cf. also *ibid.*, 3, 6, 8, pp. 500, 501, 502, 504, a clear declaration that Mary was the only one who was absolutely free from any sin.

It is interesting to see that JOSEPH BRYENNIUS, who died about 1435, and who was an avowed enemy of union with the Latins,[90] is, on the other hand, an outspoken believer in Mary's Immaculate Conception. Two short quotations will illustrate his belief clearly. In one homily on the Annunciation, he exclaimed:

> She who was inaccessible to any impurity and was free of any stain, merited to conceive the Word of God, which is immaculate by nature.[91]

Another passage is even more expressive:

> She who was to be more worthy and more pure than other (women) was sanctified by God from her mother's womb. . . . And the sovereign merit which she possessed consisted in being purified in advance by the Holy Spirit and made worthy to receive in herself the unapproachable divinity.[92]

From the context, it seems apparent that Bryennius had in mind a purification from the first instant of Mary's passive conception. This is what we call Immaculate Conception.

This survey of Byzantine mariologists may be terminated by a quotation from a treatise on the origin of the soul, written by GEORGE SCHOLARIOS, who became Patriarch of Constantinople after the conquest by the Turks and died about 1472. He is a very interesting figure, who was familiar with the work of all the great Latin theologians. Although he was himself a great admirer of St. Thomas Aquinas, and summarized the two *Summae* for his compatriots, he did not share Thomas' doubts, but expressed in a very clear way, his belief in the Immaculate Conception. It is the great merit of M. Jugie to have edited his works in collaboration with L. Petit and Siderides. This is what Scholarios has to say in the above-mentioned treatise:

> Inasmuch as she had been brought into existence through human seed, the most holy Virgin was not without part in the original sin. . . But the grace of God delivered her completely, just as if she had been conceived virginally, in order that she might provide flesh entirely pure for the Incarnation of the Divine Word. Hence, because she was completely liberated from the ancestral guilt and punishment—a privilege which she is the only one of the human race to have received, her soul is altogther inaccessible to the clouds of (impure) thoughts, and she became, in body and soul, a divine sanctuary.[93]

[90] See the study by A. PALMIERI on Joseph Bryennius in *Dict. de theol. cath.*, II, cols. 1156-1161.

[91] *Homil. III in Annunt.*, ed. BULGARIS (Leipzig, 1768), II, p. 231.

[92] *Homil. II in Annunt., ibid.*, p. 152: Ἄλλη μὲν ταύτης οὐ προτετίμηται, ὅτι πάσας ὁ Θεὸς προγινώσκων, τὴν τῶν λοιπῶν ἐσομένην ἀξιωτέραν ἐκ μήτρας ἡγίασε στείρας· ἀπεβάλετο δὲ τὰς εἰς τοῦτ' ἀναξίας, ὥσπερ εἰκός· ἀρετῶν δὲ πασῶν ὑπερτέραν ἐκέκτητο, τὸ προκαθαρθῆναι τῷ Πνεύματι, καὶ δοχεῖον ἑτοιμασθῆναι δεκτινὸν τῆς ἀπροσίτου θεότητος.

[93] *Oeuvres completes de Georges Scholarios* (Paris, 1928-1936), I, p. 501: Ἡ δὲ Παναγία Παρθένος τῷ μὲν ἐκ σπέρματος γεγεννῆσθαι τῆς προγονικῆς ἁμαρτίας οὐκ ἂν ἀμέτοχος ἦν . . .

CONCLUSION

This is only a brief survey of Byzantine ideas on the greatest privilege of Our Lady. Even from this short and uneven account, however, it can be gathered how deeply many Greek theologians of the Middle Ages were convinced of the original sanctity of the *Theotokos*—Mother of God. Their Mariology is rich in ideas, profound and full of daring declarations which many would hardly expect from a Byzantine writer. It can be imagined how easy it would have been for their western confreres to disentangle their controversies and to clarify their doubts if they had known the works of Byzantine mariologists. In their own way, and almost without any opposition, the Byzantines came to similar conclusions on the degree of original sanctity of Mary, as did the western scholastics after laborious efforts and a protracted and passionate struggle.

All this shows how important the study of Byzantine theology is for western religious speculation. It has so far been undeservedly neglected, although Byzantine theologians are in many respects the continuers and guardians of our inheritance from the great patristic age. It is therefore eminently to be hoped that western specialists in dogmatic theology will in the future pay more attention to the works of Byzantine theologians.

ἀλλ' ἡ χάρις τοῦ Θεοῦ καθάπαξ αὐτὴν ἀπήλλαξεν, ὥσπερ ἂν εἰ καὶ χωρὶς ἐγένετο σπέρματος, ἵνα τῇ τοῦ θείου Λόγου σαρκώσει πάντη καθαρὰν ὑπόσχῃ τὴν σάρκα. Ὅθεν ὡς ἀπηλλαγμένη . . . καθάπαξ τῆς προγονικῆς ἐνοχῆς καὶ ποινῆς καὶ μόνη πάντων ἀνθρώπων τουτὶ λαβοῦσα τὸ δῶρον, ἀνεπίβατον καὶ τοῖς νέφεσι τῶν λογισμῶν ἔσχε παντάπασι τὴν ψυχήν, καὶ σαρκὶ καὶ ψυχῇ θεῖον οὕτω γέγονε τέμενος.

See also M. JUGIE's notice, "Georges Scholarios et l'Immaculée Conception," in *Echoes d'Orient* (1914-1915) , 17. pp. 527-530.

XVII

THE SEE OF CONSTANTINOPLE IN THE FIRST LATIN COLLECTIONS OF CANON LAW

It is well known that Pope Leo the Great strongly protested against canon twenty-eight of the Council of Chalcedon (451) in which the Greek Fathers had confirmed canon three of the Council of Constantinople (381) which gave to the see of Constantinople second place after the see of Rome. The Popes Gelasius (492—496) and Symmachus (498—514) went even further than Leo the Great and refused to regard Constantinople as a major see. Their hostile attitude can be explained by the tension which dominated both Churches during the so-called Acacian schism[1].

This negative attitude to the advancement of the see of Constantinople is generally believed to have been shared by the whole Western Church for many centuries. It is, therefore, surprising to find canon three of the Council of Constantinople in the oldest preserved Latin collection of conciliar decisions and canon law, the *Prisca*. It contains the contested canon in the following version: 'Constantinopolitanum autem episcopum habere primatum honoris post Romanum episcopum, pro quod eam esse censemus iuniorem Romam[2]'. The author of this first collection is anonymous. It is generally acknowledged that he was of Italian origin and that he compiled his collection after the Council of Chalcedon, at the end of the fifth century or at the very beginning of the sixth[3]. The main source of his work was a Greek collection of canons voted by the first general and local councils[4].

The second oldest Latin canonist was Dionysius Exiguus. Born in Scythia about 470, he came to Rome before 496 and died there in 550. In Rome he compiled three collections of conciliar canons. A Greek

---

1. See for details F. Dvornik, *The Idea of Apostolicity in Byzantium and the Legend of the Apostle Andrew* (Cambridge, Mass., 1958), pp.. 106—137.

2. See the edition by C. H. Turner, *Ecclesiae occidentalis monumenta iuris antiquissima* (Oxford, 1901), vol. 2, p. 418. Cf. *P. L.*, vol. 56, col. 809.

3. C. H. Turner, *ibid.*, p. 150.

4. See for details F. Maassen, *Geschichte der Quellen und der Literatur des Canonischen Rechts im Abendlande* (Graz, 1870, republished 1956), pp. 87—100. On the manuscripts of the *Prisca* see C. H. Turner, *ibid.*, p. 150.

collection was his source also. Two of his collections are preserved. Both contain canon three of the Council of Constantinople in the following version: 'Verumtamen Constaninopolitanus episcopus habeat honorem primatum praeter Romanum episcopum, propterea quod urbs ipsa sit junior Roma[5]'. Both these collections date from the fiirst half of the sixth century.

In the seventh century the famous collection called *Hispana* was composed. It was regarded by Pope Alexander III as the official book of canon law of the Spanish Church. This collection originated before the fourth council of Toledo (633) and was put into its final shape by this council[6]. In addition to the conciliar canons it also contains the decretals of the popes, from Damasus to Gregory the Great, to which were also added the decretals of some other popes, from Gregory the Great to Leo II (682). From the ninth century on this collection was called *Isidoriana* and was attributed to St. Isidore of Seville who was born about 560 and died in 633. Most specialists reject this attribution. It is, however, possible that Isidore influenced its composition. Because the compiler of this collection used the *Dionysiana* as his main source, he, naturally, also copied canon three of the council of 381. We read there: 'Constantinopolitanae vere civitatis episcopum habere primatus honorem post Romanum episcopum, propter quod sit Nova Roma[7].'

The fact that all the first Latin canonical collections contain canon three of the second oecumenical council is the more puzzling if we hold in mind the opposition of Leo the Great and his successors to the elevation of the see of Constantinople. Because of the protest launched by Leo against canon twenty-eight of the Council of Chalcedon, it was generally believed that Pope Damasus had already rejected canon three of the second oecumenical council. Few scholars have noticed this anomaly.

---

[5]. Turner, *op. cit.*, p. 419. The edition by A. Strewe, *Die Canonessammlung des Dionysius Exiguus in der ersten Redaktion* (Berlin Leipzig, 1931, Arbeiten zur Kirchengeschichte, vol. 16 stet. The canons two and three (Mansi, vol. 3, col. 259) are put together.

[6]. See R. Naz, „Hispana ou Isidoriana (collectio)", *Diction. du droit canonique* (Paris, 1953), vol. 5, cols. 1159—1162.

[7]. Turner, *op. cit.*, p. 418. On the manuscript of this collection see *ibid.*, pp. 402, 403. Cf. also Maassen, *op. cit.*, pp. 667—716 and P. Fournier—G. Le Bras, *Histoire des collections canoniques en Occident* (Paris, 1931), vol. 1, pp. 100 sq. A critical edition of the *Hispana* is in preparation. The collection called *Epitome Hispana* does not seem to contain the disputed canon (cf. Turner, *op. cit.*, p. 419). In his work *Dionysius Exiguus Studien* (ed. by H. Foerster, Berlin, 1960, Arbeiten zur Kirchengeschichte, vol. 33), M. Peitz advanced the theory that Dionysius, invited by Pope Gelasius, compiled a collection of the canons voted by the Eastern councils on the basis of the protocols kept in the pontifical archives. Dionysius added to this collection the canons of the second and fourth oecumenical councils and the hundred and thirty-eight canons of the African councils. To this primitive collection which was in existence about 500 were added the fifty so-called apostolic canons. According to Peitz's theory, Dionysius changed this collection several times and increased it by the addition of the pontifical decretals up to the year 384. This collection was, according to Peitz, sent by Pope Hormisdas to the bishops of Spain and called *Hispana*. In spite of considerable documentary material brought forward by the author his thesis remains a theory without any solid base. On the collection of canon law from the fifth and sixth centuries see also W. M. Plöchl, *Geschichte des Kirchenrechts* (Vienna, Munich, 1953), I, pp. 251 sq.

Recently, however, M. Peitz[8] wishing to explain the presence of the contested canon in the collection of Dionysius advanced a theory which, at first glance looks interesting. According to him, definite reconciliation between Rome and Constantinople after the Acacian schism was made only in 520—521, when the envoys of the Patriarch Epiphanius arrived in Rome with the inthronistic letter of the new patriarch. When interpreting some statements made in the documents[9] brought by the Byzantine envoys and in Hormisdas' letter to Epiphanius[10], M. Peitz comes to the conclusion that the Byzantines recognized the supreme jurisdiction of Rome over Constantinople and the whole East. In return Rome is said to have recognized the oecumenicity of the Council of 381 and to have accepted its canon three on the condition that the Byzantines rejected canon twenty-eight of the Council of Chalcedon.

This explanation, however, cannot be accepted. The most serious objection to its acceptance is the fact that there is no trace of the conclusion of such a compromise in the contemporary sources. The author of this theory has to confess, himself, that no kind of protocol was composed concerning the bargaining for this important compromise. Such a procedure would be against all the rules of the pontifical chancery. The experience which the Romans had had with the Byzantines during the Acacian schism must have made them rather careful and suspicious in dealing with the Byzantines. How could the Romans content themselves with a verbal promise in such an important matter?

Moreover, if the Romans had in 520 officially accepted Constantinople's precedence over Alexandria and Antioch, there must have remained some trace of the agreement in the archives of the Roman chancery. How could we then explain the fact that the arguments of Leo the Great against the second position of Constantinople in the Church hierachy were renewed every time there was tension between the two sees as happened in the ninth century under Nicholas I and in the eleventh century under Leo IX?

M. Peitz's theory has, thus, to be rejected, but there is a simpler and more natural explanation for the apparent anomaly. The embarrassment of the canonists facing the fact that the privileged position of Constantinople is acknowledged in the first Latin collections of canon law is explained by their belief that Pope Damasus had protested against the stipulation of the Council of 381 concerning the see of Constantinople and that a Roman synod of 382 had rejected canon three. There is, however, no evidence for this belief. As shown recently[11] Rome also accepted as a principle of the ecclesiastical organization the accomodation to the

[8]. *Op. cit.* pp. 273—316.

[9]. Epiphanius' letter to the Pope and the Acts of the synod which elected Epiphanius, in *Collectio Avellana* published in vol. 35 of the *Corpus Scriptorum ecclesiasticorum Latinorum* (Vienna, 1888), pp. 707—715.

[10]. Read durind the fifth session of a local council in Constantinople in 536, Mansi, vol. 8, cols. 1030 seg.

[11]. In my book, *The Idea of Apostolicity,* pp. 1—38.

political division of the Roman Empire. The promotion of the see of Constantinople to the second place in the Church's organization must be explained by the application of this principle to a new political situation. Constantinople had become an imperial residence and its bishop had to be promoted. In Damasus' time the principle of accomodation was still fully accepted in Rome and Damasus could not ignore it. He did not protest against the elevation of Constantinople nor did the Fathers of the Roman synod of 382[12].

Even Leo the Great seems to have accepted canon three of the Council of 381. During the last session of the Council of Chalcedon Eusebius, bishop of Dorylaeum, declared that when he was in Rome in 451 he had read the contested canon to Leo the Great and the pope had approved it[13]. Leo, in fact, could scarcely dispute the see of Constantinople's promotion because the principle of accomodation was not yet completely forgotten in Rome. What alarmed Leo and what prompted him to make such a resolute protest was not the confirmation by the Council of Chalcedon of the elevation of Constantinople by the Council of 381, but the subjection of three political dioceses — Thrace, Pontus and Asia — to the direct jurisdiction of Constantinople. He was afraid that this growth of Constantinople's influence in Church life could become dangerous to the peaceful evolution of the Church and to the prerogatives of his own see.

There does not seem to have been any special meeting in Rome with the Byzantines at which the oecumenical character of the Council of 381 was officially recognized by the Pope. It is known that this council was convoked by the Emperor Theodosius to regulate the affairs of the Eastern Church. The Western prelates were not even invited. The Easterners insisted on its oecumenical character because of important dogmatic decisions that were made concerning the Holy Ghost. Its oecumenical character seems to have been tacitly recognized by Rome at the end of the Acacian schism. In their correspondence with Pope Hormisdas the future Emperor Justinian, the Patriarch Epiphanius and the bishop of Nicopolis, counted the Council of 381 among the four oecumenical councils[14] and the Pope did not protest. Hormisdas' envoys to Constantinople also counted this council among the oecumenical councils in their report sent to the Pope on 29 June 519[15].

The explanation of how it could happen that the canon confirming the honorary status of Constantinople could be included in the first Latin

---

[12]. On the attitude of Damasus see *ibidem*, pp. 50—56. It has been thought that the protest against this canon contained in the so called *Decretum Gelasianum* was voted by the Roman synod of 382. It has been, however, shown that this document was composed only at the end of the fifth century. See P. Batiffol, *Le siège apostolique* (Paris, 1924), pp. 146—150.

[13]. Mansi, vol. 7, col. 449.

[14]. See the documentary evidence in their letters contained in the so-called *Collectio Avellana*, published in vol. 35 of the *Corpus Scriptorum ecclesiasticorum Latinorum* by the Academy of Vienna, 1888. Cf. also Migne, *P. L.*, vol. 63.

[15]. *Collectio Avellana*, p. 678.

collections of canon law of the fifth and sixth centuries is then rather simple. The canonists knew that canon three of 381 was tacitly accepted in Rome. Since the oecumenical character of the Council of 381 was also recognized in Rome, they did not see any reason why they should leave out the contested canon.

There is still one detail which deserves to be noted. It is true that the *Dionysiana* does not include canon twenty-eight of the Council of Chalcedon whose acceptance Leo had so vehemently protested against. This canon is also missing from the manuscripts of other early collections. It is, however, curious to find that two manuscripts of the *Prisca* quote not only canon three of the Council of 381 but also canon twenty-eight of the Council of Chalcedon. These two manuscripts — one from Chieti, the other called de Justel — are very ancient, datind from the sixth century. They are both of Italian origin.

F. Maassen[16] has already shown how this happened. It seems that the two compilers used a Greek manuscript which first gave the text of the twenty-seven canons of Chalcedon, then, before adding canon twenty-eight, enumerated the canons of the Council of Constantinople. It would seem, as can be judged from the context of canon twenty-eight, that before defining this canon the Fathers first ordered to be read canons of the Council of 381, which were not yet divided into numbers because canon three of the Council of 381 was an introduction to the decisions made in canon twenty-eight.

We may conclude from this that the contested canon twenty-eight must have already figured in some Greek collections of conciliar canons at the end of the fifth or at the beginning of the sixth centuries and that such a collection must have been known in Italy.

The fact that these two Italian compilers of canon law collections did not hesitate to copy this canon rejected by Leo the Great and his successors indicates that the opposition to Constantinople was not as general in Italy as has been thought. Some ecclesiastical circles do not seem to have always shared the animosity of the Curia against the rival city. This seems to have been especially the case in southern Italy where the Byzantine influence was more pronounced. In this connection it should be noted that the manuscript of Chieti is of Neapolitan origin.

Dumbarton Oaks

16. *Op. cit.*, pp. 94—99, 526—536. Cf. Migne, *P. L.*, vol. 56, cols. 809, 810, the Manuscript of Chieti.

XVIII

GREEK UNIATS AND THE NUMBER OF OECUMENICAL COUNCILS

One kind of Byzantine theological literature has hitherto attracted little interest on the part of specialists, namely the anonymous Treatises on oecumenical and local councils. So far, only one such treatise has been published by Ch. Justellus (1), but the editor only used one Manuscript from the Cologne Library. It has also been reprinted by G. A. Rhallis in his *Σύνταγμα* (2). This is a short treatise which is preserved in numerous Manuscripts in the Bibliothèque Nationale, in the Vatican Library, in Vienna, Munich and Mount Sinai. It was an important part of a kind of Byzantine catechism. Many Manuscripts start with the words: " Every Christian should know that there are seven oecumenical councils ".

Other treatises are much longer and give more detailed accounts of each oecumenical council (3). Some of them also contain short reports on the most important local councils held in the early period of Christianity. Most of these treatises do not give much new data, but some of them deserve to be published because they reveal better than other documents the Byzantine mentality and the teaching of the Eastern Church on councils and on the role of the bishops in defining a dogma (4).

---

(1) In his *Nomocanon Photii... Accessere ejusdem Photii, Nili metropolitae Rhodi et Anonymi tractatus de Synodis oecumenicis ex Bibliotheca Sedanensi*, Lutetiae Parisiorum 1615. On the treatise attributed to Nilus, see F. DVORNIK, *The Photian Schism*, Cambridge 1948, pp. 384, 385, 420, 456.

(2) Athenes (185-89), pp. 370-74. Ibid., pp. 389-395 the treatise attributed to Nilus.

(3) Especially the anonymous treatise published by S. LE MOYNE, *Varia Sacra*, Leiden 1685, pp. 81 sq. I found it in different Mss. with variations.

(4) Cf. F. DVORNIK, *op. cit.*, Appendix III, pp. 452-458. I intend to complete my study in the Mss. — so far over one hundred are known to me — and to publish some of them.

All treatises stress the fact that there are only seven councils which have an oecumenical character. The so-called Ignatian Council (869-870) which condemned Photius and which is called in the West the eighth oecumenical council is not regarded as oecumenical and is never registered, but neither is the council which rehabilitated Photius (879-880) (5).

The treatise on councils which is found in the *Greek Manuscript 1712 in the Bibliothèque Nationale in Paris* (6), presents a certain interest because its author affirms that there are ten oecumenical councils. The author is evidently a Greek Uniat and he composed his treatise after the Council of Florence. The Ms. (430 folios), which is on parchment, contains *The Chronicon of Symeon Metaphrastes*, mostly parts of historical writings (namely Symeon Metaphrastes, Leo the Deacon, Michael Psellos) and dates from the fourteenth century. The last part of the Ms. (fol. 426 sq.) is from the fifteenth century. The narrative on the councils is contained in fol. 4, 4^{v}, 5, 5^{v}. The writing is of the fifteenth century. The author's description of the seven oecumenical councils is rather short and differs in some ways from the more popular treatise published by Justellus, but he seems to have used the same version as the anonymous author of the treatise preserved, for example, in *Vindebonensis Historicus Graecus 76*, fols. 134-135^{v}, from the sixteenth century.

It is remarkable that even the Uniat writer did not dare to add the Ignatian Council (869-870) to his list, although he may have known that the Latins counted it among the universal councils. For him the eighth council is the Council of Lyons (1274) which brought about a

---

(5) There are a few exceptions. The *Synodicon Vetus*, published by J. PAPPE in J. A. FABRICIUS. *Bibliotheca graeca*, Hamburg 1809, vol. 12, pp. 360-421, registers all synods concerning the Ignatian and Photian controversy (pp. 417-420), but without giving the Synod of 869-870 an oecumenical character. These additions were made by a fanatical follower of Ignatius and used in the anti-Photian collection (*Mansi*, 16, col. 453). The treatise attributed to the Patriarch Euthymius (British Museum Arundel 528, fol. 116) calls the Photian council (879-880), the council of union. The treatise attributed to Nilus which used Euthymius' treatise as a prototype, calls this synod the eighth oecumenical council. The synod of 1341 convoked against Barlaam and Akindynos is called the ninth oecumenical council. It should also be stressed that the anonymous Uniat author mentions a synod under Theodora on the worship of images. Several other unpublished Mss. mention this synod in connection with the seventh oecumenical council.

(6) H. OMONT, *Inventaire sommaire des manuscrits grecs de la Bibliothèque Nationale*, II. Partie. Paris 1888, p. 128.

union, albeit of short duration. Here he makes a very curious blunder. He affirms that this Council was held under the reign of Pope John — only John VIII can be meant — to condemn Photius, who had uncanonically occupied the patriarchal throne, was responsible for the schism between the two Churches and taught that the Holy Spirit proceeded from the Father only.

The anonymous author knew about the condemnation of Photius by a synod, but had a very hazy idea which synod it was. It was certainly not the Council of Lyons. The Acts of this Council — if there ever were any — are no longer in existence. But from the proposals presented by Humbertus de Romanis for discussion at the Council and from the few other documents which are preserved (7), it seems that the name of Photius was not even mentioned during the synod. The pope who convoked this synod was not John VIII but Gregory X.

It was also daring on the part of an anonymous Uniat author to promote the local synod of Constantinople convoked by the Patriarch John Beccus (1277) at which the union was proclaimed, to the rank of an oecumenical council. Of course, the Council of Florence (1438, 1439) fully deserved in the eyes of a Uniat to be called oecumenical.

The short treatise is followed by another short composition entitled *στίχοι εἰς συνόδους*. The description of the first seven oecumenical councils is also short and very similar to that of the first treatise. Because it does not present any special interest, I omitted it. The description of the eighth, ninth and tenth councils, however, deserves to be published. The author is even more explicit than his colleague. He mentions Pope Nicholas, but calls John VIII his immediate successor, omitting Hadrian II who was responsible for the condemnation of Photius by the Ignatian synod. He attributes to Photius the composition of anti-Latin writings. He probably has in mind his Mystagogia, because he is most anxious to prove that the Holy Spirit proceeds from the Father and Son, a thesis denied by Photius in this work.

Both treatises reveal the mentality of the Greek Uniats in the fifteenth century. They have very hazy ideas on the origin of the schism, making Photius alone responsible for it. On the other hand they know very little about his history. Omitting the Ignatian synod which was regarded in the fifteenth century by Latins canonists as being very important and oecumenical, they let Photius be condemned by the Council of Lyons. Their main preoccupation is the Filioque. They

(7) See MANSI, 24, cols. 107-136.

are very anxious to prove that all the three last councils, which they call oecumenical, had defined it clearly.

⟨Text⟩

fol. 4 Περὶ τῶν οἰκουμενικῶν συνόδων καὶ ποῦ ἑκάστη τούτων ἐγένετο· κεφά-
λαιον γ'· κανόνες· πρώτη σύνοδος.

α' Ἡ πρώτη σύνοδος ἐγένετο ἐν Νικαίᾳ τῆς Βιθυνῶν ἐπαρχίας, ἐν ταῖς
ἡμέραις τοῦ μεγάλου βασιλέως Κωνσταντίνου, καὶ Σιλβέστρου πάπα Ῥώμης.
Συνῆλθον δὲ ἐν αὐτῇ τῇ θείᾳ καὶ ἱερᾷ καὶ μεγάλῃ συνόδῳ τριακόσιοι δέκα
καὶ ὀκτὼ θεῖοι πατέρες· οἳ καθεῖλον τὸν δυσσεβῆ Ἄριον, ὃς ἦν πρεσβύτερος
Ἀλεξανδρείας· οὗτος γὰρ τὸν Χριστὸν ψιλὸν ἄνθωπον εἶναι ἐβλασφήμει,
καὶ οὐχ' ὁμοούσιον τῷ Πατρί· Ἴβηρες δὲ τότε εἰσῆλθον εἰς τὴν θεογνωσίαν
καὶ ἐγένοντο χριστιανοί.

β' Ἡ δευτέρα γέγονεν ἐπὶ Θεοδοσίου τοῦ μεγάλου· αὕτη οὖν ἡ σύνοδος
συνηθροίσθη ἐν Κωνσταντινουπόλει· ἦσαν γὰρ ἑκατὸν πεντήκοντα ἅγιοι
πατέρες, ἀρχιστρατεύοντος Δαμάσου πάπα Ῥώμης καὶ Νεκταρίου Κωνσταν-
τινουπόλεως· ταύτης ἐξῆρχε Γρηγόριος ὁ θεολόγος, ὃς τὴν ἐπωνυμίαν ἐκ τῆς
θεολογίας ἐκτήσατο· συνήχθη οὖν κατὰ Μακεδονίου τοῦ πνευματομάχου·
οὗτος γὰρ τὸ Πνεῦμα τὸ ἅγιον οὐκ ἔλεγε Θεόν, ἀλλὰ ἀλλότριον τῆς θεότητος·
ἥτις καὶ προσέθηκε τῷ ἁγίῳ συμβόλῳ τῆς πίστεως εἰς ἀνατροπὴν τῆς αἱρέσεως
αὐτοῦ, « καὶ εἰς τὸ Πνεῦμα τὸ ἅγιον, τὸ κύριον, τὸ ζωοποιόν ».

γ' Ἡ δὲ τρίτη ἁγία σύνοδος γέγονε ἐπὶ Θεοδοσίου τοῦ μικροῦ, ἐν Ἐφέσῳ
τῇ πόλει· ἦσαν γὰρ ἐν αὐτῇ διακόσιοι θεῖοι καὶ ἱεροὶ πατέρες· οἳ συνήχθησαν
κατὰ τοῦ μιαροῦ καὶ δυσσεβοῦς Νεστορίου· τὸν γὰρ Χριστὸν οὗτος, ὁ ἄθλιος,
ψιλὸν ἄνθρωπον εἶναι ἐβλασφήμει· συνελθόντες οὖν ἀναθεμάτησαν αὐτὸν
καὶ τελείως ἐδίδαξαν τὴν καθολικήν, ἀθόλωτον καὶ εἰλικρινῆ, τελείαν καὶ
ἀμώμητον πίστιν, τὴν ἐν Τριάδι θεότητος ὑμνουμένην ἀεί.

δ' Ἐπὶ δὲ Μαρκιανοῦ καὶ Οὐαλεντιανοῦ γέγονε ἡ τετάρτη σύνοδος ἐν
Χαλκηδόνι τῶν ἑξακοσίων τριάκοντα ἁγίων πατέρων, Λέοντος πάπα Ῥώμης
καὶ Ἀνατολίου Κωνσταντινουπόλεως, κατὰ Διοσκόρου πατριάρχου Ἀλεξανδρείας καὶ Εὐτυχοῦς ἀρχιμανδρίτου· οὗτοι γὰρ τὴν ἐνανθρώπησιν τοῦ Κυρίου
ἡμῶν Ἰησοῦ Χριστοῦ παρῃτοῦντο καὶ ἐν φαντασίᾳ τὴν ἄχραντον αὐτοῦ σάρκα
ἐμυθολόγουν, καὶ μίαν θέλησιν ἐπὶ τῇ ὑποστάσει ἐφλυάρουν εἶναι· ἡ δὲ ἁγία
σύνοδος αὕτη δύο φύσεις καὶ δύο θελήματα ἐδογμάτισεν.

ε' Ἡ δὲ πέμπτη ἁγία οἰκουμενικὴ σύνοδος γέγονε ἐπὶ Ἰουστινιανοῦ τοῦ
fol. 4v μεγάλου ἐν Κωνσταντινουπόλει, | ἐν τῷ παλατίῳ τῷ ἐπονομαζομένῳ Τροῦλος·
συνῆλθον δὲ ἐν ταύτῃ τῇ ἱερᾷ συνόδῳ ἑκατὸν ἑξήκοντα πέντε πατέρες, Εὐτυ-
χίου Κωνσταντινουπόλεως ἐξάρχοντος ταύτης· οἳ καθεῖλον Ὠριγένην, Εὐά-
γριον καὶ Δίδυμον τοὺς παράφρονας. τὰ γὰρ σώματα ἡμῶν μὴ ἀνίστασθαι

ἐδυσφήμουν καὶ παράδεισον αἰσθητὸν μὴ γενέσθαι ὑπὸ Θεοῦ, μήτε εἶναι,
καὶ ἐν σαρκὶ μὴ πλασθῆναι τὸν Ἀδάμ, καὶ τέλος εἶναι τῆς κολάσεως ἀπε-
φήναντο, καὶ δαίμονας ἐλθεῖν εἰς τὴν ἀρχαίαν ἀποκατάστασιν.

Ἡ δὲ ἁγία καὶ οἰκουμενικὴ ἕκτη σύνοδος γέγονε ἐπὶ Κωνσταντίνου Ἡρα- ς'
κλείου καὶ Τιβερίου υἱοῦ αὐτοῦ· συνῆλθον ἐν αὐτῇ ἑκατὸν καὶ ἑβδομήκοντα
πατέρες, ἐπὶ Ἀγάθωνος πάπα Ῥώμης, κατὰ τῶν δυσσεβῶν αἱρεσιαρχῶν,
Κύρου Ἀλεξανδρείας, Σεργίου, Πέτρου, ἓν θέλημα ἐν μίᾳ ἐνεργείᾳ τὸν Κύριον
ἡμῶν Ἰησοῦν Χριστὸν ἔχειν καὶ μετὰ σάρκωσιν, τὸν σύνδεσμον τῆς ὀρθοδοξίας διαλύσασθαι θελήσαντες, οἱ παράφρονες· συνῆσαν δὲ αὐτοῖς καὶ Μακά-
ριος ὁ νομοθέτης Ἀντιοχείας καὶ Ἰσίδωρος μαθητὴς αὐτῶν.

Ἐπὶ δὲ Εἰρήνης τῆς μητρὸς Κωνσταντίνου τοῦ τυφλοῦ γέγονε ἡ ἑβδόμη ζ'
σύνοδος τῶν ἁγίων πατέρων, ἐπὶ Ταρασίου πατριάρχου Κωνσταντινουπόλεως,
ἐν τῇ Νικαίᾳ ἑτέρα ἐπὶ καθαίρεσιν Θεοδοσίου, παρ' ἧς ἐξέθεντο ὅροι πίστεως. Ἐπὶ δὲ Θεοδώρας αὐγούστης μετὰ θάνατον Θεοφίλου τοῦ ἀνδρὸς αὐτῆς
σὺν Μιχαὴλ τῷ υἱῷ αὐτῆς γέγονε ἡ τοιαύτη σύνοδος τῆς ὀρθοδοξίας ἥτις
ᾄδεται ἕως τῆς σήμερον.

Ἡ δὲ ἁγία καὶ οἰκουμενικὴ ὀγδόη σύνοδος γέγονε ἐν Λουγδούνῳ ἐπὶ η'
Ἰωάννου πάπα Ῥώμης· ἥτις συνηθροίσθη κατὰ Φωτίου γενομένου παρὰ τοὺς
κανόνας πατριάρχου Κωνσταντινουπόλεως· ζῶντος γὰρ Ἰγνατίου τοῦ ἱεροῦ
αὐτὸς τὸν θρόνον ἀδίκως ἥρπασεν· οὗτος γὰρ ἦν ὁ τὸ σχίσμα ποιήσας μέσον
Γραικοὺς καὶ Λατίνους· ἀπηγόρευεν τὴν ἐκπόρευσιν τοῦ παναγίου Πνεύμα-
τος μὴ εἶναι καὶ ἀπὸ τοῦ Υἱοῦ, ἀλλ' ἐκ τοῦ Πατρὸς μόνου, ὅθεν ἡ σύνοδος
αὐτὸν κατεδίκασεν, καὶ ἐκ τοῦ Υἱοῦ τὸ Πνεῦμα ὡς καὶ ἐκ τοῦ Πατρὸς ἐκπορεύεσθαι ἐθεολόγησε.

Ἡ δὲ ἐνάτη ἁγία καὶ οἰκουμενικὴ σύνοδος γέγονε ἐν Κωνσταντινουπόλει θ'
ἐπὶ Γρηγορίου πάπα Ῥώμης καὶ Βέκκου πατριάρχου Κωνσταντινουπόλεως· καὶ
αὕτη ὑπὲρ τῆς αὐτῆς ταύτης ὑποθέσεως συνηθροίσθη· ἡ συναθροισθεῖσα
τὸ Πνεῦμα τὸ ἅγιον καὶ ἐκ τοῦ Υἱοῦ ἐκπορεύεσθαι ὥσπερ καὶ ἀπὸ τοῦ Πατρὸς
λαμπρῶς καὶ περιφανῶς δογματίσασα τῇ ἐκκλησίᾳ |παρέδωκε πιστεύειν,
ὁμολογεῖν καὶ σέβεσθαι.

Ἡ δὲ δεκάτη ἁγία, μεγάλη καὶ οἰκουμενικὴ σύνοδος γέγονε ἐν Φλωρεντίᾳ ι'
τῇ πόλει ἐπὶ Εὐγενίου πάπα Ῥώμης καὶ Ἰωάννου Παλαιολόγου τοῦ περιφανοῦς
βασιλέως τῶν Ῥωμαίων καὶ Ἰωσὴφ πατριάρχου Κονσταντινουπόλεως· ἣ
συνήχθη καὶ αὐτὴ ὑπὲρ τῆς αὐτῆς ὑποθέσεως· ὅθεν τὸ Πνεῦμα τὸ ἅγιον καὶ
ἐκ τοῦ Υἱοῦ ἐκπορεύεσθαι ἀνεκηρύχθη ἐν τῷ αὐτῆς ὅρῳ εἰ καὶ ἐν τῷ συμβόλῳ
τῆς πίστεως ἐν τῇ ἀνατολικῇ ἐκκλησίᾳ οὐ προσετέθη.

[. . . . .]

Στίχοι εἰσὶν ἐπίλοιποι τρεῖς· fol. 5

Ἡ δὲ ὀγδόη γέγονε σύνοδος ἐν Λουγδούνῳ, Ῥώμης πρωτεύοντος σεπτῶς η'
τοῦ θείου Ἰωάννου μετὰ Νικόλαον λαμπρῶς τὰς κλεῖς ἐκδεξαμένου, κατὰ

Φωτίου πρώτου τε τοῦ σχίσματος αἰτίου, ὃς ἀναιδῶς συνέγραψε κατὰ τῆς ἐκκλησίας τῆς πρεσβυτέρας δηλαδὴ Ῥωμαϊκῆς τῆς θείας, καὶ πρῶτος ἐξηρεύξατο λέγειν κατὰ Λατίνων ὡς οὐκ εἰσὶν ὀρθόδοξοι οἳ ψάλλοντες ἐν συμβόλῳ καὶ τὴν προσθήκην ὥς φασί, «τὸ ἐκ τοῦ Πατρὸς Υἱοῦ τε», ἥτις σαφήνειά ἐστιν μᾶλλον καὶ οὐ προσθήκη· αὕτη οὖν κατεδίκασε τὴν ἀναίδειαν τούτου, καὶ ἐξ Υἱοῦ ἐδίδαξε τὸ Πνεῦμα ὀρθοδόξως.

fol. 5v θ' *Ἡ δὲ ἐνάτη γέγονε ἐν Κωνσταντινουπόλει, Ῥώμης ἱερατεύοντος τοῦ θείου Γρηγορίου δεκάτου τε ὑπάρχοντος τὸν ἀριθμὸν ἐκείνων· ταύτης δὲ ἐξῆρχεν ἱερῶς καὶ εὐσεβῶς ὁ θεῖος Βέκκος, ὁ τρισμακάριος, ὁ θαυμαστὸς ἐκεῖνος, ἀρχιεπίσκοπος αὐτῆς ὑπάρχων Βυζαντίδος· ἡ τὴν αὐτὴν ἐδίδαξεν πίστιν τε καὶ λατρείαν ὡς ἡ λαμπρὰ καὶ πανύσεμνος σύνοδος ἐν Λουγδούνῳ.*

Ἡ δὲ δεκάτη γέγονε ἐν Φλωρεντίᾳ πόλει, Ῥώμης ἱερατεύοντος τοῦ θείου Εὐγενίου, τὰ σκῆπτρα δὲ κατέχοντος τῆς βασιλείας τότε Παλαιολόγου τοῦ χρηστοῦ, μεγάλου, Ἰωάννου καὶ Ἰωσὴφ τοῦ θαυμαστοῦ καὶ θείου πατριάρχου· ὑπῆρχον δὲ τὸν ἄριθμὸν οἱ ἱεροὶ πατέρες ἑπτάκις καὶ λ' πρὸς τοῖς ὀκτακοσίοις· αὕτη γὰρ κατεδίκασε τοὺς ἀμαθῶς ληροῦντας τὸ Πνεῦμα τὸ Πανάγιον ἐκ τοῦ Υἱοῦ μὴ εἶναι, ἀλλὰ ἐκ μόνου τοῦ Πατρός, ὢ φεῦ τῆς ἀμαθίας· εἰ γὰρ τῶν πάντων ἀγαθῶν φυσικῶν τοῦ Πατρός τε ὑπάρχων κοινωνὸς ἀληθῶς ὁ Χριστός μου, ἔχει καὶ τὸ Πνεῦμα οὖν κατὰ τοῦτον τὸν τρόπον, καθ' ὃν καὶ ὁ Πατὴρ νοεῖται καὶ οὐκ ἄλλως τοῦ ἐκπορεύεσθαι ὁ Υἱὸς ὥσπερ καὶ τὸν Πατέρα Κύριλλος ἐν τοῖς θησαυροῖς ὁ θεῖος ἐκδιδάσκει καὶ ἄλλοι πλεῖστοι πανταχοῦ τῶν ἱερῶν βιβλίων ἐκήρυξαν, ἐδίδαξαν, ἐτράνωσαν ὡσαύτως· ὃ μὴ καταδεξάμενοι ἐφθάρημεν μετ' ἤχου.

⟨Translation⟩

On the oecumenical councils and where each of them had been assembled.

The first Synod was assembled in Nicaea, in the eparchy of the Bithynians, in the days of the Emperor Constantine the Great and of Silvester, the Pope of Rome. In this divine, holy and great Synod three hundred and eighteen divine Fathers had gathered. They condemned the impious Arius who was a priest of Alexandria, for the same taught the blasphemous doctrine that Christ was a simple man and that he was not of the same nature as the Father. At that time the Iberians were acquainted with the (true) knowledge of God and became Christians.

The second (Synod) took place under Theodosius the elder. This Synod had been assembled in Constantinople. There, one hundred and fifty holy Fathers were present under the highest leadership of Damasus, the Pope of Rome and Nectarius of Constantinople. The prominent role in this Synod was played by Gregory the Theologian, who obtained this title because of (his) theology. It was thus assembled against Makedonios, the enemy of the Holy Spirit, for the same did not call the Holy Spirit God, but a being without divine nature. This Synod added to the holy Symbol of the Faith, in order to destroy his heresy, (the words) "and in the Spirit, the Holy, the Lord, the Giver of Life".

The third holy Synod took place under Theodosius the Younger in the city of Ephesus. Two hundred divine and holy Fathers were present at this Synod. They were convened against the impure and impious Nestorius. The latter, the miserable man, held the blasphemous doctrine that Christ was an ordinary man. Assembling together thus, they anathematized him and definitely proclaimed the catholic, limpid and pure, perfect and irreproachable faith, which is hymned in a Trinity of divinity for ever.

Under Marcian and Valentinian took place the fourth Synod, in Chalcedon, of six hundred and thirty holy Fathers, (with) Leo, Pope of Rome and Anatolius of Constantinople, against Dioscurus, patriarch of Alexandria and the archimandrite Eutyches. These namely repudiated the incarnation of our Lord Jesus Christ, pretending fictitiously that his unsullied body was imaginary, and claimed idly that in (his) nature was only one will. But this holy Synod defined the dogma of two natures and two wills.

The fifth holy oecumenical Synod took place under Justinian the Great in Constantinople, in the palace, called Troulos. In this holy Synod gathered one hundred and sixty five Fathers. Eutychios of Constantinople held the leadership in it. They condemned Origen, Euagrius and Didymus the demented, because they held outrageous doctrines that our bodies would not be resuscitated, that a visible Paradise was not made by God in reality, and does not exist, and that Adam was not created bodily; and declared that there would be an end of punishment and that the devils would be restored to their former status.

The holy and oecumenical sixth Synod was held under Constantine, Heraclius and Tiberius, his son. One hundred and seventy Fathers gathered in it, under Agathon, the Pope of Rome, against the impious heretical chiefs, Kyros of Alexandria, Sergius, Peter (teaching) that our Lord Jesus Christ possessed one will in one energy even after His incarnation, trying, the demented men, to dissolve the unity of orthodoxy. With them were also Macarius, the lawgiver of Antioch and their disciple Isidorus.

Then under Irene, the mother of Constantine the Blind, was held the seventh Synod of the holy Fathers, under Tarasius, the Patriarch of Constantinople, in Nicaea for the second time to depose Theodosius. This synod promulgated the rules of the faith.

Under Theodora, the Augusta [i.e. who became Empress], after the death of Theophilus her husband, with her son Michael, was held that Synod of Orthodoxy, which is in vigour until our days.

The eighth holy and oecumenical Synod was held in Lyons under John, the Pope of Rome. This Synod was convened against Photius who had become patriarch of Constantinople in defiance of the canons. He had namely, unjustly usurped the throne when Ignatius, the holy, was still alive. Indeed, it was he who effected the schism between the Greeks and the Latins. He denied that the most Holy Spirit proceeds also from the Son, but only from the Father. Because of that the Synod condemned him and defined that the Spirit proceeded from the Son as also from the Father.

The ninth holy and oecumenical Synod was held in Constantinople under Gregory, the Pope of Rome and Bekkos, the patriarch of Constantinople. This Synod also was assembled for the same matter. After being assembled (this Synod) decreed in a very clear and plain way that the Holy Spirit proceeded also from the Son as from the Father, and presented it to the Church to believe (in), to praise and to worship.

The tenth holy, great and oecumenical Synod was held in the city of Florence, under Eugenius, the Pope of Rome, John Palaeologus, the most glorious emperor of the Romans, and Joseph, the patriarch of Constantinople. This also had convened for the same matter. Because of that (the Synod) declared solemnly that the Holy Spirit proceeded also from the Son in its own definition, although this was not added to the symbol of the faith in the Eastern Church.

[. . . . .]

Three are three other notes:

The eighth Synod was held in Lyons when in Rome the divine John was presiding with dignity, having splendidly taken over the keys after Nicholas. (It was assembled) against Photius who is the first to be responsible for the schism. He wrote insolently against the Old Church, i. e. that of Rome, the divine, and was the first who came forward with affirmations against the Latins as if they were not orthodox, when singing in the Symbol also the addition, namely " from the Father and Son ". This is rather an evident truth and not an addition. This

Synod condemned his insolence and defined in an orthodox way that the Spirit proceeded also from the Son.

The ninth (Synod) was held in Constantinople when in Rome the divine Gregory the tenth in number of those (Gregories) was holding the pontificate. This Synod was directed, in saintly and pious fashion by the divine Bekkos, this blessed and wonderful being then archbishop of Byzantium. This Synod defined the same faith and worship as did the glorious, most venerable Synod of Lyons.

The tenth (Synod) was held in the city of Florence, when in Rome the divine Eugenius was holding the pontificate and the scepter of kingship was then in the hands of John Palaeologus, the righteous, the Great, during the patriarchate of admirable and divine Joseph. As concerns numbers, seven times and thirty holy Fathers were present (added) to the eight hundred. This (Synod) condemned those who were unreasonably raving that the most holy Spirit was not from the Son, but only from the Father, alas such ignorance. Because if our Christ happened to participate truly in all good qualities of the Father's nature, the Spirit thus also has (them) in this same way in which the Father is thought, and not otherwise. That the Son participates in the proceeding as the Father, is taught by the divine Cyril, and very many others everywhere in the holy writing, had in this way, proclaimed, defined, clarified. Those who do not accept this, we have condemned with vehemence ([8]).

Washington. Dumbarton Oaks.

([8]) This passage in the Greek text is not clear.

XIX

PATRIARCH IGNATIUS AND CAESAR BARDAS

There is one problem in the life story of St. Ignatius, Patriarch of Constantinople (847—858, 867—877), which has not yet been satisfactorily resolved—namely, the relationship between the Patriarch and Bardas, the brother of the Empress Theodora. Bardas became regent for his nephew Michael III in 856, having ended the regency of his sister after the murder of her prime minister Theoctistus. He is regarded as having been instrumental in the replacement of Ignatius by Photius on the patriarchal throne in 858.

The reason for the hostile attitude of the new regent towards Ignatius is said to have derived from he Patriarch's refusal to give Holy Communion to Bardas, because he had been informed that the latter had repudiated his wife and was living with his daughter-in-law. Many Byzantine chroniclers praise Ignatius for this deed and most modern Church historians agree with them.

The famous English Byzantinist J. B. Bury,[1] however, was of the opinion that the patriarch was acting rather indiscreetly in giving too much credit to the gossip which the enemies of Bardas were spreading in the capital. It will not perhaps be without interest to re-examine the sources recording the scene and the behavior of Bardas in order to throw more light on the affair.

The report of Theognostus must first be examined. He was a most zealous supporter of Ignatius and escaped to Rome after the synod of 861 which, together with the papal legates, had confirmed the illegality of Ignatius' patriarchate, because he was not elected by the synod but appointed by the Empress Theodora herself. Theognostus presented an appeal to Pope Nicolas I in the name of the deposed Patriarch. This appeal is preserved in the so-called anti-Photian collection which was circulated in Constantinople by Photius' opponents after the latter's reconciliation with Rome which is attested by the synod of 879—880.[2]

It is now known that Theognostus acted on his own because Ignatius

[1] I. B. Bury, *A History of the Eastern Roman Empire.* London, 1912, pp. 188 seq.

[2] The collection follows the Life of Ignatius and extracts from the Council of 869—870 which had condemned Photius. It is published in Mansi's Collection of Councils, vol. 16, cols. 296 seq.

had declared at the synod of 861: "I have not appealed to Rome, neither do I do so now."[3] In his false 'appeal' Theognostus enumerates in a very pathetic way all the evils which Ignatius had to suffer at the hands of Bardas. He lets Ignatius say that the reason for the persecution by the regent was Bardas' Herodian behavior and incest. "Because he was contumacious and disobedient, I excommunicated him from the Church" so we read in the appeal. In spite of the Emperor's threats and demands Ignatius is said to have refused to change his verdict.[4]

It is interesting to see that Theognostus does not mention here Bardas' divorce from his wife, although this would have made Ignatius' case stronger in the eyes of the Pope—let us remember the Pope's defense of the holiness of the marriage in the case of King Lothair—nor does he elaborate the accusation of incest. He depicts rather the physical suffering which Ignatius is said to have endured when banisched by Bardas. This appears to him to be a stronger argument than a description of the moral misbehavior of the persecutor.

Another contemporary document is the letter addressed to the logothete Manuel[5] by another passionate follower of Ignatius, the Metropolitan of Smyrna Metrophanes. It was written after the council of 869—870 at the request of this high functionary who wanted a more detailed report of the reasons which led to the condemnation of Photius by the Council. It is a biased but important report giving interesting details, distorted by the author, but which we learn only from this document. Metrophanes mentions Bardas twice, but does not say anything about his moral behaviour or about the famous scene in the church of the Holy Wisdom on the feast of the Epiphany—Ignatius' refusal to administer Holy Communion to Bardas—which, as we shall see, was regarded by Ignatius' biographer Nicetas as the main reason for Bardas' hostility to Ignatius. This seems rather significant.

We can also quote a third contemporary report of the fateful events by Stylian, Bishop of Neocaesarea. Stylian was one of the heads of the schismatic "little Church" which not only had refused obedience to Photius after his rehabilitation by the synod of 879—880, but also to his successor, the Patriarch Stephen, brother of the Emperor Leo VI, because Stephen had been ordained deacon by Photius. Stylian addressed a letter to Pope Stephen[6] in which he explained the reasons for the obstinate attitude of his group. In it he accused Photius and his partisans, who had appealed to Rome against Ignatius' judgement, of having won over Bardas

[3] An extract from the Acts of this synod was preserved by Deusdedit. See W. J. Glanvell, *Die Kanonessammlung des Kardinal Deusdedit.* Paderborn, 1905, pp. 603—610.
[4] Mansi, 16, cols. 224, 225.
[5] *Ibid.*, col. 416.
[6] *Ibid.*, col. 428 D.

whom they had persuaded to replace Ignatius by Photius. The report is very biased and distorts the true situation. When speaking of Bardas Stylian limits himself to the short remark "who was accused by the Patriarch Ignatius of a shameful union".

So far it has been thought that the most important contemporary document was the Life of St. Ignatius written by Nicetas the Paphlagonian. It was believed that this biography was composed between 880 and 890.[7] A more thorough research has shown, however, that this cannot be accepted.[8] The Life could have been written only after the death of Photius, and he died most probably on February 6, 893. When explaining the reasons why he decided to write the Life of his hero, Nicetas says[9] that the Photians were claiming for Photius the "honor of sainthood". This clearly indicates that Photius was indeed dead and that Nicetas wished to put before the eyes of his compatriots the figure of a true saint-Ignatius. In another passage[10] Nicetas says that his hero appeared "later in time than the stalwarts of old but still before this generation of ours. Since his death (in 877), the cloud of ignorance about him has grown thick during many years." If we count about thirty years for a generation, this would indicate that the Life was written about the year 907.

Furthermore, in the same passage, Nicetas indicates that he was not a contemporary of Ignatius, when declaring that he intended to describe the life of Ignatius from the beginning to the end.[11] He confesses that he has learnt about him from both written and oral testimony. His reports are, thus, not as genuine as those of a contemporary. Among the written documents used by him were most probably the excerpts from the Greek Acts of the Ignatinan Council of 869—870, which are preserved in the anti-Photianist collection. Only a Latin translation of the original Greek Acts; made by Anastasius, Librarian of Hadrian II who was, at that time, in Constantinople as envoy of the Emperor Louis II, is preserved.[12]. The report of Metrophanes and the letter of Stylian may also have been known to Nicetas. For the rest he relied upon the reports given to him by still living partisans of Ignatius who, like Stylian, had also refused to recognize the legitimacy of the second patriarchate of Photius and that of his successor Stephen.

Professor Jenkins, to whom we owe these discoveries, has also determined that the author of the Life should be identified with Nicetas

---

[7] K. Krumbacher, *Geschichte der byzantinischen Literatur.* Munich, 1897, pp. 167, 679.

[8] R. J. H. Jenkins, *A Note on Nicetas David Paphlago and the Vita Ignatii,* Dumbarton Oaks Papers 19 (1965) 241—247.

[9] I am quoting the *Vita* in the edition by Migne, *P. G.,* 105, col. 541 A, B.

[10] *Ibid.,* col. 489 A.

[11] *Ibid.,* col. 489 B.

[12] Published in vol. 16 of Mansi's Collection of Councils.

the Philosopher, a noted author of numerous hagiographical works who, so far, was regarded as a different personage.[13] Thanks to the publication of some letters of Photius' disciple Arethas,[14] we are now able to fill in some hitherto unknown details of Nicetas' career. He was a nephew of Paul the Sacellarius and was born in Paphlagonia about 885. He studied in Constantinople under Arethas who had become archbishop of Caesarea about 903. He was a great admirer of his master whom he described in a letter to his uncle Paul as his ideal.[15] He belonged, with his master, to the "anti-marriage" party opposing the legitimacy of the fourth marriage contracted by Leo VI.

This relationship was ended, however, in the spring of 907 when Arethas changed his attitude. After the deposition of the Patriarch Nicholas Mysticus, Arethas had followed Nicetas' successor Euthymius, the leader of the anti-marriage party. Won over by the Emperor, Euthymius abandoned his opposition to the legitimacy of the emperor's tetragamy.

Disgusted by the "betrayal" of Euthymius and Arethas, Nicetas left the capital and took refuge in a hermitage near Media, on the Bulgarian frontier, in order to "philosophize", namely, to lead a contemplative life. Arrested by the imperial police on suspicion of spying for the Bulgarians, he was brought to Constantinople.[16] He was under threat of very severe punishment because of his writings against the Emperor and the patriarch, in his fanatical opposition to the tetragamy. He was saved by the patriarch who allowed him to become a monk in his monastery of Agathos where Nicetas stayed until 910. After that he devoted his talents to composing numerous hagiographical writings. One of them being the Life of Ignatius.

An interesting passage at the end of Nicetas' writing shows us that the Life must have been written, not only some time after the death of Photius, but also after the reigns of several of his successors. When describing the disasters which befell the Empire after Photius had been reestablished as patriarch—the death of Basil's son is regarded as the first of them—Nicetas continues:[17] "And then even the great city of

[13] Cf. H. J. Beck, *Kirche und theologische Literatur im byzantinischen Reiche.* Munich, 1959, pp. 503, 504.

[14] R. J. H. Jenkins, B. Laourdas, *Eight Letters of Arethas on the Fourth Marriage of Leo the Wise,* Hellenika, 14 (1956) 293—372.

[15] Published by S. Lambros in Neos Hellenomnenon, 19 (1926) 189.

[16] We learn these details from the *Vita Euthymii* published by C. de Boor (Berlin, 1888); his commentary on Nicetas, pp. 194—196. New edition with English translation by P. Karlin-Hayter, Byzantion, 25—27 (1955—1957) pp. 1—172.

[17] *P. G.,* 105, col. 573. Syracuse was lost in 878. It was generally thought that the author of the *Life* must have written it soon after this event. Jenkins has shewn, however, that this is not the case. The loss of Syracuse was only the beginning of disasters which continued to strike the Empire up to the time of Nicetas' writings.

Syracuse fell after a terrible defeat, and every island, and every city and country continues to be ravaged and destroyed even down to this day, for no prayer of those who claim to be priests can win God's favor, but, as it is written, we are in truth become sheep for whom there is no shepherd. For the mischief has become inveterate, and is confirmed by numerous exampes and is a law unto the lawless, and the habit of unrightousness is, as it were, a second nature to the scoffers and draws down all wrath of God. But to recount each of the injuries and crimes of Photius himself, the first in the line of hypocrites and perjurers, and of all his successors, one after the other, that is the task of an historian, and beyond the scope of this writing."

If we have in mind that Nicetas was a fierce opponent of the tetragamy, he must have had meant Photius' successors who played a role in this affair. It was the Patriarch Anthony Cauleas (893—901) who permitted the third marriage of the Emperor Leo VI on the insistence of the latter. Nicholas Mysticus (901—907) had endeavored to win over the anti-tetragamy party, including Arethas and his disciple Nicetas, to recognizing the legitimacy of the fourth marriage of the Emperor, and Euthymius (907—912) who, although a leader of the anti-tetragamists, allowed himself to be persuaded by the Emperor and abandoned his opposition. The reward for this "betrayal" was the patriarchal see offered to Euthymius after the deposition, or forced resignation of Nicholas Mysticus.

These are the main "hypocrites and perjurers" who had imitated the "injuries and crimes" of their predecessor Photius. Of course, he might also have had in mind Arethas, his former master, who had betrayed the good cause. These are the men to whom, as Nicetas writes in another passage and which seems to be out of place in his narrative of Ignatius' history, the words of the Lord could be applied,[18] "It is needful that scandals should come; but woe unto him through whom scandal cometh". And he continues,[19] "Now, for all the heresies which, since the presence of His incarnate Divinity even unto this present day, have crept in to defile the Churches, the heresiarchs themselves, as authors of the scandals, are deservedly the first to share in their miseries also; and I suppose that, equally with the famous heretics of older days, those who have played the villain in this our generation, as authors of ten thousand scandals to the world, will be the objects of the heavenly

---

The reason for this was, according to Nicetas, because the successors of Photius had been unable to avert the Lord's wrath, being unworthy of being called high priests. Nicetas has again in mind the partiarchs Cauleas, Nicholas, and Euthymius and perhaps also Stephen, who was appointed by his imperial brother.

[18] *Ibid.*, col. 505 D.

[19] *Ibid.*, col. 508 A, B.

wrath". They may pretend to confess the orthodox faith, they may "put on a semblance of piety, and some form and empty fiction of regard for religion in all their doings and traffickings". This will not justify them in the eyes of the Savior. "Rather, because they deserted the stronghold of piety, and life according to the Gospel, and sold themselves for love of self and money and all kinds of pleasure and power, and indulged in all kinds of unrighteousness, perjuries, broken promises, and crimes and injuries against the innocent, and dissolved and confounded all ecclesiastical order; because by their manifold irregularities and illegalities they profaned the divine substance and name of Holy Church, so that the mystery of religion (one might almost say) runs the risk of being understood as mere verbiage, and no longer a reality and truth; for these reasons they shall receive God's most righteous condemnation."

In this passage Nicetas speaks about heresies which were defiling the Church "unto this present day". He can have in mind only one "heresy" that of the tetragamy. No heresy was involved in the mistreatment of Ignatius by Bardas which Nicetas was describing before this outburst. We learn, however, from a letter by Arethas that the opponents of the tetragamy had regarded it as a practice involving a heresy.[20] Arethas himself was of that opinion before he had changed his attitude. This seems to have been the conviction also of Nicetas, and it was so profound that he refused to follow the example of his master, and continued his fight against this "heresy" in writing against Euthymius and the Emperor Leo VI. He must have had Leo in mind when declaring that "sometimes God allows to govern and to be great in worldly authority, men through whom (as Divine Scripture has it) the thoughts of many hearts may be manifest, so that the grain may be divided from the chaff". All this is, of course, a work of the Devil.

All this shows clearly that the Life of Ignatius was written after the "betrayal" of Euthymius and Arethas, in the spring of 907. This also throws some new light on the purpose of Nicetas' biography of Ignatius. Disillusioned by the subservience to the will of the court by the patriarchs whom he expected to be stalwart defenders of the Church's laws, Nicetas was anxious to put before the eyes of his contemporaries the glowing example of a high priest able to resist the whims of secular rulers in defending the rights of the Church. This could only be Ignatius.

His choice of Ignatius seems to have been inspired also by the circumstance that the reason for Ignatius' removal from the patriarchal

---

[20] Ed. by R. J. H. Jenkins, B. Laourdas, *op. cit.*, pp. 299, 300. R. Jenkins found even a striking similarity in the vocabulary used by Nicetas when speaking of present heresies, with that of Arethas. Jenkins thinks rightly that Nicetas was here copying his former master.

see was his condemnation of the sexual misbehavior of Bardas, the uncle of Michael III and his regent. Ignatius' uncompromising attitude should have been followed by his successors when they were confronted with a similar situation such as the violation of moral precepts concerning marriage, by an emperor. Let us see how Nicetas described the moral misbehavior of Bardas and how Ignatius condemned it by refusing Holy Communion to the regent, the most prominent person at the court in whose hands was concentrated all political power.

Nicetas describes the famous scene in the following way:[21] "I suppose you have all heard of Bardas, that he was the brother of the good Empress Theodora, not however a good one, but very bad and inhuman. Although he was excellent and efficient in handling political affairs, nobody said that he was well disposed towards the Church. They say that he was so infatuated with his daughter-in-law that the whole city was buzzing with rumors about it. Rumors about the ugly affair reached not only the many, but also the archbishop himself. What did he do? He took no account of the high position of the person, nor did he cover the sin with silence, but reproved, according to the precept. He not only censured it, but also implored (him) to have consideration for his soul and to clean himself from this awful defilement (pollution). He however not only did not avoid the sin but not even the Church. There came the feast of the holy Epiphany, and he shamelessly went forward in order to receive the divine mysteries. What does the archpriest do? He excludes him from Communion, judging him unworthy to receive the body of the Lord. He thus raged with great madness and armed himself against his own soul. He threatened to pierce the intestines of the hierarch with his own sword. The latter however, threatens also, invoking Him who can point the sword against him (Bardas). This was the beginning of all the scandalous events."

It was to be expected that Nicetas was anxious to give the most eulogistic picture of his hero and to depict the attitude of Ignatius on that occasion in the most favorable and striking light. When we have this in mind and when we remember the real purpose which had inspired Nicetas to present Ignatius as an example which his successors, faced with similar situations should have followed, we are rather surprised that he is not as categorical as might be expected after the accusations launched against Bardas proved to be true. He speaks only of the rumors which circulated in the city and which reached the ears of Ignatius. He should also have mentioned that Bardas repudiated his wife, but this does not seem to appear to him as too serious.

Nicetas' biography of Ignatius survived due to the interest which the "little Church" of anti-Photians had in the biased account of Photius'

---

[21] *P. G.*, col. 105, col. 504.

career in the *Vita.* This circle continued to regard the actions performed by Photius during his second patriarchate as illegitimate, and his ordinations invalid. Evidence of this attitude is to be found in the correspondence of Stylian with Popes Stephen V and Formosus.[22] One group of the "little Church", led by Stylian, ended its opposition and its members recanted. This took place most probably in 899.[23] But this was not the end of the opposition. A number of stalwart opponents remained outside the Church and continued to collect evidence to support their negative attitude. The Life of Ignatius by Nicetas was added to the Greek extracts of the Ignatian Council as one of the main arguments. Other documents mentioned above, and the correspondence of Stylian with the Popes were added, with a postscript in which one of the intrasigeants blamed Stylian for his betrayal. It is true that Nicetas succeeded in making Photius the target of fierce attacks, because, in his mind, Photius "in his lust for power, was the first of a series of patriarchs who became subservient to the whims of the court".

We can have doubts, however, about Nicetas' anti-Photianism. Arethas was a disciple of Photius and it is probable that Nicetas shared the esteem which his master had for Photius. One might expect that it was Arethas' "betrayal" of the cause in which Nicetas so firmly believed which not only turned him against his master, but also against his master's teacher, whose bad example in submitting to the whims of the court was followed by the successors of Ignatius.

So it happened that Nicetas' description of the famous scene became a prototype that was followed by other hagiographers. One of them, named Michael, said to have been a monk and to have occupied the position of syncellos at the patriarcheion, wrote an encomion of the Patriarch Ignatius. It attracted the attention of the anti-photians who inserted an extract from it in their collection.[24] It is difficult to say anything definite about the author of this panegyric. There are two known writers of homilies and panegyrics both of whom are called Michael, and neither of whom attained the dignity of syncellos, either in Jerusalem or in Constantinople.[25] It is not impossible, however, that the author of the above-mentioned panegyric was another Michael, the one who wrote a Life of Theodore of Studios in the second half of the ninth century.[26] If this is the case, his panegyric might be a contemporary document.

---

[22] Mansi, 16, cols. 425 seq., 440, 441.

[23] *Ibid.,* col. 455. For more details, see F. Dvornik, *The Photian Schism, History and Legend.* Cambridge, 1948, pp. 237 f.

[24] Mansi, 16, cols. 292, 293.

[25] Cf., H. J. Beck, *Kirche und theologische Literatur in byzantinischen Reiche.* Munich, 1959, pp. 503, 504.

[26] A. Ehrhard, *Überlieferung und Bestand der hagiograph. und homilet. Literatur,* Texte

We do not learn much from this extract. Michael attributes the downfall of Ignatius to Bardas. The devil himself had incited Bardas against Ignatius because the latter "had prevented him from participating in the mystical and tremendous (sacrament), because he was having unlawful intercourse with a woman". If Michael was a contemporary of Ignatius, his testimony would again indicate that the history of Bardas' misbehavior was based only on rumors. The report is very vague.

I prefer to think, that this panegyric is not a contemporary document but was written by another Michael who had been inspired by Nicetas' Life of Ignatius composed in 907. His report on Bardas would thus be based on what Nicetas said of him and of his conflict with Ignatius. If this is so, his account is watered down considerably.

Nicetas had other followers. The most prominent of them being the anonymous biographer of St. Nicholas of Studios, successor of St. Theodore. Nicholas died in 868 and his Life was not written until the first half of the tenth century. It was certainly composed after the year 907, for when describing the famous scene which took place on the feast of the Epiphany, the anonymous author follows almost word for word the account given by Nicetas. He describes the incident in the following manner:[27] "See thus how the thing happened. The Caesar Bardas, the miserable man, made unlawfully after the bedchamber of his son, a strange bed-fellow of his own daughter-in-law, he was known as revelling in the incestuous union. Thus the archpriest of God, called after the godly one (Ignatius), trying to put straight as well as possible what was happening, did not stop, according to the divine precept, in reminding, appealing, admonishing. He hoped that, in this way, the perversion would be completely cut out. But the lover of unlawful intercourse did not in the least permit the pitiful one to come to his senses. Thus, when he saw the wretched man persist in his pertinacity, and completely enslaved to sin, he cut him off from the threshold of the Church, giving him, thereby, an occasion for amendment. He, however, unreasonably permeated with anger and passion, proceeds haughtily from authority to tyranny. In the presence of all the people, roaring, with excited mind, he enters the church and penetrating into the innermost sanctuary, he requested the archpriest's permission to participate in the awe-inspiring mysteries. But the zealous man, holding before him publicly with the lance of his words, the refutation of his transgression, stabbed him terribly in his innermost being and banished him empty-handed and ashamed from the church".

---

und Untersuchungen zur altchristlichen Literatur, Serie IV, vol. 5 (1937), pp. 486, 489, 680, 682.

[27] *P. G.,* vol. 105, cols. 905, 908.

The anonymous biographer was, of course, an admirer of his hero, Abbot Nicholas and shared his bitterness against the memory of Photius and of all who were held to be responsible for the misfortunes of Ignatius. Nicholas was one of the latter's zealous followers and had left Constantinople after Ignatius's resignation and the election of Photius.[28] If the biography had been written earlier, an extract from it would certainly have been added to the anti-Photianist collection. Following the recital of Nicetas, he omits all mention of Bardas' divorce and also does away with the caution still observed by Nicetas. He does not speak of rumors circulating in the city; for him the incestuous behavior of Bardas is a fact.

Since all of these authors are hostile to Bardas, their biased accounts should be read with care. As we have seen, the report of Nicetas is the most elaborate, but even he speaks only of the rumors concerning the misbehavior of Bardas which circulated throughout the capital and which reached the ears of the patriarch.

Fortunately we can appeal to another witness, less biased, and also a contemporary of Bardas, Ignatius and Photius, namely, the author of the Life of St. Eustratius, Abbot of the Monastery of Agauron, near the city of Brussa in Asia Minor.[29] Eustratius died in 867 or 868 while visiting Constantinople and his Life was written by an anonymous disciple. It may have been Sabas who was the author of the Life of St. Joannicius. Eustratius and Joannicius spent some years together when forced to leave their monasteries and go into hiding as a result of the iconoclastic persecution. St. Eustratius returned to his monastery after the restoration of image worship by the Empress Theodora,[30] but since the iconoclastic monks who had occupied the monastery during his exile, had dissipated the monastic wealth, he was obliged to visit Constantinople in order to make an appeal for funds from among the friends of the monastery. He returned with one hundred noumismata, but on learning that the poor of Brussa who were unable to pay their taxes were being thrown into prison, he offered the money to the tax collector. This sum was insufficient, however, and the situation was saved by the Empress herself, who added a further two hundred noumismata. Thus the saint

---

28 See J. B. Bury, *op. cit.*, p. 192.

29 Published by A. Papadopoulos-Kerameus in Ἀναλέκτα ἱεροσολ. σταχυολογίας (St. Petersburg) vol. 4 (1897), pp. 367—400. I wish to thank my colleague, Professor R. J. H Jenkins who drew my attention to this *Vita* which, so far, has been overlooked by all historians of this period.

30 On the monastery of Agauron see the short study by A. Hergès, *Le monastère des Agaures,* Echos d'Orient 2 (1898—1899) 230—238. On the role of Theodore of Studios and of Eustratius during the iconoclastic period, cf. F. Dvorník, *Les Légendes de Constantin et de Méthode vues de Byzance,* Prague, 1933, pp. 119—145.

was enabled to pay all the tax due from the poor of Brussa and from his monastery.[31]

The biographer speaks of another journey by the saint to Constantinople, again in the interests of his monastery.[32] This must have taken place in 866, and he is said to have visited the patriarch after disembarking. Unfortunately, we do not learn what he did in the patriarcheion. Several folios are missing in the manuscript following the mention of Eustratius' visit to the patriarch, who could only have been Photius, and one is entitled to think that some of the Ignatians were responsible for this lacuna in the manuscript. They could not have borne the thought that such a great saint enjoyed cordial relations with the detested Photius.

The biographer gives us precious information about the relations of the saint with the wife of Bardàs, and due to him we also learn that the name of this lady is Theodosia. When listing the miracles attributed to Eustratius the biographer speaks of two which took place in Constantinople. The second one concerned a servant of Theodosia and the account of this event is as follows:[33] "The most blessed woman called Theodosia, who had been injured by her own husband, namely, Bardas, who at that time held the title of Caesar, and had been banished from cohabitation (in marriage) with him, often invited the holy father and enjoyed his heavenly directed prayers. She had a servant, suffering terribly from quartan fever, who had been plagued by it for four years, and was cured in the following way. One day when the thrice-blest man happened to be there, as he was passing through the middle of the house, this most faithful servant, bending forward, and licking with her own tongue the dust from his holy and most graceful feet was forthwith delivered from her illness, surpassing in her faith the woman with an issue of blood (Matt. 9.20) and plucking a most wonderful fruit of that faith".

The first miracle is said to have happened in the port of Triton when the saint miraculously provided an immense fish for the shipowner and merchant who was unwilling to provide a meal for the saint from his own supplies. This seems to have happened during the first sojourn of Eustratius in Constantinople, because on his second trip he disembarked "at the port of Julian which is ordinarily called port of Sophia".

The second miracle cannot be dated from the first year's of Theodora's regency, since, at that time, Theodosia was not yet married to Bardas. The marriage could have been concluded in or after 855.[34] Theodosia had a sister, Irene who is said to have participated in the bride-show

---

[31] A. Papadopoulos-Kerameus, *op. cit.*, p. 378.
[32] *Ibid.*, pp. 391 seq.
[33] *Ibid.*, p. 389.
[34] A. Bury, *op. cit.*, p. 156.

organized, according to a Byzantine custom, by Theodora who wished to choose a wife for her son Michael from among the beautiful candidates assembled in Constantinople belonging to the best families of the Empire. Theodosia was apparently also one of the candidates. The biographer of Eustratius says that Bardas was Ceasar when he abandoned his young wife. He was created Caesar in April, 862, but the separation may have taken place earlier.

In spite of her divorce, Theodosia appears to have lived quite comfortably in Constantinople in a large house with servants. We learn the name of another of her servants from the biographer of her sister, as we shall see. She is also said to have provided day and night illumination during the funeral service and while the body of St. Eustratius lay in state in the monastery where he died. She does not seem to have become a nun and abbess as did her sister.[36]

It should be stressed that the biographer of St. Eustratius does not speak about the incestuous relations of Bardas. One would expect him to include such a detail since it would enhance the sympathies of the reader for Theodosia, who had shown such veneration for his hero.

Neither does the biographer of Irene say anything of this kind. He had no special admiration for Bardas. When mentioning Irene's sister, without giving her name, as accompanying Irene to the bride-show, he says:[37] "Her sister who later contracted a marital union with the uncle of the Emperor Michael, Bardas. He was quite an unworthy man, completely consumed by ill-will, enjoying robbery and killing." He may have had in mind the murder of Theoctistus by the accomplices of Bardas.

According to the biographer, the two sisters remained in intimate contact even after Theodosia's marriage. The messenger between them was the eunuch Cyril, the most faithful and devoted servant of Theodosia.[38] One day Irene sent a prophetic message to her sister by him, advising her to look after herself, because her husband, and Irene's brother-in-law, would be trapped by someone and killed. The same man would also kill the Emperor Michael. Irene's sister was forbidden to disclose this prophecy to anyone. But Theodosia, who knew that the prophecies of her sister were always fulfilled, "overcome by the love of her husband", revealed to him the secret message of her sister. The latter "instead of taking refuge with God", is said to have insisted that

---

[35] *Acta Sanct.*, July 28, p. 604.

[36] Papadopoulos-Kerameus (p. 557) thinks that she became abbess of a convent, but there is no indication of that in the Life of Eustratius. She seems to have been well known in the monastery where the Saint died, because she is said to have given permission to a crippled woman to take some hair of the Saint's beard. The woman was cured when she put the hair on the sick member of her body.

[37] *Acta Sanct.*, July 28 (vol. 6), p. 604.

[38] Ibid., p. 616.

Irene should reveal to him the name of the man who was to become emperor. He sent several messengers to Irene, but in vain.[39]

We may have some reservations about the genuineness of such a prophecy. The biographer, of course, knew the sequence of events, because he must have written his description towards the end of the tenth century. At least, he says, in the second passage, that the dynasty of Basil, the murderer of Bardas and Michael, stayed on the imperial throne down to the fourth and fifth generations. It is interesting, nevertheless, to note how he pictures the relations between Theodosia, Irene and Bardas. He is silent even about the separation, which had been pointed out by the biographer of Eustratius. If we would follow the two biographers, we should date the separation of Theodosia from her husband after the year 862. As already mentioned, this was the year when Bardas became Caesar.

The biographer of Irene also confirms that Bardas must have been a widower when he remaried. In the same passage he states clearly that Theodosia was the last wife of Bardas. This is confirmed by the information provided about Bardas by the Byzantine historians. He had two sons and a daughter by his first marriage. His younger son Antigonus was given the position of Domesticus of the Schools after the death of Theoctistus, while his elder son, whose name is unconfirmed, was invested with the command of several western themes. His son-in-law Symbatios became logothete of the drome.[40]

George the Monk,[41] and Pseudo-Symeon add a curious detail to this report, namely, that the Emperor Michael chose a wife for the elder son of Bardas, a wife "who was reviled". Both authors use the same phrase when relating this detail. The bad reputation of this lady mentioned by the two authors should be postdated, as both authors probably had in mind the rumors which circulated about her relations with Bardas after the death of her husband. It does not mean that she was previously the mistress of Michael. Such slanderous information would certainly have been invented by the enemies of Michael, as were other similar reports.[42]

We learn from these two informants that the elder son of Bardas died prematurely, and that the Emperor raised Bardas to the dignity of Caesar during Easter week of 862. The date of the death of Bardas' son is not

[39] The biographer reveals on this occasion Byzantine ideas on kingship. He lets Irene say: "Although this man (the future Emperor Basil I) will be responsible for murder, he is adorned with religious and imperial privileges. Because of that even God favors him and no adversary will profit from it."

[40] Theophanes Continuatus (ed. Bonn), pp. 180, 205; Pseudo-Symeon (ed. Bonn), p. 665.

[41] Ed. Bonn, p. 824.

[42] Cf. F. Dvorník, *The Photian Schism*. Cambridge, 1948, p. 135. Especially M. N. Adontz, *La portée historique de l'Oraison funèbre de Basil Ier*. Byzantion, 8 (1933) 501—513.

told us, but it seems that it must have happened soon after his father's elevation to Caesar.

Pseudo-Symeon also gives us the name of the widow of Bardas' elder son, which is Eudocia. He reports in the following manner on Bardas' misbehavior: "In this [Michael III] seventh year rumor was spreading that the Caesar Bardas was having illegitimate sexual relations with his own daughter-in-law Eudocia. The Patriarch Ignatius often admonished him to abstain from such an evil. He, however, did not comply, but rather bore a grudge against the patriarch who wanted to bring him to his better senses. Therefore, one day when Bardas desired to participate in the holy mysteries, the patriarch rejected him as unworthy. The latter, struck with scorn in his soul, chases his admonisher from the Church as lawless and corrupt, and inflicts on him innumerable torments in order to force him to abdicate".

The Pseudo-Symeon belongs to the circle of writers gathered around the Emperor Constantine VII Porphyrogenitus [912—959]. Their works were inspired by the Emperor who was anxious to place the life and deeds of his grandfather, Basil I, the founder of the Macedonian dynasty, in the best light. Of course, Michael III and Bardas, who were both murdered by Basil, had to be described in their works as evil men, who had to be disposed of in the interests of the state and of the Church. Basil acted as the instrument chosen by Providence to remove them. In describing Bardas, Pseudo-Symeon has used as his main source the Life of Ignatius by Nicetas the Paphlagonian, whose reliability is doubtful, as we have seen. However, he was not alone. An almost identical report on this incident is given by George the Monk,[43] and by the continuator of Theophanes.[44] The latter also mentions Bardas' divorce. They were preceded by Joseph Genesios,[45] one of the writers gathered around Porphyrogenetus. Genesios wrote his history between 945 and 959. Although he, too, used Nicetas as one of his sources, he is the least outspoken among all the historians of Porphyrogenetus' circle. He accused Bardas of wanting to dominate not only the state, but also the Church. He says simply that Bardas wanted to depose Ignatius because the patriarch had excluded him from Holy Communion because of an abdominable defect of which he had been suspected."

It is useless to look for more precise information in the works of Cedremus[46] who wrote in the eleventh, or at the beginning of the twelfth century. His compilation from the beginning of the ninth century on, is only a copy of the chronicle written by John Scylitzes in the eleventh

[43] Ed. Bonn, p. 826.
[44] *Ibid.*, p. 193.
[45] Ed. Bonn, p. 99.
[46] Ed. Bonn, p. 172.

century. He repeats almost word for word what George the Monk and the continuator of Theophanes say about Bardas. The same can be said about another chronicler of the twelfth century named Zonaras.[47] This review of the historical reports concerning the relations between Ignatius and Bardas shows that all their accounts of the famous incident go back to the "biographer" of Ignatius, who is Nicetas of Paphlagonia. We have already pointed out that his work is extremely biased and must be used with caution. Less biased writers, such as the biographers of St. Eustratius and of St. Irene, do not say anything about the incestuous relations of Bardas. Two contemporary writers, Theognostos and Stylian, who could have exploited this incident in their appeals to the Pope, limit themselves to a short remark, and Metrophanes says nothing about it. Moreover, all those who followed Nicetas, like him speak only of rumors which were circulating in the capital. There is but one exception, the biographer of St. Nicholas of Studios. The recital is a rhetorical and exaggerated version of Nicetas' report.

What conclusions can be derived from all these accounts? If the incident which Nicetas describes really did happen, it could have taken place only in 857 or 858, after the change of regent. Even if Bardas had misbehaved before that date, his morals would not have attracted great attention in the capital because he did not hold a position of great importance in the government. Since his elder son, who was married to Eudocia, is said to have died early, we can date his marriage in 856, after his promotion by Michael III and his death in 857. It appears that after the death of his son, Bardas introduced the widow, his daughter-in-law, into his household. He himself married Theodosia in, or immediately after, 855. Theodosia and Eudocia were about the same age. Then the rumors began to spread in the capital that Bardas was guilty of an incestuous union with his daughter-in-law; rumors spread by his political enemies who hated the new régime and who were desirous of bringing Theodora back to the palace.

It is not even established that Bardas was separated from his young wife, Theodosia at that time. The biographers of both Eustratius and Irene seem to date this separation from the time when Bardas had become Caesar, and that would be after 862. It would not be too daring to suggest that the occasion of this separation was the jealousy of Bardas' wife, who had listened too readily to gossip. We have seen that there is little evidence in the reports we have quoted which point to a formal divorce, and that Theodosia, although separated from her husband, continued to live comfortably in a house most probably provided by Bardas himself. If we may give credit to the biographer of Irene, even the saintly sister of Theodosia continued to enjoy relations with Bardas. This may

---

[47] Ed. Bonn, vol. 3, pp. 402, 403.

be imagination on the part of the author, but it should be stressed, however, that neither of the two biographers accuse Bardas of incestuous relations with his daughter-in-law.

We are entitled, therefore, to conclude from all this that Ignatius was the victim of intrigues hatched by the political enemies of the new régime. Appearances would seem to indicate that the rumors spread by the enemies of Bardas were based on fact. The knowledge that Eudocia was living in the house of her father-in-law was sufficient evidence for his enemies to invent the slander, even if Bardas, in 857 and 858, was still living with his second wife. We know the kinds of tales which were circulating in the capital about the relations between the Emperor Michael and Eudocia Ingerina, the wife of Basil. New research has revealed to us that this ménage à trois was the slanderous invention of Michael's political enemies.[48] A similar manœuver may have been plotted against Bardas.

Perhaps we may be permitted to consider the scene depicted by Nicetas as somewhat exaggerated, although there must be some truth in it. Maybe the description of the threat with the sword was added by Nicetas in order to have a better effect on the pious reader, but the threat of refusal of Holy Communion, or of a real refusal, might have taken place. Let us not forget, however, that Ignatius did not later condemn Basil who reached the throne by committing two murders, that of Bardas and of his benefactor Michael III. The violent scenes described by Nicetas did not often happen in Byzantium.

Ignatius certainly acted in good faith. He owed everything to Theodora and intended to remain faithful to the Empress who had restored the custom of venerating the saints, their pictures and relics. Her piety was well established, but Bardas, the new regent, was certainly not a saint. However, it was not the scene described by Nicetas which brought about the downfall of Ignatius, but rather his refusal to tonsure Theodora and her daughter, who, in the autumn of 858, were ordered to take monastic vows by authority of the new régime. It is for this noble gesture that Ignatius merits our respect.

---

[48] M. N. Adontz, *op. cit.*, pp. 402, 403.

XX

WHICH COUNCILS ARE ECUMENICAL?

It is generally expected that, after the conclusion of the Second Vatican Council the atmosphere will be favorable for dialogues between the representatives of Roman Catholics and the leaders of other Christian churches with a view to finding ways towards a better understanding and a more intimate rapprochement which could lead finally to a reunion.

Many Catholic leaders think that a dialogue with the Eastern Orthodox Churches should begin as early as possible and hope for positive results since there are no fundamental dogmatic differences between the Roman and Orthodox Churches.

This may be true, but it is premature to expect a speedy agreement between the Eastern Churches and Rome. There are many other aspects in the constitution, historical development, the mentality and spiritual life of Eastern Christianity which are not sufficiently understood by the West, and which will make the dialogue much more difficult than is expected by the optimistic observer.

In this paper I would like to call attention to a difference between the Catholics and the Orthodox which could be regarded as minor—namely, the number of ecumenical councils which are accepted by these Churches. But it is not minor, for it bears within it another question: by what criteria may a council be called truly ecumenical?

It is known that the Orthodox recognize only seven councils as ecumenical, the first being that of Nicaea (325) and the last the second of Nicaea (787), which condemned the iconoclastic heresy regarding representations of Christ and the saints and the worship of their images as unlawful.

The Roman Church added to the Seven Ecumenical Councils the Synod of 869-870 which condemned the Patriarch Photius as a usurper of the patriarchal throne of Constantinople and confirmed the reinstatement of St. Ignatius in his stead, as the Eighth Ecumenical

Council. This Council called itself ecumenical because it was convoked by an Emperor—Basil I—as were all previous ecumenical councils. The invitations to assist at it were addressed to the bishops of the Empire and it was attended by the representatives of Pope Hadrian II and four other Patriarchs. In spite of this it was opened in the presence of only twelve bishops, and its Acts were signed by only the one hundred and ten Fathers who had responded to the repeated exhortations of the Emperor to appear at its sessions. The reason for this meagre attendance was that the great majority of Byzantine prelates considered the accusations launched against Photius as unjust, since he had been canonically elected by a local synod after the resignation of Ignatius in 856. Because the majority of the clergy had ignored the decisions of this Council Ignatius had difficulties in the administration of his patriarchate. Fortunately, this situation was cleared up when the Emperor brought Photius back from exile and entrusted him with the education of his sons. Then both Ignatius and Photius were reconciled. Another council was planned in order to seal the reconciliation of the followers of Ignatius and of Photius and to end the schism in the Byzantine Church. The Emperor and Ignatius asked Pope John VIII to send his representatives to the new council. Unfortunately, before the Papal legates reached Constantinople, Ignatius died, and Photius was reinstated as Patriarch. The Council took place in November of 879 and ended in March, 880. Photius was reinstated by the numerous conciliar Fathers with the assent of the papal legates and the representatives of the other Patriarchs. The Council of 869-870 which had condemned Photius and his followers was abrogated. This explains why we do not have the Greek original of the Acts of this Council, but only a Latin translation made by the papal librarian Anastasius who, in 870, was in Constantinople as envoy of the Emperor Louis II. There exists also a Greek extract of the Acts compiled by an opponent of Photius who had refused to accept him as patriarch even after his reconciliation with Ignatius and restoration by the Council of 879-880 confirmed by John VIII. This extract was incorporated into the so-called anti-Photian collection compiled in a very biased manner by a zealot who wished to justify the refusal of the extremist party to accept the decisions of the Council of 879-880 and to recognize Photius as their legitimate Patriarch.

The Photian Council was also convoked by the Emperor Basil I, and representatives of all five patriarchs were present together with

380 Fathers. The Fathers were thus fully entitled to designate the assembly as a "holy and ecumenical synod." In the Acts this council is called "a holy Synod convoked under the most holy and ecumenical Patriarch Photius for the union of the holy and apostolic Church of God."

A similar title is given to this synod by the Patriarch Euthymius (907-912).[1] In his treatise on synods the Patriarch gives it the designation of "holy and ecumenical synod," but it is called the Eighth—it merely remains the "Union Synod." This means that it was assembled in order to seal the union between Rome and Constantinople, disrupted by the condemnation of Photius, which had been regarded as unjust by the great majority of the Byzantine clergy, and also to end a schism in the Byzantine patriarchate by reconciling definitely the pro-Photian and the pro-Ignatian clergy.

Of course, no mention is made in this treatise of the Ignatian Council of 869-870 which was cancelled ten years later by the synod of 879-880. Euthymius gives the ecumenical character only to the preceding seven councils quoting the definitions of Catholic doctrines which these councils had confirmed. This treatise was written only about three decades after the Photian Council and its author knew the Acts of this council in the version that has come down to us.

It should not surprise us that Euthymius regarded only seven councils as ecumenical. We can quote a document which reveals that even Photius himself did not add to the seven ecumenical the council which had reinstated him as the Eighth. In the Greek Manuscript 47 of the National Library in Paris I found the text of a profession of faith (fols. 231, 231a), composed by Photius, which was to be recited by all candidates to the episcopate. The future bishops had to subscribe to the Seven Ecumenical Councils and profess their dogmatic definitions. Even if Photius had composed this profession during his first patriarchate, there is no reason not to suppose that he used this formula also after the council of 879-880. We shall see presently that Photius was primarily interested in the ecumenicity of the seventh council and wished that it should be solemnly proclaimed by the representatives of all the patriarchs.

The treatise on synods composed by Euthymius was reedited in the fourteenth century by Neilos Diasorenos, metropolitan of Rhodes

---

[1] The treatise is preserved in Ms. Arundel 529 of the British Museum. See my book, *The Photian Schism* (Cambridge, 1948), pp. 383, 456-457.

(1357).[2] Neilos was an ardent supporter of the Patriarch Philotheus and of Gregory Palamas, the protagonists of the hesychast movement.[3] The monk Barlaam, the adversary of their doctrine on the living light of Mount Tabor which the mystics were supposed to see when reaching the highest degree of their ascetic practice, was condemned by a synod convoked by the Patriarch John XIV Aprenos in 1341. This synod marked the victory of the hesychasts and was regarded as an important milestone by all adherents of this movement. It is not surprising that they placed it alongside the Seven Ecumenical Councils, the basis of the orthodox faith.

Neilos therefore adapted the treatise of Euthymius to the needs of the fourteenth century by adding to the seven councils that of Photius (879-880) as the Eighth Ecumenical, and the synod of 1341 as the Ninth, giving also an extract from the Acts of this synod. He was not alone in this practice. In the Greek Manuscript 968 (fols. 392-395) in the National Library of Paris, I found an anonymous treatise on councils, also based on Euthymius' tractate, in which the Photian Council is added to the seven ecumenicals as the Eighth, and that of 1341 as the Ninth. However, the author concedes ecumenical character only to the first seven synods. Another version of Euthymius' treatise is preserved in the Manuscript Historicus Graecus 34 in the National Library of Vienna (fols. 359 ff.).[4] These two treatises must have been composed soon after 1341 by anonymous zealots propagating the hesychast doctrine. I would be tempted to date them before the writings of Neilos, because they are not as emphatic concerning the ecumenicity of the two last councils as was the Archbishop of Rhodes who, because of his zeal for hesychasm, was promoted by the Patriarch Philotheos Kokkinos to an exarchos in 1366. He lost this distinction under the Patriarch Makarios (1376-1379) who was an adversary of the hesychasts.

As said before, it is not surprising that the hesychasts were anxious to promote the synod of 1341 to that of an ecumenical council, but why did they add to the seven councils described in their prototype, the Photian Council as the Eighth? One is tempted to perceive in these later editions an echo of the anti-Latin polemic which was very acute

---

2 See K. Krumbacher, *Geschichte der Byzantinischen Literatur* (Munich, 1897), p. 109, and H. G. Beck, *Kirche und Theologische Literatur im Byzantinischen Reich* (Munich, 1959), p. 787.

3 Cf. G. Ostrogorsky, *History of the Byzantine State* (New Brunswick, 1957), pp. 456ff.

4 Cf. F. Dvornik, pp. 384, 420, 456.

in the fourteenth century. Did the Byzantines of this period know that the Latins had added to the seven councils the Ignatian synod of 869-870 which had unjustly, in their opinion, condemned Photius? It is possible, although we find in the polemics of the twelfth and thirteenth centuries very few references to general councils. In the twelfth century Hugo Etherianus or his brother Leo Tuscus was aware of the difference between the Greeks and the Latins in the matter of general councils.[5] But the Latins were, in general, not much interested in the problem of the councils and their number. They insisted on the primacy of the pope alone, and many of them were wary of speaking about the councils, being uncertain how to reconcile their authority with the papal primacy. Moreover, the case of Photius played a very small role on the polemics of this period.[6]

However, a strong echo of the anti-Latin polemic can be detected in Neilos' treatise on another point in contest: the question of Filioque. He insists on the condemnation of the addition of Filioque to the Creed said by the papal legates in their profession of faith at the end of the Photian synod and he adds to his account on the Photian council an extract from the famous letter of John VIII to Photius in connection with the Filioque incident, which is said to have been sent to Constantinople after the Photian council, and the authenticity of which is doubtful. Moreover, it should be stressed that many prominent supporters of hesychasm, especially Gregory Palamas, Philotheos, Neilos of Rhodes, Neilos Kabasilas, were very much engaged in anti-Latin polemics. Thus, we must not exclude the thought that the addition of the Photian council to the seven ecumenicals as the Eighth could be interpreted as a condemnation of the Latin practice of regarding the censures proclaimed against Photius by the synod of 869-870 as just and still valid.

It is possible that a similar operation was made in the new version of the Synodicon Vetus.[7] Its first and most important version contained in the Manuscript of Mount Sinai[8] and edited, most probably on the basis of an older treatise by an Ignatian between the years 886-891, regards the Ignatian council as the Eighth ecumenical. The second version contained in some manuscripts of the fourteenth cen-

---

[5] *Ibid.*, p. 347. (See also below, footnote #25).
[6] *Ibid.* 348ff., 397ff.
[7] Published by J. Pappe in J. A. Fabricins' *Bibliotheca Graeca* (Hamburg, 1809), vol. 12, pp. 360-421.
[8] *Sinaiticus Graecus*, No. 418 (1117), fols. 357a-365a. Cf. F. Dvornik, *The Patriarch Photius in the Light of Recent Research* (Munich, 1958), pp. 35ff.

tury speaks of the Eighth ecumenical as that "of the union between Photius and John VIII."[9]

However, there is also another explanation of the promotion of the two synods to ecumenical councils. The partisans of the hesychasts were naturally interested in stressing the importance of the synod of 1341. When promoting it to an ecumenical council they could not overlook the synod of union described in their prototype. In the Byzantine tradition it was regarded as an important assembly. They could thus not place their synod of 1341 immediately after the seven councils as the Eighth. This place was given to the Photian synod, and the hesychast synod was numbered as the Ninth. The Ignatian synod of 869-870, of course, did not exist for them, as for all Byzantines, because it was cancelled in 880.

In a similar way we can explain the designation of the Photian synod as the Eighth ecumenical in the fourteenth century versions of the Synodicon Vetus. Their prototype, reedited by an Ignatian at a time when the Photian controversy was still a passionate topic, stopped at the synod of 869-870 which he called the Eighth Ecumenical. The Byzantines of the fourteenth century looked at this incident from a long way off. If a council could be called the Eighth Ecumenical it could be in their minds only the synod of 879-880, which had cancelled the Ignatian council. This explains why in the new version of the Synodicon the Eighth council is that which marked the reconciliation between Photius and John VIII.

These are the few exceptions from the general rule accepted by the Byzantine Church which admits only seven ecumenical councils, exceptions which might have been inspired by anti-Latin trends in the fourteenth century or, at least, which show the mentality of this period. Otherwise, in all official and private documents from the eighth century to modern times it is stressed that the Orthodox Church admitted only seven ecumenical councils as the basis of the orthodox faith. This is particularly documented by the numerous short treatises on councils which are found in manuscripts in all major European libraries.[10] Some of them can be regarded as a sort of catechism teaching the main dogmas of the orthodox faith.

---

9 A new edition of the Synodicon and its versions on the basis of all available manuscripts is being prepared by John Parker.

10 Cf. Dvornik, *The Photian Schism,* pp. 452ff. Only one such treatise has been published by Ch. Justellus in his *Nomocanon Photii . . . Accessere ejusdem Photii, Nili metropolitae Rhodi et Anonymi tractatus de synodis oecumenicis* (Paris, 1615). This treatise and that of Neilos are reprinted by G. A. Rhallis in his *Syntagma* (Athens 1885-1889), p. 370-374, 389-395.

The conviction that only the first seven councils can be regarded as ecumenical, and that this character can in no way be attributed to the council of 869-870, was so firmly imbedded in Greek minds that even those Greeks who had accepted the union with Rome, concluded at the councils of Lyons and of Florence, hesitated to accept the Latin practice of regarding the Ignatian council of 869-870 as the Eighth Ecumenical. This is especially illustrated by two treatises on ecumenical councils written by Greek Uniats after the Council of Florence. I found them in the Greek Ms. 1712 in the National Library in Paris, and I published the main passages concerning our question in "Mélanges Eugène Tisserant."[11]

After enumerating the seven ecumenical councils, and after mentioning the synod of orthodoxy under Theodora, the widow of the last iconoclastic Emperor Theophilus, the author of the first treatise continues: "The eighth holy and ecumenical synod was held in Lyons under John the Pope of Rome. This synod was convened against Photius who had become patriarch of Constantinople in defiance of the canons. He had unjustly usurped the throne when Ignatius the holy was still alive. Indeed, it was he who effected the schism between the Greeks and the Latins. He denied that the most Holy Spirit proceeds also from the Son, but only from the Father. Because of that the Synod condemned him and defined that the Spirit proceeded from the Son as from the Father.

"The Ninth holy and ecumenical Synod was held in Constantinople under Gregory, the Pope of Rome, and Bekkos, the patriarch of Constantinople. This Synod also was assembled for the same matter. After being assembled [this Synod] decreed in a very clear and plain way that the Holy Spirit proceeded also from the Son as from the Father, and presented it to the Church to believe [in], to praise and to worship.

"The Tenth holy, great and ecumenical Synod was held in the city of Florence, under Eugenius, the Pope of Rome, John Palaeologus, the most glorious emperor of the Romans, and Joseph, the patriarch of Constantinople. This also had convened for the same matter. Because of that [the Synod] declared solemnly that the Holy Spirit proceeded also from the Son in its own definition, although this was not added to the symbol of the faith in the Eastern Churches."

The second short treatise gives also first the description of the seven ecumenical councils adding to them the council of Lyons as

[11] *Studi et Testi*, No. 232 (1964), vol. 2, pp. 93-101.

the Eighth, that under the Patriarch Bekkos as the Ninth, and the council of Florence as the Tenth. The author attributes the convocation of the Council of Lyons to Pope John VIII whom he regards as immediate successor to Pope Nicholas, omitting Hadrian II, who was responsible for the condemnation of Photius at the Council of 869-870. Both authors knew about the condemnation of Photius by a synod, but had a very hazy idea which synod it was. In this respect they were influenced by the tradition deeply rooted in Byzantine minds that only the first seven councils could be given the ecumenical character. None of the numerous treatises on councils, which they must have known, said anything about the Ignatian synod of 869-870.

It was natural for a Greek Uniat to regard the two councils which had proclaimed the union between the two Churches—that of Lyons (1274) and that of Florence (1438, 1439)—as ecumenical and to add them to the first seven councils. However, it was daring to promote even the local synod convoked by Bekkos in 1277 to an ecumenical council. One understands this promotion, because it was this synod which had to proclaim the union concluded at Lyons, in Constantinople.

The Orthodox Church is proud of this tradition.[12] We can detect an echo of this glorious past of the Eastern Church in the encyclical letter of the ecumenical Patriarch Athenagoras written in 1950 on the occasion of the feast of Orthodoxy, in which the Patriarch thanked most solemnly his predecessors for having preserved uncorrupted the faith proclaimed by the seven ecumenical councils during the turbulent stages of history.[13]

How and when did it happen that the Western Church abandoned the primitive tradition, common to East and West, adding to the first seven ecumenical councils the synod of 869-870 as the Eighth Ecumenical? I studied this problem in my book on the Photian Schism,[14] and I came to the conclusion that even the Roman curia had accepted the decisions of the council which had restored Photius, and which continued to recognize as ecumenical councils binding all Christians, only the seven primitive synods. Among other documents we can

12 Cf. H. Alivisatos, "Les Conciles Oecuménique V, VI, VII et VIII," *Le Concile et les conciles*, edition de Chevetogne (1960), p. 120.

13 It was published in the official review of the Patriarchate, *Orthodoxia* (1950), No. 2, p. 39-41. A French translation appeared in the *Istina* (1954), No. 1, pp. 46, 47.

14 *Ibid.*, pp. 314ff.

quote a letter of Pope Marinus II (942-946) to Sicus, Bishop of Capua, and that of Pope Leo IX to Peter, the Patriarch of Antioch. Both Popes knew only the seven general councils. Equally important is the formula of the profession of faith which every Pope had to recite and sign after his election. This formula is preserved in the so-called Liber Diurnus,[15] a kind of school-book intended for the training of papal notaries, containing copies of most of the formulae and instructions. The official formulary used is in the papal chancery. The formula for the profession of faith enumerated originally only four councils, but the Fifth, Sixth and the Seventh were added after these councils had been accepted in Rome. The Seventh Council could have been added only after the Photian council of 879-880. During this council Photius asked that the ecumenical character of this council should be officially recognized by the whole Church.[16] It can be shown that before this date the Seventh Council had not yet been added to the six ecumenical councils in Rome.

The latest edition of the formula containing the profession of faith of the newly elected popes is preserved in the collection of Canon Law composed by Cardinal Deusdedit during the reign of Pope Gregory VII (1073-1085). He copied it from the Liber Diurnus which then must have been reedited in the eleventh century, most probably during the reign of Leo IX. It is very significant that in this new edition of the formula only seven councils are enumerated as ecumenical and binding upon all Christians. Also, the so-called *Cautio Episcopi*, or the profession form recited by bishops after their election, contained in the new edition of the Liber Diurnus, enumerates only seven ecumenical councils. All this shows clearly that up to the end of the eleventh century the Roman chancellery recognized only seven ecumenical councils, excluding the council of 869-870, and that of 879-880. Both Churches were thus in perfect accord on this important matter.

I have tried also to explain why the Ignatian Council had been added in the West to the list as the Eighth Ecumenical. This happened during the reign of Gregory VII, who had opened the Lateran archives to his canonists who were looking for new arguments for the papal primacy and who were against the intervention of laymen

[15] Cf. *Ibid.*, pp. 318ff., 435ff.

[16] At the beginning of the fifth session Photius asked that Rome and all other Patriarchs should regard the council of 787 as ecumenical and should add this council to the six others. All representatives of the patriarchs did so solemnly when signing the decisions of the Photian Council. Mansi, *Concilia* 17, col. 493, 508ff.

in the appointment of bishops and abbots. They needed a strongly worded official document which they could use in their fight against the investiture, or appointment of clergy to ecclesiastical dignities by influential laymen. They found such a document in Canon twenty-two voted by the Ignatian Council, which forbade laymen to influence the appointment of prelates. All canonists and reformists of the Gregorian period used this canon as their most powerful weapon in their struggle for the freedom of the Church in the election of prelates. To give more weight to this argument they promoted the Ignatian Council to one of the most important ecumenical synods, overlooking the Acts of the Photian Council which had cancelled the Council of 869-70, although the Acts of this council were also kept in the Lateran Archives. Only Cardinal Deusdedit copied a part of the Acts of the Photian Synod of 861 and of 879-880. He was followed by Ivo of Chartres, who, in the famous prologue to his collection of Canon Law, quoted a long passage of the letter of John VIII to Basil I concerning the restoration of Photius in the "doctored" version read at the council.[17]

The controversy between Latins and Greeks concerning the number of ecumenical synods was begun very late, only in the fifteenth century, during the Council of Ferrara-Florence. During the discussion on the Filioque use was made of the Acts of the first councils. When, at the beginning of the sixth session, Cardinal Julian Cesarini asked the Greeks to lend him the book containing the Acts of the Eighth Council,[18] the metropolitan of Ephesus answered that the Greeks did not possess these Acts. This is understandable because these Acts were destroyed when the Council of 869-870 was abrogated. "But even were it [this book] in our possession," said the metropolitan, "we could on no account be asked to number among the ecumenical councils a synod which not only was never approved, but was even condemned, for the synod mentioned by Your Holiness drew up Acts against Photius . . . ," but another synod was subsequently held which reinstated Photius and abrogated the first synod. This council, also called the Eighth, met under Pope John. It also

[17] I discussed Ivo's prologue in my book, *The Photian Schism*, pp. 302-308. On pp. 335-341 I quoted some canonists who had copied parts of Ivo's prologue. Since then I found Ivo's prologue with the letter of John VIII in several other collections of canon law which are not yet published. This shows that Ivo's prologue with the papal letter rehabilitating Photius exercised a greater influence on Western canonists than has been thought.

[18] Mansi, *Concilia*, vol. 31, cols. 528-551; cf. Dvornik, *The Photian Schism*, pp. 362ff.

dealt with the question of addition to the Synod, deciding that nothing should be added . . . . Since then the Acts of that council were annulled, it is not these, but rather the Acts of the subsequent council that should be looked for. The Cardinal, surprised by this outburst, assured the Metropolitan that nothing should be read from the Eighth Council. However, five days later, in the course of the seventh session, the Archbishop of Rhodes, speaking in the name of the Latins, attacked the Metropolitan of Ephesus in a very passionate way. He maintained that Photius was an enemy of the Roman Church and was rightly condemned by the Eighth Council. "As to what you recently affirmed," continued the Archbishop, "namely, that a synod was summoned later and condemned the Eighth Council, I say that this seems very unlikely. It will not do to come forward with any doubtful argument to prove the contrary, that the synod did pass such a condemnation, for neither the Pope nor his representative were present." "Because the Latins had no knowledge of such a synod, therefore, the council you mentioned never took place."[19]

In spite of this sharp encounter, the question of the number of ecumenical synods was left open. The Greeks continued to count only seven ecumenical councils and in the council's definitions every reference to the Eighth Council was intentionally omitted.

It should be stressed that even the Greek Uniats did not accept the Latin thesis concerning the Eighth Council. This is illustrated by the attitude of the Greek Bishop Bartholomew Abraham of Crete. Because the Latin text of the Acts of the Council of Florence was lost, the Archbishop of Ravenna asked the Bishop of Crete to translate the Greek Acts into Latin. He did it in an abridged form, but in his preface he called the Council of Florence the Eighth Ecumenical. He did so with the full approval of the papal chancellery given to the translation under Pope Clement VII (1523-1534), in 1526. This title was given to the Council of Florence also by one of the first editors of conciliar Acts, Laurence Surius, in 1567, although with some hesitation.[20]

Most of the famous theologians of the fifteenth and sixteenth century were impressed by the edition of the Acts of the Florentine

---

[19] Cf. also *Quae supersunt Actorum Graecorum Concilii Florentini*, part I, ed. J. Gill (Rome 1953, Concilium Florentinum, series B. vol. V, 1), p. 90.

[20] See Dvornik, *The Photian Schism*, pp. 364ff. More detailed description is given by V. Peri, "Il numero dei concili ecumenici nella tradizione cattolica moderna," *Aevum* 37 (1963), pp. 472ff., and *I consili e le chiese* (Rome, Cultura 29, 1964), pp. 55ff.

Council by the Bishop of Crete, although some of them remained faithful to the Latin tradition designating the Ignatian Council as the Eighth Ecumenical. Therefore, they referred to the Council of Florence as the Ninth. This can be traced in the writings of Fantino Vallaresso, Juan de Torquemada, Reginald Pole, Antonio Agustin, Gasparo Contarini, Michael Eparco.[21]

From the beginning of the seventeenth century, however, another practice had started. First of all, the Ignatian Council came more and more into prominence among church historians. In 1602 appeared the tenth volume of the *Annales Ecclesiasticis* by the first modern Catholic historian Cardinal Cesare Baronius who vehemently rejected the title given to the Council of Florence, arguing that this title should be given only to the Council of 869-870 which had condemned Photius who, in Baronius' eyes, was the most dangerous enemy of the Roman Primacy and a detested Father of the schism between East and West. In 1604 M. Rader published in Innsbruck the Acts of this council with the anti-Photianist collection which was regarded as containing the most reliable documents concerning the affair of Photius. This was intended to end the practice inaugurated by the Bishop of Crete.

On the other side already the Archbishop of Rhodes in his speech during the seventh session of the Council of Florence, when refusing the Greek thesis concerning the annulment of the Eighth Council, hinted that from the Eighth Council on many important assemblies were convoked by the Popes, meaning the Western councils, the four Lateran, those of Lyons, Vienna and Constance. These councils more and more attracted the attention of the canonists. For example, the famous Spanish canonist Antonio Agustin (1517-1586) counted nine councils common to Greeks and Latins—the Ninth the Council of Florence—and seven Latin councils, namely, the Third, Fourth and Fifth Lateran, the Second of Lyons, that of Vienna, of Constance and of Trent. Jacobazzi (1538) also added to the eight first councils the Latin assemblies, but left out in his list the first and second councils of Lateran and that of Basel.

All these hesitations and uncertainties concerning the number of ecumenical councils were put aside by Bellarmin. In the first volume of his main work *Disputationes de Controvertus Christianae Fidei* (Innsbruck, 1586-1593) Cardinal Robert Bellarmin added to the eight first councils all Western assemblies, giving to the Council of

21 See V. Peri, *I Concili e le Chiese,* p. 57.

Florence the sixteenth place. He had some reserve concerning the validity of the Council of Basel. At the same time he gave a new definition of a general council, and discussed the conditions which would give a council its ecumenical character and authority binding on all Catholics. The first condition was the convocation by a Pope who should preside in person or through a representative. He mentioned also that at the first councils all five patriarchs were present representing the bishops of their patriarchates. Now, however, defined Bellarmin, the absence of the oriental patriarchs does not affect the ecumenicity of a council convoked by the Pope, because "these patriarchs are heretics, or certainly schismatics."

Bellarmin's definition put aside the most important objection which could be raised against the ecumenical character of the councils held in the West from the twelfth century on. His work was reprinted several times and the Cardinal became a leading authority on theological and conciliar matters. No wonder that another editor of the Conciliar Acts, S. Bini (Cologne, 1606), following Bellarmin, regarded the designation of the Council of Florence as the Eighth, which had been retained, although with some reserve, by his predecessor Surius, as spurious and declared that the designation "Sixteenth" should be substituted for "Eighth."

What hastened this new trend in conciliar matters was the preoccupation of the canonists to assure the ecumenical character to the Council of Trent (1545-1565), opposed and denied by the Protestants. To achieve this it seemed necessary to add to the old list of ecumenical councils also the Latin councils held in the West.

When Pope Paul V had ordered a new publication of the Conciliar Acts, a special congregation was formed to direct the preliminary work of the editors. Examining the differences concerning the Council of Florence, the congregation decided in its session of October 21, 1595, that the Council of Florence should not be called the Eighth, but the Sixteenth Ecumenical Council.[22] The way for such a decision was prepared by Bellarmin and Bini. So it happened that the *Collectio Romana,* the Roman edition of the Conciliar Acts, with the preface of I. Simond (*Concilia Generalia* 4 vols. Rome 1608-1612)[23] accepted Bellarmin's numbering of the ecumenical councils

[22] The history of this edition was examined in detail by Peri in his study *Il Numero dei Concili,* pp. 484ff. He used the archives of the Vatican and reproduced the most important decisions of the Congregation.

[23] On the Roman Edition see for details V. Peri "Due protagonisti dell *Editio Romani* dei concili ecumenici." *Studio Testi,* 237, pp. 131-232. See also G. Leonardi "Per la storia dell 'edizione romana." *Ibid.* pp. 583-637.

and their example was followed by all editors of Acts of the following period up to the present time.

This decision is, of course, not a pronunciamento on dogmatic matters. It was made rather for practical reasons and was based on works of canonists and theologians of that period. It had not solved the problem of the Ignatian and the Photian councils, making its solution rather more difficult. There is only one way to achieve an understanding. The Western Church has to revive the tradition which she herself had followed up to the twelfth century, and the memory of which was alive in the West up to the seventeenth century, as is illustrated by the history of the Council of Florence, and recognize only the seven primitive councils, excluding the so-called Eighth.

Concerning the Western councils, the Orthodox will have two objections to the value the Latins give them. According to the orthodox teaching, only a council which makes a dogmatic decision can be regarded as ecumenical.[24] All other councils are local. This was one of the reasons that the councils of 869-870 and of 879-880 were not regarded as ecumenical because they were convoked to decide on a matter of discipline and canon law. When we apply this ruling we see that many of the Western councils do not qualify.

As to the acceptance of Western councils by the Orthodox, let us recall the words which Nicetos, the Bishop of Nicomedia, addressed in 1136 to Anselm, Bishop of Havelberg, during their discussion of the Roman primacy.[25] "The Roman Church, whose primacy among its sisters we accept, to which we give the first place of honor as president of a general council, separated itself [from us] . . . . When therefore, because of these circumstances, this Church assembles a council with its Western bishops, without our knowledge of what is happening, it is right that its bishops should accept its decrees and observe them with the veneration due to them . . . . But, we, although we are in accord with the Roman Church concerning the Catholic faith, how could we, because we do not keep assemblies at the same

[24] Already in 1177 Hugo Etherianus, or his brother Leo Tuscus, gave such a definition of an ecumenical council according to the Greeks. See the quotation in Dvornik, *The Photian Schism*, p. 347. This definition is given in many Greek manuscripts containing treatises on councils. Let me quote here the Ms. 1319 of the Bibliothèque National in Paris. The Ms. is of the thirteenth century. On fol. 9 we read: "The Ecumenical Councils are [Synods] which were assembled on the order of an Emperor, which included bishops from all the Roman Empire, which discussed a problem of the faith and proclaimed a symbol of faith. All other councils are local." This Ms. gives the list of general and also local synods.

[25] *Dialogi,* Migne, *Patres Latini,* vol. 188, col. 1217ff. (chs. 7-8).

time she does, accept decisions which had been taken without our advice, and of which we even do not know anything?"

These words recall another mark or character which a council must have in order to be called ecumenical, according to the Orthodox Church, namely that all five patriarchs should be present at such an assembly and that its decisions should be accepted by the whole Church. Because of this reason, says the Greek specialist of canon law, H. Alivisatos,[26] the Eastern Church, although it considers itself a continuation of the primitive and indivisible Church, has abstained from convoking an Eighth Ecumenical Council for the reason that it would not be accepted as such by the Roman Church. A council which is not accepted in unanimous fashion does not possess the character of catholicity.

In the discussion of this and other problems dividing Eastern and Western Christianity we should recall the recommendation given by the Fathers during the fourth session of the Synod of Union (879-880).[27] The holy Synod said: Every Church has certain old usages which it has inherited. One should not quarrel and argue about them. Let the Roman Church observe its usages; this is legitimate. But let also the Church of Constantinople observe certain usages which it has inherited from old times. Let it be likewise so in the Oriental sees. . . . Many things would have not happened if the Churches had followed this recommendation in the past.

---

26 *Ibid.*, p. 120.
27 Mansi, XVII, Col. 489.

XXI

ORIGINS OF EPISCOPAL SYNODS

Some of the faithful, and even a few of the bishops, may have thought that something new was being introduced into the structure of the Church when the Second Vatican Council, in the Decree on the Pastoral Office of Bishops, spoke of "the Synod of Bishops," which "acting on behalf of the entire Catholic episcopate . . . will demonstrate that all bishops in hierarchical communion share in the responsibility for the universal Church."

This impression may have been caused by the fact that such episcopal synods have been almost non-existent in the recent history of the Church. However, when we study more closely the development of the Church throughout its early history, we find that proofs of the practice recommended by the Decree are to be found in the decisions of the first Councils of the Church.

It is now known that the synodal practice had developed in the early Church long before Constantine the Great. Practical reasons impelled the bishops to gather together whenever a problem arose requiring the consultation of several bishops to deal with it in such a way as to arrive at a solution consonant with the accepted Creed and ecclesiastical practice. It is also established that such meetings were held, also for practical reasons, in the capitals of the provinces of the Roman Empire, and that with time the bishops of such capitals acquired a certain supremacy over their confreres from the provinces. Thus originated the metropolitan organization of the primitive Church. The same political division of the Roman Empire into dioceses each containing a number of provinces motivated the development of patriarchates in the three most important political dioceses, namely, that of Italy in Rome, of Egypt in Alexandria, and of the Orient in Antioch. This development in ecclesiastical organization was clearly sanctioned by the First Ecumenical Council of Nicaea in 325.[1]

METROPOLITAN AND PROVINCIAL SYNODS

So far, Church historians have concentrated primarily on the study of the origins of the metropolitan and patriarchal organization of the primitive Church. Among the canons of the First Ecumenical Council, Canon Six,[2] which establishes the jurisdiction of the three Patriarchs, has attracted the gen-

1. For details see F. Dvornik, *The Idea of Apostolicity in Byzantium and the Legend of the Apostle Andrew* (Cambridge, Mass., 1958), pp. 3 sq.

2. Mansi, *Sacrorum conciliorum collectio* (Florence, Venice, 1759-1798), vol. II, col. 669 sq.

eral attention of Church historians and of canonists. Canon Five,[3] however, has escaped the scrutiny of most specialists, although it contains the first official regulation regarding the convocation of episcopal synods. It is addressed to the bishops of provinces, and asks them to hold two reunions each year, one on the fourteenth day of the Paschal period, and the second in the autumn. The main object of these synods would be to examine the excommunications pronounced by the bishops of the provinces, and to ascertain that this ecclesiastical censure was not launched "by narrowness of mind, by pertinacity, or any other vice of a bishop." The assembly of provincial bishops, after examination, was to make the sentence of excommunication definitive, provided the assembly, or the bishop who had originally pronounced the sentence, had not decided to impose a milder sentence. It should be stressed that Canon Five does not mention that any confirmation of the decision of the synod was necessary, either by the metropolitan of the province, or by any other authority. The decision made by the synod was forceful and final.

This Canon was confirmed and further expanded by the Council of Antioch, one of the most esteemed first synods of the early Church. Twenty-five canonical decisions are attributed to this synod. Canonists have long debated the date of its convocation, and many have proposed the year 341, a date when Constantius called a synod in Antioch on the occasion of the consecration of the great, new church of that city. The contents of the canons, however, indicate that the synod must have been assembled soon after that Council of

3. *Ibid.*, col. 687.

Nicaea, perhaps in 332, for the purpose of electing a successor to Bishop Paulinus.[4]

Most of the canons purpose to regularize the relations of priests with their bishops, and those of bishops with their metropolitans. Canon Nine confirms Canon Four of Nicaea which declares that the bishop of the capital of a province must have similar rights to those of a metropolitan, over all the bishops of his province. Without his permission, a bishop is unable to act outside the limits of the district, but, on the other hand, a metropolitan may make no decision without consulting his bishops. Canon Fifteen is more precise as to the authority of episcopal synods. Should a bishop be accused of trespassing and be found guilty by his confreres assembled in the provincial synod, the decision of that synod is definitive, and no appeal is admitted.

If, however, the bishops of the province are not unanimous in pronouncing their sentence, the metropolitan of that province must invite to the synod the bishops from the neighboring provinces, who must deliberate with the others. Thus we see that for the first time, the principle of collegial jurisdiction, wider than that of a provincial synod, was introduced into Church practice. This canon completed a disciplinary procedure already indicated in the Council of Nicaea.

Canon Twelve goes even further, and introduces another type of synodal assembly, the character of which is not clearly defined. It states, "If a priest or deacon has been deposed by his bishop, or a bishop deposed by a synod, and they wish to solicit the Emperor, they must present their

4. See G. Bardy, "Antioche (Concile et canons d')", *Dictionnaire de droit canonique* (Paris, 1935), vol. I, cols. 589-598. The canons in Mansi, II, col. 1308-1320.

cause at a more general council; they must state their reasons before a larger assembly of bishops, and they must submit to the inquest and the decision. But, if they neglect these legitimate provisions, and if they insist on going before the Emperor, they are not worthy of any pardon, for they will have no means of presenting their defense and must lose all hope of reintegration."

The Fathers of the synods had in mind another type of synod more competent than the provincial ones, and even more important and higher than those synods reinforced by the assistance of bishops from other provinces. Most probably they were thinking of the synods so often assembled by the Emperors during the Arianist crisis and which, although not ecumenical, consisted of bishops from many provinces. It would seem reasonable to expect that a further important synodical meeting would be convened in order to specify clearly the character of this higher synod.

It seems that the logical institution would have been the creation of diocesan synods which would serve as an instance of appeal from the decisions of the provincial synods. Surprisingly, the Second Ecumenical Council of 381 in Constantinople, which was a council in the oriental part of the Empire, did not take this step. Canon Two of the Council says simply:[5] "According to the canons, the bishop of Alexandria should limit himself to the administration of Egypt, the bishops of the Orient should administer only the Orient, provided that the rights of the church of Antioch described in the Canons of Nicaea be respected, the bishops of the dioceses of Asia, Pontus and Thrace, respectively, should ad-

5. Mansi, III, cols. 572, 573.

minister the affairs of only those dioceses." This canon shows only that the Fathers were anxious to keep the organization of the Church in strict conformity with the framework of the political division of the Empire. The sixth canon confirms the impression that Church organization was progressing along the lines of the political division of the Empire towards the formation of supra-metropolitan units corresponding to imperial dioceses. This same canon establishes that complaints against a bishop must first be examined by the provincial synod. The plaintiff could appeal the judgment of the provincial synod to a larger synod composed of bishops from the civil diocese.

Canon Six is couched in rather general terms and does not state by whom this larger synod is to be convoked. But, even if we admit that the larger synod is to be convoked by the same metropolitan who had presided over the first provincial synod, it must be admitted that the tendency to create a supra-metropolitan organism as a second instance of appeal is clear. It was to be applied to all civil dioceses of the eastern part of the Empire, not only to Egypt and the Orient, but also to the minor dioceses of Asia, Pontus and Thrace. That such was the tendency is also indicated in the ordinance issued by Theodosius I in July, 381.[6] The principle of adaptation to the administrative organization of the Empire is fully applied in the ordinance, and it can be rightly assumed that the bishops of the diocesan capitals soon became the most prominent leaders. There is no doubt about Alexandria and Antioch, but, in point of fact, the bishops

6. *Codex Theodisianus*, 16, 1, 3; ed. P. Krueger, Th. E. Mommsen (Berlin, 1905), p. 834.

of Caesarea, Ephesus and Heracleia, the capitals of the three minor dioceses, are listed at the head of the Klesis of 218 as metropolitans.[7] Their prominence is indicated, too, by the circumstance that each of them bore the title of exarch, a title found also in the signatures of the Council of 680.[8]

CONSTANTINOPLE AND THE PERMANENT SYNOD

Although the above-mentioned tendency of the Fathers is quite clear, they did not extend the privileges of the three major dioceses of Italy, Egypt and the Orient to the three minor dioceses. We cannot even deduce from the canons voted on by the first Councils that diocesan synods had ever been introduced as a last instance of appeal.

The main reason which explains this fact seems to be Canon Three which attributes to the See of Constantinople an honorary primacy as the second see after Rome because, as residence of the Emperors, Constantinople had become a second Rome. This promotion was accepted in the East without protest as it was a logical consequence of the adopted principle of adapting Church organization to that of the Empire. As I have shown, not even Pope Damasus rejected this canon,[9] which is also found in the first Latin collections of Canon Law.[10]

7. E. Gerland, *Die Genesis der Notitiae episcopatuum* (Kadiköy, 1931), p. 8.
8. Mansi, XI, cols. 688, 689.
9. F. Dvornik, *The Idea of Apostolicity*, pp. 1-38.
10. *Idem*, "The See of Constantinople in the First Latin Collections of Canon Law," *Recueil des travaux de l'Institut d'Etudes byzantines*, no. VIII (Beograd, 1963), pp. 97-101.

There is a question which cannot be answered easily. Did the Fathers of the Council of 381 decline to extend the patriarchal privileges to the three exarchs because, in 381, Constantinople was already thought of as the supra-metropolitan instance of appeal for Thrace and all of Asia Minor? There is no doubt that once Constantinople became the residence of the Emperors, the prestige of her bishops had risen. It was certainly felt in the diocese of Thrace.

It should be noted that in the ordinance of July 30, 381, Theodosius I omitted to mention the diocese of Thrace, and it is justifiable to suppose that already in 381, the Bishop of Constantinople was regarded as the most competent authority in that diocese. The bishop of Heracleia, Sisinnius, is referred to in the *Acts* of the Council of 680 as only "bishop of the metropolis of Heracleia of the European eparchy," although the bishops of Caesarea and Ephesus still held the title of eparch. In spite of this, Constantinople does not appear to have played any marked role in the Church before the year 380. The prestige granted to Constantinople by the honorary primacy only began to grow after the Council. The fact that the introduction of a diocesan synod was never completed helped, of course, to increase the prestige of Constantinople and of her bishop, and he was regarded as a natural intermediary in conflicts among the bishops of minor dioceses. On the other hand, the Easterners recognized the need for a synod of bishops possessing greater authority than that of the provincial synods. This is clearly indicated in Canon Six of the same Council. We have also seen in Canon Twelve of the Synod of Antioch that a bishop wishing to appeal to the Emperor must first present his case before a larger assembly of bishops. The Fathers of Antioch and of

Constantinople were most anxious to protect their rights of jurisdiction, and to prevent appeals to the Imperial Court. Since the Emperor resided in Constantinople, it would seem logical to suppose that the larger synod, whose function was to hear appeals intended for presentation to the Emperor, should be convened in that city. Such was the custom during the Arianist struggles, for the Emperors summoned the bishops to the cities in which they resided. So it came about that the "permanent" synod, *synodos endemousa,* in Constantinople was born. Synods were not assembled with any regularity, unlike the provincial synods, but only when a matter of general interest had to be decided upon. Any bishop, present in Constantinople, had the right to assist and to decide on the case with the Patriarch.

This was sanctioned by the Council of Chalcedon in 451: "If a cleric is in conflict with his own bishop or another bishop, he must present his affair to the provincial synod. But, if a bishop or a cleric is in conflict with the metropolitan of the province, he must present his affair either to the exarch of the diocese, or to the See of Constantinople."[11] It has sometimes been thought that according to this canon, appeals from all the Eastern patriarchates were to be sent to the Patriarch of Constantinople. In reality, the Fathers had in mind only those dioceses without exarchs, which means patriarchs. This was the case of the three minor dioceses. The bishops of Egypt or the Orient had their own exarchs-patriarchs and presented their appeals only to them. Canon Seventeen contains a similar instruction. This tribunal of Constantinople became thus the last instance in the chain of ecclesiastical tribunals of appeal in the Orient.

11. Mansi, VII, col. 361; cf., canon 17, col. 365.

It should be stressed that the delegates of Rome who protested vehemently against Canon Twenty-eight which had placed the three minor dioceses under the direct jurisdiction of Constantinople, accepted without protest Canons Nine and Seventeen although both canons increased the prestige of the bishop of Constantinople.[12]

Although these two canons make no reference to the "permanent synod," this institution was mentioned, and sanctioned, during the fourth session[13] of the Council which was set apart to deal with the jurisdictional conflict between Photius, metropolitan of Tyre, and Eustathius of Beyrouth, who had obtained the elevation of his See from both the Emperor and from the "permanent synod" to the detriment of the titulary of Tyre. When the Imperial judges asked the Fathers if Anatole of Constantinople was entitled to excommunicate Photius, and if the synod which he had assembled for this occasion could be regarded as a veritable synod, the Fathers declared this procedure legitimate, with the consent of the pontifical legates. From that time on the "permanent synod" became a canonical and permanent institution in the Eastern Church.

The "permanent synod" should not be regarded as an instrument of supreme appeal. It was convoked and presided over by the Patriarch of Constantinople. It was a straightforward synod which exercised legislative, judiciary, and also administrative authority. It was exclusively a tribunal of superior instance. It had to respect all ordinary instances of ecclesiastical judiciary power, and judged only major causes of general interest to the Church. It had also to de-

12. Cf., F. Dvornik, *The Idea of Apostolicity*, pp. 88 sq.
13. Mansi, VII, cols. 85-96.

fend the purity and integrity of the traditional faith. In disciplinary matters, the synod together with the Patriarch, usually followed the Byzantine principle of "economy"—which meant avoiding a sentence which might provoke bitterness, or re-open old wounds. It was inclined to compromise as far as ecclesiastical law and dignity allowed. Administrative functions were exercised only in a later period.[14]

The synod was unthinkable without a patriarch, as the patriarch also was unthinkable without his synod. He convoked it, he presided over it, but the decisions were made by him only in collegiality with the bishops. The relationship between the Patriarch and his permanent synod is very well characterized by the declaration of Patriarch Pyrrhus, as preserved in the *Acts* of the Roman synod of 840, which assembled in the Lateran.[15] He says, "We have decided in accord with our most holy bishops assembled by us. . . ." Even more telling is the declaration of Patriarch Paul II in his letter to Pope Theodore in 646. This is how he begins his profession of faith:[16] "Because that we, that is the jurisdiction of our church and the synod are confessing. . . ."

Photius on several occasions described in his *Responsa Canonica*,[17] the functioning of the episcopal perpetual synod and its relations with the Patriarch. Let us quote only his letter to the archbishop of Calabria: "The questions which your Piety have sent us have been made known to our most

14. On the functioning of the synod see J. Hajjar, "Patriarche et Synod dans l'Eglise byzantine," *Proche-Orient Chretien*, 4 (1954), pp. 118-140, and especially the work of the same author *Le Synode permanent*, Orientalia Christiana Analecta, vol. 164 (1962), especially pp. 52 sq.

15. Mansi, X, cols. 1001-1004.

16. *Ibid.*, col. 1024.

17. P. G. 120, cols. 773-781. Cf. also *ibid.*, col. 891.

pious metropolitans and they have been asked to examine them. . . ." After replying to the questions, Photius ends his letter thus, "This is the decision given by our most pious metropolitans in unanimous approval, which our Mediocrity has found just, and confirming it, is sending it to your Holiness."

From similar expressions made by other patriarchs we see that the permanent synod was a deliberative assembly which pondered in collegiality important ecclesiastical problems, making decisions which the presiding patriarch pronounced.

The question arises whether or not there was any appeal possible against the decision of this synod. We have seen that the Fathers of the first synods mentioned the possibility of appeal to the Emperor. Although he was regarded as the highest authority in many ecclesiastical matters, we cannot find an example of any Emperor changing a disciplinary judgment of the synod. In this respect the Fathers of the Eastern Church succeeded in safeguarding their rights concerning ecclesiastical discipline and other matters.

However, there was yet another possibility of appeal, namely, to the See of Rome. The Synod of Sardica (modern Sofia) in 343, which was rather a synod of the Western part of the Empire and thus of the Western Church, decided in Canon Three:[18] "If any among the bishops has been accused, but thinks his cause is just and that a new synod should be called, let us, if you consent, honor the memory of the Apostle St. Peter, and let them who examined the case write to Bishop Julius of Rome." The Pope's decision should be ac-

18. Mansi, III, col. 40. Cf. also canon three, *ibid.*, col. 8.

cepted. It must not be forgotten that some of the canons of Sardica, and Canon Three among them, were included in the Greek canonical collection of John Scholasticus in the sixth century.[19]

In spite of this, appeals from Byzantium to Rome concerning disciplinary matters were rare. Appeals which involved doctrinal questions had, of course, been quite numerous, as is understandable. Most interesting is the case of the priest, John of Chalcedon, and of the monk, Athanasius, who appealed to Pope Gregory the Great with the authorization of their superior, Patriarch John IV of Constantinople who had sent to the Pope the documents which contained without doubt the decision of the perpetual synod in this matter. Gregory actually gave a definite decision on the case, confirming the innocence of John and recommending mercy for the monk Athanasius.[20]

In has been said that in the ninth century, the Patriarch Ignatius appealed to Pope Nicholas I against the "usurpation" of Photius, but recent discoveries have shown that Ignatius did not make any appeal, and this is proved by his own categorical declaration at the Synod of Constantinople in 861: "*Ego non appelavi Romam, nec appello.*" The appeal made to Rome by the monk Theognostus in 863, allegedly in the name of Ignatius, was therefore false. But some of the bishops in the group supporting Photius, such as Gregory Asbeatas of Syracuse, Zacharias, later Metropolitan of Chalcedon, Peter of Sardis, Eulampius of Apama, and Theo-

19. *Syntagma L Titulorum,* ed. V. Beneśevic, Abhandlungen der bayerischen Akademie, Phil. hist. Kl. (1937), Heft 14.

20. *Gregorii papae Epistolae,* VI, pp. 15-17, P. L. 77, cols. 807 sq.

philus, Bishop of Amorium whom Ignatius judged for canonical reasons, had appealed to Rome on the basis of the Canons of Sardica.[21]

The Synod of 861, convened to judge Ignatius in the presence of the pontifical legates, appears to have finally accepted the Canons of Sardica. Following the declaration of the legates that they came to reexamine Ignatius' case because the Fathers of Sardica had decided that the Bishop of Rome was possessed of the power to reopen the case of any Bishop, Bishop Theodore replied in the name of the church of Constantinople, "This is a source of pleasure to our church; we have no objection to it and we find it in no way offensive." Unfortunately the Synod was rejected in 863 by Nicholas I, and its *Acts* destroyed. Only a Latin extract containing these important declarations has been preserved.[22] It is on this basis that the Roman church should commence her promised dialogue with the Eastern Church, but, so far, no action of this kind has been taken.

From all this we must conclude that the organization of the primitive Church was built on a synodal basis of bishops who, in collegiality, were bound to deliberate with their metropolitans and patriarchs on important questions concerning the faith and its disciplinary measures. The Byzantine church continued this practice in the East by means of its permanent synod of bishops united with the Patriarch.

21. For details see F. Dvornik, *The Photian Schism* (Cambridge, 1948), pp. 16-19, 21-36, 48-52, 70-90.

22. Deusdedit, Cardinal, *Canonical Collection*, ed. V. Wolf von Glanvell (Paderborn, 1905), pp. 603-616.

SYNODS IN THE PERSIAN CHURCH

There were, however, other Christian churches outside the Roman Empire, and it is valuable to know how they organized their religious life. The most important of these was the Persian church. What were its main features? Because of the hostility which for centuries had divided the Roman and Persian Empires, it had become a necessity for the Persian Christians to build their own independent ecclesiastical organization, and to maintain the least possible contact with the Christian churches of the Roman Empire. Thus the Persian church had become a kind of national church over which the Bishop of Seleucia-Ctesiphon wielded well-nigh unlimited authority.[23] It adopted, none the less, the organization it had grown up with, that of Roman Christianity complete with patriarch, metropolitans, synods and bishops, ruling from definite sees over carefully delineated dioceses as the necessary framework to carry on its Christian mission to the East. This organization the Persian church owed to the assistance of Marutha, Bishop of Maniferkat, between the Tigris and Lake Van, who went to Persia as the ambassador of Theodosius II, and represented the "Western Fathers" at the Persian synod of 410. Seleucia-Ctesiphon had all the makings of a patriarchate for Persia and for the communities that were to spring from the Persian missions.

And yet the sense of unity with the Western Christians was very much alive, and more than once in the first period of Persian church history found adequate expression. The

23. On the Persian Church see F. Dvornik, *National Churches and the Church Universal* (London, 1944), pp. 6-13. For more details see K. Lübeck, *Die altpersische Missionskirche* (Aachen, 1919).

Persian church was certainly conscious of its old connexion with Edessa and Antioch, so much so that Papa Bar Aghai (Jahbalaha) (415-420) considered it necessary to reduce opposition to his authority by appealing to the "Western Fathers," the Patriarch of Antioch and the Metropolitan of Edessa. It is questionable whether or not the Persian church was represented at the Council of Nicaea, but at its general synod of 410 the decisions of Nicaea were accepted by the church of Persia. The Western Fathers sent Bishop Akakios to Persia to settle the difficulties, and to their decisions the Persian church submitted at a synod held in 420. At that synod the Persian church also accepted the canons of some other Western synods, even admitting into her legislation other decrees on religious matters issued by the Roman Emperors.

But in all other things, the Persian church followed the direction of her own growth. The works of her greatest priest, Father Afrahat, written in the first half of the fourth century, reveal a mentality all its own. Christian, no doubt, yet Syriac and Persian for all that, and unaffected by the course of Greek Christianity. The head of the church was the bishop of the capital city who did not take the title of Patriarch, but of Katholikos. He reigned over the church in collegial union with his bishops assembled at numerous synods, to discuss with him major matters. In 424, the Persian synod decreed that thereafter there would be no appeal from the judgment of the Katholikos to the Western Fathers: "Easterners shall not complain of their own Patriarch to the Western Patriarch. Any case that cannot be settled by him shall await the tribunal of Christ."

This decision of the Persian synod which proclaimed a kind of autocephaly was made after a persecution of the

Christians by the Persian King of Kings. It did not mean a separation of Persian Christianity from the Church Universal, but was dictated by the desire to show that the Persian church should not be suspected of a relationship with the Roman Emperors, who were thought of as enemies of the King of Kings. It should be stressed that these synods were assembled when the Persian church still professed the Orthodox faith, which reveals to us that the basis of its organization was that of collegial union with the bishops at their synods, presided over by their Katholikos or Patriarch. Nestorianism was introduced only in 486 in Persia. But even the Nestorian church considered the assemblies of bishops in union with the Katholikos[24] to be the basis of its organization.

ARMENIAN SYNODAL STRUCTURE

The Armenian church[25] was founded by the missionary efforts of Gregory the Illuminator, who was consecrated bishop in Cappadocia. He converted King Tiridates III at the end of the third century. The bishopric was at Valarshapat, and was considered a suffragan of Cappadocia, but remained hereditary in Gregory's family. The church at Valarshapat also accepted the synodal practice as it had developed in the Byzantine Empire. Gregory's son assisted

24. "The Acts of the Persian Synods" were published by J. B. Chabot, *Synodicon Orientale,* Notices et Extraits de Mss. de la Bibliothèque Nationale et autres Bibliothèques (Paris, 1902), vol. 37.

25. Cf., F. Dvornik, *The National Churches,* pp. 13 sq.; H. Gelzer, "Die Anfange der Armenischen Kirche," *Berichte* of the Sächs. R. Academy. Cl. Phil. Hist., vol. 47 (1895), pp. 109-174. T. Markwart, *Die Entstehung der armenischen Bistümer,* Orientalia Christiana, no. 80 (Rome, 1930).

at the Council of Nicaea, and Bishop Isaak was present at a synod of Antioch and signed a letter addressed to the Emperor Jovian (363-364). Nerses the Great, who became bishop in 353, held an important synod in Ashtishat, which voted on canons concerning certain Armenian customs. Another national episcopal synod held in Ashtishat (435) accepted the decrees of the Ecumenical Council of Ephesus. The synodal practice continued during the time when Armenia was Orthodox, and during the struggle surrounding the acceptance or rejection of the Council of Chalcedon. The church became more and more national, possessing its own alphabet, and its own translation of Greek religious literature. In the fifth century, the Metropolitan of Armenia took the title of Katholikos, and his relationship with his bishops was characterized by collegiality in the synods. And so it went on, also after the rejection of Chalcedon by the Armenian synod of Ctesiphon in 614.

SYNODS IN AFRICA

We have less information concerning the synodal practice in the church of Ethiopia, which depended hierarchically on the Patriarchate of Alexandria. In the Western world of Christianity the synodal practice first developed in North Africa.[26] Christianity penetrated into the African provinces mainly through Carthage, the chief commercial and administrative center most frequently in touch with Rome and Italy in general. The episcopal sees were numerous. In 225,

26. Cf. H. Leclercq, *L'Afrique chretienne* (Paris, 1904); F. Heiler, *Altkirchliche Autonomie und papstlicher zentralismus* (Munich, 1941), pp. 3-50.

there were seventy bishops in Africa Proconsularis and Numidia. By the year 411, there were two hundred and seventeen bishoprics and their number increased to nearly six hundred by 430. St. Cyprian of Carthage with his genius for organization, firmly established the supremacy of the see over the whole of third-century Africa. This predominant position of Carthage remained untouched even after the administrative division of Africa into nine provinces by Diocletian.

In one respect, however, the church organization of Africa differed from that of other churches. The bishops of the provinces together formed a synodal unity, but when they convened in synods the chairmanship was reserved, not to the bishops of the provincial capitals, but to the oldest bishops. The provincial assemblies were, however, very much overshadowed by the universal synods of the whole African church, which were convoked and directed by the bishop of Carthage. Although his jurisdiction over the entire African church was absolute, extending over all bishoprics, he had to content himself with the modest title of *primae sedis episcopus,* as was decreed in Canon Twenty-six of the third Carthaginian synod.[27]

The African synods introduced the old Roman senatorial system into the internal structure of its assemblies.[28] This can be traced in Cyprian's letters and in the Acts of the first African synods that have come down to us. The same forms of convocation and procedure were used for the synods as for the Senate: *convocare, concilium, vocare, convocare*

27. H. T. Bruns, *Canones apostolorum et conciliorum* (Berlin, 1839), I, p. 127.

28. F. Dvornik, "Emperors, Popes and General Councils," *Dumbarton Oaks Papers,* 6 (1951), pp. 4-23.

senatum; habere concilium, habere senatum. Like the Senate under the Emperors, the council was a deliberative assembly, and the bishops had equal rights as did the senators. When Cyprian, as a bishop of the capital city, summoned a synod, he followed the procedure once used in the Senate. He read his *relatio,* or outline in the discussion, as the magistrate who represented the Emperor did in the Senate, then added a few words of explanation. Then followed the discussion and the *interrogatio* of all the bishops present, each of whom gave his *sententia,* using the senatorial formula: *censeo, decerno, mea sententia est, existimo.* The *sententia* was subsequently announced in a synodal letter addressed to the parties concerned. It was thus with this senatorial procedure, that the ecclesiastical gatherings built up their system. It was further developed at the first four General Councils.

Although in constant contact with Rome, the church of Africa spiritedly defended its autonomous status, as shown by Cyprian's attitude regarding the question of the Christians during Decius' persecution who had denied their faith, and particularly by the decision of the African Synod of 418 forbidding any appeal to Rome from the judgment of African bishops,[29] a canon which was strongly reaffirmed in a synodal letter of 426, in which the synod of Carthage forbade any further Roman intervention in African ecclesiastical matters.[30] The Africans protested, in the same document, even against the sending of legates from Rome to Africa, "We found no synodal decree which would authorize such a practice." From that time on Rome no longer inter-

29. Canon 17, Mansi, III, col. 822.
30. H. T. Bruns, *Canones,* I, p. 202.

vened in the interior affairs of the African church. Unfortunately, any further development of this African synodal practice was stopped by the invasion of Africa by the Vandals. The African synodal practice elaborated by Cyprian, by Aurelius, Allippius, and Augustine rendered great service to the Church in the struggle with Donatism, Manicheism, and Pelagianism.

COUNCILS IN SPAIN

The early Spanish church also accepted the synodal practice as is illustrated by the Acts of the Synod of Elvira, about 305.[31] The synod represented all five provinces of Spain, and its numerous canons are important for the study of early Spanish Christianity. With the nineteen bishops, twenty-four priests attended and were seated with the bishops. Other clerics attended, but they stood. The canons, however, are announced only in the names of the bishops. Sulpicius Severus speaks in the second book of his *Chronica*[32] of the synod of bishops from Spain and Aquitania who assembled in Saragossa in 380. The bishops condemned those of their number who adhered to the doctrine of Priscillianism. The synod voted on eight canons. The first synod of Toledo[33] convoked in 400 by the bishop of that city together with eighteen other bishops, voted on twenty canons but had still to deal with the Priscillianists. This was also the main

31. Mansi, II, col. 1 sq.

32. Ed. C. Halm in *Corpus scriptorum ecclesiast. latin* . . . , vol. 1 (Vienna, 1866), II, cap. 47, p. 100. On Spanish Church, see H. Leclercq, *L'Espagne chretienne* (Paris, 1906).

33. For decrees of all Councils of Toledo see H. T. Bruns, *Canones*, I, pp. 203 sq.

subject of the provincial synods of 563 and 572.

The synodal system of the Spanish church was thus well developed in the early period of its expansion. It suffered a setback during the invasion and occupation by the Visigoths (507). However, the invaders were a small minority, and were quickly romanized. When in 587 the Visigothic King Reccared had become a Catholic, abandoning the Arianist creed, the synodal system of the Spanish church flourished again displaying very interesting and particular features.[34] The bishops of the provinces formed a provincial council presided over by the Metropolitan. His see was the first tribunal of appeal for the whole province. Besides the provincial councils there existed a national council, as in the African church, called *concilium universale* or *generale*, presided over by the Archbishop of Toledo, capital of the Visigothic Kingdom. It was assembled by the King who also proposed the agenda. He often interfered in the debates, and would sign the decrees before the bishops, publishing them as state laws. The council often concerned itself with state affairs, but the King claimed juridical power over the bishops, especially the Metropolitans of Toledo. The general council was the most important institution of the Visigothic state, exercising an authoritative influence not only in the church, but in matters of State as well. The most important of the national councils is that of 589 which hastened the process of unification between the two nations.

At this council the Visigothic nation embraced the Catholic faith, even including some of the Arianist bishops. It was at this council that the *Filioque* was added to the Creed.

34. Cf., K. Ziegler, *Church and State in Visigothic Spain* (Washington, 1930).

In spite of a nationalistic particularism which this synodal system presented, the Visigothic church respected the primatial position of Rome, and the decisions made by other councils, general or particular. The bishops were well aware of their high position in the church and any intervention in their internal affairs by Rome or anyone else was repugnant to them. When in 638 Pope Honorius reproached the Spanish bishops for their laziness in suppressing heresy, the Sixth Council of Toledo (638) delegated Bishop Braulio to reply to the Pope's charge. Braulio accused His Holiness of slandering the Spanish church, as long ago the Spanish King had ordered the persecution of heretics, and thus Rome had nothing to fear.[35] On another occasion, Pope Benedict II reproached Bishop Julian of Toledo for certain inaccuracies in one of his theological commentaries. Bishop Julian made a self-confident defense of his declarations at the Fourteenth Council of Toledo (684), asserting at the finish that "to all lovers of truth, his answer, by divine judgment, will appear sublime, even if considered by ignorant, covetous men as unteachable."[36] The bishops present agreed with the speaker. We can see that the Spanish bishops at their synodal meetings evinced a similar, energetic reaction against the intervention of Rome as did the Bishops of Africa at their synods.

The Visigothic Spanish church produced several prominent ecclesiastical figures, such as Leander of Seville, Isidore of Seville, the encyclopaedist, theologian and canonist, Braulio of Saragossa, and especially Ildefonsus of Toledo, a great churchman and theologian. But intimate relations with the State sapped its energy and secularized its life. With the

35. Braulionis *Epistulae*, P. L. 80, letter 21, cols. 667-669.
36. Mansi, XII (XV. Conc. Toled.), cols. 10-18, especially col. 17

destruction of the Visigothic Kingdom by the Arabs in 711, the national, synodal system of the Spanish church broke down.

EPISCOPAL SYNODS IN GAUL

In Gaul, ancient Gallia, Christianity had from its beginning a character not Roman, but rather oriental and Greek in character. The first bishop of Lyons, about the year 130 A.D., was Photinus, from Asia Minor, and he was succeeded by his compatriot, St. Irenaeus, rightly called the father of Catholic dogmatics. His theological thinking was Eastern in character, and continued contact with the East gave the early Gallic church rather an eastern and Greek stamp. This oriental influence is seen particularly in the tendency to independence in theological thinking, ecclesiastic administration and discipline in the church of Gaul. It was more attracted to the church of Milan than to that of Rome.[37] Many of her bishops took part in synods organized by the Metropolitans of Milan, and this contact with Milan was of assistance to the church of Gaul in developing its metropolitan organization during the fourth century. But it was never so well organized as in Africa or Spain, chiefly because of the continuous rivalry between the sees of Vienne and Arles for primacy in Gaul.[38] However, the system of episcopal synods progressed well in Gaul. The first synod was held in Arles

37. Cf., T. Scott Holmes, *The Origin and Development of the Christian Church in Gaul during the First Centuries* (Cambridge, 1911). H. Leclercq, 'Gallicane (Eglise) *Dictionnaire d'archéologie chrétienne et de liturgie*, vol. 6 (Paris, 1924), cols. 310-473.

38. Cf., on this rivalry F. Dvornik, *The Idea of Apostolicity*, pp. 36-39, 46.

in 314 A.D. The synods held in Paris in 335 and in 360 voted for strong measures against Arianism. The synod of Agde (506) stressed the obligation of celibacy of priests, and the obligation of the faithful to assist at Mass on Sundays. It was presided over by Caesarius of Arles, who also directed the Second Synod of Orange (529) known for its rejection of Semi-Pelagianism and for the definition of the doctrine on grace according to St. Augustine. During the second and third centuries, Roman authority, although respected, was hardly felt in Gaul. But by the fourth century, Rome had succeeded in eliminating the influence from Milan and thus restored her lost authority. The elevation by the popes of the bishop of Arles to a kind of apostolic vicar of Gaul provoked strong protest from the bishops of Vienne and Marseilles. The Synod of Turin (417) convoked on their initiative, rejected the pope's decision, but a compromise was reached and a break with Rome was avoided. The bishop of Marseilles, Proculus, persisted in his opposition in spite of his excommunication, which illustrates the independent spirit of the bishops of Gaul.[39]

The furtherance of more intimate relations between the church of Gaul and Rome were interrupted by the occupation of Gaul by the Franks. The independent position of the Frankish national church is illustrated by the fact that the Frankish Kings approved, or appointed, the bishops, and placed the synodal system under their sovereignty. They convoked the national councils, prepared the agenda and confirmed the canons and conclusions. Provincial episcopal synods also came under their authority and were convened

39. On the Councils of Gaul and of the Franks see H. Leclercq, *op. cit.*, col. 457-467 with all documentation.

by them. The vicariate of Arles lost all importance for Rome and the primatial rights were transferred to the See of Lyons, where the bishops presided over the national episcopal synods and even pretended to the title of Patriarch. This spirit of independence in the Frankish church, shown so often in its episcopal synods, was completely broken during the Carolingian period. The political alliance of the papacy with Pepin and Charles the Great naturally had its consequences in the ecclesiastical organization of the Frankish church. Charlemagne, anxious to unify the different customs and particularities in the life of the Frankish church, introduced Roman canon law and customs, including the Roman liturgy, and he strengthened Roman jurisdiction in the church. The decadence of the Frankish church which had commenced in the seventh century helped him to bring the church completely under his control. The synods became provincial and national assemblies in which, beside the bishops and the abbots, counts and barons discussed ecclesiastic and state affairs. The decisions were promulgated by the Emperor and called *Capitularia.*

There was a certain amount of resistance to this wholesale romanization and secularization of the Frankish church. An heroic, solitary figure was that of Hincmar, Archbishop of Rheims, who defended the rights of the metropolitans to convoke provincial synods, the rightful tribunal of appeal, and he protested against appeals directed by bishops and priests to the papal Curia, without reference to their Metropolitans. His work *De jure metropolitarum* was his swan-song on the decline of the episcopal synods, once a respected organ in the administration of the early Church.

SYNODS IN THE ROMAN CHURCH

We must stress the fact that even the Bishops of Rome followed the synodical practice, at least during the early period. As a matter of fact, Pope Miltiades (311-314) had explained to Constantine the Great that the episcopal synods were the customary procedure by which the Church solved her problems. When the heretical Donatists, and the schismatics of northern Africa, dissatisfied with their condemnation by the African bishops, petitioned Constantine the Great to appoint independent judges from Gaul to examine their case, the Emperor agreed and appointed five bishops, including the Bishop of Rome. This was the first ecclesiastical case submitted to him, and he applied to its solution Roman juridical procedure by setting up a court of investigation empowered to give judgment. Pope Miltiades transformed the court into a council to which he invited fourteen Italian bishops (313). Once Constantine had learnt of the church's method, he adopted it, and when the Donatists repudiated the decision of the Roman synod, he decided to summon another council at Arles (314).[40] This was presided over by one of the judges, Marinus, Bishop of Arles; Pope Sylvester (314-335) sent only two priests and two deacons, as his representatives. At the conclusion, Constantine confirmed the decision of the Synod of Arles, and after that the Emperors used the synodical procedure in all doctrinal disputes.

Pope St. Damasus (366-384) is known to have convoked four synods for the purpose of confirming his election and for the condemnation of heretics. A fifth synod was assem-

40. For details see F. Dvornik, "Emperors, Popes, . . ." pp. 4 sq.

bled by Damasus in 385.[41] Innocent I held another in 402 which voted on sixteen canons in reply to questions sent to Rome by the bishops of Gaul. It is known that Pope Celestine[42] condemned Nestorius in 430 at a Roman synod and inaugurated the same decision made by the Ecumenical Council of Ephesus in 431.

With the growth of papal authority based on the petrine tradition, which Damasus had already begun to stress, the popes inaugurated a new custom, that of making decisions alone as the holders of the *Cathedra Petri,* and by promulgating their *Decretalia* and *statuta sedis apostolicae.* Siricius (384-398) is the first known author of such a *Decretale,* which was addressed to Bishop Himerius of Tarragona.[43] Innocent I (402-417) in one of his *Decretale* claimed that all important decisions of episcopal synods should be sent to the Roman See for approval.[44] The pattern of the *Decretalia* changed gradually, and often emulated the style and form of imperial constitutions. Gelasius went even further than Innocent I when he claimed full papal sovereignty over all episcopal synods.[45]

In spite of this new development the old synodal practice was not forgotten in Rome. For example, Leo the Great (400-461) is said to have held a synod in Rome in 444, to discuss the case against a Manichaean sect discovered in the city. The *Acts* are not preserved. He also condemned the Latrocinium of Ephesus at a Roman synod. Pope Hilarius (461-468) convoked a synod in 465 together with forty-eight

41. Mansi, 111, cols. 459-462, 485, 624.
42. *Ibid.,* col. 1019.
43. P. L. XIII, col. 1146.
44. *Epistolae,* P. L. 20, col. 473.
45. P. L. 59, col. 66.

bishops, which dealt with questions presented to the Pope by the Spanish synod of Tarragona. Pope Felix II (III), when dealing with the Patriarch Acacius who had accepted the Henoticon which favored Monophysitic ideas, did not content himself with letters or decretals. Instead he convoked a synod of seventy-seven bishops in 484, excommunicated not only Patriarch Acacius himself but also the papal legates suspected of intercourse with partisans of the Patriarch. Another synod of forty-three bishops sent its synodical decree to the oriental monks. Another Roman synod of 487 protested against the persecution of Catholics in Africa.[46] Even Gelasius (492-496) held a Roman synod in 494 to deal with Italian ecclesiastical matters. A further synod assembled by Gelasius in 495 rehabilitated the legate excommunicated by Felix II. *Acta* are preserved.[47] However, the famous *Decretum* on the Holy Books is not a decree of the Gelasian synod as is still believed by many, as it was composed in the sixth century by an anonymous author.

The synods during the reign of Symmachus (498-514) of 499, 501, and 502 dealt with the election of popes and of accusations against Symmachus. They contributed to the declaration that the first See cannot be judged by anyone.[48] Hormisdas (514-523) who ended the Acacian schism, followed the new method, fighting and defending his rights by letters and *Decretalia* sent to the Church in the East. There is no evidence that Roman synods were held on the Acacian affair. It appears, however, that the reconciliation may have been confirmed in 517 by a Roman synod. From the seventh century on let us mention especially the Roman synod under

46. Mansi, VII, cols. 1106, 1137, 1166, 1171.
47. Mansi, VIII, cols. 145-151, 178-184.
48. *Ibid.*, 230, 246, 247, 262, 295.

Severinus in 640, which condemned the imperial decree, the Ecthesis, and the first great Lateran synod convoked by Martin I in 649 to condemn Monotheletism.

The synodal practice was again revived in the ninth century by Pope Nicholas I during the Photian affair. His example was also followed by Hadrian II, who condemned Photius and reinstated Ignatius at a Roman synod in 868. The *Acta* of this synod were brought by the legates to the Ecumenical Council (869-70) and were read during the seventh session. The legates simply asked that all the bishops should accept the decision of the Roman synod without further inquiry. This simple request caused great astonishment because, according to the easterners, only an ecumenical synod could deal with a case of this kind. This embarrassed Ignatius who was reinstalled as Patriarch, and angered the Emperor Basil who intended to convoke a council in Constantinople to discuss and reach a decision on this question. This explains why only about one hundred and ten bishops assisted at that Council, and why the great majority of the bishops ignored the decision of the Council and remained faithful to Photius even though he had been condemned by both synods.[49]

PAPAL AUTHORITY AND THE DECLINE OF SYNODS

As regards the provincial episcopal synods, their importance declined in the same measure as the prestige of the Roman Curia increased in the eighth and ninth centuries. The centralization of Church administration in the Roman

49. See for details and documentation, F. Dvornik, *Photian Schism*, pp. 132, sq.

Curia was accelerated by the appearance of one of the biggest falsifications of the Middle Ages, namely, the *Pseudo-Isidorian Decretals.*[50] The falsification originated somewhere between 847 and 852 in the Frankish Empire, probably in the diocese of Rheims, and was directed against Hincmar's defense of the rights of the Metropolitans. Pope Nicholas I accepted them as genuine documents. Among the false papers was a decree that any major synod could be assembled only with permission from the Holy See. The falsity spread rapidly in Gaul and in Germany during the tenth century, and was rediscovered in Rome by the reformists under Pope Leo IX and Gregory VII. The sixteenth principle of Gregory's *Dictatus Papae*[51] declares that no synod can be called "general" without permission from the pope. Applied to the provincial synods this dictum meant the disappearance of this old institution, and ended the last remnants of the old Christian autonomous direction of ecclesiastical affairs by the episcopal synods.

The many synods held by the reformist popes, from Leo IX to Paschalis II, had quite a different aspect. The struggle against Investiture forced the popes to hold their synods outside Rome, and to invite to the gatherings those counts and barons whose help in the struggle with the Emperor was most welcome. The papacy won its struggle for the reform of the Church, and this was publicly proclaimed in the First Council of the Lateran in 1123. It was also the first Ecumenical Council of the Western Church.

This short study shows how the administration of the early Church was based on the synodical system. The

50. Ed. Paul Hinschius (Leipzig, 1863).

51. Ed. E. Caspar, *Das Register Gregors VII,* vol. 1, (Berlin, 1920), pp. 201, sq.

56

bishops assembled in collegiality in either provincial or national synods, together with their Metropolitans, possessed equal rights in the discussions and decisions on problems that had arisen in their churches. Their common faith united them with the bishops of Rome whose primacy in the Church was reverently respected by them. In matters of faith, the bishops looked to Rome for guidance, regarding her as the highest tribunal of appeal.

This system, which also made the bishops responsible for the development of religious life in their dioceses, ecclesiastical provinces, and in their nations, slowly disappeared in the Middle Ages in proportion to the growth of Roman centralization of administration. The almost complete disappearance of the primitive system of episcopal synodical rule in ecclesiastical affairs has not been of advantage to the Church as the present crisis in the Roman Catholic Church manifests.

XXII

Preambles to the Schism of Michael Cerularius

The break between the Roman and Eastern Churches in 1054 did not come unexpectedly. The full responsibility for this unfortunate happening cannot be laid only at the feet of the haughty Patriarch of Constantinople, Michael Cerularius.[1] The figures of the Patriarch and of Cardinal Humbert appeared only at the end of a long list of Eastern and Western spiritual leaders and statesmen who laid the ground for the estrangement which ended in the condemnation of Michael Cerularius by Cardinal Humbert. Nor can we consider these leaders as always personally responsible for its development.

Political ideology and political events influenced this estrangement more than dogma. Even the last act of this tragic drama had a more political than religious background. The political philosophy of the early Christians was an adaptation of the Hellenistic system to Christian belief. The Hellenistic king was deprived of his divine character, but he was regarded as chosen by God to be his representative on earth. Constantine the Great (306-337) accepted this adaptation and regarded the care for the Church and protection of the true religion as the main part of his imperial duties.[2] The Roman Empire was the *oikumene,* the only part of

[1] Cf. A. Michel, *Humbert und Kerullarios—Duellen und Studien zum Schisma des XI. Jahrhunderts,* I-II (Paderborn, 1925, 1930).

[2] For details, cf. F. Dvornik, *Early Christian and Byzantine Political Philosophy: Origins and Background* (Dumbarton Oaks Studies, 9) (Dumbarton Oaks: Washington, D.C., 1966).

the world known at that time, and the Church adapted its own organization to the political divisions of the Empire. Rome remained its base, even when the residence of the emperor was transferred to Constantinople. The Byzantines called themselves not Greeks but Romans. The papacy accepted the political supremacy of the emperor and often sanctioned even his interventions in religious affairs.

As long as the idea of one emperor appointed by God and of one Empire was generally accepted, the relations between Rome and Constantinople were normal. Not even the tempests raised by the christological disputes could disrupt these relations. The schism provoked by the adherence of Patriarch Acacius (472-489) to monophysitism accepting the existence of only one nature in the incarnate Word was ended by Justinian (527-565) in favor of Pope Hormisdas (519-523). Confirming the privileged position of Rome in the Empire, Justinian declared: "Old Rome has the honor of being the mother of law and none will doubt that she is the head of the supreme pontificate." He called Rome "the head of all holy Churches" and asserted that he could not tolerate "that anything concerning the ecclesiastical order should be settled independently of his Holiness (the pope), since he is the head of all the sacred priests of God".[3]

However, Justinian's renovation of the Roman Empire lasted only a short time. The foundation of a new Germanic kingdom in northern Italy by Lombard invaders raised unforeseen obstacles in the improvement of good relations between Rome and Constantinople. The progress of the Lombards toward Rome was becoming increasingly menacing. Gregory the Great (590-604) defended Rome, remaining loyal to the emperor, although he was unable to help Gregory in the defense of Italy. Emperor Phocas confirmed the privileged position of Rome in the Empire (607) and the incidents provoked by the monotheletistic heresy were forgotten when the Sixth Ecumenical Council (680-681) had

[3] F. Dvornik, *Byzance et la Primauté Romaine* (Unam Sanctam, 49) (Paris, 1964), pp. 61ff.: Eng. tr.: *Byzantium and the Roman Primacy* (Fordham University Press: New York, 1966).

approved the dogmatic missives of Pope Agatho on the two wills in Christ.

The popes elected by the Roman clergy continued to inform the representatives of the emperor at Ravenna of their election, asking the emperor's confirmation.[4] In 710 Pope Constantine was received in Constantinople with great respect by the emperor and the people of the capital. Justinian II confirmed anew the Roman primacy in ecclesiastical matters as had Justinian I and Phocas.[5]

The ambitions of the Lombard King Aistulf provoked a new crisis. In 751 he took Ravenna and threatened to annex Rome. Zachary, the last pope who had announced his election to Emperor Constantine V and asked for its confirmation, was unable to stop the Lombard advance. By giving his moral sanction to the elevation of Pippin to the Frankish throne, he put the new dynasty into obligation to Rome. This was exploited by his successor, Stephen II (752-757).

The emperor, unable to provide troops for the protection of Rome, sent the pope with his envoy to Aistulf with the request to stop the menace to Rome and to restore Ravenna to the Empire. When the king had refused the pope's request, Stephen II went to Pippin asking for help. After defeating Aistulf, Pippin donated the exarchate of Ravenna and the duchy of Rome to the pope.[6] But this was not yet the end of the old tradition that there was only one emperor, residing in Constantinople. Pippin remained in good rapport with the emperor, and in the territory given by him to the pope the authority of the emperor continued to be recognized at least outwardly.

Not even the storm provoked by the iconoclastic emperors brought an end to the peaceful relations between Rome and Constantinople. Good relations were restored on the occasion of the Seventh Ecumenical Council (787), and Empress Irene

[4] The diplomatic formulas are preserved in *Liber Diurnus Romanorum Pontificum* (ed. H. Foerster) (Bern, 1958).

[5] *Liber Pontificalis*, I (ed. L. Duchesne) (Paris, 1886), p. 316.

[6] For details, cf. A. Fliche and V. Martin, *Histoire de l'Eglise*, V-VI (Paris, 1947).

called the pope in her letter the "truly first priest, who presides instead of the holy and all-praised apostle Peter and in his chair".[7]

The fateful break occurred in the reign of Pope Leo III (795-816). Opposed by the Roman aristocracy and needing the support of an emperor, the pope threw himself completely into the arms of Pippin's successor, Charlemagne, who had made a definite end to the Lombard kingdom, and he proclaimed him emperor of the Romans on Christmas night in the year 800. Probably he regarded the imperial throne in Constantinople as vacant when Constantine VI had been deposed by his mother Irene. He also might have been influenced by the famous falsification—the *Donatio Constantini*—according to which Constantine the Great, before moving to Constantinople, had bestowed on the pope all imperial possessions in Italy. This falsification was probably fabricated by some Roman clerics, anxious to give to Pippin's donation a more legal base, because they were conscious that only the Emperor of Constantinople could have made such a disposition.

In the eyes of the Byzantines such an act was regarded as treachery and insurrection against the lawful Roman emperor. Charlemagne was well aware of this and tried to legalize the papal action by a marriage with Empress Irene. Her deposition by Nicephorus I (811-813) ended this compromise. The war initiated by Nicephorus against the usurper ended with Charlemagne's victory, and Charlemagne was greeted by Byzantine envoys as *basileus*—co-emperor of Nicephorus.

The unity of the Roman Empire was thus saved, but Charlemagne, not at all impressed by the *Donatio Constantini,* regarded himself as master of Italy and Rome. Inspired by Augustine's writing on the City of God on earth which he misunderstood, and the theory that a Christian king, another Melchisedech, was not only king but also priest, he introduced another political theory in the West and ruled not only over the Western part of the former Roman Empire, but also over the Church and the pope.[8]

[7] Mansi, *Concilia,* 12, col. 985.

[8] A. Fliche and V. Martin, *op. cit.,* VI. For the political theories of

All this endangered the freedom of the Church and the old practice of the papal election by the Romans. Louis I confirmed to the Romans their right to elect the sovereign pontiff, but limited this freedom in 824, demanding that the pope should take an oath of loyalty to the emperor before his consecration. Lothar decreed that one could proceed to the consecration of a pope only after an order given by the emperor and in the presence of his envoys. Louis II provoked a short schism, favoring his own candidate against Benedict III, who had been chosen by the Romans. Benedict's successor Nicholas I was elected and ordained in the presence of Louis II.

The Romans disliked this intervention. Stephen V (885-891) was elected and consecrated without the knowledge of Charles the Fat, the last Carolingian emperor, and afterward the election of the popes was in the hands of Roman aristocracy. This kind of *modus vivendi* was acceptable to Constantinople, the more so as a great part of the aristocracy was rather pro-Byzantine.

However, this *modus vivendi* was ended by Otto I. Irritated by John XII and in difficulties with Roman parties, Otto I crossed the Alps, had himself crowned in Pavia as king of Italy, and was anointed in 962 in Rome by the pope as emperor. Otto wanted to become master even of the Italian provinces which were under Byzantine sovereignty. He sent Bishop Liutprand of Cremona to Constantinople with the request for a Byzantine bride for his son, expecting that Emperor Nicephorus Phocas would give away the Byzantine provinces as a dowry with the bride. The offer was received with the greatest displeasure, and the chapters in which Liutprand describes the reaction of the Byzantines to this outrage illustrate better than anything else how large the gap between East and West had grown.[9]

Otto I renewed the constitution of 824, replaced John XII by Leo VII and forced the Romans to promise not to ordain any pope before he had taken an oath of fidelity to the emperor

---

Charlemagne, cf. F. Dvornik, *The Making of Central and Eastern Europe* (London, 1949), pp. 39ff.

[9] *Monumenta Germaniae Historica* (Scriptores, 3), pp. 273-339, 347-63.

in the presence of his envoys. This meant abolition of free election. Two popes—Leo VIII and John XIII—were elevated to the papal throne by Otto.

This almost complete control of the Roman pontificate by the Franks displeased the Byzantines. In order to protect his Italian provinces—attacked in 968 by Otto—against the Franks and against the popes under Frankish obedience, Emperor Nicephorus Phocas forbade the use of the Latin rite in the provinces of Apulia and Calabria, and he created a new metropolitan See in Otranto with five bishoprics, which was put under the jurisdiction of Constantinople. It should be stressed that the tragic drama in 1054 had also a prelude in Apulia, provoked by similar reasons.

Pope John XII, in a letter in which he recommended Otto I to Nicephorus, called the latter "emperor of the Romans". This shows that the Westerners were forgetting the old idea of a single Roman Empire, recognizing a Roman Empire of the West with a Western emperor who should be crowned by the pope in Rome.

In spite of these dissensions, it seemed that the two Empires might again become united. Emperor John Tzimisces (969-976) consented to the marriage of his niece Theophano with Otto I's son in 972. Rome and Constantinople seemed again in good relations. However, the Byzantines did not renounce their right to influence the elections of popes. They favored the national party in Rome which had elected Boniface VII and offered him asylum when he had to cede his throne to Benedict VII, a candidate of Otto II. Theophano, the imperial widow (983), let the Romans elect their candidate, John XV (985-990), who was also supported by the pro-Byzantine party. Otto III (991-1002) chose his relative Gregory V as successor to John XV, but the pro-Byzantine party supported the Greek Philagathos from Calabria as John XVI. He was deposed by Otto III who appointed as Gregory's successor the learned Gerbert as Silvester II (999-1003).[10] In spite of all this, it is

[10] For details and bibliography, cf. V. Grumel, "Les préliminaires du schisme de Michel Cérulaire, ou la question romaine avant 1054," in *Revue des études byzantines* 10 (1953), pp. 1-23.

possible that, had Otto III lived longer, Constantinople and Rome would have been able to come to a new and durable understanding. He was a son of a Byzantine princess, knew Greek, introduced Byzantine ceremonial at his court, and his second request for a Byzantine bride, transmitted by Arnulf, Archbishop of Milan, was received in Constantinople very favorably; but before his bride could reach Rome, Otto III died.[11]

Under Otto's successor, Henry II (1002-1024), the rivalry between the imperial and the pro-Byzantine parties continued. John XVII and John XVIII were certainly accepted by Byzantium, and perhaps also Sergius IV. After his death (1012) Emperor Henry II confirmed the candidate of the pro-imperial party, Benedict VIII, who crowned Henry II in 1014 according to a new ceremonial, symbolically giving him suzerainty over the universal empire.

Under the reign of Benedict VIII events took place which brought a new actor on the Italian political field and which were to have a direct influence on the tragic events of 1054. Melo, a rich merchant of Bari, led an insurrection against the Greek governor of Apulia. When defeated, he took refuge in Capua. At the famous shrine of the Archangel Michael on the Mount of Gargano, Melo became acquainted with a group of Normans who had stopped there when returning from Jerusalem. Seeing that the Norman knights were interested in profitable adventure in Italy, he persuaded them to organize an expedition which he would lead to Apulia; there they could gain a rich booty after defeating the Greeks.[12]

A band of adventurous Normans arrived in Capua in 1015 or 1016. During their visit in Rome, the pope put the Normans in contact with Lombard princes who were also jealous of the Byzantines. Melo succeeded in recruiting some Lombard contingents and, with the Normans, invaded Apulia in 1017. However, Melo's army was defeated. Melo took refuge at Henry's

[11] For details, cf. F. Dvornik, *The Making of Central and Eastern Europe*, *op. cit.*, pp. 136ff.

[12] J. Gas, *L'Italie méridionale et l'empire byzantin* (Paris, 1904), pp. 399ff.

court in Bamberg, but the Norman adventurers stayed in Italy in the service of Lombard principalities waiting for another, more favorable occasion.

In spite of the growing estrangement between the Byzantine East and the Latin West in the 10th and 11th centuries, there is no reliable indication that Rome and Constantinople were already in open schism. The emperors of Constantinople continued to regard themselves as the only rulers appointed by God as leaders of Christianity. Rome was regarded as part of their empire. Naturally, they were interested in the person of the pope whose leading position in the Church was recognized by their legislation from Justinian I on. They were ready to accept the pope elected by the Romans, but they resented the growing influence of the Frankish kings—whose imperial title they did not recognize—in the elections of the bishops of Rome. This explains the frictions between Rome and Constantinople since the Franks had taken over the rule of Italy and Rome. Basically, however, the Byzantines recognized the primacy of Roman bishops in the Church.

With the Frankish rule over a great part of Italy and especially over Rome, some Frankish and Germanic features penetrated into the Roman Church which became more dangerous for the union between East and West than the political bickering between the two powers. One of the most important innovations—which could only increase the estrangement, since it touched upon the teaching of the Church—was the introduction of the *Filioque*[13] into the Nicene Creed. The Franks had taken over this custom from Spain where it had originated, but the popes, respecting the belief of the Greeks who regarded any addition to the Nicene Creed as unacceptable, resisted their request that

[13] *Filioque* means "and from the Son". It concerns here the formulation and the doctrine of the proceeding of the Holy Spirit from the Father *and from the Son* (*Filioque*). While the ancient Byzantine Church accepted the doctrine, although with detailed differences in the declaration, the formula *and from the Son* was not incorporated into the Creed. In the East the conception prevailed that after the Council of Ephesus (431) not a single change could be brought into the text of the Creed.

this addition should be declared as obligatory for the whole Church.

It apears that Pope Sergius (1009-1012) after his consecration was the first to send to the Byzantine patriarch with his enthronement letter, as was the custom, the Nicene Creed with the addition of *Filioque*. The Patriarch of Constantinople Sergius II (999-1019) rejected this. It is possible that the names of the popes ceased to be listed in the *dyptika*—lists of commemoration—in Constantinople from this time on. Nicetas of Nicaea who in the 11th century had composed a treatise on the Greek schism[14] speaks about a schism under the patriarchate of Sergius, but he confesses his ignorance of the reasons for this rupture. This indicates that if there were any, they had no durable consequences on the relations between East and West.

Another Germanic custom introduced into the Church administration profoundly transformed Western Christianity. Unable to conceive of the possibility of any property being vested in a society or organization as was recognized by Roman law, the Germanic nations regarded all ecclesiastical institutions founded by a layman as the property of the founders (*Eigenkirchen*—proprietary churches). Naturally, the founders claimed the right to invest anybody whom they chose with the property of their foundations. The consequence of this was the curtailment of the power of the bishops who could dispose freely only of churches and abbeys which they had founded.

This custom of proprietary churches, combined with the Germanic feudal system, strengthened the hands of the secular princes. It helped the Ottos to make of the Church a *Reichskirche,* absolutely devoted to the king, and curtailed the rights of the popes in Church administration.

This practice was bound to generate many abuses—appointment of laymen to richly endowed abbeys, simony, marriage of priests—abuses responsible for the decadence of the Western Church in the 10th and 11th centuries. This situation provoked

[14] *Patrologia Graeca (P.G.)*, 120, cols. 717ff.; cf. F. Dvornik, *Byzance et la Primauté Romaine, op. cit.*

reform movements. The Abbey of Cluny started the reform of monastic life. Unfortunately, the other reformist movement which attacked the abuses among the secular clergy did not start in Rome, but in Lorraine and Burgundy where the French and German kings did not possess enough power to stop a movement dangerous to their pretensions.

The reformers saw the root of the abuses in the theocratic system of priest-kings introduced by Charlemagne, and the only remedy in strengthening the power of the papacy not only over the Church, but also over the princes. In giving to the idea of the Roman primacy the largest definition, they extended the direct jurisdiction of Rome over all patriarchs and clergy in the East, having little comprehension of the exceptional position Byzantium occupied in the Christian world. They also ignored that there were no proprietary churches in the East, no feudal system hampering the activity of the bishops, no spread of simoniacal practice, and that the Eastern clergy was legally married, only the monks and bishops being bound to celibacy. Had the reform movement started in Italy, it is possible that such a generalization would not have developed.

Thus it happened that the reformers had contributed to the collapse of the last serious attempt to regularize the relations between Rome and Constantinople. In 1024 Emperor Basil II (976-1025) and Patriarch Eustathius addressed themselves to Pope John XIX with a proposal to end the frictions between Rome and Constantinople by a declaration that both Churches were ecumenical in their own spheres. At that time, Basil II was at the height of his power. He was making preparations to invade Sicily, then in the hands of the Arabs, and he was also anxious to strengthen his position in central Italy. An entente with the pope was desirable and he hoped that peaceful relations between Rome and Constantinople would be assured by the proposed declaration. This could also end the frictions between the Latins and Greeks in Italian Byzantine provinces.

If we can trust Raoul Glaber, whose chronicle is our main source for this episode, the Byzantines had in mind a declaration that would confirm the ordinances given to Rome and Constantinople by Justinian I, Phocas and Justinian II, because Glaber affirms that the Greeks were ready to recognize the supreme power of the first patriarch over the whole Church.

The news of these negotiations spread among the reformers; ignorant of the religious developments in the East and anxious to strengthen the power of the papacy, they claimed that the Greeks wanted to buy the primacy over the Church from the pope. The pope was attacked by many reformers and, intimidated by this emotion, refused the Greek offer.

After the death of John XIX the struggles for the possession of the pontifical chair continued. Henry III (1039-1056) convoked synods for the deposition of three popes and directly appointed three others. The third of his nominees was his own uncle, Leo IX (1049-1054), former bishop of Toul. The new pope was an ardent reformer, and in order to regularize his nomination, he asked to be elected by the Roman clergy and people. With him the reformative movement had reached Rome. The pope chose his most intimate councillors—the monks Humbert and Hildebrand and Archbishop Frederick of Lorraine—from among the most zealous reformers.

Leo IX started feverish activity for introduction of the reformers' principles in Italy, convoking synods, deposing simoniac bishops and defending ecclesiastical property against the pretensions of nobles. He was determined to strengthen his authority and to impose his reforms even in Latin communities under Byzantine political suzerainty. The most important synod was held in 1050 in Siponto. From the reports of the activities of his reformers we can conclude that some of the decrees voted at this synod were directed against certain Greek usages adopted in southern Italy and especially in Apulia. This was a dangerous move because Byzantium was jealously watching for any Frankish or papal activity in this part of its empire.

Leo's partner in Byzantium was Patriarch Michael Cerularius (1043-1058), perhaps the most ambitious and strong-willed prelate in Byzantine history. As a layman he instigated a conspiracy against Emperor Michael IV, hoping to replace him on the imperial throne. After the collapse of the revolt he was exiled, became a monk and turned his ambition to a supreme career in the Church. He became patriarch under the ineffective Emperor Constantine IX Monomachus; fully conscious of the dignity of his office and biased against the Latins, he was determined to strengthen his authority in Byzantine Italy.

There were some indications that his relations with Rome could have developed peacefully. Leo IX regularized his position by accepting the papal dignity only after having been elected by the Romans. This made him acceptable in Byzantium. Michael Cerularius seems to have been favorably impressed by the personage of Leo because visitors from Italy had informed him about the piety, noble sentiments and learning of the new pope.[15] However, he might have become suspicious when he learned that the pope had appointed Humbert "archbishop of all Sicily", probably in 1050.[16] Sicily was a Byzantine possession then occupied by the Arabs, and the Byzantines were making great efforts to recover the island. We know that Humbert's main argument for the extension of papal power was the *Donatio Constantini* which also included Sicily. This might have been the first stumbling block in the relations between the two prelates.

However, Michael seems to have been more alarmed by the activity of the reformers in Byzantine possessions in Italy. In order to defend his rights in Italy, which he thought menaced by the Latins, he started an offensive. As a countermeasure he ordered all Latin institutions in Constantinople to accept the Greek rite, closing monasteries and churches which had refused to comply. Such a measure was not warranted, even if we accept the possibility that some parishes in Apulia which were of the Greek rite had been persuaded to return to Roman obedience and liturgy.

At the same time Cerularius invited the Archbishop of Achrida to warn the Greek and Latin communities agains the offensive

[15] *P. G.*, 120, col. 784 for Michael's letters.
[16] A. Michel, *op. cit.*, I, p. 77.

movement. Leo of Achrida addressed a letter to the Latin bishop of Trani in Apulia, in which he attacked some Latin customs, especially the use of unleavened bread in the eucharist.[17]

The circulation of the latter in Byzantine possessions of Italy stirred up the sentiments of the inhabitants, and this was very unwelcome even to the emperor because a new danger had started to menace his Italian possessions. The Normans were again invading Apulia. Invited by another adventurer, Ardonine of Milan, who had been given command of some cities in Apulia by the Greeks, the Normans, whose numbers had grown, defeated the Byzantines and took possession of a great part of the province. Not content with this conquest they started to pillage and annex other cities, and they plundered the territory of the papal patrimony as well.

The pope was forced to take some protective action. He occupied Benevento and made preparations for a war against the Normans. Being unable to collect an army which could curb the Normans, he looked for an ally. The most logical one was the Emperor of Constantinople whose possessions were also in danger. Probably in order to strengthen the loyalty of the Latin population, the Emperor appointed as the commander-in-chief and governor of Apulia a Latin, Argyros (1051). Unfortunately, Argyros was especially disliked by Cerularius. Fearing that such an appointment might spell the end of Byzantine ecclesiastical sway in southern Italy, the patriarch strove to the utmost to prevent it, but without success. Argyros started negotiations with the pope and Leo IX welcomed the offer. However, their troops were routed in June, 1053, by the Normans who took the pope prisoner and placed him under a strong guard for a year in Benevento.

Seeing that anti-Latin sentiments had grown among the Greeks in Italy as a consequence of Leo of Achrida's letter, the pope asked Humbert to refute Achrida's accusations. The cardinal composed a very bitter and biased treatise; however, this was not published because, in the meantime, the emperor sent an embassy

[17] *P.G.*, 120, cols. 835-44.

to the pope; this embassy also brought a conciliatory missive to the pope from the patriarch. Leo IX decided to conclude an alliance and to send Humbert, Frederick of Lorraine and the Bishop of Amalfi as legates to the emperor. Humbert was charged to answer the patriarch's letter. However, Cerularius refused to receive the legates because the letter contained an attack against his title of ecumenical patriarch, a denial of the second place in the hierarchy to the patriarch of Constantinople and an expression of doubt about the legitimacy of Cerularius' elevation.

The cardinal, offended by the patriarch's behavior, published his treatise against Leo's letter in which he attacked violently many customs of the Greek Church; furthermore, in his disputation with the monk Stethatos, he accused the Greeks of suppressing the *Filioque* in the Creed. He probably thought that, in discrediting the patriarch to the clergy, he could, with the help of the emperor, overthrow him. Contrary to his expectations, the Greek clergy, offended by this attack, gathered in support of the patriarch. The emperor's attempt at restoration of good understanding remained unsuccessful and the embittered Humbert deposited the famous bull of excommunication of the patriarch on the altar of Hagia Sophia and left Constantinople.[18]

The contents of the bull profoundly shocked not only the patriarch but also the emperor. The latter allowed the patriarch to convoke a local synod which condemned the bull as full of unjust attacks against Greek customs and excommunicated the legates, calling them envoys not of the pope but of Argyros.[19]

Thus it happened that the papal action, meant to conclude an alliance and strengthen the union with Constantinople, ended with a new rupture more fateful than any other in the past. Cerularius was greatly responsible for it, and he was blamed by Peter, patriarch of Antioch, for his anti-Latin animosity. Humbert who misunderstood so tragically the mentality of the Byzan-

[18] *Patrologia Latina*, 143, cols. 930-74, 1001-4.

[19] *P.G.*, 120, cols. 736ff. The documents concerning the schism of 1054 were republished by C. Will, *Acta et Scripta quae de controversis ecclesiae graecae et latinae saeculo undecimo composita extant* (Leipzig/Marburg, 1861) (reprint: Frankfurt a M., 1963).

tines carries an even heavier responsibility for his rash and offensive action.

Only the patriarch was excommunicated by Humbert, and the validity of this act is doubtful because Leo IX was already dead at that time. The synod excommunicated only the legates, abstaining from any attack on the pope or on the Latin Church. Thus, the schism between Rome and Constantinople was not yet concluded, and in the following period several popes and emperors reopened negotiations toward a union.[20] They could not succeed because the Byzantines, faithful to their political ideology, could not understand the development of the Latin political speculation which, under Gregory VII, had culminated in a new theocratic theory, proclaiming the superiority of spiritual power over the temporal. The Crusades, although originally intended to promote a union, at the end made the rift even deeper. The first open schismatic act happened in Antioch, reconquered by the Crusaders, when their leader Bohemond I appointed a Latin patriarch. The most fateful event was the conquest of Constantinople in 1204 by the Fourth Crusade, followed by the plundering of the city and its churches. The destruction of the Byzantine Empire by the Crusaders and the elevation of a Latin patriarch in Constantinople consummated the schism for centuries to come.

[20] For details cf. W. Norden, *Das Papsttum und Byzanz* (Berlin, 1903). Cf. also F. Dvornik, "Constantinople and Rome," in *Cambridge Mediaeval History*, 4 (1966).

INDEX